ENGLISH MEDIEVAL SHRINES

BOYDELL STUDIES IN MEDIEVAL ART AND ARCHITECTURE

ISSN 2045–4902

Series Editors
Dr Julian Luxford
Professor Asa Simon Mittman

This series aims to provide a forum for debate on the art and architecture of the Middle Ages. It will cover all media, from manuscript illuminations to maps, tapestries, carvings, wall-paintings and stained glass, and all periods and regions, including Byzantine art. Both traditional and more theoretical approaches to the subject are welcome.

Proposals or queries should be sent in the first instance to the editors or to the publisher, at the addresses given below.

Dr Julian Luxford, School of Art History, University of St Andrews, 79 North Street, St Andrews, Fife, KY16 9AL, UK

Professor Asa Simon Mittman, Department of Art and Art History, California State University at Chico, Chico, CA 95929–0820, USA

Boydell & Brewer, PO Box 9, Woodbridge, Suffolk, IP12 3DF, UK

Previously published titles in the series are listed at the back of this volume.

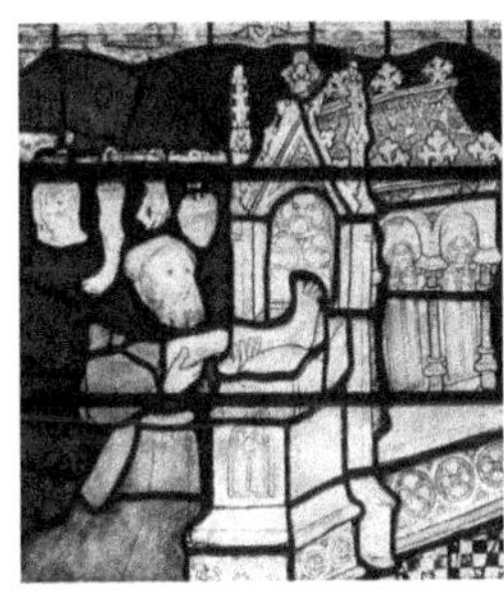

ENGLISH MEDIEVAL SHRINES

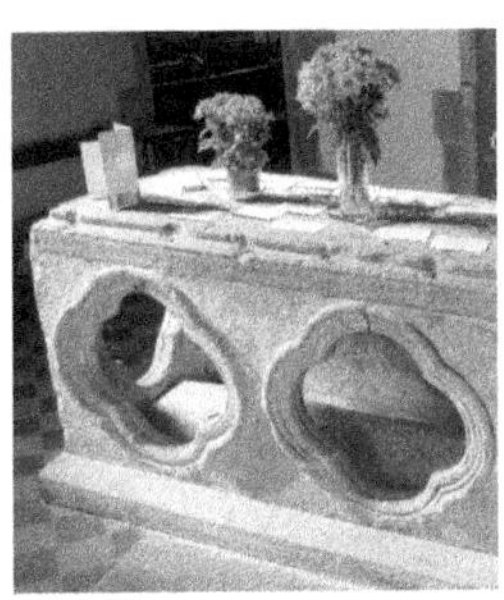

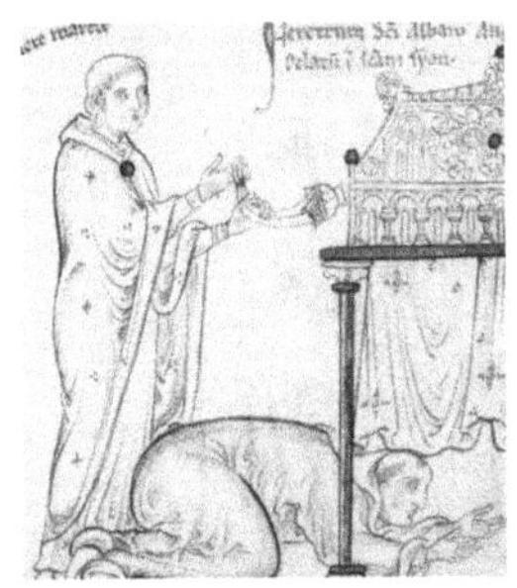

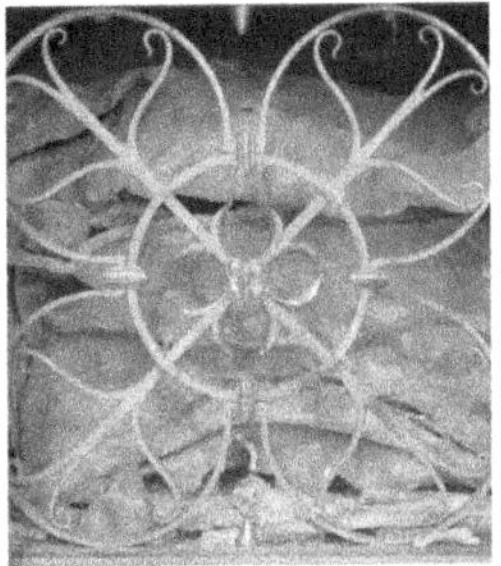

John Crook

THE BOYDELL PRESS

First published 2011
The Boydell Press, Woodbridge
Paperback edition 2016

ISBN 978 1 84383 682 7 hardback
ISBN 978 1 78327 093 4 paperback

The Boydell Press is an imprint of Boydell & Brewer Ltd
PO Box 9, Woodbridge, Suffolk, IP12 3DF, UK
and of Boydell & Brewer Inc.
668 Mt Hope Avenue, Rochester, NY 14620–2731, USA
website: www.boydellandbrewer.com

A CIP catalogue record for this book is available from the British Library

Designed and typeset by Tina Ranft, Woodbridge, Suffolk

CONTENTS

IN MEMORIAM MATRIS
DILECTISSIMÆ

LIST OF ILLUSTRATIONS

FIGURES

PLATES

Except where otherwise credited, all plates are © Dr John Crook

INTRODUCTION

The cult of saints is one of the most enduring features of medieval Christianity. Indeed, in many parts of western Christendom, the faithful still maintain devotional practices with which their medieval forebears would have been instantly familiar. From the late second century, and perhaps a good deal earlier than that, the graves of holy people—martyrs, bishops, later joined by saintly women such as abbesses and anchorites—became regarded as places of particular holiness, attracting pilgrims who believed that the earthly remains of the saintly departed formed a channel of communication, a spiritual information highway, between earth and heaven.

The cult of saints was an unashamedly physical affair, involving close access to, even contact with, human bodily remains. It engendered a material response in the architecture and internal arrangement of those churches where the saintly cults were located. The principal subject of this book is the development of those specialised monuments, loosely known as 'shrines', that flourished in medieval England from the early Anglo-Saxon period until the 1540s, when the reforms of Henry VIII brought the cult of saints to an abrupt end.

It is perhaps worth stressing at this stage that most of the cults examined are of actual departed human beings. The very word 'saint', which means no more than 'holy', has acquired supernatural resonances, and for many people saints, angels, and archangels are probably no more real than images from a nineteenth-century stained glass window. Many of the cults examined in this book involved deceased clerics of some distinction, such as abbots or bishops, whose lives on earth are usually adequately recorded, though the focus of interest in the present study is what happened to their bodily remains after their deaths.

The approach is mainly chronological, but also thematic as far as possible; many of the cults that I have studied evolved over the ages, so several individual cults tend to recur throughout the book as their physical settings underwent changes in response to new artistic styles or liturgical fashions. The cult of Alban, England's protomartyr, is a case in point: we first encounter the cult in Germanus's mission of 429, then in the Anglo-

Saxon and post-Conquest periods, and finally in the great reconstruction of his final shrine—still the best example of a medieval high shrine—in the fourteenth century.

The opening chapters trace the evolution of the cult of saints and religious practices at their graves, first in Rome, then Merovingian Francia. Both areas influenced the ways saints' cults would be pursued in Anglo-Saxon England. The focus then moves to these shores. There are some slender indications of Romano-British and post-Roman cults, notably those of Alban and the mysterious Aaron and Julius, but discernible patterns of saints' cults, still dependent on continental practice, begin to emerge in the late seventh century, notably those of St Æthelthryth of Ely and her sisters, and St Cuthbert.

The Rome-inspired architectural response to saints' cults that was a feature of the Carolingian renaissance found its echoes in crypts created at English churches such as Repton, Brixworth, Wing, and, ultimately, Anglo-Saxon Canterbury. Meanwhile structures that we would recognise as 'shrines' were being erected at main level within churches, a trend that flourished above all during the monastic reforms of the tenth century. Older cults such as those of Æthelthryth and Cuthbert were relaunched, joined by new ones such as Swithun, St Edmund of Bury and other minor royal saints. The monastic reform created its own saints, notably Oswald of Worcester. In the early eleventh century the saints of Northumbria were vigorously promoted. During the whole of the middle and late Saxon periods England could indeed claim to be called the 'Island of Saints'.

The effects of the Norman Conquest on the English Church were of course considerable, and this affected the cult of local saints, many of whom were initially regarded with suspicion by the new churchmen. Soon, however, English saints were being promoted by Norman prelates, and the near total reconstruction of this island's cathedrals and major churches was accompanied by the creation of new reliquary arrangements. The translation of St Cuthbert in 1104 demonstrates the enthusiasm with which native cults were now promoted. Just one shrine, albeit reconstructed, survives from that period—that of St Melangell, in North Wales. It is worth mentioning at this stage that although this book is entitled *English Medieval Shrines*, it includes those Welsh cults where there is evidence of shrines, notably the cult of St David. Unfortunately many Welsh cults, and indeed those of the Celtic saints of Cornwall, are represented only by place-names, church dedications, or holy springs, and to have broadened the book's title would have unduly raised expectations west of Offa's Dyke.

In the post-Conquest period and throughout the twelfth century, the usual arrangement was either for the saint's reliquary to be placed on an altar, or in some cases raised above it on a reliquary beam; or to be supported on a monument resembling a table-tomb, consisting of a stone slab supported on columns. Similar arrangements were to be found on the Continent at the same period, where indeed they persisted throughout the middle ages and beyond. In late twelfth-century England a new kind of monument came into being connected with the cult of saints: the 'tomb-shrine', notable for the provision of porthole-like openings in the sides giving limited access to the tomb beneath. The origins of these monuments seem to be found in the pierced panels that in the early eleventh century had been installed around the tomb of Christ in Jerusalem to protect the holy rock from pilgrims. Fittingly, the design was used for the first monument to the greatest saint of medieval England, Thomas Becket, whose cult outshone all others for the rest of the middle ages.

Tomb-shrines proved to be something of an evolutionary blind alley, however, and from the thirteenth century onwards the norm was for saintly reliquaries to be raised on high on tall shrine-bases, typically provided with niches along the sides at which pilgrims could pray to the saint. These high shrines began to evolve towards the end of the twelfth century and especially during the thirteenth. Their decoration was a small-scale expression of the developing styles of English architecture. Several major shrines were reconstructed during the fourteenth century, when the embellishments of the Decorated style were particularly appropriate for shrines; most of the physical remains of shrines that have been rediscovered date from this period.

The cult of saints was a convenient target for Henry VIII, and the destruction of so many shrines in major churches, many of which were monastic, was the prelude to the dissolution of those monasteries a year or two later. Religious practices of over 1200 years' standing were swept away, and the glee of the commissioners is evident from the reports they left behind. It does them no credit.

A NOTE ON ORIGINAL SOURCES

Much of the evidence is literary, and of course in Latin. I have not always translated each reference, but often paraphrased them in the main text and provided the original source in footnotes.

ACKNOWLEDGEMENT

My sincere thanks are due to the many friends and colleagues, too numerous to mention by name, who have helped me during the many years this book was in preparation. I am especially grateful to the team at Boydell & Brewer, who undertook its editing and production with gentle efficiency.

SHORT TITLES AND ABBREVIATIONS

The works listed here are those cited more than two or three times in the text, except where such citations immediately follow one another.

AASS (plus month and volume no.)	*Acta Sanctorum*, ed. J. Bollandus, and others (Antwerp and Brussels, from 1643).
Adam of Eynsham, *Magna Vita*	Adam of Eynsham, *Magna Vita S. Hugonis*, ed. D. L. Douie and D. H. Farmer, 2 vols., rev. edn., OMT (Oxford, 1985).
Ailred, *Saints of Hexham*	Ailred of Rievaulx, *De Sanctis Ecclesiæ Haugustaldensis*, in *The Priory of Hexham, its Chroniclers, Endowments, and Annals*, ed. J. Raine, Surtees Soc., 44 (1864), 173–203.
Alban and St Albans	*Alban and St Albans. Roman and Medieval Architecture, Art, and Archaeology*, ed. M. Henig and P. Lindley, *BAA Trans.*, 24 (Leeds, 2001).
Antiq. J.	*Antiquaries Journal*, Society of Antiquaries of London.
Arch. Aeliana	*Archaeologia Aeliana*, Society of Antiquaries of Newcastle upon Tyne.
Arch. Cant.	*Archaeologia Cantiana*, Kent Archaeological Society.
Arch. J.	*Archaeological Journal*, Royal Archaeological Institute of Great Britain and Ireland, London.
Archaeol.	Archaeological.
ASC	*Anglo-Saxon Chronicle*.
BAA Trans.	Conference Transactions of the British Archaeological Association.
Barlow, *Edward the Confessor*	F. Barlow, *Edward the Confessor* (London, 1970).
Battiscombe, *St Cuthbert*	*The Relics of St Cuthbert*, ed. C. F. Battiscombe (Oxford, 1956).
Bede, *HE*	Bede, *Bede's Ecclesiastical History of the English People*, ed. B. Colgrave and R. A. B. Mynors, OMT (Oxford, 1969).

Bede, *Metrical Life of Cuthbert*	*Bedas Metrische Vita Sancti Cuthberti*, ed. W. Jaager (Leipzig, 1935).
Bede, *Prose Life of Cuthbert*	Bede, *Vita Cuthberti*, in *Two Lives of Saint Cuthbert*, ed. Bertram Colgrave (Cambridge, 1940), 142–307.
BHL	*Bibliotheca hagiographica latina antiquæ et mediæ ætatis*, Subsidia Hagiographica, 6, 2 vols., new edn. (Brussels, 1949).
Biddle, 'Alban and the Anglo-Saxon Church'	M. Biddle, 'Alban and the Anglo-Saxon Church', in *Cathedral and City: St Albans Ancient and Modern*, ed. R. Runcie (St Albans, 1977), 23–42, 138–42.
Biddle, 'Cult of Saints'	M. Biddle, 'Archaeology, Architecture, and the Cult of Saints in Anglo-Saxon England', in *The Anglo-Saxon Church; papers on history, architecture, and archaeology in honour of Dr H. M. Taylor*, ed. L. A. S. Butler and R. K. Morris, CBA Research Report No. 60 (London, 1986), 1–31.
Biddle, 'Remembering St Alban'	M. Biddle, 'Remembering St Alban: the site of the shrine and the discovery of the twelfth-century Purbeck marble shrine table', in *Alban and St Albans; Roman and Medieval Architecture, Art and Archaeology*, ed. M. Henig and P. Lindley, *BAA Trans.*, 24, for 1999 (Leeds, 2001), 124–61.
Biddle, *Tomb of Christ*	M. Biddle, *The Tomb of Christ* (Stroud, 1999).
Binski, *Westminster Abbey*	P. Binski, *Westminster Abbey and the Plantagenets: Kingship and the Representation of Power, 1200–1400* (New Haven and London, 1995).
Blockley, *Canterbury Nave*	K. Blockley, M. Sparks, and T. Tatton-Brown, *Canterbury Cathedral Nave: Archaeology, History and Architecture*, Archaeology of Canterbury, n.s., i (Canterbury, 1997).
Bonner, *St Cuthbert*	*St Cuthbert, his Cult and his Community to A.D. 1200*, ed. G. Bonner, D. Rollason, and C. Stancliffe (Woodbridge, 1989).
Brooks, *St Oswald*	*St Oswald of Worcester, Life and Influence*, ed. N. Brooks and C. Cubitt (Leicester, 1996).
Brown, *Cult of Saints*	P. Brown, *The Cult of the Saints* (London, 1981).
Byrhtferth, *Vita S. Oswaldi*	*Byrhtferth of Ramsey: The Lives of St Oswald and St Ecgwine*, ed. M. Lapidge, OMT (Oxford, 2009).
CCSL	*Corpus Christianorum Mediævalis, Series Latina* (Turnhout, from 1954).

Coldstream, 'Decorated shrine bases'	N. Coldstream, 'English Decorated Shrine Bases', *JBAA*, 129 (1976), 15–34.
Cole and Johnston, 'St Hugh'	R. E. G. Cole and J. O. Johnston, 'The Body of St Hugh', *Associated Architectural Soc. Reports and Papers*, 36.1 (1921–2), 47–72.
Colgrave, *Two Lives of St Cuthbert*	*Two Lives of Saint Cuthbert*, ed. B. Colgrave (Cambridge, 1940).
Crook, *Architectural Setting*	J. Crook, *The Architectural Setting of the Cult of Saints in the Early Christian West, c.300–1200* (Oxford, 2000).
CSEL	*Corpus Scriptorum Ecclesiasticorum Latinorum* (Vienna, from 1866).
CVMA	Corpus Vitrearum Medii Aevi.
Delehaye, *Origines*	H. Delehaye, *Les origines du culte des martyrs*, *Subsidia Hagiographica*, 20, 2nd edn. (Brussels, 1933).
Delehaye, *Sanctus*	H. Delehaye, *Sanctus: Essai sur le culte des saints dans l'antiquité*, *Subsidia Hagiographica*, 17 (Brussels, 1927).
DNB	*Oxford Dictionary of National Biography*, ed. H. C. G. Matthew and B. Harrison, 60 vols. (Oxford, 2004).
Duffy, *Stripping of the Altars*	E. Duffy, *The Stripping of the Altars: Traditional Religion in England, c.1400–c.1580*, 2nd edn. (New Haven and London, 2005).
Eadmer, *De reliquiis S. Audoeni*	*De reliquiis sancti Audoeni et quorundam aliorum sanctorum quæ Cantuariæ in Æcclesia Domini Salvatoris habentur*, in *Edmeri Cantuarensis Cantoris noua opuscula de sanctorum ueneratione et obsecratione*, ed. A. Wilmart, *Revue des Sciences Religieuses*, 15 (1935), 362–70.
Eadmer, *Lives*	*Eadmer of Canterbury, Lives and Miracles of Saints Oda, Dunstan, and Oswald*, ed. and trans. A. J. Turner and B. J. Muir, OMT (Oxford, 2006).
Eadmer, *St Anselm*	*The Life of St Anselm, Archbishop of Canterbury, by Eadmer*, ed. R. W. Southern, rev. edn. (Oxford, 1962).
Eadmer, *Vita Bregwini*	'Eadmer's Life of Bregwine, Archbishop of Canterbury, 761–764', ed. B. W. Scholtz, *Traditio*, 22 (1966), 127–48.
Eadmer, *Vita Wilfridi*	*The Life of Saint Wilfrid by Edmer*, ed. B. J. Muir and A. J. Turner (Exeter, 1998).
Eddius Stephanus	*The Life of Bishop Wilfrid by Eddius Stephanus*, ed. B. Colgrave (Cambridge, 1927, reprinted 1985).

EETS	Early English Text Society
EHR	*English Historical Review.*
Evesham Chronicle	*Chronicon Abbatiæ de Evesham*, ed. W. D. Macray, RS, 29 (1863).
Farmer, *Dictionary*	*The Oxford Dictionary of Saints*, ed. D. H. Farmer, 3rd edn. (Oxford, 1992).
Flight, *Bishops and Monks*	C. Flight, *The Bishops and Monks of Rochester*, Kent Archaeol. Soc. Monographs, 6 (1997), 55–69.
Flores Historiarum	*Flores Historiarum*, ed. H. R. Luard, 3 vols., RS, 95 (1890).
Fouracre and Gerberding, *Merovingian France*	P. Fouracre and R. A. Gerberding, *Late Merovingian France: History and Hagiography, 640–720* (Manchester, 1996).
Frend, '*Ecclesia Britannica*'	W. H. C. Frend, '*Ecclesia Britannica*: Prelude or Dead End?', *Jnl. of Ecclesiastical History*, 30 (1979), 129–44.
GA	*Gesta Abbatum Monasterii Sancti Albani*, ed. H. T. Riley, 3 vols., RS, 28.iv (1867–9).
Gerald of Wales	*Giraldi Cambrensis Opera*, ed. J. S. Brewer, J. F. Dimock, and G. F. Warner, 8 vols., RS, 21 (1861–91).
Gervase	*The Historical Works of Gervase of Canterbury*, ed. W. Stubbs, 2 vols., RS, 73 (1879–90).
Gildas, *De Excidio*	*Gildæ sapientis, De Excidio et Conquestu Britanniæ*, in *Chronica Minora Saec. iv. v. vi. vii.*, vol. iii, ed. T. Mommsen, *MGH*, *Auctores Antiquissimi*, xiii, pt. i (Berlin, 1898), 25–85.
Goscelin, *Saints of Ely*	*Goscelin of Saint-Bertin, The Hagiography of the Female Saints of Ely*, ed. R. C. Love, OMT (Oxford, 2004).
Gransden, *Historical Writing, I*	A. Gransden, *Historical Writing in England, I, c.550–c.1307* (London, 1974).
Greatrex, *Common Seal*	*The Register of the Common Seal of the Priory of St Swithun, Winchester*, ed. J. Greatrex, Hampshire Record Series, vol. II (Winchester, 1978).
Greg. Tur.	Gregory of Tours
Greg. Tur., *GC*	*idem*, *Liber in Gloria Confessorum*: *MGH*, *SRM*, i, ed. W. Arndt and B. Krusch (Hannover, 1884), 745–820.
Greg. Tur., *GM*	*idem*, *Liber in Gloria Martyrum*: ibid. 487–561.
Greg. Tur., *HF*	*idem*, *Historia Francorum*: ibid. 1–450.
Greg. Tur., *VJ*	*idem*, *De Virtutibus Sancti Iuliani*: ibid. 562–84.
Greg. Tur., *VM*	*idem*, *De Virtutibus Sancti Martini*: ibid. 584–661.
Greg. Tur., *VP*	*idem*, *Vita Patrum*: ibid. 661–744.

Hist. Church of York	*Historians of the Church of York and its Archbishops*, ed. J. Raine, 3 vols., RS, 71 (1879–94).
Jancey, *Thomas Cantilupe*	*St Thomas Cantilupe, Bishop of Hereford: Essays in his Honour*, ed. M. Jancey (Hereford, 1982).
JBAA	*Journal of the British Archaeological Association.*
Jnl.	Journal.
John of Worcester	*The Chronicle of John of Worcester*, ii, *The Annals from 450 to 1066*, ed. R. R. Darlington and P. McGurk, trans. J. Bray and P. McGurk, OMT (Oxford, 1995); iii, *The Annals from 1067 to 1140 with the Gloucester Interpolations and the Continuation to 1141*, ed. and trans. P. McGurk, OMT (Oxford, 1998)
Knowles, *Heads*	*The Heads of Religious Houses, England and Wales*, 3 vols. (Cambridge, 1972–2008); i [940–1216], ed. D. Knowles, C. N. L. Brooke, and V. C. M. London; ii [1216–1377], ed. D. M. Smith and V. C. M. London; iii [1377–1540], ed. D. M. Smith.
L & P Henry VIII	*Letters and Papers, Foreign and Domestic, Henry VIII*, 21 vols. and *addenda* (London, 1864–1932).
Lapidge, *St Swithun*	M. Lapidge, *The Cult of St Swithun*, Winchester Studies 4.ii (Oxford, 2003).
Le Blant, *Inscriptions*	E. Le Blant, *Inscriptions Chrétiennes de la Gaule*, 3 vols. (Paris, 1856–92).
Leland	*The Itinerary of John Leland in or about the years 1535–1543*, ed. L. Toulmin Smith, 5 vols. (London, 1906–10).
Letters relating to the Suppression, ed. Wright	*Three Chapters of Letters Relating to the Suppression of Monasteries*, ed. T. Wright, Camden Soc., o. s., 26, (1843).
Liber Eliensis	*Liber Eliensis*, ed. E. O. Blake, Camden Soc., 3rd ser., 92 (1962).
Love, *Three Saints' Lives*	*Three Eleventh-Century Anglo-Latin Saints' Lives*, ed. R. C. Love, OMT (Oxford, 1996).
Malden, *St Osmund*	*The Canonization of St Osmund*, ed. A. R. Malden, Wilts. Record Soc. (Salisbury, 1901).
Malmesbury, *GP*	William of Malmesbury, *Gesta Pontificum Anglorum: the History of the English Bishops*, ed. and trans. M. Winterbottom and R. M. Thomson, 2 vols., OMT (Oxford, 2007).
Malmesbury, *GR*	William of Malmesbury, *De Gestis Regum Anglorum*, i (1998), ed. R. A. B. Mynors, R. M. Thomson, and M. Winterbottom; ii (1999), *General Introduction and Commentary*, by R. M. Thomson in collaboration with M. Winterbottom, OMT (Oxford, 1998–9).

Malmesbury, *Miracula Wulfstani*	*The Vita Wulfstani of William of Malmesbury*, ed. R. R. Darlington, Camden Soc., 3rd ser., 40 (1928), 115–80.
Malmesbury, *Vita Dunstani*	*Vita Dunstani of William of Malmesbury*, in *William of Malmesbury, Saints' Lives*, ed. M. Winterbottom and R. M. Thomson, OMT (Oxford, 2002), 157–303.
Malmesbury, *Vita Wulfstani*	*The Vita Wulfstani of William of Malmesbury*, in *William of Malmesbury, Saints' Lives*, ed. M. Winterbottom and R. M. Thomson, OMT (Oxford, 2002), 10–155.
Materials for the Study of Becket	*Materials for the Study of Thomas Becket*, ed. J. C. Robertson, *et al.*, 7 vols., RS, 67 (1875–85).
Matthew Paris, *Chronica Maiora*	*Matthæi Parisiensis ... Chronica Maiora*, ed. H. R. Luard, 6 vols. and index, RS, 57 (1872–83).
Memorials of Bury	*Memorials of St Edmund's Abbey*, ed. T. Arnold, 3 vols., RS, 96 (1890–6).
Memorials of St Dunstan	*Memorials of St Dunstan, Archbishop of Canterbury*, ed. W. Stubbs, RS, 63 (1874).
MGH	*Monumenta Germaniæ Historica.*
MGH, SRM	*MGH, Scriptores rerum Merovingicarum*, ed. W. Arndt, B. Krusch, and W. Levison, 7 vols. (Hannover, 1884–1920).
Miracula Ithamari	'The Miracles of St Ithamar', ed. D. Bethell, *Analecta Bollandiana*, 89 (1971), 421–37.
Nat. Hist.	Natural History.
Nilson, *Cathedral Shrines*	B. Nilson, *Cathedral Shrines of Medieval England* (Woodbridge, 1998).
Nova Legenda Anglie, ed. Horstmann	*Nova Legenda Anglie: as collected by John of Tynemouth, John Capgrave, and others, and first printed ... by Wynkyn de Worde a.d. mdxui*, ed. C. Horstmann, 2 vols. (Oxford, 1901).
n.s.	new series.
OMT	Oxford Medieval Texts.
Orderic, *Historia*	Ordericus Vitalis, *The Ecclesiastical History of Orderic Vitalis*, ed. M. Chibnall, 6 vols. (Oxford, 1969–80).
o.s.	old series.
Osbert, *Vita Edwardi*	'La Vie de S. Édouard le Confesseur par Osbert de Clare', ed. M. Bloch, *Analecta Bollandiana*, 41 (1923), 5–131.
Pat. Grec.	*Patrologiæ Cursus Completus, Series Græca*, ed. J.-P. Migne, 161 vols. (Paris, 1857–66), plus indices (1928–36).
Pat. Lat.	*Patrologiæ Cursus Completus, Series Latina*, ed. J.-P. Migne, 221 vols. (Paris, 1844–65), plus supplements and indices (1958–74).

Paulinus, *Letters*	*The Letters of St. Paulinus of Nola*, ed. and trans. P. G. Walsh, Ancient Christian Writers, 35–6, (Westminster Maryland, and London 1967).
Paulinus, *Poems*	*The Poems of St. Paulinus of Nola*, trans. P. G. Walsh, Ancient Christian Writers, 40 (New York, 1975).
Potts, 'Tombs'	R. U. Potts, 'The Tombs of the kings and archbishops in St. Austin's Abbey', *Arch. Cant.*, 38 (1926), 97–112.
Proc.	Proceedings.
Raine, *Hexham Priory*	*The Priory of Hexham, its Chroniclers, Endowments, and Annals*, ed. J. Raine, Surtees Soc., 44 (1864).
Raine, *St Cuthbert*	J. Raine, *St Cuthbert: with an Account of the State in which his Remains were Found upon the Opening of his Tomb in Durham Cathedral in the year MDCCCXXVII* (Durham, 1828).
Ramsay, *St Dunstan*	*St Dunstan; his Life, Times, and Cult*, ed. N. Ramsay, M. Sparks, and T. Tatton-Brown (Woodbridge, 1992).
Reginald, *Libellus*	*Reginaldi monachi Dunelmensis Libellus de Admirandis Beati Cuthberti Virtutibus quæ novellis patratæ sunt temporibus*, ed. J. Raine, Surtees Soc., 1 (1835).
Registrum Roffense	*Registrum Roffense*, ed. J. Thorpe (London, 1769).
Ridyard, '*Condigna Veneratio*'	S. J. Ridyard, '*Condigna Veneratio*: Post-Conquest attitudes to the saints of the Anglo-Saxons', *Anglo-Norman Studies*, 9, Proc. of the Battle Conference for 1986, ed. R. Allen Brown (Woodbridge, 1987), 179–206.
Ridyard, *Royal Saints*	S. J. Ridyard, *The Royal Saints of Anglo-Saxon England* (Cambridge, 1988).
Rollason, 'Lists'	D. W. Rollason, 'Lists of Saints' Resting-Places in Anglo-Saxon England', *Anglo-Saxon England*, 7 (1978), 61–93.
Rollason, 'Murdered royal saints'	D. W. Rollason, 'The cult of murdered royal saints in Anglo-Saxon England', *Anglo-Saxon England*, 11 (1983), 1–22.
Rollason, *Saints and Relics*	D. W. Rollason, *Saints and Relics in Anglo-Saxon England* (Oxford, 1989).
RS	Rolls Series.
s.a.	*sub anno.*
ser.	series.
Sharpe, 'Late antique passion'	R. Sharpe, 'The Late Antique Passion of St Alban', in *Alban and St Albans*, 30–7.
Soc.	Society.

Southern, *Anselm and his Biographer*	R. W. Southern, *Saint Anselm and his Biographer* (Cambridge, 1966).
Stancliffe, *St Martin*	C. Stancliffe, *St Martin and his Hagiographer* (Oxford, 1983).
Stocker, 'Mystery'	David Stocker, 'The Mystery of the Shrines of St Hugh', in *Saint Hugh of Lincoln*, ed. H. Mayr-Harting (Oxford, 1987), 89–124.
Stocker, 'Tomb and shrine'	D. A. Stocker, 'The Tomb and Shrine of Bishop Grosseteste in Lincoln Cathedral', in *England in the Thirteenth Century: Proceedings of the 1984 Harlaxton Symposium*, ed. W. M. Ormrod (Harlaxton, 1985, reissued Woodbridge, 1986), 143–8.
Sumption, *Pilgrimage*	J. Sumption, *Pilgrimage: an Image of Mediæval Religion* (London, 1975).
Sym. Op.	*Symeonis Monachi Opera Omnia*, ed. T. Arnold, 2 vols., RS, 75 (1882, 1885).
Symeon, *Libellus*	Symeon of Durham, *Libellus de exordio atque procursu istius, hoc est Dunhelmensis, ecclesie*, ed. D. Rollason, OMT (Oxford, 2000).
Tatton-Brown, 'Pilgrimage shrines'	T. Tatton-Brown, 'Canterbury and the Architecture of pilgrimage shrines in England', in *Pilgrimage: The English Experience from Becket to Bunyon*, ed. C. Morris and P. Roberts (Cambridge, 2002), 90–107.
Taylor, *Anglo-Saxon Architecture*	H. M. Taylor and J. Taylor, *Anglo-Saxon Architecture*, i–ii (Cambridge, 1965); iii by H. M. Taylor (Cambridge, 1978).
Thacker, '*Membra disjecta*'	A. Thacker, '*Membra Disjecta*: the division of the body and the diffusion of the cult', in *Oswald: Northumbrian King to European Saint*, ed. C. Stancliffe and E. Cambridge (Stamford, 1995), 97–127.
Toynbee and Ward Perkins, *Shrine of St Peter*	J. M. C. Toynbee and J. Ward Perkins, *The Shrine of St. Peter and the Vatican Excavations* (London, 1956).
Trans.	Transactions.
VCH [plus name of county]	*The Victoria History of the Counties of England.*
Visitation articles, ed. Frere	*Visitation Articles and Injunctions of the period of the Reformation*, ed. W. H. Frere, 3 vols. (London, 1910).
Vita Ædwardi	*Vita Ædwardi regis: The Life of King Edward who rests at Westminster*, ed. F. Barlow, 2nd edn. (Oxford, 1992).
Vita Gundulfi	*The Life of Gundulf, Bishop of Rochester*, ed. R. Thomson, Toronto Medieval Latin Texts, 7 (Toronto, 1977).

Wall, *Shrines*	J. Charles Wall, *Shrines of British Saints* (London, 1905).
Wallace-Hadrill, *Commentary*	J. M. Wallace-Hadrill, *Bede's 'Ecclesiastical History of the English People': A Historical Commentary*, OMT (Oxford, 1988).
Wharton, *Anglia Sacra*	*Anglia Sacra sive Collectio Historiarum*, ed. H. Wharton, 2 vols. (London, 1691).
Wilson, *St William*	C. Wilson, *The Shrines of St William of York* (York, 1977).
Winchester Annals	*Annales Monastici*, ii (Winchester and Waverley), ed. H. R. Luard, RS, 36 (1865), 3–125.
Worcester Annals	*Annales Prioratus de Wigornia*, ed. H. R. Luard, *Annales Monastici*, iv, RS, 36 (1869), 355–564.
Wulfstan, *Vita Æthelwoldi*	*Wulfstan of Winchester: The Life of St Æthelwold*, ed. M. Lapidge and M. Winterbottom, OMT (Oxford, 1991).

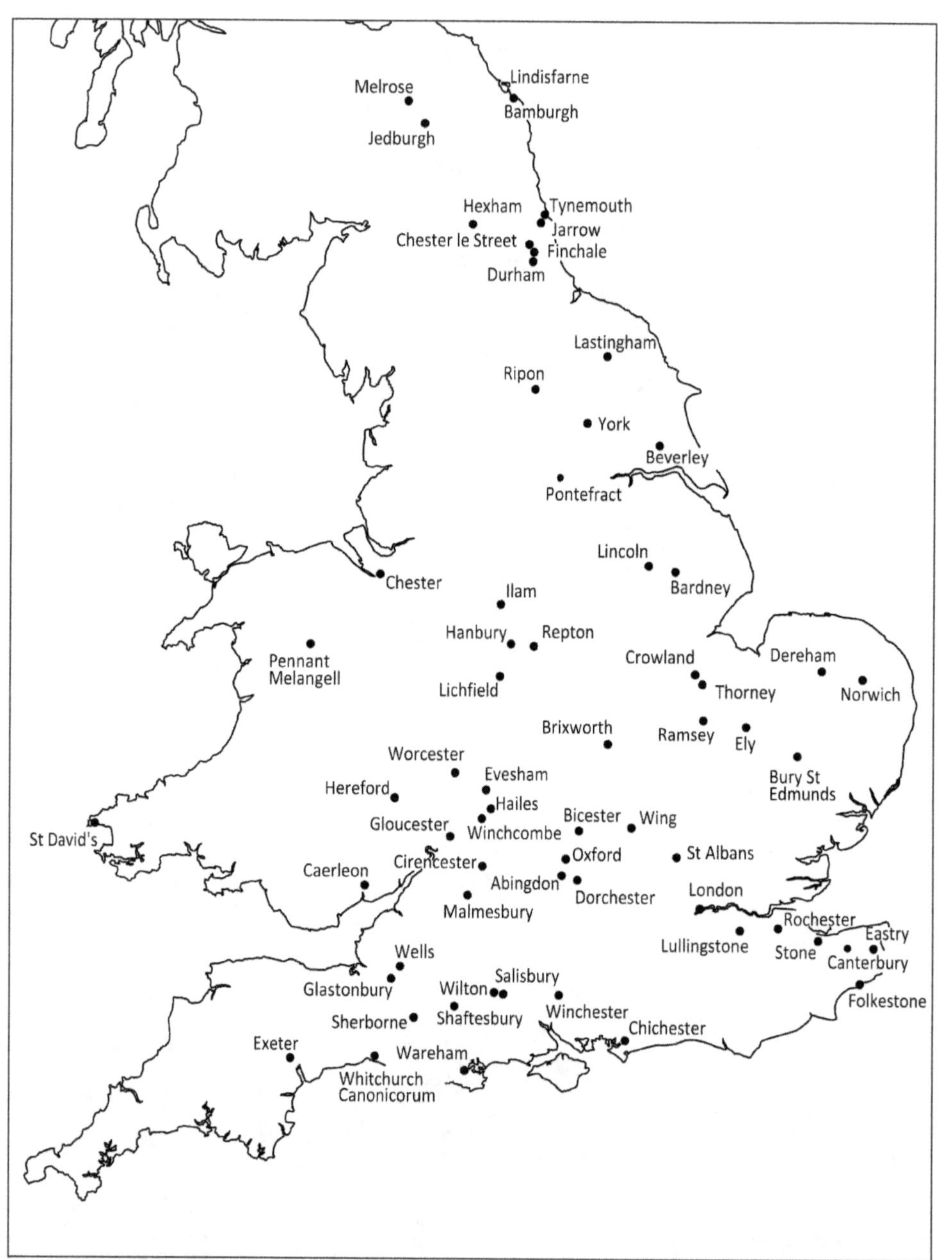

MAP OF SHRINE LOCATIONS

RELICS, SHRINES, AND PILGRIMAGE 1

Desiderius Erasmus was decidedly unimpressed by the relics of St Thomas Becket. His scorn, aroused during a trip to Canterbury in 1512–15,[1] is put into the mouth of 'Ogygius', an imaginary visitor to the shrine. The fictitious pilgrim describes being shown 'some linen rags ... with which the holy man [St Thomas] wiped the sweat from his face or neck, the dirt from his nose, or whatever other kinds of filth human bodies have'.[2] Erasmus's low opinion of these admittedly unlikely relics seems to foreshadow the distaste expressed so forcibly by the English reformers some twenty years later, in order to justify the destruction of English shrines. One wonders what he would have made of the activities of Alfred Fitz-Westou, sacristan of the Anglo-Saxon cathedral at Durham in the first half of the eleventh century. It seems that Alfred frequently opened the coffin of St Cuthbert, who had been dead for over three hundred years, combing the saint's hair, and even cutting off locks in order to demonstrate to his friends that they were non-inflammable.[3] Or how would Erasmus have judged the attentions of Oswen, the sacrist at Bury St Edmunds, who used to give the patron saint of that monastery an annual haircut and manicure?[4] The Dutch humanist, one feels, could scarcely have comprehended Paulinus of Nola's enthusiastic evocation of the intense joy people felt in the late fourth century when touching, or even kissing, the bones of saints; or St John Chrysostom's description, at the same date, of the way in which the faithful embraced and wept over caskets

[1] For information on Canterbury in Erasmus's day, see notes to J. G. Nichols' translation (2nd edn., London, 1875); C. E. Woodruff and W. Danks, *Memorials of the Cathedral and Priory of Christ in Canterbury* (London, 1912), 272–3.

[2] *Peregrinatio Religionis Ergo*, in *Opera Omnia Desiderii Erasmi Roterodami*, ed. L. E. Halkin, F. Bierlaire, and R. Hoven (Amsterdam, 1972), i.3; p. 491. For an English translation, see 'A Pilgrimage for Religion's Sake', in *The Colloquies of Erasmus*, trans. C. R. Thompson (Chicago, 1965), 285–311.

[3] Reginald, *Libellus*, 57. An ivory comb was indeed found in the coffin when it was opened in 1827, but this is now thought to be contemporary with Cuthbert rather than Alfred—it was possibly a liturgical comb: Peter Lasko, 'The comb of St Cuthbert', in Battiscombe, *St Cuthbert*, 336–55, pls. XX–XXII. Both comb and scissors had been seen in the coffin when it was previously opened in 1104; the scissors appear to have vanished when the shrine was destroyed in 1539.

[4] Abbo of Fleury, *Passio S. Eadmundi*, cap. 15; *Memorials of Bury*, i. 20.

containing the remains of martyrs.[5] He would have scorned the activities of that great churchman, St Hugh, bishop of Lincoln from *c.*1156 until his death in 1200, an inveterate relic collector, who whilst at Fécamp obtained two fragments of an arm-bone said to be that of St Mary Magdalen by chewing them off, 'first with his incisors and finally with his molars'.[6] Erasmus would have considered equally unseemly an experiment carried out by Leofstan, abbot of Bury (1044–65) and the monk Thurstan, when the shrine of St Edmund was restored. When the coffin was opened Edmund's formerly severed head seemed miraculously to have reattached itself to his body, and the investigators tugged at the corpse in order to check how firmly the head was now attached.[7] In somewhat similar fashion, Abbot Ralph of Sées tested the body of St Cuthbert during the translation at Durham in 1104, firstly moving his head around and pulling his ear back and forth (... *aurem trahens et retrahens*);[8] two years previously, Bishop Gundulf of Rochester had tweaked the beard of Edward the Confessor, thirty-six years in his grave, in an attempt to pull out a hair.[9] As for miracle stories, Erasmus would no doubt have endorsed the scorn of the Durham Cathedral librarian and founder of the Surtees Society, James Raine, who wrote in 1833 that the *miracula* attributed to his local saints were 'intended as so many romantic tales, to take their turn with stories of ghosts, and giants, and fairies, and amuse the people of the palatinate during their winter nights'.[10] He would certainly have laughed at the notion of more esoteric, though widespread, relics, such as the Virgin's milk or the holy foreskin.[11]

This veneration of body parts such as bones or teeth, or of scraps of bloodstained cloth, certainly seems to stand in stark contrast with what today, by believers and non-believers alike, would be regarded as proper respect for the dead. It certainly did not find favour with Anglicans of the nineteenth century. The antiquary Thomas Wright, for example, roundly condemned the contemporary enthusiasm for publishing saints' Lives, describing them as 'the most ridiculous and most disgusting portions of the belief of the middle ages' and pouring scorn on 'the trash in which "devout

[5] St John Chrysostom, *Homily on the Holy Martyrs*, cap. 3; *Pat. Grec.*, l. cols. 645–54, at 649. Idem, *Homily on the Martyrs Juventinus and Maximinus*, cap. 3; ibid., cols. 571–8, at 576.

[6] Adam of Eynsham, *Magna Vita*, v.14; ed. Douie and Farmer, ii. 169. On another occasion Bishop Hugh cut for himself a sinew from the incorrupt arm of St Oswald, preserved at Peterborough; ibid., ii. 170. For Oswald's cult in the twelfth century see below, pp. 65–7.

[7] *Samsonis Abbatis opus de Miraculis S. Ædmundi*, cap. 8; *Memorials of Bury*, i. 107–208, at 134.

[8] *Capitula de Miraculis et Translationibus S. Cuthberti*, cap. 11; *Sym. Op.*, i. 229–61, at 259. See below, p. 151.

[9] Osbert, *Vita Edwardi*, cap. 30; ed. Bloch, 122. Ailred of Rievaulx, *Vita S. Edwardi regis et confessoris*; *Pat. Lat.*, cxcv. cols. 737–90, at 782.

[10] J. Raine, *A Brief Account of Durham Cathedral with Notices of the Castle, University, City Church, Etc.* (Newcastle, 1833), 5.

[11] For some of these unlikely relics, see, in particular John of Glastonbury's list, *De sanctis in ecclesia Glastoniensi quiescentibus* in his *Chronica sive Antiquitates Glastoniensis Ecclesie*; *The Chronicle of Glastonbury Abbey*, ed. J. P. Carley (Woodbridge, 1985), 22–9.

minds" are required to believe'.[12] But the medieval cult of relics is the product of a long evolution that started as early as the second century AD. Many beliefs about saints, and patterns of veneration of their relics, may be traced back more than a thousand years before the Reformation. Indeed, it is scarcely possible to appreciate the essential role played by the cult of saintly relics in the English middle ages, or to understand its manifestations, without an understanding of the early background. So let us first trace the genesis of the cult of holy relics and explore its development in the early middle ages. What follows can be no more than a summary of a subject for which there is an impressive corpus of published material, including the writings of that great pioneer, the Bollandist Hippolyte Delehaye,[13] and important studies by Paul Ernst Lucius, André Vauchez, and Peter Brown.[14]

THE ORIGINS OF SAINTS' CULTS

In around AD 155 Bishop Polycarp of Smyrna was martyred in the local amphitheatre during a pagan festival. He was an old man of eighty-six, said to have been a disciple of St John the Evangelist, and he was evidently an influential leader of the flourishing Church in Asia Minor. In an attempt to make him abandon his faith, the Roman governor threatened Polycarp with lions, then proposed what was presumably perceived as an even crueller end, namely death by fire, the manner of execution that had miraculously been foretold to the bishop. The crowd would, it seems, have preferred to see him mauled by the big cats, but the formal games had officially closed, so burning was the only option. The cry obligingly changed to a demand for Polycarp to be incinerated. Initially he proved incombustible and had to be stabbed; the flow of blood quenched the flames. The centurion then cremated the lifeless body for fear of the Jews. It is the fate of his physical remains that is significant: in a letter to the Christian community at Philomelium the faithful of Smyrna later fondly recalled how they had gathered up his bones, 'more valuable than precious stones and finer than gold, and laid them where it was fitting. There the Lord will permit us, as shall be possible to us, to assemble ourselves together in joy and gladness, and to celebrate the birthday of his martyrdom, alike in memory of them that have fought before, and for the training and preparation of them that are to fight hereafter.'[15]

[12] T. Wright, 'On Saints' Lives and miracles', in *Essays on Archaeological Subjects*, 2 vols. (London, 1861), i. 227–67, at 227 and 255.

[13] Delehaye, *Sanctus*, idem, *Origines*.

[14] P. E. Lucius, *Die Anfänge des Heiligenkults in der christlichen Kirche* (Tübingen, 1904). A. Vauchez, *La Sainteté en Occident aux derniers siècles du Moyen Âge: d'après les procès de canonisation et les documents hagiographiques* (Rome and Paris, 1981). Brown, *Cult of the Saints*.

[15] The passage is preserved in Eusebius of Cæsarea, *Historia Ecclesiastica*, iv.15; *Pat. Grec.*, xx. col. 361. For the date of Eusebius's text, see A. Louth, 'The Date of Eusebius' Historia Ecclesiastica', *Jnl. of Theological Studies*, 41 (1990), 111–23. This translation from *A New Eusebius*, ed. J. Stevenson (London, 1963), 24–5.

There is nothing strange in the notion of annual visits to Polycarp's tomb: in the same way Romans visited the graves of their deceased relatives on their birthdays, and ate commemorative meals, *refrigeria*, in the open air. Tombs were even provided with 'libation holes'—openings or tubes through which food and wine could be poured to nourish the dead person—and such kindly sustenance was afforded not only to whole bodies but also to cremated remains which had been interred.[16] But the activities which the Smyrna Christians intended to pursue in Polycarp's case varied from traditional Roman custom in two significant ways. Firstly, the celebration was to take place on the anniversary of Polycarp's martyrdom rather than on his birthday; secondly, this was not a simple family commemoration but one performed by the local religious community as a whole, for whom the grave of the martyr had become a focus of a religious devotion that was evidently as powerful as any affection due to kinship.

The case of Polycarp is the first for which we have written testimony, but it may well reflect practices that were already well established. Meanwhile at the same period in Rome a grave identified as that of the Prince of the Apostles, St Peter, seems to have been the scene of activities similar to those recorded at Smyrna. Excavations at the Vatican which began in 1939 and continued for a decade after World War II revealed evidence for a first monument (*tropaion*), perhaps dating from as early as AD 160.[17] The earliest surviving reference to it dates from the end of that century, in a fragment of a letter which a Roman priest named Gaius had written to Proclus, leader of the Montanist cult. Gaius's comments are preserved in the writings of Eusebius of Caesarea, who refers to a 'written discussion' with Proclus, perhaps over where SS. Peter and Paul were buried, or the superiority of Rome as a cult centre. Gaius claimed that at the Vatican or on the road to Ostia one could see the 'memorials' (*memoriæ* or *tropaia*) of those who founded the Church, that is to say, St Peter and St Paul.[18] From such modest beginnings developed the Vatican basilica of St Peter and the great church of S. Paolo fuori le Mura.

The *memoria* of St Peter discovered during the Vatican excavations consisted essentially of an altar over a grave, originally located in an open courtyard; this relationship between an altar and a saintly tomb is an abiding feature of relic cults. Some authorities have even identified a passage in the Book of Revelation as an early allusion to the practice: 'I saw under the altar the souls of them that were slain for the word of God, and for the testimony which they held.'[19]

Cult centres were established at the graves of other Roman saints, and because Roman laws prohibited burials within towns, these devotional hot-

[16] J. M. C. Toynbee, *Death and Burial in the Roman World* (London, 1971), 51.

[17] Toynbee and Ward Perkins, *Shrine of St Peter*, 135–67. E. Kirschbaum, *The Tombs of St. Peter and St. Paul* (London, 1959), 133–43.

[18] Eusebius of Cæsarea, *Historia Ecclesiastica*, ii.25; *Pat. Grec.*, xx. col. 209.

[19] Revelation, 6:9.

spots were normally located in cemeteries beside the main highways leading out of Rome and outside the city walls, as the very name of the church of S. Paolo fuori le Mura still indicates. Thus the early basilicas which continue to encircle the ancient limits of Rome had their origins in extramural cemeteries over the graves of saints: S. Sebastiano, S. Pancrazio, and S. Lorenzo are typical examples, and the last-mentioned is still on the site of an active Roman cemetery on the Verano hill. Extramural burial was a practice that would spread throughout the Christian world, even to Verulamium on the northern fringes of the Roman Empire. There, the present abbey church stands, like its predecessors, over or at least close to the site long venerated as that of the grave of St Alban, on the opposite side of the river Ver from the Roman town; indeed, the town itself has moved northwards and Verulamium is represented only by a few upstanding stubs of Roman brickwork. Much of it, appropriately, was used in the construction of the present great abbey church dedicated to the saint, as well as for other monastic buildings.

As for the status of these holy men of Rome, they were all 'martyrs', literally 'witnesses' (the exact connotations of the term are much discussed) who had given up their lives for their faith. Indeed, as we shall see, until the late twelfth century the saints of Rome were mainly restricted to martyrs and early popes, Gregory the Great being the last saint of this group. In this early period Rome did not need to participate in the creation of 'confessors', a practice that became characteristic of the Church of Gaul and later of Anglo-Saxon England.

It is clear from the testimony of early Christian writers that what impelled the devout to visit these holy graves was a belief that in some mysterious way the saint, though dead in body, continued to maintain contact with the earthly sphere through the physical remains that he had left behind. The bones provided a channel of communication, a 'holy hot-line', between earth and heaven. Furthermore, the relics of a saint were a source of spiritual power (*uirtus* or *potentia*) which could be used, for example, in healing infirmities; this power was accessible at the grave of the saint. Indeed, by the end of the fifth century, perhaps much earlier, the saints were conceived as actually dwelling at their tombs, as well as being present in heaven. This was an effective reversal of a comment made in the anonymous *Letter to Diognetus* (perhaps by the Christian apologist Justin Martyr, †*c.*165) that Christians were 'passing their days on earth but were citizens of heaven'.[20] Many examples could be cited of the belief in the actual presence (*præsentia*) of saints at their graves, the best-known being an inscription close to the late fifth-century tomb of St Martin of Tours, proclaiming that, though his soul was in the hand of God, Martin was totally present there (*anima est in*

[20] *The Epistle to Diognetus*, cap. 5, para. 9, ed. E. H. Blakeney (London, 1943), 23. For a discussion of the text, see *A Dictionary of Christian Biography*, ed. W. Smith and H. Wace, 4 vols. (London, 1880–7), ii. 162–7.

manus Dei sed hic totus est).[21] A fragment of the inscription has actually survived, but the full text is known only from literary sources.[22] At Glastonbury in the mid-fourteenth century the chronicler John of Glastonbury felt able confidently to state that various saints 'lay' in the old church there, including SS. Patrick, Benignus, Pincius, Gildas, David, and Dunstan—all of whom had been originally buried elsewhere, and could only have been represented by small relics of dubious authenticity.[23] Miracle stories use the language of visitation: the faithful 'went to see St Martin' or other saints. Chaucer's pilgrims were in no doubt that they would meet the 'holy blissful martyr' at his shrine in Canterbury Cathedral, not in some remote celestial sphere.[24]

The leaders of the early Church were well aware of the novelty of the cult of relics. A third-century text, the *Didascalia Apostolorum*, stressed the contrast between Old Testament practice—where elaborate rituals of purification had been prescribed for those who even inadvertently touched human remains or entered a tomb—and the way tombs were becoming cult centres:

> For in the Second Legislation, if one touch a dead man or a tomb, he is baptised; but do you, according to the Gospel and according to the power of the Holy Spirit, come together even in the cemeteries, and read the Holy Scriptures ... For this cause therefore do you approach without restraint to those who are at rest, and hold them not unclean.[25]

TRANSLATION AND FRAGMENTATION

By the later third century a new practice was emerging in some areas, though not in Rome. If sanctity was concentrated in holy bodies, why should the bodies not be moved to a more convenient place? From there it was only a small step to the notion that the sphere of a saint's influence might be widened still further by removing parts of his body from the grave and distributing them. Here, then, we have the concepts of translation (moving a body from one place to another) and of fragmentation. Previously the moving of bodies had been allowed only in exceptional circumstances; for example, when Pliny the Younger, governor of Bithynia, consulted the emperor Trajan on whether he should allow the exhumation of tombs threatened by dilapidation due to age or by flooding, Trajan wrote back that

[21] Le Blant, *Inscriptions*, i. 240.

[22] The earliest MS of the 'Martinellus' containing the inscriptions at Tours is Quedlinburg, Codex 79, fos. 167r–173r: the inscription in question occurs at fo. 171v.

[23] John of Glastonbury, *Chronica*, cap. 5 (*De sanctis in ecclesia Glastoniensi quiescentibus*); *Chronicle of Glastonbury Abbey*, ed. Carley, 16–21, at 16–17.

[24] Geoffrey Chaucer, *The Canterbury Tales*, prologue.

[25] *Didascalia Apostolorum*, ed. R. H. Connolly (Oxford, 1929), 253–4.

Pliny (and, indeed, other local governors) should use his own discretion.[26] But now the notion was arising that bodies might be translated to satisfy religious aspirations. Successive emperors tried to resist this trend and attempted to preserve from disturbance bodies buried in the extramural cemeteries. By 386 it was necessary for the Roman emperor Theodosius I, a pious Christian, to pass a decree stating that 'No person shall transfer a buried body to another place. No person shall sell the relic of a martyr; no person shall traffic in them. But if any of the saints has been buried in any place whatever, persons shall have it in their power to add whatever building they may wish in veneration of such a place, and such a building is to be called a *martyrium*.'[27]

The Theodosian Code epitomised the Roman attitude to the translation of relics. Disturbing a tomb (*violatio sepulchri*) was still a criminal offence. The idea of touching human remains was abhorrent to the Roman mind. Yet the very fact that such legislation had to be made suggests that orthodox Roman practice was already under threat, perhaps being actively infringed. In the sixth century, when first Pope Hormisdas then, at the tail end of the century, Pope Gregory the Great tried to revive imperial prohibitions of the disturbance of bodies, they blamed 'the Greeks', that is to say, the Eastern Churches, for starting the undesirable trend. Thus, in 519 Pope Hormisdas refused to the Emperor Justinian pieces of the bodies of Peter and Paul which he had requested for the consecration of a new basilica dedicated to those apostles at Constantinople; the papal legates explained to the emperor that this demand, though conforming with Greek custom, ran contrary to Roman ways (*secundum morem Græcorum ...contra consuetudinem sedis apostolicæ*), but suggested to the pope that contact relics, *sanctuaria*, should be sent instead. It was also agreed that he might be given a fragment of the grid-iron on which St Lawrence had been martyred.[28] Likewise, when the Empress Constantina wrote to Pope Gregory in 594, requesting 'the head of St Paul or another part of his body' in order to consecrate yet another church in Constantinople dedicated to that apostle, she met with a firm refusal. Horrible things had happened to those who had previously interfered with the saint's grave. For good measure Gregory added an anecdote about the deaths of those who in his predecessor's time had tried to elevate the body of St Lawrence. In short, giving away relics or interfering with bodies was 'not the Roman way'; instead, the custom was to create contact relics, *brandea*. Gregory knew that dismembering bodies was a practice current amongst the Greeks, though he protested he could hardly believe it.

[26] *C. Plinii Cæcilii Secundi Epistulæ*, ed. E. G. Hardy (London, 1889), bk. x, letter 68.

[27] Codex Theodosiani, ix.17, '*De Sepulchri Violati*', in *Theodosiani Libri XVI*, ed. T. Mommsen and P. M. Meyer, 2 vols. (Berlin, 1905), i. 466: *Humatum corpus nemo ad alterum locum transferat; nemo martyrem distrahat, nemo mercetur. Habeant uero in potestate, si quolibet in loco sanctorum est aliquis conditus, pro eius ueneratione quod martyrium uocandum sit addant quod uoluerint fabricarum.*

[28] *Hormisdæ Papæ Epistolæ et Decreta*; *Pat. Lat.*, lxiii. cols. 367–534, at 474–5.

Constantina must be satisfied with a contact relic (though not St Paul's winding-sheet, which she had also demanded), namely some filings from the chains with which the apostle was said to have been bound.[29] A set of chains is still preserved in the relic chapel at S. Paolo fuori le Mura; they are displayed in the church on certain feast-days.

It is true that translation and fragmentation of saintly bodies does seem to have begun in the Eastern Empire, rather than the West. Sometimes the manner of a martyr's death meant that all that remained was ashes or fragments of bone, which facilitated their distribution: Gregory of Nyssa (331–94) tells us that relics of the Forty Martyrs of Sebaste were shared 'throughout the world'.[30] But perhaps the earliest recorded translation of a whole body occurred in the early 350s when Gallus Caesar (351–4) moved the body of St Babylas into a new church at Daphne, a suburb of Antioch, in order to silence an oracle of Apollo.[31] Babylas did not stay at Daphne for long; ten years later Julian the Apostate moved him out, in an attempt to revive the oracle. Then in 356–7 Constantius II brought the bodies first of St Timothy, then of SS. Andrew and Luke, to the church of the Apostles in Constantinople, where they were buried beneath or close to the altar, close to Constantine's tomb.[32] In his poem 'On Martyrs', composed in 405 (the eleventh of an annual series of 'birthday poems' (*Natalicia*) addressed to his deceased patron St Felix), Paulinus of Nola expressed the view that this was the first time Christian saints had thus been moved. He wrongly believed the translation to have been ordered by Constantine himself, when he founded Constantinople in 330, rather than by his son Constantius.[33] He also sought to explain why saintly translations had become necessary: because the Christian faith had not initially spread through the whole world, many areas were without martyrs. Later, however, Christian leaders were inspired to 'summon martyrs from their earliest homes and to translate them to fresh lodgings on earth'.[34] Interestingly, the development of the tomb of Paulinus's beloved patron, St Felix of Nola, closely followed the Roman tradition. In another *Natalicium*, composed for the saint's feast-day in 407, Paulinus described in some detail how the monument was examined owing to concerns on the part of the Church

[29] *MGH, Gregorii I Papæ, Registrum Epistolarum*, vol. i, pt. i, ed. P. Ewald (Berlin, 1887), 263–6.
[30] Gregory of Nyssa, Homily 3, 'On the Forty Martyrs of Sebaste'; *Pat. Grec.*, xlvi. cols. 749–88, at 783–4.
[31] Sozomen, *Historia Ecclesiastica*, v.19; *Pat. Grec.*, lxvii. col. 929. Gregory of Nanzianus, *Contra Julianum*, i.25; ibid., xxxv. col. 552.
[32] *Chronicon Pascale, sub annis* 356–7; *Pat. Grec.*, xcii. col. 733. Cf. Philostorgios, *Ecclesiasticæ Historicæ*, iii.2, in *Historiarum Epitome a Photio patriarcha confecta*; *Pat. Grec.*, lxv. cols. 480–1, who gives a different order: first Andrew, then Luke (both from Achaia), and finally Timothy, from Ephesus. The relics were discovered under the altar enclosure when the church of the Apostles was rebuilt by Justinian, as described in Procopius, *Buildings*, bk. i, cap. 4; *Procopius*, ed. H. B. Dewing, 7 vols., The Loeb Classical Library (London and Cambridge, Mass., 1914–40), vii. 48-55.
[33] Paulinus of Nola, *Carmina*, XIX (*Natalicium* No. 11), lines 317–24: *CSEL*, xxx. 129; this translation from Paulinus, *Poems*, 131–56, at 142. The relocation of the apostles' bones was correctly attributed to Constantius by Jerome, *Contra Vigilantium*, i.5; *Pat. Lat.*, xxiii. col. 343.
[34] Paulinus, *Carmina*, XIX.

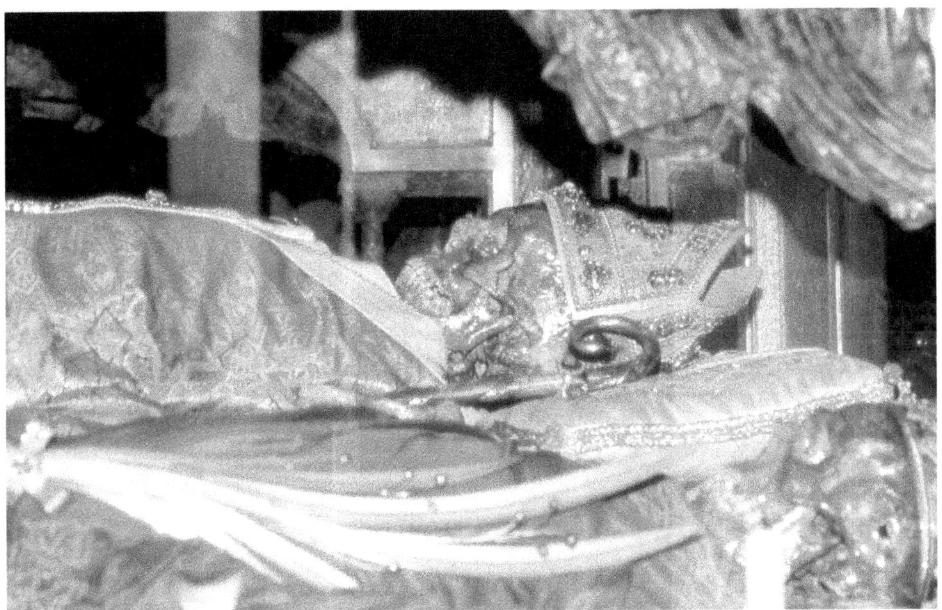

PLATE 1.1 MILAN, CHURCH OF SANT'AMBROGIO The mummified body of St Ambrose, in the crypt, flanked by those of SS. Gervasius and Protasius.

authorities. It had been discovered that 'dust', including fragments of bone, was being scooped out by pilgrims—instead of the oil which they were accustomed to retrieve, having poured it in through holes in an upper slab. After the removal of its superstructure the sarcophagus was actually exposed to view for a short while, but Paulinus emphasises that the body was not disturbed; they left Felix's inner tomb unmolested and 'carefully protected, so that his bones may rest undisturbed in their bed until that day of the Lord on which the saints will be aroused together to have the shining honour they deserve under Christ's presidency. So the same peace which awaits his holy soul in the heavens possesses also his revered body in the earth.'[35]

With the exception of Rome, activities which Pope Gregory might have condemned as 'the Greek way' had begun to make their appearance in the west as early as the late fourth century. Thus, in 386 St Ambrose of Milan explained in a letter to his sister Marcellina how he had miraculously discovered and elevated the bodies of SS. Protasius and Gervasius.[36] He was inaugurating a new church, forerunner of the present cathedral, and the local population had asked him to dedicate it 'like a Roman basilica', which

[35] ibid., XXI (*Natalicium* No. 13); *CSEL*, xxx. 179 (lines 636–42); this translation from Paulinus, *Poems*, 173–201, at 194.

[36] *St Ambrose, Epistolæ*, xxii; *Pat. Lat.*, xvi. cols. 1019–26, at 1023. Cf. St Augustine, *Confessions*, bk. ix, cap. 7. For Hippolyte Delehaye, however (*Origines*, p. 65), far from being the 'Roman manner', the translations at Milan were influenced by the Eastern Churches.

he agreed to do if he found the remains of martyrs. During excavation of the area in front of the chancel screens (*cancelli*) of the church of SS. Nabor and Felix the complete skeletons of two individuals conveniently came to light. They were identified by some aged local inhabitants as Protasius and Gervasius. The bones were translated to the new basilica and placed under the altar, and miracles began to occur. Ambrose expressed his desire to be buried next to the new saints, and his emaciated corpse still reposes between those of the two saints in the crypt of the present, late eleventh-century basilica of Sant'Ambrogio, beneath the high altar, though the crypt itself is, alas, an eighteenth-century reconstruction.

It is clear from the testimony both of Paulinus and Ambrose that the bones of saints were becoming regarded as indispensable for the dedication of a church. It was felt that they should be buried beneath or within the altar, just as altars at Rome had been constructed over holy graves, effectively, a reversal of Roman practice. At the Council of Carthage, in 401, indeed, it was enacted that altars without the proven body of a bishop or relics of a martyr should if possible be destroyed.[37]

So, just as Paulinus indicated, relics began to be disseminated. Relics of Gervasius and Protasius, together with those of St Nazarius, another Milanese saint whom Ambrose also elevated a little later, were sent to Bishop Victricius of Rouen in two batches. After the second consignment had arrived the bishop used them to consecrate the 'church of the city of Rouen' (*ecclesia ciuitatis*)—presumably a new cathedral—dedicated in 396, and he preached a sermon 'On the Praise of the Saints' (*De Laude Sanctorum*).[38] The consecration relics consisted of blood-soaked earth: St Ambrose had indeed mentioned 'much blood' being discovered at the exhumation of 385–6. According to a letter written to him by his friend Paulinus of Nola, Victricius was instrumental in putting Rouen on the map as a major cult centre. 'Your deserving sanctity has transformed Rouen into the entire appearance of Jerusalem', he wrote.[39] Victricius also seems to have visited Britain, probably preceding St Augustine by two centuries in bringing Christianity to Canterbury. It is just possible that he initiated the cult there of St Martin, for when Augustine arrived in 597 he was allowed to use the redundant church of St Martin as his mission developed.[40] The church in question is identified as the church of St Martin, beside the Sandwich road, on the hillside east of Canterbury.[41]

[37] *CCSL*, cxlix. 204 (*Concilia Africæ*).
[38] *CCSL*, lxiv. 53–93.
[39] Paulinus, *Epistula* 18, 'To Victricius', para. 5; *CSEL*, xxix. 128–37, at 132. For English translation, see Paulinus, *Letters*, vol. 35, 167–77 at 171.
[40] Bede, *HE*, i.26; ed. Colgrave and Mynors, 76–7.
[41] T. Tatton-Brown, 'St Martin's Church in the 6th–7th century', in *The Parish of St Martin and St Paul, Canterbury*, ed. M. Sparks (Canterbury, 1980), 12–18. M. Sparks and T. Tatton-Brown, 'The History of the Ville of St. Martin's, Canterbury', in J. Rady, 'Excavations at St. Martin's Hill, Canterbury, 1984–85', *Arch. Cant.*, 104 (1987), 123–218, at 200–12. But Charles Thomas, in *Christianity in Roman Britain to A.D. 500* (London, 1981), 170–4, has argued that the church in which Queen Bertha was already accustomed to pray when Augustine arrived was in fact St Pancras's rather than St Martin's. See also Wallace-Hadrill, *Commentary*, 36–7.

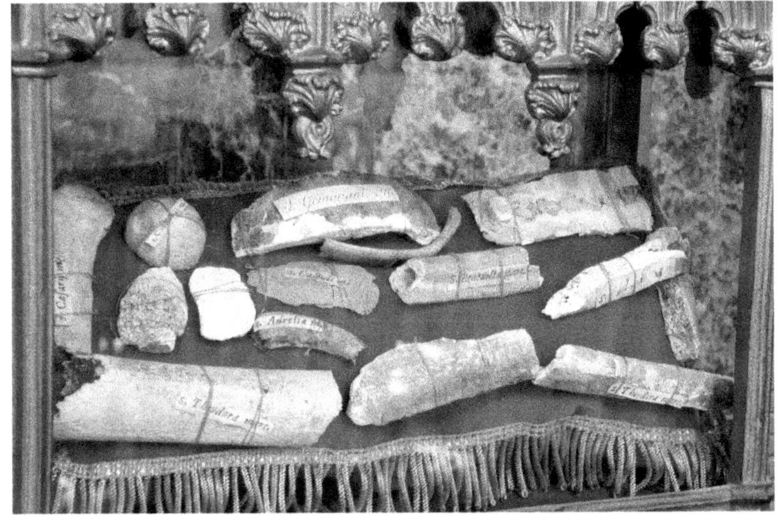

PLATE 1.2
MORTAIN (DEPT. MANCHE, FRANCE), ÉGLISE SAINT-ÉVROULT
A typical collection of fragmentary relics, removed from their reliquaries.

Another feature of relic cults is illustrated by Victricius's reception of the Milanese saints. The relics he had received were small, the bishop told his congregation, but 'the whole was in each part. Each particle was linked to all of eternity'. In other words, a fragment of a saintly body, or even a contact relic, was considered just as powerful as a whole body, and worthy of the same veneration. A slightly later churchman, Theodoret, bishop of Cyrrhus (†*c.*460), at first seemed sceptical on this point: church congregations were in the habit of claiming that they possessed the whole body of, for example, 'Julian', 'Romanus', or 'Timothy' (three martyrs whose cult was practised at Antioch), when in fact they only had tiny fragments.[42] But he also acknowledged elsewhere that even the smallest fragment of a relic of a martyr possessed the entire grace of the whole body.[43] St John Chrysostom had already said much the same thing a couple of decades previously.[44]

Four years after the exhumation of SS. Gervasius and Protasius, Florence received its own hitherto unknown saints, Vitalis and Agricola, whom St Ambrose had exhumed at Bologna.[45] Then in the late 390s Ambrose opened the tombs of SS. Nazarius and Celsus, which were located in a 'garden' outside Milan, and translated the bodies into the Basilica of the Apostles,

[42] Theodoret, Letter 130, 'To Bishop Timothy'; *Pat. Grec.*, lxxxiii. cols. 1341–8, at 1347–8. Cf. the similar idea (using different martyrs, probably from Cyrrhus) expressed in Letter 144, 'To the soldiers'; ibid., cols. 1369–76, at 1373–4.

[43] Theodoret, *Græcarum Affectionum Curatio (The Cure of Greek Afflictions)*, Book 8 ('On Martyrs'); *Pat. Grec.*, lxxxiii. cols. 775–1152, at 1011–12: 'Even though the body is cut up, all of its grace (ἡ χάρις) remains, and each tiny fragment of a relic retains as much power as the whole body of the martyr if he had not been thus divided ...'.

[44] St John Chrysostom, *Homily on Holy Martyrs*, cap. 2; *Pat. Grec.*, l. cols. 645–54, at 649.

[45] *Vita S. Ambrosii a Paulino eius notario ... conscripta*, cap. 29; *Pat. Lat.*, xiv. col. 37.

within the city.[46] Although Nazarius's head and body were still separated (he had died by decapitation), his head was miraculously incorrupt, and the blood was as fresh as though it had been spilt that very day. Furthermore, the body exuded a smell which 'exceeded all aromatic perfumes in sweetness'. Celsus's body also proved to be a treasure which 'neither moth nor rust doth corrupt, nor thieves break in and steal'.[47] These are early examples of a tradition of incorruptibility that would feature prominently in later saints' cults, especially in Merovingian Francia. Nearly a century later, in 488, the unblemished body of St Severinus, Apostle of Austria (†482), was exhumed, and, like St Cuthbert two hundred years after that, was carried about for a time by his followers, working miracles until a resting place was provided for him at Naples.[48]

Individual Christians were also beginning to obtain personal relics during this period. Again, Paulinus of Nola tells us in his eleventh *Natalicium* that these early pilgrims were increasingly inclined to

> break off some keepsakes from the holy bones as their deserved reward, so that they could individually bear back home for their personal protection the reward for their service and the payment for their toil. As a result, the sacred ashes have been scattered over different areas like life-giving seeds. Wherever a drop of dew has fallen on men in the shape of a particle of bone, the tiny gift from a consecrated body, holy grace has brought forth fountains in that place, and the drops of ashes have begotten rivers of life.[49]

Paulinus had himself obtained 'a fragment of dust' from the bodies of the apostles, which were kept in a church at Fundi.[50] Gregory of Tours, that great promoter of the cult of saints whose influence we shall study in Chapter 2, inherited from his parents a gold medallion (*lupinus aureus*) containing the 'ashes' (*cineres*) of unknown saints, which proved effective against fire and storm.[51] Another frequently cited early example of such personal mementos is the bone of a martyr kept by an early fourth-century Spanish resident of Carthage called Lucilla, a 'foolish woman', *femina factiosa*, according to St Optatus, bishop of Milevis in Numidia (now in modern Algeria). He criticised her for touching the chalice with this private relic before receiving the eucharist, condemning it as 'a bone of some unknown dead man'.[52] Here we are evidently on the boundary between orthodox veneration of relics and the realm of charms and talismans. Such hocus-pocus was denounced by St John

[46] ibid., caps. 32–3; cols. 38–9.
[47] Matthew, 6:19.
[48] Eugippus, *Vita S. Severini*, cap. 46; *CSEL*, ix.2, pp. 65–6.
[49] Paulinus of Nola, *Carmina*, XIX (*Natalicium* No. 11); *CSEL*, xxx. 129, lines 353–62. This translation from Paulinus, *Poems*, 131–56, at 143.
[50] ibid., lines 363–77; Paulinus, *Poems*, 143–4.
[51] Greg. Tur., *GM*, cap. 83; *MGH, SRM*, i. 544–5.
[52] *Sancti Optati Milevitani Libri VII*, i.16; ed. C. Ziwsa, *CSEL*, xxvi (1893), 18–19: … *os nescio cuius hominis mortui.*

Chrysostom at the end of the fourth century: he reminded his catechumens that the Cross had the strength of a wonderful amulet, and scorned people who tied bronze coins of Alexander the Great around their heads and feet.[53]

THE FIRST RELIQUARIES

Fragmentary relics had to be housed in suitable containers, and we see here the beginnings of reliquaries which were such an important class of precious religious object in the middle ages. As one would expect, the first recorded examples are from the Eastern Church, reflecting the beginnings of fragmentation there. In the late fourth century St John Chrysostom (347–407) was urging the faithful to kiss the *thecæ* containing saintly relics; even these caskets had great power, which they had absorbed from the bones within.[54] At about the same period, Gregory of Nyssa (331–94) buried his parents close to a presumably much larger *theca* containing the relics of the Forty Martyrs of Sebaste.[55] According to St Augustine, after the discovery in 415 of the tomb of St Stephen at Caphar Gamala, north of Jerusalem, Bishop Evodius of Uzala (a diocese in North Africa) sent a fragment of the saint to a colleague in a little silver box (*capsella argentea*), which cured a blind man during the journey.[56] It is clear, however, that most such reliquaries were small in size, as befitted their modest contents: Gregory of Tours's writing makes it clear that even where saintly bodies were moved in his day they were rehoused in tombs (*sepulchra*) or sarcophagi rather than full-sized reliquaries of the kind that we shall encounter in the later middle ages.

INCORRUPTIBILITY

During the early centuries of Christianity a belief gradually developed that saintly bodies, unlike those of ordinary mortals, did not decay in their tombs: an understandable inference, given that the faithful believed that the saints were in some way still alive and present at their graves. Furthermore, justification for the belief could be found in holy Scripture: 'Thou shalt not suffer thy Holy One to see corruption';[57] or 'The dead shall be raised incorruptible.'[58] The incorruption of saintly bodies prefigured that state which all bodies might experience at the resurrection.

[53] St John Chrysostom, *Catacheses ad Illuminandos (Baptismal Catacheses)*, ii.5; *Pat. Grec.*, xlix. cols. 231–40, at 239–20. English version in *St John Chrysostom, Baptismal Instructions*, xi.25, ed. P. W. Harkins, Ancient Christian Writers, xxxi (Westminster, Maryland and London, 1963), 168; ibid., xii.57, ed. Harkins, 190.

[54] St John Chrysostom, 'Homily on the Holy Martyrs Bernice and Prosdoce', cap. 7; *Pat. Grec.*, l. cols. 629–40, at 640.

[55] Gregory of Nyssa, Homily 3, 'On the Forty Martyrs of Sebaste'; *Pat. Grec.*, xlvi. cols. 749–88, at 783–4.

[56] Augustine of Hippo, *De miraculis S. Stephani*, i.8; *Pat. Lat.*, xli. cols. 833–54, at 839.

[57] Psalms, 16:10.

[58] I Corinthians, 15:52.

The beginnings of the tradition are perhaps apparent in the activities of St Ambrose: the bodies of Gervasius and Protasius miraculously oozed blood, as did that of St Nazarius; and the head of the latter saint was miraculously undecayed. Gregory of Tours gives several examples: when his great-grandfather Bishop Gregory of Langres was translated, the lid of his sarcophagus came loose, revealing the saint's intact face like that of a sleeping man.[59] Here are early examples of an alleged phenomenon which we shall frequently encounter in the saints' cults of Merovingian Francia, and indeed in medieval England with cults of 'incorrupt' saints such as Cuthbert of Durham, Æthelthryth of Ely, and Edmund of Bury. These three cults of incorrupt bodies, together with Fursey of Peronne, are particularly cited by Bede.[60] Later other incorrupt English saints, such as Edward the Confessor, would join the sanctoral.

As already noted, saintly bodies also often demonstrated their sanctity by exuding a marvellous smell. A very early example was the body of St Nazarius of Milan, exhumed by St Ambrose. When Gregory of Tours's contemporary Bishop Eberigisilus exhumed the body of St Mallosus at Birten, he knew he was digging in the right place when a sweet fragrance reached his nostrils.[61] Gregory himself records a marvellous smell at the tomb of St Julian of Brioude, 'like roses, even though it was the ninth month'.[62] At the death of St Gertrude of Nivelles in 659 a 'most pleasant odour, as if a fragrant mixture of scents' (*suavissimus odor, quasi flagrantia unguentorum mixta*) filled her cell.[63] The same phenomenon occurred in 716 at Langres, where St Ceolfrith, abbot of Jarrow, was initially buried, having died on his way to Rome. There 'the fragrance of a wonderful odour filled the whole church; and it was followed by a supernatural light, which remained no little time, and finally rose to the roof of the church'.[64] Ceolfrith's incorrupt body was eventually brought back to England.[65] The body of St Eorcengota, a Kentish princess who died at Faremoutiers-en-Brie (Seine-et-Marne) *c.*660,[66] was elevated after only three days and gave off a sweet scent 'as if stores of balsam had been unsealed'.[67] This link between incorruptibility and a pleasant, aromatic odour has suggested to some authorities that the

[59] Greg. Tur., *VP*, cap. 7, *De Sancto Gregorio Episcopo*, para. 4; *MGH, SRM*, i. 689–90.

[60] Bede, *HE*; ed. Colgrave and Mynors, 240–1, note 2.

[61] Greg. Tur., *GM*, cap. 62; *MGH, SRM*, i. 530.

[62] idem, *VJ*, cap. 46b; *MGH, SRM*, i. 562–84, at 583.

[63] *Vita Sanctæ Geretrudis*, Version 'A' (written before 670), cap. 7; *MGH, SRM*, ii. 447–64, at 464.

[64] 'The anonymous life of St Ceolfrith, abbot of Jarrow', in *English Historical Documents c.500–1042*, ed. D. Whitelock, 2nd edn. (London, 1979), item 155, pp. 758–70, at 770. For an earlier example of the *topos* of miraculous light, see Paulinus of Nola, *Carmina*, XVIII (*Natalicium* VI, composed in 400), lines 154–80; English translation in Paulinus, *Poems*, 119–20.

[65] Alcuin, *Versus de Patribus, Regibus et Sanctis Euboricensis Ecclesiæ*, lines 1299–300; idem, *The Bishops, Kings, and Saints of York*, ed. P. Godman, OMT (Oxford, 1982), 102–3.

[66] See below, p. 59.

[67] Bede, *HE*, iii.8; ed. Colgrave and Mynors, 240–1: … *quasi opobalsami cellaria esse uiderentur aperta.*

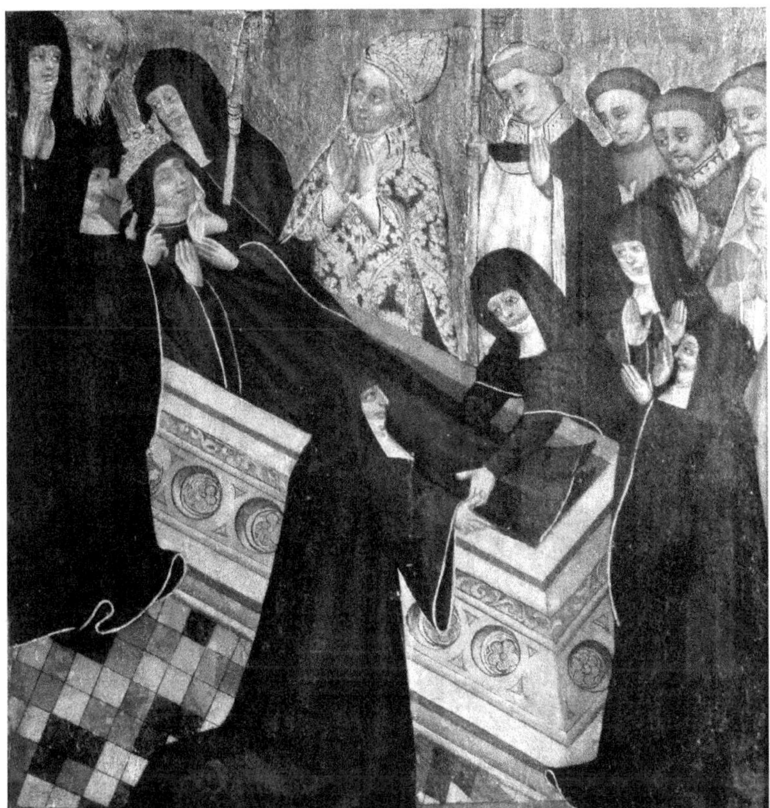

PLATE 1.3 ST ÆTHELTHRYTH AT ELY The exhumation of her incorrupt body.

bodies of potential saints might have been embalmed.[68] In twelfth-century England, William of Malmesbury made a list of incorruptible saints: Æthelthryth and Wihtburh of Ely, King Edmund the Martyr, Archbishop Ælfheah, and Bishop Cuthbert, 'all with skin and flesh inviolate and joints yet supple … as though they meant only to seem asleep'.[69]

The miraculous light that accompanied Ceolfrith's death was another hagiographical commonplace: Bede relates, for example, that one of the nuns in St Hilda's convent of Whitby became aware of her abbess's death in 680 when she saw the saint's soul ascending to heaven, borne aloft by angels.[70] But at much earlier date Gregory of Tours had noted the 'great light' (*magna claritas*) in a crypt containing saintly bodies at Lyon, which he thought indicated the merit of the martyrs.[71]

[68] See below, p. 62.
[69] Malmesbury, *GR*, ii.207; ed. Mynors, i. 386–7: *omnes inuiolatis cute et carne, flexibilibus articulis … spetiem dormientium mediantes.*
[70] Bede, *HE*, iv.23; ed. Colgrave and Mynors, 412–13.
[71] Greg. Tur., *GM*, cap. 49; *MGH, SRM*, i. 522.

Although incorruptibility provided useful corroborative posthumous proof of the sanctity of an individual, it did not necessarily qualify him or her for sainthood on its own. For example, the chronicler John of Hexham includes a lengthy account of the life and works of Archbishop Thurstan of York (1114–40), whom he considered as having lived an exemplary life, and who died amongst the Cluniac brethren at Pontefract in 1140. He was buried in a prestigious location in the church of St John, in front of the high altar. Many years later, when the monks were carrying out repairs in that area, his tomb was opened, and his body and the vestments in which he had been laid to rest were found to be quite unaffected by their long interment.[72] Yet Thurston never became a saint; nor did Archbishop Theobald when his body was exhumed in Canterbury Cathedral in 1180 and was found to be incorrupt.[73]

CONTACT RELICS

A relic did not have to be a fragment of bone. Much of the distribution of relics involved '*sanctuaria*' or secondary relics: objects that had themselves come into contact either with a saint during his or her lifetime, or with his body after death. Some of the earliest examples are provided by St Augustine, and reflect contemporary practice in North Africa. In that rich account of saints' cults, chapter 8 of the final book of Augustine's *City of God*, he describes how a Spanish priest called Eucherius was brought back from the dead (they were already 'tying up his thumbs') when his own tunic, which had been laid on a shrine of St Stephen, was laid over his prostrate body;[74] a nun living near another shrine was similarly cured.[75] Oil from yet another shrine of St Stephen, at Augustine's natal town of Hippo, served to cure the son of Irenæus the tax collector.[76] A blind woman was cured by pressing to her eyes flowers that had merely been briefly touched by a bishop who was bringing a relic of St Stephen to another North African town.[77]

Paulinus of Nola has left us a fascinating description of the way visitors to the tomb of St Felix created holy oil by pouring oil through two holes in an upper slab above the coffin and scooping it out from the bottom.[78] In the later middle ages, the miraculous production of holy oil was a feature of the shrine of St William at York Minster.[79] Even dust from the tomb of a martyr

[72] *Symeonis Historia Regum, continuata per Johannem Hagustaldensem*, cap. 10; *Sym. Op.*, ii. 305.

[73] See below, p. 137.

[74] *De Civitate Dei*, xxii.8; *CCSL*, xlviii, 822. English translation in Augustine, *The City of God against the Pagans*, 7 vols., vii (books xxi–xxii), trans. W. M. Green, Loeb Classical Library (Cambridge, Mass. and London, 1972), 232–3.

[75] *De Civitate Dei*, xxii.8; *CCSL*, xlviii, 823; trans. Green, 236–7.

[76] ibid.

[77] ibid., xxii.8; *CCSL*, xlviii, 821; trans. Green, 232–3.

[78] Paulinus of Nola, *Carmina*, XXI (*Natalicium* No. 13); *CSEL*, xxx. 177 (lines 586–95). English translation in Paulinus, *Poems*, 173–201, at 192–4. See the section 'Holy Oil', in Crook, *Architectural Setting*, 28–31 for this and other examples.

[79] See below, pp. 247–8.

was heavy with power. In the later middle ages such dust was frequently employed to create sanctified water, a contact relic two stages removed from the primary relic of the saint's body. Gregory of Tours records that his elder brother, Peter the Deacon, was cured by means of dust that had settled around the tomb of St Julian of Brioude.[80] Gregory recounts how people were cured of epidemics by infusions of water left over from the annual Eastertide cleansing of St Martin's tomb.[81] In the late twelfth century increasingly dilute potions of St Thomas's water, originally infused with his blood, were said to be effecting miracles at Canterbury.[82]

In the Church of Rome, the use of contact relics provided the answer to local reluctance to disturb the bodies of martyrs. Many of the classic examples date from the late sixth century, when Pope Gregory the Great strove to maintain, or perhaps regain, control over the major Roman cults. One of the best-known cases is Gregory of Tours's famous description of the way pilgrims to the tomb of St Peter used to lower pieces of cloth on strings down the shaft above the grave. These were left overnight and when they were drawn up next morning it was believed that they had actually become heavier with the weight of the power (*uirtus*) that they had soaked up. Creating secondary relics in such a way was the preferred, essentially Roman option, as Pope Gregory had explained in his famous letter to the Empress Constantina in 594. To obtain a relic for the consecration of a church, Roman practice was to place a cloth on a holy body; these *brandea* were considered to have acquired as much holiness as the actual body of the saint. Indeed, it was recalled that in the time of Pope Leo certain 'Greeks' had doubted the efficacy of such contact relics: the Pope had cut one of the cloths and blood had oozed out.

It may be suspected that Pope Gregory was at least partially motivated by notions of self-interest: by refusing to dismember Rome's prestigious holy remains, the papacy could maintain control over their cults. To emphasise the point still further, Gregory had, as we have noted, pointed out to Constantina the dangers of disturbing the graves of saints: the tomb of St Lawrence had accidentally been opened, and those who had seen the holy body, even though they had not touched it, had died within ten days.

But the consequence of the exclusive attitude practised by Rome was a duality in the treatment of holy relics which persisted throughout the middle ages. In the Carolingian period, when Charlemagne looked to Rome for inspiration, new architectural forms would emerge which were inspired precisely by the desire to avoid disturbance to saintly remains—in contrast with practice in Merovingian Francia, where elevation and fragmentation had become the rule. Such influences affected the form that shrines would take in England. Here, centres inspired by Rome, notably Canterbury, tended

[80] Greg. Tur., *VJ*, cap. 24; *MGH, SRM*, i. 562–84, at 575. The dust around the tomb is also mentioned in ibid., caps. 33 and 46a; pp. 578, 582.
[81] Greg. Tur., *VM*, ii.51, ii.34: *MGH, SRM*, i. 626, 640.
[82] P. A. Sigal, 'Naissance et premier développement d'un vinage exceptionnel: l'eau de saint Thomas', *Cahiers de Civilisation Médiévale*, 44 (2001), 35–44.

to adopt a more conservative approach to their relics. This conservatism perhaps goes right back to the time of St Augustine: when Mellitus, Justus, Paulinus, and Rufinianus arrived in Canterbury as reinforcements in the conversion of southern England, they brought with them 'relics of the holy apostles and martyrs' that Pope Gregory had provided for the consecration of the new churches,[83] and these must have been contact relics.

THE PSYCHOLOGY OF RELIC CULTS

So far in this chapter I have focused on the official establishment of saints' cults, the way Church leaders promoted local saints and used their relics as a focus when establishing churches and setting up altars. As we shall see, this institutional character remained an abiding feature of the cult of saints; despite the best efforts of hagiographers, the impetus for initiating a new saint's cult came from churchmen rather than the church congregations. This is an aspect of such cults which has been explored in some detail by Peter Brown, who has aptly characterised bishops who established local saints' cults as 'impresarios'.[84] As we shall see, the term has a particular relevance in the cults of Merovingian Francia and those deriving from it, notably the medieval cults of England.

But the success of the cult of saints was undoubtedly the way it appealed to the hearts of those who were drawn to the graves and relics of saints. The cult of relics seems to have met a very basic human need. Contact relics may be considered as holy 'comfort objects': items which in a mysterious way retain the presence of their original owner. Just as a child clings to a scrap of blanket or a dog in kennels is calmed by an item of its master's clothing, so on a higher spiritual plane the faithful drew solace from objects which had touched the body of a saint.

EARLY PILGRIMAGE

If a body remained relatively undisturbed, the saint's powers could not be widely distributed, and people wishing to venerate the saint would have to make a journey in order to reach the grave. Such people became known as 'pilgrims' from the Latin *peregrinus*, a word itself deriving from *per* plus the locative case of *ager*, literally meaning 'one who travels through the fields', and by extension a traveller in (or from) foreign lands.

The first examples of such special journeys, 'pilgrimages', were not specifically to the graves of saints, but to the biblical sites of the eastern Mediterranean. Interest in places associated with the life of Christ began with St Helena, mother of Constantine the Great, and was vigorously promoted by Bishop Eusebius of Caesarea from whose episcopate we have

[83] Bede, *HE*, i.29; ed. Colgrave and Mynors, 104–5.
[84] Brown, *Cult of Saints*, 10, 30, 38, 67.

the first written account of a pilgrimage to Jerusalem, by the 'Bordeaux Pilgrim', in 333. At the end of the century an anonymous nun, subsequently identified as 'Egeria', travelled from her convent on the Atlantic coast, in Spain or Gaul, to the holy places.[85] The account she wrote in debased Latin for her fellow sisters back home has partially survived, and provides an insight into the preoccupations and interests of an early pilgrim.[86] She visited, for example, the site of the 'tomb of Moses' on Mount Nebo,[87] and related how an altar and a church had been erected over the 'tomb of Job' at Carneas, 'that the body should rest under the altar';[88] she described a *martyrium* over the 'entire body' of St Thomas the Apostle at Edessa;[89] she also gave a vivid description of the Holy Week ceremonies at Jerusalem, centred around the greatest contact relic of all, the empty Tomb of Christ.[90]

Not all churchmen shared Egeria's enthusiasm. In an attack on those who abused the Jerusalem pilgrimage, Gregory of Nyssa enquired in somewhat sceptical vein what advantage there could be in visiting such places;[91] quite different was the attitude of St Jerome, who, in a letter written *c.*392–3 on behalf of Paula and Eustochium to the Roman noblewoman Marcella, emphasised the special sacredness of the tomb of Christ, making a specific link between the cult of saints and the primary cult: '... everywhere in the world we venerate the tombs of the martyrs, and hold their holy ashes to our eyes or, if we may, kiss them—then how can anyone think we should neglect the tomb in which they placed the Lord!'[92] In 404, following the death of the aristocratic Roman widow Paula, St Jerome recalled having witnessed her fervent response on entering the Tomb of Christ during a tour of the Holy Land nineteen years previously. 'As for that very place where the body of the Lord had been placed, as if her thirst had been quenched by the water she had so long desired, she smothered it with kisses.'[93]

At the same time it is clear from contemporary descriptions that on the feast-days of saints people were flocking to the cemeteries in order to visit the graves and their associated *memoriæ*. In Rome, for example, Prudentius

[85] The evidence for Egeria's homeland is found in a letter by a seventh-century Galician monk, Valerius, who tells us that she was 'a native of the Ocean's western shore'. See *Egeria's Travels*, trans. J. Wilkinson, 3rd edn. (Warminster, 1999), p. 177.

[86] *Itinerarium Egeriæ: Peregrinatio Ætheriæ*, ed. O. Prinz (Heidelberg, 1960), 20; *CCSL*, 175 (*Itineraria et alia Geographica*), 27–90. English translation in *Egeria's Travels*, trans. Wilkinson.

[87] *Itinerarium Egeriæ*, 12.1; trans. Wilkinson, 121.

[88] ibid., 16.5; p. 129.

[89] ibid., 17.1; p. 130.

[90] ibid., 30.1–41; p. 151–9.

[91] Gregory of Nyssa, *Epistola* II ('On those who go on pilgrimage to Jerusalem'); *Pat. Grec.*, xlvi. cols. 1009–16.

[92] Jerome, *Epistolæ*, xlvi.8: *CSEL*, liv. 338: ... *martyrum utique sepulchra ueneramur et sanctam fauillam oculis adponentes, si liceat, etiam ore contingimus: et monumentum, in quo dominus conditus est, quidam æstimant neglegendum?*

[93] Jerome, *Epistolæ*, cviii.9 (*Ad Eustochium, Epitaphium Sanctæ Paulæ*); *CSEL*, lv. 306–51, at 315: ... *et ipsum corporis locum, in quo domino iacuerat, quasi sitiens desideratas aquas, fide, ore lambebat.*

described how '... with equal ardour patricians and the plebeian host are jumbled together, shoulder to shoulder, for the faith banishes distinctions of birth'.[94] As already noted, the cemeteries were located outside the towns, usually along the roads leading to the countryside, so a journey of at least a short distance was necessary. Thus the idea that a journey was involved when visiting a cult centre was established at an early date.

Likewise in the late fourth century, individuals were already resorting to saintly tombs in expectation of a cure or in the hope of begetting children. The first examples seem to be from the East. In another letter about Paula's experience, addressed to her mother, the lady Eustochium, in the form of a funeral eulogy, St Jerome recalled the younger noblewoman's experiences at Sebaste during a tour of the Holy Land in 385. There Paula had witnessed the horrifying noises and contortions of demoniacs in front of the saintly tombs: 'She saw devils moaning under the influence of various torments, and before the tombs of saints she heard men howling like wolves, barking like dogs, roaring like lions, hissing like snakes, bellowing like bulls; some with their heads thrown back, touching the ground behind them with the tops of their heads, women hanging by their feet without their dresses slipping over their faces.'[95] Jerome's account prefigures by seven centuries the lurid tales of literally colourful cures wrought at English centres such as Worcester, where 'St Wulfstan's water' caused one young sufferer to vomit 'a large quantity of multicoloured worms' (*diuersis coloris et quantitatis uermes*).[96] At around the same time as Jerome, St John Chrysostom was preaching sermons on the saints and urging his congregations to visit shrines.[97]

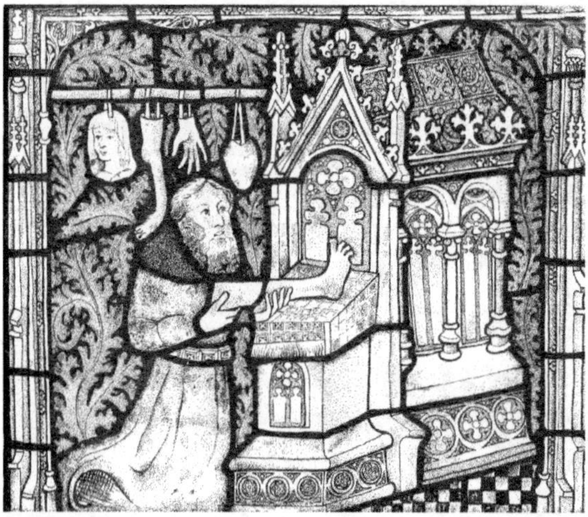

PLATE 1.4 YORK MINSTER, THE FIFTEENTH-CENTURY 'ST WILLIAM WINDOW'
A man presents an ex-voto to the shrine, in the form of a wax model of his leg.

Even fragmentary relics could work a cure, according to Gregory of Nazianzus.[98] Likewise Theodoret of Cyrrhus listed the benefits expected by people who visited martyrs: those who were healthy prayed to retain their health; the

[94] Prudentius, *Peristephanon*, poem XI, lines 199–202; *Pat. Lat.*, lx. cols. 275–596, at 552–3, discussed in Brown, *Cult of Saints*, 42–3.
[95] Jerome, *Epistolæ*, cviii.13; *CSEL*, lv. 306–51, at 323: *Namque cernebat dæmones uariis rugire cruciatibus et ante sepulchra sanctorum ululare homines luporum uocibus, latrare canum, fremere leonum, sibilare serpentum, mugire taurorum, alios rotare caput, et post tergum terram uertice tangere, suspensisque pede feminis uestes non defluere in faciem.*
[96] *Miracula Wulfstani*, Durham Cathedral Library, MS B.iv. 39b, i.20; ed. Darlington, 127–8.
[97] St John Chrysostom, 'Homily to St Ignatius, Martyr'; *Pat. Grec.*, l. 587–96, at 595–6. Idem., 'Homily on Martyrs'; ibid., cols. 661–6, at 664–6.
[98] *Contra Iulianum*, i.69; *Pat. Grec.*, xxxv. col. 589.

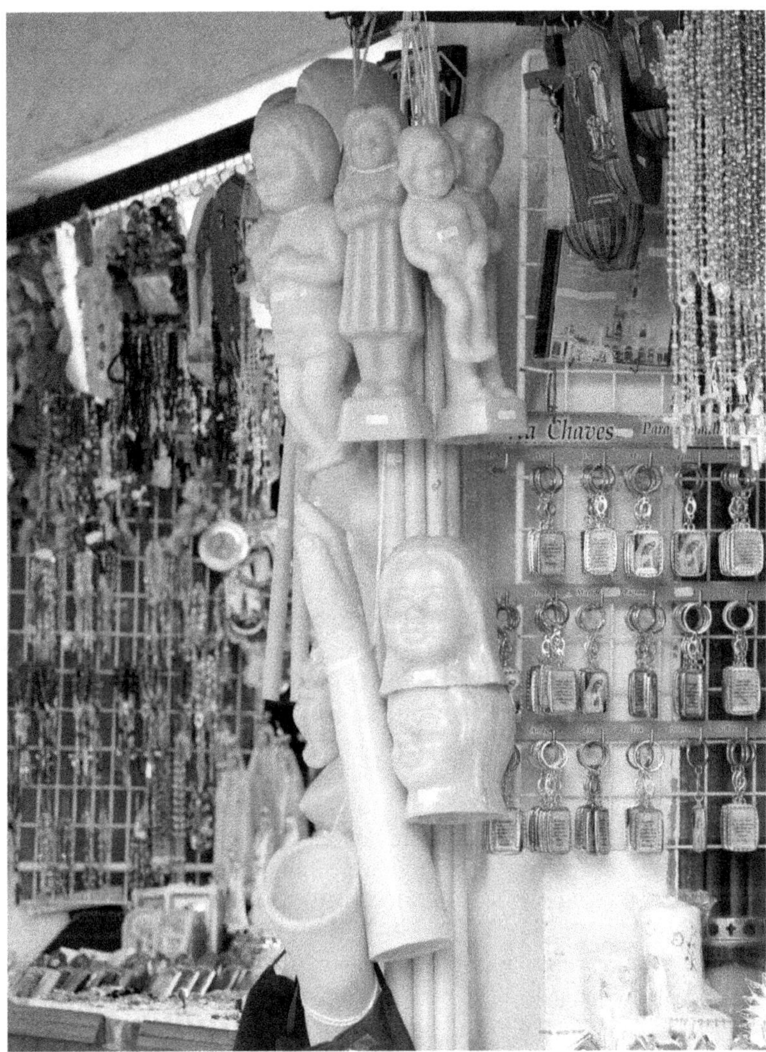

PLATE 1.5
PORTUGAL
Ex-votos on sale for presentation to the shrine of Our Lady of Fatima.

sick asked to be cured. Those without children asked martyrs to grant them; those who had children prayed that they should keep them.[99] He also mentions another interesting feature, ex-votos: silver or gold models of affected parts, such as eyes, feet, or hands;[100] for Theodoret these were the symbols of cures accomplished rather than hoped for. The use of ex-votos had simply been adopted from pagan religious practice, and Gregory of Tours comments on a 'temple' at Cologne where the local 'barbarians' used

[99] Theodoret, *Græcarum affectionum curatio*, *Sermo* viii ('On Martyrs'); *Pat. Grec.*, lxxxiii. cols. 775–1152, at 1031–2.
[100] ibid.

to adore the idols, placing wooden models of parts of the human body whenever some part of their anatomy was touched by pain.[101] From time to time attempts were made to curb the practice, and at the Council of Auxerre in the late sixth century an injunction about the proper keeping of saints' days included the clause 'nor let anyone dare to make feet or images of men out of wood'.[102] Such pronouncements fell on deaf ears, and similar ex-votos may still be seen at Continental shrines, where dismembered dolls represent the diseased limbs of petitioners to the saint. References abound to the practice in England: in the late twelfth century Adam of Yarmouth is said to have sent to the shrine of St William in Norwich Cathedral a 'candle' which was as tall and wide as himself, and therefore might be considered as a crude representation of his body,[103] and people were still sending large numbers of wax models to Our Lady of Walsingham on the eve of the Reformation.[104] Over two thousand images in silver or wax of human body parts were noted at the tomb of St Thomas Cantilupe of Hereford.[105] The St William window (*c.*1415) at York Minster depicts a man offering a full-size wax leg,[106] and silver ex-votos in the shape of various body parts were recorded in around 1509.[107] Gerald of Wales cites the case of a knight called Milo, who developed a horrifyingly swollen arm after blood-letting, presumably an infection. The doctors despaired of a cure, but he implored the help of St Hugh of Lincoln and was cured; he then went to the tomb where he left an accurate wax model of his arm (*formam brachii sui curati de cera expressam et effigiatam*).[108] One of the miracles of St Osmund concerns a man who was instructed in a vision to offer a wax bust at the tomb of the saint in order to cure a serious injury incurred while playing sport.[109] Some of these objects have survived. At Exeter Cathedral in 1943 a cache of wax ex-votos deposited at the tomb of Bishop Edmund Lacey (1420–55)—subject of a local cult, but never canonised—was discovered amongst debris on top of the choir-screen which rises above the monument: they included human feet and fingers, and animal legs and hooves, and the figure of an entire woman; attached strings suggested they were intended to be hung up.[110] More recent silver ex-votos stamped out of metal are displayed in the Pitt-Rivers Museum in Oxford. At Fatima in Portugal wax breasts, hands, legs, and other body parts bearing a notable resemblance to a scene from the St William window

[101] Greg. Tur., *VP*, cap. 6, *De Sancto Gallo*, para. 2; *MGH, SRM*, i. 681.

[102] *The Conversion of Western Europe 350–750*, ed. J. N. Hillgarth (Englewood Cliffs NJ, 1969), 97–9 at 97.

[103] Thomas of Monmouth, *Miracula Willelmi Norwiciensis* v.19; *The Life and Miracles of St William of Norwich*, ed. A. Jessopp and M. R. James (Cambridge, 1896), 210–11.

[104] *Letters relating to the Suppression*, ed. Wright, 138.

[105] R. C. Finucane, *Miracles and Pilgrims* (London, 1977), 98, citing Vatican, MS Latin 4015.

[106] For ex-votos see also Sumption, *Pilgrimage*, 157.

[107] See below p. 280.

[108] Adam of Eynsham, *Magna Vita*, iii.5. *Gerald of Wales*, vii. (ed. J. F. Dimock), 81–147, at 142–3.

[109] Malden, *St Osmund*, 71–2.

[110] U. M. Radford, 'The Wax Images found in Exeter Cathedral', *Antiq. J.*, 29 (1949), 164–8.

are bought by today's pilgrims at stalls just outside the sanctuary. At Copacabana, a Marian shrine on the shores of Lake Titikaka (Bolivia), the ex-votos are of a more worldly form: models of expensive cars or opulent houses bear witness to the material aspirations of the donors.

BURIALS 'AD SANCTUM'

It was not just the living who sought proximity to a saintly tomb. Just as the aim of the devout was to get as close as possible to a holy body, so too early Christians sought to bury their loved ones *ad sanctum*: close to a saint. We have already seen that St Ambrose arranged to be buried next to Gervasius and Protasius, but numerous grave inscriptions proclaim that humbler churchmen and ordinary laymen aspired to the same privilege.[111] The epitaph on a grave in the cemetery of SS. Paulinus and Maximinus at Trier vividly demonstrates the hoped-for advantages of such burial: 'The bones of Ursinus the sub-deacon rest under this tomb, who deserved to be associated with the burials of the saints, and whom neither the fury of Hell not the fierce punishment will harm.'[112]

A few random examples of early burials *ad sanctum* must suffice here. Lupus ('Saint-Loup'), bishop of Sens (†623) was buried 'at the feet of St Columba', legendary patroness of the monastery (his body was discovered in 1160).[113] St Eustella, a princess who had been baptised by Bishop Eutropius of Saintes, was buried beside her patron.[114] St Paulinus of Nola buried his own son, Celsus, only a week old, near to the martyrs Justus and Pastor at *Complutum* (Alcalá de Henares, Spain), 'so that with the blood of the saints close by he may sprinkle our souls when they are in the fire after death'.[115]

FROM MARTYR TO CONFESSOR

The Peace of the Church that resulted from Constantine's edict of toleration in 313 meant an end to martyrdom; in theory at least, for sporadic persecutions and political murders were responsible for later martyrs. But in the fourth century the concept of sainthood was being extended to 'confessors': people who had lived exemplary lives but who had died naturally.[116] The earliest saints of this category were the great bishops and fathers of the Church, such as St Basil (†379), St Ambrose (†397), St Martin

[111] Crook, *Architectural Setting*, 14–16 for further examples and references.
[112] Le Blant, *Inscriptions*, i. 396.
[113] *Vita Lupi Episcopi Senonici*, cap. 26; *MGH*, *SRM*, iv. 176–87, at 186.
[114] *AASS*, *Aprilis III*, 735E.
[115] Paulinus of Nola, *Carmina*, XXI, lines 607–10; *CSEL*, xxx. 329; this translation from Paulinus, *Poems*, 309–29, at 329. The poem concerns another young Celsus, who had died at the age of eight. For the martyrs of *Complutum* see Prudentius, *Peristephanon*, poem IV, lines 41–4; *Pat. Lat.*, lx. cols. 275–596, at 364.
[116] The most complete study of the implications of the words 'martyr', 'confessor', remains Hippolyte Delehaye's *Sanctus*.

of Tours (†397), and St Jerome (†420). Soon many more saintly bishops, ascetics, scholars, and virgins would be added to the sanctoral. Their cults were indistinguishable from those of the martyrs who in earlier days had died for their faith. The point was well made by the seventh-century author of the Life of St Audoenus of Rouen (Saint-Ouen):

> And just as the martyrs of Christ in the time of the persecution … poured forth their precious blood in the name of Christ, so too this man, in a time of peace when the persecution had stopped, urged himself on as a fiery soldier and, being very famous for his faith, he earned the palm of a martyr by emulation.[117]

Similarly in the twelfth century the compiler of the *Liber Eliensis* applied to St Æthelthryth the concept of 'bloodless martyrdom': had she lived in the time of Nero or Diocletian she would undoubtedly 'have climbed up on to the torturers' rack of her own accord'.[118]

Some confessors certainly seem to have earned their place in the ranks of the saints through narrowly escaping actual martyrdom, such as St Victricius of Rouen, whose biography is known from a letter written to him in 397–8 by Paulinus of Nola.[119] A one-time Roman soldier, he had thrown down his weapons on the parade ground, and declared for Christ; he was flogged and condemned to death. As Victricius was on his way to this fate the executioner was struck blind. Victricius's bonds miraculously fell off; the official ordered to execute him was converted. But sufferings for Christ could be self-imposed. The pillar saints, the most famous of whom is St Symeon Stylites (†459), achieved sanctity (admittedly in the Eastern rather than Western Church) through bodily privations and mind-boggling discomfort; and St Symeon attracted large crowds who regarded him as a saint during his lifetime. Later even chastity was considered a sufficient suffering to qualify appropriately born people for the sainthood, such as virgins, usually of royal blood, who had refused sexual relations with their husbands, and espoused a second career as abbesses. Inevitably, the extension of the sanctoral ran the danger of devaluation, and one suspects that in the high middle ages some bishops were sanctified more to enhance the prestige of their successors than as a result of any special holy virtues on their own account.

There were thus many ways a person could become recognised as a saint. In the following chapter we shall examine further the way in which the sanctity of Christendom's holy dead found expression in the physical setting of their earthly remains.

[117] *Vita Audoini Episcopi Rotomagensis*, cap. 6; *MGH*, *SRM*, v. 536–67, at 557. This translation from Fouracre and Gerberding, *Merovingian France*, 157. *Et velut persequutionis tempore martyres Christi, agentibus tyrannis […] pro Christi nomine pretioso sanguine fuderunt, ita et hic in pacis tempore, desinente persequutione, ipse sibi fervidus milis instinterat; confessione præclarus, martyrii palmæ consectando promeruit.*

[118] *Liber Eliensis*, i.12; ed. Blake, 29: *sine cruore martyrium*.

[119] Paulinus, *Epistula* 18, 'To Victricius', para. 7; *CSEL*, xxix. 128–37, at 133–5. English translation, in Paulinus, *Letters*, vol. 35, 167–77 at 172–5.

2

GRAVES, SHRINES, AND CRYPTS

The physical setting of saints' cults on the Continent

In the previous chapter we saw how the major saints' cults of the Christian West were initially located at the site of their undisturbed graves. This was the 'Roman custom', as Pope Gregory later called it, blaming 'the Greeks' for the development of what he viewed as an undesirable habit of disturbing saintly relics. For a time other parts of Western Christendom conformed with the Roman model. It is however clear that, with the exception of Rome itself, where conservatism long prevailed, new practices were emerging around the 370s and particularly during the century after that. Holy graves were increasingly being opened and saintly bodies dismembered to provide relics, allowing the saint's cult to be more widely disseminated. Nevertheless, the resting place of the greatest part of the body would normally have the pre-eminence: thus Milan could proudly claim possession of Gervasius and Protasius, even though relics of those saints were widely distributed soon after their discovery, even reaching Rouen within a very short time.[1]

These developments are apparent in England's earliest cult, that of St Alban, whose long and involved history we shall trace throughout this book. In 429 Germanus, bishop of Auxerre, later to be elevated to the sainthood himself, visited Alban's grave. According to Bede, the bishop opened the martyr's grave (*sepulchrum*), placing within it 'limbs of saints (*membra sanctorum*) that had been gathered from various regions'; presumably not from Rome, for Bede's choice of the word *membra* seems to indicate that primary relics in the form of major bones were involved, which would have been contrary to Roman practice. In the early twelfth century the monks of St Albans claimed that Germanus had given them

[1] Above, p. 10.

'relics of the twelve Apostles and of several martyrs', and Abbot Richard provided a new chest or *feretrum* to house them.[2]

The events of 429 seems to prefigure the decidedly non-Roman practices that characterised the majority of English saints' cults from the end of the seventh century. The meaning of the word *sepulchrum* is crucial: the fact that Germanus was apparently able to 'open' the 'sepulchre' without any sort of exhumation may perhaps indicate that the grave was already marked by a *memoria*, constructed over it, and that this monument, rather than the grave itself, was what Germanus actually opened.[3]

SAINT-MAKING IN SIXTH-CENTURY GAUL

The main influences on the physical expression of saints' cults in early medieval England were to come from Gaul, more specifically from the northerly kingdoms of the Merovingian Franks, collectively known as 'Francia', so to understand English cults we must first look across the English Channel. Francia was a region which, with a few exceptions, lacked martyrs, but Church leaders made up for this deficiency by creating new cults of local bishops. First of these was St Martin, the former Roman soldier popularly remembered for cutting his cloak in half to share it with a beggar. He had left the Roman army in 356, and within about fifteen years was bishop of Tours, a post that he held until his death in 397.[4] His holiness was recognised even during his lifetime, attracting an important pilgrim, Sulpicius Severus, in 393–4. A friend of Paulinus of Nola, Sulpicius was the wealthy owner of a late Roman estate somewhere in Aquitaine, at a place called *Primuliacum*.[5] His visit to Tours seems to have been a life-changing experience. Hitherto he had lived like a late Roman aristocrat. Now he renounced the world, and by 396 had completed a Life of Bishop Martin, taking as his exemplar a *Vita* of St Anthony written by Athanasius *c.*375. This text was evidently available to Sulpicius in a Latin translation by his contemporary the bishop and writer Evagrius of Antioch (†392 or later).[6] Sulpicius's saintly biography of Martin (which cannot strictly speaking be defined as 'hagiography', as it was completed a year before the death of its subject) was to establish a pattern for saints' *vitæ* throughout the middle ages.[7]

[2] *GA*; ed Riley, i. 69–70: ... *Abbas Ricardus fecit thecam unam, quam 'feretrum' appelamus, aureis imaginibus redimitam; in qua recondidit Duodecim Apostolorum reliquias, et Martyrum plurimorum, quas Sanctus Germanus, Autissiodorensis Præsul, in sepulcro Sancti Albani reverenter collocavit.*

[3] See below, p. 45.

[4] The date is disputed, but Clare Stancliffe argues in favour of 397: Stancliffe, *St Martin*, 111–33.

[5] For the location of *Primuliacum*, a Latin name which would have developed into 'Prémillac' (or 'Prémilly' if it was in the *langue d'oïl* region), see ibid., 30. Clare Stancliffe argues that it was somewhere west of Toulouse.

[6] Evagrius's translation is printed in *Pat. Lat.*, lxxiii, cols. 125–70.

[7] For both Martin and Sulpicius, see Stancliffe, *St Martin*.

Much of our knowledge of saints' cults during the sixth century derives from a later bishop of Tours, Gregory. He was born in around 538, probably in the Auvergne, and amongst his family connections he could boast several influential, aristocratic churchmen who were eventually recognised as saints—as he was himself. Born Georgius Florentius Gregorius, he presumably took his name from his maternal great-grandfather, St Gregory, bishop of Langres from 506 to *c*.539. An uncle on his mother's side was Nicetius (St Nizier), bishop of Lyon (552–73). Gregory's paternal uncle was Bishop Gallus of Clermont (525–51), and his father's family claimed descent from Vettius Epagatus, one of the forty-eight Christians martyred at Lyon in AD 177.[8] Saints were thus in Gregory's blood. In 565 he made a pilgrimage to the shrine of St Martin, as we know from a passage in his Life of that saint,[9] and eight years later he himself became bishop of Tours. During his twenty-year episcopate he wrote a number of important works on the cult of saints. As well as biographies of St Martin and of St Julian of Brioude, and a Life of the Fathers (*Vita Patrum*), he composed *In Gloria Martyrum* (The Glory of the Martyrs), and *In Gloria Confessorum* (The Glory of the Confessors), and a History of the Franks (*Historia Francorum*). Gregory died in about 594.

Gregory of Tours's writings are marked by an intensely personal interest in saints' cults. As an adolescent he had been cured of a serious illness at the tomb of St Illidius (Allyre) of Clermont, another former bishop.[10] He records in *De Virtutibus Sancti Martini* no fewer than six personal cures at the tomb of St Martin, including relief from fevers, from a sore throat caused by a fish-bone, and from a swollen tongue; this was cured when he stuck it through the wooden bars of the screen around the tomb.[11] In his *Historia Francorum* he relates how St Martin had saved him from drowning when an overloaded boat began to sink,[12] and elsewhere he recalls how during a visit to Dijon he was cured of an eye complaint by water sanctified by contact with a stone on which St Benignus had allegedly been tortured.[13]

Gregory was writing at a time when the physical setting of saints' cults was undergoing change. Some of the saintly bodies that interested him were still in their original locations, and several lay in late Roman burial-chambers or hypogea, to which pilgrims could obtain limited access. But by the end of the sixth century such structures were evidently going out of fashion, and saint-making in Gaul was evolving into a new pattern, with important architectural consequences. Typically a bishop would decide to give greater prominence to a local saint; the body would therefore be

[8] M. Heinzelmann, *Gregory of Tours* (Cambridge, 2001), 10–22. Gregory names forty-five of the martyrs in *GM*, cap. 48.

[9] Greg. Tur., *VM*, i.32; *MGH*, *SRM*, i. 603.

[10] idem, *VP*, cap. 2, *De Sancto Illidio Confessore*, para. 2; *MGH*, *SRM*, i. 668–72, at 670.

[11] idem, *VM*, i.32; *MGH*, *SRM*, i. 603. Ibid., ii.1 (pp. 608–9); ibid., ii.60 (pp. 629–30); ibid., iii.1 (p. 632); ibid., iv.1–2 (pp. 649–50).

[12] idem, *HF*, viii.14; *MGH*, *SRM*, i. 333.

[13] idem, *GM*, cap. 50; *MGH*, *SRM*, i. 523.

transferred, usually to a prestigious position behind the high altar of the principal church. Here the cult of St Martin of Tours provided an exemplar: in 472 Perpetuus, bishop of that city, had constructed a new basilica over the saint's grave, and St Martin's body had been moved into the apse of the enlarged church.[14]

By Gregory's day such elevations were more common. When he visited Vienne to see the relics of the martyr St Ferreol, he learned that when Bishop Mamert rebuilt the church there, he had exhumed three sets of relics. The incorrupt body of St Ferreol was identified by the fact that the burial included the head of St Julian of Brioude, which according to local tradition had been placed in the same *sepulchrum* so the two saints could lie together.[15] Not all saints were willing to be elevated however: St Quintinian of Rodez was rebuked by his deceased predecessor, St Amantius, when he moved his body to a new church dedicated to that saint (now Saint-Amans).[16] A fifth-century marble sarcophagus in Rodez Cathedral is claimed as that of the saint. Early in the sixth century Bishop Gregory of Langres had elevated the body of St Benignus of Dijon, by that date revered as a third-century Christian martyr. But now Bishop Gregory was to become a saint himself. His son, Tetricus, who had succeeded him as bishop in 539, was evidently responsible for creating the cult, thus continuing a chain of saint-making typical of the period (Tetricus was in turn later regarded as a saint after a long episcopate of thirty-three years). The church of St John was inadequate as a cult setting, and Tetricus added an apse to its east end as a more suitable location for his father's body. Gregory of Tours relates in some detail how it had been possible to form the apse outside the church before the east wall was pierced, and how a new arch had been formed, linking the new apse to the pre-existing building.

> Because the blessed pontiff had been buried in a corner of the basilica, and it was a restricted space, people were unable to get in there as their devotion required, St Tetricus, his son and successor, seeing these things and witnessing miracles happening there, laid a foundation in front of the altar of the basilica [i.e. outside the east end where the altar was located], constructed an apse, and vaulted it over with wonderful workmanship. Once it was vaulted, and the wall broken through, he constructed an arch. When everything was completed and decorated, he excavated a *loculus* in the middle of this apse, and desiring to translate the body of the holy father there he convened priests and abbots to this duty, who, keeping vigil, prayed that the blessed confessor

[14] idem, *HF*, x.31; *MGH*, *SRM*, i. 444. Bishop Perpetuus 'pulled down the earlier basilica which Bishop Brice had erected over St Martin, and built another of great size and wondrous workmanship, into whose apse he translated the blessed remains of that venerable saint'.

[15] idem, *VJ*, cap. 2; *MGH*, *SRM*, i. 562–84, at 564–5.

[16] idem, *VP*, cap. 4, *De Sancto Quintiano*, para. 1; *MGH*, *SRM*, i. 673–7, at 674.

> would allow himself to be transferred into this new dwelling. The next morning, singing psalms, they translated the sarcophagus into the apse which the blessed bishop had built.[17]

This unusually detailed account suggests that the saint's sarcophagus was at least partly submerged in its new position below the floor of the apse (Tetricus had to excavate a *loculus* to receive it). Frequently, though, larger and presumably more opulent monuments were provided, which rose up above pavement level. Thus, towards the end of the sixth century, Avitus, bishop of Clermont († after 592) moved the bones of his distant predecessor St Illidius (†*c.*385) from a restricted and inaccessible vault (*cripta*) into the splendid new 'apse' which he had built around it (*in circuitu*). Avitus discovered the bones in a coffin of wooden planks (*capsa tabulis formata ligneis*); he took them out, wrapped them in a shroud, and placed them 'as was the custom' (*iuxta morem*) in a sarcophagus.[18] The vault was then filled up and the sarcophagus placed at higher level (*altius*), presumably above its original location. Another of Gregory of Tours's contemporaries, Bishop Palladius of Saintes, elevated the remains of the first bishop of the diocese, St Eutropius (Eutrope), placing the 'holy ashes in the place that he had prepared'.[19] Likewise, St Gallus, who had died in around 640 at Arbon in Switzerland, was buried 'between the altar and the wall' within the oratory of one of his hermitages. Some forty years later, after the first sepulchre had been damaged by Germanic invaders, Bishop Boso of Constance replaced the remains in a 'worthy sarcophagus' in the same location, constructing a *memoria* over it.[20] The town of Saint-Gall developed around the cult centre.

LITERARY CONVENTIONS

Gregory's writings demonstrate an awareness of the literary conventions that were beginning to accumulate around saints' cults. A few miraculous elements appear in his accounts, but they are not as repetitious as in later hagiography, where conformity with standardised routines was understood as confirming the authenticity of the saint. Yet Gregory must surely have been aware of the story of the translation in 415 of the relics of St Stephen,

[17] idem, *VP*, cap. 7, *De Sancto Gregorio Episcopo*, para. 4; *MGH, SRM*, i. 686–90, at 689–90: *Cum beatus pontifex in angulo basilicæ fuisset sepultus, et parvus esset locus ille, nec ibi populi sic possent accedere, ut devotio postulabat, sanctus Tetricus, filius et successor eius, hæc cernens et virtutes ibidem assidue operari prospiciens, ante altare basilicæ fundamenta iacet, erectaque absida, miro opere construit et transvolvit. Qua transvoluta disruptoque pariete, arcum ædificat. Quod opus perfectum atque exornatum, ut in medio absidæ loculum fodit, ubi corpus beati patris transferre volens, convocat presbiteros et abbates ad istud officium; qui vigilantes orabant, ut se beatus confessor ad hanc præparatam habitationem transferri permitteret. Mane autem facto, cum choris psallentium adprehensum sacofagum ante altare in absidam, quam beatus episcopus ædificaverat, transtulerunt.*

[18] idem, *VP*, cap. 2, *De Sancto Illidio Confessore*, para. 4; *MGH, SRM*, i. 668–72, at 671.

[19] idem, *GM*, cap. 55; *MGH, SRM*, i. 526.

[20] *Vita Galli, auctore Wettino*, ii.36; *MGH, SRM*, iv. 277.

which would set the pattern for 'invention' narratives,[21] just as Sulpicius's Life of St Martin, compiled some twenty years earlier, had set the pattern for saintly biography.

This seminal event was claimed to have been recorded at the time by a priest called Lucian in an encyclical letter 'to every church about the revelation of the bodies of Stephen the first martyr and others', written in Greek *c.*AD 415 and subsequently translated into Latin by Avitus of Braga and relayed to posterity by the holy biographer Gennadius of Marseilles (†*c.*496).[22] Lucian was dozing in bed when an old man, with a long beard and dressed in white robes marked with golden crosses, and shod in gilded boots, appeared and struck him with a golden wand uttering his name three times. He revealed himself as Gamaliel, who, according to the *Acts of the Apostles*, had instructed St Paul in the Faith. The saintly visitor told Lucian to go to Jerusalem and instruct a certain 'Bishop John' to seek out the bodies of St Stephen, Nicodemus, and indeed Gamaliel himself, all of whom had been buried at Gamaliel's villa at Caphar Gamala. In some doubt about the authenticity of the vision, Lucian had to be told the same message three times before visiting the bishop. After further set-backs a simple-minded monk revealed the site of the grave; at this point Bishop John sent for other Church leaders, and finally the saint's coffin (*theca*) was revealed. There was an earthquake, a wonderful smell as though of paradise, and seventy-three sick people were cured on the spot.

Then, 'with psalms and hymns they carried the relics of most blessed Stephen to the holy church of Sion where he had been ordained archdeacon; leaving to us [at Caphar Gamala] a few small pieces from the saintly limbs, albeit great relics, namely earth with dust which had absorbed all his flesh; they carried away the rest'.[23]

As Michael Lapidge has emphasised, Lantfred, the author of the first translation account of St Swithun in the late tenth century, was undoubtedly familiar with Lucian's *Epistola*.[24] But such repetition began over four centuries previously. If we now look at Gregory of Tours's account of the case of St Ursinus, the parallels are not hard to perceive.[25] Ursinus was the first bishop of Bourges, apostle to that city, sent by 'disciples of the apostles'. Initially he was buried among the tombs of other people. The graveyard became redundant and a vineyard was planted on top of it. Many years later, in the 540s, Ursinus appeared in a dream to Agustus, abbot of the church of Saint-Symphorien, near Bourges; he asked to be exhumed and led him to the grave.

[21] The parallel is discussed in detail in Lapidge, *St Swithun*, 12–13.

[22] *Epistola Luciani ad omnem æclesiam de revelatione corporis Stephani martyris primi et aliorum*; *Pat. Lat.*, xli. cols. 807–18.

[23] ibid., para 8; col. 815: *Et tunc cum psalmis et hymnis portaverunt reliquias beatissimi Stephani in sanctam ecclesiam Sion, ubi et archidiaconus fuerat ordinatus: dereliquentes nobis de membris Sancti parvos articulos, imo maximas reliquias, terram cum pulvere, ubi omnis ejus caro absumpta est, cætera asportaverunt.*

[24] Lapidge, *St Swithun*, 13–14.

[25] Greg. Tur., *GC*, cap. 79; *MGH, SRM*, i. 796–8.

Agustus in turn informed Bishop Probianus, who showed no interest in the search. Then Bishop Germanus of Paris came to stay with Probianus: Ursinus obligingly appeared in a dream to both bishops. Germanus and Agustus went to the designated spot next night and discovered the incorrupt body. They told Probianus what they had seen. Abbots and clergy were assembled and psalms were sung whilst the *sepulchrum* was raised. This was presumably a stone sarcophagus, and the men carried it on bars (*vectes*): but these were so long that when they arrived at the church porch they could not get through the door. Germanus invoked the aid of Ursinus. The sarcophagus became so light that a few of the men could carry it by hand without the bars. After the celebration of mass Ursinus was buried next to the altar while the people rejoiced, and many miracles subsequently occurred.

Gregory's account of the discovery of the relics of St Mallosus of Birten in the late sixth century follows a somewhat similar pattern: there Bishop Eberigisilus († before 614) had constructed a church whose apse enclosed the saint's oratory, though it was not certain where Mallosus had been buried. The location of the body was miraculously revealed to a deacon who came to Birten and, though he had never been there before, told the bishop where to excavate. As noted in Chapter 1, a miraculous odour indicated the presence of the saint, and on digging further down the intact body was discovered.[26]

Needless to say, the development of such hagiographical commonplaces makes the interpretation of the physical setting of saints' cults more difficult; it is to Gregory's credit that in most cases he relates directly what he had observed without recourse to *topoi*.

SAINTLY SARCOPHAGI

It is likely that some of the stone sarcophagi which, in several of the cases related by Gregory, were provided for the saints were reused Roman ones. Several examples of such *spolia* are known to have housed the remains of saints. At Aire-sur-Adour (Landes) the body of St Quiteria (Sainte-Quitterie) reposed in a fine Roman marble sarcophagus, and this is still displayed in the crypt of the church dedicated to her; the body of St Lusor (Saint-Ludre) was similarly enshrined in a Roman sarcophagus which survives in the south-east crypt of the church of Saint-Étienne, Déols (Indre). Gregory of Tours almost certainly saw this actual sarcophagus, characterising it as 'a tomb wonderfully sculpted in Parian marble' in his book *In Gloria Confessorum*.[27] The sarcophagus is pagan, adorned with hunting scenes, but this evidently did not worry those who reused it for the saintly burial. In England, the body of St Æthelthryth was similarly rehoused at Ely, after her elevation in 695, in a 'beautifully made sarcophagus of white marble' which the monks of the double monastery had dug up from the Roman cemetery

[26] Greg. Tur., *GM*, cap. 62; *MGH, SRM*, i. 530.
[27] idem, *GC*, cap. 90; *MGH, SRM*, i. 805–6.

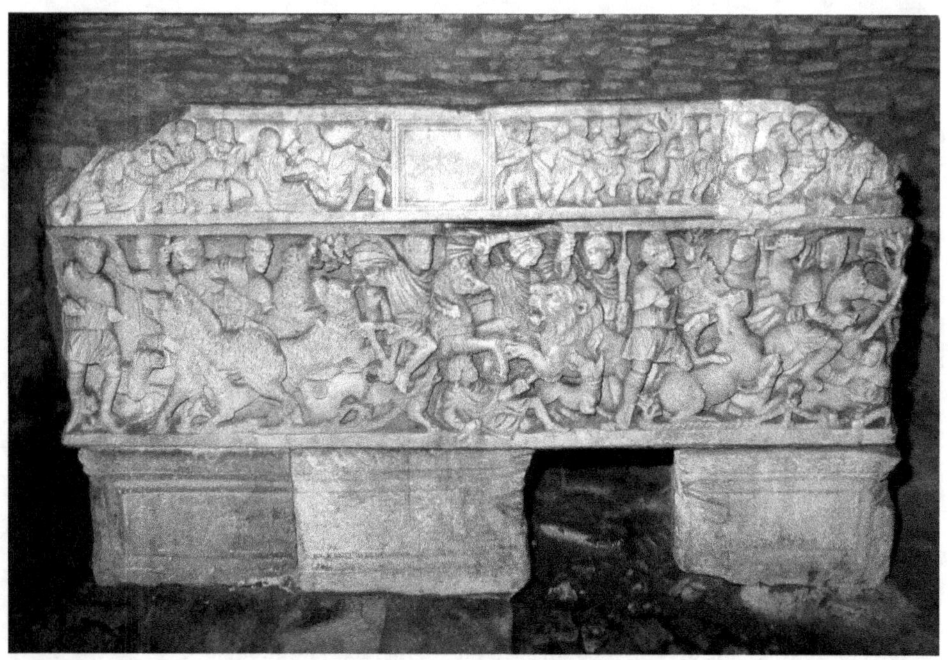

PLATE 2.1
DÉOLS (DEPT. INDRE, FRANCE), ÉGLISE SAINT-ÉTIENNE
The supposed tomb of St Lusor, a reused Roman sarcophagus.

outside Cambridge.[28] The reused Roman coffin of St William of York is now displayed in the crypt of York Minster. A Roman lead funerary coffer was used to hold the remains of St Eanswyth of Folkestone, described below.[29]

A single coffin was insufficient for the kind of monument which was envisaged for St Radegundis of Poitiers following her death in 587: her body, packed in spices, was placed in a wooden coffin (*capsa lignea*) that was itself placed within a larger stone monument made by removing one side from each of two normal-sized sarcophagi and joining them together.[30]

The description of Radegundis's new tomb shows that a simple coffin was by that date beginning to be considered inadequate as a worthy setting for a new saint, and it is likely that larger monuments were already being created to contain the bodies of saints, possibly including a superstructure above the actual coffin or at least some kind of monument built around it. Indeed, Gregory's description of the resting place of St Martin suggests that Perpetuus had provided a structure of some sort around the saint's sarcophagus, for Gregory relates that, when he was cured of a headache there, he 'came out of the tomb, cured'.[31] There are other indications that at this

[28] Bede, *HE*, iv.19; ed. Colgrave and Mynors, 394.
[29] pp. 68–70.
[30] Greg. Tur., *GC*, cap. 104; *MGH*, *SRM*, i. 816.
[31] idem, *VM*, ii.60; *MGH*, *SRM*, i. 630: ... *sanus recessi de tumulo.*

period the graves of saints were being enclosed within or surmounted by suitable monuments. At Clermont, for example, Gregory tells us that the tomb of St Venerandus was placed beneath what he called an *analogium*, a term used by a number of hagiographers to denote a structure created over a grave.[32] According to Gregory, '... when someone decides to put his head into a small window over the tomb and prays for what his situation requires, soon, if he has made a just petition, he obtains a result'.[33] The arrangement seems to prefigure Bede's account of the tomb of St Chad (†672) at Lichfield, discussed in the following chapter.[34] The tomb of St Julian of Brioude, was covered by a tall monument with a screen (*cancellus*) around it; it stood in a church which Bishop Illidius (Allyre) seems to have built to replace a small structure which Gregory of Tours calls a *cellula*.[35] The *cancellus* is mentioned in a miracle story about the attempted theft of a cross studded with jewels that had been placed on the monument on the saint's feast-day. Having hidden in the church at night, the thief jumped over the screen (*super cancellum beati sepulchri cursu prosilit rapido*) and went back to his corner bearing his stolen goods.[36] He was foiled (presumably through the power of the saint) when the sacristan saw a glint of light from one of the jewels.

The earliest monuments constructed to mark the translated remains of saints (or sometimes merely erected over their tombs) appear to have been quite simple affairs. Only occasionally were they more richly decorated. A forerunner of the sumptuous monuments which became a commonplace in the following century was the tomb of the mid-fifth-century bishop of Saintes, St Vivian. In one of his poems Venantius Fortunatus described how it had been embellished in the mid-sixth century by a rich aristocratic lady called Placidina, who had raised over it a gleaming silver superstructure (*argentea tecta*) incrusted in gold, with vivid representations of wild animals, presumably in repoussé work.[37]

SAINT-MAKING IN SEVENTH-CENTURY FRANCIA

The saintly bishops of the sixth century whose activities are chronicled by Gregory of Tours had been the product of the Gallo-Roman aristocracy, wealthy villa-dwellers who passed their days writing elegant poetry and

[32] C. de Fresne, *Glossarium mediæ et infimæ Latinitatis*, new edn., 10 vols. (Niort, 1883–7), i. 238, cites uses of the term at Verdun and Saint-Riquier.
[33] Greg. Tur., *GC*, cap. 36; *MGH, SRM*, i. 770–1: *Est ibi et sepulchrum ipsius sancti Venerandi episcopi a quo hæc ædes nomen accepit, sub analogio conpositum, super quod per fenestellam quique vult inmittit, precans quæ necessitas cogit, obtenitque mox effectum, si iuste petierit.*
[34] See pp. 64–5.
[35] Greg. Tur., *VJ*, caps. 5–9; *MGH, SRM*, i. 562–84, at 566–9.
[36] ibid., cap. 20; p. 573.
[37] Venantius Fortunatus, *Carmina*, bk. i, no. 12, *De basilica S. Bibiani*, lines 15–19; *MGH, Auctores Antiquissimi*, vol. iv, pt. i, *Venantii Fortunati Opera Poetica*, ed. F. Leo (Berlin 1881), 14: *sacra sepulchra tegunt Bibiani argentea tecta,| unianimis tecum quæ Placidina dedit.| quo super effusum rutilans intermicat aurum| et spargunt radios pura metalla suos;| ingenio perfecta novo tabulata coruscant| artificemque putas hic animasse feras.*

perhaps brooding on the decline of the Roman Empire and the approach of Germanic invaders. St Paulinus of Nola was an exception, who surprised his contemporaries by his apparent retreat from the world. Such men had become bishops because of who they were rather than what they did. Their successors in the seventh century on the other hand were increasingly political appointees, men connected with the Merovingian court and enjoying royal patronage; their appointment to bishoprics reflected their political influence and power.[38] The elevation to the sanctoral of these seventh-century bishops may be seen as the posthumous continuation of political patronage by members of the Merovingian royal families and nobility. Indeed, there was sometimes a price to pay for political allegiance, as in the case of the seventh-century bishops Leodegar of Autun (St Leger, †679) and Præjectus of Clermont (Saint-Prix, †676), who were murdered for political reasons and were regarded as martyrs. A further twist to the story of St Leodegar is the fact that he was put to death by a faction which included two other future Frankish saints, Audoenus of Rouen (Saint-Ouen) and Eligius of Noyon (Saint-Éloi). Furthermore, some members of the royal family, notably females, themselves became saints through their association with the abbeys that they founded.

Take, for example, the case of Balthildis (St Bathild). She was a slave-girl from 'across the sea' given in marriage to King Clovis II of Neustria by the mayor of the palace, Erchinoald. It is likely that she was of noble birth, as hinted in the *Liber Historiæ Francorum*, and that she was an Anglo-Saxon.[39] She acted as regent for her son, Clothair III, then retired to the monastery that she had founded at Chelles, where she died in 680. She was also an important benefactress of the abbey of Faremoutiers-en-Brie. As we shall see in the following chapter, the links between this abbey and those in Anglo-Saxon England may have played a part in the transmission of Frankish patterns of saintly veneration to England.

Such royal patronage was reflected in the increasing opulence of the monuments enclosing the saintly remains. For in the seventh century it became fashionable to decorate the monuments of saints more elaborately than the modest structures described by Gregory of Tours. Previously decoration was restricted to lavish textiles on the walls surrounding the tomb and over the tomb itself. Gregory gives many examples: at the tomb of St Martin, a woman was cured from a haemorrhage by wiping her ears and eyes on the pallium,[40] in a clear parallel to the cure of the woman with an issue of blood in the Gospels,[41] and people were similarly cured simply by touching the cloth covering the remains of St Nicetius of Lyon.[42] Gregory tells us, too, that it was impossible to cover the close-huddled tombs

[38] For this period, see especially Fouracre and Gerberding, *Merovingian France*.

[39] ibid., 97–104.

[40] Greg. Tur., *VM*, ii.10; *MGH*, *SRM*, i. 612.

[41] Luke, 8:43–8.

[42] Greg. Tur., *VP*, *De Sancto Nicetio Lugdunensi Episcopo*, cap. viii, para. 12; *MGH*, *SRM*, i. 701.

(*coniunctis sarcofagis*) of the companions of St Martial of Limoges with pallia as the faithful desired until the burials miraculously moved apart, ending up next to the opposite walls of the chamber.[43]

A key monument in the history of the development of shrines is the structure built to enshrine the remains of St Fursey (or Fursa/Furseius), one of a group of Irish missionaries who were established in the monastery of Lagny and at Péronne in northern France by Erchinoald, mayor of the Neustrian court. Fursey died at Péronne in around 650 (the date is uncertain). When his body was elevated four years later it was found to be miraculously incorrupt and giving off a marvellous smell. The text known as the *Virtutes Sancti Furseii* describes the creation of his monument, which the author calls a 'little house' (*domuncula*):

> All those present, filled with great joy, took up his body with great rejoicing and buried it on the right-hand side of the altar of the prince of the apostles (St Peter). There he remained buried for four years where many miracles were displayed. Meanwhile the *domuncula* was being prepared into which after as many years the body was translated by the illustrious bishops Eligius, Autberthus, and Medardus. And so at that time he was discovered to be incorrupt, as if he had only just left his body. There with great perfumes they cover the clear limbs; and there many miracles shine forth through the merits of the saint.[44]

Elsewhere in the *Virtutes* we learn that Bishop Eligius had 'diligently wrought the sepulchre of the venerable St Fursey with his own hands'.[45] Eligius (St Eloy), Apostle to the Belgians, and patron saint of metalworkers, was bishop of Noyon at the time of Fursey's translation. He was an immensely important figure in the development of shrines and reliquaries. His biographer, Bishop Audoenus of Rouen, attributed to him 'notable sepulchres … and many others besides' and, above all, 'a sepulchre of marvellous workmanship in gold and gems for blessed Martin of Tours', the tomb of St Briccius (Brice), and 'the mausoleum of St Denis of Paris, and a monument (*tugurium*) over that tomb, marvellously made in gold and jewels'. The writer concludes that 'he so exercised his craft … that he created almost every fine piece of ornamental work in Gaul'. In these activities he was supported by Queen Balthildis who, after his death in 659,

[43] idem, *GC*, cap. 27; *MGH, SRM*, i. 764–5.

[44] *Virtutes S. Fursei*, cap. 22; *MGH, SRM*, iv. 440–9, at 448: *Cuncti adstantes, gaudio magno repleti, elevaverunt corpus cum magna exultatione et condiderunt dextra parte altaris apostolorum principis, ubi conditum iacuit annis quattuor, ubi et multa patuerunt miracula. Interim parabatur domuncula, in qua post tot annos ab inlustribus viris Elegio, Autberto et Medardo episcopis translatum est. Sicque tunc inventum est inlesum, quasi eadem hora migrasset e corpore. Ibi cum odoribus magnis clara tegunt membra; ibi et virtutes multæ clarescunt per merita sancti.*

[45] ibid., cap. 24; p. 449: *sanctus Dei vero Elegius diligenter fabricavit manibus venerabilis sancti Fursei sepulchrum.*

provided for him a sumptuous monument of the kind he had himself created for the earlier saints.[46] Needless to say, miracles at the tomb were not slow in coming.

In the past scholars have had difficulty with the notion that a bishop might really have created works of art with his own hands, suggesting that Eligius was merely the patron of the works rather than the actual artificer. Of course this may be partly true; the role of the bishop, given his early training, might have been that of an overseer of workshops creating a product with which he was familiar. But several later examples of such versatility may be cited: according to the Evesham Chronicler, Abbot Mannig (or Manny) was the greatest craftsman of his time, producing a shrine of gold, silver, and gems, which eventually housed the relics of St Ecgwine.[47] St Dunstan, too, was renowned as a metalworker though only the most credulous would accept the tongs displayed at Mayfield church, said to be those with which he seized the devil by the nose. That anecdote was recounted by Osbern, precentor of Canterbury, but it occurred at Glastonbury, not in Sussex. According to Eadmer, 'He so excelled in the arts of writing, of painting, of sculpting whatever he wished in wax, wood, or bone, and of casting in gold, silver, iron, or bronze, that he was held in great admiration by many people.'[48] Æthelwold, abbot of Abingdon (and later bishop of Winchester), is said to have been 'a great builder of churches and other buildings', who personally worked on the construction of the new church at Abingdon.[49] Eadfrith, later bishop of Lindisfarne, is said to have copied and illuminated the Lindisfarne Gospels.

The novel nature of monuments such as the shrine (and we may at last use this term) of St Fursey proved a linguistic challenge to contemporary writers, who fell back on vague expressions like 'little house' (*domuncula*) or 'cottage' (*tugurium*). What the terms do suggest is that the structure was gabled, a shape presumably deriving from Roman sarcophagi. The shrine of St Dionysius (Saint-Denis), more or less contemporary with that of Fursey, was evidently also covered by an arrangement resembling a pitched roof. Gregory of Tours tells us that, during an Austrasian incursion in 574, a soldier climbed on to the top of the monument in order to try to seize a golden dove. His feet slipped and he appears to have landed painfully astride the roof: *compressis testiculis*, he stabbed himself in the side and was found lifeless. In the light of this description it is interesting that a late, possibly twelfth-century, example of this type of integrated shrine, consisting of a substantial monument enclosing the reliquary, has survived in France in the

[46] *Vita S. Eligii*, ii.41; *MGH, SRM*, iv. 725.

[47] *Evesham Chronicle*, 86–7, discussed in C. R. Dodwell, *Anglo-Saxon Art* (Manchester, 1982), 65ff. See below, pp. 105–6.

[48] *Vita S. Dunstani*, cap. 7; Eadmer, *Lives*, 50–159, at 59.

[49] Wulfstan, *Vita Æthelwoldi*, cap. 15; ed. Lapidge and Winterbottom, 28. See also *Chronicon Monasterii de Abingdon*, ed. J. Stevenson, 2 vols., RS, 2 (1858), i. 344; which simply says that he 'built' (*construxit*) the church there, without hinting at personal activity.

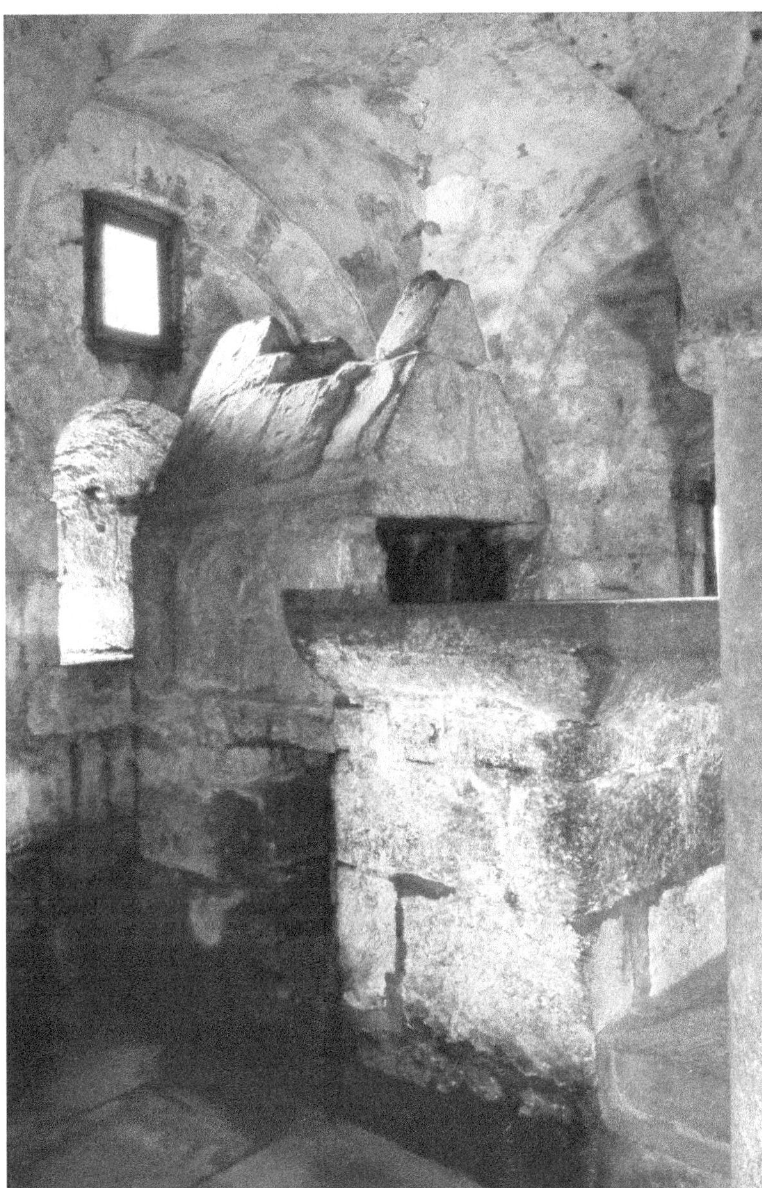

PLATE 2.2
AHUN
(DEPT. CREUSE,
FRANCE),
ÉGLISE SAINT-
SYLVAIN
The shrine of
St Sylvanus, the
titular saint.

crypt of the church of Saint-Sylvain at Ahun (Creuse).[50] Another example is found nearer home: the twelfth-century shrine of St Melangell (Monacella), at Pennant Melangell (Powys).[51]

[50] Crook, *Architectural Setting*, 276–7.
[51] See below, pp. 166–9.

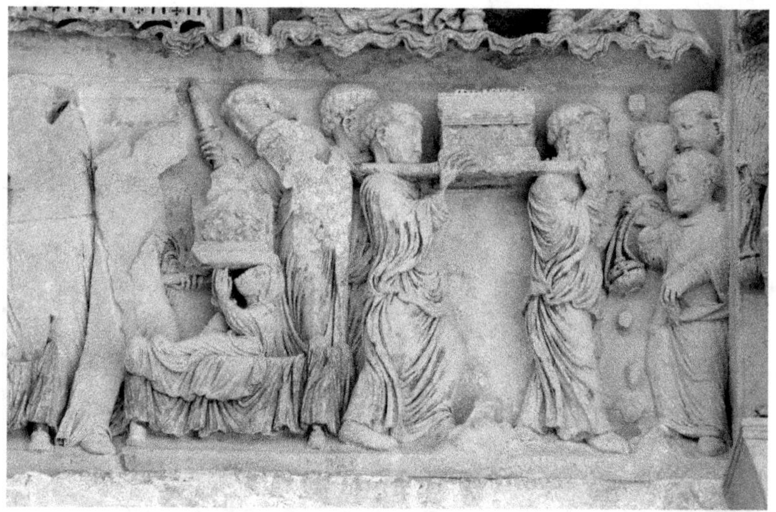

PLATE 2.3 SAINT-BENOÎT-S/LOIRE (DEPT. LOIRET, FRANCE), ABBAYE DE FLEURY
A thirteenth-century bas-relief frieze above the north door, portraying the ceremonial arrival (adventus) of St Benedict's relics.

THE *INVENTIO* AND *ADVENTUS* OF ST BENEDICT

In the examples cited above, the creation of a new saint was a domestic affair, undertaken typically by his successors. Another type of saint-making was beginning to emerge by the late seventh century: the commandeering of relics of holy men by a distant community, usually in the face of opposition from the locals. The translation of the relics of St Benedict of Nursia from Monte Cassino to Fleury-sur-Loire in the seventh century was of crucial importance. All the *topoi* established at this time were employed by the compiler of his *translatio*, the Fleury monk 'Adalberht' two hundred years later.[52] The monastery at Monte Cassino, where the relics lay, had been destroyed by the Lombards; Abbot Mummulus of Fleury sent a team led by Aigulf (Abbot of Lérins, and a future saint, †*c.*676) on a mission to claim the bodies of Benedict and his sister St Scholastica. The monks stopped off in Rome then continued to Monte Cassino, where, following hints provided by an old man, the graves revealed themselves by means of a marvellous light. Then, pursued both by the pope and the Lombards, the monks made their escape; they were saved by a miraculous fog. Miracles occurred along the route: a man's sight was restored and a paralytic was able to stand again, and when they reached Fleury another blind man was miraculously able to see again.

The arrival at Fleury is presented like the triumphal return, the

[52] *Historia Translationis SS. Benedicti et Scholasticæ in Galliam, auct.* Adalberto; *AASS, Martii III*, 302–5. Adalberht is perhaps identical with Adrevald, the better-known author of Benedict's *miracula*.

adventus, of a Roman emperor.[53] This treatment is perhaps prefigured by Victricius's arrival at Rouen with Roman relics, but the *adventus* of St Benedict's remains was on a far grander scale. Crowds of monks and the entire population of the Orléans region came to meet the party,[54] and with great joy and rejoicing they reached the monastery. At first Abbot Mummolus was uncertain where the saintly remains should be placed: but a miraculous shaft of light made it clear to the community that God had chosen the church of St Mary for this purpose.[55]

SAINTS' CULTS AND THE CAROLINGIAN RENAISSANCE

With the establishment of the dynasty of the Pippinids, later known as the Carolingians, new ways of housing local saints evolved in France and indeed throughout the empire. The Carolingians looked towards Rome, consciously regarding themselves as the inheritors of the Roman tradition, and the early Christian architecture of Rome was a major influence on ecclesiastical architecture north of the Alps from the mid-eighth century onwards.[56]

The most important manifestation of this new Roman influence was the diffusion of the 'ring-crypt'. This novel solution to the problems of organising pilgrim movement around the body of a saint had first been devised at St Peter's, Rome, almost certainly by Pope Gregory the Great in around 600.[57] At St Peter's the supposed grave of the Prince of the Apostles was buried deep underground, at the geometrical centre of the western apse of the basilica that Constantine the Great had constructed in the early fourth century, and beneath a high altar which itself appears to have incorporated the cut-down remains of the second-century monument (*ædicula*) marking the burial place of the saint. Pope Gregory's builders inserted a platform into this apse, raising the altar higher; the platform incorporated a curved passage running around the inner face of the apse, with a straight passage that returned eastwards from the apex. This allowed pilgrims to walk around the apse in order to approach the grave from the west.

The innovative design evidently proved successful, and was taken up in the Roman church of St Pancratius (S. Pancrazio) when it was reconstructed under Pope Honorius I (625–38). But the great resurgence of interest in the form occurred from the eighth century, with similar ring-crypts in Rome at S. Crisogono (usually dated to the papacy of Gregory III (731–41) and, during the early years of the following century, at S. Cecilia and S. Prassede

[53] For the concept of *adventus* see A. Thacker, 'Cults at Canterbury: Relics and Reform under Dunstan and his Successors', in Ramsay, *St Dunstan*, 221–45, at 227–31.
[54] *Historia Translationis SS. Benedicti etc.*, cap. 2; *AASS, Martii III*, 304B: … *agmina monachorum cum plebe territorii Aurelianensis obuiam eis processerunt …*
[55] ibid., cap. 3; pp. 304F–305B.
[56] Crook, *Architectural Setting*, 80–134.
[57] ibid.

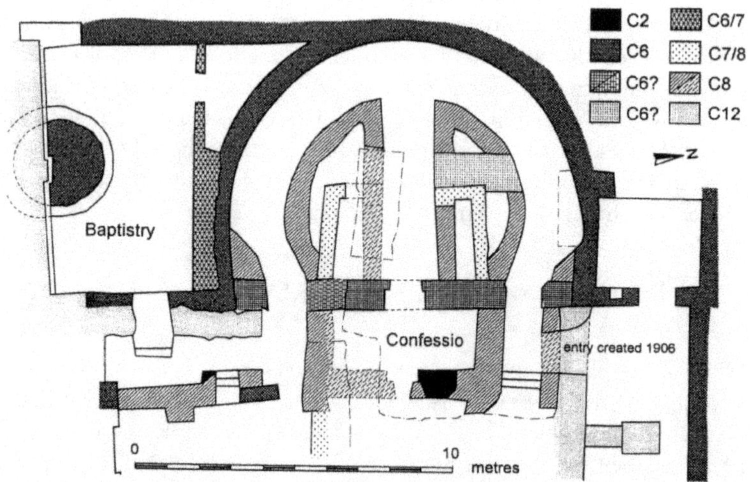

FIG. 2.1
ROME,
CHURCH OF SAN CRISOGONO IN TRASTEVERE
The eighth-century ring-crypt, derived from that of St Peter's basilica.

(both built by Pope Pascal I (817–24)), at S. Marco (Gregory IV, 827–44), S. Martino ai Monti (Sergius II, 844–47), and at SS. Quattro Coronati and S. Stefano degli Abessini (Leo IV, 847–55).

Meanwhile similar ring-crypts were being constructed away from Rome, and the new enthusiasm for the design may have been two-way: the ninth-century Roman ring-crypts were themselves perhaps a product of the Carolingian renaissance. Two of the earliest examples are found in the Alpine regions, close to the main routes over the mountains from Italy: St Luzius's church at Chur, and Saint-Maurice d'Agaune. The latter example is particularly significant in that when it was remodelled in around 787, its orientation was changed to make it even more 'Roman'. By that date altars were normally located at the east end of churches, as is the norm today, but at Saint-Maurice the liturgical focus was moved to the west end. This meant that the church now conformed with early Roman exemplars, such as St Peter's, which had retained the ancient orientation. The western ring-crypt at Saint-Maurice accommodated the remains of St Mauritius, which had been brought to that settlement at the foot of the St Bernard Pass in the mid-fourth century.

The great ring-crypts of Rome and the derivatives constructed in Charlemagne's empire during the so-called Carolingian renaissance are perhaps the most obvious examples in the early middle ages of the architectural influence of saints' cults.[58] As we shall see in the following chapter, such influences were to extend across the English Channel, where they influenced the design of Anglo-Saxon churches housing cults of local saints.

[58] Other Continental examples are discussed and illustrated in Crook, *Architectural Setting*, 95–103.

3

'BUT LO! THERE BREAKS A YET MORE GLORIOUS DAY'

Saints' cults in early Anglo-Saxon England

Any account of saints' cults on these shores should rightly begin with England's proto-martyr, St Alban. Here Bede's dramatic portrayal of the martyrdom, in Book I of his *Ecclesiastical History*, is of strictly limited value,[1] apart from the light that it sheds on the cult in the author's own day. It must be remembered that Bede's story of the cult's origins was written at least as long after Alban's martyrdom as the period now separating us from the reign of Elizabeth I. The Jarrow historian relied mainly on a *passio* (martyrdom narrative) of the saint which survives in a ninth- or tenth-century manuscript in the Bibliothèque Nationale in Paris. Pre-dating Bede's source text is a rather different *passio* preserved in a manuscript at Turin. Professor Richard Sharpe has convincingly argued that both these texts were independently amplified from a much shorter version (known as 'E') whose origins were perhaps a copy made in the early fifth century of explanatory inscriptions, *tituli*, displayed within a basilica at Auxerre dedicated to the saint.[2] The existence of this church is attested as early as the ninth century;[3] it was thought to have been founded by Germanus, bishop of that city, whose visit to Alban's tomb in 429 is the earliest evidence we have for the cult of the saint.

Professor Sharpe's findings mean that little or no reliance can be placed on the extended versions of the *Passio* as evidence for the much argued

[1] Bede, *HE*, i.7, 18; ed. Colgrave and Mynors, 28–35 and 58–61.

[2] Sharpe, 'Late antique passion'. Sharpe's chronology is a reversal of that of the nineteenth-century philologist Wilhelm Meyer, for whom version 'E' (Excerpts) was an abridgement of the Turin Manuscript: W. Meyer, 'Die Legende des h. Albanus des Protomartyr-Angliæ in Texten vor Beda', in *Abhandlungen der Königlichen Gesellschaft der Wissenschaften zu Göttingen, Philologisch-Historische Klasse*, n.s., viii.1 (Berlin, 1904), a discussion and edition in parallel of the Turin and Paris *passiones* and 'E'.

[3] Sharpe, 'Late antique passion', 36, citing the *Gesta episcoporum Autissiodorensium*, para. 7, ed. L.-M. Duru, *Bibliothèque historique de l'Yonne* (Auxerre, 1850–63), 2, 315–21.

question of the date of Alban's death.[4] The Turin manuscript places his martyrdom under Septimius Severus (193–211) and was notably used by John Morris in an ingenious attempt at pinpointing the saint's execution to the specific date of 22 June 209,[5] but Morris's conclusions have been invalidated by Sharpe's new interpretation: text 'E' does not mention the name of the emperor at all. As for Bede, he employed a version of the *Passio* closer to the Paris manuscript, which likewise does not identify the emperor at the time of Alban's death. The dating of the saint's martyrdom to the early fourth century, which was thereafter adopted by medieval hagiographers and long persisted in the local traditions of medieval and post-medieval St Albans, appears to have been taken from the well-known Dark Ages text *De Excidio Britanniæ,* a homiletic work written by the British monk Gildas *c.*530–40. Gildas evidently did not have access to any firmer dating evidence than we possess today, for he merely conjectured (*ut conicimus*) that Alban and other British saints had been put to death during the persecution of Christians at the end of the reign of the emperor Diocletian (284–305).[6] In short, there is no good evidence for the date of Alban's martyrdom, and several modern historians, shunning the precision both of the Turin *Passio* and Bede, favour a vaguer, mid-third-century date, the period of the persecutions of the emperors Decius (250–1) and Valerian (257–9).[7]

Gildas was also the first authority to hint at the place of Alban's martyrdom, somewhat ambiguously referring to him as *sanctum Albanum Verolamiensem*. The phrase might be translated something like 'St Alban the man of Verulamium', but it is not clear whether Gildas used the epithet *Verolamiensis* because Alban was a citizen of that town or because that was where his cult was later practised. If we accept the legend, both were true. But Gildas makes it clear that neither he nor his fellow British Christians were able to visit the saint's grave, either because it was in a region occupied by 'barbarians' or perhaps because getting there involved crossing barbarian territory. He therefore lacked first-hand knowledge of the geography of Verulamium, and in his version of events Alban did not cross the river Ver on the way to his martyrdom but the Thames, whose waters miraculously separated like the Red Sea, allowing him to pass dry-shod.[8] Nor is further light shed on the matter either by text 'E' of the *Passio* or the expanded versions. All three are silent on the location of the martyrdom and grave, though it is true that the description of the topography of the martyrdom site given in the Turin version perfectly matches the geography of Verulamium. It seems accurately to describe the spatial relationship between

[4] For discussion, notes, and a bibliography of this thorny issue, see Biddle, 'Alban and the Anglo-Saxon Church'.
[5] J. Morris, 'The Date of Saint Alban', *Hertfordshire Archaeology*, 1 (1968), 1–8.
[6] Gildas, *De Excidio*, para. 10; ed. Mommsen, 31. An English translation is available: *Gildas, The Ruin of Britain and Other Works*, ed. and trans., M. Winterbottom (Chichester, 1978).
[7] For Charles Thomas, *Christianity in Roman Britain to A.D. 500* (London, 1981), 50: '... the middle of the third century is still the least improbable period'.
[8] Gildas, *De Excidio*, para. 11; ed. Mommsen, 31–2.

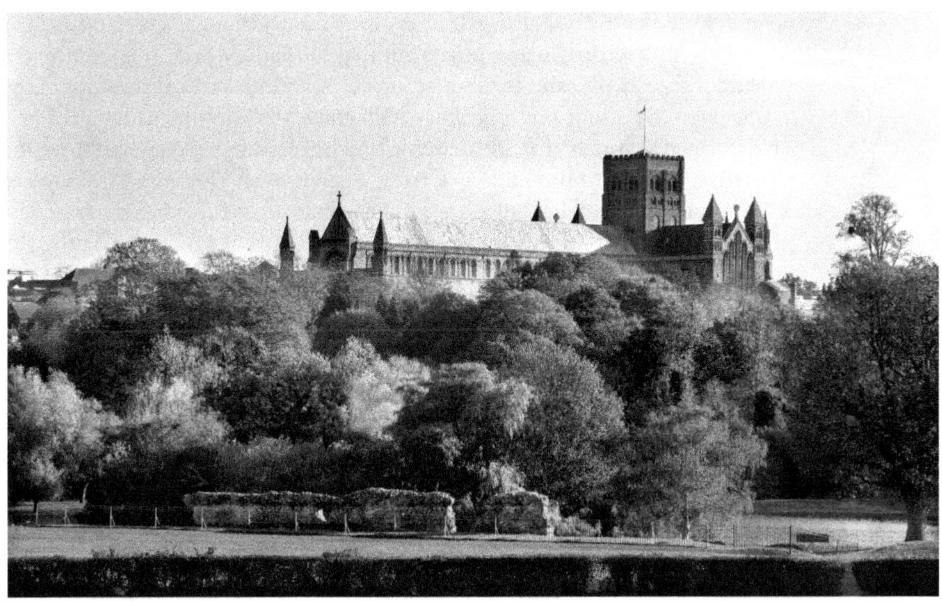

PLATE 3.1 ST ALBANS, THE PRESENT ABBEY CHURCH, built over the saint's legendary place of martyrdom, seen from Roman Verulamium, on the south side of the river Ver.

the Roman town and the hill opposite, over the Ver river crossing, where the cult was undoubtedly located several centuries later.

That Alban's grave was already the focus of a cult in the early fifth century is not in doubt. Famously, it was visited by Bishop (later Saint) Germanus of Auxerre (†446), probably in 429, an event briefly alluded to within a few decades by his biographer, Constantius of Lyon, who mentions that Germanus and Bishop Lupus of Troyes (†678) went to St Alban's tomb to give thanks for the success of their attempt to eradicate the Pelagian heresy from this land. Infuriatingly, Constantius does not say where the tomb was located.[9] Germanus's visit is also recorded in the 'E' version of the *Passio Sancti Albani*; indeed, Sharpe speculates that Constantius may have used 'E' for this part of his biography. The passage in 'E', copied in both the longer versions, relates how Germanus came to 'Alban's basilica';[10] there he was able to open the *sepulchrum* in order to add further relics which he had brought with him, and he took a lump of earth from the place where the martyr's blood had been spilt (not necessarily from the tomb itself).[11] One may

[9] *Vita Germani Episcopi Autissiodorensis, auctore Constantio*, cap. 16; ed. B. Krusch and W. Levison; *MGH, SRM*, vii.i (Hannover, 1919), 225–83, at 262: *sacerdotes* [*scil. Germanus ac Lupus*] *beatum Albanum martyrem, acturi Deo per ipsum gratias, petierunt.* See also W. Levison, 'St. Alban and St. Albans', *Antiquity*, 15 (1941), 337–59.

[10] 'Die Legende des H. Albanus', ed. Meyer, 44–5: ... *ad cuius basilica...* ('E' and 'T'); ... *ad eius basilica* ... ('P').

[11] ibid: *de loco ipso ubi martyris sanguis effluxerat massam pulveris rapuit.* Bede *HE*, i.18; ed. Colgrave and Mynors, 58–9. See W. H. C. Frend, '*Ecclesia Britannica*: Prelude or Dead End?', *Jnl. of Ecclesiastical History*, 30 (1979), 129–44.

speculate that he took this relic back to Auxerre, though Constantius does not say so. Richard Sharpe points out that the earliest known reference to a cult of the British saint in Germanus's see is a ninth-century account of the deeds of the bishops of Auxerre, which states that Germanus founded and dedicated a church of St Alban there: 'and he honourably disposed there the relics that he had brought back from England'.[12] A clod of earth may not seem much of a relic, but we have seen that thirty-three years previously Victricius of Rouen was able to justify bringing from Milan to his own city equally modest relics of SS. Gervasius and Protasius.[13]

Bede inferred, quite reasonably, that the basilica visited by Germanus, with its active cult, was a church still standing in his own day, a building 'of wonderful workmanship ... a worthy memorial of his martyrdom' that had been constructed 'next to the city of Verulamium' (*iuxta ciuitatem Uerolamium*). It is not clear from his ambiguous wording whether he believed the church stood over the place of martyrdom or the grave, though of course the latter proposition is more likely. Medieval writers subsequently supposed that the two sites were close together if not one and the same. Bede added that 'To this day sick people are healed in this place and the working of frequent miracles continues to bring it renown'.[14] Even though the earlier writers (the author of the 'E' version of the *Passio,* then Constantius, and later Gildas) failed to give the precise position either of the grave or the place of execution, it would be perverse to argue that the cult in the fifth century was located in a different place from that known to Bede's informant two centuries later. All the comparative evidence available from Continental exemplars points, indeed, to the focus of the cult being the alleged grave of the saint. Excavations carried out by Martin and Birthe Biddle have shown that the present abbey church lies just north of a Roman cemetery, and they have reasonably argued that St Albans was another example of the classic occupation pattern observed at cult sites such as Xanten and Bonn, where the cities actually changed location in response to saints' cults established in originally extramural graveyards. Thus, in all probability, when Bede was completing the *Ecclesiastical History* in around 730 the grave of St Alban had been a focus of continuous veneration since the late Roman period.[15]

The form of the *sepulchrum* opened by St Germanus is unknown. The term is often translated 'grave', which is misleading. The fact that (if we accept the testimony of the *Passio* and the implication of Constantius's allusion) the place where Alban's body was thought to lie was so obviously marked by a basilica 'of the saint' in the fifth century could indicate that the grave was further embellished by a monument within that church; the

[12] Sharpe, 'Late antique passion', 36.

[13] Above, pp. 10–11.

[14] Bede, *HE*, i.7; ed. Colgrave and Mynors, 34–5: *ecclesia ... mirandi operis atque eius martyrio condigna ... in quo uidelicet loco usque ad hanc diem curatio informorum et frequentium operatio uirtutum celebrari non desinit.*

[15] As argued by Biddle in 'Alban and the Anglo-Saxon Church'.

author's statement that Germanus opened the *sepulchrum* should perhaps not necessarily conjure up visions of grave-digging. The *sepulchrum* may have been an early variety of 'tomb-shrine': a *tropaion* with an altar-like structure over the actual grave and a shaft providing limited access to the relics below, the sort of structure postulated on archaeological evidence for the tomb of St Peter at the Vatican. However, the earliest, though admittedly dubious, evidence for a reliquary shrine of St Alban purports to date from after 793. In that year his earthly remains were said to have been rediscovered by King Offa of Mercia when he founded the religious community that was the forerunner of the medieval monastery; we will discuss this evidence in the following chapter.[16]

Bede's extensive treatment of the cult of St Alban should not blind us to the fact that other Romano-British cults may also have survived the Anglo-Saxon invasions. When Augustine reached Canterbury in 597 he found there a church dedicated to St Martin (†397), which, according to the Canterbury tradition relayed to us by Bede, had been built 'while the Romans were still in Britain'. This was arguably the present church of St Martin on the road to Sandwich.[17] Even so, Augustine had effectively to refound the church at Canterbury 'from scratch', as William Frend has written.[18] Bede does briefly mention the martyrdom of 'Aaron and Julius', and of 'many others of both sexes in various other places', again taking his information from Gildas.[19] The latter author was writing shortly before 547,[20] and he attributed to the emperor Diocletian the martyrdom not only of 'Alban of Verulamium' but also of 'Aaron and Julius, citizens of Caerleon, and the rest, of both sexes, who in different places stood their ground in the Christian contest'.[21] Within ten years of the end of these persecutions, Gildas adds, Christ's recruits (*tirones*) 'renewed the churches that had been razed to the ground, and founded, constructed, and completed the basilicas of the holy martyrs'.[22] But, as Richard Sharpe has pointed out, this statement is merely a reworking of a passage from Eusebius's *Ecclesiastical History*, and cannot be relied on at all as a report of what happened in England.[23]

The cult of Aaron and Julius at Caerleon, site of the Roman fortress of *Isca* (known to medieval chroniclers as the 'City of the Legions'), is attested

[16] Below, pp. 78–81.
[17] See above, p. 10.
[18] Frend, '*Ecclesia Britannica*', 129.
[19] Bede, *HE*, i.7; ed. Colgrave and Mynors, 34–5.
[20] But Thomas D. O'Sullivan, *The* De Excidio *of Gildas: its Authenticity and Date* (Leiden, 1978), argues for an earlier date of *c.*515–20 ±10 years, rather than the 'orthodox date' of shortly before 547.
[21] Gildas, *De Excidio*, para. 10; ed. Mommsen, 31: ... *sanctum Albanum Verolamiensem, Aaron et Iulium Legionum urbis cives ceterosque utriusque sexus diversis in locis summa magnanimitate in acie Christi perstantes dico.*
[22] ibid., para.12; ed. Mommsen, 32: *Renovant ecclesias ad solum usque destructas; basilicas sanctorum martyrum fundant, construunt, perficiunt, ac velut victricia signa passim propalant.*
[23] Sharpe, 'Late antique passion', 31.

in a charter of *c.*864 preserved in the *Book of Llandaff*, by which the *Merthir* (*martyrium*) of the two saints was granted a *territorium* on the south side of the river Usk.[24] The *martyrium* seems to have been located within the site of one of the three cemeteries of the Roman fortress, and may have been in existence well before that.[25] There is even some slight archaeological evidence for the church in the form of a fragment of 'a ninth-century sculptured cross slab' which turned up in the vicinity in around 1860. In the twelfth century the name of St Alban was added to the dedicatees when the church was granted to the newly founded priory at Goldcliff (five miles to the south of Caerleon), and the dedication to Alban seems subsequently to have eclipsed that to the other two martyrs.[26] The chapel at Caerleon was demolished at the Reformation, though its site—and, indeed, the original dedication to Julius and Aaron—was known to the antiquary William Camden;[27] today the only indication of its existence is the name of the site, 'Mount St Albans', a hill north-east of the modern town. A suggestion has been abandoned that one of several small chambers excavated in the entrances to the amphitheatre just outside the Roman fortress was a *cella memoria* to the two martyrs who perhaps met their deaths in the amphitheatre.[28]

Despite many uncertainties, Gildas's early testimony perhaps bears witness to the survival of a cult which may well go back to the mid-third century. The Roman fortress of *Isca* was destroyed at the end of that century and abandoned for about 250 years, apart from sporadic and small-scale civilian occupation.[29] Assuming, then, that the cult recorded by Gildas *c.*540 had a genuine basis in the martyrdom of two individuals who had been put to death for practising a prohibited faith, it must have started while *Isca* was still occupied by the Second Augustan Legion.[30] G. R. Stephens has noted that the martyrdom might not necessarily have taken place during one of the great persecutions, as Gildas believed; the practice of Christianity remained a capital offence until the early fourth century.[31] As to the identity

[24] *The Text of the Book of Llan Dâv*, ed. J. Gwenogvryn Evans and J. Rhys (Oxford, 1893), 225–6 and 377. Wendy Davies, *The Llandaff Charters* (Aberystwyth, 1979), 121, accepts the charter as genuine.

[25] J. K. Knight, 'Britain's Other Martyrs', in *Alban and St Albans*, 38–44; a reworking of the analysis by Levison in 'St. Alban and St. Albans', 333–44. For the site, see G. C. Boon, *Isca: The Roman Legionary Fortress at Caerleon, Monmouthshire*, 3rd edn. (Cardiff, 1972). The cemetery in question was on the south side of the river Usk, due east of the Roman fortress.

[26] Levison, 'St. Alban and St. Albans', 341–3. Knight, 'Britain's Other Martyrs', 41.

[27] William Camden, *Britannia* (London, 1586), 362, described the ruins of Isca, and stated that *Iacent hic duo nobiles, & post Albanum & Amphibalum præcipui Britanniæ maioris protomartyres, & ibidem martyrio coronati, Iulius, scilicet & Aaron, quorum uterque ecclesiam in urbe insignem habebat.* In the Latin edition of 1607 (London, 1607), 492, he referred also to a house called 'St Julian's', which allegedly stood on the site of the church of St Julius the martyr, about a mile out of town.

[28] Boon, *Isca*, 137, note 350.

[29] ibid., 62–4.

[30] See G. R. Stephens, 'Caerleon and the martyrdom of SS. Aaron and Julius', *Bulletin of the Board of Celtic Studies*, 32 (1985), 326–35, for the legal context of the martyrdom.

[31] ibid., 327.

of the martyrs, Gildas calls them *cives*, citizens, rather than soldiers; they might indeed have been civilians living in the protective shadow of the walls of the Roman fortress.[32]

The recording of the cult of the two saints of Caerleon, even that of Alban, was incidental to Gildas's main purpose, so it is quite possible that other Romano-British cults were active which he did not mention. Evidence for the survival in the late sixth century of another cult which may date from as early as the Romano-British period is found in the so-called *Obsecratio Augustini*. This forms part of a series of written replies, known as the *Libellus Responsionum*, supposedly supplied by Pope Gregory to questions posed by Augustine concerning the practices he should establish in the new English Church, though the authenticity of the document is disputed; much of it appears to have been compiled at Canterbury by Archbishop Nothelm *c*.731.[33] Many of the *responsiones*, though not the *obsecratio*, were transcribed by Bede in what reads like a lengthy digression in his *Ecclesiastical History*.[34] In the *obsecratio* Pope Gregory (if he be indeed the author) wrote that, at Augustine's request, he was sending him relics of St Sixtus (the martyred pope Sixtus II), to replace those of another 'Sixtus' who was the subject of a local cult.[35] Gregory evidently had his doubts about the cult of the British Sixtus: nothing was known about him, nor had any miracles been recorded at the place of his burial. Unfortunately the location is not specified: the cult was located 'in a certain place' (*in loco quodam*), which was presumably within the areas reached by the Augustinian mission. If the *obsecratio* indeed pre-dates Nothelm's compilation and was an authentic letter from Pope Gregory preserved in the Canterbury archives in 731, it would provide further evidence for the survival of Christian cults during the so-called Dark Ages of early Anglo-Saxon England. It is unfortunate, or perhaps significant, that Bede does not mention these cults, apart from repeating Gildas's statement that after the Diocletian persecutions, the Christians 'endowed and built shrines to the holy martyrs'.[36] David Rollason has speculated that Bede might deliberately have played down such cults in consequence of his prejudice against the British Church,[37] though his silence may simply reflect

[32] ibid., 328.

[33] *Libellus Responsionum*; *MGH, Epistolæ*, vol. ii, pt. i, ed. L. M. Hartmann (Berlin, 1899), 331–43. For the question of its authenticity, see P. Meyvaert, 'Les Responsions de S. Grégoire à S. Augustin de Cantorbéry', *Revue d'Histoire Ecclésiastique*, 54 (1959), 879–94.

[34] Bede, *HE*, i.27; ed. Colgrave and Mynors, 78–103.

[35] M. Deanesly and P. Grosjean, 'The Canterbury edition of the Answers of Pope Gregory I to Saint Augustine', *Jnl. of Ecclesiastical History*, 10 (1959), 1–49, at 28–9. The *Obsecratio* is accepted as genuine by P. Meyvaert: 'Les Responsions de S. Grégoire', p. 88, and idem, 'Bede's text of the *Libellus Responsionum* of Gregory the Great to Augustine of Canterbury', in *England before the Conquest; Studies in Primary Sources presented to Dorothy Whitelock*, ed. P. Clemoes and K. Hughes (Cambridge, 1971), 24. For further discussion, see N. Brooks, *The Early History of the Church of Canterbury: Christ Church from 597 to 1066* (Leicester, 1984), 20.

[36] Bede, *HE*, i.8; ed. Colgrave and Mynors, 34–5.

[37] Rollason, *Saints and Relics*, 17–18.

the paucity of the source material available to him. As far as Canterbury is concerned, Bede is quite clear: Christian worship had ceased, and Queen Bertha had brought her own Frankish chaplain with her. Æthelberht allowed Augustine to repair redundant Christian churches for the newly established faith; there is no suggestion they were still in use. Furthermore, despite his veneration of the English proto-martyr St Alban, Germanus was careful to bring with him relics of 'all the apostles and various martyrs'; these, Bede tells us, the bishop used in the miraculous cure of a little blind girl.[38] Relics of English saints were not yet available (the first evidence we have is the blood-soaked earth that Germanus removed from the site of Alban's execution, but he probably took that contact relic back to Auxerre) and visiting missionaries had to import their own relics from abroad. Likewise, Augustine's reinforcements, headed by Mellitus, arrived in Canterbury in 601 equipped with a kind of holy starter kit, comprising 'relics of the holy apostles and martyrs' which would be used in the consecration of the altars of the new Roman-style churches.[39] Some of these churches were on former pagan sites, as mentioned in a letter of Gregory the Great to Mellitus, where he told him to 'build altars and place relics in them'.[40]

It is unlikely that new texts relating to Romano-British saints' cults will come to light, whereas archaeology continues to enhance our knowledge of the physical setting of possible early cults. Excavations at St Albans have so far failed to unearth material evidence of the cult before the Conquest: investigation of the area beneath the present shrine has revealed that the east end of Paul of Caen's church was built on a virgin site. But relevant discoveries are claimed to have been made elsewhere.

Warwick Rodwell has argued, for example, that the origins of Wells Cathedral lie in a forgotten cult there. The hypothesis relies on discoveries made in 1980 towards the end of the three seasons of archaeological excavations in the Camery, the area east of the former cloister.[41] There, an empty 'rectangular chamber' was excavated, measuring about 1.6m wide internally by at least 2.1m long. It was aligned approximately NNW–SSE. Initially timber lined, the chamber had subsequently been relined in stone but retained from the original structure six timber posts which were interpreted as supports for a canopy. Rodwell argued that the chamber was a Romano-British *cella*, of late fourth- or early fifth-century date and that it had originally been located within a mausoleum, whose original dimensions,

[38] Bede, *HE*, i.18; ed. Colgrave and Mynors, 58–9.
[39] ibid., i.29; pp. 104–5.
[40] ibid., i.30; pp. 106–7.
[41] W. Rodwell, 'The Origins of Wells Cathedral', *Antiquity*, 56 (1982), 215–18; idem, 'From Mausoleum to Minster: the Early Development of Wells Cathedral', in *The Early Church in Western Britain and Ireland: Studies presented to C. A. Ralegh Radford*, ed. S. M. Pearce, British Archaeol. Reports, British Ser., 102 (Oxford, 1982), 49–59; idem, *Wells Cathedral: Excavations and Discoveries*, 3rd edn., revised (Wells, 1987); idem, *The Archaeology of Wells Cathedral: Excavations and Structural Studies, 1978–93*, English Heritage Archaeol. Reports, 21, 2 vols. (London, 2001).

allowing for circulation space around the *cella*, might have been in the order of 5.2m by 4.1m. By the mid-tenth century the mausoleum had been demolished and the chamber was infilled with the remains of about fifty coffined burials that the excavators thought had probably been housed within the mausoleum.[42] By the late tenth century a new mortuary chapel had been constructed, still oriented more or less north–south, overlapping one corner of the *cella*. The replacement mortuary chapel was then enlarged with the addition of a western 'nave' to form 'St Mary's chapel', a building resembling a simple church with nave and chancel. The main Anglo-Saxon church probably built by Bishop Aldhelm in the early eighth century followed the same alignment as the chapel; its replacement, Reginald FitzJocelin's collegiate church (mid-1190s), was, however, regularly aligned east–west, and in 1476 the anomalously aligned St Mary's chapel was replaced by a regularly oriented chapel, the 'Lady Chapel by the Cloister'. This chapel continued to be used for the burial of clergy and influential lay benefactors until it was demolished in 1477. Rodwell's interpretation has not been accepted by all scholars, notably John Blair who questioned the proposed early date of the *cella*; could such a structure really have remained open for nearly five hundred years, and during that period would Christian burials have continued on an irregular alignment within the mausoleum?[43] Blair dismissed the notion of a Roman mausoleum as 'a chimera'; his interpretation was that a much later circular feature with burials had given way to a square mortuary chapel, and he noted that there was no firm evidence for north–south burials within the supposed mausoleum. If Romano-British, and if it attracted early Christian burials, the *cella* might indeed have been the focus of a cult, though it is difficult to envisage that, given the long history of the site, the identity of the saint should have been lost.

Similar difficulties of identification are encountered in the interpretation of the early church at Stone-by-Faversham (Kent). There, the lower parts of the walls of an originally almost square chamber of Roman date were first excavated within the ruins of the western half of the chancel of the medieval church by the Kent Archaeological Society in 1872.[44] The remains were surveyed by J. T. Irvine in 1874, investigated again by W. Hawley in 1926,[45] and were re-excavated by Sir Eric Fletcher and Lt.-Col. G. W. Meates in 1967–8, again revealing the square structure which David Rollason has likened to 'the type of chapel built on the continent around a martyr's tomb'.[46]

[42] Rodwell, *Archaeology of Wells Cathedral*, 85.
[43] J. Blair, 'Wells : Roman Mausoleum or just Anglo-Saxon Minster?' (review of Rodwell, *Archaeology of Wells Cathedral*), *Church Archaeology*, 5–6 for 2001–2 (2004), 134–7.
[44] J. T. Irvine, 'On the Remains of Saxon or early Norman work in the church of Stone juxta Faversham', *JBAA*, 31 (1875), 249–58.
[45] H. M. Taylor and D. D. Yonge, 'The ruined church at Stone-by-Faversham: a re-assessment', *Antiq. J.*, 138 (1981), 118–45, at 123.
[46] Rollason, *Saints and Relics*, 15. For the excavations, see E. Fletcher and G. W. Meates, 'The ruined church of Stone-by-Faversham', *Antiq. J.*, 49 (1969), 273–94; idem, 'The ruined church of Stone-by-Faversham: Second report', ibid., 57 (1977), 67–72.

The excavators found no signs that the structure was originally Christian, and argued that it had most probably been adapted for Christian worship soon after the Augustinian mission of 597.[47] The square chamber might, however, have been a non-Christian Roman *cella* or burial chamber which was reused as part of a Christian church in the early Saxon period.[48] There is no other evidence for a local saint's cult at Stone.

A somewhat similar development occurred at the Roman villa at Lullingstone (Kent), where a timber-lined tomb chamber was eventually surrounded by a stone mausoleum that was finally supplanted by a Christian church. Originally a flint and mortar structure dating from the late first century, the villa was rebuilt in stone and extended during the second century. In the early fourth century a mausoleum was constructed north of the main building; this was incorporated as the foundations of a late Saxon church.[49] It had been constructed over a tomb-chamber containing the lead coffins of two individuals, buried *c.*300, and comprised a typical *cella* eventually surrounded by an ambulatory. Nothing suggested that the mausoleum was originally Christian, but the villa itself contained a house-church constructed over a small pagan temple and redecorated with Christian wall-paintings. Meates saw the construction of the late Saxon church over the pagan burial site as an example of 'the precept of Pope Gregory to St. Augustine to utilize the places of former pagan worship'.[50] But there were absolutely no indications that the individuals buried within the mausoleum were ever venerated as Christian saints; indeed, the fact that the tombs were apparently robbed whilst the villa was in Christian occupation suggests that the mausoleum did not play an important part in their religious life. The building decayed: in Meates's words, 'by the last quarter of the fourth century … the inhabitants of the villa had embraced Christianity, doubtless giving no further attention to the preservation of this pagan building …'.[51]

Yet, as David Rollason and Richard Morris have pointed out, several ancient English church sites are located on former Roman cemeteries, which might indicate that they were first established over the graves of those regarded as martyrs. The best examples are the suburban churches of St Cecilia and St Lawrence at Cirencester; St Mary de Lode and St Oswald at Gloucester; far less certain are the Canterbury churches of St Martin, St Dunstan, St Sepulchre, and perhaps St Paul.[52] If such speculation is correct,

[47] Fletcher and Meates, 'Stone-by-Faversham' (1969), 283–4.

[48] The view of Thomas, *Christianity in Roman Britain to A.D. 500*, 183–4. Taylor and Yonge, 'Stone-by-Faversham', 120, also considered the square structure to have been 'used for religious purposes, more probably pagan than Christian'.

[49] Lt.-Col. G. W. Meates, *The Roman Villa at Lullingstone, Kent*, 2 vols., Kent Archaeol. Soc. Monograph Ser., 1 (1979) and 3 (1987).

[50] ibid., i. 19.

[51] ibid., i. 130.

[52] Rollason, *Saints and Relics*, 17–18. R. Morris, *Churches in the Landscape* (London, 1989), 13.

the origins of these churches would be consistent with what happened in many Continental examples, beneath some of which Gallo-Roman hypogea still exist.[53] But it has to be said that the arguments for a neat transition from Roman cemetery to Anglo-Saxon church are, in most cases, based on little more than theorising and wishful thinking.

CONTINUATION OF ROMAN INFLUENCE

The Roman imprint given to Christianity at Canterbury also marked funerary practices there, and the burials of the first archbishops of Canterbury followed the Roman tradition. This is scarcely surprising: St Augustine had been prior of the monastery of St Andrew founded by Pope Gregory on the Celian Hill in Rome, and had been sent to England by that conservative pope, who, as we have seen in Chapter 1, was fighting a rearguard action against, in his eyes, undesirable practices of saintly veneration that were developing away from Rome. True, even Pope Gregory seems to have been pragmatic when it came to adopting local religious traditions; the version of the *responsiones* quoted by Bede includes a letter to Augustine in which the pope told the bishop that he should feel free to adopt local customs if they were 'more pleasing to Almighty God'.[54] But such concessions did not apparently extend to burial practice, and all the early archbishops of Canterbury were buried in the north *porticus* of St Gregory at St Augustine's Abbey, outside the city walls, where their bodies remained undisturbed, in true Roman fashion, until 1091. The remains of their empty tombs, archaeologically excavated in 1916–17,[55] are still to be seen.[56] About 125 years after Augustine's death *c*.605, the position of his grave and that of many of his successors was briefly described by Bede, who presumably obtained his information about St Augustine's from Abbot Albinus whose help he acknowledges in his preface.[57] The archbishop had been temporarily buried outside the church, until it was consecrated in 613 by Archbishop Laurence.[58] Then,

> ... as soon as [the church of SS. Peter and Paul] was consecrated, the body was carried inside and honourably buried in the chapel

[53] A possible example is at Saint-Maximin (Var): Crook, *Architectural Setting*, 52–4. There, however, the hypogeum was not originally Christian, but was later refurbished during the establishment of the cult of St Mary Magdalen.

[54] Bede, *HE*, i.27; ed. Colgrave and Mynors, 80–3. Cf. *Libellus Responsionum*, ed. Hartmann, p. 334.

[55] W. H. St. John Hope, 'Recent discoveries in the Abbey Church of St Austin at Canterbury', *Arch. J.*, 32 (1917), 1–27.

[56] See below, pp. 133–6.

[57] Bede, *HE*, preface and v.20; ed. Colgrave and Mynors 2–3 and note 4, and 530–1.

[58] Bede, *HE*, i.33; pp. 114–15 does not give the date of this consecration. The year 613 was proposed by the late fourteenth-century historian William Thorne, in Twysden col. 1767. Cf. Thomas of Elmham's account, written in the early fifteenth century, *Historia Monasterii S. Augustini Cantuariensis*, ed. C. Hardwick, RS, 8 (1858), 131–2.

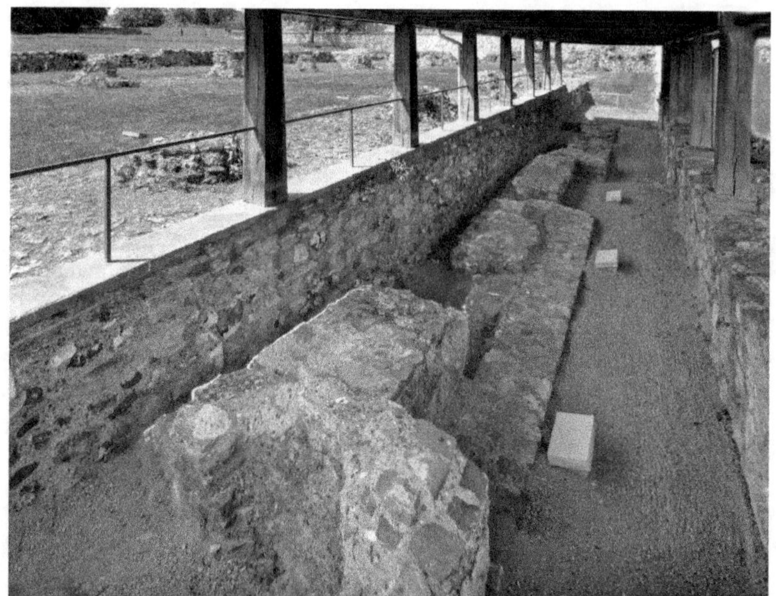

PLATE 3.2
CANTERBURY, ST AUGUSTINE'S ABBEY
The burial place of the early archbishops, in the north *porticus* of the Anglo-Saxon church.

> [*porticus*] on the north side. In it the bodies of all succeeding archbishops have been buried, with the exception of two, Theodore [669–90] and Berhtwold [693–731], whose bodies were placed in the church itself because there was no more room in the chapel.[59]

The next two archbishops after Berhtwold, namely Tatwin (731–5) and Nothelm (735–*c*.740), were also buried at St Augustine's, probably also within the body of the church, though in 1091 Nothelm's remains were said to have been found beneath the altar of St Gregory in the north *porticus*. It is not certain, however, that this was his first burial-place: Thomas of Elmham's statement that Nothelm was buried 'with his predecessors' (which could be taken as implying that he had indeed been interred in the *porticus* from the outset) was probably simply based on Goscelin's account of the discoveries of 1091.[60] The first archbishop to be buried in his own cathedral precincts at Christ Church Canterbury was Cuthbert (*c*.740–58), who built for himself and his successors a funerary chapel, dedicated to St John the Baptist, immediately east of the cathedral. Later it was claimed that

[59] Bede, *HE*, ii.3; ed. Colgrave and Mynors, 142–5: *Mox uero ut dedicata est, intro inlatum et in porticu illius aquilonali decenter sepultum est; in qua etiam sequentium archiepiscoporum omnium sunt corpora tumulata præter duorum tantummodo, id est Theodori et Berctualdi, quorum in ipsa ecclesia posita sunt, eo quod prædicta porticus plura capere nequiuit.*
[60] Thomas of Elmham, *Historia Monasterii S. Augustini Cantuariensis*, 312: *sepultusque est in præsenti ecclesia cum prædecessoribus suis.*

Archbishop Cuthbert had sought the permission of Pope Gregory III for this change in burial custom.[61]

Roman influences may also be discerned in the cult of St Paulinus at Rochester. He had arrived in England a few years after Augustine, in a second wave of Roman missionary activity. A native of Rome, he may well have been a monk at St Andrew's monastery on the Celian hill, founded by Augustine, its first abbot. Paulinus is remembered as the apostle to Northumbria, having accompanied Æthelberht's daughter Æthelburh to the northern kingdom as her chaplain when King Edwin sought the princess's hand in marriage. He was consecrated bishop for this purpose in 625, and two years later became the first archbishop of York, but he returned to Kent with Queen Æthelburh after Edwin's defeat at Hatfield Chase in 633, ending his days as the third bishop of Rochester. Pope Honorius sent him the archiepiscopal pallium after he had left York, and Paulinus later bequeathed it to the cathedral at Rochester.[62] He died on 10 October 644, and this day (his *obit*) would later be celebrated as his feast-day. According to Bede, at his death in 644 Paulinus was buried in the 'sanctuary' (*secretarium*) of his cathedral church, which King Æthelberht had built.[63] As for Æthelburh, she was buried in 647 in the Anglo-Saxon church at Lyminge, twelve miles south of Canterbury, where she is said to have founded a nunnery in 633. The approximate site of her grave was very inexpertly excavated by the Revd Robert Jenkins in the late nineteenth century, but it is certain that St Æthelburh's relics had been elevated long before the present church was constructed by Lanfranc alongside its Saxon predecessor.[64]

Bede merely calls Paulinus *reuerentissimus* (most reverend) and there is no suggestion that he was regarded as a saint in that author's day. The cult seems, however, to have developed during the eighth century, and in 788 King Offa of Mercia granted land 'to the church of blessed Andrew the Apostle and the bishopric of the castle which is called Rochester, where blessed Paulinus lies' (*ad ęcclesiam beati Andreę apostoli et ad episcopium castelli quod nominatur Hrofescester ubi beatus Paulinus pausat*).[65] This charter is qualified by its most recent editor, Alistair Campbell, as 'sound'; he describes, however, as 'highly suspicious' a charter of 823 by which Ecgberht of Wessex granted privileges *pro amore Sancti Andreę et beati Paulini archiepiscopi cuius corpus in predicta ęcclesia requiescit.*[66] There is no doubt, however, about the inclusion of the feast of St Paulinus (10 October) in pre-Conquest calendars used at a variety of locations: it occurs in fifteen

[61] Brooks, *Early History of the Church of Canterbury*, 81–3.
[62] Bede, *HE*, ii.20; ed. Colgrave and Mynors, 204–5.
[63] ibid., iii.14; pp. 254–7: *sepultusque est in secretario beati apostoli Andreæ, quod rex Ædilberct a fundamentis in eadem Hrofi ciuitate construxit.*
[64] [R. Jenkins] 'Remarks on the early Christian basilicas, in connection with the recent discoveries at Lyminge', *Arch. Cant.*, 10 (1876), ci–cii (with plan).
[65] *Charters of Rochester*, ed. A. Campbell, British Academy Anglo-Saxon Charters, i (London, 1973), no. 12, p. 14.
[66] ibid., no. 18, p. 21.

of the nineteen pre-1100 calendars printed by Francis Wormald.[67] The cult features also in the important pre-Conquest Old English list of saints' resting places, *Secgan be þam Godes sanctum þe on Engla lande ærost reston*, first published as a scholarly edition by Felix Liebermann in 1889 but now better known thanks to David Rollason's careful analysis.[68] The earlier of the two principal surviving manuscripts of the *Secgan* is dated to *c.*1031.[69] The so-called 'Kentish Royal legend', which precedes the *Secgan*,[70] refers to Paulinus's mission to Northumbria, while the actual list of saints states that 'Đonne resteð Sanctus Paulinus on Hrofe ceastre.'[71] The continued presence of Paulinus's body at Rochester was also noted in an *addendum* to an Old English homiliary based on the homilies of Ælfric. The addition, which was evidently written at Rochester in the early eleventh century, mentions that St Paulinus 'was buried here and here yet lies'.[72]

There is no evidence that Paulinus's body was ever elevated from its grave within the *secretarium*; it seems to have remained in its original position deep in the earth, in Roman fashion. There is, of course, no way of telling what the tomb of St Paulinus might have looked like. One may perhaps postulate some sort of monument over the grave, which would allow the faithful to get near to the remains beneath. Possible Continental parallels include the raised tomb of St Lotharius (Saint-Loyer) near Argentan, but further speculation is futile. All one can say is that the tomb appears to have remained an identifiable feature of the Anglo-Saxon church of Rochester from 644 until the 1080s. As we shall see, a cult later developed at Rochester of Paulinus's successor, St Ithamar, but this seems to have been an early twelfth-century innovation, at a time of renewed interest in local saints' cults and Ithamar does not feature in Anglo-Saxon sources such as the *Secgan*.

Away from Canterbury and Rochester Roman traditions also re-emerged sporadically throughout the Anglo-Saxon period. Thus in the 670s St Wilfrid constructed two extraordinary crypts at Hexham and, almost certainly, at Ripon,[73] which are nothing less than artificial Roman catacombs, probably

[67] F. Wormald, *English Kalendars before A.D. 1100*, Henry Bradshaw Soc., 72 for 1933 (London, 1934).

[68] F. Liebermann, *Die Heiligen Englands: angelsächsisch und lateinisch* (Hannover, 1889). Rollason, 'Lists', 61–93.

[69] BL, Stowe MS 944 (formerly 960 until the MSS were renumbered before the 1895 catalogue was published), 34v–39r, publ. in *Liber Vitæ: Register and Martyrology of New Minster and Hyde Abbey, Winchester*, ed. W. de Gray Birch, Hampshire Record Soc. (London and Winchester, 1892), 87–96. A later MS is Corpus Christi College Cambridge, MS 201, pp. 147–51, which Liebermann dates to the third quarter of the century.

[70] *Liber Vitæ*, ed. de Gray Birch, 83–7, at 83.

[71] ibid., 92. Cf. Liebermann, *Die Heiligen Englands*, 15.

[72] *Sanctus Paulinus ... wearð þa her bebyrged, 7 her gyt aligð and nis nan ...* : K. Sisam, 'MSS Bodley 340 and 342: Ælfric's "Catholic Homilies", part I', *Review of English Studies*, o.s., 7 (1931), 7–22, at 10–11.

[73] R. Bailey, 'St. Wilfrid. Ripon and Hexham', in *Studies in Insular Art and Archaeology*, ed. C. Karkov and R. Farrell, American Early Medieval Studies, i (Oxford Ohio, 1991), 3–25. Bailey stresses that there is no contemporary documentary evidence that Wilfrid built the Ripon crypt, but the constructional similarities (notably the idiosyncratic use of rib-like

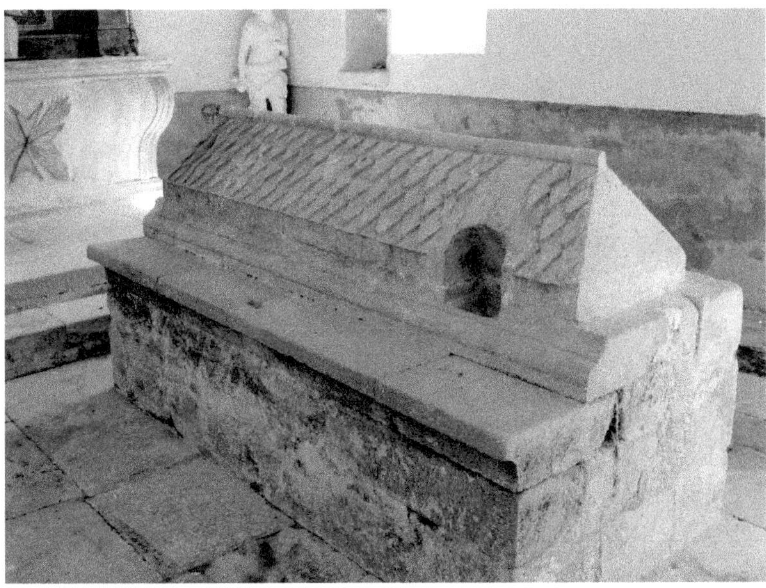

PLATE 3.3 SAINT-LOYER-DES-CHAMPS, NEAR ARGENTAN (DEPT. ORNE, FRANCE) Chapel. The tomb-shrine of the saint.

inspired by his first visit to Rome as a twenty-year-old in 654–5. Later (in 680, and 704–5) he travelled to Rome again, and Wilfrid's biographer, Stephen of Ripon ('Eddius Stephanus'), tells us that during these latter trips, before setting off back home, Wilfrid visited the extramural churches of the principal Roman cults, obtaining relics, and taking care to record their details;[74] these relics were 'for the edification of the churches of Britain'. They were presumably small, contact relics, intended to be placed within church altars at their consecration, but it is plausible to suppose that some of them might have been placed in the two surviving crypts attributed to him. In one important respect the relationship between relics and the churches over them was diametrically opposed to Roman practice: in Rome the churches housing major saints' cults were built over the undisturbed remains of those identified as saints, sometimes lying in their burial *loculi* within extramural catacombs (as at the churches of S. Pancrazio or S. Agnese);[75] at Hexham and Ripon it was the relics themselves that were moved, so as to hallow churches the choice of whose position was presumably arbitrary.

reinforcements for the tunnel vaults of both crypts) suggests that both crypts were Wilfrid's work. Moreover, Eadmer twice states in the *Vita S. Wilfridi* that Wilfrid built the church at Ripon 'from the foundations'. For the structure of the Hexham crypt see P. Bidwell, 'A Survey of the Anglo-Saxon crypt at Hexham and its reused Roman stonework', *Archaeologia Aeliana*, 5th ser., xxxix (2010), 53-145.

[74] *Eddius Stephanus*, 12–13, 66, 120.

[75] In the mid-seventh century, however, Pope Paul I (757–67) rescued a number of saintly bodies from the extramural Roman cemeteries, bringing them within the walls where they would be less vulnerable to Lombardic invaders: *Le Liber Pontificalis*, ed. L. Duchesne, Bibliothèque des Ecoles Françaises d'Athènes et de Rome, 3 vols. (Paris, 1886–1957), i. 464.

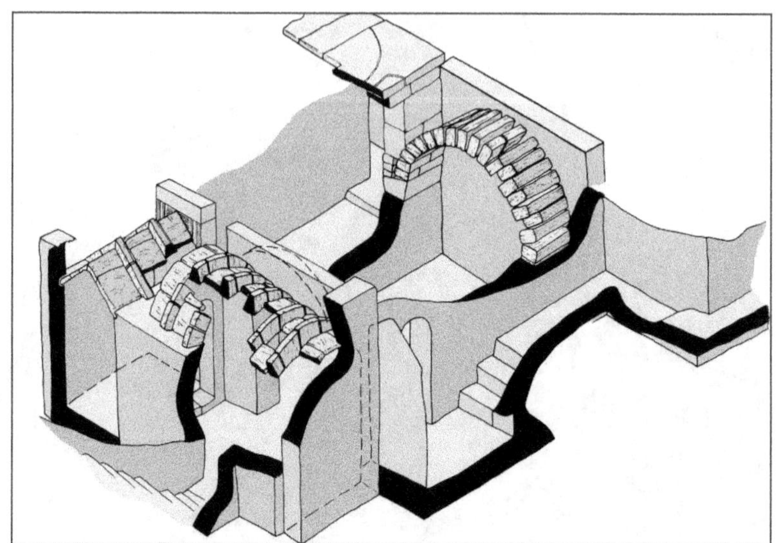

FIG.3.1
HEXHAM PRIORY
Cutaway view of St Wilfrid's crypt from the south-west.

The impression still produced by Wilfrid's crypts (and especially Hexham, which is the more complicated) is one of disorientation, particularly as in each case the passages leading to the central chamber, probably located beneath the high altar of the earliest church,[76] are asymmetrical. This effect seems to have been deliberate, and it is likely that the aim was to reproduce something of the atmosphere of a Roman catacomb. But the catacombs were hollowed out of solid rock, whereas excavation has shown that the Ripon and Hexham crypts were constructed by a 'cut-and-cover' process. Interestingly, recycled Romano-British masonry, some of it bearing inscriptions, was employed in the walls, so Wilfrid's crypts were Roman in fabric as well as in design.

At around the same period, in 674 AD, shortly after his fourth visit to Rome, Benedict Biscop had founded the monastery at Wearmouth. Like St Wilfrid, Benedict was an avid collector of Roman relics 'of the apostles or martyrs of Christ', which were distributed amongst the churches of England.[77] The influence of Rome was even apparent in the very architecture of the monastery, for in a well-known passage Bede recalled that Benedict had summoned masons from Gaul in order to build a church 'according to the Roman manner' (*more Romano*).[78]

The other crypt which may be related to early Christian burial practices

[76] On this difficult issue, now see Bailey, 'St. Wilfrid', 11–17 (discussion of Wilfrid's church at Hexham). See also R. N. Bailey, 'The Anglo-Saxon Church at Hexham', *Archaeologia Aeliana*, 5th ser., 4 (1976), 47–67.
[77] Bede, *Historia Abbatum*, in *Venerabilis Baedæ Opera Historica*, ed. C. Plummer (Oxford, 1896), 364–87: esp. cap. 4 (p. 367), cap. 6 (p. 369).
[78] ibid., cap. 5; p. 368.

now lies beneath the east end of the church of St Wystan at Repton, which excavations have indicated may have formed from the first part of a larger building to the west.[79] Measuring approximately 5m × 5m on plan, with rectangular niches in the walls to east, north, and south, and in its original form probably with a single access stair in the centre of the west side, it certainly resembled a hypogeum of Gallo-Roman type. It was possibly constructed as a royal mausoleum for Æthelbald of Mercia, whose burial at Repton in 757 is recorded in the *Anglo-Saxon Chronicle*,[80] though it might equally have been built as a baptistry.[81] The crypt certainly served for the burial of Wiglaf, king of Mercia (*c.*828–40).[82] If it were a mid-eighth-century mausoleum, it would be a remarkably late example of the sort of structures that were already going out of fashion when Gregory of Tours described them in the late sixth century. But another possible hypogeum of Gallo-Roman type was excavated at Glastonbury in 1928. Alfred Clapham, one of the directors of that investigation, considered it earlier than the church built above it during the abbacy of St Dunstan (940–57). He speculated that it might have served for the burial of King Ine of Wessex (688–726), likening it to the 'Hypogée des Dunes' at Poitiers.[83] Harold and Joan Taylor, on the other hand, considered that the crypt was contemporary with an 'eastern tower' built above it by Abbot Dunstan when Ine's church was extended, and that its function was to house the bones which had been collected during the construction of that tower and its flanking *porticus*.[84] But the excavators were clear that the crypt formed a 'smaller' building within the eastern structure (whether chancel or tower), describing how the space between the walls of the crypt and those surrounding them had been carefully filled with rubble to provide a bedding for the floor.[85] On balance, the crypt may well predate Dunstan's work but could still have been used (as Clapham believed) to house the bones exhumed during Dunstan's building works. A large stone coffin, containing the relocated remains of some seventeen individuals, might have been the central feature of the crypt. The excavators judged that it was ex-situ, as it had been placed on the likely site of the stair leading down into the crypt.

There is also some slender evidence for an even later mausoleum of this type at Winchcombe (Glos), where the site of a chapel dedicated to the Roman boy martyr St Pancrace (Pancratius) was seen by the antiquary John

[79] Blockley, *Canterbury Nave*, 106, citing Martin Biddle, *pers. comm.*
[80] *ASC*, *s.a.* 757. Cf. *John of Worcester*, ii. 198–9.
[81] As suggested by Birthe Kjølbye-Biddle, in Biddle, *Cult of Saints*, 16.
[82] See below, p. 72.
[83] A. Clapham, 'Note on the burial chamber', in C. R. Peers, A. W. Clapham, and Dom E. Horne, 'Glastonbury Abbey Excavations, 1928', *Proc. Somerset Archaeol. and Nat. Hist. Soc.*, 74 (1928), 1–9, at 5–7, and Pl. III. C. R. Peers, A. W. Clapham, and Dom E. Horne, 'Interim Report on the Excavations at Glastonbury Abbey', *Antiq. J.*, 10 (1930), 24–9.
[84] Taylor, *Anglo-Saxon Architecture*, i. 252–5. For Dunstan's works at Glastonbury, see Malmesbury, *Vita Dunstani*, i.xvi; ed. Winterbottom and Thomson, 204–7.
[85] Peers and others, 'Glastonbury Abbey Excavations', 2.

Leland during his tour of Gloucestershire in 1542; he was told that the chapel 'at the west end of the abbey', near the local red-light district, Gropecunt Lane, was replaced by the parish church in the time of Henry VI.[86] A document drawn up in 1320 mentions a 'chapel with a cellar under it', and if this chapel was indeed the one dedicated to Pancrace, the *cellarium* under a chapel is likely to have been a crypt.[87] It has tentatively been identified as the mausoleum of another royal boy saint, whose body is said in the *Secgan* to have lain at 'Wincelescumbe', namely St Cynhelm (Kenelm), allegedly murdered by order of his sister Cwenthryth between 811 and 821. In William of Malmesbury's day (early twelfth century) his 'tiny body' enjoyed a very active cult: William says that 'hardly any place in England is honoured by larger crowds of people coming to the saint's festival'.[88] But David Rollason has expressed grave doubts as to the authenticity of the accounts of the origins of the cult (Cynhelm is not even mentioned in the *Anglo-Saxon Chronicle*), and it is by no means certain that he was murdered at his accession in childhood as claimed in the earliest, mid-eleventh century version of his *Passio*.[89]

MEROVINGIAN PATTERNS OF VENERATION REACH ENGLAND

These late survivals of Roman-style *mausolea* no longer represented normal practice: they were certainly completely outmoded in Francia, where, as we saw in the previous chapter, saintly bodies were being elevated from simple burial chambers during the sixth century. By the late seventh century the features relating to saint cults that we have traced in Merovingian Francia were fully operational in Anglo-Saxon England, and abbesses and bishops were enthusiastically elevating their predecessors in very much the same way as their Continental counterparts had raised saintly bodies from their first graves. Various channels of communication are apparent, the most obvious being the influence of Queen (later Saint) Balthildis (d. 680), the English-born wife of the Neustrian king Clovis II, whom she married in 649. As well as founding the abbey of Chelles, now on the edge of the suburbs of eastern Paris,[90] she was an important benefactress of the monastery of Faremoutiers-en-Brie (Seine-et-Marne), and may have been responsible for

[86] Leland, ii. 54–5.
[87] S. R. Bassett, 'A Probable Mercian royal Mausoleum at Winchcombe, Gloucestershire', *Antiq. J.*, 65 (1985), 82–100.
[88] Malmesbury, *GR*, ii.211; ed. Mynors *et al.*, i. 390–3: *Corpusculum sancti celebriter colitur, nec ullus fere locus in Anglia maiori ad festum aduentantium ueneratur frequentia.* For Malmesbury's racy story of how Cwenthryth's crime was revealed, see Malmesbury, *GP*, iv.156; ed. Winterbottom and Thomson, i. 448–9.
[89] Rollason, 'Murdered royal saints', 9–10.
[90] According to the Life of Bertila of Chelles (*c.*658–705), 'kings of the Saxons' sent to Chelles for teachers and people who might found monasteries in England: *MGH, SRM*, vi. 106–7, quoted in Wallace-Hadrill, *Commentary*, 101.

the presence and eventual cults there of the Anglo-Saxon princesses Sæthryth, Æthelburh, and Eorcengota.[91] Sæthryth is the least known of the three. Bede identifies her as a step-daughter of Anna, king of the East Angles, who had been killed by the pagan king Penda of Mercia in around 654;[92] he calls her *filia uxoris Annæ*.[93] Anna's 'natural daughter' (*filia naturalis*) Æthelburh (*Ethelburga/Aedilberg*), the third abbess of Faremoutiers, was buried in 664 within the completed part of a church dedicated to the Apostles that she had begun building. Seven years later, when the community abandoned that construction project, they decided to translate her remains into an existing church dedicated to St Stephen. On opening her coffin the participants discovered that her body was incorrupt; it was washed, dressed in new clothes, and carried into the church.[94] In this way her remains joined those of her niece Eorcengota, daughter of her sister Queen Seaxburh and King Eorcenberht of Kent. Eorcengota, who was evidently the subject of an important cult at Faremoutiers, had also become a nun there during Æthelburh's time as abbess; she died about four years before her aunt, *c.*660, and was buried in the church of St Stephen. Her body was elevated only three days later, and was found to be exuding a marvellous sweetness.[95]

The way in which the cult of Æthelburh came into being at Faremoutiers prefigured very similar saint-making activity at the English abbey church of Ely, some twenty-four years later. This is scarcely surprising, for the two abbeys were linked by the patronage of three powerful Anglo-Saxon princesses, all daughters of King Anna.[96] As already noted, Æthelburh became abbess of Faremoutiers in succession to her half-sister, St Sæthryth. Æthelburh's other two sisters remained in England.[97] One of them, Seaxburh (*Sexburga*), whom Bede identifies as Anna's oldest daughter, sought retirement in the abbey which she had founded at Sheppey following the death of her husband, King Eorcenberht of Kent, in 664; the other, Æthelthryth (*Etheldreda* or 'Audrey'), retired from the world after two unsuccessful marriages, and, after a period

[91] Bede is our source for these details: *HE*, iii.8; ed. Colgrave and Mynors, 236–41. He explains that 'because few monasteries had yet been founded in England, numbers of people from Britain used to enter the monasteries of the Franks or Gauls to practise their monastic life'.

[92] *ASC*, MS 'C', *s.a.* 654 (MS 'E' has 653). For the date of Anna's death (not given by Bede), see B. Yorke, *Kings and Kingdoms of Early Anglo-Saxon England*, 2nd edn. (London, 1997), 63.

[93] For St Saethryth, see *AASS*, *Januarii I*, 626–7.

[94] Bede, *HE*, iii.8; ed. Colgrave and Mynors, 240–1.

[95] ibid.

[96] As the compiler of the *Liber Eliensis* pointed out in the twelfth century, 'many people from Britain ... even sent their daughters [to the Frankish monasteries] to be educated ... particularly to Brie, Chelles, and the monastic community at Les Andelys'. *Liber Eliensis*, i.2; ed. Blake, 13. This translation from *Liber Eliensis*, trans. J. Fairweather (Woodbridge, 2005), 15.

[97] The youngest of this family of holy sisters was allegedly Wihtburh, abbess of East Dereham (Norfolk), whose body was brought to Ely by Brithnoth, the first abbot after the refoundation of Ely Priory during the tenth-century monastic reforms. See below, pp. 87–8.

of training at the abbey of Coldingham under her aunt Æbbe, founded the monastery of Ely in 673. When Æthelthryth died in 679 Seaxburh succeeded her as abbess of Ely, and Seaxburh's younger daughter Eormenhild became abbess of Minster-in-Sheppey, where she had been a nun since the death in 674 of her husband, King Wulfhere of Mercia; then, on the death of Seaxburh (which is unrecorded, but was presumably within a few years of the translation of St Æthelthryth in 695),[98] Eormenhild became the third abbess of Ely. The date of Eormenhild's death is not known either; indeed doubt has been cast on her very existence and even on that of her daughter Wærburh (Werburg).[99] It is pleasant to relate that King Anna, the progenitor of this extraordinary family of saintly women, also became the subject of a local cult, still active in the twelfth century, at Blythborough (Suffolk), where he had been buried.[100]

Sixteen years after her arrival at Ely, on 17 October 695, Seaxburh elevated Æthelthryth's remains in a ceremony which differed little from the elevation at Faremoutiers of her other sister, Æthelburh, twenty-four years previously. The saint-making process was recorded in some detail by Bede,[101] and was repeated in somewhat expanded form in Book I of the twelfth-century compilation of historical texts relating to Ely known as the *Liber Eliensis*.[102] The first challenge was to find suitable materials from which to make a new tomb. This was evidently considered a task for the male members of the double monastery of monks and nuns; the brethren returned bearing a marble sarcophagus, presumably Roman, which they had discovered near the walls of the deserted Roman fortress of 'Grantacæstir' (Cambridge).[103] The miraculous discovery of a suitable coffin was another hagiographical commonplace (*topos*), and Roman sarcophagi were frequently reused to house saintly bodies, as noted in the previous chapter.[104] The next part of Bede's account is taken verbatim from the eye-witness description by Cynefrith, a doctor who had tended Æthelthryth towards the end her life, when she was suffering from an abscess or even a cancer (*tumorem maximum*) in the lower jaw. A tent was erected over the grave of the future saint, and the members of the monastery divided into separate choirs of men and women around the tent, chanting psalms. Abbess Seaxburh and a few chosen confidants entered the tent expecting to wash a disarticulated skeleton, but shortly afterwards the abbess was heard to exclaim, 'Glory be to the name of the Lord!' Seaxburh had discovered that

[98] A Life of Seaxburh (which its most recent editor argues was not by Goscelin) is printed in Goscelin, *Saints of Ely*, 134–89.

[99] See Goscelin, *Saints of Ely*, xv, citing C. Fell, 'Saint Æthelþryđ: a historical dichotomy revisited', *Nottingham Medieval Studies*, 38 (1994), 19–34.

[100] *Liber Eliensis*, i.7; ed. Blake, 18: *usque hanc diem pia fidelius devotione veneratur*.

[101] Bede, *HE*, i.19; ed. Colgrave and Mynors 390–7.

[102] *Liber Eliensis*, i.25–31; ed. Blake, 42–8.

[103] Colgrave and Mynors comment (Bede, *HE*, 394, n. 1), 'Doubtless a Roman sarcophagus taken from the Roman town on Castle Hill, Cambridge.'

[104] See above, pp. 31–2.

the body of her predecessor was incorrupt, a phenomenon which Bede attributed in part at least to her having avoided sexual contact with her second husband, Ecgfrith, king of Northumbria.[105] Indeed, as with Gregory of Langres, the saint seemed to be merely asleep. Other miracles were apparent: the wound caused by the draining of the abscess had miraculously healed, and the newly discovered sarcophagus proved to fit Æthelthryth's body as though it had been made for her.[106] This was another hagiographical *topos*: in the case of the holy Sebbi, king of the East Saxons, for example, a stone sarcophagus miraculously adapted itself to the size of the body when he was buried outside St Paul's Cathedral, London in 694.[107] The clothes in which Æthelthryth had first been buried were powerful contact relics, used in exorcisms, and the original coffin proved efficacious in curing eye diseases. The original grave site continued as a secondary focus of veneration, marked by a miraculous spring which appeared there and seems still to have been evident in the third quarter of the twelfth century.[108] She was placed in the church, though Bede does not specify the exact location, stating only that in his day Æthelthryth's body was still held in great veneration there. There is, however, no documentary evidence that the relics were moved from their first place within the Anglo-Saxon church. The *Liber* provides a little circumstantial detail about the nature of the tomb. At the second translation of 1106, the participants are said first to have processed 'to the holy and reverend virgin Æthelthryth's tomb of most white Parian marble, as was appropriate for [her] virginal purity', and for a time no-one dared open the monument.[109] The author adds that a hole had been made in the sarcophagus during the Danish ('pagan') invasions, through which a rash priest had attempted to extract a relic of the saint.[110] We may infer from these circumstantial details, and from the fact that no excavation of the sarcophagus is mentioned, that the *tumba* stood on the pavement of the Anglo-Saxon church in the manner of a tomb-shrine. In the early twelfth century the tomb was described as a *turris*, suggesting it may have been surmounted by some sort of superstructure, but it is uncertain whether this arrangement dated from the late seventh-century translation.[111]

As David Rollason has pointed out, the theme of incorruptibility appears to have been a Continental import.[112] So was the *topos* of the marvellous

[105] Bede, *HE*, iv.19; ed. Colgrave and Mynors, 392–3.
[106] Even the head cavity was said to be of the perfect shape. Head cavities are not a feature of Roman sarcophagi, so the detail was probably added by an author more familiar with early medieval sarcophagi.
[107] Bede, *HE*, iv.11; ed. Colgrave and Mynors, 366–9.
[108] One of the miracles, recorded in *Liber Eliensis*, iii.118; ed. Blake, 367, had occurred 'recently' (*nuper*).
[109] ibid., ii.144; p. 229: ... *ad sancte ac reverende virginis Ætheldrede tumulum, pario de marmore candidissimum, uti decebat candorem virgineum.* [...] ... *nemo ipsius tumbam pandere ... presumpsit.*
[110] As also recorded in ibid, i.49; pp. 60–1.
[111] See below, pp. 155–6.
[112] Rollason, *Saints and Relics*, 50–1.

smell that so often accompanied the exhumation of saintly remains. Thus the fragrance, 'as if stores of balsam had been unsealed', that occurred when St Eorcengota's body was exhumed, or at the elevation of St Fursey of Péronne, finds many parallels in the writings of Gregory of Tours.[113] As already noted, this phenomenon has been interpreted by some scholars as evidence that the bodies of potential saints may have been embalmed and that what observers were smelling was the fluids used in the preservation of the corpse. Indeed, when the bundles containing relics of the saints of Hexham were opened in the mid-twelfth century and a marvellous fragrance was apparent, the participants' first thought was that the bodies had been buried with spices (*aromata*).[114]

Another allegedly incorrupt member of the 'saintly sisterhood', as the closely related group of female royal saints has picturesquely been called, was St Werburg (Wærburh). According to Ely legend she was the granddaughter of St Seaxburh, and the daughter of Queen Eormenhild, who, as we have seen, had married Wulfhere, king of Mercia, ending her days as abbess first of Minster-in-Sheppey then of Ely.[115] Wærburh also took the veil when Wulfhere died in 674, retiring with her mother to the convent founded at Ely by her great-aunt St Æthelthryth, still abbess there. This was no secluded existence, however, for Wærburh established and superintended monastic houses throughout Mercia, notably at Weedon (Northants), Threekingham (Lincs), and Hanbury (Staffs). She died at Threekingham on 3 February, possibly in 690 (as held in Chester tradition)[116] or in 699. In accordance with her wishes her body was moved to Hanbury. Nine years later King Ceolred of Mercia (709–16) elevated her mortal remains, considering that they should no longer lie hidden under a bushel. (This phrase, taken from a well-known parable, would become formulaic, and was used in papal bulls announcing canonisations from the time of Pope Innocent III (1198–1216), if not earlier.) It was expected that Wærburh's body would have decayed, but, as Henry Bradshaw wrote in his English version of Goscelin's Life of the saint,

> The corps hole and sounde was funde, verely
> Apperyung to them on slepe as she had ben…[117]

The date at which Wærburh's remains reached Chester is uncertain. According to the Chester Annals, the body was exhumed and carried there

[113] See above, p. 35.
[114] See below, p. 183.
[115] Wærburh's Life by Goscelin is printed in Goscelin, *Saints of Ely*, 28–51. See also *John of Worcester*, iii. 126–7, the probable source of the same details in *Liber Eliensis*, i.7; ed. Blake, 19.
[116] *Annales Cestrienses*, ed. R. C. Christie, Lancs. and Cheshire Record Soc., vol. 14 for 1886 (London, 1887), 10: *dcxc Obiit beata Werburga.*
[117] 'The Life of St Werburghe of Chester by Henry Bradshaw. Englisht A.D. 1513, Printed by Pynson A.D. 1521, and now re-edited by Carol Horstmann', EETS, o.s. 88 (1887), 122. Cf. Goscelin, *Vita S. Werburge*, 11; Goscelin, *Saints of Ely*, 48–9: *inventa est potius uirgo integerrima quasi in dulci stratu obdormire.*

in 875, as a precaution against the Danes, then wintering at Repton: the annalist says that it was at this date that they were reduced to 'dust' (i.e. disarticulated) for the first time.[118] However, the reform of the minster was of later date, being a pet project of King Alfred's daughter Ethelfleda, queen of the Mercians; Ethelfleda dedicated the Chester community to her saintly forebear. It is possible that the relics did not in fact reach Chester until the early tenth century.[119]

One of the most famous examples of saintly incorruptibility is that of St Cuthbert, whose body was judged by some observers to be still substantially intact when it was exhumed in 1827 (little was made of this phenomenon at the second opening in 1899, when the skeleton was so obviously fragmentary).[120] Again, the original elevation in 698 clearly followed Merovingian practice. It was recorded in detail very soon after the event by an anonymous monk of Lindisfarne, writing between 699 and 705;[121] and by Bede in a metrical Life,[122] a subsequent prose Life of the saint,[123] and also in Book IV of his *Ecclesiastical History*. Bishop Cuthbert had initially been buried in a stone sarcophagus in his cathedral church of St Peter the Apostle on Lindisfarne in 687, on the south side of the high altar.[124] This position within a church was considered prestigious in Merovingian Gaul, and was also a location of special sanctity in England, as Bede stresses when describing the final burial place of St Aidan, whose bones were 'buried on the right side of the altar, with the honour due to so great a bishop'.[125] St Cedd was buried at Lastingham in a similar location.[126] Cuthbert began to work miracles almost immediately, when a demoniac boy on the Lindisfarne estate was cured by a particle of earth from the place where the water used to wash the saint's body had been poured.[127] Eleven years after Cuthbert's death the brethren sought the permission of Bishop Eadberht to elevate the body. In this case the impetus for the elevation appears not to have come directly from the saint's successor, but from his monastic community. This represented a slight divergence from Frankish practice, but Eadberht was evidently closely involved in proceedings. As with Æthelthryth, the monks expected that the body would have decayed to dust,

[118] *Annales Cestrienses*, ed. Christie, 12: *tunc primum in pulverem resolutum*.

[119] For the uncertainty over the date see Goscelin, *Saints of Ely*, xvi.

[120] Raine, *Saint Cuthbert*. J. T. Fowler, 'On an examination of the grave of St Cuthbert in Durham Cathedral Church, in March, 1899', *Archæologia*, 57 (1900), 11–28, at 19–24 ('Notes on the bones').

[121] Colgrave, *Two Lives of St Cuthbert*, 60–139. For the date of the Anonymous Life, see ibid., 13.

[122] *Bedas metrische Vita sancti Cuthberti*, ed. W. Jaager (Leipzig, 1935). There is also a fifteenth-century English metrical life: *The Life of St. Cuthbert in English Verse*, ed. J. T. Fowler, Surtees Soc., 87 for 1889 (Durham, 1891).

[123] Colgrave, *Two Lives of St Cuthbert*, 142–307.

[124] ibid., 288–9.

[125] Bede, *HE*, iii.17; ed. Colgrave and Mynors, 264–5.

[126] ibid., iii.23; p. 288–9.

[127] Bede, *Prose Life of St Cuthbert*, cap. 41; Colgrave, *Two Lives of St Cuthbert*, 288–91.

but it proved to be incorrupt: '... intact and whole as if it were still alive, the joints of the limbs flexible and more like a sleeping than a dead man'.[128] The corpse was reclothed and placed in a wooden reliquary-coffin, described as a 'light chest' (*leuis theca*). During the nineteenth-century openings of the saint's post-Reformation tomb at Durham pieces of this reliquary-coffin were discovered, together with numerous fragments of other wooden coffins, making a total of some six thousand pieces of oak.[129] About 170 fragments from the reliquary-coffin have been reassembled and are now splendidly displayed in the Treasury of the present cathedral. The style of its incised decoration was closely related to contemporary art on the Continent, and is strikingly similar to that found on stone panels in a Frankish monument, the Roman-style hypogeum of Abbot Mellebaudis just south of Poitiers, known as the Hypogée des Dunes, dated to the early eighth century.

Bishop Eadberht died on 6 May 698, only a few weeks after the elevation of St Cuthbert. On the point of death, he requested to be buried in Cuthbert's empty tomb, and the saint's reliquary-coffin was placed over it.[130] Some of the miracles reported at the double monument were ascribed to Eadberht's presence, and he also quickly became regarded as a saint.

The reliquary arrangement at Lindisfarne served to elevate Cuthbert's coffin, which was evidently visible above ground level, but it is hard to find parallels for this double-decker arrangement. At first sight, it is reminiscent of the tombs of the abbesses at Jouarre, each of which consisted of a sarcophagus containing the actual body, surmounted by an empty, coffin-like superstructure: some of these upper cenotaphs were of gabled form. The sarcophagi at Jouarre were not originally intended to be seen, but were buried beneath a platform (*estrade*) running along the east side of the crypt, only the superstructure of each tomb being visible. The masonry between the burials was removed in 1884, making the two-decker arrangement more obvious.[131] The difference between this format and the Lindisfarne example is that the upper coffin of St Cuthbert was not an empty superstructure but actually contained the body of the saint. It is not quite clear from Bede's account whether Eadberht's body was within the sarcophagus previously occupied by Cuthbert, though this seems the most likely interpretation.

Other burial arrangements described by Bede are perhaps closer to Jouarre, notably the tomb of St Chad at Lichfield. Bede tells us that the bishop's bones (the body was not incorrupt) had been translated from his original burial place outside the church of St Mary into the church of St Peter,

[128] ... *inuenerunt corpus totum, quasi adhuc uiueret, integrum et flexibilibus artuum conpagibus multo dormienti quam mortuo similis* ... : Bede, *HE*, iv.30; ed. Colgrave and Mynors, 442.

[129] J. M. Cronyn and C. V. Horie, 'The Anglo-Saxon coffin: further investigations', in Bonner, *St Cuthbert*, 247–56.

[130] Bede, *Prose Life of Cuthbert*, cap. 43; ed. Colgrave, 296–7. Cf. Bede, *HE*, iv.30; ed. Colgrave and Mynors, 442–5.

[131] M.-J. Maillé, Marquise de la Tour-Landry, *Les Cryptes de Jouarre* (Paris, 1971), 221–38, 252–5.

and he describes the new *sepulchrum* in some detail; it was only a few decades old at the time of writing, for the saint had died as recently as 672, though the year of his translation is not recorded. It was 'covered by (*coopertus*) a wooden coffin made in the shape of a little house (*domunculus*)' over the tomb, with a hole in one side, through which the faithful could gather 'dust' as a contact relic (it could be used to make healing infusions).[132] The wooden construction of the monument over the tomb links it with the *leuis theca* of Cuthbert's shrine; but because the *domunculus* was empty, the arrangement bears a closer resemblance to the Jouarre tombs or the large number of Merovingian monuments where the grave was surmounted by a superstructure. It was, indeed, an early version of a 'tomb-shrine'; a monument giving limited access to the faithful people who sought to touch the primary contact relic which was the tomb of the saint. Bede's terminology reminds us of the tomb of St Fursey (Fursa) at Péronne, where the monument over the tomb of the saint behind the high altar, built following his elevation in the mid-seventh century, was called a *domuncula*.[133]

Chad's brother, Cedd, bishop of the East Saxons, also became the subject of a saint's cult. He died during a great plague epidemic in 664 while visiting the monastery of Lastingham (North Yorks) which he had founded, and was initially buried there 'outside the walls' (of the church, presumably), but was elevated within a few years and, as we have seen, was placed to the right of the altar in the new monastery church.[134] Later his cult was pursued at Lichfield, whither his relics had been translated by the eleventh century, rejoining those of his brother, but the memory of Cedd is kept alive at Lastingham, where the important Norman crypt, begun *c.*1078 by Stephen, first abbot of St Mary's York, is sometimes called 'St Cedd's crypt'. There is, however, no evidence that relics of St Cedd ever featured in the post-Conquest church, which is dedicated to St Mary the Virgin, presumably after the parent church at York.

The cults of Æthelthryth, Cuthbert, Chad, and Cedd were official, set up by major figures of the Anglo-Saxon Church hierarchy. But Bede also describes more popular manifestations of the cult of saints. He devotes a considerable number of pages to the somewhat earlier cult of King Oswald of Northumbria, effectively writing a *Vita* and *Miracula* of that saint. As Alan Thacker argues in an important paper, Bede seems to have regarded Oswald as foremost amongst those Northumbrian leaders through whose guidance the entire English people might achieve salvation.[135]

Before Oswald's great victory over the British tyrant Cadwallon near Hexham, at 'Heavenfield' in 634, the Northumbrian king set up a hastily made wooden cross, holding it with both hands while his soldiers fixed it in position. The wood of Oswald's cross acquired the sanctity of its prototype

[132] Bede, *HE*, iv.3; ed. Colgrave and Mynors, 344–7.
[133] See p. 35.
[134] Bede, *HE*, iii.23; ed. Colgrave and Mynors, 288–9.
[135] Thacker, '*Membra disjecta*'.

in Jerusalem: even in Bede's day, people were 'in the habit of cutting splinters from the wood ... and putting them in water' to create a curative potion.[136] Equally impressive were the contact relics deriving from the place of Oswald's violent death in battle in 642 at *Maserfelth* (traditionally identified with Oswestry, though the point is debated):[137] sick men and beasts were cured at the spot. Bede relates that a certain 'Briton' identified the place as holy because the grass there was unusually green: surely the earliest recorded example of an archaeological crop-mark.[138] He tells us, too, that so much earth was removed from the spot, to be used in healing infusions, that a large hole developed, 'as deep as a man's height'.[139] The story of Oswald's contact relics did not end there: after Queen Osthryth and her husband King Æthelred of Mercia translated the remainder of Oswald's body to the monastery of Bardney between 679 and 697 the bones were washed, and the water was poured into a corner of what Bede calls the *sacrarium*, presumably the sacristy. Again, the earth which had received that holy water could be used in exorcisms.[140] The treatment of Oswald's remains at Bardney conforms closely to the patterns noted above at Ely; despite the loss of the head and arms, the process was identical to that for a whole-body cult.

In Bede's account the miracles wrought by contact relics seem to outshadow the corporeal relics. But the latter were unusual, for the king had been hacked to death and dismembered;[141] his severed arms (including his miraculously incorrupt right hand and arm) were taken to Bamburgh by his brother, King Oswiu, who founded a church there, where the relics were enshrined.[142] Five centuries later the compiler of the *Historia Regum* attributed to Symeon of Durham described the 'costly and precious reliquary' (*scrinium speciosum et preciosum*) within the 'most beautifully constructed church' on the top of the rock at Bamburgh, where the king's right hand reposed wrapped in a cloth.[143] By then, however, the monks of Peterborough also laid claim to the relic. They claimed to have acquired the arm (presumably by *furtum sacrum*, holy theft) in the tenth century; and, as we have seen, Bishop Hugh of Lincoln cut himself a small fragment from it. Oswald's head was taken to Lindisfarne, whence it eventually accompanied Cuthbert's body to Durham, and it was replaced in the coffin at the translation of 1104. As Alan Thacker has emphasised,[144] this was an

[136] Bede, *HE*, iii.2; ed. Colgrave and Mynors, 214–17.
[137] Thacker, '*Membra disjecta*', 99.
[138] Bede, *HE*, iii.10; ed. Colgrave and Mynors, 244–5.
[139] ibid., iii.9; pp. 242–3.
[140] ibid., iii.11; pp. 246–7.
[141] See especially Thacker, '*Membra disjecta*'.
[142] ibid., 100, citing *Alcuin: The Bishops, Kings, and Saints of York*, ed. P. Godman, OMT (Oxford, 1982), 28–30 (lines 304–9).
[143] Symeon of Durham, *Historia Regum*, cap. 48; *Sym. Op.*, ii. 45. Cf. Symeon, *Libellus*, 22–5, where Symeon notes (bk. I, cap. 2) that Oswald's right arm and hand were still incorrupt right down to his own age, though his bones [i.e. the main part of his body] had been translated to 'a monastery situated in the kingdom of Lindsey' (i.e. Bardney).
[144] Thacker, '*Membra disjecta*', 101.

exceptionally early example of a cult where various parts of a saintly body were separately venerated at different locations. The distribution was the result of the exceptional circumstances of his death. Later multiple focuses of veneration would become more usual.

One other feature of Oswald's cult should be noted. The bones at Bardney were laid, with due honour, in a *theca*—a container constructed for the purpose—and his banner was placed above it. Just what the initial shrine arrangement at Bardney consisted of is unclear; a minimalist interpretation is that it comprised a simple tomb-chest on which the banner was laid as a pall. A century later it would be lavishly decorated by King Offa; it is perhaps more likely that the monument at Bardney was a *domuncula*, the kind of tomb-shrine which, as we have seen, developed in the mid-seventh century at Péronne and Lichfield. There is no record that Offa rehoused the bones, and it is quite possible therefore that Oswald's monument was recognisably a shrine, rather than a conventional tomb.

Rather more information was provided by Felix, author of the *Life of St Guthlac*, about the *memoria* erected at Croyland Abbey (Lincs) over the tomb of that saint, whom David Farmer has called 'after Cuthbert ... England's most popular pre-Conquest hermit saint'.[145] Guthlac, a member of the Mercian royal dynasty, had died on 11 April 714,[146] and was buried in a lead coffin sent to him by Edburh, abbess of Repton.[147] His incorrupt body was elevated by his sister, the anchoress Pega, exactly one year later. According to the *Historia Croylandensis* compiled by Ingulph, the first post-Conquest abbot (†1109), the abbey was founded at that time by Æthelbald of Mercia and the foundation charter was sealed at Guthlac's tomb in 716.[148] 'Now,' Felix affirmed within two or three decades, 'built around it we behold wonderful structures and ornamentations put up by King Ethelbald in honour of the divine power.'[149] What sounds like an elaborately decorated tomb-shrine was saved from the Danes in 870, when Abbot Theodore and some of the stronger monks fled to the fens in a boat taking the abbey's principal relics (including the *sacratissima gleba corporis sancti Guthlaci*), treasures, and manuscripts with them; but the tombs of other Croyland saints who had been buried beneath tall marble monuments *ad sanctum* to right and left of Guthlac's tomb were destroyed.[150] As we shall see, there was a resurgence of interest in Guthlac's cult during the twelfth century, when the body was finally elevated and enshrined.[151]

An important group of new saints was indeed provided by kings such as

[145] Farmer, *Dictionary*, 221.
[146] H. Mayr-Harting, in *DNB*, xxiv. 301–2, refers, however, to 'his death in 715, probably on 3 April'.
[147] Probably the St Edburh mentioned in the *Secgan* as 'resting at Southwell-on-Trent'; see Farmer, *Dictionary*, 145.
[148] *The Chronicle of Croyland Abbey by Ingulph*, ed. W. de Gray Birch (Wisbech, 1883), 3–7.
[149] *Felix's Life of Saint Guthlac*, ed. B. Colgrave (Cambridge, 1956), 162–3.
[150] *Chronicle of Croyland Abbey*, ed. Birch, 35–6.
[151] See pp. 164–6.

Oswald, who had died in battle or as a result of political conflicts and came to be regarded as martyrs.[152] They include such royal saints as Æthelberht, king of the East Angles (†794), beheaded by King Offa and venerated at Hereford; Wigstan (Wystan) of Repton;[153] and Cynhelm (Kenelm) of Winchcombe.[154] As Rollason has pointed out, the number of English royal saints far exceeded those on the Continent, and those who had died unnaturally formed a significant number.

Other royal cults remain shrouded in obscurity. Amongst these is that of St Eanswyth of Folkestone (*c.*614–*c.*640), grand-daughter of King Æthelberht of Kent and daughter of Æthelberht's successor, Eadbald (†640). Her mother was Emma, a Frankish princess (probably the daughter of the Austrasian king Theodeberht).[155] According to the probably unreliable, late sources for her cult, she renounced the marriage with a Northumbrian prince planned for her by her father (then a pagan) and founded a nunnery at Folkestone where she later became abbess, but died at a young age;[156] these elements of the story are, however, familiar both in Gaul and Anglo-Saxon England and could be mere hagiographical commonplace: Bede, it would appear, had never heard of her.

According to John Capgrave, who claimed to cite a lost Life of the saint, the site of the original monastery vanished through coastal erosion, and a new church of St Peter was established further from the chalk cliffs.[157] The monastery is mentioned in a charter purporting to have been issued by King Æthelstan in 927 granting to Christ Church, Canterbury land at Folkestone 'where there was once a monastery and abbey of holy virgins and where St Eanswyth was buried'; but this document is not considered genuine in its surviving form.[158] Æthelstan's involvement is therefore open to question. A later tradition states that in 1095 Nigel de Muneville refounded it some two centuries after it had been devastated by the Danes, but that following further coastal erosion the priory was moved further inland by William d'Avranches in 1138, and the relics were again translated.[159] The priory was dissolved in 1535 and the church became the parish church of Folkestone, still dedicated to 'St Mary and St Eanswythe'.

The cult is especially interesting because the relics have survived. In June 1885, during building works in the thirteenth-century chancel, workmen

[152] Rollason, 'Murdered royal saints'. Ridyard, *Royal Saints*.
[153] See pp. 72–4.
[154] See above, p. 58.
[155] See S. E. Kelly, 'Eadbald', in *DNB*, xvii. 521–2. Eanswyth is also mentioned in the so-called 'Kentish Royal Legend': Liebermann, *Die Heiligen Englands*, 1–9, as discussed in Rollason, 'Lists' 73.
[156] Dame Eanswythe Edwards, *St Eanswythe of Folkestone* (Folkestone, 1980).
[157] *AASS, Augusti VI*, 685–7, at 685E.
[158] P. H. Sawyer (ed.), *Anglo-Saxon Charters: An Annotated List and Bibliography* (London, 1968), 168 (No. 398).
[159] E. Hasted, *The History and Topographical Survey of the County of Kent*, 2nd edn., 12 vols. (Canterbury, 1797–1801, reprinted East Ardsley, Wakefield, 1972), viii. 180. See also S. E. Rigold, 'The "Double Minsters" of Kent and their analogies', *JBAA*, 31 (1968), 27–37.

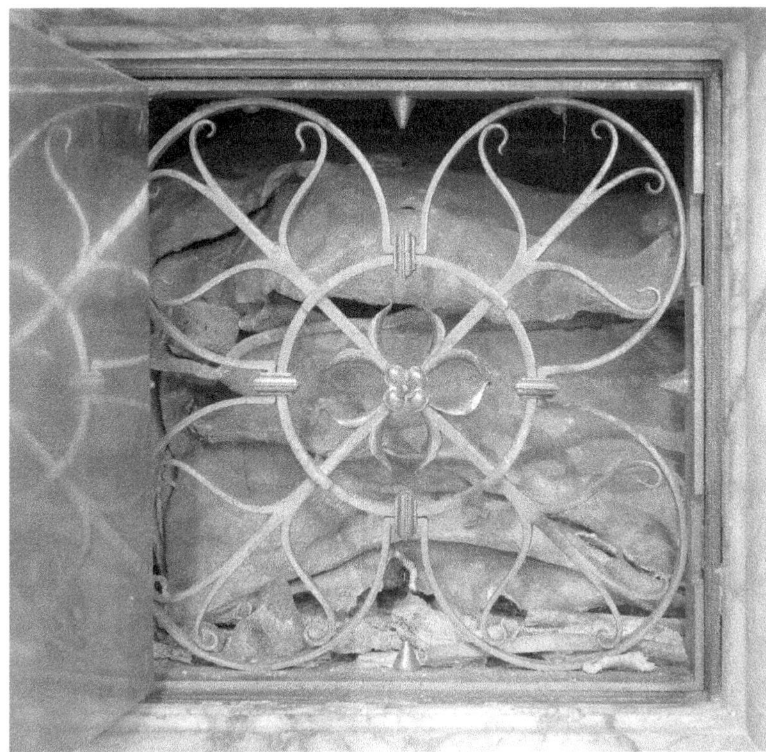

PLATE 3.4 FOLKESTONE (KENT), CHURCH OF ST MARY AND ST EANSWYTHE The *loculus* housing the crushed lead coffer said to have contained the relics of St Eanswyth.

exposed a blocked recess in the north wall, enclosing the deformed remains of a lead casket.[160] Although no inscription was present, it was supposed that this was the reliquary of St Eanswyth, which had been concealed at the Dissolution. The casket proved to contain bones, which were subjected to a medical examination in 1980: the fragmentary remains were identified as those of a young woman and were therefore consistent with the legend of St Eanswyth.[161] The crushed lead coffer and relics are now housed in a *loculus* in the sanctuary.

Whether the relics are indeed those of the saint cannot be ascertained. However, the casket is of particular relevance in our study of shrines. It measures approximately 350 × 220 × 200mm (14 × 9 × 8 inches), but is very deformed. When Canon Scott Robertson examined it in 1885 he concluded that it was of two dates. He considered that the best parallel for the actual coffer, adorned with lozenge-shaped decoration in the form of rows of small

[160] Canon Scott Robertson, 'St Eanswith's reliquary in Folkestone Church', *Arch. Cant.*, 16 (1886), 322–6.

[161] Edwards, *St Eanswythe*, 22–3, Appendix 2: 'Report of an examination of the relics of St. Eanswythe in Folkestone Parish Church by Dr. P. H. Garrard, M.B., B.S., on 29.2.1980'.

pellets, was the lead cist of Gundrada de Warenne (†1085) at Lewes; the lid, however, he considered to have been adapted from a Roman coffin decorated with cable-moulding. This seems to make the history of the construction of the coffin unduly tortuous: all the decoration could in fact be Roman, and it is possible therefore that the coffer was formed from a Roman lead sarcophagus. If so, it may be another example of the reuse of prestigious Roman materials for the relics of a saint. Militating against this, however, is the fact that the coffer would have been too short to accommodate even the femora of a disarticulated skeleton: the remains, which are far from complete, must have suffered damage before they were placed within the coffer. It is conceivable therefore that they were placed in the coffer only in the post-Conquest period: either at the refoundation of the monastery in 1095 or at the time of the construction of the third church and final translation of the relics in 1138.

The physical evidence for early Anglo-Saxon saints' cults is sparse, and for their interpretation one must perforce rely mainly on literary sources. As we shall see in the following chapter, physical evidence survives more abundantly in the middle and late Saxon periods: the golden age of pre-Conquest saints.

‘THE ISLAND OF SAINTS’ 4

Saints’ cults in mid- to late Anglo-Saxon England

LATER ANGLO-SAXON CRYPTS AND SAINTS’ CULTS

As we saw in Chapter 2, a revived architectural response to the cult of local saints flourished during the reign of Charlemagne and his successors. This architecture looked back to late sixth-century Rome, and drew particular inspiration from the crypts built by Popes Gregory the Great and Honorius I. The late Anglo-Saxon crypt at Canterbury, discussed below, appears to have been inspired by the ring-crypt of St Peter’s, Rome. A somewhat disparate collection of surviving Anglo-Saxon crypts may also have been associated with saints’ cults.

At Brixworth (Northants) the apse at the east end of the church is surrounded by an external ring-crypt, which was rediscovered and excavated by the incumbent in the mid-nineteenth century.[1] Victorian churchmen with antiquarian tastes were evidently less scrupulous than their modern successors, and the Revd Charles Watkins unashamedly ‘[took] occasion of the burial of a parishioner in the chancel to make excavations there’.

> I observed in the north-western corner of the exterior two sides remaining of a former polygonal structure, and noticed that the interior of that part curved a little. This led me to infer that it was part of an original apse, polygonal without and semi-circular within, and probably with an underground crypt, as in the oldest forms. I therefore made the masons prolong their excavations, till they reached, as I suspected, a subterranean wall, ten feet deep, which I made them lay open in its whole extent, till it came to view a perfect semicircle …

[1] C. F. Watkins, *The Basilica or Palatial Hall of Justice and Sacred Temple; its Nature, Origin, and Purport: and a Description and History of the Basilican Church of Brixworth* (London, 1867).

At the apex of the Saxon apse, whose interior wall he had exposed, Watkins observed a doorway, and inferred that it led to 'a subterranean chamber or corridor on the outside of the wall' and that if there was indeed an external ambulatory other entries to it should be found at the east end of the main body of the church. This proved to be the case, and eventually the external ring-crypt was opened up as seen today.

To conform with Continental exemplars, however, a central passage returning westwards from the head of the apse would be expected. Watkins's excavations revealed no evidence of this: 'Contrary to expectation, I found the original floor of the chancel on a level with that of the church, and unbroken ground beneath: so that there could have been no crypt under the church, but only the ambulatory around it and beneath.' It is of course not clear that Watkins excavated the whole area of the original chancel down to floor level, and the doorway that Watkins discovered at the apex of the apse certainly sounds like an entrance to a central corridor. Until the apse is re-excavated the question will remain uncertain. No known local saint's cult existed at Brixworth, however, and the resemblance of its crypt to architectural forms normally associated with such cults may be fortuitous. Possibly the cultic origins of the design had been forgotten by the late eighth or early ninth century, which seems the most likely date for this structure.[2]

We can be more certain about the use of another crypt, which appears to have been adapted to suit a new saint's cult. As already noted, the crypt at Repton may originally have been built as a royal mausoleum for King Æthelbald of Mercia (†757) in the mid-eighth century. There is no evidence that he was ever considered a potential saint, despite his promotion of the cult of St Guthlac, which might have had the usual knock-on effect. Æthelbald's son Wiglaf was buried in the same crypt in 839. Wiglaf was in turn succeeded, not by his son Wigstan (Wystan), who declined the throne for religious reasons, but by Beorhtwulf, whose relation (possibly his son) Beorhtfrith subsequently sought to marry Wiglaf's widow and inherit the kingdom of Mercia. Wigstan naturally objected to these power-seeking manoeuvres, a criticism which led to his murder in 849; thereafter he was quickly regarded as a saint.[3] Like his father and, possibly, his grandfather, he was buried in the crypt at Repton,[4] which was soon adapted so as to reflect its new function as the focus of a saint's cult. As already noted, the original crypt consisted of a square chamber with recesses on three sides and (it is conjectured) a single access stair leading down, either from the outside or from a building to the west, to an entrance in the west wall. In a second, probably mid-ninth-century, phase of building, the central opening on the west side of the crypt was blocked to form a fourth recess. Entrance

[2] The crypt did not form part of the excavations described in E. D. C. Jackson and E. G. M. Fletcher, 'Excavations at Brixworth, 1958', *JBAA*, 3rd ser., 24 (1961), 1–15, where the church (though not necessarily the crypt) is attributed to St Wilfrid (late seventh century).

[3] Rollason, 'Murdered royal saints', 5–9.

[4] *John of Worcester*, ii. 262–3.

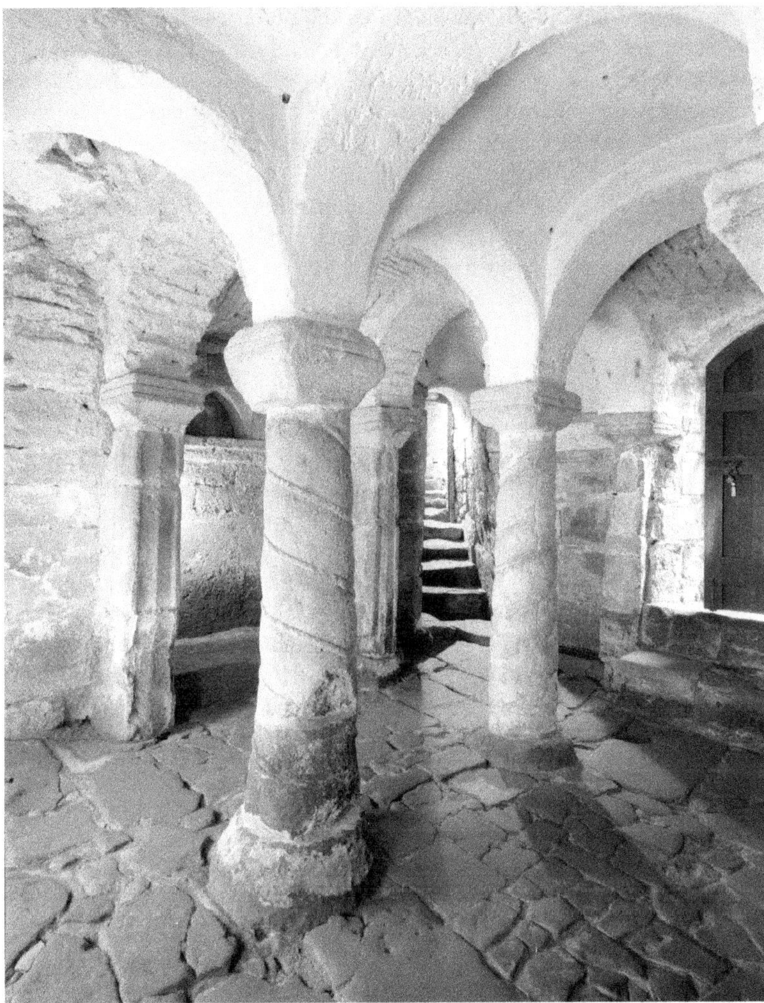

PLATE 4.1 REPTON (DERBYSHIRE) The crypt as remodelled, probably following the murder of King Wigstan (St Wystan) in 849.

tunnels were created in the north-east and north-west corners, containing stairs descending from the east end of the church, which had been built immediately to the west of the crypt. A new vault was formed, comprising nine domed cells supported on four pillars decorated with a spiral twist design. This motif had been associated with saints' cults ever since Constantine the Great imported six porphyry barley-sugar twist columns from the 'east' (*de Grecias*), four of which served to support the canopy over the tomb of St Peter in Constantine's new basilica at the Vatican.[5] The most

[5] As illustrated in the fifth-century 'Pola casket': Toynbee and Ward Perkins, *Shrine of St Peter*, 204 and Figs. 20–1 and 247–51. See also J. B. Ward Perkins, 'The Shrine of St. Peter and its Twelve Spiral Columns', *Jnl. of Roman Studies*, 42 (1952), 21–33.

likely context for the alterations to the Repton crypt was the burial of St Wigstan, and the whole arrangement appears to have been designed to emphasise the sanctity of his tomb. This presumably lay in a central position between the four pillars, which formed a kind of *baldachino* above the burial; the new access stairs allowed pilgrim circulation. The body of St Wigstan remained at Repton until the time of Cnut (1016–35), who translated it to Evesham at the request of Abbot Ælfweard.[6] There, despite initial reservations on the part of the first Norman abbot, the cult would flourish, particularly in the thirteenth century.[7]

The other important Anglo-Saxon crypt to have survived is that of the marvellously complete pre-Conquest church at Wing (Bucks), but this case presents several problems of interpretation.[8] As originally built, the crypt was polygonal, with recesses, rather like those at Repton, to east, north, and south; there is some slight evidence that the builders' original intention was to form an exterior ambulatory around it, as at Brixworth.[9] The crypt was subsequently remodelled when extra, elongated piers were inserted giving a plan somewhat reminiscent of a ring-crypt, though retaining its polygonal form. The vault was reconstructed at the same time. The crypt was later filled with earth (perhaps after the Reformation) and was rediscovered by Sir Gilbert Scott in the mid-nineteenth century. In about 1880 his son George Gilbert Scott supervised the removal of the infill. This permitted an examination of the entrance passages and other features at the end of the crypt. Notably, Scott discovered, behind the western wall of the central vessel of the crypt, a feature that he described as the 'remains of the *jugulum*, *cataracta*, or *fenestra* ... which clearly connected with the nave of the church'.[10] Scott's use of Latin terms obscures his meaning: *jugulum* is a throat in classical Latin, *cataracta* a waterfall or sluice, and *fenestra* a window. The term *cataracta* can, however, also mean an underground passage in medieval Latin, and this is presumably what he had in mind. He seems to have interpreted his discovery as a deep recess at the east end of the nave, located beneath the high altar platform and between the two flights of stairs leading up to that platform, with an opening (for which the Latin term *fenestella* is appropriate) at the end, looking down into the crypt. The western wall of the crypt, which Scott had evidently broken through, was subsequently made good, and no further archaeological discoveries were made for nearly a century. Speculation by a local antiquary, Arthur Vere Woodman, who was understandably confused about Scott's alleged discoveries, did not

[6] *Evesham Chronicle*, 83, 325–6.

[7] See below, pp. 228–9.

[8] The best introduction to this crypt remains Taylor, *Anglo-Saxon Architecture*, ii. 665–72.

[9] ibid., 669.

[10] G. Gilbert Scott, *An Essay on the History of English Church Architecture prior to the Separation of England from the Roman Obedience* (London, 1881), plate X.iii and pp. 46 and 189–90, at 190. The discoveries were also reported in [G. G. Scott] 'Re-opening of a Roman basilica under the chancel of Wing Church', *Records of Bucks*., 5 No. 3 (1880), 147–8.

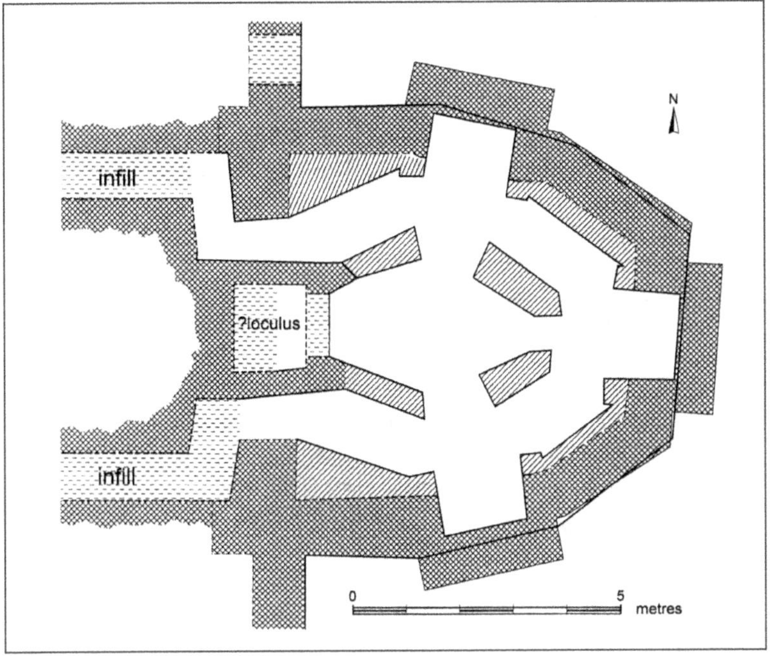

FIG.4.1 ALL SAINTS' CHURCH, WING Plan of the crypt showing possibly mid-tenth-century modification of the original eighth-century structure (single hatch), conjectural position of the loculus housing a saint's relics (cross-hatch), and modern infill (dashed).

significantly increase knowledge of the crypt.[11] Then in around 1960 Dudley Jackson and Eric Fletcher took up an area of pavement at the entrance to the chancel, where the incumbent had reported that the floor sounded hollow. What they discovered was initially identified by Vere Woodman, influenced no doubt by Scott's earlier interpretation, as 'a squint about 4 ft. 6 in. wide and in fair condition'. But Jackson and Fletcher had in fact discovered a rather different structure. Having lifted a few tiles within the chancel, they slid down a rope into what they described as a 'cavity' within the earth fill behind the west wall of the crypt. The fill here had presumably been partly removed when the west wall was pierced as part of Scott's investigations, though the authors never mentioned this. The cavity proved to be part of a larger, infilled space west of the main crypt, certainly with masonry walls to north and south; it was presumably Scott's '*cataracta*'. Investigation must have been difficult (the cavity tapered downwards to only 21in. wide), but the pair were able to ascertain that the internal dimension from north to south was 5ft. Probing within the earth fill, which was however not removed, indicated that the cavity extended at least 3ft towards the west, and it was 'approximately 7 ft. 6 in. deep below the chancel floor'.[12]

[11] A. V. W. [Arthur Vere Woodman], 'Wing Church', *Records of Bucks*., 16 pt. 5 (1960), 367–8, at 367; A. Vere Woodman, 'Wing Church', ibid., 17 pt. 2 (1962), 130–1.

[12] E. D. C. Jackson and E. G. M. Fletcher, 'The apse and nave at Wing, Buckinghamshire', *JBAA*, 3rd ser., 25 (1962), 1–20, at 13.

But Jackson and Fletcher's sectional drawing shows that the level of the bottom of the tapering cavity roughly corresponded to the crypt floor, which seems to disqualify Scott's suggestion that the chamber was a sloping access tunnel descending eastwards from the nave. It is more likely to have been a western *loculus* similar to a number of known Continental exemplars. This was also Jackson and Fletcher's conclusion: they postulated a western wall behind the earth fill, 'thus constituting an enclosed chamber'.[13] If there was a *fenestella* it would have been at the west end of the cavity, looking upwards into the nave through the head of the western wall of the chamber, which the investigators did not reach.

Such an arrangement, together with the existence of a pair of entrance stairs (now blocked) formerly leading down into the crypt from the east ends of the nave,[14] could reasonably be associated with a saint's cult; but unfortunately there are no records that such a cult existed at Wing church, apart from a rather dubious reference to relics there mentioned in the will, datable to the period 966 × 975, of a certain royal lady called Ælfgifu. Amongst other property, she bequeathed her estate at Wing to her royal lord (King Edgar), and 'the shrine with her relics' (*hire scrín mid hiræ haligdomæ*) to Old Minster, Winchester, where she desired to be buried.[15] Dorothy Whitelock conjectured that Ælfgifu might have been the divorced wife of King Eadwig.[16] The remodelling of the crypt was dated by Jackson and Fletcher to Ælfgifu's time, a chronology accepted by Harold and Joan Taylor. The Taylors considered, however, that the western loculus and dog's-leg entrance passages formed part of the first phase of the crypt rather than the later, possibly mid-tenth-century, modifications.

Another possible ring-crypt has been excavated at Cirencester,[17] but again there is no good documentary evidence for a saint's cult there. These ring-crypts may have been introduced simply because the patrons liked the sophistication of the form, even though they had lost sight of their original function.

The best example of a ring-crypt arguably connected with a saint's cult in England is the most tantalising: the eastern ring-crypt of the Anglo-Saxon cathedral at Canterbury, known only from a description by the Anglo-Saxon monk Eadmer.[18] His text has been the subject of intense debate amongst architectural historians,[19] but despite the efforts of some scholars to prove otherwise, it cannot be denied that his description is precisely what a non-

[13] ibid., 14.
[14] Rather than from the aisles, as supposed by Scott; see Taylor, *Anglo-Saxon Architecture*, ii. 669 and note 3.
[15] BL, Add. MS 15350 (the *Codex Wintoniensis*) fo. 94, printed in *Anglo-Saxon Wills*, ed. D. Whitelock (Cambridge, 1930), item VIII, pp. 21–3 and 118–21.
[16] ibid., 119.
[17] Crook, *Architectural Setting*, 104–5 and Fig. 32.
[18] Eadmer, *De reliquiis S. Audoeni*.
[19] For the bibliography of the debate, see Crook, *Architectural Setting*, 105–6; and Blockley, *Canterbury Nave*, 107–10.

specialist might have written when attempting to set down on paper a verbal picture of a Roman ring-crypt. Indeed, Eadmer actually stated that the crypt had been built 'in imitation of the crypt (*confessio*) of St Peter'.[20] He also said that the church as a whole had been built 'to a certain extent in imitation of the church of the prince of the Apostles'. Investigations undertaken when the nave floor of Canterbury Cathedral was relaid in 1993 showed that the western end of the church was extensively remodelled at the beginning of the eleventh century, with the addition of a new western structure comprising a deep apse, polygonal externally and semi-circular within, flanked by hexagonal stair-turrets.[21] It is possible therefore that the eastern end was also modified at the same time, and that the ring-crypt was introduced then. Unfortunately the site of the east end of the Anglo-Saxon cathedral lies beneath the central crossing tower (and, perhaps, within the west end of the present crypt) of Archbishop Lanfranc's new church; little if any physical evidence is likely to survive. We may speculate that the central corridor led to the tomb of St Dunstan, which Eadmer says was surmounted by a *pyramis*, a term meaning little more than a raised monument. According to this interpretation, the crypt may have been formed by Archbishop Ælfric or his successor Ælfheah in order that St Dunstan's undisturbed body should be appropriately venerated.[22] On the other hand, the accounts of St Dunstan's miracles compiled by Osbern, a young boy while the Anglo-Saxon church was still standing,[23] do not suggest that suppliants needed to enter the crypt in order to reach the tomb of the saint. For example, Osbern recounts how three blind women visited the church in search of a cure: they came to the church door, joined hands, and threw themselves on the ground in front of the *memoria*.[24] Osbern personally witnessed another miracle, the cure of a girl blind from birth. She had obtained permission to spend the night praying next to Dunstan's tomb, and Osbern and the monks were singing lauds when they noticed the girl rubbing her eyes, her sight restored.[25] On yet another occasion the young Osbern and a little boy of the same age had been serving at the 'altar of Christ' when a woman with a crippled daughter appealed to them for aid.[26] They sent the pair to Dunstan's tomb, where the girl was cured. Then 'we ran up, saw, and wept', says Osbern.[27] All these examples suggest that the *tumba* or *memoria*, which several suppliants are recorded as having touched

[20] *De reliquiis S. Audoeni*, 365.

[21] Blockley, *Canterbury Nave*, *passim*.

[22] As I have argued in Crook, *Architectural Setting*, 105–6.

[23] *Miracula S. Dunstani, auct. Osberno*, in *Memorials of St Dunstan*, 129–61. Osbern mentions (p. 138) that he was a small boy (*puerulus*) while Godric was dean, (*c.*1050 × *c.*1070), acc. Knowles, *Heads*, i. 33.

[24] *Miracula S. Dunstani, auct. Osberno*, 131.

[25] ibid., 136–7.

[26] ibid., 138–9.

[27] ibid., 139: *Itaque accurrimus, vidimus, flevimus, et facto mane cum exultatione totius urbis, Dominicum Deum Jesum nostrum Jesum Christum laudavimus.*

in order to obtain a cure, was located in an accessible place, where the goings-on were visible to all, rather than in the seclusion of a crypt. Dunstan's actual sarcophagus may have been situated at the end of the central corridor of the ring-crypt, but it seems to have been at the *pyramis* constructed over it that the faithful sought his aid. The crypt was perhaps accessible only to the monks. Debate over the form of the crypt will no doubt continue. Nevertheless, the eastern ring-crypt at Canterbury would seem to be an example of the influence that Rome has always had on that cathedral, founded as it was by the Roman delegation led by St Augustine on the orders of Pope Gregory the Great.

There is documentary evidence for another late Saxon crypt at Evesham, which was dedicated to St Ecgwine, founder of the abbey. Shortly before the Conquest a monk named Sperckwulf from the newly founded abbey of Coventry was in the habit of spending time wandering alone around the church. On one occasion he was in the crypt, where he witnessed a ghostly procession of monks making their way to the altar of St Ecgwine, where they recited the night offices.[28] A similar saintly manifestation subsequently occurred in what was probably the Lady chapel (it is called *ecclesia Dei Genetricis*), where Sperckwulf saw St Ecgwine and the Blessed Virgin processing to the Lady altar, where the saint celebrated mass. Although these events illustrate the power of the cult in the time of Prior Dominic, it is perhaps unlikely that the saint's main reliquary, created two to three decades earlier under Abbot Mannig,[29] was located within the crypt itself. Comparative evidence suggests that it is more likely to have been at main level.

'St Cedd's crypt' at Lastingham, as it was once known, must reluctantly be deleted from the list of Anglo-Saxon crypts connected with saints' cults. Its architectural detail (such as the volute capitals crowning its stumpy piers) show that it was started soon after the arrival in 1078 of Stephen, abbot of Whitby. As the Taylors have shown, the pier bases are reused pre-Conquest fabric from the earlier church.[30] After his death in 664 Cedd had initially been buried 'outside the walls' of Lastingham during a time of plague, but was moved to the right-hand side of the (high) altar in a stone church dedicated to the Virgin Mary.[31] Later, his relics would be claimed by Lichfield.

KING OFFA AND THE LEGENDARY FOUNDATION OF ST ALBAN'S ABBEY

As well as being credited with embellishing the shrine of St Oswald *c.*792, and granting a generous endowment to the church of Rochester in 788,[32] King Offa of Mercia (757–96) was also remembered by the monks of St

[28] *Evesham Chronicle*, 51–2.
[29] see pp. 105–6.
[30] Taylor, *Anglo-Saxon Architecture*, i. 373.
[31] Bede, *HE*, iii.23; ed. Colgrave and Mynors, 288–9.
[32] above, p. 53.

Alban's Abbey in the later medieval period as the founder of their community. This belief required playing down the well-recorded earlier history of the cult which, as we have indicated, went back at least to the time of St Germanus of Auxerre. Even at the beginning of the twentieth century when Charles Peers and William Page were writing their description of the abbey church for the *Victoria County History*, they confidently asserted that 'The history of the Abbey begins with its foundation by Offa in 793', making little of the evidence for an earlier church.[33]

Later commentators have been more circumspect, pointing out that there is very little pre-Conquest evidence for Offa's involvement with St Albans, and certainly no contemporary evidence connecting him with the refoundation of the community there.[34] As Julia Crick, editor of the St Albans charters, has emphasised, all the charters purporting to record Offa's endowments to St Albans are forgeries dating from the early twelfth century. The *Anglo-Saxon Chronicle* contains an annal relating the foundation in 793, but this addition to the text was presumably made when the 'F' (Canterbury) version was compiled at the end of the eleventh century. Some evidence has, however, emerged that traditions about Offa's involvement were perhaps developing at St Albans at the time of the late tenth-century monastic reforms,[35] and the association with Offa is explicitly stated in diplomas of King Æthelred dating from *c*.1000.[36] Given the gap in time between the purported events and the later, no doubt highly embellished accounts, it is hard to discern what may be a core of truth. One may perhaps speculate that Offa, with his proven interest in at least one other major saint's cult, did indeed translate Alban's body, but given that Bede describes miracles at the tomb only sixty years before Offa's alleged translation it is unlikely that the grave was unknown, as later tradition maintained. Like so much hagiography, this was a *topos* intended to emphasise the sanctity of the community's patron saint.

Our best source for the Offa tradition is the *Life of the Two Offas*, attributed to the thirteenth-century St Albans monk Matthew Paris (*c*.1200–1259),[37] and although his version of events appears to stand on

[33] *VCH Herefordshire*, ed. W. Page, ii (1908), 483–510 (Architectural description of 'St Albans Cathedral' by C. R. Peers and W. Page).

[34] W. Levison, 'St. Alban and St. Albans', *Antiquity*, 15 (1941), 337–59, at 350–8. Biddle, 'Alban and the Anglo-Saxon Church', 30–1. Julia Crick, 'Offa, Ælfric and the Refoundation of St Albans', in *Alban and St Albans*, 78–84.

[35] S. Keynes, 'A Lost Cartulary of St Albans Abbey', *Anglo-Saxon England*, 22 (1993), 253–79.

[36] Crick, 'Offa, Ælfrid and the Refoundation', 79, citing *Charters of St Albans*, ed. eadem (Oxford, 2007), 167–98.

[37] Especially the *Vita Offæ Secundi*, in *Matthæi Parisiensis ... Historia Major*, ed. W. Wats (London, 1640). In that edition 'The Lives of the Two Offas', and other material, is separately paginated (it started life as a volume published in 1639); the story of the invention of Alban's relics and the foundation of the monastery is on pp. 26–32. For the authorship of the *Lives of the Two Offas*, and Matthew's use of Roger of Wendover's *Flores Historiarum* as a source, see R. Vaughan, *Matthew Paris* (Cambridge, 1958), 41–8, 189–94.

shaky historical foundations, it reveals much about contemporary attitudes to the abbey's patron saint, whose alleged translation in 793 is portrayed as central to the supposed foundation of the abbey. For this reason, we shall only briefly summarise his version of events here.

According to Matthew, an angel appeared to Offa in a dream whilst he was at Bath, telling him that he should raise the proto-martyr, Alban, from the earth and place him more worthily in a shrine (*in scrinio dignius collocaret*), the usual formula.[38] He sought the advice of Humbert, archbishop of Lichfield, and, together with his suffragan bishops and a great number of lay folk, the king hurried to Verolamium. This was about 344 years after Germanus's visit, i.e. around 793, and the church that Bede described had allegedly been demolished during the Saxon invasions, which meant the place of burial had been lost. Fortunately the saint miraculously indicated his presence by a great shaft of light; the wooden *theca* containing Alban's remains was quickly located, together with many other relics which Germanus had deposited there. All were moved to tears. Then the relics, 'more precious than gold and precious jewels, and long hidden under a bushel', were reverently taken out of their grave and transferred to a small church (*ecclesiolam*), conveniently built by his neophytes on the place where the martyr had died. Needless to say, this detail is inconsistent with the site's having being lost. Miracles occurred, in the account of which Matthew resorts to *topoi*: the dead were brought to life, the half-killed were restored unscathed, lepers were cured, the paralysed walked again.[39] Then,

> ... the most Christian king Offa gave orders that the aforesaid shrine (*locellus*) should be fittingly adorned with gold and silver plates and precious stones, which he bountifully provided from his treasury at his own expense; and that the same church in which, as we have already said, the body was laid should be decorated with pictures, curtains and other ornaments until that same church, worthy of adornment, should be built larger when it was endowed with many possessions and honours.[40]

Offa's advisors counselled him to seek papal ratification of Alban's sanctity and permission for the construction of a monastery where the martyr would be venerated; and the king determined to travel to Rome personally. Pope Hadrian I approved Alban's canonisation and agreed to the construction of a new monastery. He endowed an English school in Rome, to be funded by 'St Peter's Pence' (but the new monastery would be exempt). On Offa's return to England the king endowed the monastery with suitable property, and construction began. Willegod, who had been present at the invention, was

[38] *Vita Offæ Secundi*, ed. Wats, 26.
[39] ibid., 27.
[40] ibid., 28: *Rex igitur* Offa *Christianissimus, locellum memoratum laminis aureis & argenteis, gemmisque pretiosis, de thesauro suo munifice sumptis, decenter adornari, et ecclesiam ipsius, in qua ut iam dictum est, corpus collocabatur, picturis, aulæis, et aliis ornamentis, donec amplior multis ditanda possessionibus et honoribus ædificaretur, iussit decorari.*

appointed first abbot. Offa himself laid the foundation stone. The penultimate section of Matthew's narrative is concerned with the abbey's endowments (there being no better place to confirm possessions than in hagiography) and the work ends with Offa's death. The fact that Offa was not buried at St Albans must have been an embarrassment; Matthew explains that he was buried in a chapel by the river Usk outside Bedford, but that both chapel and tomb were destroyed in a flood.

THE INFLUENCE OF THE DANISH INVASIONS ON ENGLISH SAINTS' CULTS

As we have seen, costly decoration seems to have been an important feature of Anglo-Saxon shrines. It is a commonplace to state that the marvellous metalwork of shrines, reliquaries, and crosses attracted the attention of the Danes during the Viking invasions. Indeed, the creation of the see of Durham is indirectly linked with Danish depredations, and the story of St Cuthbert may conveniently be pursued here. Of the development of his monument at Lindisfarne for nearly two centuries after the translation of 698 we have no evidence. Lindisfarne was, however, especially vulnerable to marauders crossing the North Sea, and was sacked in 793, when on 7 June the Danes 'pillaged all the treasures of the church'.[41] The shrine of Cuthbert evidently escaped destruction. During the second wave of Viking invasion, which began in 866, Bishop Eardwulf 'foresaw that the church of Lindisfarne would be finally destroyed', and, after discussion, he and Abbot Eadred 'Luisc' resolved to evacuate the monastery, taking Cuthbert's body and other relics with them.[42] By 883 the small group had reached Chester-le-Street, where they stayed until 995.[43] There, Cuthbert's shrine was visited by both King Æthelstan (in 934) and King Edmund (in 945), who presented gifts, some of which were placed within the coffin.[44] Finally in 995 the community moved again to the peninsula at Dunholm, modern Durham. According to Symeon of Durham, once the saint had miraculously indicated that this was where he wished to stay, he was placed first in a temporary church made of 'branches' (perhaps wattle), then for three years in another one, called the 'White Church', and finally he was translated into the new Anglo-Saxon church of Bishop Ealdhun, where his body was enshrined with due honour in the place prepared for it.[45]

According to St Albans tradition recorded by Matthew Paris, the relics of that saint were also affected by the Danish invasions. In the time of Wulnoth, said to be the fourth abbot since the 'foundation' of 793, the abbey

[41] Symeon, *Libellus*, 89.
[42] ibid., 101–3. For the date of the invasion, ibid., 96–8, note 41.
[43] E. Cambridge, 'Why did the Community of St Cuthbert settle at Chester-le-Street?', in Bonner, *St Cuthbert*, 367–86. G. Bonner, 'St Cuthbert at Chester-le-Street', ibid., 387–95.
[44] Anon., *Historia de sancto Cuthberto*, caps. 26–32; *Sym. Op.*, i. 196–214, at 211–13.
[45] Symeon, *Libellus*, 148–54.

was allegedly plundered by the Danes, who removed the relics to 'Owense', i.e. Odensee in Denmark. It is claimed they were retrieved by the St Albans sacrist, Egwyn, who infiltrated himself into the Odensee community and after a few years became sacrist there as well. This gave him the opportunity of surreptitiously removing the relics through a hole in the bottom of the wooden reliquary. He then wrapped the bones in a parcel, and got a merchant to carry them back to St Albans, saying they were a packet of books which he was sending to the abbot. Once he heard the relics had arrived safely he set sail for England, thoughtfully writing to the Odensee monks on his return to tell them what he had done.[46] It is a marvellous tale, but the degree of historical truth must be regarded as strictly limited.

This was only the beginning of prolonged disagreements about the location of the relics of England's proto-martyr. Ælfric II, the eleventh abbot (his dates are unknown but the early eleventh century seems probable), is alleged to have tried to preserve the relics from the Danes by burying them beneath an altar dedicated to St Nicholas. In a curious bit of double bluff he sent a set of bones to Ely, claiming that they were those of St Alban. When the Danish threat subsided, the St Albans monks asked for the bones to be returned, whereupon the Ely monks substituted yet another batch of false relics. Eventually the buried bones were disinterred and displayed again within the abbey church; the Ely monks, however, continued to claim that they possessed the genuine relics of the saint.[47]

SAINTS' CULTS AND THE TENTH-CENTURY MONASTIC REFORMS

The cult of saints played an important part in the monastic reforms of the tenth century, when another wave of Continental influences affected religious practices in Anglo-Saxon England. The key figures behind the English reforms, encouraged by King Edgar, were Bishops Æthelwold of Winchester and Oswald of Worcester. Recent scholarship has tended to play down the influence of Archbishop Dunstan.[48] All three prelates would become saints.

Winchester provides the best example of the way saints' cults were an inseparable component of the monastic reforms. Old Minster, the Anglo-Saxon cathedral, had been founded in the late seventh century by St Birinus, apostle of Wessex, and could lay claim to at least some of his relics, as discussed below. Shortly after his consecration in 963 Bishop Æthelwold expelled the secular canons who hitherto had occupied Old Minster, installing in their place monks from Abingdon, where he had previously

[46] *GA*; ed. Riley, i. 12–18.
[47] ibid., i. 34–7.
[48] e.g. Nicholas Brooks, in 'The Career of St Dunstan', in Ramsay, *St Dunstan*, 1–23, at 1: '... in recent scholarship Dunstan's role has waned as that of his younger contemporaries, Æthelwold and Oswald, has grown'.

been abbot. The Abingdon monks were themselves imports from Fleury, one of the Continental centres of the monastic reform movement.

Æthelwold evidently felt that a new saint was required as the *persona* of the monastic community. He therefore promoted the cult of one of his predecessors, Swithun,[49] bishop of Winchester from 852–63, now known mainly for a late medieval weather myth. Swithun was probably a former secular canon of Old Minster, and the choice may have been intended to appease the canons ejected in 964, but very little is known about him; indeed, he may have been selected precisely because his career, good or bad, was unknown.

St Swithun's elevation was described, some twenty-five years later, by Wulfstan, cantor of Old Minster (writing in 994–6), who was present at the ceremony as a young oblate. His account therefore provides precious witness to the elevation, though much of his poem consists of a metrical adaptation of a prose *Translatio et Miracula* probably composed in 972 × 974 by the monk 'from overseas' (most likely a native of Francia and perhaps a monk of Fleury), Lantfred, whose account of the actual *elevatio* is far briefer.[50]

Swithun had been buried in the forecourt of Old Minster, between the west end of that small church and a tower-porch dedicated to St Martin. According to the familiar *topos*, the saint made known his wish to be translated by miracles. Michael Lapidge has emphasised that Lantfred's account of the events leading up to the miraculous discovery of the saint, the *revelatio*, was heavily dependent on an early fifth-century Greek prototype, the *Revelatio Sancti Stephani*, discussed in Chapter 2.[51] First Swithun, 'comely with attractive white hair and resplendent in the likeness of an angel, being clothed in a linen robe and wearing golden sandals on his feet, appeared in the quiet of a dream to a certain trustworthy smith', waking him by lightly touching him on the head three times with a golden staff.[52] Such details are identical with Gamaliel's appearance to Lucian.[53] The smith was instructed to go to Eadsige, one of the recently dispossessed canons, and inform him that he should in turn tell Bishop Æthelwold that Swithun desired his body to be elevated. The second miracle involved a hunchbacked priest who was instructed by two angelic youths to visit the tomb of the unknown saint. The authors provide some interesting detail: the tomb was covered by a four-sided structure, described by Lantfred as a *tugurium* (a 'little hut') and by Wulfstan as a *tumulare sacellum* or 'tomb-house'; it resembled a sarcophagus, with a gabled roof (*culmine tectum*). The

[49] His name should really be 'Swithhun' ('strong bear-cub'), but the traditional spelling has prevailed.

[50] Roger Quirk's perceptive analysis of these sources, R. N. Quirk, 'Winchester Cathedral in the Tenth Century', *Arch. J.*, 114 (1957), 28–68, written before the excavation of Old Minster in the 1960s, is now superseded by Lapidge, *St Swithun*.

[51] See above, pp. 29–30. Lapidge, *St Swithun*, 232–3.

[52] ibid., 261.

[53] See above, p. 30.

description calls to mind the *domuncula* of Bishop Fursa at Péronne,[54] or the monument over the grave of St Dionysius at Saint-Denis, and it seems that the authors were attempting to describe an early example of a tomb-shrine, resembling a small house rather than an actual building such as a chapel over the grave. This structure gave limited access to the lid of the actual sarcophagus, which was apparently visible: both Lantfred and Wulfstan mention that it was possible to touch iron rings set in the coffin-lid. The monument was evidently imposing, which is at variance with the authors' insistence that Swithun had been buried in a humble grave whose location had been forgotten. These circumstantial details are best interpreted as hagiographical *topoi*: the bishop seems in fact to have been buried in the most prestigious place possible, and the fact that the monument over his grave appears to have been designed to give access to the coffin raises the interesting possibility that some sort of cult was already envisaged or in progress.

The translation took place on 15 July 971, a date that was to become the major feast of St Swithun. As with the elevation of St Æthelthryth two centuries previously, a tent, or at least cloth screens (*tentoria*), were erected around the monument to give some privacy during the exhumation: a detail which supports the notion that the *tugurium* was the actual tomb monument rather than a chapel. If the term had referred to a building over and around the tomb there would have been no need for screens. Then the coffin was opened. Unlike some of the cults already described, it was never claimed that Swithun's body was incorrupt, for when the corpse was taken out the bones were washed 'limb by limb' (*membratim*). They were placed in a temporary chest (*locellus*) which was set on an altar (not necessarily the high altar) whilst a suitable reliquary was being prepared. Michael Lapidge's careful analysis of the chronology of Lantfred's text indicates that the miracles described as occurring after the translation all happened within months of that event, which means that any information that may be gleaned from Lantfred about the position of the saint's temporary reliquary relates only to the architecture of the church as it was before Æthelwold embarked on a project nearly to double its size.[55] Once the bones of the saint had been exhumed, work began on a large-scale remodelling of the west end of the small original church, over the empty grave. Excavations during the 1960s revealed two phases of construction. An initial intention to create a western structure with flanking apses to north and south was abandoned, and in its place a 'westwork' was built, probably to a design similar to surviving examples in the Rheinland.

Meanwhile a sumptuous reliquary was produced at King Edgar's expense. It was the work of royal artificers at a royal *vill* called 'the great', which was not far from Winchester: possibly King's Somborne. Lantfred does not

[54] See above, p. 35.

[55] Lapidge, *St Swithun*, 235–7.

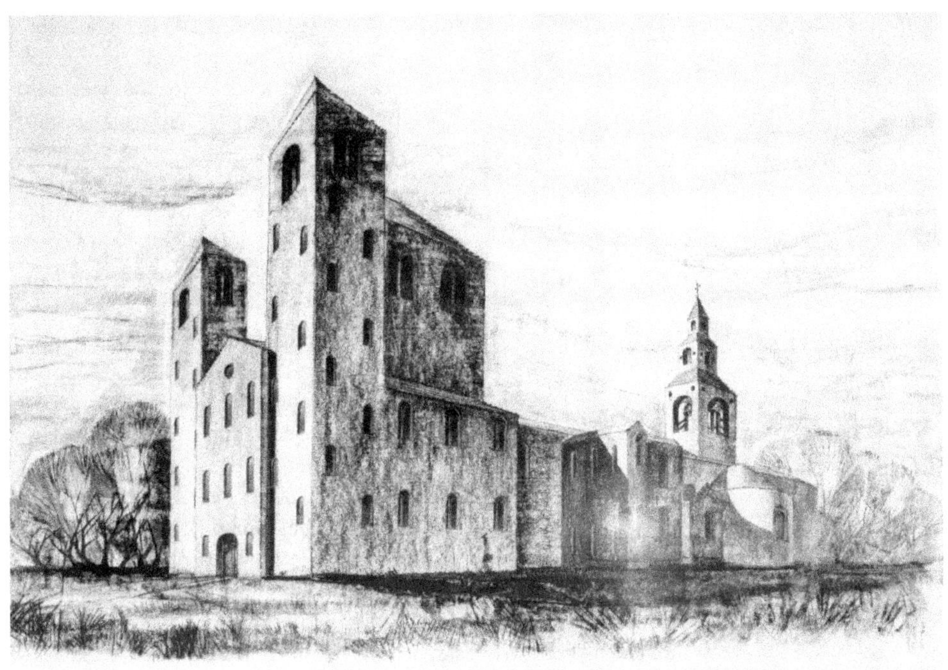

PLATE 4.2 WINCHESTER Old Minster in its final form, showing the westwork erected over the grave of St Swithun.

mention the reliquary, which post-dated his account, but Wulfstan describes it in some detail. It required silver, precious jewels, and three hundred pounds of gold, 'carefully weighed out on a balance', and featured scenes, presumably in relief, portraying Christ's Passion, Resurrection, and Ascension. Part of the saint's body was placed in the reliquary when it was inaugurated, probably in 974 and certainly before Edgar's death the following year. Amazingly, this important Anglo-Saxon artefact appears to have survived until around 1450, when it was melted down.[56] The reliquary may, indeed, be illustrated in an early thirteenth-century wall-painting in the former sacrist's room (now the cathedral library) at Winchester Cathedral.[57]

The church as remodelled by Æthelwold was presumably more or less complete (though his successor would enlarge it further) by 20 October 980, when the martyrium which he had constructed at the west end of the church was dedicated in the presence of King Æthelred and most of England's bishops.[58] Just where the reliquary was placed is not certain. There are tantalising references in Lantfred to the altar of the saint, said to be within an inner chamber *aditum*/*sacellum*; this does not sound like the high altar

[56] See below, p. 283.
[57] J. Crook, 'King Edgar's reliquary of St Swithun', *Anglo-Saxon England*, 21 (1992), 177–202.
[58] Wulfstan, *Vita Æthelwoldi*, cap. 40; ed. Lapidge and Winterbottom, 60.

PLATE 4.3 WINCHESTER CATHEDRAL Detail from an early thirteenth-century wall-painting in the cathedral library, showing the reliquary of St Swithun.

area.[59] Roger Quirk considered that the passage might refer to an altar in the westwork, immediately above the saint's original grave, but this interpretation relies on the assumption that the westwork was indeed completed by the time of the undated miracle.[60]

Swithun was chosen as Winchester's patron saint in preference to St Birinus, apostle of Wessex, who might have laid equal claim to this title. Birinus had died at Dorchester-on-Thames, but Bede informs us that during the episcopate of Hæddi (bishop of Winchester, 676–705) his body was translated to Winchester, where it was buried in Old Minster.[61] Later in the middle ages Winchester and Dorchester would dispute their respective claims to the body of the saint.[62] According to a late eleventh-century Life of St Birinus, Æthelwold raised up the body of the saint, placing it 'next to the high altar' (*iuxta maius altare*).[63] The latest editor of the Life plausibly argues that this translation took place after the reconstruction of the east end of Old Minster *c.*980,[64] a conjecture supported by Wulfstan the Cantor's assertion, in the *Narratio metrica, epistola specialis*, that Birinus's remains lay in the church as rebuilt by Æthelwold, though Wulfstan does not indicate the precise location.[65]

Bishop Æthelwold's activities at Winchester were not restricted to Old Minster, or his saint-making to former bishops. The cult of a royal saint, St Eadburh ('Edburga'), was promoted as part of the reform of Nunnaminster, a convent which had probably originally been founded by Ealhswith, King Alfred's wife.[66] Eadburh (not to be confused with several

[59] See especially Lantfred, cap. 22, in Lapidge, *St Swithun*, 303–4.
[60] Quirk, 'Old Minster', 63. For Lapidge, however (*St Swithun*, 302–3, n. 212), 'The passage is probably best understood as referring to the high altar within the chancel of the original two-cell Old Minster ...'.
[61] Bede, *HE*, iii.7; ed. Colgrave and Mynors, 232–3.
[62] See below, pp. 227–8.
[63] *Vita S. Birini*, cap. 21, in Love, *Three Saints' Lives*, 2–47, at 46–7.
[64] ibid., lxi.
[65] *Narratio metrica*, lines 265–6, in Lapidge, *St Swithun*, 392–3: *Qua uir apostolicus iacet almus et ille Birinus/has lauacro gentes qui lauit occiduas.*
[66] For what follows, see especially Ridyard, *Royal Saints*, 96–139, including her edition of Osbert of Clare's *Vita Edburge*, ibid., 253–308.

namesakes, including St Eadburh of Thanet *alias* St Bugga (†751) and Eadburh of Bicester) was the daughter of Edward the Elder. According to the Life which Osbert of Clare composed in the early twelfth century, she rejected the trappings of royalty in favour of the monastic life at the age of three, remaining at Nunnaminster until her early death twenty-seven years later. Her cult developed both at Winchester and at Pershore, where the monks also laid claim to her relics. Like Swithun, she is said to have been buried in a 'humble tomb' outside the church,[67] and like Swithun her desire to be elevated was made known by a miracle. At first, the prospective saint was reburied 'outside the choir' of Nunnaminster. She was unsatisfied with this position, and after a further appearance to the nuns she was moved to a more prestigious location beside the high altar. At the time of the monastic reforms Eadburh was elevated still higher, for Bishop Æthelwold ordered that her body should be placed in a splendid shrine, decorated with gold and silver flowers, interspersed with precious stones.[68] The shrine fared worse than that of St Swithun: following the Danish invasions of the 980s it was stripped of its gold and silver in order to pay the ransom of captives.[69]

Bishop Æthelwold's encouragement of the cult of Eadburh meant that the two neighbouring monastic institutions, Old Minster and Nunnaminster, each enjoyed saintly patronage, and for the virgin's biographer the two saints could be regarded as equals.[70] The two cults were evidently the subject of a certain rivalry which expressed itself in hagiography: in his Life of Eadburh Osbert of Clare comments that 'the confessor and the virgin as it were alternately in disputation brought to conclusion novel miracles, while in alternate writings in prose and verse they strove among themselves, locked in mutual disputations'.[71]

Bishop Æthelwold was also responsible for renewing the cult of St Æthelthryth at Ely, when that monastery was refounded *c.*970 by King Edgar with Byrhtnoth as first abbot. According to the *Liber Eliensis*, Æthelwold discovered her body 'in the church, near the high altar' (*in ecclesia secus altare maius*) where she had been placed by Seaxburh, raising her up so that she would no longer lie neglected underground but would be visible on high (*super eminentem*).[72]

Æthelwold is also said to have encouraged Abbot Byrhtnoth to translate the relics of St Wihtburh from Deorham (usually identified as East Dereham,

[67] *Vita Edburge*, cap. 12; ed. Ridyard, 283: *foris in atrio humilem elegit sepulturam.*
[68] ibid., cap. 19; p. 293.
[69] ibid., cap. 20; pp. 293–4.
[70] ibid., cap. 18; p. 291: ... *beatus confessor Dei Suuithunus diuersis in urbe Wintonia fulgurabat usquequaque miraculis, et gloriosa uirgo et felix Eadburga preclaris et innumeris rutilabat signis.*
[71] ibid., *Certatim namque confessor et uirgo quasi quibusdam successibus noua determinabant miracula, dum tanquam reciprocis apicibus in prosa et uersu inter se confligerent, et mutuis disputationibus altercarent.* See also Ridyard's comments, ibid., 30.
[72] *Liber Eliensis*, ii.52; ed. Blake, 120.

Norfolk) to Ely. Wihtburh is claimed to have been the youngest daughter of Anna, king of the East Angles (†654). There are, however, problems in identifying this saint. She is first mentioned in the late eleventh-century 'F' version of the *Anglo-Saxon Chronicle*, in an annal for 798, where she is identified as the first abbess of Deorham; the chronicler claims that her incorrupt body was discovered there fifty-five years after her death.[73] If she died in 743 she must have been conceived at the very end of Anna's life, dying eighty-nine years after him: not biologically impossible, but perhaps improbable. Furthermore, she is not mentioned by Bede, who makes much of the other descendants of Anna in his *Ecclesiastical History*.

The community at Ely must have enjoyed the racy account given in the *Vita Wihtburgæ* of the saint's translation in 974 when it was read each 8 July as one of the Lections for her feast day.[74] It is a classic account of a 'holy theft', with Abbot Byrhtnoth cast in the role of a 'faithful pirate' (*fidelis predo*), whose duty was to transfer the saint's incorrupt body into a 'more exalted bridal-chamber' (*ad sullimiorem thalamum*). The abbot set off for Deorham with a picked band (*cum militari manu*). There he threw a party for the townsfolk, and after they had retired, exhausted by the feast, he and his monks kept watch in the church. Having opened the stone coffin, revealing the intact body, they replaced the lid and, using rollers and levers, transferred the sarcophagus to a wagon and set off back to Ely by land and water. Finally, the holy body reached the monastery where, as the writer imagined, Wihtburh was met by her sisters Æthelthryth and Seaxburh, and her niece Eormenhild. The sarcophagus was a feature of the Anglo-Saxon church at Ely until the translations of 1106 under Abbot Richard; it was eventually retained, despite set-backs during the removal process.[75] Of the cult at Dereham there remains only 'Withburga's Well'; this appears to be on the site of a baptistry—there is antiquarian evidence that the original well was further away.

The author of *Liber Eliensis* was less informed about Æthelwold's treatment of the remains of the other two holy women, Seaxburh and her daughter Eormenhild. All we are told in the *Liber* is that Seaxburh was buried in a suitable position 'behind' her most blessed sister (Æthelthryth) —*post beatissimam sororem suam*;[76] a statement which seems at variance with the compiler's observation that before being translated in 1106 the two saints lay 'within the tower' to left and right of the high altar. When Seaxburh's remains were translated in 1106 it was inferred that Æthelwold had disturbed the body when he rebuilt the minster church: the bones and dust were placed separately in individual wooden boxes, within a stone 'memorial' (*in monumento*). As for Eormenhild, Abbot Richard found her

[73] This version of the *Anglo-Saxon Chronicle* (perhaps incorporating a Life of the saint), was cited by the compiler of *Liber Eliensis*, ii.147; ed. Blake, 233.

[74] *Vita S. Wihtburge Virginis*, caps. 8–14; Goscelin, *Saints of Ely*, 53–93, at 66–75. The passage was copied in *Liber Eliensis*, ii.53; ed. Blake, 120–3.

[75] See below, p. 155.

[76] *Liber Eliensis*, i.35; ed. Blake, 51.

body 'in an unadorned pavement-tomb, without covering, buried in this way by St Æthelwold'.[77]

Relic collecting was also evident in the monasteries formed or reformed by that other great churchman of the later tenth century, St Oswald of Worcester.[78] Alan Thacker has characterised him as an 'elusive personality', and much of our knowledge of the bishop comes from the *Vita Oswaldi* now attributed to Byrhtferth of Ramsey.[79] Oswald was a regular visitor to Byrhtferth's monastery, where, as we shall see, he encouraged the cult of SS Æthelred and Æthelberht.

Julia Barrow has examined the long-held view (first propounded by Armitage Robinson) that, unlike the dramatic 'big bang' at Winchester, the replacement of secular canons at Worcester was a slow process, perhaps completed only after Oswald's death in 992. Between 966 and 977 Oswald introduced monks from Ramsey into the new church of St Mary built in 966–83; for a time secular canons remained at St Peter's, though under a head chosen from amongst the monks.[80] So Oswald's activities at Worcester in promoting saints' cults were less linked to monastic reform than those of Æthelwold at Winchester. According to Byrhtferth, who compiled Oswald's *vita* shortly after the archbishop's death, he elevated the relics of St Wilfrid and other saints at Ripon.[81] This seems unlikely, as the relics of St Wilfrid had probably been taken to Canterbury a generation previously by Oswald's uncle, Archbishop Oda.[82] At the same time he is said to have created another equally fine reliquary, sending it to Worcester. When asked whom it was for he replied that it was 'for someone known only to himself'. It was in this reliquary that his own relics were said to have been placed when his body was elevated by Archbishop Ealdwulf in 1002.[83]

Finally, of the trio of reformers, St Dunstan seems to have been the least interested in saints' cults; indeed his role in effecting monastic reform at Canterbury has also been called into question.[84] His cult, and indeed the introduction of monks to Christ Church, seems to have developed only at the very end of the tenth century; as already noted, it is possible that the eastern arm of the cathedral was remodelled with a ring-crypt focused on the grave of the saint.

[77] ibid., ii.145; ed. Blake, 231: *Reliquias vero sanctissimæ Ærmenilde in nudo sepulcri pavimento absque velamine invenit, a beato sic Æðelwoldo repositas.*

[78] A. Thacker, 'Saint-making and relic collecting by Oswald and his communities', in Brooks, *St Oswald*, 244–68.

[79] M. Lapidge, 'Byrhtferth and Oswald', in Brooks, *St Oswald*, 64–83. *Byrhtferth of Ramsey: The Lives of St Oswald and St Ecgwine*, ed. M. Lapidge, OMT (Oxford, 2009).

[80] J. Barrow, 'The community of Worcester, 961–c.1100', in Brooks, *St Oswald*, 84–99.

[81] Byrhtferth, *Vita S. Oswaldi*, v.9; ed. Lapidge, 170–1.

[82] For the rival claims for Wilfrid's body, see below, pp. 127–8, 138.

[83] Eadmer, *Vita S. Oswaldi*, cap. 28 [formerly 26], in Eadmer, *Lives*, 215–89, at 272–3: *Seruatum est itaque Wigornæ feretrum idem, ac reliquiæ ipsius admirandi patris Oswaldi a terra post multos annos leuatæ magno cum honore sunt in eo collocatæ.*

[84] A. Thacker, 'Cults at Canterbury: Relics and Reform under Dunstan and his Successors', in Ramsay, *St Dunstan*, 221–45.

ROYAL CULTS: ST EDMUND OF BURY

The cult of St Edmund of Bury is best regarded as a belated product of the tenth-century reform. The origins of the cult are not as clear-cut as its earliest hagiographers would have us believe. According to the earliest account, written for the monks of Ramsey in the late 980s by Abbo of Fleury (†1002), Edmund had been martyred by the Danes in 869. Like St Sebastian he had been pierced with arrows until his corpse resembled a hedgehog or a thistle, then his head had been cut off. The Christians recovered his body, minus the head, which was soon miraculously discovered in a wood at *Haglesdun* guarded by a huge wolf; the head then miraculously reunited itself with the body. The remains were placed in a tomb, over which a chapel was built. After many years, and following further miracles, the body was translated to a new large wooden church at Beadricesworth. At that time the body was found to be miraculously incorrupt, only a thin red line round the neck bearing witness to the decapitation.[85] As the editor of this narrative, Thomas Arnold, emphasised in 1890, all this is the stuff of legend,[86] a judgement more recently endorsed by Antonia Gransden.[87] Perhaps all one can safely say is that by about 1000 a shrine, allegedly containing the body of King Edmund, was the centre of a cult at Bury.[88]

The Anglo-Saxon church was rebuilt in the 1020s, and consecrated, according to John of Worcester, in 1032.[89] In his *Liber De Miraculis* Hermann the archdeacon (writing, however, at the very end of the eleventh century) places this reconstruction in the context of the refounding of the community as a Benedictine monastery, under the patronage of Cnut. There is no other secure evidence for this, and Antonia Gransden has suggested that the king was cast in the role of a kind of latter-day Edgar in order to boost the monastery's prestige as an allegedly royal foundation.[90]

Of the appearance of the late Anglo-Saxon church we have little knowledge. At the end of the eleventh century Archdeacon Hermann recalled that it had not been 'as sophisticated in its design as some of those being built these days'.[91] Two miracles related by Hermann indicate that Edmund's wooden reliquary or coffin stood east of the choir of the pre-Conquest church, in a screened-off area called the *sancta sanctorum*. In one

[85] Abbo of Fleury, *Passio S. Eadmundi*, caps. 10–15; *Memorials of Bury*, i. 3–25, at 15–20.
[86] Introduction, *Memorials of Bury*, i. xviii.
[87] A. Gransden, 'The legends and traditions concerning the origins of the Abbey of Bury St Edmunds', *EHR*, 100 (1985), 1–24, at 6 and 7: a 'hotch-potch of hagiographical commonplaces' … ' a patchwork of borrowings from well-known hagiographies'.
[88] ibid., 8.
[89] *John of Worcester*, ii. 518–19, *s.a.* 1032: *Ecclesia sancti Eadmundi regis et martyris hoc anno dedicata est.*
[90] Gransden, 'Legends and traditions', 10–12.
[91] Hermannus, *De Miraculis S. Eadmundi*, cap. 43; *Memorials of Bury*, i. 85: *Hæc quoque simplici facta schemate, non sic artificialis ut quædam construuntur hoc tempore …*

miracle the saint emerged (passing through a locked door) in order to cure a crippled woman at the far (west) end of the church;[92] in another, a Dane called Osgod Clapa was struck down by the saint for the casual way he strolled through the choir, still carrying his battle-axe, on his way to the 'holy of holies'.[93]

As for the monument, Hermann calls it a *lectica* (litter), a word synonymous with *feretrum*.[94] It was evidently made of wood. In the mid-eleventh century a dumb Winchester woman, Ælfgeth, was cured of her infirmity (Hermann compares her new gift of speech with the miracle of Balaam's ass). Taking on an unofficial role as shrine-keeper, she informed the monks that the saint was displeased at the way they had neglected the monument, which was riddled with woodworm and covered in spiders' webs. Consequently the brethren decided to view the body: its incorrupt nature was confirmed and the head was found to be still attached to the body. A marvellous smell pervaded the monastery, and the body was reclothed.[95] It was subsequently replaced in the same *locellus*. The aged shrine-keeper Egilwine was brought in to witness proceedings; in 1010 he had taken charge of the body when it was evacuated from Bury during Danish invasions.

MURDERED ROYAL SAINTS

St Edmund was martyred by foreign foes, but a sizeable group of Anglo-Saxon English saints comprised members of the various dynasties who had met unpleasant ends during internecine feuds. King Edgar's successor Edward the Martyr was murdered at Shaftesbury in 978–9 after a short reign of three years.[96] The motive was undoubtedly political, and the murder occurred in the context of the so-called 'anti-monastic reaction' that followed Edgar's death. The anti-monastic faction supported Edward's half-brother, Æthelred, whose involvement may therefore be suspected. The event was recorded in the 'D' manuscript of the *Anglo-Saxon Chronicle*: '979: In this year King Edward was killed at the gap of Corfe on 18 March in the evening, and he was buried at Wareham without any royal honours.'[97] The same source explains that in the following year '980: Ealdorman Ælfhere fetched the holy king's body from Wareham and bore it with great honour to Shaftesbury.' This was an appropriate resting place given that Edward was the grandson of the foundress of that monastery, Ælgifu, first wife of Edmund, son of Edward the Elder. By the late eleventh century a suitable *Passio* had been composed (possibly by Goscelin of Canterbury), pinning

92 ibid., cap. 18 ; i. pp. 49–50.

93 ibid., cap. 21; i. pp. 54–6.

94 ibid., caps. 18, 21; i. pp. 50, 56.

95 ibid., cap. 20; i. pp. 52–4.

96 For this cult see especially Ridyard, *Royal Saints*, 44–50, 154–75; and Rollason, 'Murdered royal saints'.

97 *The Anglo-Saxon Chronicle: a Revised Translation*, ed. D. Whitelock (London, 1961), 79.

the blame on Edward's step-mother Ælfthryth.[98] William of Malmesbury used the *Passio* to create a more elaborate version of the legend, explaining, that after Edward's murder by his stepmother at Corfe Castle his body was first buried at nearby Wareham. There a miraculous light from heaven was seen and miracles of healing occurred. Two or three years later, perhaps at the instance of Archbishop Dunstan, who had supported Edward in the struggle for the throne, the body was translated to a more fitting monument at Shaftesbury.[99] Æthelred the Unready, who had benefited from his murder, subsequently raised the saint's incorrupt body from the grave.[100] This translation occurred in 1001, when Æthelred granted the *cœnobium* of Bradford upon Avon (Wilts) and other lands to the monastery at Shaftesbury and indeed to Edward as the monastery's *patronus*, significantly calling him 'Christ's saint'.[101] Seven years later Æthelred and the Witan decreed that the day of Edward's death should be commemorated annually. There is little evidence for the way in which Edward was enshrined. None of the legends suggests that his body was regarded as incorrupt, and it is most likely that the disarticulated bones were preserved in a house shrine decorated with precious metal plates bearing scenes in bas-relief.

Another cult of the late tenth century has more dubious beginnings. In the opening chapters of his *Historia Regum*, Symeon of Durham incorporates part of a Life of two Kentish princes, Æthelberht and Æthelred. The account was probably adapted from earlier sources by Byrhtferth of Ramsey in around 1000, when their cult developed at that monastery. They were great-grandsons of King Æthelberht, the first Christian king of Kent; the murder must therefore have occurred in the early to mid-seventh century.[102] The author praises the victims' outstanding spiritual qualities, and tells how when they were orphaned they were entrusted to King Ecgberht, their cousin, who had taken over the kingdom. But, the hagiographer continues, Ecgberht was persuaded by an evil counsellor, Thunor, to strangle the two boys, who evidently had a rival claim to the throne. In the end, Thunor personally did away with the boys, burying their bodies beneath the royal palace at Eastry. The king became aware of the crime when a miraculous column of light appeared over the palace; Thunor confessed to the murder and later was swallowed up by the earth at a place

[98] The *Passio Edwardi* is printed in C. F. Fell, *Edward King and Martyr*, Leeds Texts and Monographs, n.s., 3 (Leeds, 1971), 1–17.

[99] Malmesbury, *GP*, ii.86, ed. Winterbottom and Thomson, i. 294–7. Matthew Paris, *Chronica Maiora*, i. 471, attributes the translation to the Mercian eaoldorman Ælfhere.

[100] *Passio Edwardi*, ed. Fell, 12.

[101] J. Kemble, *Codex diplomaticus Aevi Saxonici*, iii (London, 1845), 318–22, charter 706, at p. 319: *sancto suo, germano scilicet meo, Eadwardo.*

[102] Symeon of Durham, *Historia Regum*, paras. 1–8; *Sym. Op.*, ii. 3–12. For the date of Symeon's source, see Malmesbury, *GR*, ii. 198. The legend is also preserved in an addition to the 'A' MS of *Anglo-Saxon Chronicle*, where the date is given as 640: *Anglo-Saxon Chronicle*, ed. D. Whitelock, 19, n. 7, who calls it a 'late Canterbury legend'. See also *Nova Legenda Anglie*, ed. Horstmann, i. 429–31.

thereafter called 'Thunerhleaw' (Thunor's Mound). Such was the official version of events, but it is perhaps more probable that Ecgberht himself was responsible for his cousins' death; they may even have been older than him, which would rob the story of much of its charm.[103] It is the development of their cult that concerns us here. The bodies were disinterred; an attempt to take them to Canterbury failed, and they ended up at a certain *monasterium*, perhaps Wakering (Essex), where they were placed 'behind the high altar' (*principalem retro altarem*). Later Bishop Oswald of Worcester is said to have translated their relics to Ramsey Abbey, after which miracles occurred.[104] David Rollason has suggested that Ramsey's promotion of the cult of the princes may have been a tacit comment on Ealdorman Ælfhere's anti-monastic stance and his failure really to make proper atonement for the murder of St Edward.[105] A later version of the legend was written by Thomas of Elmham, which included an account of how Ecgberht compensated the cousins' sister with an estate on Thanet which eventually became the initial endowment of the minster church there.[106]

EPISCOPAL SAINTS OF THE MONASTIC REFORM

The churchmen most closely associated with the tenth-century reforms were all eventually recognised as saints. Æthelwold died at his episcopal estate of *Beaddingtun* (modern Beddington, two miles west of Croydon) on 1 August 984, and his body was transported to the Old Minster at Winchester, where, according to Wulfstan the Cantor, it was buried in a crypt on the south side of the high altar.[107] Twelve years later the prospective saint appeared to a blind man, Ælfhelm of Wallingford; Wulfstan himself was involved in the subsequent elevation. The body was raised up on 10 September 996 by Bishop Ælfheah, and was placed in the choir of the church: Wulfstan assured his readers that the relics were 'held in great veneration [there] to the present day'.[108]

Oswald, bishop of Worcester (and concurrently archbishop of York from 972), appears to have been recognised as a potential saint immediately after his death in 992. In the Life of the saint which Byrhtferth of Ramsey compiled within five years of his death (certainly by 1005), the biographer claimed, following a hagiographical *topos* that may be traced back to several

[103] K. P. Witney, *The Kingdom of Kent* (London, 1982), 142–3.
[104] Malmesbury, *GR*, ii.209; ed. Mynors *et al.*, 388–91: *Iacuere ibi usque ad tempus regis Edgari; tunc enim a beato Oswaldo archiepiscopo Wigorniensi levata et ad cenobium Ramsiæ deportata sunt, ex qua die multis se miraculis manifestarunt supplicum uotis exorabiles.*
[105] Rollason, 'Murdered royal saints', 18–19.
[106] D. W. Rollason, 'The date of the parish boundary of Minster-in-Thanet (Kent)', *Arch. Cant.*, 95 (1979), 7–17.
[107] ... *in crypta ad australem plagam sancti altaris*: Wulfstan, *Vita S. Æthelwoldi*, cap. 41; ed. Lapidge and Winterbottom, 64–5.
[108] ibid., cap. 43; pp. 66–7.

Merovingian exemplars, that at the funeral some women mourners witnessed a dove and a miraculous light. These manifestations were taken as a sign of Oswald's sanctity.[109] He was buried in a sumptuous tomb within his cathedral, over which a monument of 'marvellous workmanship' (*mausoleum mirabile operis opus*) was constructed. It may have been a 'tomb-shrine' providing access to his sarcophagus, and Eadmer states that the monument was located on the south side of the high altar, the spot indicated by the dove and the ball of light.[110] Then on 15 April 1002,[111] Oswald's body was elevated by Archbishop Ealdwulf, and was placed in a *feretrum* located in a yet more worthy place to which, it was claimed, the irreverent could not gain access.[112] A position behind the altar seems most probable. The *feretrum* appears to have been a reliquary that Oswald himself had originally created to hold the relics of saints which he had brought to Worcester from Ripon (including, as it was claimed, St Wilfrid).[113] Later it would be enlarged when Oswald's remains were translated into Bishop Wulfstan's new cathedral.[114]

The cult of St Dunstan was rather slower to develop. He died on 19 May 988, having chosen his burial-place: Eadmer tells us in his Life of the saint, that 'when he had indicated the place in which he wished to be buried he ordered a tomb to be prepared for himself'.[115] Canterbury retained its Roman imprint, and a Roman-style ring-crypt may have been provided at the end of the century, as already described.

OTHER ROYAL SAINTS OF THE LATE TENTH CENTURY

Other royal cults developed during the later tenth century. Somewhat surprisingly, King Edgar, royal supporter of the monastic reform, who is shown in the centre of the well-known drawing of the promulgation of *Regularis Concordia*,[116] never became widely regarded as a saint. As Ann Williams has, however, commented, 'the king's devotion to the Benedictine

[109] Byrhtferth, *Vita S. Oswaldi*, v.18; ed. Lapidge, 194.
[110] Eadmer, *Vita S. Oswaldi*, cap. 38 [formerly 3]; Eadmer, *Lives*, 215–89, at 286–7: ... *uisio quæ apparuit in australem æcclesiæ plagam prope altare diuertit, quasi locum designans corporis sepeliendi.*
[111] According to 'Florence' of Worcester: *John of Worcester*, ii. 452–3, though William of Malmesbury and Eadmer wrongly place the event two years later; Ealdwulf died later in 1002.
[112] Eadmer, *Miracula S. Oswaldi*, cap. 4; Eadmer, *Lives*, 290–323, at 300–1: ... *in loco sæcularium personarum frequentia uacuo irreuerentique accessu remoto.*
[113] See above, p. 89.
[114] Malmesbury, *Vita Wulfstani*, iii.10.4; ed. Winterbottom and Thomson, 122–3, later emphasised that 'the shrine was made earlier by Oswald, though Wulfstan enlarged it': *scrinium a beato Oswaldo factum, sed a Wlstano ampliatum.*
[115] *Vita Dunstani Auct. Eadmer*, cap. 66; Eadmer, *Lives*, 43–159, at 154–5: ... *designatoque loco in quo sepeliri uolebat, sepulchrum sibi præparari præcepit.*
[116] BL, Cotton MS Tiberius A.iii, fol. 2*v*.

reform movement should not be taken as evidence of high personal morals'.[117] According to William of Malmesbury, his body was buried in the earth, but was subsequently honoured with a silver and gilded *scrinium* on account of his personal merits.[118] Later versions of Malmesbury's account bear witness to a local attempt at promoting his cult. When the tomb was opened in 1052 by Abbot Æthelweard the body was found 'clear of all stain' and still capable of spurting blood. It was placed in a casket which he had given to the church, over the altar, with the head of St Apollinaris and relics of Vincent the martyr.[119]

It was perhaps easier for royal princesses who had become heads of monasteries to achieve sanctity. Edgar's daughter Edith (Eadgyth) had entered the nunnery of Wilton where she died between 984–7, at the age of twenty-three, and was buried in an oratory dedicated to St Dionysius (St Denis), built at her own expense.[120] Her body was elevated thirteen years after her death with the enthusiastic backing of her half-brother Æthelred. Goscelin's Life, our principal source for the cult, was written almost a century later, in 1078–87. It claims that the saint miraculously summoned St Dunstan (who had actually died nine years previously) to Wilton to carry out the translation of her body to a shrine in the *porticus* dedicated to the Archangel Gabriel,[121] where miracles soon took place. Later King Cnut provided a golden shrine, and the cult was also supported by Edith's namesake, the daughter of Earl Godwin.

ROYAL PATRONAGE OF ENGLISH SHRINES

The support given to new saints by Edgar, Æthelstan, and Cnut continued a tradition of royal promotion that had been apparent from earlier in the tenth century. Some kings distinguished themselves in this regard. William of Malmesbury thought highly of Æthelstan for his many contributions to Malmesbury Abbey, notably for providing an evidently opulent reliquary (*scrinium*) for the relics of a sixth-century bishop of Avranches, St Paternus.[122] One can get some idea of the appearance of the latter shrine from a miracle story involving a thief who stole its gold plates: apart from what was presumably repoussé decoration, the shrine bore an inscription proclaiming that it was the king's gift.[123] He was also responsible for enriching the monastery of Milton Abbas (Dorset) with the relics of St

[117] A. Williams, 'Edgar', *DNB*, xvii. 698–703.

[118] Malmesbury, *GR*, ii.160; ed. Mynors *et al.*, 260: *scrinio argenteo et inaurato locatum pro merito personæ honoratur.*

[119] ibid. This detail occurs in MSS C and B.

[120] B. Yorke, 'Edith', *DNB*, xvii. 737–8.

[121] 'La Légende de Ste Édith en prose et en vers par le moine Goscelin', ed. A. Wilmart, *Analecta Bollandiana*, 56 (1938), 5–101; 265–307, at 269.

[122] Malmesbury, *GP*, v.247–9; ed. Winterbottom and Thomson, i. 594–7.

[123] ibid, v.248; pp. 596–7: *Hoc opus rex Ethelstanus, totius Britanniæ multarumque gentium in circuitu positarum imperator, in honorem sancti Paterni fieri iussit.*

Sampson.[124] William says that Æthelstan also provided a rich shrine for St Aldhelm, and implies that he was responsible for that saint's elevation,[125] but this is at variance with other traditions.[126] When Æthelstan died at Gloucester on 27 October 940 his body was taken to Malmesbury, where it was buried under the high altar in the church of St Mary (*ibique sub altari sanctæ mariæ in turri sepultus est*).[127]

During the following century Cnut evidently wished to show himself as keen a promoter of English saints' cults as the descendants of Cerdic, and the *Encomium Emmæ* contains many examples of his generosity towards indigenous cults. A famous letter recalled how he would visit shrines, weep copious tears, and leave gifts.[128] One of his main achievements in this field was transporting the body of St Ælfheah from St Paul's to Canterbury, as related by Osbern.[129] Likewise Queen Emma is said to have bought the body of St Audoenus in Rouen (a transaction at which William of Malmesbury professed himself horrified) and transported it to England: *corpus reliquum Cantuariæ cointulit, caput in secreto suo habuit.*[130]

THE LIST OF SAINTS AND THE PLACES WHERE THEY DWELT

A kind of snap-shot of the state of saints' cults and the location of pilgrimage centres in Anglo-Saxon England in around 1000 is provided by the well-known *Secgan*, which we have already mentioned with reference to St Paulinus.[131] As David Rollason has shown, the document in its surviving form is a fusion of two sources: the first a pre-Viking list of twenty-nine saints at twenty-seven sites, the second comprising additions made when the extant text was compiled *c.*1031.[132] The combined list mentions eighty-nine saints in all.

One cult mentioned in the first (pre-Viking) group is that of John of Beverley, an early eighth-century archbishop of York: *Đonne resteð sanctus Iohannes biscop on þare stowe Beferlic, neah þare ea Hul.*[133] A native of Yorkshire, he had been appointed bishop of Hexham in 687, where he ordained Bede first deacon, then priest: Bede remains the main source for

[124] ibid., v.250; pp. 598–9.

[125] ibid., v.236 and 249; pp. 582–3 and 596–9.

[126] See below, p. 104.

[127] Malmesbury, *GP*, v.246; ed. Winterbottom and Thomson, i. 592–5.

[128] F. Liebermann, *Die Gesetze der Angelsachsen* (Halle, 1903), i. 276.

[129] See the annotated edition and translation by A. R. Rumble and Rosemary Morris in *The Reign of Cnut*, ed. A. R. Rumble (Leicester, 1994), 283–315. Cf. Malmesbury, *GR*, ii.181; ed. Mynors *et al*, i. 322.

[130] Malmesbury, *GP*, v.263; ed. Winterbottom and Thomson, i. 626–9.

[131] See above, p. 54. The *Secgan* was published by F. Liebermann, *Die Heiligen Englands: angelsächsisch und lateinisch* (Hannover, 1889).

[132] Rollason, 'Lists', 61–8.

[133] Liebermann, *Die Heiligen Englands*, 10.

Bishop John's career.[134] In 705 he was translated to the see of York, where he remained bishop until 717, when he retired to his monastery of *Inderauuda* (Beverley),[135] where he died on 7 May 721 and, according to Bede, was buried in the *porticus* of St Peter. Alcuin commented that 'although his body remained on earth, his spirit was entirely in heaven', a phrase appropriate for a potential saint.[136] Bede recounts several miracles of healing during Bishop John's lifetime, some of which he had heard from Abbot Berhthun, and the *Secgan* shows he was regarded as a saint of national importance by the year 1000. Even so, John's cult must have been given a major boost in 1037, when Archbishop Ælfric elevated the body. There are some indications that the earlier tomb was already decorated in the manner of a shrine: it was described as a 'wonderfully and ingeniously carved wooden sepulchre' (*ligno mirabili artificio insculpto*), a phrase which calls to mind the coffin of St Cuthbert. However, the tomb continued as a secondary focus of veneration at Beverley, and the phrase, if it is not simply a literary borrowing from Bede's account of Cuthbert's tomb, might reflect the appearance of the monument after the elevation of 1037. The new reliquary was a more lavish affair as befitted a saint. It was, needless to say, a 'shrine, of gold and silver and precious stones, of incomparable workmanship'.[137]

A little later, shortly before the Norman Conquest, Archbishop Ældred (1061–70) commissioned a Life of the saint from Folcard, to which were gradually added collections of *miracula*.[138] The latter provide a few tenuous indications of the progress of the cult in the post-Conquest period and, together with the anonymous *Chronica Pontificum Ecclesiæ Eboracensis*, were used as the main basis of Richard Morris and Eric Cambridge's analysis of the early architectural development of the church before the collapse of the crossing tower *c.*1213 and the start of the long process of construction of the present church.[139] In the absence of archaeological evidence it is doubtful whether more light will be shed on that period of the building's history, which included the destruction of much of it by fire in 1188 and the loss, for a time, of the relics. By contrast, the construction of St John's final shrine is wonderfully documented, as we shall see in a later chapter.[140]

[134] Bede, *HE*, v.2–6; ed. Colgrave and Mynors, 456–69.
[135] R. Morris and E. Cambridge, 'Beverley Minster before the early thirteenth century', in *Medieval Art and Architecture of the East Riding of Yorkshire*, *BAA Trans.*, vol. 9, for 1983 (Leeds, 1989), 9–32, at 9–10.
[136] *Alcuin: The Bishops, Kings and Saints of York*, ed. P. Godman (Oxford, 1982), 96–9.
[137] *Chronica pontificum ecclesiæ Eboracensis, pars prima, auct. anonymo*, in *Hist. Church of York*, ii. 343: *capsam auro et argento et lapidibus pretiosis opere incomparabili apud Beverlacum fabricari fecit.*
[138] *Hist. Church of York*, i. 239–60. The Life is followed (ibid., 261–47) by a long series of *Miracula*, the first group of which are attributed to a clerk called William Ketell (early twelfth century), followed by later additions: a first group datable to *c.*1180, followed by two undatable groups of miracles.
[139] Morris and Cambridge, 'Beverley Minster'.
[140] See below, pp. 256–7.

ALFRED WESTOU AND THE SAINTS OF NORTHUMBERLAND

One of the best recorded and influential promoters of Anglo-Saxon saints' cults in the eleventh century was that 'arch-relic-hunter'[141] Alfred son of Westou, sacrist of Durham Cathedral (fl. *c*.1025–60). His principal responsibility there was the shrine of St Cuthbert, and to enhance the cult he sought relics of other saints throughout Northumbria, intending that they should play a supporting role to his beloved spiritual master. He was particularly active at Hexham, a town with which he had strong family links. He was one of the hereditary priests who held the church of Hexham from the bishops of Durham, rather like a prebend. A priestly dynasty of this sort was still possible at that time, when Pope Clement VII's injunctions concerning clerical celibacy had not yet reached the north of England. Alfred was indeed the great-grandfather of Ailred of Rievaulx, so sanctity ran in the family blood.[142] Alfred was highly respected by the three bishops under whom he served. He was still active during the episcopate of Æthelwine (the last Anglo-Saxon bishop of Durham, 1056–71) and probably died shortly before the Norman Conquest.

Our earliest source for Alfred's activities is the *Libellus de Exordio ... Dunhelmensis Ecclesie* ('Tract on the Origins ... of the Church of Durham'), compiled by the Durham monk Symeon between 1104 and, at the latest, 1115.[143] On the evidence of his handwriting Symeon was from Normandy, so possibly he came to Durham with William of Saint-Calais in 1091 when the bishop returned to his see from exile.[144] Symeon rose to the position of cantor to the Durham monastic community. He cannot have known Alfred personally but relayed what a monk called 'Gamel' had told him before he died. This was presumably the Gamel whose name is listed as one of the first monks of Durham after the monastic reforms of 1093;[145] he also came from Hexham, where Alfred had appointed as his deputies two successive clerks of that name, *Gamel elde* (also known as *Gamel Hamel*) and *Gamel iunge*.[146]

Symeon emphasises Alfred's piety and his exemplary duty as guardian of Cuthbert's relics; he also relates how Alfred had extracted a hair from the saint's head which proved incombustible, a miraculous property which he

[141] Bertram Colgrave's phrase in his *Two Lives of Saint Cuthbert*, 318.

[142] Symeon, *Libellus*, lxxxix, and 162, n. 26, citing, *inter alia*, [W. H. D. Longstaffe], 'The Hereditary Sacerdotage of Hexham', *Arch. Aeliana*, n.s., 4 (1860), 11–28. For the genealogy of Westou's family see Raine, *Hexham Priory*, li–lii.

[143] Symeon, *Libellus*, iii.7 ; ed. Rollason, 160–7. For the date and attribution of the *Libellus* to Symeon, see ibid., xlii–xliv.

[144] M. Gullick, 'The Hand of Symeon of Durham: Further Observations on the Durham Martyrology Scribe', in *Symeon of Durham: Historian of Durham and the North*, ed. D. Rollason (Stamford, 1998), 14–31, at 18. This contrasts with the view of Thomas Arnold that Symeon came from Jarrow in 1083.

[145] Symeon, *Libellus*, preface; ed. Raine, 6. For Rollason, Gamel was perhaps 'a descendant' of the Hexham priests, rather to be identified with one or other of them.

[146] Longstaffe, 'Hereditary Sacerdotage', 14.

enjoyed showing off to his fellow monks. Conceivably it was a gold filament from one of the rich textiles which had been placed within Cuthbert's coffin long after the first translation. The same story was repeated by another Durham historian, Reginald, in the third quarter of the twelfth century; he added further details, which he claimed to have received from Alfred's great-grandson, Ailred of Rievaulx.[147] He told how Alfred used to open the saint's wooden reliquary-coffin, combing the hair and clipping the fingernails of the incorrupt body, and he included a charming tale of a weasel which chose to rear its family within the coffin. Such anecdotes should be regarded as entertaining stuff to be read to the Durham monks on Cuthbert's feast-days, but add little to our historical knowledge.

Symeon was closer to events, and perhaps had even spoken to eye-witnesses such as the monk Gamel. He describes how Alfred Westou moved around the north of England, elevating the bodies of Northumbrian saints.

> ... he set out at the command of a vision and visited the former sites of monasteries and churches in the kingdom of the Northumbrians. He raised from the earth the bones of those saints whom he knew to be buried in these places, and enshrined them above ground so that they might be better known to the people and venerated by them. The bones in question were those of the anchorites Balthere and Billfrith, the bishops of Hexham Acca and Alchmund, and King Oswine, together with those of the venerable abbesses Æbbe and Æthelgitha.[148]

The passage demonstrates the wide area covered by Alfred. St Balthere was a hermit from Tyninghame (East Lothian), who died *c.*756;[149] St Billfrith may also have come from there, and achieved renown as the binder of the Lindisfarne Gospels.[150] Acca and Alchmund were buried at Hexham, where they remained enshrined; King Oswine (murdered in 651) had a cult at Tynemouth; and St Æbbe was a seventh-century abbess of Coldingham (where Æthelgitha, about whom nothing else is known, may also have been abbess).[151]

The fullest accounts of Alfred's activities were, however, probably not written by Symeon, though they occur in two interpolated passages in the *Historia Regum* attributed to him.[152] As the *Historia*'s nineteenth-century editor, Thomas Arnold, pointed out, the interpolations deal not with English kings but Hexham saints, which led Arnold to suppose that the entire work

[147] Reginald, *Libellus*, cap. 26; ed. Raine, 57–60.
[148] Symeon, *Libellus*, iii.7; ed. Rollason, 162–5.
[149] ibid., ii.2; ed. Rollason, 80–1. Symeon of Durham, *Historia Regum*, para. 42, in *Sym. Op.*, ii. 41.
[150] Symeon, *Libellus*, ii.12; ed. Rollason, 120–1.
[151] For these details, see ibid., 163–5, nn. 29–33.
[152] ibid., xlviii–xlix, citing P. Hunter Blair, 'Some observations on the *Historia Regum* attributed to Symeon of Durham', in *Celts and Saxons: Studies in the Early British Border*, ed. N. K. Chadwick (Cambridge, 1963), 63–118.

had actually been compiled at Hexham.[153] But the only surviving manuscript seems more likely to be a product of the Durham scriptorium, and dates from the last quarter of the twelfth century.[154] This is well after Symeon's death in 1128, but the interpolations could have been copied from an earlier source.

One of the interpolated passages concerns that cosmopolitan scholar Acca, bishop of Hexham (709–31). We learn that at his death *c.*740 he had been buried outside the church. His grave was marked with two marvellously carved Anglo-Saxon stone crosses, one of which was inscribed with his name.[155] A surviving cross-shaft fragment with a luxuriant double vine-scroll decoration has long been identified as one of Acca's grave-markers though the attribution cannot be regarded as certain.[156] The interpolator states that, 'more than three hundred years after his death' (i.e. the mid-eleventh century), thanks to a revelation to 'a certain priest' (presumably Alfred Westou, though he is not mentioned by name), his relics were elevated and placed within the church, in a *feretrum*. His chasuble, dalmatic, and maniple (*sudarium*) had survived for three centuries within the tomb, and his winding-sheet was also undamaged. Another Hexham writer, Prior Richard (1141–*c.*1160), observed that his maniple, chasuble, and silken 'tunic' were still displayed in his church, all as beautiful as ever and, even more surprising in Richard's view, as strong as if they were new;[157] and these contact relics were also known to the author of the tract on Hexham saints attributed to Ailred of Rievaulx.[158] Parts of them found their way to Durham Cathedral, where they were noted in a relic list of 1383: 'an ivory casket with relics of St Acca the Bishop, with portions of his face-cloth and chasuble, which were in the ground for 300 years'.[159] The *Historia Regum* interpolator adds the other interesting detail that a portable altar was found within Acca's tomb, made of two hinged wooden panels, bearing the legend '*Almæ Trinitati, agiæ Sophiæ, sanctæ Mariæ*'.[160] Perhaps Acca acquired it during one of his travels abroad with St Wilfrid, whom he accompanied to Rome. This artefact, alas, has not survived.

A second, somewhat shorter, interpolation in the *Historia Regum* tells of the similar elevation of Alchmund, bishop of Hexham from 767 to 780/1, and here Alfred Westou is named.[161] Alchmund had been buried next to St

[153] See also H. S. Offler, 'Hexham and the Historia Regum', in *Trans. of the Architectural and Archaeol. Soc. of Durham and Northumberland*, 2 (1971), 51–62.
[154] See Rollason's introduction to Symeon, *Libellus*, xlviii–xlix, discussing Corpus Christi College Cambridge, MS 139.
[155] Symeon of Durham, *Historia Regum*, para. 36, in *Sym. Op.*, ii. 32–3.
[156] Raine, *Hexham Priory*, xxxiv and plate on facing page; more recently discussed by Rosemary Cramp, *County Durham and Northumberland*, British Academy Corpus of Anglo-Saxon Stone Sculpture in England, 1 (Oxford, 1984), 176.
[157] 'Prior Richard's History of the Church of Hexham'; Raine, *Hexham Priory*, 8–62, at 36.
[158] Ailred of Rievaulx, *De Sanctis Ecclesiæ Haugustaldensis*, cap. 6; Raine, *Hexham Priory*, 184–6.
[159] Printed in Raine, *St Cuthbert*, 121–30, at 126.
[160] Symeon of Durham, *Historia Regum*, para. 36; *Sym. Op.*, ii. 33.
[161] ibid., paras. 51–2; ii. pp. 47–50.

Acca. More than 250 years later Alchmund appeared in a dream to a pious local resident, instructing him to ask Alfred to translate his remains into a worthier place within the Anglo-Saxon church built by St Wilfrid. The elevation accordingly went ahead in the presence of a large crowd of onlookers: the bones were raised from the earth, wrapped in a cloth, and placed in a casket (*scrinium*) on top of a *feretrum* (the word is here used in its proper sense of a bier), and taken into the *porticus* of St Peter, on the south side of the church, where it would rest for a night before the translation into the body of the church. Whilst the other watchers were dozing, Alfred removed a single finger joint from the holy remains, intending to take it back to Durham. But next morning the saint foiled his intentions by causing the bier to become immovable; only when Alfred returned the bone was it possible to carry the relics into the church. Later a very similar story would be told at Hexham concerning Alfred's grandson, Aldred (Aluredus) the shrine-keeper, who also tried to abstract a bone of St Acca when the Hexham saints were again translated in the late eleventh or early twelfth century.[162] One should not necessarily conclude from this that relic theft evidently ran in the family; rather, the story of the saints' desire to remain at Hexham in as complete a form as possible is a hagiographical commonplace, presumably intended to reinforce Hexham's claim to the saints.

The location within the church of the Hexham saints translated by Elfred Westou is uncertain. It is probably unwise to place too much reliance on accounts compiled up to 150 years after the events, and in any case the layout of the Saxon church at Hexham is highly speculative. The interpolated passages in the *Historia Regum* state simply that the *feretra* of Acca and Alchmund were placed within the church, where they were held in great veneration to that day. Prior Richard, writing in the mid-twelfth century, commented merely that Elfred had translated the two sets of remains into 'the more remote parts within the church' (*intra ecclesiam in remotioribus partibus*), but thought (perhaps wrongly) that they had subsequently been placed in the sanctuary: Acca to the right (south side) of the high altar, and Alchmund to the left.[163] The Life of St Eata, probably a twelfth-century compilation, also mentions the translation of Acca and Alchmund, stating that Alfred had placed their relics in *feretra* 'within the church' there.[164]

Eata was arguably Hexham's most prestigious saint. Trained by St Aidan on Lindisfarne, he rose to the position of abbot of Melrose, where his pupils included two future saints: his prior, Boisil, and the young Cuthbert. Subsequently Eata was appointed bishop of Lindisfarne then, for little more than a year, of Hexham where he died in 686. His cult appears to have

[162] The story occurs in Symeon's *Historia Regum*, para. 36; *Sym. Op.*, ii. 33–5, and was also recounted by Ailred of Rievaulx, *De Sanctis*, cap. 101; Raine, *Hexham Priory*, 192.
[163] 'Prior Richard's History', cap. 4; Raine, *Hexham Priory*, 49.
[164] Raine, *Hexham Priory*, 211–15, at 214. The Life of Eata was first printed by Raine from a York MS that he dated to the fourteenth century, as *Vita S. Eatæ Haugustaldensis Episcopi*, in *Miscellanea Biographica*, ed. J. Raine, Surtees Soc., 8 (1838), 121–5.

followed a somewhat different course from Acca and Alchmund, the bones remaining separately enshrined. According to his Life, he was originally buried 'next to the sanctuary of the aforesaid church of Hexham, on the south side, and a small stone chapel was built over his tomb'; later his remains were placed together with due honour within the church (*intra ecclesiam*). The author of the Life thought it likely that Alfred Westou was also responsible for this translation.[165] But Prior Richard seems to imply that after they had been elevated, Eata's relics still lay enshrined within a *porticus* on the south side of the sanctuary.[166] It seems likely that the 'stone chapel' and the '*porticus*', both on the south side of the sanctuary, were one and the same; Eata's remains may therefore have initially been raised into a *feretrum* above his original grave, but there is no reason to suppose that Alfred was necessarily responsible. It will be noted that Eata is not mentioned in Symeon of Durham's account of Alfred's activities at Hexham, quoted above; nor, for what it is worth, did Ailred of Rievaulx, his great-grandson, credit Alfred with translating that saint. But Symeon's failure to mention Eata's translation is perhaps not surprising: as David Rollason has observed, the *Libellus de Exordio* is 'suspiciously silent' about Hexham, perhaps reflecting continuing tensions between Durham and the Hexham community.

A unified theme underlies the activities of Alfred Westou: his desire to enhance the cult of St Cuthbert by bringing relics of the saints of Northumbria to Durham, now the episcopal see. Alfred was unsuccessful with Alchmund's relics, as we have seen, but he evidently brought relics of several of the other saints that he elevated back to Durham, and some of them appear in a relic list appended to one of the manuscripts of Symeon's *Libellus* in the late twelfth century.[167] These secondary relics remained close to the tomb-shrine of St Cuthbert throughout the middle ages, preserved in reliquary cupboards, *armoires*, on the feretory platform.

Westou also brought two complete sets of saintly bodies back to Durham, namely the disarticulated bones of the Venerable Bede and St Boisil. Bede had been buried in the monastery of St Andrew which he had founded at Jarrow; Symeon relates that Alfred made many visits to that monastery on the anniversary of Bede's death.[168] One year he returned home unusually early, and never went to Jarrow again. He had evidently fulfilled his purpose, for towards the end of his life he revealed to his fellows at Durham that the bones of Bede now reposed with those of Cuthbert. This claim was later supported by Symeon, who describes how, when Cuthbert's body was translated in 1104

[165] ibid., 124. The *Vita S. Eatæ* was reprinted in Raine, *Hexham Priory*, 211–15.

[166] 'Prior Richard's History', cap. 4; in Raine, *Hexham Priory*, 8–62, at 49: *In quadam enim porticu iuxta secretarium eiusdem ecclesiæ, versus australem partem, decenter in una theca collocatæ, quiescebant.*

[167] Cambridge University Library, MS Ff i.27 p. 194. The MS is discussed by David Rollason in Symeon, *Libellus*, xxiv–xxix. The relic list is printed in *Sym. Op.*, i. 168–9.

[168] Symeon, *Libellus*, iii.7; ed. Rollason, 164–7.

(at which he was the youngest monk present), Bede's relics, separately located in a linen bag, were discovered in the reliquary-coffin.[169] The discovery of Bede's bones and other relics is more fully described in one of the anonymous 'Chapters on the Miracles and Translations of St Cuthbert' (*Capitula de miraculis et translationibus sancti Cuthberti*),[170] which explains that the relics of Bede, the head of St Oswald, and other relics were then removed from the coffin and enshrined elsewhere in the church.

As for St Boisil, he had been Cuthbert's spiritual master at Melrose and prior of that community in succession to Eata. Cuthbert, indeed, was with Boisil when he died of the plague in around AD 660–1.[171] Alfred brought the relics from Melrose to Durham, and placed them close to Cuthbert; they were still there when Symeon was writing the *Libellus de Exordio* in around 1104–9.[172]

> At the bidding of revelation he went to the monastery of Melrose, and from there he translated the bones of St Boisil, who had once been the blessed Cuthbert's teacher in that same monastery, to the church of his former disciple, where he installed them fittingly in another shrine near to Cuthbert's body, just as they are preserved to this day.[173]

Symeon's account seems to conflict with the identification of a fragment of what appears to have been a gabled 'house-shrine' at Jedburgh as the shrine of St Boisil.[174] Ralegh Radford has estimated that the monument measured about 2134mm long, 768mm wide, and 1422mm high. In the absence of documentary evidence, the attribution to St Boisil must remain speculative.

FORM AND DECORATION OF ANGLO-SAXON RELIQUARIES

At this stage it will be helpful to sum up the evidence for the appearance of a 'typical' Anglo-Saxon shrine, if such a thing ever existed. It is more probable that there was a great variety. Possibly a basic distinction existed

[169] ibid.

[170] BL, Harley MS 1924; printed in *Sym. Op.*, i. 229–61, at 252–3. Other chapters in ibid., ii. 333–62. Though undoubtedly the work of Durham monks, there is no reason to attribute the *capitula* to Symeon (see Symeon, *Libellus*, lxxv–lxxvi).

[171] For Boisil as Cuthbert's master, see Bede *HE*, iv.27; ed. Colgrave and Mynors, 430–5. For Boisil's death, see Bede, *Vita S. Cuthberti*, cap. 8, in Colgrave, *Two Lives of Saint Cuthbert*, 180–5.

[172] Simeon, *Libellus*, iii.7; ed. Rollason, 164–5: ... *ossa sancti Boisili ...in ipsius discipuli ecclesiam transtulit, et iuxta illius corpus in altero scrinio decenter sicut hactenus habentur condidit.*

[173] ibid., iii.7; pp. 164–5.

[174] C. A. Ralegh Radford, 'Two Scottish Shrines: Jedburgh and St. Andrews', *Arch. J.*, 112 (1955), 43–60. Also illustrated and discussed in *Royal Commission on the Ancient Monuments of Scotland, Inventory: Roxburghshire*, 2 vols. (London, 1956), i. 207–8, where it is dated to *c.*700.

between shrines where the body was deemed intact, and smaller reliquaries containing disarticulated bones. Where the body was reputedly intact, the *feretrum* resembled a full-sized, decorated coffin: the reused Roman sarcophagus of Æthelthryth, or the light wooden *theca* of Cuthbert. The *feretrum* of St Edmund of Bury appears to have also been a wooden coffin, located east of the high altar.[175]

Other reliquaries containing disarticulated bones were probably placed on the altar. William of Malmesbury has left a good description of a reliquary in his own abbey church, which was believed to have been presented by King Æthelwulf of Wessex in 837 in order to house the relics of St Aldhelm, the first bishop of Sherborne.[176] Aldhelm was the most important saint of the monastery of Malmesbury, whither his body had been translated by Bishop Ecgwine of Worcester a few years after his death at Doulting in 709. The accounts of the movements of his relics are somewhat confused. William of Malmesbury, internally inconsistent, asserts elsewhere that Aldhelm was laid to rest in the church of St Michael, where his body remained buried for 246 years,[177] i.e. until around 955, when the secular canons whom King Eadwig of Wessex had installed in the church in place of monks raised the body from the ground (*de terra*).[178] This is clearly at variance with the construction of a shrine *c.*837. The confusion seems to have originated with Faricius's Life of the saint. Rod Thomson argues that the shrine was in fact rebuilt in Eadwig's time, using the old front and back plates.[179] Within a few years, however, at Dunstan's instigation the bones were removed from the shrine for fear of the Danes and reburied in a stone tomb on the right-hand side of the altar. William has an unlikely story that the empty shrine was the only object left in the church, where it was protected from the Danes by the saint's power. Thomson argues that it is more likely that Dunstan had the shrine dismantled and that the precious front and back plates were preserved, eventually to feature in the late eleventh-century translation under Abbot Warin and Bishop Osmund of Salisbury, as described in the following chapter.[180]

Despite the vicissitudes suffered by the shrine, Malmesbury has left a first-hand description of an Anglo-Saxon shrine, elements of which may indeed have gone back to the time of Æthelwulf. The reliquary was embellished on the 'front' with images of the saint in solid silver, and on the 'back' with scenes in relief showing miracles wrought by the saint. 'Front and back' must refer to the long sides of the shrine, showing that, unlike a tomb and the later high shrines which derived from them, it was oriented

[175] see above, pp. 90–1.
[176] Malmesbury, *GP*, v.236; ed. Winterbottom and Thomson, i. 582–3.
[177] ibid., v.232; pp. 578–9.
[178] ibid., v.251; pp. 602–5.
[179] Malmesbury, *GP*; ed. Winterbottom and Thomson, ii. 327–9, Appendix A 'The Tomb and Shrine of St Aldhelm'.
[180] See below, p. 114.

north–south. William also noted a knob or finial (*fastigium*) of rock crystal, given by Æthelwulf, featuring the king's name in gold letters.[181]

There is a fair amount of documentary evidence for the ways reliquaries were decorated. Official *vitæ*, such as Felix's *Life of Guthlac*, with its description of the 'wonderful structures and ornamentations' which adorned the tomb of that saint in the second third of the eighth century,[182] provide the best source of information about Anglo-Saxon saints' cults after Bede. They suggest that the shrines of saints with royal connections in the eighth and ninth centuries were as richly adorned as their Continental counterparts. For example, Goscelin records that when Ceolred of Mercia elevated the incorrupt body of his cousin St Wærburh at Hanbury *c*.709, he placed it 'in a *theca* fittingly provided for her, where in full view she illuminates the faithful people with her most brilliant light'.[183] At the end of that century (perhaps in 792) King Offa decorated the tomb of St Oswald at Bardney 'with silver, gold, gems, and much finery'.[184] This kind of embellishment, which may be traced back to practitioners like Eligius of Noyon,[185] provided an opportunity for Anglo-Saxon craftsmen to display their skills. In the mid-eleventh century Abbot Mannig or Manny (*Mannius*) of Evesham created a new reliquary (*scrinium*) for St Ecgwine. The relics of that saint had had a narrow escape in the time of Abbot Osweard (*c*.970–*c*.975), when the church had 'fallen down' and the relics were buried under the rubble; the receptacle (*vasculum*) containing the bones was, however, miraculously undamaged.[186] Presumably Abbot Mannig's new shrine was intended as a replacement for this receptacle and as a reliquary worthy of the newly embellished church which Mannig had 'rebuilt' (more probably, enlarged).

Although Mannig was himself renowned as a craftsman, some of the work on St Ecgwine's reliquary was subcontracted, and the chronicler includes a revealing anecdote describing how one of the *artificiosi*, called Godric, who had been hard at work heating and beating out the metal decoration, and was creating a tiny image (*imaginula*) with a sharp tool, cut himself when the *scalprum* slipped, but was miraculously cured by the

[181] Malmesbury *GP*, v.236; ed. Winterbottom and Thomson, i. 582–3.
[182] See above, p. 67.
[183] *Vita S. Werburge*, cap. 11; Goscelin, *Saints of Ely*, 25–51, at 48–9: ... *in theca sibi competenter parata, ubi conspicue fideles populos illustrat preclara lampade sua.*
[184] *Alcuin: The Bishops, Kings, and Saints of York*, ed. Godman, 34–5. Alcuin's poem was possibly written (or at least revised) in the 790s, shortly after the event.The occasion of this embellishment may have been Offa's marriage to the daughter of Æthelred, king of Northumbria, in 792: A. Thacker, 'Kings, Saints, and Monasteries in Pre-Viking Mercia', *Midland History*, 10 (1985), 1–25, at 4.
[185] See above, pp. 35–6.
[186] Byrhtferth, *Vita S. Ecgwini*, iv.11; ed. Lapidge (ed.), 300–1. Cf. the version compiled *c*.1100 by Dominic, an Evesham monk, printed in *Evesham Chronicle*, 41–2. This version was in turn recycled by Thomas of Marlborough, *History*, ii.68; *Thomas of Marlborough: History of the Abbey of Evesham*, ed. J. Sayers and L. Watkiss, OMT (Oxford, 2003), 78–81.

saint.[187] Evidently what he was doing was putting the fine detail on an image created in repoussé work (*opus ductile*) in the way later described by the German technical writer Theophilus.[188] The *scrinium* of St Ecgwine was made of silver and gold, and incorporated three precious stones which 'lit up' the church at night. It would seem, therefore, to have been displayed within the body of the Anglo-Saxon church, rather than in the crypt dedicated to the saint.[189]

The late Anglo-Saxon period was a golden age for saints' cults; indeed, England could perhaps claim to be then called 'the island of saints', a sentiment that was taken up by in the mid-nineteenth century by the archbishop of Westminster, Cardinal Wiseman, who in his well-known prayer for England prayed: 'Remember our holy martyrs, who shed their blood for Christ: especially our first martyr, Saint Alban, and Thy most glorious bishop, Saint Thomas of Canterbury. Remember all those holy confessors; bishops, and kings, all those holy monks and hermits, all those holy virgins and widows, who made this once an island of saints, illustrious by their glorious merits and virtues.' But the cult of local saints, like so many other aspects of English life, was about to be rudely shaken.

[187] *Evesham Chronicle*, 44, 86. Cf. Thomas of Marlborough, *History*, ii.72; ed. Sayers and Watkiss, 84–7.

[188] For Theophilus and the technique of *opus ductile*, see below, p. 142.

[189] For the crypt, see above, p. 78.

ENGLISH SAINTS AND THE 'NEW ENGLISHMEN' 5

Anglo-Saxon shrines and relics after the Norman Conquest

Less than a hundred years after the tenth-century monastic reforms, the Church in England underwent an even greater upheaval as a result of the Norman Conquest. In some ways, the previous decades had been an 'Indian summer' for the Old English Church, especially for monastic communities. Thanks to royal support (and despite the so-called 'anti-monastic reaction) these flourished in the wake of the tenth-century reforms.[1] But within a few years of the Norman invasion, Stigand, the pluralist archbishop of Canterbury, had been deposed. William the Conqueror began to pursue in England the ecclesiastical policies which had proved so successful in mainland Normandy, impressing a particularly Norman stamp upon the Church in his conquered territory.[2] Just as the dukes of Normandy had exercised tight control over the Church there, so the new Norman king of England took charge of the English Church. True, the Old English Church had also been subject to royal control well before the Conquest; in the late Saxon period appointments to bishoprics and abbacies were effectively royal prerogatives, exemplified by the way Anglo-Saxon kings had referred in official documents to 'their' archbishops, bishops, and abbots.[3] Indeed, under the terms of *Regularis Concordia* the king and queen had been given a special, personal responsibility for the abbeys and nunneries of the realm. From the reign of Alfred onwards, royal and ecclesiastical councils went hand-in-hand. The Conqueror turned this royal control to his own ends, maintaining the ecclesiastical institution as

[1] C. Brooke, 'Bishop Walkelin and his inheritance', in *Winchester Cathedral: 900 Years*, ed. J. Crook (Chichester, 1993), 1–12, at 1.

[2] For more on this matter, see D. C. Douglas, *William the Conqueror: The Norman Impact upon England* (London, 1964), 317–45 (cap. 13); and, for a different view, A. Williams, *The English and the Norman Conquest* (Woodbridge, 1995).

[3] F. Barlow, *The English Church, 1000–1066: A Constitutional History* (London, 1963), 4–6.

an even more tightly integrated component of feudal power. But with the accession of the reformist Pope Gregory VII in 1073 tensions began to develop which would reach breaking-point during the following century in the form of the 'Investiture' quarrel: the question as to whether heads of monasteries should be appointed by the king or the bishop.

Another feature of the post-Conquest Church in England was the rapid succession of Church councils under royal supervision (William attended most if not all of them), which determined Church policy and appointments. Thus, the Norman control of ecclesiastical institutions found physical expression in the ecclesiastical building explosion that followed Lanfranc's Council of London in 1075, when ordinances were passed requiring episcopal sees to be moved from villages to more populous towns.[4] This process had in fact started in 1050, when the diocese covering Devon and south-west England was transferred from Crediton to Exeter by Bishop Leofric. Several sees had been relocated in larger towns soon after the Conquest; for example, the diocese based on Dorchester-on-Thames had begun its slow transfer to Lincoln *c.*1072, when King William issued a writ, allegedly authorised by Pope Alexander II (†1073), ordering the transfer of Bishop Remigius's see.[5] The 1075 council gave impetus to the trend, and was followed almost immediately by a flurry of activity and *déménagement*. The see of Sherborne (combined with Ramsbury since 1058) moved to Old Sarum, Selsey to Chichester, Lichfield to Chester, and North Elmham (the see for East Anglia) to Thetford. Later in the century further moves took place: Wells transferred (for a time) to Bath in 1090, and by 1095 the former see of Lichfield had been relocated yet again, moving from Chester to Coventry.[6] Also in 1095 the East Anglian diocese moved from Thetford to Norwich, thirty miles up the road. A new cathedral was founded at the abbey of Ely in 1109.

Other cathedrals were rebuilt on the same site: the rebuilding of fire-damaged Christ Church Canterbury began in 1070 shortly after Lanfranc's arrival, and the reconstruction of Hereford, Worcester, and Durham cathedrals started shortly afterwards. The rebuilding process also affected abbey churches (such as St Augustine's Canterbury, Bury St Edmunds, and St Albans), minsters, and local churches. Consequently no English cathedral contains any Anglo-Saxon architecture, apart from the crypt of Ripon—which became a cathedral only in 1836—and one fragment at Sherborne, which stopped being a cathedral in 1078. Within half a century every cathedral church in England had been rebuilt.

These changes in the architectural setting were accompanied by a

[4] H. Loyn, *The English Church, 940–1154* (Harlow, 2000), 75.

[5] D. Bates, *Bishop Remigius of Lincoln, 1067–1092* (Lincoln, 1992), 11–12, with photograph of the writ. In the record of the Council of London (1075) Remigius was described as 'bishop of Dorchester or Lincoln' (ibid.).

[6] Lichfield would attain cathedral status again by the early thirteenth century, the diocese being called 'Coventry and Lichfield'; Chester became a cathedral city again in 1541, but in a different church.

change in personnel, as Anglo-Saxon prelates were progressively replaced by Normans. Edward the Confessor had already introduced some Norman and other foreign clergy, notably churchmen from Lorraine, to higher posts in the English Church. The most significant pre-Conquest Norman churchman was Robert, formerly abbot of Jumièges, appointed bishop of London (1044–51) then, for a time, archbishop of Canterbury, until the purge of Norman clergy under Earl Godwin and his sons. He was replaced in London in 1051 by another Norman, William (†1075). The Lotharingians included Ulf, appointed bishop of Dorchester in 1049 (but, like Archbishop Robert, driven out of England in 1052), and Giso, bishop of Wells from 1061 to 1088, formerly one of Edward's chaplains, a native of St Truiden, a village in the region of Hesbaye in modern Belgium. Giso imposed a canonical rule on his community at Wells, perhaps the rule compiled by St Chrodegang for his cathedral community at Metz (†764) or the later rule established for the canons of Aachen by St Benedict of Aniane. Another of Edward's chaplains, Hereman (or Hermann), perhaps a native of the Low Countries,[7] who had taken his vows at the monastery of Saint-Bertin in Flanders, had been appointed bishop of Ramsbury in Wiltshire in 1045, and Queen Edith's chaplain Walter had been appointed to Hereford in 1060. Finally, Abbot Baldwin of Bury, a former monk of Saint-Denis, had been brought to England by Edward as the court physician; he was set in charge first of the newly refounded monastery of Deerhurst, then (from 1065 until his death in 1097) the abbey at *Beadricesworth*, modern Bury St Edmunds.[8]

Despite this early ecclesiastical immigration, nothing can have prepared English clergy for the wholesale takeover by Norman prelates that followed the Norman Conquest. In 1070 the pluralist Stigand was deposed and replaced as archbishop of Canterbury by Lanfranc, abbot of Caen, and as bishop of Winchester by Walkelin, a canon of Rouen. Stigand's brother, Æthelmær, bishop of the East Anglian diocese at Elmham, was deposed at the same time, as was Æthelric of Selsey, who had been closely associated with Stigand. Within ten years of the Battle of Hastings almost all bishoprics were in foreign (mostly Norman) hands, with the exception of Worcester, where the Saxon Wulfstan occupied the episcopal throne to the end of his days.[9] These men continued the work of the pre-Conquest 'foreign' prelates in transmitting to the Church in England the reformist ideas which had been brought to Normandy by William of Volpiano at the beginning of the eleventh century.

[7] Malmesbury, *GP*, ii.83; ed. Winterbottom and Thomson, i. 286–7. William calls Hereman '*natione Flandrensi*'. If so, he was not a Lotharingian *stricto sensu*.

[8] A. Gransden, 'Baldwin, abbot of Bury St Edmunds, 1065–1097', *Anglo-Norman Studies*, 4, Proc. of the Battle Conference for 1981, ed. R. Allen Brown (Woodbridge, 1982), 65–76.

[9] F. Barlow, *The English Church, 1066–1154* (London, 1979), 57–8. Of fifteen bishops in 1086, eleven were Normans, two were Lotharingians, while Lanfranc himself was Italian. See also Loyn, *English Church*, 72. Hereman had died in 1078 being replaced by Osmund, a Norman.

NORMAN ATTITUDES TO ENGLISH SAINTS

What, then, did the new rulers of England, both secular and ecclesiastical, make of Anglo-Saxon saints? The question has long been debated by students of the period, and the consensus of opinion has swung back and forth. Dom David Knowles cited examples of the 'disrespectful attitude' of the new Norman abbots towards the Old English saints: 'even the great name of St Cuthbert was not proof against Norman scepticism' (he was thinking of Prior Turgot's examination of the relics in 1104).[10] Knowles's adumbration of the problem was amplified by Antonia Gransden, for whom 'the Anglo-Saxon saints and their relics were on trial'.[11] She argued that there was a hiatus in the cult of Anglo-Saxon saints after the Conquest, resulting from distrust on the part of the new churchmen of indigenous saints, about whom they knew little. On the other hand, Susan Ridyard has contended, in an important and influential study of post-Conquest attitudes to Anglo-Saxon saints, that Norman abbots quickly became aware of the advantages that promoting a local saint's cult might bring—for example, in supporting claims to land tenure, the saints being potential supernatural guardians of monastic assets whom it might be unwise to displease—and she has characterised Norman scepticism of the cult of saints as a 'myth'.[12] She is supported by David Rollason, who has concluded that, 'however we analyse it we discern no real disruption with the Anglo-Saxon past'.[13] Rollason points out, however, that the new, albeit short-lived, cults of Waltheof and Hereward the Wake, and the less certain cult of King Harold, were not exploited for political ends: if there had been so much official, Norman hostility to indigenous saints, one might have expected these cults in particular to have formed a rallying point for opposition, but such cults as did develop around those political 'martyrs' appear to have remained local affairs.[14] While supporting Ridyard's general thesis, Rollason departs from her contention that some Anglo-Saxon saints were regarded as patrons of the English political cause, questioning, for example, her view that St Æthelthryth's shrine 'became a rallying-point for rebellion'.[15]

In this shift of scholarly opinion, adherents of the rival views have clearly interpreted the evidence in surprisingly different ways. Thus, some of those who perceive discontinuity have suggested that the main difficulty faced by the first Norman churchmen in England was the lack of documentation about local saints. Sir Richard Southern, for example, wrote,

[10] D. Knowles, *The Monastic Order in England* (Cambridge, 1949), 118–19.

[11] Gransden, *Historical Writing, I*, 105, and *eadem*, 'Cultural Transition at Worcester in the Anglo-Norman Period', in *Medieval Art and Architecture at Worcester Cathedral*, *BAA Trans.*, vol. 1, for 1975 (Leeds, 1978), 1–14, at 1.

[12] Ridyard, '*Condigna Veneratio*', 183–5 and 204. Cf. Rollason, *Saints and Relics*, 222–3.

[13] Rollason, *Saints and Relics*, 217.

[14] ibid., 217–20.

[15] Ridyard, '*Condigna Veneratio*', 182.

> Like every other great and ancient English church, Christ Church Canterbury was rich in the relics of native saints, but poor in writings about them. From this state of affairs there followed a large part of the contempt in which these saints were held by the Norman conquerors. Not only did the saints have uncouth names and enjoy an apparently exaggerated local veneration, but for many of them there was nothing beyond vague tradition to testify to their activity or even existence.[16]

A quite different view on Southern's last point was advanced by David Rollason, for whom the composition of English saints' Lives and *Miracula* was already flourishing at the time of the Conquest:

> The real take-off point for hagiographical writing was the late tenth century and the flourishing of the genre which began then continued undisturbed through the eleventh century and into the twelfth ... it is true that the volume of hagiographical composition seems to have increased in the late eleventh and twelfth centuries but that was only a further development of a process which had begun in the tenth century and was well under way in the early to middle eleventh ...[17]

It can scarcely be held, however, that the influential Flemish hagiographers Goscelin and Folcard (both former monks of the monastery of Saint-Bertin, at Saint-Omer in Flanders) were hard at work on Lives of Anglo-Saxon saints during a period which overlapped the arrival of the Normans.[18] As Antonia Gransden has emphasised, the main period of Goscelin's hagiographical activity began eleven years after the Conquest and continued to the end of the century.[19] Goscelin appears to have been persuaded to come to England by a fellow-Fleming, Bishop Hereman. As explained earlier, Hereman had been bishop of Ramsbury since 1045, but when his desire to add Malmesbury to his diocese and relocate his *cathedra* there was thwarted by the king (under pressure from Earl Godwin), he went into three years' voluntary exile at his former monastery of Saint-Bertin.[20] It is therefore possible that Goscelin accompanied Hereman back to England in 1058, when the diocese of Ramsay was reunited with that of Sherborne with Hereman at its head; Goscelin was certainly resident in England in the early 1060s. In around 1075 work began on the new cathedral at Old Sarum, within the ancient hill-fort which the Conqueror had taken as the site of his new castle.[21] On Hereman's death in 1078 and the appointment of the royal

[16] Southern, *Anselm and his Biographer*, 249.
[17] Rollason, *Saints and Relics*, 228.
[18] ibid., 230: 'Goscelin's career in England, if not also Folcard's, spanned the Conquest and shows that it had no really disruptive effects on the veneration of English saints.'
[19] Gransden, *Historical Writing, I*, 64 and 107–12.
[20] Malmesbury, *GP*, ii.83; ed. Winterbottom and Thomson, i. 288–9.
[21] ibid; pp. 288–9. Malmesbury accurately describes the site as 'on a hill and mightily walled': *locatum in edito, muro uallatum non exiguo.*

chaplain, Osmund, as bishop, Goscelin left the episcopal *familia*, finding Osmund less congenial than his predecessor. For some years Goscelin followed a peripatetic existence, ending up by 1090 at St Augustine's, Canterbury, where he lived well into the eleventh century. His known output of saints' lives is impressive,[22] and the choice of subject-matter seems to have been determined by the various monasteries at which he resided, but he does not appear to have embarked on writing saintly *Vitæ* until 1077, when Bishop Hereman commissioned a Life of St Wulsige (Wulsin), a late tenth-century bishop of Sherborne. This was quickly followed by a Life of St Edith of Wilton (written between 1078 and 1087 at the latest), reflecting his work as chaplain to the nuns of that monastery; he has also been credited with writing a Life of St Cynhelm for the monastery of Winchcombe,[23] and a cycle of five Lives for the nuns of Barking. Between 1087 and 1090 he wrote a *Vita* and *Miracula* of St Ivo for the 'whole convent' of Ramsey.[24] During that period Goscelin also stayed at the abbey of Ely,[25] for which he compiled Lives of the principal female saints, Seaxburh, Eormenhild, Wærburh, and Wihtburh, and indeed a *prosa* in honour of St Æthelthryth which does not appear to have survived.[26] In 1093–4 he wrote the Life of another Anglo-Saxon female saint, Mildred of Thanet, sister of the murdered brothers Æthelberht and Æthelred.[27] He has sometimes also been credited with the late eleventh-century Lives of SS. Swithun and Birinus,[28] but undoubtedly his most interesting work for the architectural historian is his account of the saintly translations at St Augustine's in the 1090s.[29]

As for Folcard, who seems to have come to England in the 1050s from Saint-Bertin (having already written the Life of the founder of that monastery), he was abbot of Thorney from 1069; but his first known Life of an English saint was that of Archbishop Ealdred of York who died in 1069.[30] In short, a few years seem to have elapsed between the Conquest and Goscelin and Folcard's first extant Lives of English saints. It is true that these

[22] *Vita Ædwardi*; ed. Barlow, 133–49, Appendix C, 'Goscelin of Saint-Bertin and his Works'. For an analysis of several of Goscelin's Lives, see P. A. Hayward, 'Translation-narratives in post-Conquest hagiography and English resistance to the Norman Conquest', *Anglo-Norman Studies*, 21, Proc.of the Battle Conference for 1998, ed. C. Harper-Bill (Woodbridge, 1999), 67–93, at 73–85.

[23] *Vita S. Kenelmi*, in Love, *Three Saints' Lives*, 49–89. Rosalind Love states (p. ci) that 'the case for admitting this text into the canon of [Goscelin's] works does seem quite strong'. For an analysis, see Hayward, 'Translation-narratives', 73–7.

[24] *AASS*, *Iunii II*, 288A–92F. For the date, see Hayward, 'Translation-narratives', 84.

[25] As recorded in *Liber Eliensis*, ii.133; ed. Blake 215–16.

[26] Goscelin, *Saints of Ely*.

[27] 'Goscelin of Canterbury's account of the Translation and Miracles of St. Mildreth (*BHL* 5961/4): An Edition with Notes', ed. D. W. Rollason, *Medieval Studies*, 48 (1986), 139–210, at 140–1. For the two Kentish martyrs, see above p. 92.

[28] As discussed by Rosalind Love in Goscelin, *Saints of Ely*, lviii–lx.

[29] See below, pp. 133–6.

[30] R. Love, 'Folcard of Saint-Bertin', in *The Blackwell Encyclopaedia of Anglo-Saxon England*, ed. M. Lapidge, J. Blair, S. Keynes, and D. Scragg (Oxford, 1999), 189.

two hagiographers are the most likely candidates for the authorship of the *Vita Ædwardi Regis*, Book I of which appears to have been started before the king's death in January 1066 (arguably in 1065).[31] The first part of the *Vita* cannot, however, be considered a work of hagiography but rather, as the prologue makes clear, a celebration of Edward's wife, Queen Edith (to whom the work was dedicated), and of other members of Earl Godwin's family; Frank Barlow has suggested that it would better be named *Encomium Edithæ Reginæ*.[32] Book II, apparently written very soon after Edward's death, is more hagiographical in tone.[33]

The so-called *Vita Ædwardi* apart, new English hagiographies seem to post-date the Conquest by some years. Antonia Gransden calls this new flush of saintly writing 'the third period of Anglo-Saxon biography'.[34] For Gransden, English hagiographical writing 'bridged the Conquest' only in the sense that a second wave of hagiography at the time of the late tenth-century monastic reforms lasted into the early eleventh century, took as its subject matter those bishop and abbots who lived in the mid-eleventh century, and resumed in the late eleventh century under the Normans.[35]

There are few surviving contemporary comments on the richness or otherwise of mid-eleventh-century hagiographical writings. Osbern, an English monk and precentor at Christ Church Canterbury during Lanfranc's episcopate, later said that before the Conquest local biographers had (in his fellow-monks' view at least) written 'quite elegantly but without sufficient diligence', and remarked that source material for his life of Dunstan had perished in the fire of 1067.[36] Half a century after the Norman Conquest William of Malmesbury claimed that between the time of Bede and Eadmer little had been written about the achievements of the famous men of England.[37] However, William was not discussing saints in that passage but kings, and in any case his comment may have been no more than the conventional material of a prologue. Elsewhere, however, William showed a commendable reluctance to write about saints whose lives had not been properly chronicled: of the saints whose bodies Bishop Æthelwold had translated to the fenland monastery of Thorney he commented that 'it would seem to be frivolous if you proclaim the merits of those about whom one cannot find any recorded miracles (*miracula*)'.[38]

There may have been an understandably racial element in the perceived Norman distrust of saints' cults. William of Malmesbury reported that the

[31] *Vita Ædwardi*; ed. Barlow, xxix–xxxiii. For the authorship see ibid., xliv–lix, also Rollason, *Saints and Relics*, 229, and Barlow, *Edward the Confessor*, 257–8.
[32] *Vita Ædwardi*; ed. Barlow, xxii.
[33] See below, p. 158.
[34] Gransden, *Historical Writing, I*, 87.
[35] ibid., 69.
[36] *Vita S. Dunstani, auct. Osberno*, in *Memorials of St Dunstan*, 69–128, at 69–70.
[37] Malmesbury, *GR*, i, prologue; ed. Mynors *et al.*, i. 15–16.
[38] Malmesbury, *GP*, iv.186; ed. Winterbottom and Thomson, i. 494–5: ... *friuolumque uideatur si eorum predices merita, quorum nulla inuenias miracula.*

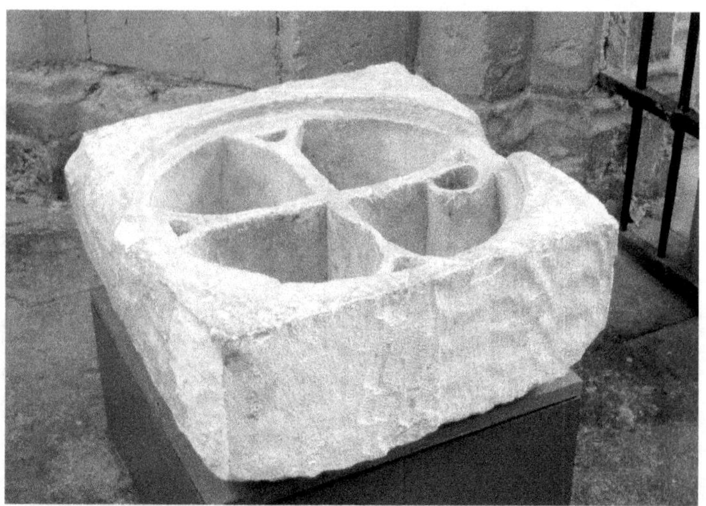

PLATE 5.1
AUXERRE (DEPT. YONNE, FRANCE), ÉGLISE SAINT-GERMAIN
A reliquary in the form of a bowl subdivided by stone partitions in the form of a *chi-rho*. The *lapideæ crateræ* containing pre-Conquest English relics at Malmesbury may have been something like this but with wooden partitions.

'uncouth ring and rough flavour' of the names of the Thorney saints just mentioned struck people (Normans, presumably) as 'barbarous'.[39] In the immediate post-Conquest years such distrust of English saints seems to have been prevalent even amongst churchmen: thus Abbot Æthelhelm of Abingdon referred to St Æthelwold and the unofficial saint Edward the Confessor as 'rustic Englishmen' (*Anglici rustici*), forbidding the celebration of their feast-days.[40] Then on his appointment in 1070 Warin, the new Norman abbot of Malmesbury, downgraded the relics of St Meidulf and other former abbots of that monastery; according to William of Malmesbury they had chosen to be buried in that abbey church even though they had been promoted to higher posts elsewhere, and their relics were displayed either side of the high altar in two unusual reliquaries in the form of stone 'bowls' (*lapideæ crateræ*) divided up by wooden partitions. But Abbot Warin moved these relics out of the main abbey church, immuring them in a corner of the new church of St Michael which was put up at his command.[41] According to Ailred of Rievaulx, Lanfranc accused Wulfstan of Worcester to his face of being simple and illiterate, almost an idiot, who knew no

[39] ibid: ... *nomina ... barbarum quiddam strident ... uocabula eorum inconditum sonant, horridum olent ...*

[40] *Chronicon Monasterii de Abingdon*, ed. J. Stevenson, 2 vols., RS, 2 (1858), ii. 284.

[41] Malmesbury, *GP*, v.265; ed. Winterbottom and Thomson, i. 628–31: *Ossa denique sanctæ memoriæ Meildulfi, et ceterorum qui, olim ibi abbates posteaque in pluribus locis antistes, ob reuerentiam patroni sui Aldhelmi se in loco tumulatum iri iussissent, quos antiquitas ueneranda in duobus lapideis crateris ex utraque parte altaris, dispositis inter cuiusque ossa ligneis interuallis, reuerenter statuerat ... hos igitur omnes in extremo angulo basilicæ Sancti Michahelis, quam ipse dilitari et exaltari iusserat, inconsiderate occuli lapidibusque precludi precepit.* For a discussion of the *crateræ*, see R. M. Thomson's commentary in Malmesbury, *GP*; ed. Winterbottom and Thomson, ii. 314.

French and could not therefore become involved in royal affairs. If we accept Osbert of Clare's well-known story, Lanfranc's view of Wulfstan rapidly changed when the deceased Edward the Confessor miraculously indicated his support for the Saxon bishop. Wulfstan's episcopal staff became firmly embedded in the saint's tomb, and only the bishop himself was able to extract it: a sure indication that the Confessor, at least, recognised Wulfstan's fitness to continue in office, despite his linguistic shortcomings.[42] We do not have to take the anecdote literally, but it may perhaps be viewed as an expression of a change in Lanfranc's attitude that was still remembered more than half a century later. Eadmer put things more succinctly: respect for older people was an Anglo-Saxon characteristic, and the reverence due to saints was simply an extension of this.[43]

The key figures in this debate are, naturally enough, the king and his new archbishop of Canterbury. There is no reason to suppose that William was inherently distrustful of local saints' cults, for there were many such cults in Normandy which might have been regarded as equally dubious. The Conqueror had good reason, for example, to be grateful to St Walaric (Valéry) of Luxeuil, whose relics he had paraded at Saint-Valéry in order to obtain a favourable wind for England in October 1066. That superb piece of propaganda, the Bayeux Tapestry, showed Harold's oath being sworn on a portable reliquary whose contents were presumably considered as potent as those on the other side of the Channel, and, according to Orderic Vitalis, William subsequently hung those same relics around his neck.[44] Amongst the possessions of Battle Abbey was a gift from the Conqueror: a 'feretory in the shape of an altar, in which were many relics, on which it was his custom to have mass celebrated when on campaign'.[45] Charles Wall speculated that this was the portable reliquary shown in the Bayeux Tapestry.[46] Actually the tapestry shows two different reliquaries, both of the gabled, 'house-shaped' variety and adorned with five bays of blind arcading. One, with cross-shaped finials, stands on a portable bier with two carrying poles from which textiles hang to the ground; the other, with a central knop on the ridge, is on a draped altar on three steps, but both the bier and the altar rest on a cobbled surface, suggesting that the oath took place in the open air and that the altar was indeed movable.[47]

[42] Osbert, *Vita Edwardi*, cap xxix; ed. Bloch, 120. Cf. Ailred of Rievaulx, *Vita S.Edwardi regis et confessoris*; *Pat. Lat.*, cxcv. cols. 737–90, at 779–81 for the same anecdote.
[43] Eadmer, *Vita Bregwini*, cap. 13; ed. Scholtz, 145: *Et quidem ut multi affirmant, hunc inter se morem Saxones pręstantius habent, ut maiores suos dignius honorent, et irreuerentię subditorum non pareant ne insolescant. Morem igitur suæ gentis et mundo exemptus filiis suis studiit bonus pater exhibere, ut eos moneret qua reuerentia se debeant erga maiores suos habere.*
[44] Orderic, *Historia*, iii; ed. Chibnall, ii. 172.
[45] *The Chronicle of Battle Abbey*, ed. E. Searle, OMT (Oxford, 1980), 90–1: ... *cum feretro in modum altaris formato, quo multe erant reliquie, super quod in expeditione missa celebrari consueuerat.*
[46] Wall, *Shrines*, 17–18.
[47] As pointed out by David Wilson, *The Bayeux Tapestry* (London, 1985), 180.

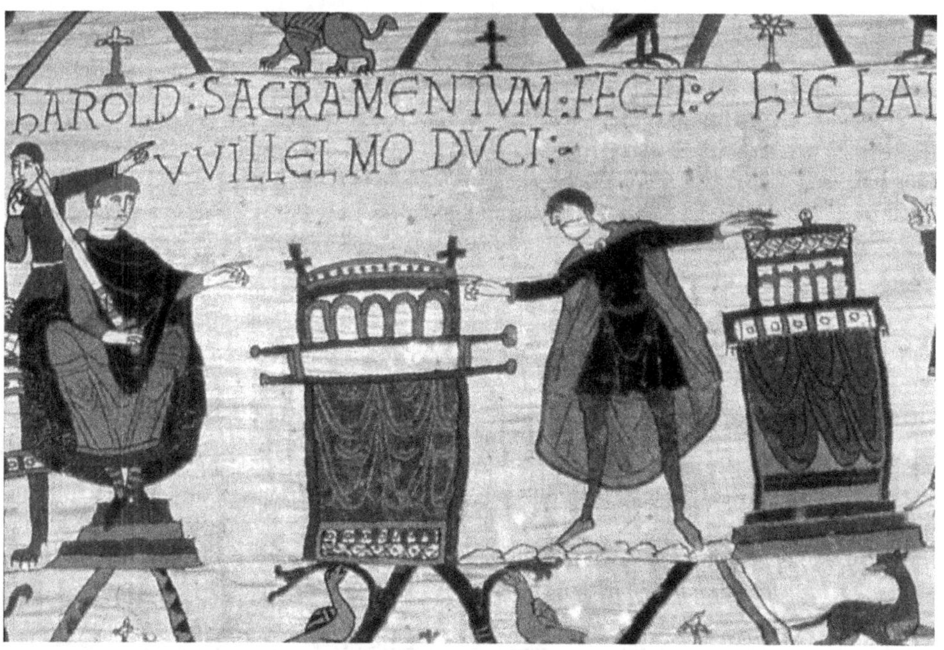

PLATE 5.2 BAYEUX TAPESTRY RELIQUARIES depicted in the scene of Harold's oath.

As for Archbishop Lanfranc, his apparently short-lived misgivings may have been the result of his personal ecclesiastical background, which would have given him little experience of local cults. The abbey of Bec had been dedicated to the Virgin Mary and the abbey at Caen to St Stephen rather than to local saints, and he had presumably long ceased to be influenced by any early experiences of local cults in his native Lombardy. Thus, as archbishop of Canterbury Lanfranc seems to have preferred to emphasise the great mysteries of the Christian faith rather than encourage the veneration of the incorrupt bodies of more recently departed holy men.[48] This is typified by the fact that the focus of his new cathedral at Canterbury was, initially at least, not the shrines of his illustrious predecessors Dunstan, Ælfheah, and Oda,[49] as had been the case in the Anglo-Saxon church, but the great Rood which dominated the nave, flanked by images of the Virgin Mary and St John the Evangelist,[50] and it was in front of the Rood that Lanfranc was buried in 1087. The relics of several of the pre-Conquest archbishops were relegated to wooden chests placed high in the north transept, though this might have been a temporary arrangement during the

[48] For more on this question, see Crook, *Architectural Setting*, 178–81.

[49] See the reconstruction plan of the Anglo-Saxon cathedral, based on Eadmer's description, in Blockley, *Canterbury Nave*, 105 (Fig. 40).

[50] Gervase, *Tractatus de combustione et reparatione Cantuariensis ecclesiæ*, in *Gervase*; ed. Stubbs, i. 3–29, at 9–10.

building works.[51] Professor Christopher Brooke makes the point strongly:

> In seven years Lanfranc built his new cathedral at Canterbury, and when it was finished neither Dunstan, nor Ælfheah—nor Wilfrid—were visible; instead, at the centre of the apse, beyond and above the high altar, one was made aware on great festivals of the presence of the archbishop himself.[52]

One other piece of evidence which seemingly supported the notion of Lanfranc's hostility to English saints' cults was a calendar found appended to the so-called 'Bosworth Psalter', edited by Cardinal Gasquet and the liturgiologist Edmund Bishop in 1907.[53] The editors believed it to have been a Christ Church Canterbury document dating from between 988 and 1023 (probably nearer the start of that date bracket), and they noted the large number of feasts of Anglo-Saxon saints within it. They compared the document with another Christ Church manuscript, a psalter containing a calendar derived from Winchester (BL, Arundel MS 155), which they believed to date from after the Conquest: here English saints' feasts numbered fewer than half of those in the Bosworth manuscript, suggesting that drastic pruning had taken place after 1066. In fact, Michael Korhammer has confirmed that the Arundel calendar also dated from the early eleventh century (*c.*1010–20).[54] Its adoption at Canterbury was the consequence not of the wish to restrict English saints' cults, but the expansion of the Winchester calendar: 'a product of the reforming impetus emanating from Winchester', as Rollason has written in an admirable summary of this complex issue.[55] Far from proving Norman reluctance to Anglo-Saxon saints, the comparison of the two Canterbury calendars shows that the English sanctoral had been subject to judicious reduction some fifty years before the Conquest. Nevertheless, Sandy Heslop has now demonstrated that some English saints' feasts were indeed removed from the earliest post-Conquest Canterbury calendar preserved in Oxford, Bodleian Library, Add. MS C.260, which he dates to the early 1120s. He qualifies these removals as a 'purge' which should be regarded in the light of Lanfranc's attitudes as expressed at the Council of Winchester (1072).[56] Thus Gasquet and Bishop seem to have

[51] See below, pp. 122–3.

[52] C. N. L. Brooke, 'Princes and Kings as Patrons of Monasteries: Normandy and England, 1066–1135', in idem, *Churches and Churchmen in Medieval Europe* (London, 1999), 139–57, at 146.

[53] F. A. Gasquet and E. Bishop (eds.), *The Bosworth Psalter* (London, 1908), an edition of BL, Add. MS 37517, a psalter formerly at Bosworth Hall, Leicestershire.

[54] P. M. Korhammer, The Origin of the Bosworth Psalter, *Anglo-Saxon England*, 2 (1973), 173–87, confirming the date of 1012–23 proposed by Francis Wormald, *English Kalendars before A.D. 1100*, Henry Bradshaw Soc., 72 for 1933 (London, 1934), 169. See also T. A. Heslop, 'The Canterbury Calendars and the Norman Conquest', in *Canterbury and the Norman Conquest: Churches, Saints and Scholars*, ed. R. Eales and R. Sharpe (London, 1995), 52–85, at 54.

[55] Rollason, *Saints and Relics*, 228.

[56] Heslop, 'Canterbury Calendars', 60–2.

drawn broadly correct inferences from the wrong source material. Additions to the Canterbury calendars show, however, that within a few decades of the Conquest more Anglo-Saxon saints were being reinstated.[57]

In broad terms, Lanfranc, the 'new Englishman' (*novus Anglus*), as he described himself in a letter written to Pope Alexander within a year of his arrival, soon appears to have accepted the local saints, and indeed promoted some local cults within his province, such as that of Paulinus of Rochester, discussed below. Lanfranc's apparent reservations were perhaps less the result of a distrust of saints' cults *per se* than of a determination that only saints whose holiness was undoubted should be venerated. This is typified by his alleged uncertainty over the cult of St Ælfheah, whom he presumably knew only as a shadowy historical figure who had met with a brutal death at the hands of the Danes; Anselm was able to persuade the archbishop of Ælfheah's sanctity, though the main point of the story was to illustrate the persuasive powers of Anselm himself.[58] Nevertheless, the tale may be taken as typifying Lanfranc's careful acceptance of an aspect of the life of the Church of which he had had little experience; later, in fact, the archbishop commissioned the English monk Osbern to compile a Life of St Ælfheah. Indeed, Ælfheah is the only Anglo-Saxon saint whose feast (17 April) Lanfranc included in the lists of festivals in the constitutions that he drew up for his metropolitan cathedral.[59] The omission of Dunstan from these lists may seem surprising (Ridyard calls this a 'short-lived hesitancy' on Lanfranc's part),[60] and by the time Osbern came to write the *Miracula Dunstani*, possibly also commissioned by Lanfranc, the archbishop had reason to be grateful to the saint for curing him from a life-threatening illness.[61] Furthermore, having completed his Life of St Edith shortly after the death of Bishop Hereman in 1078, Goscelin dedicated the work to Lanfranc, referring to the archbishop in his preface as 'the most efficacious vicar of St Dunstan' (*Dunstanu[s], cuius te efficacissimum prebuisti uicarium*), which suggests that Lanfranc would have been flattered rather than insulted to be considered the patron of an English saint.[62] As we shall see, a Rochester tradition seems to have credited Lanfranc with the first translation of their major saint, Paulinus (though another version favours Gundulf). And at Malmesbury in the early twelfth century Lanfranc was said to have proclaimed that Aldhelm was a saint following miracles in around 1080.

Lanfranc's cautious approach to Anglo-Saxon holy men was followed by other Norman Church leaders, some of whom tested the authenticity of their

[57] For example, the addition of St Paulinus to BL, Arundel MS 155 in the twelfth century.

[58] Eadmer, *St Anselm*, i.30; ed. Southern, 51.

[59] *Decreta Lanfranci: The Monastic Constitutions of Lanfranc*, ed. and trans. D. Knowles (London, 1951), 59. Lanfranc lists 'principal festivals' (p. 55), 'other festivals which are kept with solemnity' including Ælfheah's, and 'other feasts of the third rank' (pp. 64–5).

[60] Ridyard, '*Condigna Veneratio*', 203.

[61] *Miracula S. Dunstani, auct. Osberno*, cap. 20; *Memorials of St Dunstan*, 129–61, at 151–2.

[62] 'La Légende de Ste-Édith en prose et vers par le moine Goscelin', ed. A. Wilmart, *Analecta Bollandiana*, 56 (1938), 5–101, 265–307, at 38; discussed in Flight, *Bishops and Monks*, 56–7.

local saints. Walter, the first Norman abbot of Evesham (1077–1104), for example, famously had doubts about many of the relics in his church, including those of St Wigstan which Cnut had given to his predecessor Ælfweard in 1019. He therefore submitted them to the test of fire—a trial which they survived.[63] Some years later (1104), the relics of St Cuthbert were examined to ensure that they were as incorruptible as it had been claimed, though, as argued in the following chapter, this was probably an expression less of scepticism than of prudence.

OSMUND AND THE CULT OF ST ALDHELM

There is one notable exception to this tale of prudence. Osmund, who as we have seen was promoted to the new diocese of Sarum in 1078 in succession to Hereman, was responsible for developing the cult of St Aldhelm at a period when many of his fellow Norman churchmen were treating Anglo-Saxon saints with disdain. Why Osmund should be so different is unclear. Perhaps his background has something to do with the matter. Whereas the other new Anglo-Norman prelates were all related to the dukes of Normandy or were at least members of the Norman knightly class, Osmund's ancestry, though his name is Scandinavian, is never stated by contemporary chroniclers and we may perhaps infer that he rose from the ranks to the Norman ecclesiastical hierarchy.[64] His abilities were evidently recognised by William the Conqueror, and from 1070 until his appointment as bishop of Sarum Osmund held the position of royal chancellor.

One of Osmund's actions on becoming bishop was to preside over the translation at Malmesbury Abbey of the bones of St Aldhelm (d. 709), his predecessor as the first bishop of Sherborne and the most important saint of the monastery of Malmesbury. We followed the movements of St Aldhelm's remains in the previous chapter.[65] On 3 June 1078 the bones were transferred to a new reliquary. Within a year or two Osmund obtained a relic of the saint for his new cathedral, namely a fragment from Aldhelm's left arm, lavishing 'money and art on the making of a silver casket to house it'.[66] In the early thirteenth century it was listed amongst the Sarum relics: 'the arm of St Aldhelm, covered in silver, with many stones'.[67] It was presumably a reliquary in the shape of an arm extended in blessing, of which several Continental examples are still extant. Diana Greenway has suggested that Osmund adopted his Anglo-Saxon predecessor as his patron saint because he was attracted to his scholarship and the rigorous attitude to celibacy that

[63] *Evesham Chronicle*, 323 and 335–7.

[64] B. R. Kemp (ed.), *English Episcopal Acta*, 18 (Salisbury 1078–1217), British Academy (Oxford, 1999), pp. xxxiv–xxxviii.

[65] See p. 104.

[66] Malmesbury, *GP*, v.269; ed. Winterbottom and Thomson, i. 640–1: *opera sumptuosa et arte studiosa thecam parauit argenteam, qua illud induceret.*

[67] Malden, *St Osmund*, 53: *brachium sancti Aldelmi argenteum et deauratum.*

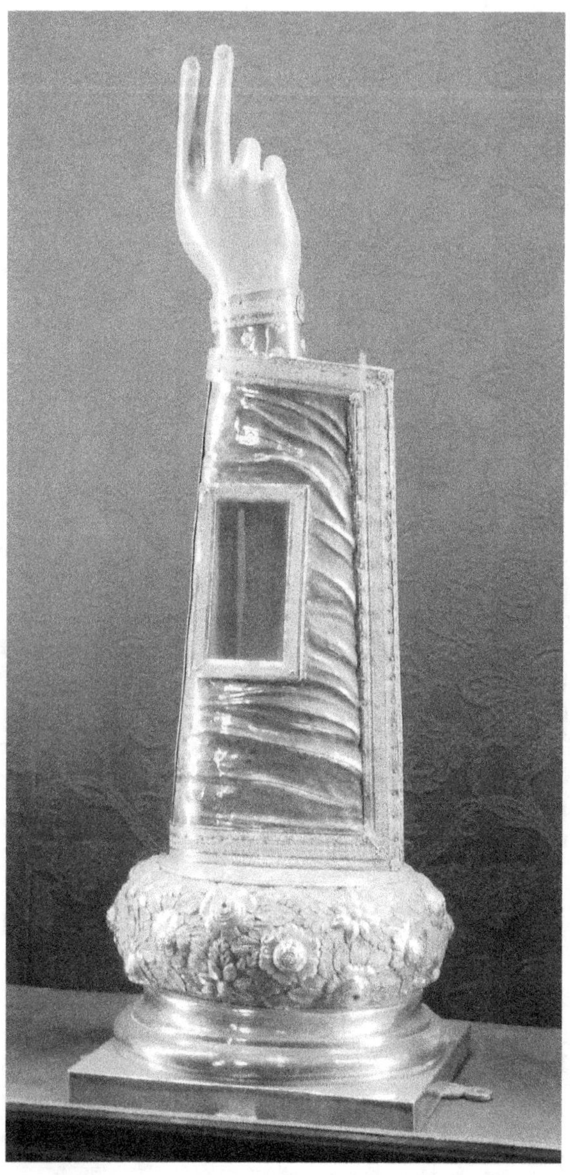

PLATE 5.3 SEVILLE CATHEDRAL, SPAIN
A post-medieval arm reliquary.

Aldhelm had displayed in his book *De Virginitate*.

In the final book of his *Gesta Pontificum*, a Life of St Aldhelm, William of Malmesbury recounts many miracles carried out by the saint in the author's own church. After one notorious miracle, involving the cure of a deformed youth called Folkwine, an account was sent to the abbot who was at the royal court. Archbishop Lanfranc himself heard of the affair and, says William, ordered that Aldhelm should henceforth be revered as a saint. An annual market on his feast-day was set up at the same time, to attract people.[68]

William's account of the cult of St Aldhelm at Malmesbury in the late eleventh and early twelfth centuries was compiled from childhood memories, and as already noted, showed some internal inconsistencies and divergence from the other account of the cult, by Faricius.[69] He recalled activities at the shrine whilst he was a boy. One event made a particular impression. On the saint's feast-day large crowds thronged to the shrine, including an irreligious rabble. One of them exposed himself at the shrine and farted loudly (*nudato inguine incestavit aera, tum deinde crepitu ventris emisso turbavit auras*). He was quickly punished for his impiety by being possessed by a devil.[70]

[68] Malmesbury, *GP*, v.269; ed. Winterbottom and Thomson, i. 636–41.
[69] See above, p. 104.
[70] Malmesbury, *GP*, v.275; ed. Winterbottom and Thomson, i. 656–7.

ARCHITECTURAL EVIDENCE FOR THE CULTS OF ANGLO-SAXON SAINTS AFTER THE CONQUEST

It is perhaps significant that throughout the high middle ages Anglo-Saxon and Celtic saints remained the principal cults in England and Wales: the Normans introduced virtually no existing Continental saints' cults, apart from St Audoenus (Ouen), venerated at Canterbury. Of course some post-Conquest cults involved 'Englishmen' of Norman origin, such as Thomas Becket, born to Norman parents living in England. Another Anglo-Norman was St Thomas Cantilupe, bishop of Hereford from 1275–82, the son of an Anglo-Norman baron and his aristocratic Norman wife. St Hugh of Lincoln (bishop 1186–1200) was a Burgundian from Avallon and a former Carthusian monk of the Grande Chartreuse. These local cults of people of Norman descent stood alongside undoubtedly home-grown products: William of Norwich, allegedly ritually murdered by the Jewish community in 1144; 'Little St Hugh' of Lincoln, who died in similar circumstances in 1255; William of Perth, murdered in 1201. In the final two centuries before the Reformation, many other local cults would develop, such as that of Sir John Shorne at St George's, Windsor. Clearly, then, the Anglo-Saxons would eventually prevail, and any misgivings that the Norman churchmen may have had about the quality of Anglo-Saxon saints seem to have been rapidly dispelled. By the mid twelfth century some pre-Conquest churchmen who had perhaps not hitherto been regarded as saints were also being venerated, such as Ithamar of Rochester and Mellitus of London.[71]

The most reliable indication of post-Conquest attitudes is not the reported political posturing and half-remembered conversations of Norman prelates, but what actually happened to the English saints in the immediate post-Conquest years, and the way their relics were treated in the rebuilt churches of Norman England. It is useful, therefore, to look at a few of the major Anglo-Saxon cult centres and examine the role played by the local saint at the time when the new Norman churches were under construction.

CHRIST CHURCH, CANTERBURY

The old cathedral church of Canterbury had burned down in 1067 and was therefore the earliest of the English cathedrals to be reconstructed. One of Lanfranc's first actions was to rescue various sets of holy bones from the ruins. Eadmer, who was a little boy (*puerulus*) at the monastery school at the time,[72] tells us that Lanfranc ordered the remains of earlier archbishops to be removed to safety (*in tuto locari constituit*).[73] The individuals included

[71] See below, pp. 179–81.

[72] As he mentioned in the letter to the Glastonbury monks concerned with their claim to possess the body of St Dunstan: *Epistola Eadmeri ad Glastonienses*, in *Memorials of St Dunstan*, 412–22, at 413: *quia cum adhuc in scholis puerulus essem*.

[73] Eadmer, *Vita Bregwini*, cap. 11; ed. Scholtz, 144–5: *prę̨fatos antistes leuari ac in tuto locari constituit, donec ea quam cę̨perat ę̨cclesia facta esset in qua decenter poni ualerent..*

Archbishop Cuthbert (†760), who had been buried in a 'church' dedicated to John the Baptist, which Cuthbert had added at the east end of the Anglo-Saxon cathedral which it 'nearly touched' (being *pene contigua*); it was perhaps linked to the south-east corner, as conjectured by Willis,[74] but had also perished in the fire. Eadmer relates that Cuthbert had built it to serve as a baptistry, a consistory court, and as a burial place for archbishops, who hitherto had been buried at St Augustine's abbey.[75] Osbern describes how the bones were first moved to an oratory dedicated to the Blessed Virgin, together with the body of St Dunstan, whose reliquary-coffin (*theca*) had been reverently exhumed.[76] Eadmer retained a more detailed childhood memory of the location of the oratory, which without doubt was the apsidal western structure added to the Anglo-Saxon cathedral *c.*1000 and excavated in 1993:

> [Lanfranc] ordered the bodies of the saints buried in the eastern part of that church to be moved to the western part where the much-visited monument of the blessed mother of God and eternal virgin Mary was located. Wherefore, after a three-day fast had been observed, in the midst of a vast multitude of people the most precious bodies of the bishops of Christ, Dunstan and Ælfheah, were elevated. They were then translated to their place of burial which had been determined and the voices of all resounded with the Lord's praise.[77]

Osbern's version of events was very similar. When the western oratory had in turn to be demolished to accommodate the foundations of the new cathedral, all the relics were removed to a building associated with the refectory (*in domum quandam refectorii*), because 'apart from that building no other could be found in which divine service could take place and where the relics of saints could fittingly and conveniently be located'.[78] But, as already noted, Lanfranc did not rescue the relics so that they might form some kind of spiritual focus of the new cathedral, even though Eadmer's comments suggest that Ælfheah and Dunstan may have received more

[74] R. Willis, *The Architectural History of Canterbury Cathedral* (London, 1845), 29–30 and fig. 2.

[75] Eadmer, *Vita Bregwini*, cap. 3; ed. Scholtz, 140: *ut … archepiscoporum corpora in ea sepelirentur, sublata de medio antiqua consuetudine, qua eatenus tumulari solebant extra ciuitatem in ęcclesia beatorum Petri et Pauli, ubi posita sunt corpora omnium antecessorum suorum*. See the schematic plans of the Anglo-Saxon cathedral in Southern, *Anselm and his Biographer*, 264–5.

[76] *Miracula S. Dunstani auct. Osberno*, cap. 17; *Memorials of St Dunstan*, 129–61, at 142–3.

[77] *Miracula S. Dunstani, auct. Eadmero*, cap. 16 (formerly 14); Eadmer, *Lives*, 160–211, at 176–7: *[Lanfrancus] iussit corpora sanctorum quæ in orientali parte ipsius æcclesiæ humata erant in occidentalem partem, ubi memoria beatæ Dei genitricis et perpetuæ uirginis Mariæ celebris habebatur, demutari.*

[78] *Miracula S. Dunstani auct. Osberno*, cap. 19; *Memorials of St Dunstan*, 129–61, at 148–9: *… nec præter illam alia domus inveniri poterat in qua vel divinum servitium fieri vel reliquiæ sanctorum congrue atque habiliter locari possent*. Cf. Eadmer's *Miracula S. Dunstani*, cap. 16 (formerly 14); Eadmer, *Lives*, 176–9, where only the bodies of Dunstan and Ælfheah are mentioned.

privileged treatment and may indeed have shortly afterwards been 'visible' in Lanfranc's church (Eadmer may have telescoped the sequence of events). These last two saints were probably exceptions. According to Eadmer the relics of the earlier archbishops of Canterbury (only Bregwine is mentioned by name, as the passage occurs in his Life) were placed 'above a vault on the north side, each within individual wooden caskets; in that place the mystery of the sacrifice of salvation is daily celebrated'.[79] This sounds like a chapel at gallery level in the north transept: indeed Gervase's much later description of Lanfranc's transepts makes it clear that each transept ended in a tribune platform,[80] whose existence has been confirmed by excavation of the footings of the supporting columns of the south transept. These platforms gave access to first-floor chapels, stilted on plan and terminating in apses, on the east side. Presumably Eadmer's purpose in adding the curious remark that mass was celebrated there daily was to emphasise that the first-floor north chapel was not a forgotten corner, but an area in liturgical use (unlike the similar space in the south transept, which was where the organ was located).

Eadmer also makes it clear that one of Canterbury Cathedral's most prestigious relics was the body of St Wilfrid, said to have been exhumed at Ripon and brought to Kent by Archbishop Oda after the Danish devastation of Ripon in 948.[81] The relics were placed in the high altar (*in maiore altari*) of the Saxon cathedral at Canterbury. When the altar was demolished after the fire, the relics were rediscovered and were placed in a *scrinium*. This was presumably a temporary location during the building works, for 'when, after a number of years there was agreement among the brothers that it would be more fitting for the relics to be enclosed in a permanent position, a tomb (*sepulcrum*) was constructed for them on the north side of the [high] altar'.[82] Later, after the remodelling of the east end of the church, they would be moved to the axial chapel of Anselm's choir.[83] A different story was, however, current at Worcester, where it was claimed that Oda's nephew St Oswald had placed the relics in a new shrine at Ripon and rebuilt the monastery as a supporting community.[84]

[79] Eadmer, *Vita Bregwini*, cap. 11; ed. Scholtz, 145: ... *in aquilonali parte super uoltum singuli sub singulis ligneis locellis ubi cotidie misterium sacrificii salutaris celebratur positi sunt.*
[80] Gervase, *Tractatus de combustione*, in *Gervase*; ed. Stubbs, i. 3–29, at 10. Gervase subsequently explains (ibid., 11) that the gallery of Lanfranc's north transept was demolished after the fire of 1174 to make a more spacious setting for the altar of the martyrdom: *Pilarius autem ille qui in medio crucis hujus steterat et fornix ei innitens, processu temporis, ob reverentiam martyris demolita sunt, ut altare in loco martyrii elevatum, ampliori spatio cerneretur.*
[81] Eadmer, *Vita Wilfridi*, cap. 63, paras 115–16; ed. Muir and Turner , 142–7.
[82] ibid., cap. 63, para. 117; pp. 146–7: *Cum ergo predictum altare subuerteretur, reliquie beati Wilfridi reperte ac leuate sunt, atque in scrinio collocate. Uerum cum post aliquot annos fratrum uoluntas in eo consentirent ut magis fixo loco clauderentur, sepulcrum eis in aquilonari parte altaris factum est ...*
[83] See below, p. 138.
[84] A. Thacker, 'Saint-making and relic collecting by Oswald and his communities', in Brooks, *St Oswald*, 244–68.

Dunstan and Ælfheah may, however, have been moved to *memoria* within the body of the church reasonably soon after its completion, for Osbern tells us that when Dunstan miraculously cured the archbishop from illness (the doctors had despaired of his life), Lanfranc asked the monks to lock themselves in the cathedral and offer up thanks for his cure 'at the monument of the saint' (*ad memoriam sancti*).[85] This suggests a rather more prestigious placement than above the vault of a north *porticus*. Indeed, the saint's body was accessible to other people seeking his aid, such as the monk Edward, who regretted his former life as archdeacon of London, and entered the cathedral in order to ask the saint's permission.[86] Even Osbern himself had overcome his litigants in a law-suit by invoking the saint 'at the tomb of the saint', throwing his arms around the middle of the monument.[87] Osbern was clearly then an adult, so the event must have taken place in Lanfranc's church, when the choir was still at the east end of the nave. It is therefore quite possible that both Dunstan and Ælfheah were enshrined within the monastic choir, as they certainly were within a few years of the remodelling of the cathedral by Prior Ernulf (1096–1107), but of this there is no record. Our best source for the cathedral at the end of the eleventh century, Gervase, writing over sixty years after the east end of the cathedral had been remodelled by Priors Ernulf and Conrad into 'Anselm's Glorious Choir', could find no information about Lanfranc's choir: 'you must realise, gentle reader, that I never saw Lanfranc's choir, nor have I been able to find any description of it'.[88]

In short, both the design and, as far as we can perceive it, the internal layout and furnishings of Lanfranc's cathedral showed little influence of the cult of saints, unless the small east crypt was used for cultic purposes. The form of the east end of its Anglo-Saxon predecessor appears to have been strongly influenced by such cults, with a ring-crypt providing direct access to Dunstan's tomb in a manner derived from St Peter's, Rome. Lanfranc's cathedral, on the other hand, followed the example of the Conqueror's church of St Stephen at Caen as far as the lack of architectural influence of saints' cults was concerned.

Canterbury was not only the first cathedral to be rebuilt by the Normans, but it was also constructed under the direct influence of Lanfranc. Although the architecture yields no hint that major saints were enshrined there, the internal furnishings, especially the tomb-shrines of Dunstan and Ælfheah that possibly were moved to more accessible locations in Lanfranc's own time, may reflect the archbishop's gradual acceptance of English saints' cults.

[85] *Miracula S. Dunstani, auct. Osberno*, in *Memorials of St Dunstan*, 129–61, at 152.
[86] ibid., 156.
[87] ibid., 159: *ad sepulcrum sancti cucurri, medium illud utrisque brachiis amplexatus sum.* Osbern 'disappears from view after 1093' (Southern, *Anselm and his Biographer*, 251), so the incident is unlikely to have occurred in the late eleventh-century Glorious Choir.
[88] Eadmer, *Tractatus de Combustione*, in *Gervase*; ed. Stubbs, i. 3–29, at 12: *Scias autem, lector bone, quod chorum Lamfranci non vidi, nec ab aliquo descriptum repperi.*

The architectural response to the cult of saints would be more obvious at Canterbury in the late 1090s, when, under the inspiration of Lanfranc's successor, St Anselm, the eastern arm of the cathedral was enlarged, as described in Chapter 6.

LINCOLN AND OLD SARUM

The next two major churches to be rebuilt were cathedrals on new sites: Lincoln, begun in 1072, and Old Sarum, begun in 1075. It is therefore interesting to note that these two cathedrals seem at first to have been characterised by a total absence of any sort of local saint's cult. Both were dedicated to the Blessed Virgin Mary, but dedication to a mainline saint of the Church Universal, such as the Virgin or one of the Apostles, was normal even in churches housing a local cult.[89] Important local cults had, on the other hand, been a feature of the Anglo-Saxon cathedrals where the sees were located before the Conquest. At Dorchester-on-Thames there was a flourishing cult of St Birinus (though his cult was also celebrated at Winchester), but this never moved to Lincoln. Similarly at Sherborne there were cults of several saintly Anglo-Saxon monarchs, but these cults did not travel to Old Sarum with the see but remained in the parent churches. It would have been perfectly possible for the relics to be translated from the Anglo-Saxon churches in order to effect the consecration, and the fact that this did not happen seems indicative of the attitude of the recently arrived Norman churchmen towards English saints. Only later would new cults emerge: first, at Old Sarum, where the developing cult of St Osmund may have influenced the form and above all the decorative scheme of the enlarged east end of the church; and later at Lincoln, with the growth of the cult of St Hugh.

WINCHESTER

According to the *Annales Wintonienses*, the monks of Old Minster moved into the new cathedral, then under construction, on 8 April 1093, in the presence of 'almost all the bishops and abbots of England'.[90] It is clear that only the eastern arm, central tower, transepts, and part of the nave can have been complete at that date: most of the nave could not be built until the Anglo-Saxon cathedral, Old Minster, had been demolished. A few months later, on the feast of Swithun, presumably his translation, 15 July, which by then had superseded the day of his death (*depositio*) as the major feast, 'having processed from the new church back to Old Minster, they took up St Swithun's *feretrum* and installed it with honour in the new church'. The

[89] St Augustine's Canterbury was dedicated at SS. Peter and Paul as was St Swithun's Winchester. Bury St Edmunds was dedicated to St James the Great, Durham and Worcester were the Cathedral Churches of Christ and the Virgin Mary. Ely was dedicated to the Holy Trinity, Rochester to St Andrew. The minster churches retained double dedications: for example, Minster-in-Sheppey was dedicated to St Mary and St Seaxburh; Folkestone to St Mary and St Eanswith.

[90] *Winchester Annals*, 37: '*in præsentia omnium fere episcoporum atque abbatum Angliæ* …'.

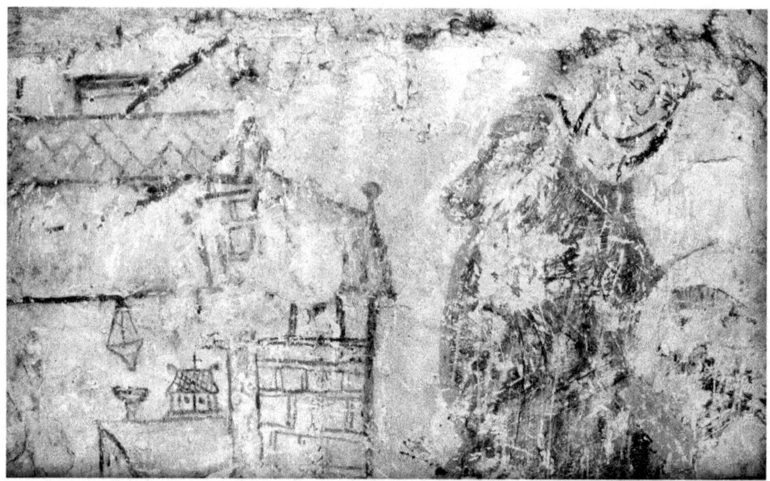

PLATE 5.4 WINCHESTER CATHEDRAL A thirteenth-century wall-painting in the Morley Library, showing (rt) the elevation of St Swithun and (left) the Romanesque cathedral, with the reliquary on an altar within the main choir apse.

very next day Bishop Walkelin gave orders for the Anglo-Saxon church to be demolished, and Old Minster was almost totally taken down within the year.[91] The translation appears to have been a less spectacular event than the first inauguration, and there is no hint that the prelates who had come to Winchester before Easter returned there in July to witness the saint's arrival in the new church.

The earlier parts of the *Annales* (certainly down to 1139 and perhaps to 1202) are attributed to the Winchester monk Richard of Devizes, writing in the late twelfth century, and were therefore compiled long after the demolition works of 1093–4.[92] Nevertheless, the surviving physical evidence and the later history of the *feretrum* suggest that Richard had access to a trustworthy source when relating the events of some ninety years previously. The annals do not say that the translation of St Swithun's relics involved the construction of a new monument to the saint. His reliquary, almost certainly that precious container which had been given to Old Minster by King Edgar at the translation of the 1070s,[93] was simply transferred to the new cathedral, in what may have been regarded as an expedient demonstration of continuity. The translation of the relics appears to have constituted above all a dedication ceremony, one which also marked the redundancy of the old church prior to its demolition (there is no evidence for a formal ceremony of deconsecration).

The annalist does not specify where the reliquary was placed; such evidence as we have suggests that it was placed on, or at least close to, the high altar, and the relics seem to have remained there until their final

[91] ibid.

[92] J. T. Appleby, 'Richard of Devizes and the Annals of Winchester', *Bulletin of the Institute of Historical Research*, 36 (1963), 70–7; J. Crook, 'Early Historians of Winchester Cathedral', *Hampshire Studies: Proc. Hampshire Field Club and Archaeol. Soc.*, 58 (2003), 226–41, at 226–7.

[93] See above, p. 000.

translation to a late medieval high shrine in the cathedral retrochoir in 1476. Indeed, the relics are apparently portrayed at the high altar in an early thirteenth-century wall-painting which adorned the walls of the sacrist's office, now the cathedral library. The painting shows a reliquary standing on the high altar of a church, within an apse, and it is likely that the painting was intended as a view of the Romanesque cathedral.[94]

WORCESTER

The next cathedral to be built was Worcester, where the Anglo-Saxon Bishop Wulfstan supervised the reconstruction. One might therefore expect that the local saints would continue to be appropriately housed. Worcester's principal saint was a former bishop, St Oswald. His remains were translated into the new Norman cathedral by Bishop Wulfstan in 1088–9, only four years after the starting date of the works given in the *Worcester Annals*.[95] The monks had moved into the cathedral during the year preceding Whit Sunday 1089. The date is known thanks to the record of a charter relating to the gift of the estate of Alveston (Warwickshire) being placed on the high altar at that time.[96] The short timescale suggests that only the eastern arm had been constructed at the time of this first dedication.

The remodelling of that part of Worcester Cathedral in the thirteenth century has obliterated any evidence for the location of his cult. There is no evidence of any sort, either documentary or archaeological, that Oswald's bones were rehoused in the crypt. Philip Barker and Christopher Guy have noted that areas of late eleventh- to early thirteenth-century plaster floor in the ambulatory at the entrance to the south-eastern chapel showed none of the wear or patching that would have resulted from the movement of a large number of pilgrims.[97] It is more probable that the reliquary was placed at main level, near the high altar.

Fortunately we have some clues as to how Oswald's bones were housed, though not their exact position within the new church. According to William of Malmesbury, Wulfstan had placed the relics, together with those of many other saints, in a reliquary (*scrinium*) which was an enlarged or remodelled version of the one that Oswald himself had originally created to house relics of St Wilfrid.[98] Oswald had allegedly brought this *scrinium* from Ripon, and it had contained his own remains since Archbishop Ealdwulf translated them in 1002.[99] But in the *Gesta Pontificum* William twice

[94] J. Crook, 'King Edgar's reliquary of St Swithun', *Anglo-Saxon England*, 21 (1992) 177–202.
[95] *Worcester Annals*, 373, *s.a.* 1084: *Inceptio operis Wigorniensis monasterii per Sanctum Wulstanum*.
[96] *The Cartulary of Worcester Cathedral Priory*, ed. R. R. Darlington, Pipe Roll Soc., 76 (n.s., vol. 38) for the years 1962–3 (1968), item 3, pp. 8–9 and facsimile, pl. 4, facing p. 8.
[97] C. Guy, 'Excavations at Worcester Cathedral, 1881–1991', *Trans. Worcester Archaeol. Soc.*, 3rd ser., 14 (1994), 1–73, at 29–30.
[98] Malmesbury, *Vita Wulfstani*, iii.10.4; ed. Winterbottom and Thomson, 122–3. Cf. Malmesbury, *Vita Dunstani*, i.15.6; ed. Winterbottom and Thomson, 204–5.
[99] See above, p. 94.

mentions the tradition that Wilfrid's body was at Canterbury, though he does suggest that the relics in question might in fact have been those of Wilfrid II, a later archbishop of York.[100]

Where, then, was this reliquary situated? There is no evidence that it was placed in the crypt, which, in any case, would at that date have been an unlikely location for a major saint.[101] I have argued elsewhere that a more likely location would be on the south side of the east arm, foreshadowing the similar placement of his shrine in the later medieval cathedral.[102] But in truth, one has to conclude that the position of Oswald's shrine in Wulfstan's east arm must remain inconclusive. Later, as explored more fully in Chapter 6, the cults of Oswald and Wulfstan went hand-in-hand.

ROCHESTER[103]

As noted in the previous chapter, at the Norman Conquest the only local saint's cult current at Rochester was that of St Paulinus: the cult of Ithamar developed later. The development of the post-Conquest cult of Paulinus is recorded in a number of documents whose reliability has been analysed by Colin Flight. He seeks to prove, partly on linguistic evidence, that the earliest of these was a lost book of miracles, *Miracula*, known to us through the fourteenth-century transcription made by John of Tynemouth in his *Sanctilogium*.[104] For Flight the *Miracula* was an early twelfth-century production, written 'within the first quarter of the twelfth century, perhaps within the first decade'. On his evidence this must be the latest possible date, for he notes the use of internal rhymes, an affectation employed by writers such as Goscelin and Osbern in the late eleventh century but abandoned soon afterwards.[105] It is certain that by the beginning of the thirteenth century the Rochester monks did indeed possess a volume entitled 'The Miracles of St Paulinus and St Ithamar', as we know from a list of the cathedral library's books dated 1202.[106] Amongst a set of books said to be 'in the precentor's chest' (*in archa cantoris*) at that early thirteenth-century date were two books of the miracles of the local saints, referred to in the list

[100] See below, p. 138.
[101] For more on this point, see J. Crook, 'The Physical Setting of the Cult of St Wulfstan', in *St Wulfstan and his World*, ed. J. S. Barrow and N. P. Brooks, Studies in Early Medieval Britain, 4 (Aldershot, 2005), 189–217.
[102] ibid., 200.
[103] This section draws heavily on J. Crook, 'The medieval shrines of Rochester Cathedral', in *Medieval Art, Architecture and Archaeology at Rochester, BAA Trans.*, vol. 27, for 2002 (Leeds, 2006), 114–29.
[104] *Nova Legenda Anglie*, ed. Horstmann, ii. 312–16.
[105] Flight, *Bishops and Monks*, 61–2.
[106] The document, published by B. Rye, 'Catalogue of the library of the priory of St Andrew, Rochester, A.D. 1202', *Arch. Cant.*, 3 (1860), 47–64, occurs as two vellum leaves at the beginning of a copy of St Augustine's *De Doctrina Christiana*, BL, Royal MS 5.B.xii, and is headed (Rue, 54) *Anno ab incarnatione Domini M.CC.II. hoc est scrutinium librarii nostri*. In a different hand on fo. 3 it is stated the list was compiled by Alexander '*quondam cantor*' of the monastery: see *British Museum: Catalogue of Western Manuscripts in the Old Royal and King's Collections*, ed. G. F. Warner and J. P. Gilson, 4 vols. (London, 1921), i. 104.

as *Miracula sancti Ythamari, i. volumen* and *Miracula sancti Paulini et sancti Ythamari, i. volumen.*[107] However, neither of these *Miracula* feature in an earlier book-list that occurs in the second part of the so-called *Textus Roffensis*, dating from the 1120s,[108] so there is some uncertainty about the date of the source of John of Tynemouth's transcription.

According to the text relayed to us by Tynemouth, Archbishop Lanfranc paid personally for the expense of translating the bones of St Paulinus:

> When a long time had passed [since Paulinus's death], when Gundulf was bishop there, Archbishop Lanfranc completely destroyed the old church of blessed Andrew and rebuilt a new church; he raised the bones of St Paulinus from the earth and placed them together honourably in a shrine (*scrinium*).[109]

This version of events must, however, be compared with that provided in the *Vita Gundulfi*, which tells a different story, crediting that bishop, rather than Lanfranc, with organising the translation, and never mentioning the archbishop's role:

> That venerable father [Gundulf], having convened with great solemnity the monks and clergy of the convent as well as a great multitude of lay people at the sepulchre of the most holy confessor Paulinus (who had been laid to rest in the old church), caused the treasure of his holy relics to be translated into the new church and to be laid in a place which had decently been prepared for this purpose.[110]

The two bishops appear in fact to have worked closely together, first at Canterbury, then at Rochester. Colin Flight has, however, argued that the change in emphasis (Gundulf, rather than Lanfranc) results from the efforts of the Rochester monks, somewhat later in the twelfth century, to distance themselves from Canterbury, and to paint a picture of Gundulf as the successor of the impresario bishops of Frankish Gaul. Flight dates the *Vita*

[107] Rye, 'Catalogue', 58, items 146–7. The library also possessed (ibid., 56, item 82) a '*Vita S. Dunstani et sancti Alfegi martyris, in 1 vol*', which also seems to be mentioned in the earlier book-list in the *Textus Roffensis* (see below).

[108] Rochester Cathedral, MS A.3.5, published in facsimile as *Textus Roffensis: Part I*, ed. P. H. Sawyer (Early English Manuscripts in Facsimile VII, Copenhagen, 1957); *Textus Roffensis: Part II*, ed. idem (Early English Manuscripts in Facsimile XI, Copenhagen, 1962). The book-list occurs on fos. 224r–228r. It was published by R. P. Coates, 'Catalogue of the library of the Priory of St. Andrew, Rochester, from the Textus Roffensis', *Arch. Cant.*, 6 (1866), 120–8.

[109] *Nova Legenda Anglie*, ed. Horstmann, 314: *Elapso autem multo tempore, Gundulpho ibidem pontificante, Lanfrancus archiepiscopus ueterem ecclesiam beati Andree funditus destruxit, nouamque basilicam reedificauit, ossa sancti Paulini de terra leuauit, et in scrinio honorifice collocauit.*

[110] *Vita Gundulfi*, cap. 18; ed. Thomson, 41–2. *Idem uenerabilis pater, collecto monachorum et clericorum conuentu necnon et copiosa multitudine plebis, cum magna solennitate ad sepulchrum sanctissimi confessoris Paulini, qui in ueteri æcclesia reconditus fuerat, et thesaurum sanctarum reliquiarum eius in nouam æcclesiam transferri et in loco decenter ad hoc præparato reponi fecit.*

Gundulfi to the time of Bishop John I (1125–37), considering the text as a piece of polemic directed against that bishop which painted a rosy picture of Gundulf as an ideal with which Bishop John had, by implication, failed to conform. This date of composition in the second quarter of the twelfth century is considerably later than the 1114 × 1124 date bracket proposed by the most recent editor of the text.[111] The respective dates of the putative *Miracula* used by John of Tynemouth and the *Vita Gundulfi* are critical. It would, however, be unwise to use the emphasis on Gundulf's role in the translation, rather than Lanfranc's, as supporting evidence for the relative dates of the *Vita Gundulfi* and the *Miracula*, for later texts revert to crediting Lanfranc with Paulinus's translation. For example, in a list of benefactors included in the early thirteenth-century Cotton MS Vespasian A.xxii, published by Thorpe under the title *Registrum Roffense*, Gundulf is remembered only for minor gifts of vestments and books, whereas the credit for the enshrinement of Paulinus's relics is given to Lanfranc alone:

> Amongst the other good deeds which Archbishop Lanfranc did for our church … he caused the body of St Paulinus to be raised up, and to be placed in a silver shrine which he himself had made. … He also gave the cross which stands over the shrine of St Paulinus …[112]

The passage was subsequently copied almost verbatim in the Rochester manuscript of the *Flores Historiarum*, dating from the early fourteenth century,[113] and here the chronicler adds another detail: silver from the *feretrum* was later used by the monks to pay the legal expenses of their dispute with Bishop Gilbert Glanville (1185–1214).[114]

Such details should evidently be accepted with caution, as they are more likely to reflect the situation at the time of writing than to be an accurate record of the state of affairs in a period long past. It is also true that the emphasis in the *Vita Gundulfi* on that bishop's role as a promoter of saints'

[111] Flight, *Bishops and Monks*, 41. *Vita Gundulfi*, 3–4: 'It does not seem possible to date its composition more precisely than between the years 1114 and 1124, and even then only the earlier date is entirely certain.'

[112] *Registrum Roffense*, 120: *Lanfrancus archiepiscopus, inter cetera bona qui fecit ecclesie nostre … Fecit etiam levari corpus S. Paulini, et in feretro argenteo quod ipse fieri fecit, poni. … Dedit autem crucem qui stat super feretrum S. Paulini, et thuribulum argenteum.* (MS fo. 87v).

[113] *Flores Historiarum*, ii. 20, *s.a.* 1088: *Lamfrancus archiepiscopus inter cætera bona quæ fecit ecclesiæ Roffensi … Fecit etiam levari corpus sancti Paulini et in feretro argenteo quod ipse fieri fecit reponi. Dedit etiam duas casulas, unam rubeam et alteram nigram de purpura, et tabulam argenteam ante maius altare et crucem quæ stat super feretrum sancti Paulini et turribulum argenteum.*

[114] ibid., 21: *Argentum vero quod idem Lamfrancus super feretrum sancti Paulini posuerat, propter placitum inter ecclesiam Roffensem et Gilbertum de Glanville eiusdem ecclesiæ episcopum, in subsidium ecclesiæ antedictæ est allatum.* See also a later passage in the same annals (fo. 127) published by Wharton, *Anglia Sacra*, ii. 346: *magna fuerat perturbacio in ecclesia Roffensi, cuius occasione prior et conuentus multa bona una cum argento quo uenerabilis Lamfrancus feretrum sancti Paulini decorauerat: in placito inter eos et episcopum uendiderunt.*

cults might be regarded as consistent with the assertion of various non-Rochester writers that he participated in a number of post-Conquest translations. In a letter to the monks of Glastonbury, Eadmer recalled that, during his own childhood, Gundulf—not yet bishop—and Abbot Scolland were present when Dunstan's body was translated at Canterbury Cathedral soon after the fire of 1067.[115] According to Goscelin, Gundulf presided at the translation of Augustine and his successors at St Augustine's Canterbury in 1091, standing in for the archbishop during the long interregnum between Lanfranc and the eventual consecration of Anselm.[116] In 1102 Gundulf is also said to have been present at the examination of the body of Edward the Confessor.[117] In the light of these interests, it might be expected that the bishop would have had a more significant part to play in the saintly translations of his episcopate, as recorded by all sources except his *Vita*.

The debate over who was responsible for the translation and the significance of the apparently rival claims are, however, side-issues. The two early accounts agree, at least, that Paulinus's body was 'honourably displayed' within the new, late eleventh-century cathedral after the translation, though the year is unknown: a date in the late 1080s seems probable, and if the *Registrum* is correct that Lanfranc organised the translation his death in 1089 provides a *terminus ante quem*.[118] None of the sources employs a commonplace of hagiography, that Paulinus's body was miraculously incorrupt, and the relics presumably consisted of disarticulated bones: John of Tynemouth's text actually calls them *ossa sancti Paulini*.[119] One would expect these to have been placed in a receptacle of the kind commonly called a *feretrum* by contemporary writers.

Despite these caveats, it is not implausible that the *feretrum* provided by Lanfranc (or Gundulf) was adorned with silver at the time of the translation. The terminology is of little help: *feretrum* means literally a bier, but by this date it was usually used synonymously with *scrinium*, a word which in its origins means a chest or box. One might postulate a wooden container, covered in repoussé silver panels, a successor to the opulent Anglo-Saxon shrines such as the one provided at King Edgar's expense for the remains of St Swithun at Winchester. As for the spoliation of the shrine to raise funds, this need not surprise us. Shrines were frequently despoiled in this way, often by churchmen: the same thing had happened at Ely in the time of Bishop Nigel (1133–69), incurring the censure of the author of the *Liber Eliensis*.[120] But of the exact appearance of the Romanesque *scrinium* of St Paulinus, we know nothing.

[115] *Epistola Eadmeri ad Glastonienses*, in *Memorials of St Dunstan*, 412–22, at 413.
[116] Goscelin, *Historia Translationis S. Augustini episcopi*; *Pat. Lat.*, clv. cols. 13–46.
[117] Osbert, *Vita Edwardi regis*, cap xxix; ed. Bloch, 118–19. Repeated by Ailred of Rievaulx, *Vita S. Edwardi regis et confessoris*; *Pat. Lat.*, cxcv. cols. 737–90, at 780.
[118] P. McAleer, *Rochester Cathedral, 604–1540* (Toronto, 1999), 17, suggests that Paulinus was translated 'as early as circa 1088', citing the *Vita Gundulfi*, fo. 56[57]r, but the year is not actually mentioned in this document.
[119] *Nova Legenda Anglie*, ed. Horstmann, ii. 314.
[120] *Liber Eliensis*, iii.50 and 89; ed. Blake, 288–96, at 290, and 334–5, at 335.

There are, however, a few isolated shreds of evidence for the location of the *scrinium* within the Romanesque cathedral, even though we are inevitably hampered by our lack of knowledge about the form of the east end of the late eleventh-century building. The most likely location for Paulinus's relics is within the eastern arm, where a measure of accessibility would have been available to suppliants. Here, such evidence as we have occurs in the form of miracle stories relating to the cult of St Paulinus, and the later one of St Ithamar. However sceptical one may be about much of the content of such stories, it is unlikely that they would have misrepresented the architectural setting. The monks who were the principal audience for the *miracula*, intended to be read at the annual feast of the saint, would have been quick to spot any such discrepancies. According to the text transcribed by John of Tynemouth, immediately after Paulinus's relics had been brought into the new cathedral church a sinful woman successfully sought a cure at the *sepulchrum*,[121] but shortly afterwards relapsed into her evil ways, 'like a dog returning to its vomit'. When further tribulations brought her back to the church she was less successful; she intended bringing a taper to the shrine (a typical activity, where a taper was made to the length of the sick person), but got no further than the first step before being violently repulsed by the saint. Only after she convinced Bishop Gundulf of her true repentance was she able to reach the relics and leave a gift. Another version of the same story occurs in the *Vita Gundulfi*.[122] We may at least infer from this that the reliquary was located in a part of the church that was at a higher level than the nave, so the east end, above the crypt, seems the most probable site.[123] If any reliance can be placed on the record of Lanfranc's gifts provided in the *Registrum Roffense*, the *feretrum* might have been placed on or, more probably, immediately behind an altar in an axial position well east of the choir, with a cross above it (perhaps supported on a transverse beam) and, as we shall see, this conjecture may be supported by the additional evidence we have for the location of the shrine of St Ithamar, who would join Paulinus later in the twelfth century. Perhaps Rochester occupies a transitional position, indicative of Lanfranc's change of heart, and the influence of Gundulf: the start of a trend which would be more pronounced after 1091.

In conclusion, the post-Conquest period was one of consolidation for English saints' cults. After the brief hesitancy caused by the arrival of the Normans with their critical attitudes towards indigenous cults, the veneration of saints was soon in full swing again, with exciting new developments in the way relics were made available to pilgrims, as we shall see in the following chapter.

[121] The word is frequently used in hagiographical texts to denote a shrine rather than a literal 'tomb', and does not indicate that the miracle took place in the Anglo-Saxon church.
[122] *Vita Gundulfi*, cap. 18; ed. Thomson, 41–2.
[123] At Worcester, too, the steps leading to the general area of the shrine of St Oswald featured in a miracle story: Crook, *Architectural Setting*, 240.

INTO THE TWELFTH CENTURY 6

From tomb to shrine

If the examples cited in the previous chapter suggest that for a short while Norman prelates were often somewhat reticent about promoting the native cults with which they were confronted, by the end of the eleventh century local saints seem once again to have regained their former prominence in the religious landscape. At the same time we see the first examples of large monuments of the sort usually denoted by the term 'shrine', essentially consisting of a substructure supporting the *feretrum* housing the saint's remains. The 1090s were a particularly busy period in this regard, especially in the important centres of Canterbury and Winchester.

ST AUGUSTINE'S, CANTERBURY

The cult of local saints received a huge boost during the early 1090s, when the abbey church of St Augustine at Canterbury was in the final stages of its Romanesque reconstruction. The works were chronicled by the hagiographer Goscelin of Saint-Bertin, who by then was resident in the monastery. The reconstruction had begun under Abbot Scolland, but in 1091 his successor, Abbot Wido, was confronted with a particular impediment in the form of the north *porticus*, a chapel dedicated to St Gregory. As we have seen,[1] this *porticus* housed the tombs of St Augustine and his immediate successors, and it needed to be taken down in order to complete the nave.[2] Some other important burials within the church (including the bodies of the scholarly African Abbot Hadrian (†709) and of King Æthelberht and Queen Bertha) had already been moved to facilitate earlier stages of the building works, but the demolition of St Gregory's chapel with its graves of saintly archbishops

[1] See above, pp. 51–3.
[2] Goscelin, *Translatio S. Augustini*, i.1, para. 2; *AASS*, *Maii VI*, 413C: *suæ dormitionis porticus obstabat.*

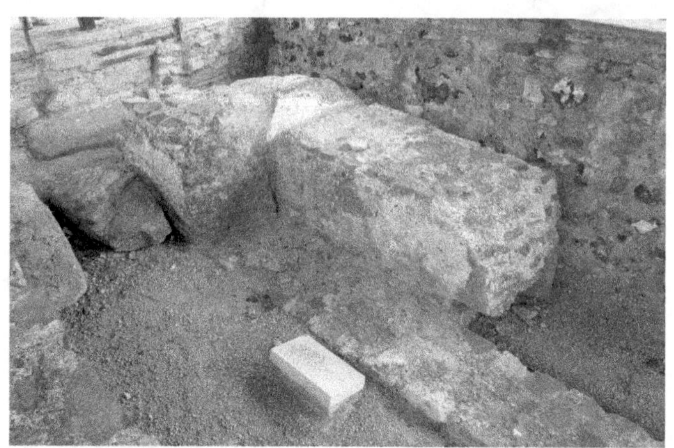

PLATE 6.1 CANTERBURY, ST AUGUSTINE'S ABBEY
The brick substructure of the tombs in the north Anglo-Saxon *porticus* still shows the damage caused when they were opened in 1091. They were re-excavated by William St John Hope in 1914. The tomb shown here was that of Archbishop Lawrence.

was evidently more sensitive, and was left until last.[3] Indeed, Abbot Scolland had clearly felt uneasy about demolishing the Anglo-Saxon church and interfering with its hallowed graves. During a visit to Rome in 1072 he had sought the advice of Pope Alexander II on the matter and had obtained papal permission to disturb the burials.[4] As things turned out, Scolland died before the tombs needed to be touched, leaving Abbot Wido with the challenge of relocating the early burials.

The opening of the tombs of the first six archbishops of Canterbury in September 1091 has often been likened to an archaeological investigation, such is the level of detail provided by Goscelin in his *Historia Translationis Sancti Augustini*. He shows an unusual interest in building materials and in what would now be called archaeological stratigraphy, even describing the layer of subsoil beneath the tombs. By September the *porticus* itself had already been demolished—apparently somewhat clumsily, for Goscelin describes the mass of brickwork and timbers which covered the tombs of St Augustine and his fellows, all of which survived the demolition to a degree which was felt to be miraculous, bearing in mind that they were fragile and formed of 'tile' (*fractiles et lateritiæ*).[5] The 'tile' (actually Roman brick) may still be seen in William St John Hope's excavation trench of 1914, left open and protected by a shed roof.[6] At the time of their burials, the wooden coffins of the archbishops had been lowered into quite shallow graves, then encased in Roman brick set in mortar, creating table-tomb-like structures, presumably plastered or marble

[3] As emphasised by Richard Sharpe, 'The setting of St Augustine's translation, 1091', in *Canterbury and the Norman Conquest: Churches, Saints and Scholars 1066–1109*, ed. R. Eales and R. Sharpe (London, 1995), 1–13, at 2–3.

[4] Goscelin, *Translatio S. Augustini*, ii.i, para. 6; *AASS*, *Maii VI*, 433E.

[5] ibid., ii.1, para. 3; *AASS*, *Maii VI*, 413D.

[6] W. St. John Hope, 'Recent discoveries at St. Austin's Abbey, Canterbury', *Arch. Cant.*, 31 (1915), 294–6; idem. 'Recent discoveries in the abbey church of St. Austin at Canterbury', ibid., 32 (1917), 1–26. Potts, 'Tombs', 97–112.

clad, rising above pavement level. Augustine's tomb (for which all archaeological evidence was destroyed in 1091) may have been more elaborate, and there was evidently an altar at the west end. It was additionally described as being decorated with 'sculptures and angelic images', including a marvellous *Maiestas* (the figure of Christ in Majesty). After the demolition of the *porticus* the monument remained out in the open for about nine weeks, covered only by a temporary structure (*tugurium*). Then on Monday 15 September Bishop Gundulf of Rochester, standing in for the archbishop of Canterbury during the interregnum that followed Lanfranc's death, struck the first, symbolic blow at the 'front' (east end) of the tomb. He thus put heart into the trembling workers, who were evidently reluctant to proceed for fear of divine retribution: Goscelin describes their furtive demeanour as 'like thieves' (*tamquam reos*). Encouraged by Gundulf, the head mason, Blitherus, continued the demolition work, dismantling the altar at the west end of the grave.[7] A white marble slab was revealed (again suggesting that Augustine's grave was more carefully constructed than his successors', whose wooden coffins were simply encased in brickwork), and finally the body of the saint was laid open to view, still clad in full pontificals. Goscelin comments that 'He looked as though he were still alive, only touch revealing his condition.' The body was carried to the altar of the Apostles in a temporary coffin. Meanwhile large crowds had arrived, attracted by a miraculous odour which had spread through the city of Canterbury and indeed the whole of Kent; they kept vigil at the empty tomb, where miracles of healing occurred. Finally, on Thursday 18 September the body was laid before the high altar pending the construction of a proper monument. Augustine's final resting place would be at the east end of the church, in the central apse, flanked by his successors, Mellitus and Lawrence.[8] This is how they are depicted in a famous drawing preserved in the Trinity Hall manuscript of the early fifteenth-century *Historia Monasterii Sancti Augustini Cantuariensis*, attributed to Thomas of Elmham.[9]

As Richard Sharpe has emphasised,[10] there was a large element of spectacle in the proceedings, which lasted full eight days. Furthermore, the fact that Augustine's translation was subsequently commemorated annually (on 13 September, octave of the translation, when all the saints translated in 1091 during that one week's frenzied activity were celebrated together) ensured that the event would not be forgotten.[11]

[7] Goscelin, *Translatio S. Augustini*, ii.1, para. 9; *AASS*, *Maii VI*, 414A ...*altareque capitis summi Augustini ad pavimentum exhaurit.*
[8] ibid., i.3, para. 24; *AASS*, *Maii VI*, 419A.
[9] Thomas of Elmham, *Historia Monasterii S. Augustini Cantuariensis*, ed. C. Hardwick, RS, 8 (1858).
[10] Sharpe, 'Setting', 1–13, 7–8.
[11] For the choice of the date see ibid., 3 and n. 11, citing the Martyrology of St Augustine's Abbey, BL, Cotton MS Vitellius C.XII, fos. 140v–141r, printed in F. Wormald, *English Benedictine Kalendars after AD 1100*, Henry Bradshaw Soc., 77 (London, 1939), i. 50: *Quia enim simul non poterant uno die transferri, placuit in octava ebdomade omnibus composita simul eos celebrari.*

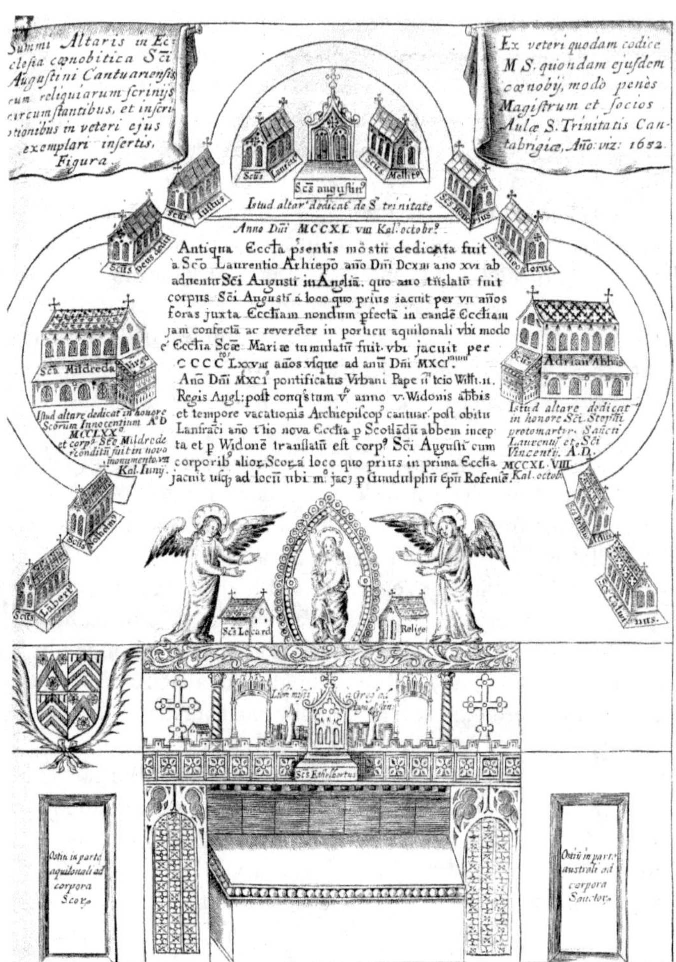

PLATE 6.2
THE SHRINES AT ST AUGUSTINE'S, CANTERBURY
from Thomas of Elmham's *History*, reproduced by William Dugdale in his *Monasticon*.

Goscelin tells us, however, that the precise site of Augustine's tomb was covered by the third pillar from the crossing: 'tiles' from his tomb were preserved, as contact relics, in a spacious cavity formed within the pillar itself.[12] Unfortunately these were not discovered during the twentieth-century excavations, the upper part of the pillar having been demolished in 1538–9, when Henry VIII was making the new lodgings for Queen Anne of Cleves.[13]

[12] Goscelin, *Translatio S. Augustini*, i.5, para. 29; *AASS, Maii VI*, 420F.
[13] Hope, 'Recent discoveries' (1917), 20–1; Potts, 'Tombs', 100.

CHRIST CHURCH CATHEDRAL, CANTERBURY

The new interest in local saints' cults was also evident at nearby Christ Church (Canterbury Cathedral), where in 1096 Archbishop Anselm (1093–1109) began to transform Lanfranc's modest eastern arm into an apse-and-ambulatory design, with a double transept reminiscent of St Hugh's new church at Cluny. The design of Anselm's remodelling is known from a lively description by the late twelfth-century Canterbury monk Gervase. His avowed aim in providing so complete an account of the church that had just perished in the fire of 1174 was to record for posterity the precise locations of the various shrines. Gervase's text is so detailed that it is possible to use it to draw a reasonably trustworthy plan of the church before the fire. Whereas the high altar was the focus of Lanfranc's cathedral, the tombs of saints appear to have been more evident in the cathedral of Anselm and his successors. The images of the saints were set on a reliquary beam slightly east of the high altar. Two important tomb-shrines were in the choir. Gervase mentions three altars: the high altar dedicated to Christ himself, and 'the altar of St Dunstan and the altar of St Ælfheah with their holy bodies'.[14] The most likely arrangement is that the two saints were enshrined to left and right in front of the high altar, as they certainly were after the repairs and rebuilding of the 1170s. Of the form of the shrines we have no evidence.

St Anselm himself was buried in the eastern arm, in the south-east chapel leading off the ambulatory, behind an altar dedicated to SS. Peter and Paul and beneath a tower; both altar and tower were henceforth known by his name.[15] It seems fitting that the man who famously persuaded Lanfranc of the sanctity of St Ælfheah, and whose Glorious Choir formed such a splendid setting for the veneration of Canterbury's principal saints, should himself be recognised as a saint—unlike Lanfranc. When that archbishop's lead coffin was opened in 1180 his corpse, dressed in full archiepiscopal vestments, at first seemed intact after a little over seventy-nine years, but the body soon proved to have fallen into dust: Lanfranc's bones had rotted away (*ossa eius multa putritudine consumpta*). The monks were more impressed by the preservation of Archbishop Theobald in the adjacent tomb. They had expected his body to have disintegrated, and its apparently incorrupt state led many people to acclaim him as a saint.[16]

The other archiepiscopal relics, which, as already noted, had been displayed in galleries and on beams in Lanfranc's cathedral, were also relocated in chapels which nevertheless continued to be dedicated to universal rather than local saints: in this respect Canterbury continued to maintain Roman practice. In other words the archbishops, most of whom were in any case not regarded as saints, were laid *ad sanctos*, close to the

[14] Gervase, *Tractatus de combustione*, 13.
[15] ibid., ed. Stubbs, 15: *Sanctus vero Anselmus, illuc translatus et retro altare positus, altari nomen dedit et turri.*
[16] ibid., 25–6.

greater saints of the Church Universal. Gervase continued his description by explaining that there were two *porticus* (actually stilted, apsidal chapels) projecting from the 'wall' of each of the eastern transepts. Off the north-east transept, the northernmost chapel contained the altar of St Martin, flanked by the tombs of Archbishops Wulfred (805–32) on the right and Lyfing (1013–20) on the left; the adjacent chapel contained the altar of St Stephen flanked by Archbishops Æthelheard (793–805) and 'the venerable Cuthbert' (741–58).[17] Likewise, leading off the south-east transept the north chapel contained the altar of St John the Evangelist, flanked by Archbishops Æthelgar (right) and Eluric (left); the southernmost chapel contained the altar of St Gregory, flanked by St Bregwine (right) and St Plegmund (left).[18] In pride of place behind the altar of the Holy Trinity (one of the cathedral's dedicatees) in the axial chapel were the relics of two bishops: St Oda (or Odo) of Canterbury (942–58) and—as it was claimed—St Wilfrid.[19] The relics of the latter saint had allegedly been translated from Ripon when that church was destroyed by the Danes *c.*947.[20] William of Malmesbury attributed the translation from Ripon of Wilfrid's body to Oda's friend King Eadred (946–58) rather than to Archbishop Oda himself. However, commenting on the rival claims of Ripon and Canterbury to possess Wilfrid's body, he added that the people of York claimed that the saint whose body Oda had brought south was Wilfrid II, bishop of York from 718.[21] Oda and 'Wilfrid' (whichever one it actually was) were flanked by two post-Conquest archbishops of Canterbury, Lanfranc (1070–89) to the south (transferred from the nave which he had built and where he was first buried) and Theobald (1138–61) to the north.[22]

Other relics took a little longer to reach their final destination. The bones of St Bregwine and other pre-Conquest archbishops of Canterbury, which had been placed high in the north transept in Lanfranc's church, were translated in around 1123. Eadmer's *Vita Bregwini* appears to have been composed in the context of this translation, which it records. He tells us that a German monk, Lambert, had shown a particular devotion to Bregwine and had even attempted to acquire the body; these designs came to nothing, and after Lambert's death in 1123 the saint's body, together with that of St Plegmund, was translated into the cathedral's south transept, and both were buried behind the altar of St Gregory.[23]

[17] ibid., 14. See the schematic plans in Southern, *Anselm and his Biographer*, 265.
[18] Gervase, *Tractatus de combustione*, 15.
[19] ibid., 16.
[20] Malmesbury, *GP*, i.15 and iii.109; ed. Winterbottom and Thomson, i. 28–9, and 372–3. See also above, pp. 89 and 123, for the rival claim of Ripon.
[21] Malmesbury, *GP*, iii.111; ed. Winterbottom and Thomson, i. 374–5. Idem., *Vita Dunstani*, i.15.6; ed. Winterbottom and Thomson, 204–5.
[22] Gervase, *Tractatus de combustione*, 16.
[23] Eadmer, *Vita Bregwini*, cap. 15; ed. Scholtz, 147: ... *reliquias ipsius patris a prȩfato loco cum reliquiis beati Plegemundi archiepiscopi in australem ȩcclesiȩ partem transtulit, et post altare beati Gregorii papȩ decentissime tumulauit.*

WINCHESTER CATHEDRAL

Neither at St Augustine's nor at Christ Church was it claimed that the mortal remains of the various saints were entire, incorrupt bodies (with the possible exception of Augustine, though Goscelin does not press the point). Likewise at Winchester, the bones of St Swithun were certainly separate, each bone having allegedly been individually washed in 971.[24] Furthermore, by the end of the eleventh century Swithun's skeleton had been somewhat depleted, for his head is said to have been taken to Canterbury by Ælfheah when the former bishop of Winchester was promoted to the archiepiscopal see in 1006; by the fourteenth century the canons of Évreux Cathedral in Normandy claimed to possess his head, and it may still be seen there.[25] Later other parts of the body would leave Winchester. In the early twelfth century the monk Reinald took one of Swithun's arms (probably just one bone) on his mission to Norway, and in 1128 work began on a cathedral at Stavanger dedicated to the Holy Trinity and St Swithun. By the mid-twelfth century his other arm was said to reside at Peterborough.[26] St Albans also claimed a relic of the saint.[27]

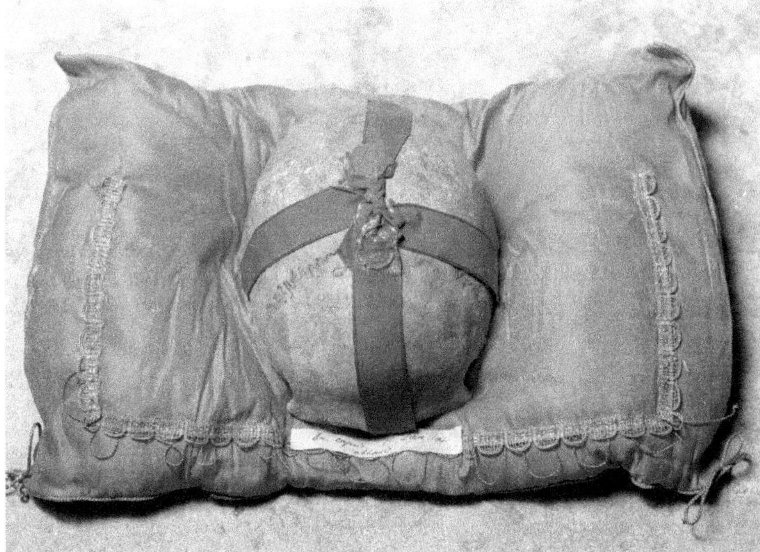

PLATE 6.3
ÉVREUX CATHEDRAL, (DEPT. EURE, FRANCE)
The top of a skull, venerated since the fourteenth century as the 'head' of St Swithun of Winchester.

[24] See above, p. 84.
[25] J. Crook, 'Appendix: The Rediscovery of St Swithun's Head at Évreux', in M. Lapidge, *The Cult of St Swithun*, *Winchester Studies* 4.ii (Oxford, 2003), 61–5 and pl. XVI.
[26] *The Chronicle of Hugh Candidus, a monk of Peterborough*, ed. W. T. Mellows (Peterborough, 1949), 54: *Brachium sancti Swithuni episcopi.*
[27] As appears in a relic list in BL, Cotton MS Claudius E.iv, fo. 379, printed in Sir William Dugdale, *Monasticon Anglicanum*, ed. J. Caley, Sir H. Ellis, and the Revd B. Bandinel, 8 vols. (London, 1846), ii. 234–6, at 235.

As noted in the previous chapter, Swithun's reliquary was carried into the new cathedral on his feast-day in July 1093. One other reference to the cult of Swithun has come down to us. In the 1120s Bishop William Giffard (1100–29) granted to his cathedral priory the Whitsuntide offerings (*Pentecostalia*) from the churches in his diocese. He specified that they were to be used 'towards the necessary functions of the church in supplying the altars as much in lights as in other ecclesiastical needs'. The transaction was later confirmed 'on 27 June', when the bishop dedicated an altar to St Swithun and placed the charter upon it. If the dedication took place, as was usual, on a Sunday, then 27 June 1126 seems the most probable date.[28]

The precise location within the cathedral of the new altar that Giffard dedicated is more problematical. The high altar was dedicated to SS. Peter and Paul, rather than the priory's new patron. There would, however, have been enough space in the apex of the main choir apse to accommodate a secondary altar. It would, though, be straining the evidence to postulate the existence within the apse of a shrine altar supporting the reliquary of St Swithun as early as the 1120s. An alternative possibility is that the altar of St Swithun dedicated by Gifford was in a gallery or tribune at the west end of the cathedral, but this must remain pure speculation.

ST ALBAN'S ABBEY

The abbey church at St Albans was rebuilt by Abbot Paul of Caen (1077–93). Work began in 1077, and within eleven years the eastern arm and transepts were complete and the monks were able to move into their new ritual choir. The nave, on the other hand, may not have been finished until Tuesday 28 January 1115, when, according to Matthew Paris, Abbot Richard had the new church dedicated by Geoffrey (Gaufridus), archbishop of Rouen (1111–28) and three other bishops. The event was witnessed by Henry I and his queen, and a large gathering of important people both laity and clergy.[29] Most of the guests stayed for the feasting and religious ceremonies, which continued from Christmas Day to Epiphany. As at Winchester, the Anglo-Saxon monastery church, traditionally said to have been founded by King Offa of Mercia in 793, must have remained in use until 1088; it cannot therefore have been beneath the eastern half of its replacement, though it might have been located under the present nave. Indeed, the Biddles' excavations have provided serious evidence that this was the case: there may have been more than one church, connected by cloister-like walkways, an arrangement similar to that at the abbey of Centula (Saint-Riquier).

As we have seen, St Albans was the location of the oldest indigenous saint's cult in England, but there is no evidence that Abbot Paul showed any

[28] *Winchester Cathedral Chartulary*, MS, Winchester Cathedral Archives, fo. 7r (item 32): M. J. Franklin (ed.), *English Episcopal Acta VIII, Winchester 1070–1204* (Oxford, 1993), 11 (item 19).
[29] *GA*; ed. Riley, i. 70–1.

particular devotion to his new country's proto-martyr. In fact documentary evidence for the translation of the saint's relics into the Norman church is entirely lacking. The earliest recorded translation occurred in 1129, but that was a rehousing of the relics. It is inconceivable that the bones of the abbey's patron saint did not accompany the monks when they entered the new building for the first time. Matthew Paris states that Abbot Richard d'Aubigny (1097–1119) presented his church with an opulent new reliquary (*theca*) to hold relics believed to be those of the apostles which St Germanus had placed within Alban's tomb in the early years of the fifth century.[30] The chronicler helpfully mentions that the *theca* was 'what we [i.e. the St Albans monks] call a *feretrum*'; the latter term seems to have been a local one to denote a portable reliquary.[31] Abbot Richard also gave a second *theca*, to house the relics of various other saints and martyrs; it was described as being 'partly gilded, and partly covered with ivory'.[32] It is reasonable to suppose that these reliquaries containing remains of unspecified saints were located near to the primary reliquary of St Alban. By placing near to the English proto-martyr those relics which St Germanus had supplied nearly seven centuries previously, Abbot Richard would in effect have been replicating an earlier, hallowed arrangement. His donation of reliquaries for secondary saints may perhaps be regarded as further evidence that Alban had already been translated into the Norman church by the end of the eleventh century.

Despite his interest in the local saint (and his participation in the translation of St Cuthbert in 1102), Abbot Richard does not appear to have contemplated replacing Alban's reliquary. This task was undertaken by Richard's successor, Geoffrey of Gorron (1119–46). According to Matthew Paris, work on the shrine started in 1124, the fifth year of Geoffrey's abbacy, but the project was temporarily abandoned after £60 had been expended. It was a time of famine—the crop seems to have failed, and wheat cost twenty shillings—and to provide money for the poor the benevolent Abbot Geoffrey ordered the shrine's silver decorative plates (as yet ungilded) to be stripped off, and the embedded jewels to be removed.[33] The following year work began again. Fortunately a craftsman with the requisite skills was available. One of the monks, a Dane called Anketill, had formerly been moneyer to the king of Denmark, and things seem to have proceeded quickly under his energetic supervision.[34]

Matthew, with his evident interest in technical matters, gives a brief account of how Dom Anketill made the decorative plates covering the

[30] ibid., 69–70.

[31] The word *feretrum* is again explained later in the *Gesta Abbatum* (ed. Riley, i. 189), when it is applied to the new reliquary chest of St Alban commissioned by Abbot Simon (1167–83): *thecam exterioram quam nos feretrum appellamus*. For Abbot Simon's *theca*, see below, pp. 204–5.

[32] *GA*; ed. Riley, i. 70: *Fecitque aliam thecam, ex una parte deauratam, ex alia vero, ebore coopertam, in qua posuit reliquias plurimorum Martyrum et aliorum Sanctorum.*

[33] ibid., 82–3, 96.

[34] Matthew provides a brief biography of Anketill in ibid., 84–5.

wooden substructure of the reliquary, which basically was simply a wooden box. 'He did it all in repoussé work, both raising it up and drawing it out; he beat out the images and consolidated them by placing filler in the hollows behind.'[35] Matthew's knowledge may partly have been gained from watching contemporary craftsmen, but he probably had access to the treatise 'On Various Arts' (*De Diversis Artibus*) by Theophilus—a priest and monk working in Germany in the first half of the twelfth century.[36] In one chapter Theophilus gives a careful description of the process for producing repoussé work (*opus ductile*) in gold or silver,[37] and Matthew's account reads like a précis of this part of the treatise. A plate of precious metal was beaten out to the required dimensions. If, as was most usual, a human figure was required, the head was first beaten out ('raised'), using a hammer and a rounded tool, proceeding in slow stages interrupted by reheating after each part of the design was raised. Then finer tools, such as the *scalprum* which slipped and cut the hand of a craftsman working on the shrine of St Ecgwine of Evesham in Abbot Mannig's day,[38] were used to create the smaller detail. Finally, before attaching the plates, the hollows behind the figures were filled up. Theophilus implies that this was necessary in order to form a flat surface which could be attached more securely to a wooden chassis; it would also have given more substance to the thin metal of the repoussé work. A filler (Matthew's '*cæmentum*') comprising two parts of crushed tile or sand, and one part of melted wax was prepared by melting the wax and stirring in the coarse components. Such was the raised work which another observer with an interest in technical matters, William of Malmesbury, referred to by its Greek term, *anaglyfum*, in an aside about historical sources.[39]

After this brief technical digression, with its verbal echoes of Theophilus, Matthew relapses into a vaguer description of how he thought Anketill might have continued: 'He drew together the elegance of the whole body of the reliquary: to put it most briefly, by working upwards towards the top. And thus he adorned all the better the substance of the whole thing.'[40]

Nevertheless, Anketill was not able to complete the reliquary. Matthew explains that there was not enough gold and silver available to finish the decorative cresting (*crista*) and implies that the lid of the reliquary was, for some years, something of a makeshift affair. The body of the reliquary, however, was adorned with several antique cameos which had formerly

[35] ibid., 83: *Fecit autem illud opere ductili, et elevato et educto, imagines impulit elevari, et concavas cæmento solidavit.*

[36] *Theophilus, The Various Arts: De Diversis Artibus*, ed. C. R. Dodwell, OMT (Oxford, 1986).

[37] ibid., cap. 74; ed. Dodwell, 131–5.

[38] See above, pp. 105–6.

[39] Malmesbury, *GP*, v.212; ed. Winterbottom and Thomson, i. 538–9: *Nec uero hæc nostra ita fide oculata carent, cum ea scrinii antiqui argento uiderimus impressa, eo genere artifitii quod anagliphum uocant.*

[40] *GA*; ed. Riley, i. 83: … *elegantiam totius corporis feretralis, in brevius culmen ascendendo, coartavit. Et sic totius rei substantiam melius venustavit.*

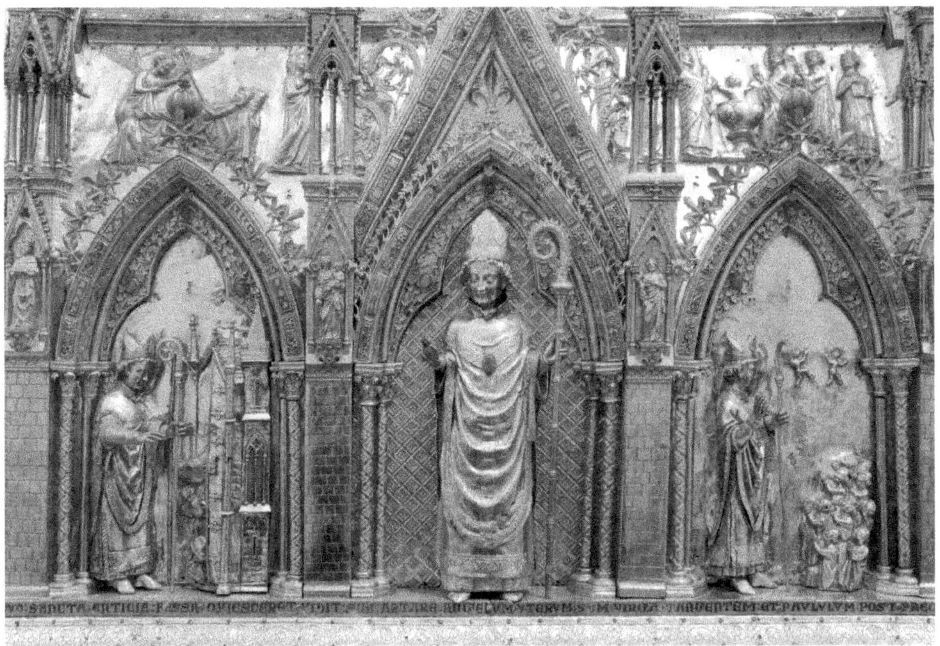

PLATE 6.4 ÉVREUX (DEPT. EURE, FRANCE), ÉGLISE SAINT-TAURIN The constructional technique of the gilt reliefs of this mid-thirteenth-century reliquary is similar to that described at St Albans in around 1125. Mounted on an oak chassis, the bas-reliefs are in silver-gilt, and the statues in gilded copper.

formed part of the treasures of the 'old church', and which Matthew implied had been discovered by a certain 'Abbot Eadmer' (about whom we know nothing apart from Matthew's comment) during his excavation of the Roman town of Verulamium.[41] They were certainly in the Anglo-Saxon abbey church in the time of the next abbot, whom Matthew names as 'Leofric' (another shadowy figure, probably in office at the end of the tenth century), for Matthew mentions that the cameos escaped being sold at that time to provide alms for the poor and were reserved for an earlier refurbishment of the shrine. One of the cameos, a massive piece of intaglio work (one could scarcely hold it in one hand, Matthew says), which Æthelred II had given to the monastery, was not used. It served as a talisman for women during childbirth and, curiously, it seems to have been feared that the cameo might lose this power if it were inserted in the shrine. It featured a woman dressed in ragged garments (*imago pannosa*) holding in one hand a spear with a serpent crawling up it and a child carrying a shield in the other. At the feet of the *imago* was an eagle spreading its wings. The

[41] ibid., i. 29.

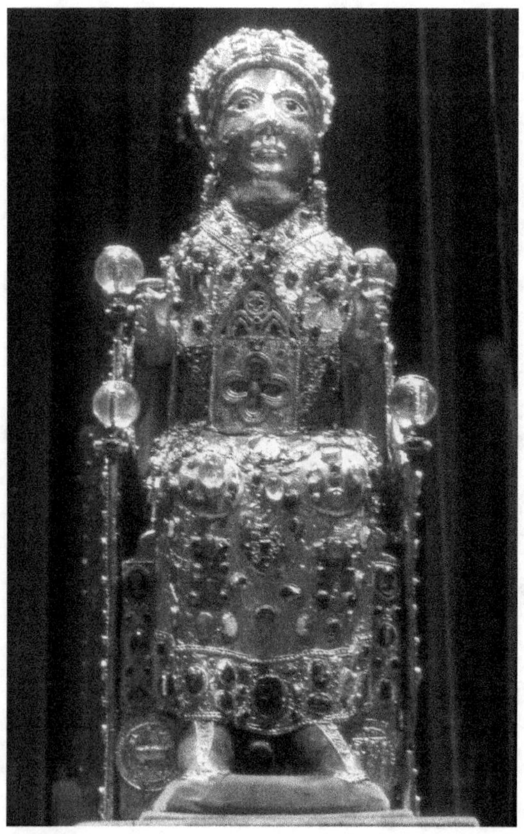

PLATE 6.5 CONQUES CATHEDRAL (DEPT. AVEYRON, FRANCE)
The 'Majesté' of St Faith, decorated with antique cameos.

use of antique cameos is of particular interest. One of the best surviving parallels is the adornment of the famous gilded statue or 'Majesté' of St Faith (Sainte-Foy) at Conques, a wonderful assemblage of a late antique head for which a new body was created, perhaps in the late ninth century, subsequently remodelled *c.*1000 when filigrane bands containing antique, Byzantine, and Carolingian intaglios were added.[42]

The shrine was sufficiently complete for Alban's relics to be placed within it on 2 August 1129. The event was attended by Bishop Alexander of Lincoln, in whose diocese St Alban's Abbey was located (though it claimed exemption from episcopal jurisdiction), and church leaders from Evesham, Thorney, Rouen, and Noyon. These witnesses were presumably invited in order to testify to the authenticity of the relics, given the unfavourable traditions that had arisen about St Alban's remains being in Denmark, or at Ely. The central event was the opening of the old shrine, the *theca antiquissima*, and the ceremonial displaying of each part of the body in turn, to prove they had all the bits: *dinumerata sunt omnia ossa Martyris, et singillatim ostensa*. The only missing item was the martyr's left shoulder-blade; Matthew explained in one of his lengthy digressions that it had been taken to Spain. The head of the saint was found to be bearing a convenient label (*scedula*) attached by a silk thread, with the words *Sanctus Albanus*. There was also a gold band (*circulus*) round the head, which the monks thought King Offa had provided, inscribed 'This is the head of St Alban the first martyr of the English' (*Hoc est caput Sancti Albani, Anglorum protomartyris*). Needless to say, such labels tended conveniently to make their appearance at translations. The chronicler adds that the gold band was later carelessly destroyed to furnish further precious metal for the shrine.

The fortunes of the yet incomplete *theca* are carefully recorded in the *Gesta Abbatum*. Under Abbot Ralph Gubion (1146–51) the gilded plates

[42] J. Taralon, 'La Majesté d'or de Sainte-Foy au trésor de Conques', *Revue de l'Art*, 40–1 (1978), 9–22, at 16–18.

were again removed to purchase a manor, but Ralph subsequently provided funds which enabled his successor, Robert of Gorron (1151–66, nephew of Abbot Geoffrey), to embellish the reliquary once again.[43] As we shall see in the following chapter, this reliquary would form part of an ensemble which has every right to be termed the first true 'shrine' of St Alban.

THREE WHOLE-BODY CULTS

We should now consider the post-Conquest development of three Saxon whole-body cults which were closely linked to the dedication of major Norman churches that were rebuilt during the period under discussion here. The late twelfth-century monk Reginald of Durham, probably writing *c.*1150–65,[44] related a miracle, said to have occurred more than seventy years previously, in which a nobleman from southern England, suddenly afflicted by leprosy, conducted an empirical experiment to determine which of England's three major whole-body cults was likely to be the most powerful in curing him; he dedicated three tapers measured to the length of his own body to Cuthbert of Durham, Edmund of Bury, and Æthelthryth of Ely, and watched to see which one burnt down soonest.[45] Needless to say, Cuthbert's candle won the contest, and our nobleman hastened northwards to receive a cure. For Reginald, at least, the three cults were the most powerful in England, and they received a tremendous boost at the turn of the eleventh/twelfth centuries when their allegedly incorrupt corpses were translated. At around the same period a completely new whole-body cult would also emerge, that of Edward the Confessor, discussed later in this chapter.

BURY ST EDMUNDS (1095)

The earliest of these translations was that of St Edmund, murdered king of the East Angles, the development of whose cult we examined in Chapter 4.[46] The cult at *Beadricesworth* might be expected to have had political implications, centred as it was around an Anglo-Saxon royal saint who had been murdered by Norsemen, and it was perhaps inevitable that the Normans should be sceptical. As for Abbot Baldwin, though of French origin (he was born at Chartres and educated at Saint-Denis), he was one of the group of foreign churchmen who had been brought to England by Edward the Confessor.[47] Furthermore, tensions had developed between the abbey

[43] *GA*; ed. Riley, i. 109.
[44] For the date of the first 111 chapters of Reginald's *Libellus*, see V. Tudor, 'The cult of St Cuthbert in the twelfth century: the evidence of Reginald of Durham', in Bonner, *St Cuthbert*, 447–67, at 449–50. See also V. Tudor, 'Reginald of Durham and St Godric of Finchale: A Study of a Twelfth-century Hagiographer and his Major Subject', unpubl. Ph.D. thesis, University of Reading, 1979.
[45] Reginald, *Libellus*, cap. 19; ed. Raine, 37–41.
[46] pp. 90–1.
[47] See above, p. 109.

and the bishops of the East Anglian diocese, then at Norwich. The monastery was threatened with the seizure of its estates, and Archdeacon Hermann, a contemporary writer commissioned by the abbot to write the *Miracula* of the saint, tells us that in 1095, when the presbytery of the new church was complete and Abbot Baldwin had requested the king's permission to translate Edmund's body and consecrate the church, some of William Rufus's 'courtiers' (*palatini*) expressed doubts about whether the martyr's body was really incorrupt or even there at all; they suggested that money intended for the shrine would be better spent on maintaining the royal troops.[48] Nevertheless, the king grudgingly agreed to a translation, whilst forbidding the consecration of the new church. Hermann's propaganda had evidently been successful.

Even though the body does not appear to have been examined at this time, most doubts about the *præsentia* of the saint were dispelled during the excitement of the translation. On 29 April 1095 a visitation comprising Bishop Walkelin of Winchester and Ranulf Flambard, the king's chaplain and later bishop of Durham (1099–1128), came to Bury to preside over the ceremony. Hermann describes the translation in some detail in the final chapters of his narrative; no doubt the events were fresh in his memory.[49] The town was seething with a huge crowd of lay folk, both men and women, who had flocked to the vill to watch. At nine in the morning Bishop Walkelin entered the church, first sprinkling the area of operations with holy water. Then the old wooden coffer (*loculus*, *sarcina*) containing the incorrupt body was 'uncovered', though not, it would seem, opened; it was taken up, and carried in glorious procession into the new church, together with the relics of SS. Botolf and Jurmin. So eager was the saint to be translated that the coffer became miraculously light, and the six monastic porters later said that it had never been an easier burden than when they carried the holy body out of the south door of the old church; previously 'forty men and more' had been required to carry him in there! This is of course a well-known hagiological *topos*. In Chapter 4 we saw how St Alchmund of Hexham managed to make his *feretrum* immobile in order to avoid losing a finger;[50] likewise at Evesham St Odulf was able to avoid being taken to Winchcombe against his will by miraculously increasing the weight of the *feretrum*.[51] Hermann adds that at Bury, in the Saxon church St Edmund had been accustomed to make himself much heavier whenever his reliquary was carried about for some reason.[52]

Some further detail was later added by Abbot Samson (1182–1211) in his account of the events surrounding the translation of 1095, notably the

[48] *Hermanni Archidiaconi Liber de Miraculis S. Eadmundi*, cap. 44; *Memorials of Bury*, i. 26–92, at 86.
[49] ibid., caps. 45–50; pp. 86–91.
[50] See above, p. 101.
[51] *Translatio et miracula S. Odulfi*; *Evesham Chronicle*, 313–20.
[52] Hermann, *Liber de Miraculis*, cap. 47; *Memorials of Bury*, i. 89.

accompanying miracles.[53] During the translation the reliquary had been placed on a temporary base, described as a 'little hill of rocks' (*saxorum colliculum*), and the eye complaint of a man from London was miraculously cured when he placed his forehead and eyes against the stones.[54] Once the reliquary had reached the 'altar of the saint', and Bishop Walkelin had preached an open-air sermon, the opportunity was taken of invoking the saint's help against the prevalent drought. Needless to say, this achieved the desired result.

With his emphasis on the high emotion of the translation, Hermann confers on the event something of the quality of an *adventus*: a ceremonial arrival of the saint, coming like a hero to his halls appointed, to what it was envisaged would be his final resting place.[55] There is little reason to doubt that the shrine was placed in the location it occupied throughout its later history, namely in the apse of the abbey church. An addition to a copy of John of Worcester's Chronicle made at Bury in the twelfth century noted, admittedly long after the event, how St Edmund's body was carried and 'suitably placed' behind the high altar.[56]

The presbytery was of apse-and-ambulatory design, and the east end of the choir was enclosed by eight closely spaced cylindrical piers.[57] The high altar lay on the chord of the apse. One may gain a fairly close idea of what this part of the abbey church looked like in the later twelfth century from the so-called Chronicle of Jocelin of Brakelond, which is mainly an account of the acts of Abbot Samson. He describes in particular a fire which caused damage in June 1198.[58] Between the shrine and the high altar (there was no separate shrine altar) was a wooden platform (*ligneus tabulatus*), with a space beneath it in which the sacrists stored 'flax, thread, wax and divers utensils'. It was this wooden structure and its inflammable contents that were set alight by a falling candle composed of recycled wax tapers which had been roughly cobbled together: Jocelin blamed the shrine-keepers for not keeping a more vigilant eye on things. The platform had what Jocelin calls 'iron walls' (*parietes ferrei*) and a door; at the time of the fire it was covered by a cloth. The 'iron walls' were presumably lateral grilles incorporating a

[53] *Samsonis Abbatis Opus de Miraculis S. Ædmundi* ii.1; *Memorials of Bury*, i. 107–208, at 155–60.
[54] The *colliculum* is depicted in an illustration of the entombment of St Edmund in Pierpont Morgan MS 736, p. 33; publ. in R. M. Thomson, *Manuscripts from St Albans Abbey 1066–1235* (Woodbridge, for University of Tasmania, 1982), ii. pl. 78.
[55] For the concept, see above, pp. 38–9.
[56] *John of Worcester*, Appendix B, 'The Bury St Edmunds Interpolations', iii. 309–26, at 316: *retro magnum altare* [*erasure*] *decenter reconditur* (Oxford, Bodleian Library, MS Bodley 297).
[57] J. Crook, 'The Architectural Setting of the Cult of St Edmund at Bury, 1095–1539', in *Bury St Edmunds: Medieval Art, Architecture and Economy*, ed. A. Gransden, *BAA Trans.*, vol. 20 for 1994 (Leeds, 1998), 34–44, at 37–9.
[58] *The Chronicle of Jocelin of Brakelond concerning the acts of Samson, Abbot of the Monastery of St. Edmund*, ed. H. E. Butler (London, 1949), 106–16.

door providing access to the shrine-keepers' store. After the fire, Abbot Samson had the space between the high altar and the *feretrum* blocked with stones and mortar as a fire precaution.[59] As at Durham, it was possible for people to crawl beneath the wooden *loculus*. Abbot Samson recalled that in around 1174, at a time of dispute between the monastery and Bishop Ridel of Ely, he had been obliged to hide beneath the monument for a time from his predecessor, Abbot Hugh (1157–80).[60]

The wooden *feretrum* evidently suffered as a result of the fire. It had been covered in silver plates, presumably repoussé work, whilst on the 'front' (i.e. the west end, facing the altar) was a golden *maiestas*, presumably a figure of Christ in Glory, though as we have seen the term could be used more widely to denote other cult statues, such as the Majesté de Sainte-Foy at Conques. Jocelin tells us that the wooden core was burnt 'to the thickness of my finger', so that the silver plates simply dangled loosely, no longer supported by their nails.[61] The golden Majesty, on the other hand, survived unscathed, as did 'certain stones'.

The repair of the shrine involved the dismantling and refixing of its heavy component panels, and this provided an opportunity for Abbot Samson to examine the saint's body.[62] The lid of the *feretrum* was fastened with sixteen long iron nails, which were removed with some difficulty. Then the body was revealed, which, as Jocelin recalled, fitted so tightly within the wooden container, 'both lengthwise and across, that a needle could scarce be placed between the Saint's head or feet and the wood'.[63] The coffin can therefore hardly have been more than six feet long. There was a hole in the lid to provide limited contact with the body for the select few, and iron rings at the end 'after the fashion of a Norse chest'. It sat in a kind of wooden trough (*ligneus alueolus*) to protect it from the stone of the shrine-base. The repairs to the *feretrum* would today be regarded as a commendable conservation exercise, even the 'self-same sixteen nails' being used to fix the lid down again after the examination, 'in the same manner as it had been before'.

DURHAM—ST CUTHBERT (1104)

Eleven years after Edmund's translation, the remains of St Cuthbert were enshrined at Durham, and the well-recorded event is central to the renewed interest in local saints at the dawn of the twelfth century. As we saw in

[59] ibid., 116: *spacium illud quod erat inter feretrum et altare, solidari fecit lapide et cemento, ne aliquod ignis periculum fieri possit …*
[60] ibid., 49.
[61] ibid., 107.
[62] ibid., 112–16.
[63] Interestingly, an early twelfth-century illustration of the entombment of St Edmund, New York, Pierpont Morgan Library, MS 736, fo. 18, shows the body being placed in a strigilated sarcophagus: C. M. Kauffmann, *Romanesque Manuscripts, 1066–1190: A Survey of Manuscripts Illuminated in the British Isles*, III, ed. J. J. G. Alexander (London 1975), 72–4, No. 33.

Chapter 3, his allegedly incorrupt body had reached Durham in 995, and after a few temporary arrangements during building works the remains were enshrined in the Anglo-Saxon cathedral by Bishop Ealdhun. There they remained until the early twelfth century. The church suffered during the 'harrying of the north' in 1069, and the contemporary writer Symeon of Durham tells us that on the approach of William's forces Cuthbert's body was temporarily taken back to Lindisfarne in 1069–70.[64] The community returned to find their church despoiled, though the king was angry at this and punished the perpetrators.[65] Sometime later, on his way back from Scotland in 1072, William ordered an examination of Cuthbert's tomb to make sure the body was still there, but before the coffin had even been opened he was punished for his presumption, falling victim to what now might be called a panic attack.[66] In a slightly different version of events, written in the late twelfth century, Roger of Howden claimed that as a result of his experiences the king confirmed all the existing privileges of the church of Durham.[67] A late thirteenth-century entry in the 'Durham Register' claimed that William had also granted the manors of Alverton and Howden 'to blessed Cuthbert and the bishops of Durham', including the symbolic gift of a talent of gold, together with gold bracelets (*armillas*), which were placed on the altar of St Cuthbert; Symeon's silence on this matter casts doubt on these later accounts.[68]

The reconstruction of the cathedral did not begin until the 1090s, under William of Saint-Calais, who in 1083 had introduced a community of Benedictine monks from Jarrow and Wearmouth to Durham, thus fulfilling, as it was claimed, the intention of his predecessor, Walcher. Amongst the group of imported monks was probably Symeon, an eye-witness during the building campaign. Work began on Thursday 11 August 1093,[69] and by 1104 the new cathedral was sufficiently complete for the relics to be translated. The preliminaries to the translation, and the translation itself, are fully recorded in the anonymous *Capitula de Miraculis et Translationibus Sancti Cuthberti*.[70] The monks at that time were in some doubt as to whether the body of the saint really was still incorrupt, and were perhaps understandably apprehensive about what might be revealed during the translation, a very public affair. To set their minds at rest a preliminary, in-house investigation was arranged, led by Prior Turgot. The witnesses included Symeon, who may indeed have been the author of the relevant chapter of *De Miraculis*.[71] If, as noted above, Goscelin's account of the exhumation of the Canterbury

[64] Symeon, *Libellus*, iii.15; ed. Rollason, 182–9.
[65] ibid., iii.15; pp. 188–9.
[66] ibid., iii.19; pp. 196–7.
[67] Roger de Hoveden, *Chronicle*, ed. W. Stubbs, 4 vols., RS, 51 (1868–71), i. 126–7.
[68] *Registrum Palatinum Dunelmense*, ed. J. D. Hardy, 4 vols., RS, 62 (1873–8), iii. 51.
[69] Symeon, *Libellus*, iv.8; ed. Rollason, 244–5.
[70] BL, MS Harley 1924. *Sym. Op.*, i. 229–61, at 247–61.
[71] The names of the participants were provided by Reginald in his *Libellus*, cap. 40; ed. Raine, 84–6, at 84.

archbishops reads like an archaeological report, the astonishingly detailed descriptions of Cuthbert's translation left to us by the Durham monks Symeon and Reginald resemble a condition survey from a conservator.

A tradition current in the sixteenth century held that a chapel was constructed in the cloister as a temporary resting place for Cuthbert's body while the new cathedral was under construction.[72] However, the insistence of Symeon, a contemporary witness, that the examination took place 'in the middle of the choir', before the body was translated into the new church, suggests that the theatre of events was in fact the Anglo-Saxon cathedral. Yet Reginald also mentions the chapel in the cloister as the place from which the body had been removed on the day of the translation;[73] it is therefore just possible that the later cloister chapel in fact marked the site of the east end of the Anglo-Saxon church. One must, however, remember that Reginald was writing at least fifty years after the destruction of the old church—so there is plenty of time for an entirely spurious tradition to have developed.

It would be expected that at least the east arm of what by now was a monastic cathedral church would be retained until its replacement was ready for occupation. True, Symeon asserts elsewhere that Bishop William of Saint-Calais had ordered the destruction of the old cathedral in 1092, but this presumably referred only to the decision to replace it, rather than to its demolition in that year.[74] After spending a suitable period of prayer and fasting, the monks—not without difficulty—opened the tomb, to disclose an outer coffin (*arca*), encased in leather and studded with iron nails.[75] Within it was revealed a wooden chest (*loculum de ligno*), wrapped in three layers of coarse linen cloth, which they identified as the *levis theca* of Cuthbert's first translation, as described by Bede. At this point the monks' courage failed them, but they were encouraged to continue by one of their number, Leofwine. Accordingly they moved the coffin from behind the altar of the Anglo-Saxon church into the centre of the choir (presumably to provide a clearer working space) and, after attempting in vain merely to peer through some crack in the coffin, they lifted the lid and revealed the incorrupt body of the saint. The coffin was packed with other relics, including—as they believed—the head of St Oswald and, in a linen bag (*in lineo sacello*), the bones of the Venerable Bede. Symeon commented that there was only room for such a collection because Cuthbert's body was resting on its right side rather than supine. The brethren resolved to store the other relics elsewhere and to replace Cuthbert on his back. In order to achieve this, two monks, one at his head and one at his feet, lifted out the corpse. They were astonished at its flexibility; a third monk was needed to support the body at the waist. For Reginald of Durham it was above all this flexibility which demonstrated

[72] *The Rites of Durham*, cap. 33, ed. J. T. Fowler, Surtees Soc., 107 for 1902 (Durham, 1903), 68–9.

[73] Reginald, *Libellus*, cap. 48; ed. Raine, 98–101, at 100: *circa tumbam, qui infra claustrum est ...*

[74] Symeon, *Libellus*, iv.8; ed. Rollason, 244–5.

[75] Hermann, *Liber de Miraculis*, 7.2; *Memorials of Bury*, i. 249.

Cuthbert's superiority over England's other whole-body cults.[76] The other relics were removed and the body was replaced.

Things might have stopped there, but Bishop Flambard was sceptical about the incorruptibility of the body, and the following night the body was yet again removed from its coffin and placed on carpets in the middle of the choir. This time various cloths in which the body was wrapped were removed, and the state of the body was again ascertained.

This was still not the end of the matter. Even while people were assembling for the translation, on 29 August 1104, one of the visiting abbots levelled a charge of deception against the monks, and a furious argument ensued. Finally Abbot Ralph of Sées, a future archbishop of Canterbury, agreed to act as mediator, and the body was examined for a third time. First the abbot moved the head of the corpse around and tugged at its ear, then he raised it into a seated position and felt the body all over, finding that its 'nerves and bones were solid, and covered in soft flesh'. Finally he pronounced to the assembled company that 'this body lies here, lifeless indeed, but as sound and entire as on that day on which the blessed soul left it on its way to heaven'.[77]

Reginald of Durham adds further details, which it is reasonable to suppose he obtained from those who had been present at the translation half a century earlier. These include a meticulous description of the various precious textiles in which the body had been enveloped,[78] and of the coffin itself.[79] Parts of the silks that had been in contact with the other relics had been affected by their decay; likewise the bottom board of the coffin, where it had been in contact with those relics, was blackened, stained, and somewhat damp. Accordingly, the brethren prepared a new false floor to serve as a damp course, a board (*tabula*) raised by means of blocks at each corner slightly clear of the original bottom of the coffin: Reginald specifies that the new floor was three inches higher than the old. The body of the saint was placed on this false floor, so that he now lay about halfway down in the coffin.[80]

After all these preliminaries the actual translation took place, described in the *Liber de Miraculis*.[81] The body was carried out of the Anglo-Saxon church, at which sight the onlookers burst into tears of joy and swarmed around the relics. Cuthbert was carried round the new cathedral, and the monks paused for a station at the east end, where Bishop Ranulf Flambard preached a sermon which the narrator judged over-long. Meanwhile it started to rain (miraculously nothing was harmed by the water), and the

[76] Reginald, *Libellus*, cap. 19; ed. Raine, 37–44 at 39, in a passage which Reginald himself calls a 'long digression'.

[77] Hermann, *Liber de Miraculis* 7.11; *Memorials of Bury*, i. 259. "*Ecce ... fratres, hoc corpus iacet hic quidem exanime, sed ita sanum et integrum, sicut ea die qua, cælestia petens, id sancta reliquerat anima.*"

[78] Reginald, *Libellus*, cap. 42; ed. Raine, 87–9.

[79] ibid., cap. 43; pp. 89–90.

[80] ibid., cap. 40; pp. 84–6.

brethren hurried to carry the coffin into the new church, where it was laid 'in the place that had been prepared for it' (*ubi decenter paratum fuerat*).

Reginald does not specify where the shrine was located, calling the area simply the 'inner church' (*basilica interior*);[82] it was closed off by doors (*valvas*) which were usually guarded.[83] There is no reason to suppose that it was ever other than in the apex of the Romanesque apse, the location of the relics throughout the high middle ages. The apse, with its shrine, was the scene of an attempted theft by a man who concealed himself in the shadows of the church in order to gain access to the shrine area when all was quiet. No-one saw him entering the 'inner church', where he attempted to steal an ivory casket that was located high on a screen (*tabula*) with other saintly relics; in order to reach it he climbed on the bishop's throne. He then remained immobile in the darkness until one of the monks, *Reginaldus nomine*, presumably the author himself, stumbled over him and led him to the altar of St Oswald where he was questioned by the sacrist.[84] Needless to say, the screen with its secondary relics might have been a later twelfth-century insertion rather than a feature of the church dedicated in 1104.

During the translation ceremony in 1104 a miracle occurred which provides precious information about the design of the new shrine. Amongst the participants was Abbot Richard of St Albans (1097–1119), who was suffering from palsy of the hand. For a long time he had been unable to celebrate mass, and had sought Cuthbert's aid shortly before the translation ceremony. The narrator observes that 'the reliquary-coffin of the incorrupt body was to be lifted up higher behind the altar on a stone, diligently wrought by the hand of craftsmen for the purpose of sustaining such a burden, which nine columns raised higher above the ground, as befitted its size'. Prior Turgot climbed on to the slab in order to set the coffin in place, and requested the abbot's assistance: 'My Lord Abbot, come up higher (*ascende citius*) and help me.' Abbot Richard climbed up and, forgetful of his infirmity, helped position the coffin; once this was achieved he remembered his paralysed hand but found that it was now cured, and that he could move his fingers with ease.[85]

Further details may be gleaned from miracle accounts recorded later in the twelfth century by Reginald. Pilgrims could evidently crawl beneath the slab in order to receive the holy radiation,[86] and one demoniac was pursued there by four demons until they were driven away by the saint.[87] A soldier

[81] Hermann, *Liber de Miraculis*, 12; *Memorials of Bury*, i. 259–60.

[82] Reginald, *Libellus*, cap. 79; ed. Raine, 164. A manacled man, seeking release from his chains, banged on the doors of the 'inner church' and was let in by the sacrist: *per vallas* [*sic*, for *valvas*, doors] *interioris basilicæ, strepitum faciens, ab secretario patefactum impetravit ingressum*.

[83] ibid., cap. 89; pp. 165–8, at 166.

[84] ibid., cap. 80; pp. 165–8.

[85] *Capitula de Miraculis et Translationibus s. Cuthberti*, cap. 20; ed. Arnold, ii. 359–60.

[86] Reginald, *Libellus*, cap. 60; ed. Raine, 119–21, at 119.

[87] ibid., cap. 114; pp. 255–9, at 259.

with toothache was able to place his cheek against the end of the slab, which must therefore have been about three feet above the top step.[88] Yet more information is provided in another miracle story, which Reginald claims he actually witnessed, and which occurs in two versions in the *Libellus*.[89] In both versions an unsupervised pilgrim placed a thick taper on the edge of the slab supporting the coffin, which evidently formed a kind of shelf: Reginald states that 'the stone on which the sarcophagus rested was no wider than a palm'.[90] The taper was presumably a 'trindle': a taper made to the length of the pilgrim, and folded many times. The fact that such tapers were placed so dangerously close to the coffin suggests a design fault, particularly as the coffin was potentially inflammable. Apart from being of wood, the coffin appears normally to have been enveloped in an outer covering of silk and an inner one of linen, which survived the flames, as did decorations of silver, gold, and gems. Reginald describes how 'the flames almost reached the very top of the tomb, and there was nothing else between so many fiery torches except the outer silk cloth, and another inner one of linen, which used to preserve the [wood]work of the sepulchre. In a wonderful way, the raging flame was unable to devour those cloths, which it was touching, and it did not even scorch the outer fibres of the cloths, nor alter the beauty of their colouring in any way from their pristine state.'[91]

There is therefore quite ample documentary evidence for the form of Cuthbert's monument, which is recognisably a shrine, rather than simply a venerated tomb or a raised reliquary. It may be regarded as the predecessor of the high shrines of the later middle ages. The 'pillared' type of shrine appears to have preceded the high shrine-bases with niches of the fourteenth century, and other twelfth-century examples are known, notably the shrine-base constructed at St Albans by Abbot Simon (1167–83) to support the body of St Alban. Parts of the decorated top slab of that monument have actually survived.[92]

Despite later alterations to the eastern arm of Durham Cathedral, it is possible to determine the appearance of the architectural setting of the shrine. Reginald's miracle stories provide information about the steps on which the coffin was raised: candle-wax from the trindle flowed down those steps and right down to the pavement.[93] Although the pavement within the apse was extended when the rectangular feretory platform was built, its

[88] ibid., cap. 130; pp. 278.
[89] ibid., caps. 45 and 66; pp. 91–2 and 134.
[90] ibid. cap., 45; p. 92.
[91] ibid., cap. 66; p. 134: *Flamma interim pene ad sepulcri fastigia suprema contigit, nichilque aliud inter tot flammarum faces interfuit nisi pannus sericus exterior, aliusque lineus interior, quorum operimento sepulcrum contegi consuevit. Mirum in modum, ardoris flamma pannos ipsos, quibus inhæsit, devorare non potuit, sed nec etiam exteriores filorum villos exustulavit, seu coloris pulcritudinem a prisca sui novitate in aliquo demutavit.*
[92] Biddle, 'Remembering St Alban', 124–61, at 146–51.
[93] ibid., cap. 45; p. 92: *Videres igitur ceras liquentes … perfusis undique gradibus, ad inferiora pavimenti latius descendisse.*

outline is still discernible in the pavement; and beneath the pavement the lowest courses of the masonry of the apse survive.[94] As Christopher Norton has pointed out, the pavement still lacks sophistication.[95] Reginald tells us, in the context of a miracle story, that at a much later date Prior Roger (1138–40) conceived a project, evidently never realised, for embellishing the cathedral with a marble pavement, and asked anyone travelling abroad to bring back suitable pieces of marble.[96] The shrine area is not specifically mentioned, but the work was to be done 'on account of the honour of St Cuthbert', and it is reasonable to suppose that the embellishment of the feretory would have been the prior's main concern; furthermore, the story mentions a piece of marble which was destined 'for St Cuthbert' and which was retained by the monks as a kind of relic. There is no surviving archaeological evidence for the steps supporting the first shrine, which presumably rested on the pavement, partially concealing it.

Second at Durham only to the remains of St Cuthbert were those of other saints, notably those of the Venerable Bede. As noted in Chapter 4, these relics had been brought from Hexham by Alfred Westou in the early eleventh century; they were removed from the Bede's coffin in 1104. The relics remained separately enshrined on the feretory platform for nearly two hundred and seventy years until they were moved to the Galilee chapel in 1370.[97] How the relics were enshrined in the early twelfth century is uncertain. A contemporary writer, Walfrith of Coldingham (a dependent priory of Durham), records that in the latter half of the century Bishop Hugh de Puiset (1153–95) provided a new shrine of gold and silver, in which to carry the bones of the Venerable Bede; it was made with such a degree of craftsmanship that it was doubtful whether either the quality of the workmanship or decoration could be bettered.[98] According to a continuator of Symeon's *Libellus de Exordio*, writing perhaps at the beginning of the thirteenth century, Bede's shrine also enclosed the relics of 'many other saints'.[99]

[94] J. Crook, 'The Architectural Setting of the Cult of St Cuthbert in Durham Cathedral (1093–1200)', in *Anglo-Norman Durham*, ed. D. Rollason, M. Harvey, and M. Prestwich (Woodbridge, 1994), 235–50, at 236–47.

[95] C. Norton, 'The Luxury Pavement in England before Westminster', in *Westminster Abbey: The Cosmati Pavements*, ed. L. Grant and R. Mortimer, Courtauld Research Papers, 3 (Aldershot, 2002), 7–91, at 8–9.

[96] Reginald, *Libellus*, cap. 75; ed. Raine, 154–7.

[97] *Rites of Durham*, 45, citing an inscription on the tomb which attributed the move to Prior Richard of Barnard Castle in 1370.

[98] *Liber Gaufridi Sacristæ de Coldingham De Statu Ecclesiæ Dunhelmensis*, in *Historiæ Dunelmensis Scriptores Tres*, ed. J. Raine, Surtees Soc., 9 (1839), 3–31, at 11 ... *feretrum quoque ex auro et argento, in quo ossa Venerabilis Bedæ presbyteri et Doctoris ferre decrevit, ex studio artificum tanta diligentia compositum, ut quid magis in eo præstet, opus an decor, [attrectantibus] merito veniat in dubium.*

[99] The passage, found only in Cambridge University Library, MS Ff.i.27, pp. 187–94, printed in Symeon, *Libellus*; ed. Rollason, Appendix B ('Continuation: variant section'), 322. For the MS see ibid., xxv, n. 40.

ELY—ST ÆTHELTHRYTH AND HER SAINTLY SISTERS

At the time of St Cuthbert's translation, the new abbey church at Ely was still under construction. In a building sequence reminiscent of Winchester, the Romanesque church seems to have wrapped around its Anglo-Saxon predecessor, so that the older abbey church could remain in use for as long as possible. Its position is not known for certain, and eighteenth-century antiquaries such as William Stukeley were very wide of the mark when they identified the remains of the Romanesque infirmary hall as the Saxon church.[100] The most likely site is between the nave and the north transept of the present cathedral. It seems that the east end of the Anglo-Saxon church was taken down before its successor was ready for use, for a quite detailed passage in the *Liber Eliensis* describes how the bones of SS. Wihtburh (Withburga) and Eormenhild had to be translated in 1102 owing to the building works.[101] Their tomb-shrines in the old church were presumably further east than those of St Æthelthryth and her successors. According to the *Liber*, the workmen involved in the temporary translation of 1102 cracked the lower part of Wihtburh's sarcophagus while carrying it down a flight of steps within the Anglo-Saxon church; subsequently the damage repaired itself. This was convenient, as the new coffin that had been prepared proved to be a foot too short.

The shrines of SS. Æthelthryth and Seaxburh were able to remain in place for four more years. The evidence is somewhat contradictory. According to the *Liber Eliensis* the two saints' reliquaries flanked the main altar of the pre-Conquest church, which evidently remained usable for liturgical purposes until the last possible minute, and were said to be *in turre*. Æthelthryth was on the south side, 'at her own altar', and Seaxburh to the north.[102] The phrase *in turre* presumably means 'within the ambit of the [crossing] tower', though an alternative interpretation is that *turris* refers to a monument. This seems improbable, though it would admittedly appear congruent with a statement in a reading (*lectio*) for Seaxburh's feast, probably written by Goscelin of Saint-Bertin before the 1106 translation, that she had 'a shared burial, gazing upon her sister Æthelthryth on one side, her daughter Eormenhild on the other, in a shared tomb and in infinite love'.[103] On balance, though, it seems more likely that the text describes separate monuments and that the 'shared tomb' is a figure of speech referring merely to the pre-1106 church as a whole.

[100] William Stukeley, 'Drawings of Religious Antiquitys before the Conquest', Oxford, Bodleian Library, MS Top. Eccles. d.6, fos. 37–8, purport to show 'Part of the old church at Ely built by S. Audry ...' and 'The manner of building of the first church at Ely by S. Audry'. Both in fact depict the surviving elements of the infirmary hall.

[101] *Liber Eliensis*, ii.146; ed. Blake, 231.

[102] ibid.

[103] Goscelin, *Saints of Ely*, 1–9 at 8–9: *Que in eadem ecclesia consepulta hinc sororem Ætheldritham, inde Eormenhildam filiam respectat consorti tumba et caritate infinita.*

The translation of St Æthelthryth in 1106 is recounted in some detail in the *Liber Eliensis*.[104] The operation was presided over by Abbot Richard (1100–7),[105] and was attended by an impressive concourse of prelates. Having formed a procession, the party made its way to the saint's shining white tomb: that recycled Roman sarcophagus which the monks of Ely had brought from Cambridge four hundred and eleven years earlier. At first no-one dared open the monument, recalling the dreadful things that had happened to those rash individuals who had previously interfered with the shrine. At last, though, the body was lifted up and borne into the new church with praise and singing. Æthelthryth was placed in her final position behind the high altar (*post autenticum altare*) while Bishop Herbert of Norwich preached a sermon on the life and miracles of the saint. Right on cue, a terrifying storm broke out. Archbishop Anselm, who had been unable to attend the ceremony despite being invited, heard the thunder from Canterbury and uttered a dire prophecy: few of the participants who had also viewed the body of St Wihtburh face to face would survive the year.[106]

The position of the saint's shrine in the Romanesque abbey church, and that of her saintly relations, is confirmed by other references in *Liber Eliensis*, always with the caveat that the monuments might have moved between 1106 and the date of that compilation *c.*1175. Æthelthryth is said to have been placed *contra* the high altar,[107] which presumably means to the east of it. It was not in an axial position, however. The arrangement was the same as in the pre-Conquest church: Æthelthryth's shrine was on the south side and Seaxburh's was on the north, perhaps a little further east (the author says she was 'towards the feet' of her younger sister).[108] Within twenty-eight years an inventory was drawn up describing the monuments.[109] Æthelthryth was said to be flanked by St Wihtburh on her left (north) and Eormenhild on her right.[110] The marble receptacle (*vas marmoreum*) containing Æthelthryth's body lay under (*sub*, which could simply mean 'within') a richly decorated *feretrum*. Facing the shrine altar at the west end was a gold-plated high relief image of Christ in Majesty adorned with precious stones. Along each of the longer sides were sixteen high relief images, presumably of saints, adorned with an astonishing number of crystals and other semi-precious stones. By the time the *Liber Eliensis* was compiled, Bishop Nigel had removed the precious decoration.

According to a marginal note in a late manuscript of the *Liber Eliensis*,

104 *Liber Eliensis*, ii.144; ed. Blake, 228–30.

105 Abbot Richard was in fact deposed in 1102 but resumed his abbacy probably the following year: Knowles, *Heads*, 45.

106 Blake comments (*Liber Eliensis*, 230, n. 3) that the statement was only true of Prior Richard, who died on 16 or 17 June 1107.

107 *Liber Eliensis*, ii.145; ed. Blake, 230.

108 ibid., ii.145; p. 231.

109 ibid., iii.50; pp. 288–94. The inventory was first compiled on 5 January 1134, but was updated before 1143.

110 ibid., iii.50; p. 290.

the bodies of the saints remained in the same place 'until Hugh of Northwold, the eighth Bishop of Ely, moved the said foursome into the new presbytery constructed by him from its foundations, without inspection of the bodies of the holy virgins Æthelthryth and Wihtburh'.[111]

One relic is said to be still in existence: the allegedly incorrupt hand of St Æthelthryth, which is preserved in a reliquary on the south side of the high altar at St Etheldreda's church, Ely Place, London. It was given to the church by the Duke of Norfolk when the church was restored by Father William Lockhart in 1874. The relic is presumably *spolia* from the Reformation; given the tradition of the saint's incorruptibility, it is unlikely that any fragmentation would have been countenanced as long as her shrine existed at Ely.

NEW CULTS OF c.1100

So far in this chapter we have concentrated on the way Anglo-Norman churchmen treated the cults of pre-existing, Anglo-Saxon saints with which they had to come to terms in the decades immediately following the Conquest. It was not long, however, before they began to initiate new English cults. In the early twelfth century two Anglo-Saxons—one king, Edward the Confessor, and one bishop, Wulfstan of Worcester—became recognised as saints.

EDWARD THE CONFESSOR

The cult of Edward the Confessor would assume an intense, albeit short-lived and essentially local, significance in the thirteenth century, but began to grow a hundred years before that.[112] At this point we need to consider in greater detail a quasi-hagiographical work, the *Vita Ædwardi Regis*.[113] As already mentioned,[114] the main purpose of the *Vita*, certainly as it was originally conceived, seems to have been to glorify the house of Godwin (and, perhaps, pave the way for Edward's successor) rather than to emphasise the saintly qualities of the last Anglo-Saxon monarch. Yet, the second book of this curious work, written after the Confessor's death and focusing on his religious qualities, has much of the character of a saint's Life. One problem in interpreting the *Vita* is that the earliest manuscript,[115] dating from around 1100, is defective; leaves are missing from Book II, shortly after the beginning of what must be a series of *miracula* attributed to the saint. Just

[111] ibid, p. 234, note 'c'. *donec Hugo de Northwold, viij*[us] *episcopus Elyensis predictas Domini quadrigas in novum presbiterium, ab ipso a fundamentis constructum, transtulit glebas sanctarum virginum Ætheldrede et Withburge inconspectas*. This translation from *Liber Eliensis*, trans. J. Fairweather (Woodbridge, 2005), 283, n. 771.

[112] For an overview of the development of the cult, see *Vita Ædwardi*; ed. Barlow, Appendix D 'The Development of the Cult of King Edward', pp. 150–63.

[113] *Vita Ædwardi*; ed. Barlow.

[114] See above, p. 113.

[115] BL, MS Harley 526, fos. 38–57.

two miracles have survived in the manuscript and the first few words of a third. They all seem to involve the legendary cure of *morbia regis* (the 'King's Evil' or scrofula) either directly by the royal touch or at least by contact with water with which Edward had himself been in contact. When Frank Barlow edited the work he therefore supplied the missing miracles from a later Life of the Confessor which Osbert of Clare wrote in 1138 in an initially rather unsuccessful attempt to launch the cult. Barlow describes the miracle stories as 'a poor collection' and 'the scrapings of the barrel'; they were certainly not the stuff which in a later age might persuade a papal commission of the eligibility of a potential saint. Thus the concluding passage of the *Vita*, assuming it is not a later interpolation, gives an entirely stylised summary of posthumous miracles allegedly recorded at Edward's tomb: 'through him the blind receive their sight, the lame are made to walk, the sick are healed ....'[116] The phraseology is entirely conventional, deriving from St Luke's gospel,[117] and should probably be regarded as an expression of hope rather than reality.

Although the matter has been debated, Barlow's dating of the *Vita* to the period 1065–7 seems most consistent with the internal evidence of the text.[118] Book II was clearly written after the king's death in January 1066, and probably after the Battle of Hastings, but before the death of Archbishop Stigand in 1070. If this date is accepted, and if the miracles and the conclusion were not added subsequently, we are left with what looks like a first, abortive attempt at launching a cult of the Confessor. This, too, was Barlow's conclusion, and he characterised the hagiographical elements as evidence for a local attempt at promoting a cult which 'fell by the wayside'.[119] Commenting on the closing passage of Book II, he made the pertinent observation that miracles were also said to have taken place at the tomb of Edward's murdered young brother, Alfred: 'many miracles occur where the tomb is, as people report who even declare most repeatedly that they have seen them'. Despite this, no cult of Alfred ever emerged.[120]

Even if the cult had taken off in the time of Eadwine, the last Saxon abbot of Westminster (1049–70), it is unlikely that much progress would have been maintained under his Norman successors, Geoffrey and Vitalis. By the time of the third Norman abbot, Gilbert Crispin (*c.*1085–1117), the edge of Norman disdain may have blunted. Emma Mason has written that Gilbert was 'by no means the first Norman abbot to see the potential for his monastery in promoting an unofficial English cult',[121] a view which is diametrically opposed to Frank Barlow's suggestion that Abbot Gilbert may

[116] *Vita Ædwardi*, ii.11; ed. Barlow, 126–7: ... *cum obtentu eius ibi illuminantur cęci, in gressum solidantur claudi, infirmi curantur* ...

[117] Luke 7:22: '... the blind see, the lame walk, the lepers are cleansed, the deaf hear, the dead are raised ....'

[118] *Vita Ædwardi*; ed. Barlow, pp. xxix–xxxi.

[119] ibid., lxxi.

[120] *Encomium Emmæ Reginæ*, ed. A. Campbell, Camden Soc., 3rd ser., lxxii (1949), 44–6.

[121] E. Mason, 'Westminster Abbey and the Monarchy between the Reigns of William I and John (1066–1216)', *Jnl. of Ecclesiastical History*, 41 (1990), 199–216, at 202.

actively have discouraged Edward's cult.[122] Certainly it was under Abbot Gilbert that the first examination of Edward's body took place in 1102.

There is, furthermore, some slight evidence that Edward's tomb might have been regarded as significant even before that examination. According to Osbert of Clare, writing in 1138, the tomb was protected by an opulent *capsa* which William the Conqueror, impressed by the miracle of Wulfstan's episcopal staff,[123] had given to the church: 'The vanquisher of the English, William, had commissioned the provision of a *capsa* made of gold and silver, which to the present day both protects and covers the glorious body in the church of blessed Peter the Apostle.'[124] In the late fourteenth century it was believed that this was one and the same as the *feretrum* into which Edward's body was elevated in 1163. It is unlikely, however, that what Osbert described was a reliquary, though the word *capsa* would normally be translated 'casket'. Yet it is difficult to conceive that Osbert would have lied about something which would have been apparent to his monks, so some sort of superstructure, which he attributed to the Conqueror, may have marked the tomb by 1138. The only other chronicler who might have shed light on the matter is the Westminster monk Sulcard, writing in the time of Abbot Vitalis (*c.*1076–*c.*1085), to whom he dedicated his work. Sulcard appears to have known the pre-Edwardian abbey church, and was therefore probably a monk at the time of the Confessor's death, but he states simply that the Confessor was buried, 'it would seem' (*ut videtur*) in front of the high altar.[125] The phrase *ut videtur* is curious, but it is surely incredible that such a prestigious burial should have been forgotten within nineteen years at the very most.[126]

In support of the contention that Gilbert Crispin promoted the Confessor's cult, Osbert asserts that the abbot took the initiative in inviting many notable men to the ceremonial opening of the tomb in 1102, including Gundulf of Rochester, who played a leading role. How much reliance may be placed on Osbert's account is, however, uncertain: he was a notorious forger of charters for his abbey church, and might have been equally unscrupulous when it came to concocting sanctity myths in order to achieve his goal of canonising the Confessor. His description of the opening of

[122] Barlow, *Edward the Confessor*, 266–7.

[123] See above, p. 115.

[124] Osbert, *Vita Edwardi*, cap. 29; ed. Bloch, 120: … *triumphator Anglorum Willelmus super sanctum regem Eadwardum ex auro et argento capse fabricam condidit, que utique in odiernum diem in ecclesia beati Petri apostoli gloriosum corpus obumbrat et tegit.* Cf. Ailred of Rievaulx, *Vita S. Edwardi Regis*; *Pat. Lat.*, cxcv. cols. 737–90, at 781. Matthew Paris, *Chronica Maiora*; ed. Luard, ii. 42, seems to place the decoration in the time of William Rufus (1095), but he copies almost verbatim the words of Ailred: *Tunc rex Willelmus in amortem cognati sui Sancti Eadwardi succensus, sanctissimum eius sepulchrum, auro et argento fabrefactum, miro studio decoravit.*

[125] Sulcard of Westminster, *Prologus de Construccione Westmonasterii*, ed. B. W. Scholtz, *Traditio*, 20 (1964), 59–91, at 91: *sepultusque est, ut videtur, ante ipsum altare principis apostolorum.*

[126] But see Barlow, *Edward the Confessor*, 263–4 and 267: 'by 1080, if we can trust Sulcard, the exact location of Edward's tomb became a matter of doubt'.

Edward's tomb in 1102 conforms with all the commonplaces of medieval hagiography; but then, hagiography was not expected to be original. However, in the 'florid magnificence' of his account, as Joseph Armitage Robinson, dean of Westminster, characterised it,[127] Osbert excelled himself. He related how the body had lain in the tomb full thirty-six years, and 'and many thought that, like other men, he had dissolved into ashes as is our common mortal lot'.[128] But others hoped that the 'virgin purity' of his life might have preserved his body in death. And so it turned out:

> So the upper stone is lifted from the sarcophagus, and his glorious body is found wrapt in a costly robe: slender hands and flexible joints, the finger with its royal ring, the sandals—all are plainly seen to shew no sign of corruption: the sceptre at his side, the crown upon his head, all the regal ornaments of his noble burial are shewn uninjured by the touch of time. So firm and bright was the flesh, so perfect all the garments, that their soundness told that God in truth was magnified in Edward, setting forth in his flesh an image of the resurrection of the saints.[129]

At first none of those present dared touch the body. Then Bishop Gundulf rearranged the Confessor's beard. He was about to pluck a single hair from it as a relic but was roundly scolded by Gilbert Crispin for his impertinence. In a later Life of the saint Ailred of Rievaulx adds that Edward's pall was replaced and the old one was displayed in the church as a relic.[130] And that was just about the end of the exercise. Unlike the opening of the tomb of St Cuthbert, where the participants were also in doubt as to whether the body would be found incorrupt, the opening of the tomb was not followed by an elevation: the stone cover of the sarcophagus was simply replaced. And there the body would remain for a further sixty-one years, until the first translation in 1163, to which we shall come in due course.

WULFSTAN OF WORCESTER

As we saw in the previous chapter, Wulfstan of Worcester, the last Anglo-Saxon bishop, was responsible for launching the cult of his distant predecessor St Oswald. Following the by now familiar pattern of saintly leap-

[127] J. Armitage Robinson (ed.), *Gilbert Crispin, Abbot of Westminster Notes and Documents relating to Westminster Abbey*, iii (Cambridge, 1911), 25.

[128] Osbert, *Vita Edwardi*, cap. 30; ed. Bloch, 121: *Sex namque et triginta annis rex delituerat Eadwardus in tumulo, eumque iuxta condicionem mortalitatis nostre arbitrati sunt nonnulli humanitus in cineres defluxisse.*

[129] ibid., cap. 30; pp. 121–2: *Remouetur ergo lapis superior a sarcofago, corpusque gloriosum pallio inuolutum reperriunt precioso; manus delicatas et flexibiles articulos, regioque digitum anulo circumdatum et sandalia contemplantur nullum putredinis preferre uestigium; sceptrum a latere et corona in capite et quecunque sepulture celebris erant regalia nulla uidebantur uetustate consumpta. Sicque caro solida et nitida erant ac inuiolata omnia uestimenta, ut integritas eorum loqueretur Deum in Eadwardo uere mirabilem, qui in eius carne representabat quandam sanctorum corporum resurrectionem.*

[130] Ailred of Rievaulx, *Vita S. Edwardi Regis*; *Pat. Lat.*, cxcv., cols. 737–90, at 783. Osbert does not mention the pall.

frogging, Wulfstan in turn would eventually be canonised, but the beginnings of his cult are to be found soon after his death in January 1095, at the age of nearly ninety. Soon after this, Wulfstan's former chaplain and chancellor, the monk Coleman, was commissioned to compose the *Vita* of the bishop. Appropriately for the Life of the last Anglo-Saxon bishop, Coleman wrote it in Old English. The date of the text is uncertain, but Coleman himself died in 1113 which provides a *terminus ante quem*. The commissioning of a Life suggests that early in the twelfth century the Worcester monks hoped that Wulfstan might become a saint, and Coleman's *Vita* was one of the documents used to support the canonisation process a century or so later. The lost Old English text, 'his life written in the English language a hundred years ago' as the papal commissioners called it in 1203, may indeed lurk somewhere in the Vatican archives.[131] The commissioners probably found William of Malmesbury's Latin 'translation',[132] the *Vita Wulfstani*, more useful.

Coleman described in detail the appearance of the corpse, its lying-in-state for two days and nights in front of the high altar while the brethren awaited the arrival of Bishop Robert of Hereford (miraculously summoned by Wulfstan himself after his death), the lengthy ceremonial attending the obsequies, and the reaction of the crowd—notably the way the wails of the onlookers echoed around the vault: 'The crowd shouted words of grief that the vaulted roof of the church re-echoed and redoubled.'[133] Then the monks placed the body in its grave, but Coleman piously concluded that 'the memory of him was never buried in their hearts'.[134]

A *Vita* of a prospective saint was normally followed by a companion piece, the *Miracula*, but Coleman had to work hard to find any miracles. The best he could come up with was the 'miraculous' retrieval of a couple of lost books.[135] These posthumous events are something of an anticlimax after the cures that Wulfstan allegedly operated during his lifetime: the cure of scrofula by water with which Wulfstan had washed his hands at mass,[136] or of a woman's chronic cramps, cured at a distance by applying to the most painful spots a letter that she had received from the bishop.[137]

Despite these shortcomings, the Worcester monks appear to have been successful in their campaign. It is clear that people were accustomed to kneel in prayer at the bishop's tomb within a few years of his death. We know this,

[131] The bull mentioning the Old English text is printed in Malmesbury, *Miracula Wulfstani*, ii.1; ed. Darlington, 148–50, at 149: … *scripturam quoque autenticam de uita ipsius ante centum annos Anglicana lingua conscriptam* …

[132] For the degree to which Wulfstan followed Coleman, see *William of Malmesbury, Saints' Lives: Lives of SS. Wulfstan, Dunstan, Patrick, Benignus and Indract*, ed. M. Winterbottom and R. M. Thomson, OMT (Oxford, 2002), xv–xvii.

[133] Malmesbury, *Vita Wulfstani*, iii.24.1; ed. Winterbottom and Thomson, 146–7.

[134] ibid., iii.24.2; pp. 146–9: *Immiserunt tandem amantissimi patris ossa sepulchro. Sed memoria numquam in eorum sepulta est animo.*

[135] ibid., iii.25–6; pp. 148–51.

[136] ibid., ii.7; pp. 74–7.

[137] ibid., ii.13; pp. 84–7.

and we have some idea of what the tomb looked like, because William of Malmesbury described it in his *Gesta Pontificum*, in his account of a fire which damaged the church in 1113. The tomb lay between two pillar-like structures (*piramides*), vaulted over with a beautiful stone arch. A timber (*lignum*) projected above it, into which were fixed iron grilles (*casses ferreos*), which the monks called 'spiders' webs' (*araneas*).[138] After the fire, the tomb itself was found to be completely undamaged and not even smoke-blackened. William was even more impressed by the survival of the woven mat (*natta*) on which people used to pray in front of the monument; the projecting woodwork supporting the grilles had also survived, though curiously William says that the ends of the beams, where they were encased in the stonework, 'dissolved into ashes'. The interpretation is obscure, but perhaps William meant that elements of the monument which had fallen to the ground had been preserved from total incineration, as often happens in fires. Describing the 1174 fire at Canterbury, Gervase noted that despite the damage to the upper parts of the columns it was still possible to recover bodies from the tombs in the choir; features at ground level had been preserved by the falling debris.[139] The *natta* at Worcester survived a second fire in 1147 in the same way.[140]

Malmesbury's description is difficult to interpret, but the tomb appears to have been free-standing, with tapering pillars on either side and an arch over it; the monument itself was protected by a grille. The fact that the faithful venerated the deceased bishop by kneeling 'in front of the tomb' (*ante mausoleum*) suggests it was one-sided, so perhaps it stood against an aisle wall. It was probably within the eastern arm, for in one miracle an insane woman had to be carried up a flight of steps to get to the tomb.[141] The most likely position was on the north side of the choir.[142] The monument was emphatically a tomb rather than a shrine. Only after the tomb was opened in 1198, four years before Wulfstan's canonisation, were the bones placed in a first, provisional reliquary, after which the cult proceeded on orthodox lines.

THE SAINTS AT HEXHAM

The community at Hexham made much of the sanctity of its line of bishops, three of whose bodies had been elevated in the eleventh century. Eventually, more than half of the bishops between Tunbert's election in 681 and

[138] Malmesbury, *GP*, iv.148; ed. Winterbottom and Thomson, i. 438–9. *Iacet inter duas piramides, arcu lapideo pulchre superuoluto. Lignum in superiori prominet, quod casses ferreos, quos uocant araneas, infixos habet.*
[139] *Gervase*; ed. Stubbs, i. 4.
[140] '*Abridgement of Vita Wulfstani*', ii.18; Malmesbury, *Vita Wulfstani*, ed. Darlington, 106.
[141] Malmesbury, *Miracula S. Wulfstani*, i.21; ed. Darlington, 128.
[142] As argued in J. Crook, 'The Physical Setting of the Cult of St Wulfstan', in *St Wulfstan and his World*, ed. J. S. Barrow and N. P. Brooks, Studies in Early Medieval Britain, 4 (Aldershot, 2005), 189–217.

Tidfrith's death *c.*821 would be regarded locally as saints (though the cults of John of Beverley and Wilfrid developed elsewhere). By the mid-twelfth century Hexham could probably boast the most complete collection of relics of local saints in northern England.[143] As we have seen, Alfred Westou was reponsible for promoting some of the cults in the eleventh century. His descendants were equally active. Ailred of Rivaulx, Alfred's great-grandson, tells us in his *De Sanctis Ecclesiæ Haugustaldensis* (probably written soon after the translation of 1155), that when the monastic community was established at Durham in 1083 Alfred's son, Eilav, was amongst the secular canons who were expelled to make room for the monks. Eilav successfully petitioned Thomas of Bayeux, Archbishop of York (1070–1100), to place him in charge of Hexham church and to restore it, for following the Danish incursions the building was roofless and weeds were growing within it.[144] However, Eilav did not live to complete the project, and the custody of the church passed to his son, Eilav II.

The younger Eilav cleaned the church, retiled it, and decorated the walls. Then he laid a pavement of stone slabs at the east end, and created a worthy new altar. The church's relics, which he intended to place in a single shrine, would be located here. During the building works the relics were stored in a *porticus* dedicated to St Michael, on the south side of the church. They were temporarily entrusted to Eilav's adolescent brother, Aldred (*Aluredus*, later one of the Augustinian canons of Hexham), who incurred St Alchmund's wrath when he tried to steal a small relic from that saint's remains. He tried three times to enter the chapel but was repelled by an intense blast of heat.[145]

These difficulties resolved, the relics were wrapped in a precious cloth and placed in a single reliquary, supported on a stone slab (*tabula*) and presumably located behind the high altar as Eilav II had intended. Given the Durham connections of the two Eilavs, it is likely that the arrangement at Hexham was similar to that at Durham, with the reliquary raised on a shrine-base of the pillared type.

St Eata's relics seem to have received separate treatment, as already noted, remaining within the *porticus* on the south side of the church until 1155. Eata's *Vita* includes a lengthy passage relating how in 1113 Archbishop Thomas II, under pressure from his cathedral chapter, sought to translate the body of the saint to York Minster, but was dissuaded when Eata himself miraculously appeared to the archbishop in a dream, whilst Thomas's party were already at Hexham about the business of collecting up the relics.[146]

143 Tunbert 681–5 (deposed), St Eata 685–6, St John of Beverley 687–705 (translated to York), St Wilfrid, †709 at Oundle, buried at Ripon, St Acca 709–32 (deposed, †740) , St Frithbert 734–66, St Alcmund (Ealhmund) 767–81, St Tilbert 781–9, Ethelberht 789–97, Eadred 797–800, Eanberht 800–13/14, Tidfrith 814–*c.*820

144 Ailred, *Saints of Hexham*, cap. 11; ed. Raine, 191.

145 ibid., 191–2. Possibly Ailred obtained this anecdote from Symeon of Durham's *Historia Regum*, para. 36: *Sym. Op.*, ii. 33-5.

146 *Vita S. Eatæ*, in Raine, *Hexham Priory*, 204–220, at 214–5.

'Why do you come together to trouble my repose, and to transfer me to other nations from the place where I sleep and rest with my brothers? This comes not from the will of God but from your presumption, for which you will now receive punishment' said Eata, before chastising the archbishop with his pastoral staff.[147] The anecdote reads like yet another attempt on the part of the Hexham community at reinforcing their claim to the bodies of their local saints.

GUTHLAC OF CROWLAND

The cult of St Guthlac, whose origins we studied in an earlier chapter,[148] received a boost in the twelfth century. During the first three decades of that century the church, which had already been reconstructed by Abbot Wulfketel in 1061–2, was being rebuilt again, having been severely damaged by a disastrous fire in 1091. The disaster was described in graphic detail in a *History* of the abbey by Abbot Ingulph. It started, as so often, when a plumber working in the tower had inadvertently left his brazier smouldering, and a strong wind fanned the flames. It was night before the conflagration became apparent. The abbot himself played a major role, saving many of the brethren, asleep in their dormitory.[149] Ingulph reconstructed his monastery as best he could,[150] but in 1114 (i.e. at the end of the Interdict), Abbot Geoffrey announced his intention of rebuilding the church in grander style.[151] Building materials had been brought together for the works, and an impressive roll-call of important people laid the foundation stones of the various parts of the building. Works must have been brought to a standstill by a severe earthquake in 1117, which damaged the south wall of the nave; the building had to be shored up with long beams.[152] By 1136 the eastern arm at least was sufficiently complete for Abbot Waltheof to preside over the translation of the relics of the monastery's patron saint. Shortly before that date the monks of Croyland had urged Waltheof to elevate Guthlac's relics from their unworthy place: they bewailed the fact that the relics were housed in 'vile earth' (*vili cespite*) and contained in a mere earthen vessel (*luteo vasculo*).[153] As we saw earlier, although Guthlac's tomb had been adorned by Æthelbald of Mercia in the

[147] Ailred, *Saints of Hexham*, cap. 15; ed. Raine, 202: *Cur convenit vobis meam infestare quietam, et a loco ubi cum fratribus meis dormio et requiesco, ad alias transferre nationes? non hoc Domini voluntatis, sed tuæ est præsumptionis, cuius iam nunc pœnas ex[s]olves.* The story also occurs in the *Vita S. Eatæ*; ed. Raine, 214–15.

[148] See p. 67.

[149] *Descriptio Compilata per Dominum Ingulphum Abbatem Monasterii de Croyland* in *Scriptores*, ed. Fulman, 1–107, at 96–7.

[150] ibid., 112.

[151] *Petri Blesensis continuatio ad Historiam Ingulphi*, in *Scriptores*, ed. Fulman, 108–32, at 118–20.

[152] ibid., 129.

[153] '*Translatio S. Guthlaci, ex MSS. Anglicanis*'; *AASS*, *Aprilis* II, 54C–60F at 55A–C.

early eighth century, the body had remained in place: the monument was a tomb-shrine. The abbot agreed to his monks' request, and after a three-day fast the four brethren who had been chosen for the task came by night to the tomb. The saint's power was manifested by a great light, the stone was removed, and the body was revealed, giving off a marvellous smell. The relics were temporarily placed next to the altar of the Blessed Virgin, where more wonderful phenomena and cures occurred. Finally, when all the local notable churchmen had been summoned, the glorious body was translated into a new monument, in a higher place in the church; the saint's head was separately enshrined. The chronicler adds considerable detail about the shrine. A nobleman had summoned the foremost goldsmiths and jewellers, who had skilfully created a shrine (*repa*) of wood and metal, sheathed in plates of gold and silver and adorned with crystals and jewels: this was the shrine still to be seen at the time of writing.[154] The coffin from which the saint's body was elevated was evidently preserved as a secondary focus of veneration. Orderic Vitalis, a monk of Saint-Évroult in Normandy who once spent five weeks at Croyland, records in his great *History* (completed shortly before his death *c.*1142) that the lead coffin was placed on the pavement of the church as a memorial to him, and was revered 'to the present day'.[155]

The church was further damaged by another fire in 1146, then yet another in 1170,[156] and the subsequent building works were possibly not completed until the time of Abbot Robert de Redynges (†1190). Then in 1196 Guthlac was moved again: the continuator notes that the translation occurred exactly sixty years since the first translation of 1136. The detailed account gives an idea of the practical difficulties involved in building works where an active cult was the centre of a church's activities. The precious *feretrum* was removed from the high altar and placed elsewhere (*alibi*), but the saint's relics were enclosed in a 'sarcophagus' which was made secure by means of six iron and lead seals and placed on a new, temporary altar on the high altar step. This allowed the abbey's workmen to dismantle the old high altar and create a new one. The final stage was the creation of a new marble shrine-base (*tabulatus*), supported on columns. When all was ready, on Thursday 1 June, a congregation of clergy and people attended the translation, and the *feretrum* was raised up on the marble base, 'as it is

[154] ibid., 56D: *Super lapidem vero decurio quidam, Robertus de Guardineto* [*sic* for *Grandineto*?], *miræ gravitatis veteranus, omnium religiosorum amato, conductis aurifabrorum et gemmariorum primoribus, elimatæ amplitudinis artificiosa sculptura repam in sublime suspensam construxit: quam ex diversorum metallorum lignorumque generibus conpactam, auri argentique laminis vestitam, crystallis variisque gemmis adornatam, ditavit sicut usque in hodiernum humanis visibus apparet.* The word *repa* seems to be a variant of *crepa*, a noun cognate with the Germanic 'crib' indicating a wooden box-like structure.
[155] Orderic, *Historia*, iv; ed. Chibnall, ii. 322–39.
[156] *Historiæ Croylandensis Continuatio* (from BL, Cotton MS Vespasian B.xi), in *Scriptores*, ed. Fulman, 451–593, at 452.

seen today'.[157] It was in the context of these works that the wonderful images of the *Vita* and *Miracula* of the saint contained in the famous 'Guthlac Roll' were drawn.[158]

ST MELANGELL AT PENNANT MELANGELL

I end this chapter with an account of the earliest surviving shrine in our island—though in deepest Wales rather than England. 'Surviving' is perhaps a misnomer, for like almost all the medieval shrines now displayed in English churches and cathedrals, the shrine of St Melangell (often known by the Latin version of her name, Monacella) was pieced together from fragments in quite recent times. The shrine was probably demolished in the period 1538–53; if the destruction occurred at the beginning of that date range it suggests that Thomas Cromwell's commissioners managed to penetrate even to the remote headwaters of the river Tanat, in deepest Montgomeryshire. It should be noted, however, that the diocesan council of St Asaph was still issuing proclamations relating to the removal of relics as late as 1561, so the shrine might conceivably have survived well into the second half of the sixteenth century.[159]

The legend of the saint, preserved in a late medieval text,[160] probably owes more to hagiographical *topoi* (commonplaces) than historical fact, though the writer appears to have had access to local traditions. Melangell was allegedly the daughter of an Irish king named Iowchel, who had fled the royal court in order to avoid marriage, living the life of a virgin ascetic in Wales. After fifteen years she was unexpectedly discovered at Pennant by a certain Brochwel, prince of Powys, when the hare that he was hunting took refuge in the folds of her garment. Brochwel gave her the lands at Pennant, and she founded a community of virgins there. While it remains just possible that the legend preserves the memory of the foundation of a remote religious community (not necessarily only of nuns) in the 'later eighth century',[161] it is perhaps more probable that the Life was written in order to maintain the church's sanctuary rights.[162] The earliest secure

[157] ibid., 463.

[158] *The Guthlac Roll. Scenes from the Life of St. Guthlac of Crowland by a Twelfth-Century Artist reproduced from Harley Roll Y.6 in the British Museum*, ed. Sir George Warner, Roxburghe Club (Oxford, 1928). See also G. Henderson, 'The Imagery of St Guthlac of Crowland', in *England in the Thirteenth Century*, Proc. of the 1984 Harlaxton Symposium, ed. W. M. Ormrod (Harlaxton, 1985), 76–94, at 84.

[159] R. B. Heaton and W. J. Britnell, 'A Structural history of Pennant Melangell Church', *The Montgomeryshire Collections*, Jnl. of the Powysland Club, 82 (1994), 103–26, at 113.

[160] C. A. Ralegh Radford and W. J. Hemp propose a late fourteenth- or fifteenth-century date, 'when the church was modernised': 'Pennant Melangell: The Church and the Shrine', *Archaeologia Cambrensis*, 108 (1959), 81–113, at 82. The editor of the latest edition of the *Historia Divæ Monacellæ* refines this to 'between the late fifteenth century and 1548': H. Pryce, 'A new edition of the *Historia Divae Monacellæ*', *The Montgomeryshire Collections*, Jnl. of the Powysland Club, 82 (1994), 23–40, at 28.

[161] Radford and Hemp, 'Pennant Melangell', 85.

[162] Pryce, 'New edition', 31–2.

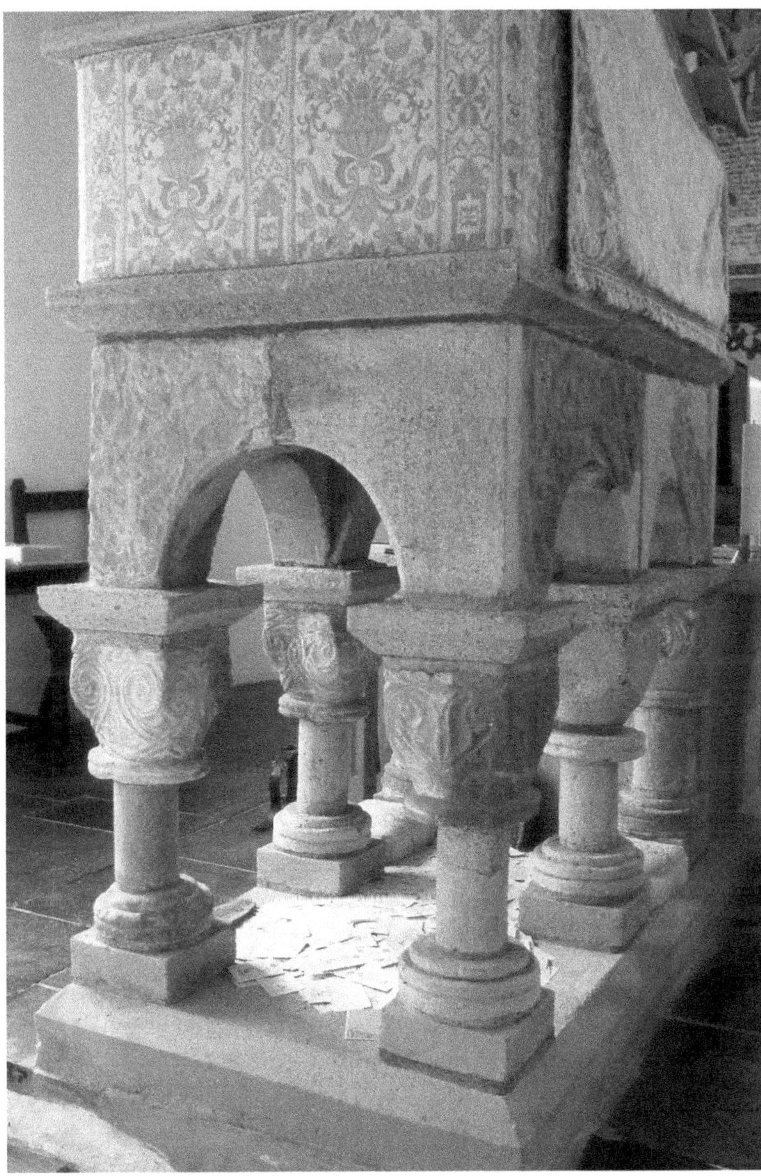

PLATE 6.6 PENNANT MELANGELL (POWYS, NORTH WALES) The reconstructed twelfth-century shrine of St Melangell (Monacella).

documentary evidence for the cult occurs only in the late fourteenth century, in later recensions of the originally early thirteenth-century genealogical tract known as the *Bonedd y Saint*.[163]

[163] Pryce, 'New edition', 33–4, correcting Radford and Hemp, 'Pennant Melangell', 83–4, who dated the *Bonedd y Sant* to the twelfth century citing A. W. Wade Evans, *Vitæ Sanctorum Britanniæ et Genealogiæ*, xvii.

The best evidence for the early cult of Melangell at Pennant is in fact the remnants of her shrine. However dubious her biography, there is no doubting the importance of the physical remains of the cult, which demonstrate in microcosm the change from grave to shrine. The earliest parts of the present church date from the twelfth century.[164] The legendary site of Melangell's grave was within a small annexe to the main body of the church, significantly known as the *Cell-y-Bedd*, 'cell of the grave'. In the mid-nineteenth century, when the cult first attracted serious antiquarian attention, the *Cell-y-Bedd* was a post-medieval structure variously used as a schoolroom or a vestry.[165] During conservation works in 1958 the floor was excavated and the footings of an earlier version of the *Cell-y-Bedd* were discovered: an apsidal structure, with an empty grave on the south side.[166] This chamber, which appeared to form part of the Romanesque church, was rebuilt in that form in 1989. During the works a narrow doorway providing access from the body of the church was discovered. It was off-set to the north, apparently to take account of the grave or, as we shall examine below, to the twelfth-century shrine.

The architectural discoveries have plausibly been linked to the surviving fragments of a twelfth-century monument, identified as the Romanesque shrine of St Melangell. The worked stones were identified as part of the shrine as early as 1893, when members of the Cambrian Archaeological Association were shown 'A large number of sculptured fragments ... built into the walls of the church and stone porch over the lych-gate, which are conjectured to have formed portions of the shrine of the Saint.'[167] Several of the pieces were removed from these locations during the works of 1958 and were reassembled in the post-medieval *Cell-y-Bedd* to a design by Ralegh Radford; in 1989–90 they were again reassembled in the body of the church, behind the high altar.

In its present form, the shrine consists of an arcaded base in two bays, supporting a chamfered, composite slab. Above this, to east and west, rise steep crocketed gables, suggesting that the structure terminated in a pitched roof whose form is now indicated by the fictive *feretrum*; some undecorated, trapezoidal blocks could have formed part of such a roof. The principal decorative elements comprise a number of pieces of the arcade, three complete four-sided capitals (and a possible fragment of a fourth), one demi-capital, one complete column base and a second fragment, and

[164] For the church, see Heaton and Britnell, 'Structural history'.

[165] Anon., 'Pennant Melangell, Montgomeryshire', *Archæologia Cambrensis*, 2 (1848), 137–42, 324–8 [erroneously numbered 224–8], at 138 and 334.

[166] Radford and Hemp, 'Pennant Melangell'. W. J. Britnell and others, 'Excavation and recording at Pennant Melangell Church', *The Montgomeryshire Collections*, Jnl. of the Powysland Club, 82 (1994), 103–26.

[167] Anon., report on expedition of 23 August 1879, *Archæologia Cambrensis*, 11 No. 42 (April 1894), 139–51, at 140.

one demi-column base.[168] The capitals are decorated with interlaced palmettes and volutes; related devices adorn the arch fragments, and although K. Watson admitted that no exact *comparandum* for the structure was known, the general *parti* of the decoration implied a late twelfth-century date, perhaps with Irish influences.[169] Somewhat similar elements are to be found at the nearby churches of Llanrhaeadr-ym-Mochnant and Llangollen, implying perhaps a local school of carving.

The limited number of surviving elements means that they may be reassembled in several different configurations, and the material has been examined in this light by Bill Britnell.[170] Although the present reconstruction within the body of the church has much to commend it, it is equally possible that the shrine in fact stood over the original grave of the saint, on the south side of the *Cell-y-Bedd*, and that the demi-shafts stood not against an altar, but against the west wall of that grave-chamber. This interpretation requires the arrangement of the surviving stones to be reconfigured as a two-sided three-bay structure, rather than the 'all-round' two-bay shrine of the reconstruction now in the apse. Furthermore this interpretation requires one of the two surviving gable elements to have been mounted along the north roof-slope of the monument, rather than at the end of the roof. Britnell is circumspect in his conjectural reconstructions, reasonably pointing out that several interpretations are possible. The fact that the door to the *Cell-y-Bedd* is displaced northwards lends weight to the hypothesis that it was here that the saint was venerated, and that the shrine and the shrine chamber were constructed at the same period. Whether the relics remained within the grave (in which case the monument should be classed a 'tomb-shrine'), or whether they were housed in the gabled superstructure, is uncertain. Whatever its original position, the monument is important as the only surviving (albeit reconstructed) example of a Romanesque shrine in a church in the British Isles.

[168] See the catalogue of the fragments in W. J. Britnell and K. Watson, 'Saint Melangell's Shrine, Pennant Melangell', *The Montgomeryshire Collections*, Jnl. of the Powysland Club, 82 (1994), 147–66, at 148–57.
[169] ibid., 157–9.
[170] 'Towards a reconstruction of the shrine', ibid., 160–5.

7 'GIVING LIGHT TO THE WHOLE HOUSE'

The new enthusiasm for saints' cults in the later twelfth century

It is often claimed, and with some justification, that the murder of Archbishop Thomas Becket in 1170, followed by his rapid canonisation, was the cause of an intense new interest in local saints, with wide-ranging consequences throughout England. In fact, the upsurge of interest in local saints displayed by certain leading churchmen seems to have begun two decades before that, though there was undoubtedly another wave of enthusiasm for saints' cults after Becket's final translation in 1220. The 1150s were, indeed, a particularly active time for the cults of local saints, and the surviving documentation gives an impression that churchmen and laity at that time moved from one splendid translation ceremony to another in a breathless whirl of hagiological frenzy.

LONDON: ST EARCONWALD (ERKENWALD)

Amongst the first examples of this revived enthusiasm for local saints is St Earconwald (Erkenwald), 'the capital's nearest to a patron saint',[1] whose cult has faded from popular consciousness since the reconstruction of his cathedral church following the Great Fire of London. The church which perished in 1666 was of course a Gothic remodelling of a Romanesque predecessor, itself a reconstruction of an Anglo-Saxon cathedral that had also been destroyed by fire in 1087.[2] The first bishop, Mellitus, had been translated to Canterbury in 619, dying there five years later. He was buried at the monastery of SS. Peter and Paul (i.e. St Augustine's, as it was subsequently known). In the later middle ages London also claimed to

[1] P. Wormald, 'Earconwald', *DNB*, xvii. 559–60, at 559.

[2] R. K. Morris, 'The new work at Old St Paul's Cathedral and its place in English thirteenth-century architecture', in *Medieval Art, Architecture and Archaeology in London*, ed. L. Grant, *BAA Trans.*, vol. 10, for 1984 (1990), 74–100, at 74.

possess some of his relics, which were housed in a *feretrum* at the high altar.[3] However, the main cult in London's cathedral quickly developed around a later bishop, Earconwald, a wealthy churchman perhaps of royal birth, founder of Chertsey monastery and the nunnery of Barking, where he died in 693. Such was his prestige that both those monasteries and his cathedral church claimed his relics; in the end St Paul's obtained the honour. By the eleventh century he was regarded as the diocese's principal saint.

The most fruitful source for the development of Earconwald's cult is a group of miracle stories compiled in the mid-twelfth century, probably by Arcoid, a scholarly canon of St Paul's who originally came from Auxerre.[4] The *Miracula* are not presented chronologically, but through the confusion it is possible to perceive something of the cult's evolution. It was, for example, remembered that in the Anglo-Saxon cathedral the saint's body lay 'behind the altar of the Lord in a wooden coffin (*theca*) which, resting on a stone plinth, stood higher than the height of a man and was covered with an ancient altar cloth (*palliolum*)'.[5] This sounds like a remarkably early example of the sort of high shrine that would become a commonplace in the later middle ages. Unfortunately, in the summer of 1087 a fire broke out in the western part of the city of London in the middle of the night, eventually reaching the church. The building was engulfed. As at Canterbury, one of the first concerns of the London canons following the fire was the condition of the relics. Earconwald's bones had in fact survived to a degree that they were able to claim was miraculous. Despite the torrent of molten lead and burning coals from the roof, and a great burning beam which had crashed down, not a single thread of the pall covering the *feretrum* had been lost: it had not even been scorched.[6] When Bishop Maurice (1086–1107) had completed the reconstruction of the church he ordered the saint's body to be placed in the crypt,[7] a location which would not have been unusual in Carolingian Gaul and later Saxon England but was decidedly outmoded by the late eleventh century. This may have been intended as a temporary setting. The reliquary was on the 'right-hand' (south) side of the altar of St Faith, to whom the crypt was dedicated.[8] One miracle from this period in the cult's development occurred when a painter decorating the crypt vault insisted on continuing to work on Earconwald's feast-day, even when people were coming to pray at the relics. The saint paralysed him as a fitting punishment.[9]

[3] See below, p. 173.

[4] *The Saint of London: The Life and Miracles of St. Erkenwald*, ed. and trans. E. Gordon Whatley (Binghampton, New York, 1989), 100–65. For Arcoid, see C. N. L. Brooke and G. Keir, *London 800–1216* (London, 1975), 356.

[5] Miracle 4, ed. Whatley, 120–9, at 120: ... *post altare dominicum sub theca lignea quiescebat, que altius quam statura sit hominis, super structuram lapideam in altum porrecta, ueteri palliolo tegebatur.*

[6] ibid., 126.

[7] Miracle 5, ed. Whatley, 128–33, at 128: *Peractis denique criptis, sanctissimi corpus Erkenwaldi ibidem collocari precepit.*

[8] Miracle 16, pp. 158–9.

[9] Miracle 17, pp. 158–61.

The crypt proved rather too secluded a location (though it presumably ensured the survival of the relics during the great fire of 1133), and in 1140/1, after an attempt had been made at stealing the relics, the canons resolved to move the shrine to a safer place (*in tutiori loco*).[10] Eight priests were accordingly appointed custodians during the three days required to arrange the translation. On 16 February 1140/1 the canons raised the lid of the wooden shrine, and 'found the most sacred body still protected by the same seals with which it had long before been secured'.[11] Later in this miracle story it is made clear that the body resided in an inner chest made of lead (*plumbeum sepulchrum*). Owing to some design fault, the new stone receptacle (*edificio*) built to house the lead coffin was not big enough, but fortunately the stonework miraculously adjusted itself to receive the relics: a common hagiographical *topos*.[12]

It was presumably in the context of this elevation that the shrine was refurbished, and a lively account of a miracle claimed to have occurred during these proceedings provides useful detail about its appearance. The wooden *cista* was being covered with silver and gold plates. A certain silversmith called Eustace, drunk as usual, came into the workshop and started fooling about with the other workers. Then he raised the lid of the chest, got into it, and impersonated the saint, saying 'I am the most holy Earconwald: bring me gifts, request my help, prepare for me a silver shrine (*ferculum*)!'[13] Needless to say he expired soon after. The story indicates that during the refurbishment the wooden *cista* was empty, so possibly the lead inner coffin had temporarily been transferred to the new stone monument behind the high altar. The story also indicates that the *cista* was the size of a full human body, even though the skeleton of the saint was presumably disarticulated. It was never claimed that Earconwald's remains were incorrupt.

Arcoid died *c.*1145, and thus did not live to see the inauguration of the final shrine, effectively a second translation, which took place on 14 November 1148.[14] It was then that the refurbished *feretrum* containing the relics was splendidly displayed behind the high altar of Bishop Mauritius's church. A century later, in 1245, Dean Henry of Cornhill described how the cathedral's principal relics were housed before the remodelling of the cathedral in the second half of the thirteenth century:

> The *feretrum* of blessed Eorcenweald is made of wood inside and covered on the outside with silver plates with images and [precious] stones. It is said that the stones total 130 … At the two

[10] Miracle 14, pp. 150–5, at 152.

[11] ibid., 152: … *cuius loculo ligneo subleuato, repperimus corpus sacratissimum isdem sigillorum munitionibus quibus iam pridem fuerat premunitum.*

[12] ibid., 152.

[13] Miracle 10, ed. Whatley, pp. 142–5, at 142: *Ego sum erkonwaldus sanctissimus: mihi munera deferte! A me auxilium postulate! Michi argenteum ferculum preparate!*

[14] Matthew Paris, *Chronica Maiora*, *s.a.* 1148; ed. Luard, ii.183: *Translatio sancti Erkenwaldi episcopi, decimo octavo kalendas Decembris.*

> ends (*capita*) of the same *feretrum* are placed two silver angels with iron brooches: they cost 40s.
>
> The *feretrum* called St Mellitus's is all of wood, only the front being covered in silver plates and images, over which stands a copper angel, completely gilded. These two [*feretra*] stand each side of the high altar.
>
> The *feretrum* above the high altar is of wood and old, covered all over with white silver, in which are various relics acquired from various collections.[15]

Sparrow Simpson, citing Dugdale, thought that these *feretra* were simply portable reliquaries standing on a beam over the altar, and that Earconwald's main shrine was elsewhere, east of the high altar. However, the account of the 1326–7 translation in the *Annales Paulini* specifically states that the relics had previously been transferred to 'near the high altar' (*prope magnum altare*), so it is perhaps reasonable to suppose that the *feretrum* of Earconwald described by Dean Henry was the same reliquary that featured in the earlier miracle accounts. It is however regrettable that our source, though rich in detail on the *feretra*, provides no information about the way they were supported.

HENRY OF BLOIS AND THE BENEFACTORS OF WINCHESTER

Henry of Blois, abbot of Glastonbury from 1126 and concurrently bishop of Winchester from 1129 until his death in 1171, was one of the most significant figures of the English Church in the twelfth century, and as sub-dean of the province of Canterbury second only to Thomas Becket, at whose archiepiscopal consecration he presided. Henry was the younger brother of King Stephen, being the Conqueror's grandson through his mother, Adela. Inevitably, given his royal connections, he was deeply involved in the politics of his day; unlike Becket, he did not die a martyr's death and there was never any question of his becoming a saint. He was renowned in his own times as being both 'monk and soldier' (*monachus et miles*), displaying his prowess in the twelfth-century Civil War.[16] With the accession of Henry II, and following a period of exile at Cluny, Henry turned increasingly to charitable

[15] 'Two Inventories of the Cathedral Church of St. Paul, London, dated respectively 1245 and 1402 ...', ed. W. Sparrow Simpson, *Archæologia*, 50, pt. ii (1887), 439–524, at 469–70. *Feretrum beati Erkenwaldi est interius ligneum extra coopertum platis argenteis cum ymaginibus et lapidibus. Est autem summa lapidum, ut dicitur, C. et xxx. ... Ad duo capita feretri eiusdem apponuntur duo angeli cum brochis ferreis; ponderant lx. solid. Feretrum quod dicitur Sancti Melliti totum ligneum, fronte solum cooperto platis argenteis et ymaginibus, cui imponitur angelus de cupro totus deauratus, et hæc duo sunt collateralia in magno altari. Feretrum supra magnum altare ligneum est et vetus, et coopertum albo argento undique, in quo sunt diversæ reliquiæ collectæ e diversis collectionibus.* (Details of other *feretra* and relics follow.)

[16] Henry of Huntington, *De Contemptu Mundi*, cap. 15; *Henry, Archdeacon of Huntingdon: Historia Anglorum, The History of the English People*, bk. viii, ed. D. Greenway, OMT (Oxford, 1996), 584–619, at 601–11. Henry calls his namesake 'a new kind of monster, composed part pure and part corrupt, I mean part monk and part knight'.

works. He is especially remembered at Winchester Cathedral for the lavish gifts which he bestowed upon his church,[17] and for his services as a great patron of the arts. The renowned Winchester Bible was almost certainly produced under his patronage; the Tournai marble font dates from his episcopate; and he probably commissioned the famous wall-paintings of the Holy Sepulchre chapel, though he may not have lived to see the completion of that project.

Such is the context of several significant translations of saintly bones in Winchester Cathedral in the mid-twelfth century. According to the *Winchester Annals*, '1150. In this year relics were translated of the holy confessors Birinus, Swithun, Hæddi, Beornstan, and Ælfheah.'[18] Whether Bishop Henry was involved is uncertain. He had recently returned from Rome, whither he had gone to seek pardon from Pope Eugenius III for failing to attend the Council of Rheims in 1148. At that time the local affairs of Winchester Cathedral were probably of secondary concern to him. As we shall see,[19] a fifteenth-century Winchester historian made use of a lost document describing the deeds (*Acta*) of Bishop Henry, and if the translations of 1150 had been really significant they would presumably have been chronicled in that text and relayed to us by the later historian.

Apart from the annal nothing else is known of the 1150 translations. Its wording and the fact that relics of so many Anglo-Saxon saints were involved probably indicate that only fragments of the various saints' bodies were moved: *reliquiæ* could be translated 'some relics' as well as 'the relics'. In any case, the greater part of Archbishop Ælfheah's body was at Canterbury. There is no reason to suppose that the reliquary containing the main group of Swithun's bones changed its location. In the later middle ages St Birinus (for whom a rival claim was held by the monks of Dorchester-on-Thames) was commemorated in his own chapel at the south-east corner of the rebuilt east arm of Winchester Cathedral, and his altar may have been situated in the corresponding chapel of the Romanesque cathedral. As for Bishops Hæddi and Beornstan, we know only that their tombs were a prominent feature of Winchester's Old Minster, and the 1150 annal is the last time we hear of their relics at Winchester. In short, the translations of 1150 were probably a modest affair, of local interest only.

Nevertheless, these translations, however insignificant, may be regarded as a prelude to a much more extensive reordering of Winchester Cathedral's illustrious dead in 1158, immediately after Bishop Henry's return from

[17] E. Bishop, 'Gifts of Bishop Henry of Blois, Abbot of Glastonbury to Winchester Cathedral', *Downside Review* (1884), 33–44, reprinted in *Liturgica Historica* (1918), 392–401. See also the more recent study by P. Ward, 'Saint-seducing gold; Henry of Blois and two accounts of his gifts to Winchester Cathedral', unpubl. dissertation for University of London Diploma in Medieval History, May 2006.

[18] *Winchester Annals*, *s.a.* 1150; ed. Luard, 54. *Hoc anno translatæ sunt reliquiæ sanctorum confessorum Birini, Swithuni, Æddæ, Birstani, Elfegi.*

[19] Below, p. 175.

Cluny. He is said to have raised 'from a lowly place' the relics of certain unnamed kings and bishops who had previously been buried in Old Minster, placing them in lead caskets near the high altar.[20] As I have investigated in greater detail elsewhere,[21] he thus initiated a prolonged sequence of arrangements for housing the remains of pre-Conquest individuals who, though not saints, were regarded as benefactors of the church of Winchester. Even today the bones of some of the people in question almost certainly reside in the sixteenth- and seventeenth-century mortuary chests on the screen walls either side of the presbytery of Winchester Cathedral. Allegedly containing, as their inscriptions proclaim, the bones of early pre-Conquest monarchs and bishops, these chests are the direct descendants of Henry of Blois's lead caskets. The identity of the 'lowly place' from which Bishop Henry raised the remains of the Winchester benefactors is debated. It is likely that the bones of the earlier group of Anglo-Saxon kings and bishops, having been exhumed from Old Minster when that church was demolished in 1093–4, were placed within the crypt of Walkelin's new cathedral. The identity even of the earliest royal and episcopal burials in the Anglo-Saxon cathedral of Winchester probably remained known whilst that church remained standing, because the individuals concerned would have been commemorated annually at their tombs, but the situation evidently changed when their unmarked sarcophagi were transferred to the Norman cathedral. Fortunately, fragments of the lost twelfth-century *Acta* of Bishops William Giffard and Henry of Blois have survived, embedded within the so-called *Liber Historialis* of Winchester Cathedral, and this early source specifically says that the sarcophagi from which Bishop Henry removed the royal and episcopal bones bore no inscriptions. It seems, therefore, that by the 1150s the identities of the individuals concerned had been lost. Prior Robert relates that Bishop Henry simply placed in the new lead receptacles a jumble of 'kings with bishops and bishops with kings, all mixed up together'. This was the beginning of a mingling of skeletal remains that is still apparent in the way the bones are preserved today. Another, later, group of burials was however more likely to have been identifiable.[22] The bodies of recent monarchs, such as Cnut and Hardacnut, together with Queen Emma, all of whom were perhaps buried within the late tenth-century eastern extension to Old Minster, were probably not relegated to the crypt. Martin Biddle has argued that their sarcophagi were placed in the presbytery of the new cathedral, possibly on the low stylobate wall between the piers of the Norman choir arcade. There they remained until the fourteenth-century

[20] The event is recorded in a cartulary of Winchester Cathedral (MS, Winchester Cathedral Archives) item 4: *Chartulary of Winchester Cathedral*, ed. A. W. Goodman (Winchester, 1927), 3.

[21] John Crook, 'The architectural setting of the cult of St Swithun in Winchester Cathedral, 1093–1536', in *Winchester Studies*, 4.i, ed. M. Biddle, forthcoming.

[22] For this suggestion I am indebted to M. Biddle and B. Kjølbye-Biddle, 'Knud den Store og hans familie', in *Selskabet til Udgivelse af Danske Mindesmærker*, ed. K. Kryger, forthcoming.

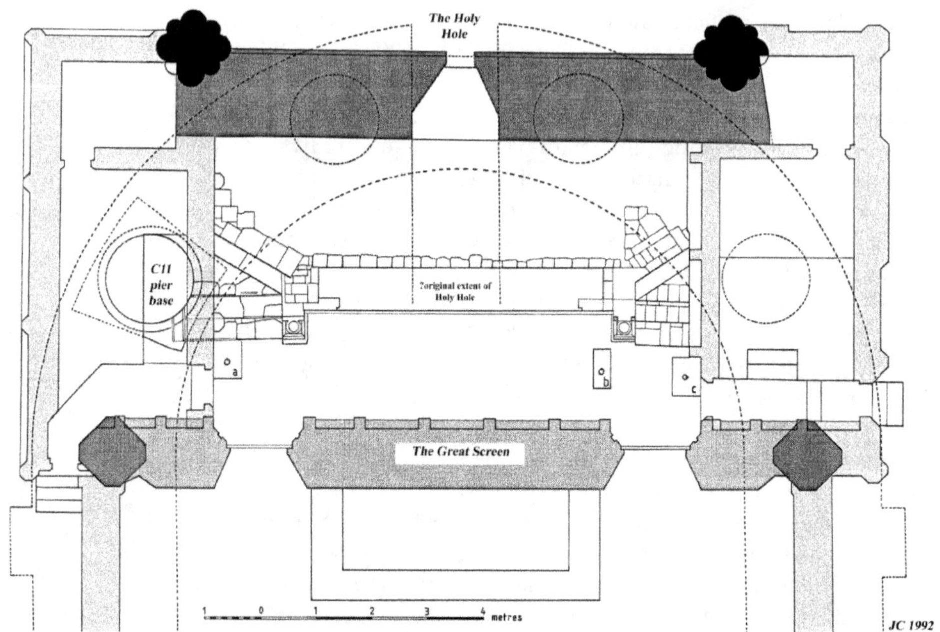

FIG. 7.1 WINCHESTER CATHEDRAL Plan of the feretory, showing position of the 'Holy Hole' formed within a platform inserted into the apse by Bishop Henry of Blois in the 1150s.

remodelling of the presbytery or perhaps even until the early sixteenth century. In support of this view is the fact that three other royal bodies, those of Hardacnut, Earl Bjorn, and Richard of Normandy, seem still to lie entombed in similar positions between the fourteenth-century piers that replaced the Norman arcade. The coffins needed to be moved only a short distance when the presbytery was reconstructed, to take account of the different spacing of the replacement piers. The argument of continuity of place is compelling.

The elevation of the royal and episcopal remains into their lead caskets is only part of the story. Surviving within the 'feretory' (a nineteenth-century term), immediately east of the Great Screen behind the high altar, are the remains of a masonry platform that was constructed within the apse of Bishop Walkelin's choir in the later twelfth century. As originally built, the floor in this area was 555mm above the pavement level of the ambulatory around the choir, an enhancement intended to give greater prominence to the high altar. The inserted platform raised the floor level at the apex of the apse by a further 1095mm. This addition is datable from its architectural detailing (including tooling and geology), and the most likely context for its construction was a major reordering of the high altar area undertaken by Bishop Henry in the 1150s, perhaps alluded to in the memorandum cited above. The platform terminated in a vertical wall on the west side, behind the high altar, and was accessed via flights of stairs on either side. These steps, which partially survive, abutted two of the cylindrical piers of the apse

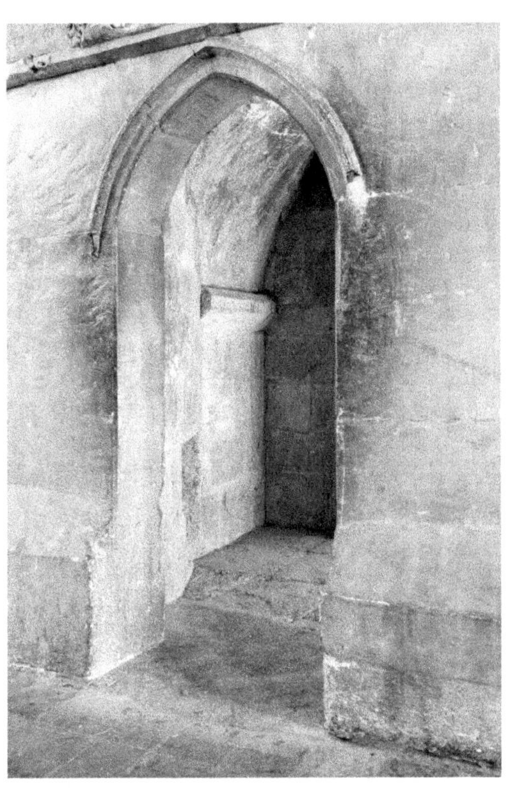

PLATE 7.1 WINCHESTER CATHEDRAL The 'Holy Hole', with twelfth-century masonry visible through the early fourteenth-century arch.

and covered their moulded bases. The most interesting feature of the platform was a tunnel leading westwards from the Romanesque ambulatory. Despite the almost complete remodelling of this part of the eastern arm in the fourteenth century, and the demolition of much of the tunnel at the Reformation, a short length of the Romanesque passage survives. It appears originally to have continued as far as the western face of the platform, though it was truncated when a reliquary *armoire* was inserted into that side of the platform, probably in the early fourteenth century as discussed below.

The tunnel has been known as the 'Holy Hole' since at least the fifteenth century, and I have long argued that its purpose was to provide limited access for pilgrims wishing to venerate the relics of St Swithun. As we have seen, the Anglo-Saxon reliquary containing that saint's bones was located within the apse, either on the high altar (as depicted in the library wall-painting) or perhaps more probably behind the altar, possibly on a secondary altar within the apse. Thus, the tunnel would have functioned in a similar way to a ring-crypt, albeit on a smaller scale, allowing the faithful to crawl westwards, in a suitably humble posture, to a location beneath the bones.

Living pilgrims were perhaps not the only individuals to benefit from the saint's presence. Although the memorandum in the Winchester Cathedral chartulary states only that the remains of a mixed bunch of early Anglo-Saxon saints and bishops were elevated 'near to the high altar', it is possible to argue that Bishop Henry's motive was also to place the bones of more certainly identified individuals closer to the cathedral's principal relic. The lead coffers containing their bones seem to have stood on the curved retaining wall enclosing the feretory platform, where the position of each coffer was marked by an inscription carved in the stonework of that wall, each stating that such-and-such an individual 'lies here'. We know this because twelve inscribed blocks, splayed on plan so as to fit together to form a curve matching the radius of the apse, have been recovered from later partition walls within the cathedral. Three inscriptions may be reconstituted from these remains by comparing them with later Winchester manuscripts such as the *Liber Historialis*, the wording of whose relevant sections may actually have been copied from the inscriptions themselves. The *tituli* relating to Cynegils of Wessex and Ecgberht are typical: 'Here lies [king] Cynegils who gave Chilcombe' (*Hic iacet Kingilsus qui dedit Chiltecombe*) and 'Here lies Ecgberht, who gave to this church Droxford, Worthy, Alton, and Bedhampton' (*Hic iacet Egbertus qui dedit huic ecclesie Droxford, Worthy, Alton et Bedhampton*). Not only was each monarch named, but also the lands which he was supposed to have settled on the cathedral priory. Likewise a later figure, Bishop Ælfwine, was commemorated by a lengthy inscription commemorating his gift of nine manors, a donation made after he had been cleared of a charge of an adulterous relationship with Queen Emma. The nine manors corresponded to the nine red-hot plough-shares on which she walked to prove her innocence. She might have preferred to have made a monetary payment like the bishop.

THE ELY BENEFACTORS

The individuals in the Winchester mortuary chests were not saints, but the arrangement ordered by Bishop Henry ensured that in death they lay *ad sanctum*, close to Winchester's principal saint. The elevation of the mixed batch of benefactors in 1158 may, in fact, have been inspired by a similar event at Ely Cathedral.[23] There in around 1154 Prior Alexander is said to have translated into the Romanesque cathedral the bones of seven men who were regarded as the foundation's greatest benefactors. Amongst their number was Archbishop Wulfstan of York, who before his death in 1023 had requested, following the promptings of a miracle, to be buried in the Anglo-Saxon priory church at Ely. Another was Ealdorman Byrhtnoth, famously slain at the Battle of Maldon in 991. There were also five other pre-Conquest bishops, who were remembered in the *Liber Eliensis* as having endowed the monastery with gifts of land.

Soon after being brought into Ely Cathedral the bones seem to have been placed in niches (*loculi*) on the north side of the wall at the rear of the choir-stalls, which at that time were located beneath the Norman tower. The compiler of the *Liber* says that each *loculus* had an inscription saying who was buried within it. The tower collapsed in 1322 and was replaced by the famous Octagon. It is possible that a short length of the choir wall containing the *loculi* was retained, to be incorporated in the fourteenth-century choir wall, but this contention depends on the stylistic analysis of a somewhat ambiguous eighteenth-century drawing. Certainly the bones remained in the wall from the early fourteenth century until 1769 when it was demolished. The eighteenth-century antiquaries who witnessed the works described the *loculi*, which were located within the sills of seven architectural

[23] For a detailed account of the Ely remains, see J. Crook, '*Vir Optimus Wlstanus*: The post-Conquest commemoration of Archbishop Wulfstan of York at Ely Cathedral', in *Wulfstan, Archbishop of York*, Proc. of the Second Alcuin Conference (York, 15–18 July 2002), Studies in the Early Middle Ages, 10, ed. M. Townend (Turnhout, 2004), 501–24.

niches of thirteenth- or fourteenth-century date. The niches themselves were adorned with mid-fourteenth-century wall-paintings and inscriptions. The bones were subsequently moved to the south-east chapel of the cathedral, where they were incorporated in the superstructure of Bishop West's tomb.

Although it cannot be held that the Ely benefactors had been moved to a position *ad sanctum* (as already noted, the relics of the Ely saints were located much further east, behind the high altar),[24] nevertheless there are clear parallels with the treatment of their counterparts at Winchester: the elevation into a worthy architectural setting, the marking of their tombs with inscriptions, and indeed the continuation of these 'cults' by subsequent architectural embellishment of their final resting places. Neither at Ely nor Winchester were there reliable charters to record the alleged donations given by the benefactors, but at both cathedrals this lack was compensated by the very presence of the donors themselves. At Winchester the inscriptions clearly stating who had given what to the priory were the lapidary equivalents of charters; at Ely the deficiency was made good by appropriate passages in the *Liber Eliensis*.

ITHAMAR OF ROCHESTER

The cult of Ithamar of Rochester seems to have come into being around 1150. Ithamar was Paulinus's successor, a Kentish man, and the first native English bishop; Bede commented that he was nevertheless 'the equal of his predecessors in learning and in holiness of life'.[25] Richard Sharpe has pointed out that the saint's unusual name was borrowed from the Old Testament, Ithamar being one of the four sons of Aaron and founder of a priestly line.[26] The name was perhaps conferred on the bishop at his consecration, and was particularly appropriate for one who was first in the succession of English prelates. He died *c.*660, but the exact year is unknown.

The first secure evidence for the cult is a collection of *miracula* preserved in Corpus Christi College Cambridge, MS 161.[27] This compilation of various saints' legends is broadly datable to the late twelfth to early thirteenth centuries in its present form, but its editor argues from internal evidence that the text relating to Ithamar was composed in the 1150s. It states that the remains of the saint had been translated at least twice during the first half of the twelfth century. The first translation was said to have been during the time of Bishop Gundulf 'from the place where he had first been buried into a certain high vault on the north side [of the new cathedral]'. Sometime later, after an elderly monk had been cured of his failing sight through the action of the saint, Gundulf moved the reliquary chest (*theca*, the Greek equivalent of *scrinium*) to a 'more honourable place' (*in loco decentiori*) in

[24] Above, p. 156.
[25] Bede, *HE*, iii.14; ed. Colgrave and Mynors, 256–7.
[26] R. Sharpe, 'The Naming of Bishop Ithamar', *EHR*, cxvii, no. 473 (Sept. 2002), 889–94.
[27] *Miracula Ithamari*; ed. Bethell, 421–37.

the presbytery, where the bones would be accessible to all; many miracles occurred there. Finally the relics were rehoused in a 'new and more worthy reliquary' (*de priore t[h]eca ... in novam et decentiorem*) by Bishop John (1125–37), who had also been cured of an eye complaint through the powers of the saint. This event took place on an unspecified 10 June, which thereafter was celebrated as the saint's feast-day. In the early fourteenth century the compiler of the Rochester version of the *Flores Historiarum* dated the third translation of the relics to 1128, but there is no corroborative evidence that it occurred in that year.[28] All one can safely infer is that the cult had almost certainly come into being by the mid-century.

The Corpus Christi *Miracula* provide a few clues as to the way Ithamar's relics were enshrined by the time those miracle accounts were compiled. In one miracle, a deformed dumb woman sought a cure from the saint: we are told that having climbed up the steps as far as the entrance to the presbytery, she was able to see Ithamar's *feretrum* 'in the distance' (*eminus*).[29] It was not long before the hoped-for cure took place. The author of the *Miracula* and his fellow monks were singing the saint's festival mass in the choir at the time, and from there they could hear the noise of the excited populace, rushing 'as if to a spectacle' (*quasi ad spectaculum*) to witness the miracle.[30] As with the first post-Conquest miracle of St Paulinus, this story preserves a precious indication of the position of the shrine, which was apparently in the raised eastern arm, above the crypt. The word *eminus* implies, furthermore, that the shrine was located at some distance eastwards from the top of the steps. In another miracle story, an aged monk claimed to have dreamt that he was standing by the [high] altar, from where he saw SS. Peter and Andrew, Paulinus and Ithamar, standing on 'the beam which overhangs the cross' (*que imminet crucem*) and pointing at the reliquary chests (*capsas*).[31]

Cumulatively, these fragmentary circumstantial details suggest that Ithamar's relics, like those of Paulinus, were located at the east end of the Romanesque church, behind the high altar. If the east end was apsidal the beam could have been located on the chord of the apse as at Bury St Edmunds;[32] the monk in the last miracle may have dreamed that the saints were pointing down at the shrines beyond the altar.

Finally, Ithamar's *Miracula* also provide some detail about the shrine itself. It is referred to as a *feretrum*, and on one side was a 'depiction' of the saint. This was used by a widow suffering from chronic fever to create holy water by contact with the image,[33] a procedure for which several parallels

[28] BL, Cotton MS Nero D.II, fo. 110v: published by Henry Wharton, *Anglia Sacra*, 343. The passage is, however, tacitly rejected by Luard in his edition (*Flores Historiarum*).
[29] *Miracula Ithamari*; ed. Bethell, 436.
[30] ibid., 437.
[31] ibid., 436.
[32] Crook, *Architectural Setting*, 192–3.
[33] *Miracula Ithamari*, cap. 7; ed. Bethell, 426.

occur in Merovingian hagiography.[34] Her action suggests that the 'depiction' was not merely painted, but might have been a bas-relief sculpture in repoussé metal. The *feretrum*, like that of Paulinus, was presumably raised up on some sort of shrine-base to form a composite monument.

CULTS OF ALLEGEDLY RITUALLY MURDERED CHILDREN

The enthusiasm for local saints' cults was also apparent at Norwich Cathedral in the early 1150s. A new cult developed around a twelve-year-old boy called William, who had allegedly been ritually murdered by Jews in 1144. For the legend we are totally dependent upon a contemporary, Thomas of Monmouth, who became a monk at Norwich cathedral priory shortly before 1150, and compiled a Life and *Miracula* of the saint in 1172–3. He dedicated it to that zealous inquisitor of the Jews, William Turbe, bishop of Norwich *c.*1146–74.[35] By then Thomas had long been sacrist, with special responsibility for the shrine. The story of William's murder, which Thomas claimed to have obtained from his fellow-monk Theobald, a Jew who had converted to Christianity, is needless to say highly suspect. William's body had been miraculously discovered lying in Thorpe Wood when first a nun then a forester spotted a column of light gleaming above it like a ladder of fire ascending to heaven. The little corpse was initially buried in the wood. Within a month, still incorrupt, it was carried to the cathedral, to be interred in the monks' cemetery on 24 April 1144.[36] All these events took place before Thomas of Monmouth joined the monastery. He claimed to have seen visions during the Lenten fast of 1150, when the long-deceased Bishop Herbert Losinga, the first bishop of Norwich (†1119), appeared to him three times in succession. As Thomas himself realised, this occurrence was reminiscent of the revelation of Gamaliel to Lucian regarding the relics of St Stephen. On the third occasion Herbert told him to pass to the present bishop a message that the saintly body should no longer rest hidden away in the cemetery, but should initially be buried amongst the boys' seats in the chapter house. The message was duly relayed via Prior Elias, and the translation took place just before Easter.[37] However, the coffin refused to remain submerged beneath the pavement, and subsequently floated up even higher. Despite these alarming manifestations the prior was reluctant to promote the cult. Following further miracles (some caused by water made holy by contact with scrapings from the tomb), and with the encouragement of Elias's successor, Prior Richard, the body was translated into the actual cathedral in 1151. It seems initially to have been placed on the south side of the high altar, but

[34] Crook, *Architectural Setting*, 27–31.

[35] *The Life and Miracles of St William of Norwich by Thomas of Monmouth*, ed. A. Jessopp and M. R. James (Cambridge, 1896).

[36] ibid., i.17–19; ed. Jessopp and James, 49–55.

[37] ibid., iii.1–2; pp. 116–27.

Thomas says that the place was not suitable to receive hordes of pilgrims, so in 1154 it was moved 'from the south side of the high altar to the north side, namely to the altar [formerly] called of the Holy Martyrs'.[38] Thomas states that their new 'quiet resting-place' was 'under the side of the high altar screen' (*sub latere magni altaris cancellus*).[39] For Jessopp and James this was the present Jesus chapel,[40] though this is on the other side of the ambulatory, scarcely close to the high altar. By the Reformation the saint's altar was at the north end of the rood screen. There does not appear to be any surviving physical evidence for the cult, and references to the medieval shrine provide little information: it was gilded and painted in 1305,[41] but by the mid-fourteenth century the cult attracted very few pilgrims and offerings at the shrine were negligible.[42]

The case of St William does little credit to the Christian church. A similar legend grew up a century later at Lincoln, where 'Little St Hugh' was said to have been martyred by the Jews in 1255. Finally, for the sake of completeness, we should mention that at Bury St Edmunds, there was an unsuccessful and unofficial cult of St Robert, also alleged to have been crucified by the Jews in 1181.[43] William Worcestre visited Bury in May 1479, and noted that the local saint's feast was held on an unnamed day in May.[44]

THE TRANSLATIONS AT HEXHAM IN THE MID-TWELFTH CENTURY

The twelfth-century enthusiasm for saints' cults spread throughout England. In the mid-century, when local saints' cults were being promoted at Lincoln, Ely, and elsewhere, the posthumous fortunes of the saints of Hexham, that great cult centre of the north, were also given a significant boost when their relics were translated on 3 March 1155.[45] Ailred of Rievaulx's account is particularly valuable as one of the most complete surviving descriptions of a major translation in the mid-twelfth century.[46]

[38] ibid., vi.i: *De quarta translatione sancti Martiris a latere magni altaris ad austrum ad latus aquilonale, ad altare scilicet quod dicebatur sanctorum martirum*; ed. Jessopp and James, 220–2. The chapter heading is the only evidence for the temporary station on the south side.
[39] ibid., ed. Jessopp and James, 221. *Cancellus* is usually second declension rather than fourth, but this is the only possible translation.
[40] ibid., lxxii.
[41] ibid., pp. lxxxiii–lxxxiv.
[42] ibid., pp. lxxxiii–lxxxiv.
[43] The so-called 'martyrdom' is mentioned by Jocelin of Brakelond, who claims to have written up the cult 'elsewhere', presumably in the form of *Miracula*: *Memorials of Bury*, ed. Arnold, i. 223. Cf. the 'Bury Chronicle', ibid., iii. 6, giving the date 10 June (*iiij. idus Iunii*), which Arnold says was obtained from Taxter.
[44] *William Worcestre, Itineraries*, ed. J. Harvey, OMT (Oxford, 1979), 162–3: *Sanctus Robertus puer crucifixus per Iudeos apud Bery dies eius agitur [blank] die mensis Iunii sed celebratur die [blank] Maii.* According to Thomas Arnold, *Memorials of Bury* i. 223, marginal note, he died on 10 June 1181.
[45] i.e. 1154 old style.
[46] Ailred, *Saints of Hexham*, caps. xi, xiii–xv; ed. Raine, 190–195, 199–203.

As we have seen, Eilav II had placed the relics of Acca and Alchmund in a single reliquary; Eata remained separately enshrined in the south *porticus*. Ailred explains that the new canons of Hexham felt that their saints were no longer worthily enshrined; they were indignant that they were housed together in boxes of common wood, scarcely a worthy or glorious sight for the common people who so often enjoyed the benefits that the saints could confer on them.[47] So, having discussed the matter and worked themselves up into a fine frenzy, they approached Prior Richard with a proposal to house the relics in a more becoming manner. Accordingly, three new reliquaries were prepared. The largest was 'of suitable size, covered with silver and gold', and adorned with jewels.[48] The two smaller reliquaries were equally finely decorated but more cheaply.[49] Prior Richard announced the date of the translation, and the brethren prepared themselves with psalms, prayers, and spiritual exercises.

The great day arrived, and at around nine in the morning the prior and brethren assembled in the church, prostrating themselves barefoot in front of the high altar. They chanted in a loud voice both the penitential psalms and suitable prayers for confessors. Then, dressed in albs and still barefoot, the brethren placed the old reliquary (that Eilav had created) on the pavement west of the altar step, a suitably spacious and sacred working area. Having taken out the relics, they laid them out on cloths (*pallia*) on the pavement. They found that there were four sets, each wrapped in a most elegant cloth. As the canons began to unroll the bundles they were conscious of a marvellous fragrance, and at first they conjectured that the bodies had been buried with spices (*aromata*). Then they realised that it they were smelling the sweet scent of Paradise, which God had conferred on the bishops as an act of grace.

On opening the first bundle, they revealed gleaming bones. Fortunately it was possible to identify which saint it belonged to, thanks to a label (*cedula*), presumably deposited as a certificate of authenticity when Eilav II translated the relics, proclaiming that the relics were those of Bishop Acca. The bones were wrapped again in clean cloths, and in order that the information provided on the *cedula* should not be lost, it was copied out on parchment and was also inscribed on a lead plate: *in membrana simul et plumbi lamina eadem scribentes et sculpentes, reliquiis apposuerunt.*

The bones of Alchmund were also conveniently identified by a similar label (Ailred does not say whether the monks recopied the information, though this must be likely). The contents of the third bundle also bore a label proving them to be relics of St Fritheberht (bishop of Hexham, 734–766). Both sets of bones were wrapped up again. But the fourth set of

[47] ibid., 193: *Indignabantur vili tectos ligno, nichil gloriæ et honoris plebis præferre conspectibus, quæ eius beneficiis sæpius iocundabatur.*

[48] ibid., 194: *Paratur theca congruæ magnitudinis, argentoque et auro vestitur. Inseruntur locis convenientibus gemmæ, et pro artificis industria opus summo decore variatur.*

[49] ibid. *Compinguntur etiam duæ minores non parvi decoris, quamvis non eiusdem pretii.*

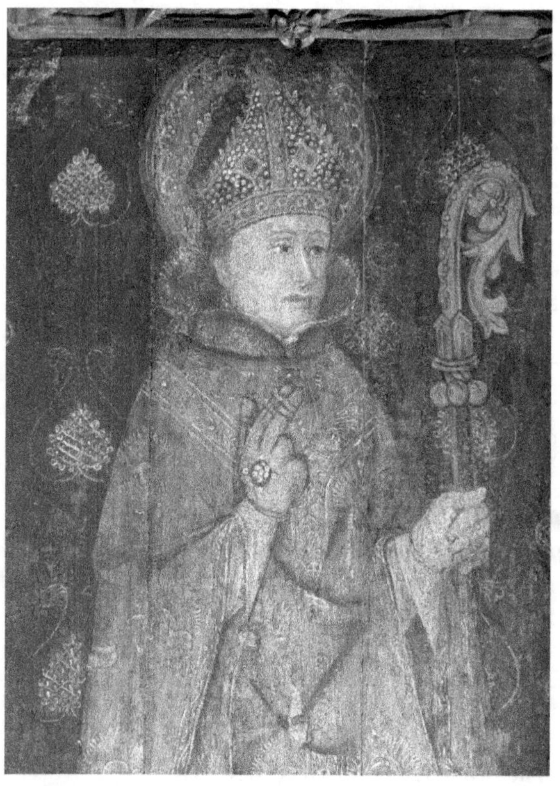

PLATE 7.2
HEXHAM ABBEY
A fifteenth-century portrait of St Alchmund from the screen on the north side of the choir.

relics was unmarked. Ailred then recalled that during his childhood it had been common knowledge that the *loculus* also contained the bones of Bishop Tilberht (†789), so everyone accepted that the unnamed relics must be his. All four sets of bones, having been individually wrapped in precious cloths, were placed in the large reliquary in order that they should remain together just as they had been found.

Next the *scrinium* containing St Eata's bones was opened. As we have seen, by the date of this translation this reliquary was probably still displayed in the south *porticus*. Again, his sanctity was manifested by a miraculous fragrance. Within the reliquary was a lead *uas* (perhaps a purse reliquary) containing a few particles from the body of St Fritheberht. The brethren replaced these in one of the reliquaries that they had prepared, together with fragments claimed to come from the body of St Babylas (a third-century bishop of Antioch), and particles from the bones of St Acca and Alchmund.

Finally, the great new reliquary arrangement was prepared. A shelf (*tabula*) had been erected just behind the high altar (Ailred says it was 'alongside' (*secus*) the altar). It was supported on three columns and was decorated with 'sculptures' (*sculpturis*, presumably bas-reliefs) and paintings. At the centre was the 'great shrine' (*scrinium maius*), containing the remains of Acca, Alchmund, Fritheberht, and Tilberht. This was flanked by the two smaller reliquaries. St Eata's *theca* was on the right; on the left (north) side was a miscellaneous collection comprising relics of Fritheberht from Eata's previous *theca*, and fragments of the bones of Babylas, Acca, and Alchmund.[50] It is therefore clear that the *tabula* was aligned north-south.

This interpretation is confirmed by what Prior Richard says about the translation in his *History of the Church of Hexham*, though he claims no credit for what must have been largely his initiative.[51] He adds elsewhere that

[50] Ailred, *Saints of Hexham*, cap. 13; ed. Raine, 200.
[51] 'Prior Richard's History', ii.4; Raine, *Hexham Priory*, 8–62, at 48–9.

he intended writing up the miracles of the saints of Hexham, which might have included more details of the translation.[52] His main concern was to stress that, despite the vicissitudes of Danish, Norman, and Scottish incursions, Hexham never lost the bodies of its major saintly bishops. He added that many other unnamed relics which had subsequently been given to the church were placed nearby, no doubt in order to benefit from the *præsentia* of the three major saints.[53] He described how the relics of SS. Acca and Alchmund had been placed in a single *theca* (also called a *loculus*) 'next to and behind the altar' (*retro et iuxta altare*). In the same chest were relics of Fritheberht and Tilberht. St Eata's relics were in another *theca* 'to the south', and further 'dust' of Acca and Alchmund 'to the north'. In another passage, Richard refers to the 'feretory of the holy relics which is behind the altar' (*feretrum sanctarum reliquiarum quod est post altare*), indicating that the word *feretrum* was used for the whole ensemble.

Unfortunately there is no archaeological evidence for the form of the reliquary arrangement, nor any documentary evidence for the later shrines of the Hexham saints. The east end of the church, where the high altar was located, was remodelled in the later twelfth century, a few decades after the translation of 1154. The earlier eastern arm appears to have been apsidal. During the replacement of the choir pavement in May 1908 two, presumably successive, apses seem to have been discovered, but the published archaeological record of that excavation is regrettably inadequate. The local architect and enthusiastic historian of Hexham Abbey, Charles Clement Hodges, referred briefly to the discovery of the 'Norman apse' in a revision of his guidebook, but his accompanying sketch depicted only the westernmost, 'Saxon' apse, which was apparently deemed of greater interest, and which was preserved beneath a trapdoor in the choir floor.[54] The position of the 'Norman apse' is shown in Hodges' plan in the same guide. However, the most complete record is a tracing, referred to as a 'composite plan', which Hodges sent to Professor Gerard Baldwin Brown for inclusion in the second edition of that author's massive work on Anglo-Saxon art and architecture. It was not actually published but formed the basis for a very poor 'sketch plan' of Wilfrid's church, in which the supposed 'Norman apse' was entirely omitted.[55] Fortunately Hodges' plan survived and was finally published by Harold and Joan Taylor.[56]

[52] ibid., ii.15; p. 36.
[53] ibid., 49.
[54] C. C. Hodges, *Guide to the Priory Church of St Andrew, Hexham* (Hexham, 1913), 32–4.
[55] G. Baldwin Brown, *The Arts in Early England*, 6 vols., 2nd edn. (London, 1925), ii (1925), 'Anglo-Saxon Architecture', 167–75. Brown excused Hodges (ibid., 167), on the grounds that 'he has unfortunately been precluded by ill-health from working up [the material] into a clearly defined form'.
[56] Taylor, *Anglo-Saxon Architecture*, i. 298–300 and fig. 130. Hodges' papers at that time were apparently in the possession of Prof. Bruce Dickens and Mr P. Hunter Blair (ibid., 299, n. 2). His plan is also reproduced and discussed in R. N. Bailey, 'The Anglo-Saxon Church at Hexham', *Archaeologia Aeliana*, 5th ser., 4 (1976), 47–67 and *idem*, 'St. Wilfrid. Ripon and Hexham', in *Studies in Insular Art and Archaeology*, ed. C. Karkov and R. Farrell, American Early Medieval Studies, i (Oxford Ohio, 1991), 3–25, at 14–15 and fig. 5.

The Taylors argued that the westernmost apse, identified as 'Saxon', may have belonged to a free-standing chapel to the east of the main church, of which Wilfrid's crypt is the sole surviving portion.[57] The apse further east is more dubious. It must be said that Hodges' identification of two rows of stones which seem to curve inwards towards each other at the eastern end could be just wishful thinking. If it really is an apse, it must be of later date than the 'Saxon' one, but there is no evidence for a [re]construction of the choir until the late twelfth century, to which some of the surviving work of the square-ended Transitional choir may be dated. When first discovered in May 1908 the supposed eastern apse was identified as 'the ancient foundation ... of a Norman choir, which must have been erected by the Augustinian canons between 1113 and 1140'.[58] Hodges later dated it on 'documentary evidence' to 1153, without citing his source,[59] while Pevsner opted for a reconstruction after the arrival of the Augustinian canons in 1113.[60]

It is a pleasant end to the story of Ailred of Rievaulx that he soon became the centre of a cult at his abbey in that remote Yorkshire valley. He died on 8 January 1166/7 and was buried in the chapter house, next to the tomb of the founder, William of Rievaulx (†1148); the body began to work miracles even before he was laid to rest.[61] Later the body was translated into a shrine within the church, presumably behind the high altar.

Another remote northern saint was the hermit Godric of Finchale, who, after a life of prayer and privation, died on 21 May 1170, aged around a hundred, in the church of St John the Baptist. The church, which towards the end of his life he used as his dwelling, was part of a small monastic community that had developed on the site of his hermitage, next to the river Wear, downstream from the parent priory of Durham. He was buried next to the altar of St John, on the south side of the church, on the spot where had died. Reginald of Durham, who wrote his Life and *Miracula*, briefly describes his tomb: it was firmly bound on four sides by double-ended iron straps curved around the corners and set in lead.[62] The main relic of the saint was the breastplate (*lorica*) which he had worn for fifty years. Godric immediately became the focus of a cult, the first miracle being when a sick woman was cured by means of water in which the rings of his breastplate

[57] As first suggested by Harold and Joan Taylor, 'The Seventh-Century Church at Hexham: a New Appreciation', *Archaeologia Aeliana*, 4th ser., 39 (1961), 103–34; idem, *Anglo-Saxon Architecture*, i. 306–8.

[58] *The Hexham Courant*, 16 May 1908.

[59] Hodges, *Guide*, 36.

[60] N. Pevsner and others, *The Buildings of England: Northumberland*, rev. edn. (Harmondsworth, 1992), 319.

[61] *The Life of Ailred of Rievaulx by Walter Daniel*, ed. and trans. M. Powicke, 2nd edn., OMT (Oxford, 1978), 62–4.

[62] Reginald of Durham, *Libellus de vita et miraculis S. Godrici, heremitæ de Finchale*, ed. J. Stevenson, Surtees Soc., 20 (1847), 332: *signatum est eius monumentum, et per regiones quatuor ferreis ligaminibus bicipiti fine aduncis, undique plumbo desuper infusis, firmius obseratum.*

had been washed.[63] Reginald enumerates some two hundred and twenty-five miracles, describing with a certain relish the unfortunate medical conditions from which suppliants obtained a cure at Godric's tomb.[64] Many of the miracles involved the cure of individuals who had sought help in vain elsewhere, and the author was at pains to portray Godric as more efficacious than his obvious southern rival St Thomas of Canterbury who had died later the same year. There is no evidence that Godric's relics were ever removed from the tomb which remained the focus of the cult throughout the middle ages.

THE TRANSLATION OF EDWARD THE CONFESSOR

As we have seen, although the body of the Confessor was examined in 1102, and the tomb had been adorned, perhaps from before 1087, with some sort of metal superstructure which Osbert of Clare called a *capsa* and Ailred of Rievaulx a *theca*, the body was not elevated from its tomb at that time.[65] The pall was replaced, and the grave slab was put back over the body. True, both Osbert and Ailred later called the ceremony a *translatio*, but it was nothing of the sort, and of course Edward had not yet been canonised. Nearly forty years later, in 1138, a petition, supported by Osbert of Clare's newly written *Vita*, was made to the pope to canonise Edward, but it came to nothing. As Frank Barlow has suggested, the failure was probably the result of the unfavourable political climate: King Stephen's illegitimate son Gervase of Blois had been appointed abbot of Westminster in that same year of 1138, but this was the time of Stephen's long struggle with Matilda. Only with the accession of Henry II in 1154, and the replacement of Abbot Gervase four years later, was the situation propitious for renewing the attempts at canonisation. King Henry lent his full backing to the project,[66] and at last in 1161 the new pope, Alexander III, issued a bull proclaiming Edward the Confessor a saint: the first Anglo-Saxon saint to be canonised by papal authority.

Two years after his canonisation Edward's body was finally elevated. A splendidly detailed account of the event was later composed by the Westminster monk Richard of Cirencester (fl. 1355–1400).[67] The actual elevation was something of a clandestine affair (Barlow has suggested the abbot was concerned about the state of the body).[68] So most of the monks went back to bed after matins (*post matutinas vigilias*), and the doors of the church were closed to the laity, but Abbot Laurence and a few of the brothers,

[63] ibid., 369 (*Aliud argumentum*, cap. 23).
[64] ibid., *Miracula*; pp. 371–481.
[65] See above, p. 160.
[66] See his letter to Pope Alexander III, printed in Barlow, *Edward the Confessor*, 310.
[67] Ricardi de Cirencestria, *Speculum Historiale de Gestis Regum Angliæ*, iv.50; ed. J. E. B. Mayor, 2 vols., RS, 30 (1863–9), ii. 319–27.
[68] Though midnight elevations were common: Hugh of Lincoln was elevated after matins. The idea was to exclude the laity in case anything went wrong.

who had prepared themselves by prayer and fasting, processed to the sanctuary, barefoot and dressed in albs, chanting the litany. At first just the abbot and two monks approached the grave, leaving the other members of the party in prayer by the high altar. They raised the slab, revealing the gorgeously arrayed body of the king, his white beard spread out over his chest. The other monks then joined them and rejoiced at what they saw. The king's clothing was quite untouched by age, though some dust and cement had fallen down upon the body when the coffin was opened, and this dust was carefully removed. Then they lifted up the body, some at his head, others at his feet, others supporting his shoulders or middle. A carpet had been laid out, on which they wrapped Edward's body in a precious silk cloth, then placed the body in a wooden chest (*cista lignea*) prepared for this purpose. Everything found within the coffin was placed in the chest, apart from the king's gold ring, which the abbot retained. By 1163 some of the other objects noted in 1102, such as the crown and sceptre, had evidently vanished.[69]

That was just the *elevatio*—the raising up of the body—a few days before the day appointed for the translation, Sunday 13 October, a date which thereafter became the saint's main feast. The wooden chest was borne into the church at the head of a procession, followed by King Henry II, Archbishop Thomas Becket, and all the great and the good of the land, including several bishops with an interest in saints' cults, such as Henry of Blois and Nigel of Ely, and two others who, like the archbishop, would become saints themselves, namely William of Norwich and Richard of Chichester. The body was carried around the cloister, then back into the church where it was set on high, 'like a candle, which should not be hidden under a bushel but set up on a lampstand to give light to the whole house'. It was placed (perhaps still in the wooden *cista*) in the precious *feretrum* which Richard of Cirencester believed was the container (*theca*) that Osbert of Clare claimed had been given to the abbey church by William I, a view echoed by Edward's later biographers.[70] Then Ailred preached a sermon, and was soon commissioned to rewrite St Edward's Life, but he drew heavily on the hagiographical fictions of Osbert.

There is some possible graphical evidence for the form of the monument created in 1163. In the thirteenth century, around twenty years before Edward's body was again translated into the magnificent shrine commissioned by Henry III, yet another Life of the saint was composed, the *Estoire de Seint Aedward le Rei*. The *Estoire*, dedicated to Henry's queen, Eleanor of Provence, was most probably written in the 1240s, when the new shrine was already envisaged.[71] Lavishly illustrated with drawings on every

[69] *Vita Ædwardi*; ed. Barlow, 153.

[70] See above, p. 159.

[71] Cambridge University Library, MS, Ee.iii.59, published in facsimile as *La Estoire de Seint Aedward le Rei*, ed. M. R. James, Roxburghe Club (Oxford, 1920); text published and translated in *Lives of Edward the Confessor*, ed. H. R. Luard, RS, 3 (1858). For James (p. 12) the MS dated from the 1240s.

page, the *Estoire* is a French adaptation of Ailred of Rievaulx's Life: the author claimed that it was a faithful translation from the Latin, though in fact it is somewhat expanded.[72] The editor of the facsimile edition in the Roxburghe Club series, Montague Rhodes James, argued that the author was the prolific St Albans monk Matthew Paris, and that the work was 'carried out at St. Alban's Abbey under his supervision, not by his own hand'.[73] This identification has not always been accepted. There was no special cult of St Edward at St Albans, and, as Paul Binski has emphasised, if Matthew Paris was the author, the work was presumably commissioned by the Westminster monks. M. R. James perceived the hand of more than one illustrator, a conclusion generally followed by later scholars, including Binski, who suggests that the illustrations were the work of 'a professional, probably metropolitan establishment with connections to the royal works at Westminster and Windsor, but almost certainly not the Benedictine abbey of St Alban'.[74] It may be, therefore, that the text was copied and illustrated at Westminster.

At least two monuments appear to be shown in the *Estoire*, though the drawings are bewilderingly inconsistent. Little help may be obtained from the six- to eight-line rubricated verse descriptions accompanying each picture. Two are usually identified as portraying the eleventh-century tomb of the Confessor from which the body was finally removed at the 1163 translation. The subjects appear to be Edward's burial in 1066 (pl. 7.3),[75] and the opening of the tomb in 1102,[76] though the images differ in their detail. But a third drawing, of miracles performed by the saint, seems to show a low, house-shrine type of reliquary on top of the monument; this might be an attempt at portraying the *capsa*, which Osbert claimed marked the tomb even before it was opened in 1102.[77] Certainly the miracle portrayed in the drawing (the cure of a blind sacristan (*uns marglers*), according to the rubricated description) was believed to have taken place before the tomb was opened, the event which ends the *Estoire*. But two other illustrations may give a clue to the appearance of the monument after 1102, and, indeed, the final page of the manuscript (after the tantalising loss of one leaf) deals with Abbot Gilbert Crispin's opening of the tomb. The translation of 1163 is probably shown in yet another drawing, where a king, presumably intended for Henry II, appears to be placing the Confessor's body in a

[72] *Lives of Edward the Confessor*, ed. Luard, xxii–xxiii.

[73] *Estoire*, ed. James, 17.

[74] P. Binski, 'Reflections on La Estoire de Seint Aedward le Rei: hagiography and kingship in thirteenth-century England', *Jnl. of Medieval History*, 16 (1990), 333–50, at 335.

[75] *Estoire*, p. 54, discussed by James, 57–8: *En la iglise de Westmuster … est si cors enseveliz.* So there is no doubt that this is the king's burial.

[76] ibid., p. 65 (left), discussed by James, 62. This drawing has no rubricated description.

[77] ibid., p. 61, discussed by James, 60–1. The picture appears also to be commented on by eight rubricated lines on p. 60, which refer in a more general manner to miracles at the *tumbe Seint rei Aedward.*

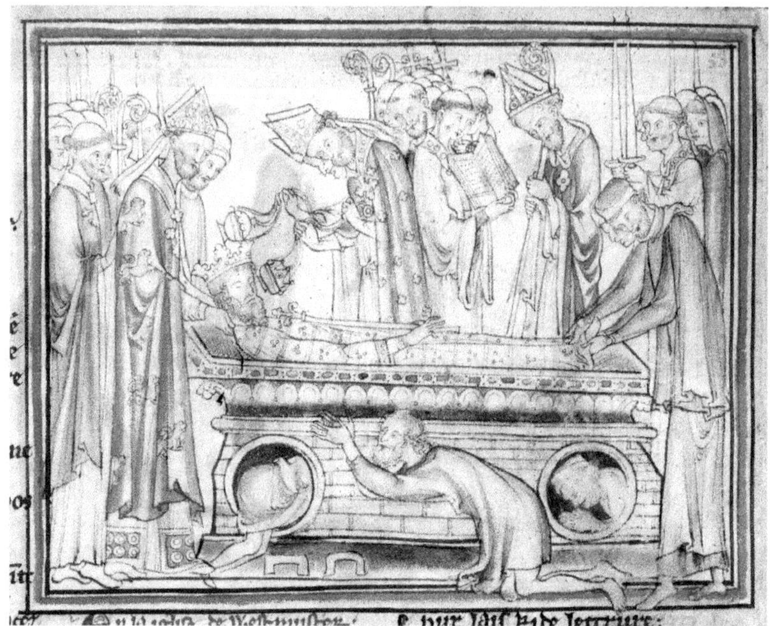

PLATE 7.3
THE TOMB-SHRINE OF EDWARD THE CONFESSOR
A thirteenth-century drawing from the *Estoire de Seint Aedward le Rei*, attributed to Matthew Paris.

decorated reliquary supported on a draped base.[78] This is one of a pair of drawings at the end of the text, lacking rubrics, and intended to stand apart from the main *Estoire*. But it seems possible that the reliquary of 1163 (or perhaps a kind of preview of the shrine of 1269) is depicted in the best-known illustration from the *Estoire*, featuring the west end of the monument. It shows a gabled structure, opulently decorated, with a vesica of Christ in Majesty and figures of saints.[79] Yet the rubric and the position of this image in the sequence makes it clear that, whatever anachronistic liberties the artist is taking, the viewer is intended to understand that what is shown is still Edward's tomb (*sun sarcu*) prior to 1163.

It is clear that one should not place too much reliance on the illustrators' attempts at depicting the first tomb of the Confessor, or, indeed the later shrine or shrines. Realistic depiction for the sake of twenty-first-century historians was not their concern, and in any case they probably had no clearer idea of the form of the pre-1163 tomb, after a lapse of nearly eighty years, than we have today. Perhaps the most interesting aspect is that when drawing the tomb, variously called *la tumbe* and *le sarcu* in the text, they tried to show a type of monument that became more widespread in the

[78] ibid., p. 65 (right), discussed by James, 62–3, who identifies it as 'replacement of the body, or the translation of 1163'. For Binski however (p. 59) both parts of this illustration show the 'first opening of the tomb of St Edward'.
[79] ibid., p. 55.

twelfth and thirteenth centuries, i.e. a 'tomb-shrine' with openings, *foramina*, in the side. As discussed in the following pages, this type of monument was normally constructed *over* a grave which remained *in situ*, thus providing some access to the grave. The tomb is shown with two or three round holes in the side and one in the end, into which pilgrims were able to crawl. In the illustration depicting the burial of Edward the artist gives the impression that the body lay on top of the tomb-shrine. But as depicted there could be no room for the body above the chamber occupied by the praying pilgrims, and the drawing is perhaps best regarded as an artistic conflation, showing the interment of the saint and the monument that, in the artists' imagination at least, was subsequently constructed over the grave. A good parallel for this sort of confusion is a scene of St Thomas's burial from the Becket window at Sens, where the archbishop is shown lying on top of the tomb-shrine, whereas the miracle accounts make it clear (as we shall see) that the monument was constructed *over* the grave.[80] The main concern of the artist of Edward's interment was to indicate that pilgrims were making their way to the grave at an early date: before the body was even placed within the tomb, if one reads the drawing literally.

Nevertheless, the monument of 1163 was presumably known to the artists who illustrated the *Estoire*, and it is perhaps possible that they used it as the model for their depiction of Edward's first tomb; they simply could not have known what the earlier monument looked like. There is regrettably little evidence for the form of the twelfth-century shrine, apart from the phrase used by the Oxford chronicler Thomas Wykes, who, describing the translation of 1269, says that the Confessor's body was raised from a low receptacle (*locellum humile*).[81] A monument of the 'port-holed' variety would certainly be entirely consistent with the mid-twelfth-century date of the translation. As for its position, the fact that on his death in 1272 it was possible to lower Henry III's body into the empty grave of the Confessor (where it remained until Henry's tomb was completed in 1290) suggests that the pre-1269 monument was located over the saint's empty grave.

TOMB-SHRINES WITH *FORAMINA* OR 'PORT-HOLES'

Although there must be much doubt as to whether either the tomb or the later shrine of Edward the Confessor as portrayed in the *Estoire* conforms with reality, the type of structure depicted in three of the illustrations is especially interesting. It appears to be a 'tomb-shrine', the sort of monument which was most usually erected over a burial which remained in place. The superstructure both protected the grave and drew attention to it. The

[80] See below, pp. 195–7.
[81] 'The Chronicle of Thomas Wykes', *Annales Monastici*, iv, ed. H. R. Luard, RS, 36 (1869), 226.

monument shown in the *Estoire* is of a particular kind: it has round or sub-round apertures or 'port-holes' in the sides, allowing limited access to the grave-cover beneath.

This type of structure, which is sometimes called a '*foramina*' shrine, from a Latin word for hole, *foramen*, has an interesting history.[82] The archetype seems to have been an eleventh-century addition to the first-century rock-cut tomb long identified as the 'Tomb of Christ' in the church of the Holy Sepulchre in Jerusalem.[83] The first certain description of the *foramina* was written by a Russian pilgrim, Abbot Daniel, relating what he had seen during a visit to Jerusalem probably in 1106–7 and certainly before 1112. 'On the side [of the tomb]', he observed, 'three small windows have been cut in order to see the holy stone, and all the Christians go there to kiss it.'[84] Sixty years later, in 1169–74, another pilgrim, Theoderic, observed, 'In the side [the sepulchre] has three round holes through which travellers give the kisses they have for so long desired to give to the stones on which the Lord lay.'[85] The arrangement survived unchanged in 1347, when a Franciscan friar, Niccolò da Poggibonsi, also described the 'three round windows, through which one can see better the Holy Sepulchre',[86] but at some date in the early fifteenth century the covering of the tomb appears to have been modified,[87] and a loquacious pilgrim in 1480, Felix Schmidt (alias *Faber*), described the previous appearance of the tomb only from hearsay.[88]

The various writers, spanning a period of over three hundred and fifty years, are quite consistent in their description of the tomb. It is clear that the three *foramina* were not cut into the stone of the actual tomb-shelf, which originally had been carved out of the solid local limestone, but in a vertical slab or *transenna* that had been set in front of the shelf, along the long, south side. The holes both protected the venerated stone and allowed limited access to it: people could put their heads through the opening to kiss the rock, but it would have been harder to use tools in order to extract pieces of stone as relics. Indeed, Niccolò da Poggibonsi suggests that in the mid-fourteenth century it was not even possible to touch the original stone.

[82] For what follows, see J. Crook, 'A hitherto undeciphered inscription from Winchester Cathedral Retrochoir', *Winchester Cathedral Record*, 66 (1997), 27–30; also idem, *Architectural Setting*, 255–67.

[83] For the development of the tomb, see Biddle, *Tomb of Christ*, an expanded version of idem, 'The Tomb of Christ, Sources, Methods and a New Approach', in *Churches Built in Ancient Times*, ed. K. Painter, Soc. of Antiquaries of London, Occasional Papers, 16 (London, 1994), 73–147.

[84] J. Wilkinson, *Jerusalem Pilgrimage, 1099–1185*, Hakluyt Soc., new ser. 167 (London, 1988), 128.

[85] ibid., 279.

[86] Fra Niccolò da Poggibonsi, *Il Libro d'Oltramare*, ed. P. B. Bagatti, *Studium Biblicum Franciscanum*, 2 (Jerusalem, 1945), 18: '... dinanzi da quelle tavole del marmo delle sepolchro, si à tre finestre tonde, per le quali puoi meglio vedere lo santo sepulchro che da niuna parte toccare non puoi'.

[87] Biddle, *Tomb of Christ*, 86.

[88] Fratris Felicis Fabri, *Euagatorium in Terræ Sanctæ, Arabiæ et Egypti Peregrinationem*, ed. C. D. Hassler, 3 vols. (Stuttgart, 1843–9), i. 332.

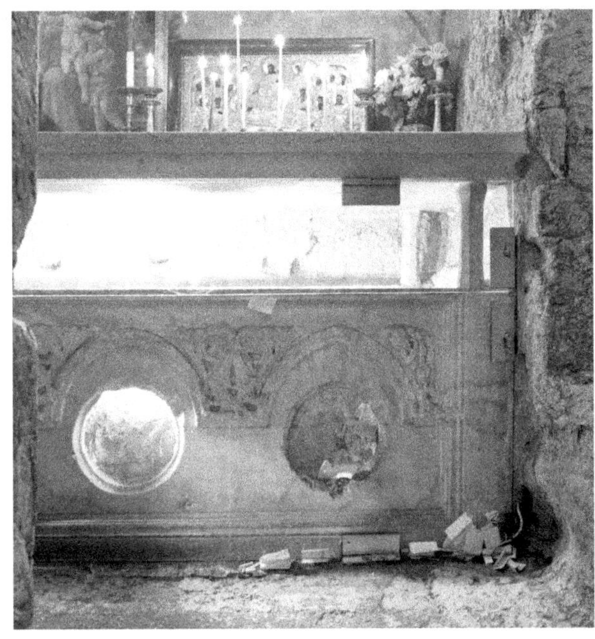

PLATE 7.4 JERUSALEM, THE 'TOMB OF THE VIRGIN' AT GETHSEMANE Detail, showing two of the three *foramina* in the *transenna* protecting the native rock.

A good local parallel for the *transenna* in front of the Tomb of Christ may be seen to this day in Jerusalem, in the underground church at Gethsemane known as the Tomb of the Virgin. Here, another rock-cut tomb-shelf on which the body of Mary the mother of Jesus was allegedly placed, until she was miraculously assumed into heaven, is still protected by a medieval slab with *foramina*. The three chamfered holes are embellished with foliate arcading above them in bas-relief, much damaged, but with rich acanthus decoration surviving in the spandrels. In 1347 Niccolò da Poggibonsi also noted the three round openings in front of this tomb, allowing the faithful to touch the rock shelf. As with the Holy Sepulchre, the slab had a protective purpose; when it was restored in 1972 great problems were caused because 'many tried to remove bits of the sacred rock so as to have a reminder of it'.[89] The slab is now covered with a second protective layer: a perspex sheet.

From the style of its acanthus decoration, the surviving *transenna* in front of the Tomb of the Virgin may be dated to the twelfth century. This raises the question of how much earlier the now vanished but evidently similar structure in front of the Tomb of Christ might have been. The 'little house' or edicule (*ædicula*), which the Emperor Constantine had built over the tomb, together with most of the church itself, was destroyed in 1009 by the mentally unstable Fatimid caliph of Egypt, Al-Hakim,[90] and it must be considered very unlikely that the pierced *transenna* predated that catastrophic event. Contemporary chroniclers, such as Raoul Glaber, specifically state that the tomb itself, the object of Hakim's fury, was broken up 'with iron hammers'. The reconstruction of the church began within three years, however, and by 1020 Al-Hakim was permitting Christian liturgy on the site of the Church of the Resurrection, that is to say the great rotunda of the Anastasis. Martin Biddle has redated the completion of the restoration

[89] B. Bagatti, M. Piccirillo, and A. Prodomo, *New Discoveries at the Tomb of Virgin Mary in Gethsemane*, Studium Biblicum Franciscanum, 17 (Jerusalem, 1975), 42–3.
[90] Biddle, *Tomb of Christ*, 72 and references there cited.

of the church to the time of the Byzantine emperor Michael IV Paphlagon (1034–41), but the edicule was almost certainly repaired long before that, and the traditional ceremony of the Easter Fire was attracting pilgrims by the late 1020s. It is therefore quite possible that the *transenna* was a Byzantine feature, introduced in the early eleventh century. In limited support of this view is the fact that a certain 'Jacinthus the presbyter', a Spanish pilgrim whose description of the tomb has now been redated on linguistic and internal evidence to the eleventh century,[91] ends his account by mentioning 'three windows round the wall of the Tomb at which masses are celebrated' (*fenestre tres ... circa murum sepulcri super quas missas* [*sic*] *celebrantur*).[92] The phrase *circa murum sepulcri* is obviously ambiguous, but as the celebration of mass on top of the tomb-slab (as is still done today) was from an early date the principal liturgical activity at the tomb, '*murum sepulcri*' may refer to the tomb-bench itself rather than the edicule. If so, the *transenna* must have been a Byzantine feature. It might, indeed, have been added to the monument with the express purpose of disguising the amount of damage that the tomb-shelf had suffered in 1009. The only other possibility is that it was introduced by the Crusaders during the short period between the capture of Jerusalem in 1099 and Abbot Daniel's visit: a period of thirteen years at the outside.

The Tomb of Christ in the form described by Abbot Daniel is well represented in Western art of the twelfth to the sixteenth centuries, and the three portholes became an iconographic shorthand for the tomb in numerous depictions of the Resurrection.[93] Only after the fifteenth century, when the *foramina* had ceased to be a feature of the tomb, did the three portholes gradually evolve in artistic representations into rosettes or other similar circular features.

ENGLISH EXAMPLES OF *FORAMINA* TOMB-SHRINES

The *foramina* structures found at Jerusalem were also to be found over saintly graves in Western Christendom from the twelfth century onwards. As argued above, the one shown in the *Estoire* was probably anachronistic. Eighty years after its replacement, the artists had no way of knowing what the pre-1163 tomb of the Confessor looked like, and fell back on depicting the kind of shrine that was becoming increasingly common in the mid-

[91] For the language, see J. Campos, 'Otro texto de Latin medieval hispano. El presbitero Iachintus', *Helmántica*, 8 (1957), 77–89, at 81. Biddle comments (*Tomb of Christ*, 152, n. 61) that '... Jachintus is clearly describing the Edicule as rebuilt after the destruction of 1009'.

[92] Leon Cathedral, Codex 14, leaf 5.

[93] For examples, see Crook, *Architectural Setting*, 257–8; and, in a more extended treatment of Russian influence, L. Beliaev, *Russkoe Spednevekovoe Nadgrobye* (Medieval Russian Graveslabs) (Moscow, 1996), 183–210; idem, 'Russian Pilgrim Art from the 12th to the 15th Century: Archaeological Elements and Problems of Romanesque Influence', *JBAA*, 151 (1998).

thirteenth century when the *Estoire* was actually composed. On the other hand, if the post-1163 shrine-base was of this type, it might have prompted the artists to include *foramina* in their depiction of the first tomb-shrine.

But other examples are known from documentary evidence. At Lincoln the tomb of St Hugh between 1200 and his canonisation in 1220 appears to have been of the 'port-holed' type. Gerald of Wales (*fl.* 1196–*c.*1220) describes how a blind woman called Matilda, who had spent more than a year near the tomb, was finally cured in 1208 ('the first year of the Interdict': *anno interdicti primo*) when she slept with her head in one of the circular openings of the marble tomb.[94] Another woman, Iveta, punished for violating the Sabbath by paralysis of the hand, was said to have been cured in a similar way after she had placed herself *in medio foramine tumbæ*.[95] The tomb appears to have been placed against a wall on the north side of a chapel, and was therefore probably one-sided.[96]

THE *FORAMINA* TOMB OF THOMAS BECKET

Another, better recorded *foramina* monument was the tomb-shrine of Becket in the crypt at Canterbury. The story of the archbishop's martyrdom on 29 December 1170 is too well known to require repeating here. Within a very short time a cult was developing. His blood was not even dry on the pavement before it was being sought as a relic. According to William Fitz-Stephen, a contemporary witness, people immediately started taking away greatly diluted blood in pewter containers (*in ampullis stanneis*);[97] so did Henry II, who left Canterbury with a flask of 'water' after his penance on 12 July 1174.[98] This 'water of St Thomas' was used for around one-third of the recorded cures wrought by the saint;[99] it was evidently diluted again and again until the chances of even one blood cell being in the tincture were infinitesimal. A similar practice is attested at Worcester where 'St Wulfstan's water' was popular with pilgrims.[100]

The monks buried their prelate beneath the pavement of the axial chapel on the east side of St Anselm's crypt, and within scarcely more than two years

[94] *Vita S. Hugonis, Dictinctio iii*, cap. 3, in *Gerald of Wales*, vii; ed. Dimock, 83–147, at 140: ... *et tunc demum fatigata, capite in uno circulari foramine tumbæ marmoreæ posito, parumper obdormivit.* The event is briefly discussed by David Stocker, 'The Mystery of the Shrines of St Hugh', in *Saint Hugh of Lincoln*, ed. H. Mayr-Harting (Oxford, 1987), 89–124, at 103.

[95] *Legenda of St Hugh*, cap. 15, in *Gerald of Wales*, vii. 172–92, at 185: she was told in a dream to place herself *in medio foramine tumbæ*. Cf. D. H. Farmer, 'The Canonization of St Hugh of Lincoln', *Lincs. Architectural and Archaeol. Reports and Papers*, 6.ii (1956), 86–117, at 110.

[96] For the location of the tomb before the translation of 1280, see below, pp. 222–3.

[97] *Vita S. Thomæ, auctore Willelmo Filio Stephani*, para. 154; *Materials for the Study of Becket*, iii. 1–154, at 150. William was writing within 2–3 years of the murder.

[98] *Gervase*; ed. Stubbs, i. 248–9.

[99] P. A. Sigal, 'Naissance et premier développement d'un vinage exceptionnel: l'eau de saint Thomas', *Cahiers de Civilisation Médiévale*, 44 (2001), 35–44.

[100] Malmesbury, *Miracula Wulfstani*, i.8, 10, 16; ed. Darlington, 120, 121, 124.

he had been canonised.[101] Shortly afterwards, a tomb-shrine was constructed over the grave. The late twelfth-century chronicler Benedict of Peterborough claimed that it had been built over the saint's coffin in order to protect it from violation, for not long after the archbishop's burial his enemies had conspired to carry off the body. Benedict described the monument in detail: it had two openings (which the chronicler called *fenestræ*, i.e. 'windows') on each side and a large slab on the top:

> Built around the marble sarcophagus was a wall of great ashlar blocks, strongly bonded with cement, iron, and lead, with two openings in each side, through which those who came, inserting their heads, were able to kiss the sarcophagus. Over it was a great marble slab, and the structure was hollow, with a gap of almost one foot between the top of the sarcophagus and the slab above.[102]

The monument shown many times in the early thirteenth-century glass in the ambulatory of the Trinity chapel at Canterbury agrees with Benedict's description, with its two apertures, rather than the three that seem to have

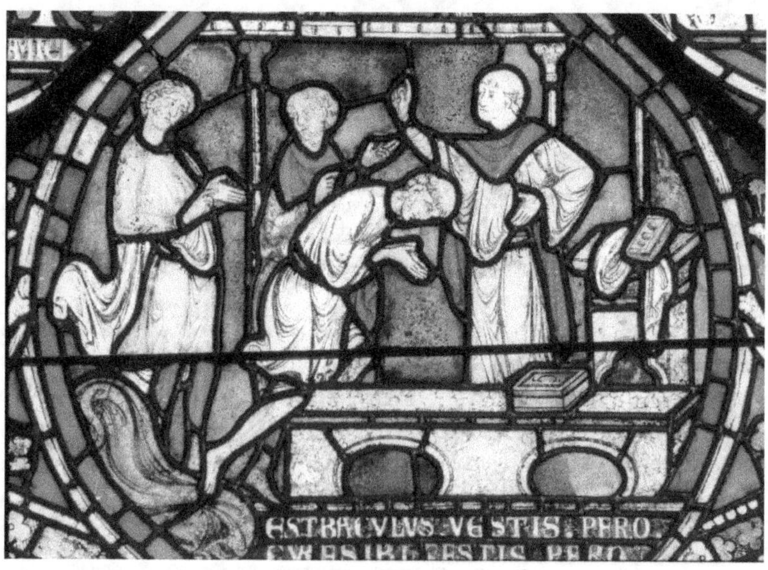

PLATE 7.5 CANTERBURY CATHEDRAL, TRINITY CHAPEL Detail from a window on the north side, (window n. IV), showing the *foramina* tomb of St Thomas.

[101] In February 1173.

[102] *Miracula S. Thomae Cantuariensis, auctore Benedicto*, ii.29; *Materials for the Study of Becket*, ii. 21–281, at 81: *Erectus est autem circa sarcophagum marmoreum paries de lapidibus magnis sectis, cæmento et ferro et plumbo firmissime consolidatis, duas in utroque parte laterum habens fenestras, quibus aduenientes capitibus immissis ad osculum sarcophagi peruenire ualerent, superposita nihilominus tabula grandi marmorea; eratque structura concaua inter sarcophagi summitatem et tabulam superpositam pæne pedalem habens distantiam.*

been more usual.[103] The tomb is similarly shown in the related Becket window at Sens Cathedral,[104] where the saint is lying on top of the tomb-shrine. As in the two Jerusalem examples, the tomb-shrine gave protection to the coffin, while still permitting pilgrims to insert their heads in order to kiss the coffin and receive maximum benefit from the curative powers emanating from the saint's body. Benedict recounts that an insane man, Ælward of Selling, actually contrived to climb into the tomb and lie on top of the coffin, to the consternation of the monks, who feared that the monument might have to be destroyed in order to set him free.[105] Eventually, having been cured, he wriggled his way out of one of the *foramina*.

The fire of 1174 did not damage the crypt, so the monument remained intact. It was presumably sheltered by a temporary roof during the rebuilding of 1180–1. Then in 1220 the relics were translated into the new shrine in the Trinity chapel. The long period between the fire and the completion of the chapel was the result of the decades of unrest at the beginning of the twelfth century, notably the Interdict of 1207–13 and the exile of the monks.

THE TOMB-SHRINE AND CULT OF ST OSMUND OF SALISBURY

At Salisbury Cathedral the *foramina* tomb-shrine of St Osmund may be seen to this day, a rare survival. The monument appears to have escaped demolition at the Reformation because by that date it was redundant, having been supplanted at the time of Osmund's belated canonisation in the fifteenth century by a more conventional high shrine.

The monument has moved twice within Salisbury Cathedral. From 1226 until 1789–90 it was on a plinth on the south side of the Lady chapel: near indeed to the site of Osmund's final shrine. In 1542 the antiquary John Leland visited Salisbury Cathedral, where he noted 'S. Osmundes first tumbe on the south side of our Lady whil the shrine a makyng.'[106] The tomb was described in 1644 by the Royalist officer Richard Symonds; by then it was thought to be that of Lord Stourton, hanged for murder in 1557.[107] Finally in 1781 'the Monument of Lord Storton [*sic*]' was sketched in the same

[103] The *foramina* tomb is shown some thirty-four times, especially in two windows in the north ambulatory of the Trinity Chapel, n.III and n.IV in the numbering system adopted by M. H. Caviness, *The Windows of Christ Church Cathedral Canterbury*, Corpus Vitrearum Medii Aevi—Great Britain, II (Oxford, 1981), 180–92. The windows are not precisely dated, but Caviness (ibid. 164) suggests a date of 1213–20: 'the lower windows at least would have been completed in time for the translation of the relics'.

[104] Reproduced in M. H. Caviness, *The Early Stained Glass of Canterbury Cathedral, c.1175–1220* (Princeton, 1977), fig. 160.

[105] *Miracula auct. Benedict*, ii.31; *Materials for the study of Becket*, ii. 82.

[106] Leland, i. 264.

[107] *Richard Symonds: Diary of the Marches of the Royal Army during the Great Civil War*, ed. C. E. Long, Camden Soc., o.s., 74 (1859), 130: '... an altar tombe of marble; on each side are three open holes in resemblance of six wells, for the Lord Stourton, who was executed (hanged) in this citty'.

position by John Carter.[108] Nine years later it was moved to the plinth of the south nave arcade, but in 1999 it was reinstated in its original position in the Lady chapel, on the new stylobate built by George Gilbert Scott.

Salisbury Cathedral was possibly not the monument's first location, however.[109] As we have seen, Bishop Osmund succeeded Hereman in 1078, and in 1075 he started to build a new cathedral at Old Sarum, where William the Conqueror had established a castle. Although Hereman supervised the transferral of the see and presumably determined the plan of the new cathedral church with his master-mason, he died within a short time of the move, and Osmund, rather than Hereman, is remembered (in Salisbury tradition at least) as 'the first bishop of Sarum'. It is true that the new cathedral in its first, modest form was completed in Osmund's episcopate; the dedication took place in 1092, though the tower was damaged a fortnight later when it was struck by lightning.[110] The plan of the cathedral church is known from excavations undertaken by William St John Hope in 1913–14. Unfortunately Hope died in 1919 and never published a full account of his investigations. Sir Alfred Clapham's much later and very brief perfunctory reworking of Hope's records appears to be inaccurate in several respects, and has been superseded by other studies.[111]

Osmund died in 1099 and was buried in his cathedral church. The location of his original tomb is unknown; possibly it lay in the choir like Lanfranc in Canterbury Cathedral, or Gundulf at Rochester. In the early twelfth century Osmund's successor, Roger le Poer, extended the first small church eastwards with a long eastern arm, perhaps in response to the eastern extension and 'Glorious Choir' that Archbishop Anselm had added to Lanfranc's modest first Norman cathedral at Canterbury. The eastern arm at Old Sarum was modified during the long episcopate of Roger's successor, Jocelin de Bohun (1142–84), who rebuilt the axial chapel.

One notable feature of the late twelfth-century chapel was an impressive geometrical pavement, the bedding patterns of which were discovered in 1913. The excavators also discovered fragments of green and purple porphyry in the same location. Porphyry was an extremely rare and expensive material, imported by the Romans from Egypt (red porphyry) and near Sparta in the Peloponnese (green porphyry). It was much recycled

[108] BL, Add. MS 29925, fo. 128, reproduced in S. Brown, *Sumptous and Richly Adorn'd*, Royal Commission on Historical Monuments (London, 1999), p. 7 (fig. 4).

[109] For this analysis of Old Sarum and the role played by Osmund's growing cult I am dependent on T. Tatton-Brown, 'The Burial Places of St Osmund', *Spire* (1999), 69th Annual Report of the Friends of Salisbury Cathedral, 19–25.

[110] Malmesbury, *GR*, iv.325; ed. Mynors, Thomson, and Winterbottom, i. 568.

[111] A. W. Clapham, *English Romanesque Architecture after the Conquest* (Oxford, 1934), 22. Idem, 'Old Sarum Cathedral', *Arch. J.*, 104 (1947), 142–3. R. Gem, 'The First Romanesque Cathedral at Old Salisbury', in *Medieval Architecture and its Intellectual Context: Studies in Honour of Peter Kidson*, ed. E. Fernie and P. Crossley (London, 1990), 9–18. See also the reworking of the evidence in Royal Commission on Historical Monuments, *The City of Salisbury* I (London, 1980).

in Italy in the medieval period; the few examples that we have in England may have come from Rome or central Italy. The excavators of Old Sarum wondered whether the pieces derived from a shrine, but Tim Tatton-Brown has more plausibly suggested that the fragments were the *tesseræ* of the geometric pavement.[112] Certainly, the size and shape of the extant fragments supports this contention. There are several English parallels for this kind of precious paving surface: the Trinity chapel at Canterbury Cathedral, Westminster Abbey, St Augustine's Canterbury, and perhaps the area in front of the shrine of St Earconwald in Old St Paul's Cathedral, London. Tim Tatton-Brown further points out that all these pavements were associated with shrines of saints.[113] It is therefore possible that the porphyry pavement at Old Sarum was also intended to embellish the area near a shrine. None of the Sherborne saints appears to have been translated to Sarum, but there was a local candidate for the sainthood in the person of Osmund, at whose tomb miracles were claimed to be occurring by the 1170s, i.e. at the period when Bishop Jocelin's works in the eastern arm were approaching completion.

On the admittedly limited stylistic evidence of its decoration, the *foramina* shrine of St Osmund, now in the present cathedral of Salisbury, might also date from this period. Tim Tatton-Brown has therefore offered the attractive suggestion that the tomb-shrine occupied a central position within the late twelfth-century eastern chapel at Old Sarum, which was located on the east side of a rectangular ambulatory around the high altar at the east end of the presbytery. The plan made in 1913 indicates that there would have been enough room to accommodate the shrine between the geometrical pavement and the altar. The provision of the ambulatory would also have provided access for pilgrims. The form of the monument, too, would be entirely consistent with a date in the 1170s, for at that time the body of England's most influential saint, the newly canonised Thomas Becket, also reposed beneath a tomb-shrine as we have seen.[114]

Such is the archaeological and comparative evidence relating to the possible position of Osmund's tomb-shrine. The admittedly limited documentation is inconclusive as to the question of whether or not the *foramina* monument preceded the move to the new site. True, a tomb is mentioned in an inventory of the 'ornaments of the church of Salisbury', compiled in 1214 and recopied in 1222, which mentions a pall which Bishop Herbert Poore (†1217) had given *ad tumbam Sancti Osmundi*;[115] but it might be thought that a pall would be an unlikely adornment to the surviving *foramina* monument as it would have prevented the access which is so

[112] T. Tatton-Brown, 'Purple and green porphyry at Old Sarum Cathedral', in *Building with Stone in Wessex over 4000 Years*, The Hatcher Review, vol. 5, no. 45 (spring 1998), 33–8.

[113] Tatton-Brown, 'Burial Places of St Osmund', 19–20.

[114] Cf. Stocker, 'Mystery of the Shrines of St Hugh', 89–124, at 103.

[115] *The Register of St Osmund, Vetus Registrum Sarisberiense alias dictum Registrum Sancti Osmundi episcopi*, ed. W. H. Rich Jones, 2 vols., RS, 78 (1883–4), ii. 127–36, at 131.

obvious a feature. More significant are the accounts of miracles at the tomb-shrine, part of the dossier relating to Osmund's canonisation published by the Salisbury Cathedral chapter clerk A. R. Malden in 1901.[116] The first group of nineteen *miracula* was drawn up at the time of the first, unsuccessful attempt by Bishop Richard Poore (Herbert's brother and successor) to canonize Osmund. His petition was submitted to Pope Gregory IX in 1228. These miracles date from the period 1188 × 1228; all take place of course at Old Sarum, and there are references to the castle there, notably to the gate of the castle where sick people used to lie.[117] There is therefore no doubt that they pre-date the move to the present cathedral. At the second inquiry in the fifteenth century the witness statements from two hundred years earlier were produced from the cathedral archives. It emerges that the *foramina* are only mentioned in the second group of thirty-three *miracula*, for which the witness records dated from 1423/4; no mention is made of the 'port-holes' in the first group of miracles. The construction of the monument is indeed scarcely mentioned in this first group. On one occasion a miraculous scent emanated from 'between two stones'.[118] Another miracle concerned the cure of a man who had been struck blind because he irreverently sat on the saint's tomb, which might imply a rather lower monument than the present tomb-shrine.[119] Then, a mad girl called Alice, daughter of Richard of Breamore, was cured after spending a night sleeping 'over the head of the tomb', again indicative of a lower monument.[120] And yet another miracle concerned a boy who had fallen down a well and drowned, who was brought back to life by being placed on top of the tomb.[121] These early thirteenth-century allusions to the tomb must be compared with the second group of miracles,[122] in which the most obvious features of the monument we now know, namely the *foramina* are twice mentioned. John Beaminster, out of his mind, was brought by his friends to the tomb at the start of the Mary mass, and remained with his head and hands *in quodam foramine eiusdem tumbe* until the Agnus Dei was sung.[123] Likewise a certain 'Loony Tom' (*Thomas furiosus*) was brought with his hands tied to the tomb; they put his hands *in foraminibus eiusdem sepulcri* and his bonds miraculously fell off.[124] Admittedly it might be argued that the absence of any reference to the holes in the first group of miracles might reflect the small sample (no mention in nineteen thirteenth-century miracles, compared with two mentions in thirty-three fourteenth-century ones), but it does cast doubt on whether the *foramina* shrine came from Old Sarum.

[116] Malden, *St Osmund*. For the witness statements, see 35–45, 56–83.
[117] e.g. ibid., 36.
[118] ibid., 37: ... *sensit suauissimum odorem exire inter duos lapides* ...
[119] ibid., 41: ... *cum quadam die sederet irreuerenter super tumbam Osmundi* ...
[120] ibid., 41: ... *cum* ... *decubuisset super caput tumbe et ibi dormitaret* ...
[121] ibid., 42–4: ... *positus erat super tumbam* ...
[122] ibid., 54–84.
[123] ibid., 57–8.
[124] ibid., 77–8.

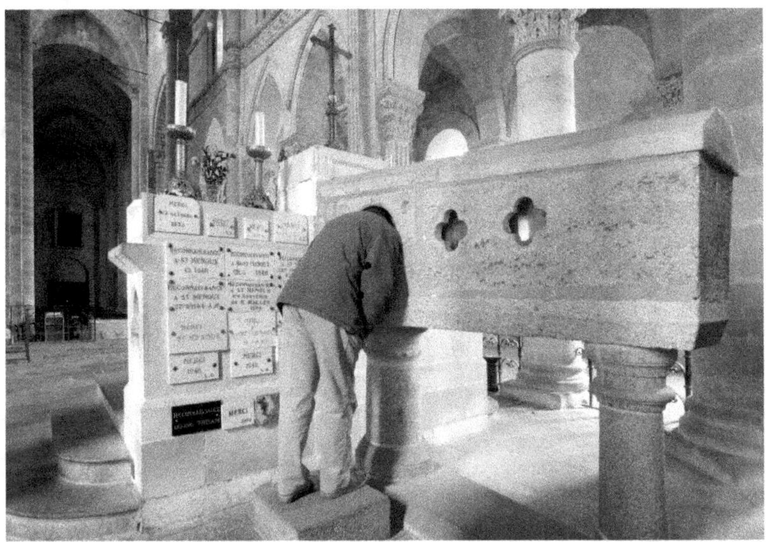

PLATE 7.6 SAINT-MENOUX (DEPT. ALLIER, FRANCE). PARISH CHURCH, THE TOMB OF ST MENULPHUS Known as the *débrédinoire*, it was still in use for cures until the early twentieth century. Suppliants inserted their heads into the holes in order to cure cerebral problems.

That having been said, Bishop Poore clearly hoped that Osmund would soon be canonised, and it is perhaps improbable that a tomb-shrine would have been created as a short-term expedient. Relevant to this question is the account in the so-called 'Salisbury Register' of the translation of the bodies of Osmund and his successors:

> In that same year [1226] on the Feast of the Holy Trinity, which then was the 14th June, the bodies of three bishops were translated from the Castle of [Old] Sarum to the New Work, namely the body of blessed Osmund, that of Bishop Roger, and the body of Bishop Jocelin.[125]

Two effigial graveslabs were undoubtedly brought to New Sarum from the castle in 1226, and these are now identified as those of Roger and Jocelin; attempts to identify the latter slab as that of Osmund are flawed.[126] This means that Osmund lacks an eleventh-century gravestone in New Sarum (the slab marked 1099 in the centre of the Trinity chapel is a post-medieval

[125] *Register of St Osmund*, ed. Rich Jones, ii. 55: *Eodem anno in festo Trinitatis, quod tunc fuit xviii° kalendas Julii, translata fuerunt corpora trium episcoporum, a castro Sarum usque ad Novam Fabricam; videlicet corpus beati Osmundi, corpus episcopi Rogeri, corpus episcopi Jocelini.*

[126] *Pace* the convoluted arguments of Daphne Stroud, 'A 12th-century effigy in Salisbury Cathedral', *Wilts. Archaeological & Nat. Hist. Magazine*, 86 (1993), 113–17, and the ingenious computations of David Howlett, *Insular Inscriptions* (Dublin, 2005), 122–4.

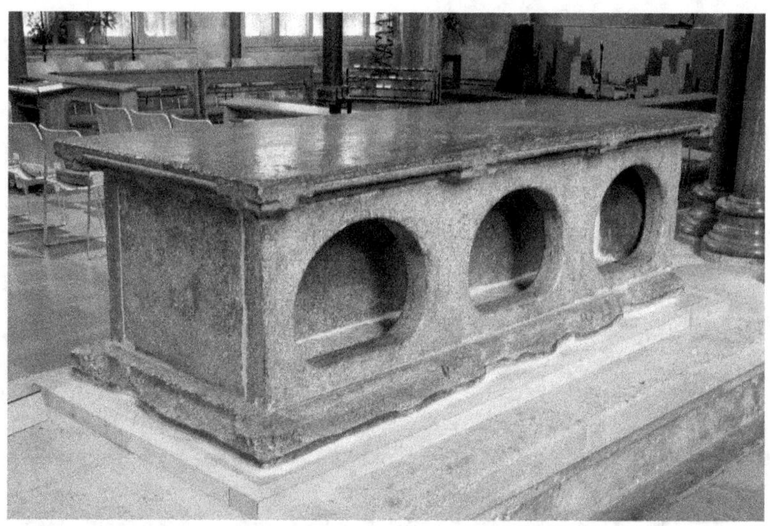

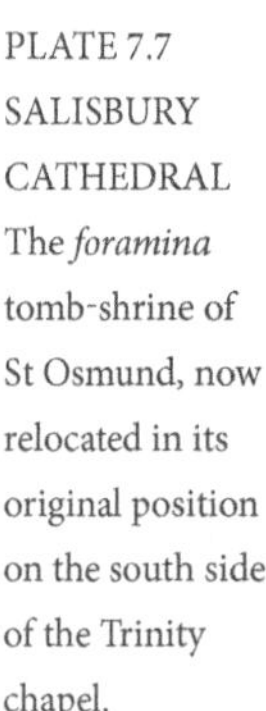

PLATE 7.7
SALISBURY CATHEDRAL
The *foramina* tomb-shrine of St Osmund, now relocated in its original position on the south side of the Trinity chapel.

modification as discussed below), which supports the idea that his tomb was indeed the *foramina* shrine, that was disassembled and brought to the new cathedral in 1226. At that time it was hoped that the bishop would soon be canonised and commemorated by an appropriate high shrine in the style of Canterbury, so the expectation must have been that the grave within the south stylobate of the Trinity chapel would be short-lived.

None of the medieval accounts specifically describes the tomb-shrine. It resembles a table-tomb, consisting of a basal slab, a central body, and an oversailing top slab. The dimensions of the latter are 2180mm long by 900mm wide at the west end, tapering eastwards to 830mm, and the monument stands about 660mm high. It is built entirely of Purbeck 'marble' from near Corfe in Dorset, which during the later twelfth century was increasingly being used for monuments and architectural decoration. Henry of Blois, bishop of Winchester (1129–71), may well have been responsible for encouraging this use of a local material as a prestigious alternative to the finely polished marbles that he would have seen during his trips to Rome. Purbeck marble comes in many different varieties, but the consistent light yellow-grey of the Salisbury tomb-shrine was all extracted from one bed. It is of course possible that the monument was created at Corfe and was reassembled at Old Sarum.

The bottom slab has inevitably suffered much damage from being stood upon, but as well as a moulding all round this element, the bases of detached shafts at each corner, and two further demi-shafts on each side of the tomb, are still discernible. All eight shafts measured about 120mm in diameter. On the underside of the overhanging top slab are corresponding capitals, which preserve rather more detail. Both bases and capitals have a pattern of fluting which must have continued on the actual shafts, none of which has survived. Whether the fluting spiralled around the shafts or continued in a straight line like an Ionic column is not certain.

The central section is a slightly tapering box formed of four Purbeck marble slabs, with perforated long sides overlapping and rebated over the plan end panels. Running up the middle of the monument is a fifth slab, a thin partition dividing the interior space in two. The wear patterns in the basal slab, either side of the partition, confirm that it was an original feature. The most interesting features are the circular 'port-holes', the *foramina* or *fenestellæ*. These are sub-round rather than strictly circular, being flat at the base. Each opening is around 480mm wide by 345mm high—a dimension which would comfortably have allowed the insertion of a pilgrim's head but only the narrowest of shoulders. Each *foramen* was originally separated from its neighbour by the demi-shafts already described.

The question of whether this monument stood over the grave of the saint or supported a coffin or reliquary needs to be addressed. If Osmund's body had indeed been translated eastwards into the twelfth-century extension at Old Sarum, it might be considered surprising that the body was reburied at the time of that first translation. On the other hand, though a saint in the making and, as already noted, called *sanctus* in 1214 and *beatus* at the time his body was carried to the new cathedral four years later, he was not actually canonised until the fifteenth century, so placing the relics in a reliquary might have been deemed premature. Furthermore, just before he was finally canonised, both ordinary folk and aristocracy (*populus et magnates*) were clamouring for his body to be raised *de terra*, 'from the earth', without even waiting for papal authorisation.[127] From all this it is clear that he had been reburied in the present cathedral; no document before the canonisation of 1457 refers to a *feretrum*, always to a tomb. The bull of canonisation refers to 'raising the tomb into a more worthy place'.[128]

In fact the question is answered by the form of the monument itself. It is clear that the *foramina* were intended to allow access to the interior of the monument, and the flat lower edge of each hole is at precisely the height which would allow pilgrims to kiss the surface of the bottom slab. This slab is indeed considerably worn, by generations of kissing, touching, and perhaps scratching away of the friable shells of which the Purbeck marble is composed. To call the lowest element a 'bottom slab' is really to do it an injustice, for in fact it was most probably the lid of the saint's second, probably late twelfth-century, coffin. This was configured precisely so that it could accommodate the superstructure we have described.

[127] Malden, *St Osmund*, 108–10, at 109. Letter to the bishop of Salisbury from Simon Huchyns, one of the two proctors sent to Rome on behalf of the bishop and chapter, dated 10 August 1452, in which he said he had told the advocate to the consistory court of this lay enthusiasm. A letter from Henry VI to the pope at around the same time referred, more vaguely, to *Osmundum cuius reliqua* [recte *reliquie*] *in ecclesia Saresburie recondita [recondite] requiescunt* (ibid., 127–8, at 128).

[128] ibid., 225–35, at 234: *et ut ad Saresberiensem ecclesiam predictam, ipsiusque venerabilem tumulum, quem in digniori loco volumus preparari* ...

It has hitherto been tacitly assumed that the 'bottom slab' was placed on top of the burial. The interpretation of the basal element as the lid of a coffin means that it is certain that the body, originally buried in 1099, was rehoused when the monument was created. The twelfth-century date of the monument on stylistic grounds means that this first translation of Osmund's remains must have taken place at Old Sarum. When Osmund's body was translated to the present cathedral, the main body of the stone sarcophagus was probably brought as well, to be set within the plinth on the south side of the Lady chapel. The sarcophagus probably survived, like many other tombs in the Trinity chapel, until the plinth was cut through at the end of the eighteenth century.

Yet the fundamental question of whether the *foramina* tomb-shrine was created for Old Sarum or specially made for the new cathedral remains unanswered. It is fairly clear that Bishop Poore hoped that Osmund would soon be canonised, and it is perhaps unlikely that a tomb-shrine would have been specially created as an interim measure. In the absence of further information, and despite the fact the *foramina* are not mentioned in the early group of miracles, the balance of probability perhaps supports the notion that the *foramina* base was built for Old Sarum and that it was that monument that was carried down to the new cathedral in 1226. The most likely period for its construction is the later 1170s when Bishop Jocelin was rebuilding the east end of the old cathedral; and the similarity with the Becket *foramina* tomb-shrine of the same period supports this dating.

As we shall see, the popularity of the *foramina* tomb-shrine continued in the thirteenth century, with an extant example at Ilam (Staffs) and Whitchurch Canonicorum (Dorset) and probable fragmentary remains of a similar monument at Winchester.

ABBOT SIMON AND THE SHRINE OF ST ALBAN

As we saw in the previous chapter, the reliquary of St Alban underwent many vicissitudes in the early twelfth century. Begun in 1124 by Abbot Geoffrey, the *theca* was still under construction when it was stripped of its precious metal casing in order to provide alms for the poor. Although the reliquary was sufficiently complete to be used in the translation of 1129, it was not finished until the abbacy of Robert of Gorron (1151–66).

But it is Abbot Robert's successor, Abbot Simon (1167–83), who is credited with creating an important new table-shrine that was the immediate predecessor of the fourteenth-century high shrine seen today. The main element of Abbot Simon's monument was the new outer chest begun by Abbot Geoffrey and completed by Abbot Robert. Matthew Paris provided another detailed description of the works, and the passage is so significant that it merits being quoted here in full.

> From that time onwards [i.e. the murder of Becket in 1170] this Abbot Simon, of holy memory, combining both foresight and

wisdom, began diligently to amass a not inconsiderable treasure store of gold, silver, and precious stones, and he commissioned the outstanding craftsman Master John the Goldsmith to work on the outer chest which we call the *feretrum*, of which we had seen no finer example at that time. And within a few years he accomplished this most painstaking, sumptuous, and highly skilled work, and the reliquary was set up in a more conspicuous position, namely east of the high altar, in front of the celebrant, so that anyone saying mass at that same altar would have the memory of the martyr both before his face and in his heart. For that reason, the decapitation of the martyr himself was depicted facing the celebrant. Moreover all around the *feretrum*, that is to say, on every side, he [Abbot Simon] caused to be depicted a series of scenes showing the life of the martyr, and the events leading up to his martyrdom. This was done in raised figures in gold and silver of repoussé work of the kind which is commonly called 'embossed'. So on the side facing west he reverently placed the scene of the Crucifixion, with images of Mary and John and carefully arranged rows of various gem-stones; on the side facing east he put the enthroned image of the Blessed Virgin holding her Son in her lap, created in relief work surrounded by gemstones and pelletwork of gold. And in this way—adorned, furthermore, with the orders of martyrs on either slope of the roof—the *feretrum* extended upwards towards a curly and artistic crest; it was squared up at the four corners with little towers with openings in them, with its marvellous domes of rock crystal. And (something greatly to be marvelled at) within this same *feretrum*, as if within an inner chamber, the [inner] *theca* of the same martyr made by Abbot Geoffrey, is suitably contained, in which one may discern his bones to be separately stored.[129]

[129] *GA*; ed. Riley, i, 189 (from BL, Cotton MS Claudius E.iv): *Iste piæ memoriæ Abbas Simon ex eo tempore coepit provide ac sapienter thesaurum non modicum auri et argenti et gemmarum pretiosarum, diligentissime coadunare, et thecam exteriorem, quam nos 'feretrum' appellamus, (qua ipso tempore nullam vidimus nobiliorem,) coepit per manum præcellentissimi artificis, Magistri Johannis, aurifabri, fabricari; et tam laboriosum, sumptuosum, et artificiosum opus infra paucos annos feliciter consummavit; et loco suo eminentiori, scilicet, supra maius altare, contra frontem celebrantis collocavit, ut in facie et in corde habeat quilibet celebrans Missam super idem altare Martyris memoriam: idcirco in obiectu visus celebrantis, Martyrium eiusdem, scilicet, decollatio, figuratum. In circuitu autem feretri, videlicet, duobus lateribus, fecit vitæ Beati Martyris seriem, quæ fuit arrha et præparatio passionis suæ, eminentibus imaginibus de argento et auro, opere propulsato, (quod vulgariter 'levatura' dicitur,) evidenter effigiari. In capite vero quod respicit orientem, imaginem Crucifixi, cum Mariæ et Johannis iconibus, cum diversarum gemmarum ordine decentissimo, veneranter collocavit. In fronte vero occidentem respiciente, imaginem Beatæ Virginis, puerum suum tenentis in gremio, eminenti opere inter gemmas et pretiosa monilia aurea, in throno sedentem incathedravit. Et sic ordine martyrum in tecto utrobique disposito, theca in crispam et artificiosam cristam consurgit; in quatuor angulis, turribus fenestratis, tholis crystallinis cum suis mirabilibus, quadratur venusta. In ipsa igitur, quæ miræ magnitudinis est, ipsius Martyris theca, (quæ quasi eius conclave est, et in qua ipsius secreta ossa recondi dinoscuntur), ab Abbate Gaufrido fabricata, convenienter reconditur.*

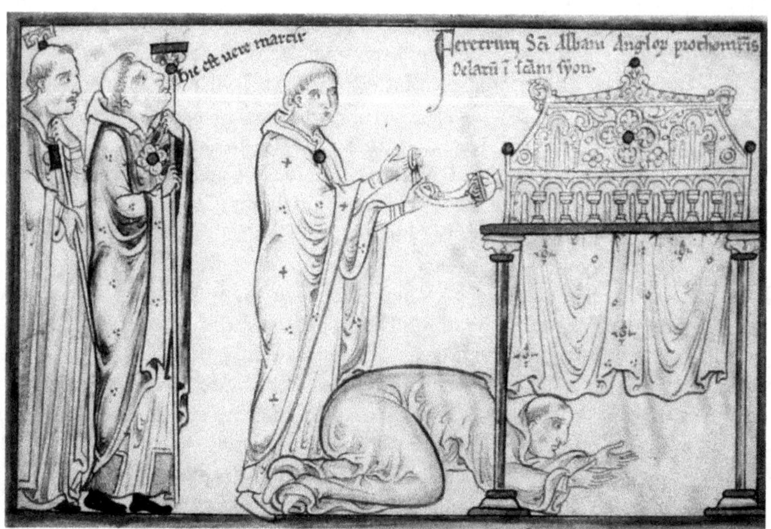

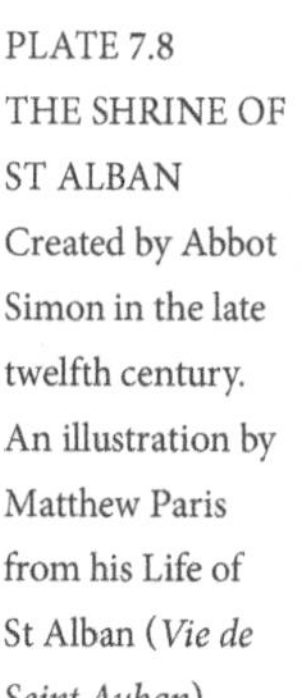

PLATE 7.8
THE SHRINE OF ST ALBAN
Created by Abbot Simon in the late twelfth century. An illustration by Matthew Paris from his Life of St Alban (*Vie de Seint Auban*).

Matthew's description of the new *theca* is probably more reliable than his drawings of the shrine. One of these, in his *Vie de Seint Auban* (more particularly in a 'tract on the Invention or Translation of St Alban'), might conceivably be intended as a view of the shrine known to Matthew, i.e. the *theca* of Abbot Simon, albeit in a late eighth-century historical context (pl. 7.8). It is labelled *feretrum Sti. Albani*. Matthew specifically notes in the passage quoted above that *feretrum* was the local name for the outer reliquary, so the drawing may be intended as a view of the one created for Abbot Simon.[130] Unfortunately the detail bears little relationship to Matthew's own description; the sides appear decorated with Romanesque arcading rather than scenes from the life of the saint; the roof slope is adorned with architectural motifs and quatrefoils; neither the towers nor the domed adornments are portrayed. Then again, a somewhat different design of reliquary is shown in Matthew's *Lives of the Two Offas*.[131] Martin Biddle has suggested that this might have been intended as a representation of the inner *theca* of Abbots Geoffrey and Robert.

Although Matthew's drawing of Abbot Simon's new *theca* is disappointing, it does provide some revealing details about how it was 'raised up', and because these at least conform with archaeological findings they may be more authentic. The *theca* is shown standing on a dark-coloured slab supported on thin pillars with moulded bases and crocketed capitals. Short curtains hang from the slab, or perhaps a cloth covering the slab and

[130] Trinity College Library Dublin, MS 177 (formerly MS E.i.40), fo. 61r, published in *Illustrations to the Life of St Alban*, ed. W. R. L. Lowe and E. F. Jacob (Oxford, 1924), 50.
[131] BL, Cotton MS Nero D.i, fo. 22r, reproduced in Biddle, 'Remembering St Alban', figs. 17 and (as a detail) 18a, and discussed in ibid., 151.

hanging down on either side is intended. To judge from the height of the bystanders the top of the slab must have been about one metre above the pavement. One monk, standing on the west side of the monument with candlebearers behind him, is censing the reliquary; another is prostrate in prayer, the upper part of his body below the slab.

In the early 1990s, during the restoration of the present shrine (i.e. the fourteenth-century monument reconstructed from fragments in 1872), it became apparent that one element of Abbot Simon's earlier shrine had probably partially survived, namely the Purbeck marble slab on which the *feretrum* was placed. Five pieces of the slab, decorated with characteristic mid- to late twelfth-century palmette decoration, had been incorporated in the nineteenth-century reconstruction. Martin Biddle has traced the fortunes of the slab, whose association with the shrine of St Alban since the later seventeenth century is indisputably demonstrated by a series of inscriptions (the last two on the slab itself). He has demonstrated that the slab was probably set in the floor beneath the final, fourteenth-century shrine, reflecting its status as an important contact relic deriving from its twelfth-century predecessor.[132] It survived, having remained in place within the basal course of the final shrine when that monument was demolished at the Reformation.

This precious survival, together with the admittedly less reliable evidence of Matthew Paris's drawing, provides some information about the twelfth-century shrine of St Alban. It was of the 'pillared' type, a rather taller version of the early twelfth-century shrine of St Cuthbert described above.[133] Only two pillars are shown, one at each end of the south side of the slab. As Biddle points out, more than two columns per side would have been required to support a slab which, from the outset, was made up of at least two blocks cramped together. They are now represented by one shorter block which has survived almost intact and a longer block now partially surviving as four fragments, one of which fortunately provides the length of this block. As with the depiction of the *theca*, Matthew's drawing of the shrine-base should probably be regarded as schematic. The shrine seems to be aligned east–west, as already noted, and in Matthew's drawing the slab abuts the frame of the picture. Biddle has suggested that this is intended to illustrate the fact that the shrine stood tight against the Romanesque apse, a contention which of course depends on the premise that Matthew really was showing the Romanesque church even whilst illustrating a scene set in the time of Offa. There is admittedly some physical evidence to support the notion that the slab abutted a wall: the palmette decoration occurs only on three sides of the slab (the fourth side being tooled but not polished), and a raised lip around the top of the slab is missing on the fourth side. It may, however, be objected that if the *theca* stood as close to the apse wall as suggested in the drawing, it would have been impossible to see the image of the Virgin at that end mentioned in Matthew's

[132] Biddle, 'Remembering St Alban'.

[133] Above, pp. 152–3.

text: he emphasises that the *theca* was decorated all round. Another interpretation might be that the undecorated side of the slab was in fact a joint with a third, shorter portion similar to the surviving shorter block at the other end. This would, however, mean that the total length of the slab was 3.3m, which is perhaps implausibly long—and the disposition of the angled holes (which Biddle believes may have held hoops over the *feretrum*) is not consistent with the idea either.

The question of the high altar's position is clearly relevant to this. Nicola Coldstream has argued that the altar remained in the same position after the thirteenth-century reconstruction of the presbytery.[134] If so, the shrine could not possibly have abutted the end of the apse, for Matthew's text implies it was very close to anyone celebrating mass at the high altar: *contra frontem celebrantis*, literally 'against his forehead'. Furthermore, as discussed below, Matthew says elsewhere that the shrine of St Amphibalus, placed in the presbytery in 1186, was to the right of the high altar, next to St Alban's *feretrum*. But if the Romanesque high altar was in its present position, with the shrines behind it, this would have left a large and inexplicable space in the main apse behind. On balance, it is perhaps more likely, *pace* Coldstream, that in the Romanesque church both the high altar and shrines were further east than they are today, but the question is incapable of proof given the replacement in the late thirteenth century of the east end of the Romanesque structure. It is perhaps significant that John de Maryns is said to have 'moved' the shrine when he rebuilt it in the early fourteenth century,[135] presumably transferring it further west.

THE TWELFTH-CENTURY FERETRUM OF ST AMPHIBALUS

Abbot Simon's interest in saints extended to a more dubious individual. In 1177 he claimed to have discovered at Redbourn (Herts) the bones of St Amphibalus, the legendary British priest hidden by Alban. His name simply means 'cloak', referring to the story that the two men exchanged garments.[136] Simon exhumed the bones, which became the focus of a cult in the abbey church. The *locellus* that he provided was soon replaced; his successor, Warin, commissioned a far more opulent and complex *feretrum*, described in some detail in the *Gesta Abbatum*.[137] It was splendidly adorned in gold and silver, including what seems to have been a repoussé image of the saint's passion on the 'front', presumably the west end, as Matthew Paris thus uses this term elsewhere. The phrase for the technique used is *arte exclusoria*.

[134] N. Coldstream, '*Cui bono*? The Saint, the Clergy and the New Work at St Albans', in *Medieval Architecture and its Intellectual Context: Studies in honour of Peter Kidson*, ed. E. Fernie and P. Crossley (London, 1990), 143–9, at 146–7.

[135] *GA*; ed. Riley, ii. 107: *Tumbam autem Sancti Albani, et feretri, amovere fecit, honorifice istud decorando.* For the fourteenth-century phase, see pp. 269–71, below.

[136] *GA*; ed. Riley, i. 192–3.

[137] ibid., i. 205–6.

The *feretrum* was subdivided by a transverse partition. Behind the image of the saint were housed the relics of Amphibalus and three of his companions, whilst the other compartment housed the remains of six other companions also found with him, each tied up in a separate bundle, together with numerous beautiful fair linen altar cloths (*corporalia*).

The subdivision of the reliquary is interesting. A small reliquary at Auxerre is similarly subdivided,[138] and a description survives of the opening in 1623 of an eleventh-century stone sarcophagus in St Servasius's church Maastricht, in which was found a lead casket divided into four compartments including the titular saint.[139]

On 24 June 1186 the reliquary was inaugurated, and, together with another similar one containing various other martyrs found in Amphibalus's grave, was placed on a wall on the south side of the presbytery, to the right of the high altar, i.e. on one of the screens separating the central and lateral apses of the triapsidal Romanesque church. As already noted, Amphibalus's *feretrum* is said to have been next to the shrine of St Alban, which must therefore have been behind the high altar.[140]

OXFORD: ST FRIDESWIDE

An important local cult which appears to have received a significant boost in the late twelfth century is that of St Fritheswitha of Oxford, better known as St Frideswide. At first sight, the legend of her life seems to be little more than a string of hagiographical commonplaces (*topoi*): she was remembered as an early eighth-century Anglo-Saxon princess who had espoused the monastic life, becoming a nun in the church which her father had built for her near the Thames crossing which later evolved into the city of Oxford. She is said to have successfully escaped the clutches of an amorous royal suitor, hiding successively at Bampton and Binsey (*Thornbiri*) before returning to Oxford, where she ended her days: she performed miracles during her lifetime and after her death. That great Anglo-Saxon scholar, Sir Frank Stenton, was dismissive even of the historical core of what he called 'one of the most nebulous of monastic legends'.[141] Fifty years later the various early recensions of the legend were studied more judiciously by John Blair, who demonstrated that, setting aside the miraculous elements and the confusion over local geography, Frideswide's Life may preserve pieces of genuine historical tradition.[142] The legend is quite consistent with what we know of late seventh-century Oxfordshire, then under Mercian domination: it is

[138] See above, pl. 5.1.
[139] Joseph Braun, *Der christliche Altar in seiner geschichtlichen Entwicklungen* (Munich, 1928), 552 and n. 34.
[140] *GA*; ed. Riley, i. 282: ... *secus maius altare, iuxta feretrum Sancti Albani, in parte aquilonari.*
[141] F. M. Stenton, 'St. Frideswide and her times', *Oxoniensia*, 1 (1936), 103–12, at 104–5, n. 1.
[142] J. Blair, 'Saint Frideswide reconsidered', *Oxoniensia*, 52 (1987), 71–127.

therefore plausible that Frideswide was indeed a Mercian princess and the first abbess of a double house at Oxford. This was one of a number of religious houses founded by her father, a local sub-king (*regulus*) whom the earliest versions of the legend call 'Didan, king of Oxford'. Her legendary escape from 'King Algar', though a hagiographical commonplace, may preserve the memory of the expansionist policies of a neighbouring local ruler, an attempt to take over the territories formerly belonging to Frideswide's father.

By the early eleventh century Frideswide's body certainly lay at Oxford, where it is mentioned in the well-known Anglo-Saxon list of saints' resting places, the *Secgan*, and in a charter of Æthelred II of 1004 referring to 'the monastery [minster] where most blessed Frideswide lies'.[143] The location of the grave, even of the church itself, is uncertain, though John Blair's argument that the Anglo-Saxon church was located on the site of the north-eastern chapels of what is now Oxford Cathedral is an attractive one. Frideswide's remains might, according to this view, have remained in the same position from the time of her burial until the first recorded translation in 1180.

The legend of the Oxford saint was widely disseminated by the early twelfth century, when an earlier, lost text appears to have been employed as a source by the authors of the two earliest extant versions: the *Vita* which Blair designates 'Life A',[144] and the account of the saint compiled *c.*1125 by William of Malmesbury in his *Gesta Pontificum*.[145] At this period the minster was reformed as an Augustinian priory (*c.*1120), with a consequent need for the reconstruction of the precincts and the church itself. The driving force behind these works seems to have been the energetic Robert of Cricklade, who was prior from before 1139 until the late 1170s. The east range of the cloister was built first, in the mid-century, and the reconstruction of the east end of the church followed, *c.*1165–70, though the rest of the building was not completed until the end of the century after Robert's death.

The cult of St Frideswide seems to have had a significant role to play in these works. During this period 'Life A' was expanded, and Blair has shown that this longer *Vita*, which he designates 'Life B', was probably written by Prior Robert himself. At the time of writing, the saint's grave was 'in the middle of the church', so the reconstruction of the chancel had probably not yet begun. John Blair has suggested that when the eastern arm of the new church was laid out, a square chapel north of the chancel was built in such a way that the grave of the saint lay axially within it, and the grave probably remained in the same position until the second translation of Frideswide's remains in the late thirteenth century.

By 1180 works were evidently sufficiently advanced for a first translation, though Prior Robert did not live to see it. Earlier in the century the canons had been concerned that the bones might have been removed by the monks

[143] idem, 'St. Frideswide's monastery: problems and possibilities', *Oxoniensia*, 53 (1988), 221–58, at 226.
[144] BL, Cotton MS Nero E.1 (ii), fos. 156–7v.
[145] Malmesbury, *GP*, iv.178; ed. Winterbottom and Thomson, i. 478–81.

of Abingdon, who had held the church 'for a certain time' (*per aliquot tempora*) in the early eleventh century. An investigation had taken place at dead of night, and the canons had at first been dismayed to unearth an empty stone coffin. One of their number astutely suggested that the empty coffin might have been a ruse to foil thieves. Heartened by this they dug deeper and discovered a body. It was identified as that of the saint when the canons' candles blew out then miraculously relit themselves.[146]

Subsequently—it is not clear how soon afterwards, though there was time for 'many miracles' to take place at the grave—the bones were raised up, in a typical ceremony of elevation, recorded in the preface to a miracle collection compiled by Prior Philip, Robert's successor.[147] The usual reason was given: that such a great light should be elevated on a candlestand rather than remain hiding under a bushel, but in fact the elevation of the relics may well have formed part of the late Prior Robert's plans for his church, marking in effect the new consecration of the building. An impressive crowd of invited bishops and nobles was present when the tomb was opened 'where the blessed body had lain for about 480 years'. When the archbishop of Canterbury lifted out the bones and placed them in an appropriately decorated reliquary, a marvellous smell filled the air.

Where the reliquary was placed in the church is not specified, but the most economical explanation is that it normally resided on top of the site of the supposedly original grave. The accounts of post-translation miracles show that sick people in search of a cure normally resorted to the grave (*sepulchrum*); activities involving the *feretrum* often occurred in the context of processions or other liturgical activity, when the portable *feretrum* might have temporarily been located elsewhere. Yet the fact that the late thirteenth-century shrine was constructed not far from the grave lends weight to the argument that grave and relics remained close to one other after the translation of 1180. It is certainly unlikely that the relics were displayed in the usual position behind the high altar only to be relegated to the north-western chapel a century later. All in all, John Blair's suggestion seems the most plausible: 'the position of St. Frideswide's shrine [i.e. *scrinium*] is more easily explained if we assume that it stood over her former grave than if we assume that it did not'.[148] The fact that suppliants were able to prostrate themselves over the grave is not necessarily an impediment to this hypothesis; twelfth-century shrines frequently were of the 'pillared' variety, like the shrine of St Cuthbert described in the previous chapter, allowing pilgrims to crawl beneath the relics.

Arrangements for the display of relics in the twelfth century were not dissimilar from those encountered on the Continent at the same period.

[146] BL, Lansdowne MS 436, fos. 103–3v, printed in Blair, 'Frideswide reconsidered', 117–18.
[147] Oxford, Bodleian Library, MS Digby 177, fos. 1v–2, printed in Blair, 'Frideswide reconsidered', 118–19.
[148] Blair, 'St. Frideswide's monastery: problems and possibilities', 251.

Either the reliquary stood on or immediately behind the high altar; or, in order to provide better access for pilgrims, it might be raised up on a monument resembling a table-tomb, supported on columns. Similar structures were to be found in France and Italy at the same period. However, England began to part company with Continental practice during the later twelfth century with the development of *foramina* shrines: tomb-shrines with port-holes. These continued into the thirteenth century as we shall see, but were increasingly superseded by monuments that were much more architectural in their conception: the high shrines of the later middle ages that would persist until the Reformation.

THE LEGACY OF THOMAS BECKET 8

The thirteenth century

An entry in the *Winchester Annals* provides an amusing glimpse of attitudes to the cult of saints at the beginning of the thirteenth century. It relates how certain holy confidence tricksters, whom the annalist calls *speudo-sacri* [sic], wandered through the towns and villages of England persuading gullible locals that they were saints.[1] The rogues had worked out a highly effective routine, which involved sending accomplices on ahead in order to identify their victims. Thus, when one of them knocked on the door of a moderately well-off but evidently simple man, the 'pseudo-saint' was able to name both the householder and his wife. Overwhelmed, the man fell at the feet of the imposter, who identified himself as 'St Nicholas'. The charlatan stayed the whole day with his victims, enjoyed a good meal into the bargain, and by means of further trickery made off with their modest savings. Another of these confidence tricksters claimed to be St Andrew, and persuaded his victims to give him all that they possessed by means of a little sleight-of-hand involving a chicken which he claimed to have brought back to life. The episode is reminiscent of the much later 'miracle' attributed to this day to St Dominic at San Domingo de la Calzada in northern Spain, where a pair of rather gloomy hens cooped in the south transept recall the memory of the life-restoring power of the local saint.

THE TRANSLATION OF THOMAS BECKET

The translation of Thomas Becket in 1220 was without question a highly significant factor in stimulating interest in local saints throughout Western Christendom. In the immediate aftermath of his translation a large number of other local saints were also enshrined, or re-enshrined.

There is little contemporary documentary evidence for the appearance

[1] *Winchester Annals*, 74–7. Perhaps the annalist half recalled Christ's warning against *pseudochristi et pseudoprophetæ*, Mark 13:22.

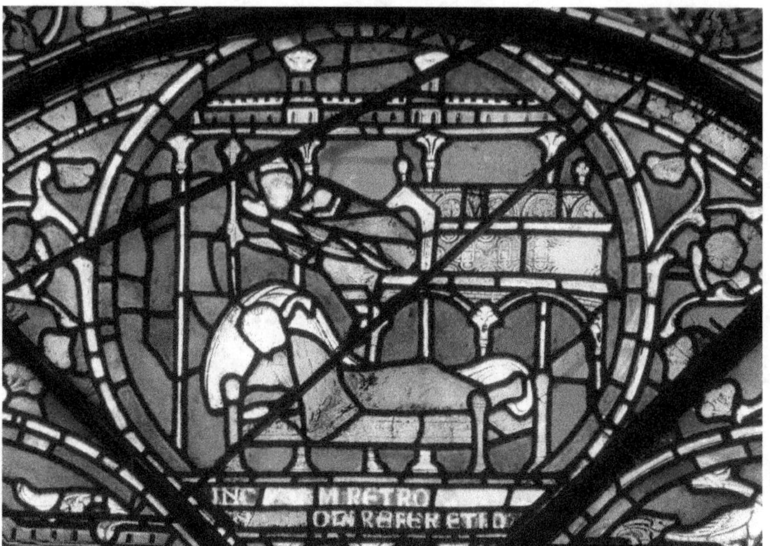

PLATE 8.1 CANTERBURY CATHEDRAL, TRINITY CHAPEL Window n.III (detail). St Thomas emerges from his first shrine.

of the shrine into which St Thomas's remains were translated by Archbishop Stephen Langton on 7 July 1220. Matthew Paris simply resorts to a conventional phrase, that the *theca* was composed 'of the finest refined gold and most precious stones' (*de auro obrizo purissimo et gemmis pretiosissimis*).[2] One piece of more or less contemporary graphical evidence is perhaps not as reliable as is sometimes supposed. A scene from the early thirteenth-century glass in the Trinity chapel ambulatory at Canterbury shows the saint emerging from a *theca* or *feretrum* supported on pillars to appear to a sleeping monk, perhaps one of the authors (Benedict or William) of the early *Miracula*, written in 1172–4.[3] The piers of an arcade are clearly visible behind both the monument and the bed in front of it, so there is no doubt that the artist was trying to show a simple six-legged table type of shrine-base. The shrine also features in the westernmost window of the Trinity chapel ambulatory,[4] where a woman is depicted kneeling before a draped altar with a lamp above and a small reliquary raised on pillars with capitals and moulded bases on the east side.[5] It would, however, be unwise to conclude from these images that the shrine inaugurated in 1220 consisted simply of a slab raised on pillars like the twelfth-century shrines at Durham and St Albans. It is surely likely that the windows were glazed before the

[2] Matthew Paris, *Historia Anglorum* (*alias Historia Minor*), ed. F. Madden, 3 vols., RS, 44 (1866–9), ii. 241.

[3] M. H. Caviness, *The Windows of Christ Church Cathedral Canterbury*, CVMA—Great Britain, II (Oxford, 1981), 187.

[4] Window s.VII.

[5] Caviness, *Windows*, 214, fig. 366.

translation ceremony,[6] and the artist's representation might have been based on typical extant examples rather than the new monument.[7] If so, the depiction of the shrine need not be taken as proof that the glass dated from after 1220. On the other hand, the windows do include representations of the tomb-shrine in the crypt, but as this monument remained in place after the translation, its portrayal does not necessarily imply that the glass was painted before 1220.

One thing seems reasonably certain: there are no accounts of a major reconstruction of the shrine after the first translation, and there is little reason to doubt that the monument consecrated in 1220 survived until 1538, though it was undoubtedly refurbished and embellished from time to time.[8] We are hampered in our analysis by the lack of early illustrations of the structure; many depictions were probably destroyed at the Reformation as part of the attempt to erase Becket's memory. A rare survival is at St Mary's church Nettlestead (Kent), where a window in the nave, datable to 1425 × 1439, portrayed episodes from the Life of Becket and miracles at the shrine. The window was severely damaged, either at the Reformation or in the great storm of 19 August 1763, but fragments were preserved. They were first assembled in the east window then reset in the westernmost window on the

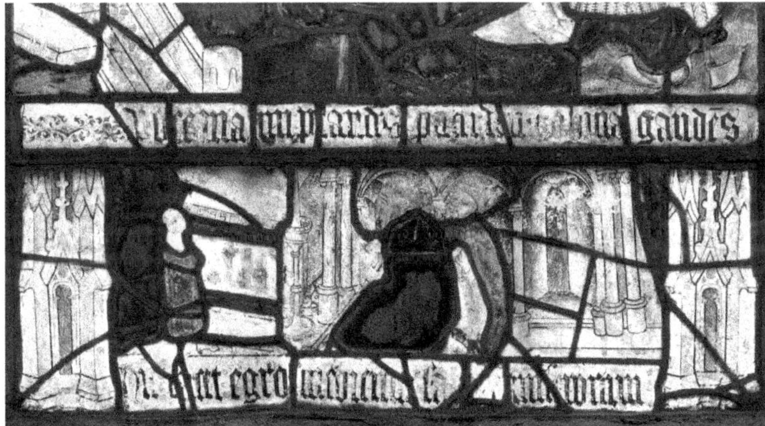

PLATE 8.2 NETTLESTEAD (KENT) Window on north side of nave (detail) showing the shrine of St Thomas.

[6] For the relationship between the shrine and its representation, and the value of the depictions as dating evidence, see M. H. Caviness, *The Early Stained Glass of Canterbury Cathedral, c.1175–1220* (Princeton, 1977), 23–35, where she concludes that the glazing of the Trinity chapel was certainly completed by 1220, but could have begun somewhat earlier.

[7] Caviness, ibid., 34, suggests, however, that 'the design of the shrine, if not the shrine itself, was available to the glass painter as a model'.

[8] According to his 'Memorandum Book', BL, Cotton MS Galba E.iv, in 1314 Prior Eastry added a new gold 'crest' to the shrine: *Pro nova cresta auri feretrum Sancti Thomæ faciendum £7 10s 0d.* At the same time the prior expended £115 12*s* 0*d pro corona sancti Thomæ, aurum et argentum et lapides preciosi ornanda.* Printed in J. Dart, *The History and Antiquities of Canterbury …* (London, 1726), Appendix, item v, p. iii.

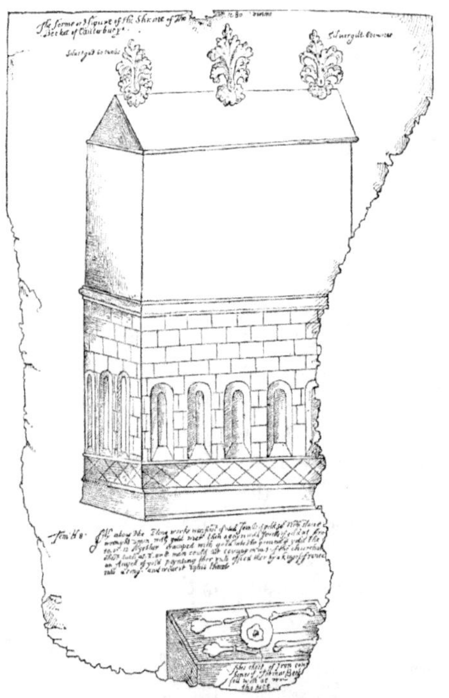

PLATE 8.3 DRAWING PURPORTING TO SHOW THE SHRINE OF ST THOMAS OF CANTERBURY From BL, Cotton MS Tiberius E.viii. It is based solely on written descriptions after the monument had been demolished and is of little evidential value.

north side in 1909.[9] One scene seems to show the lower part of the shrine-base from the south, with three vaulted niches behind round-headed arches springing from single shafts. The corners of the monument are formed of shaft clusters and there is an altar at the west end. Even had the entire image survived, its accuracy as a representation would have been open to question. Nevertheless, Becket's translation took place at a time when the pillared type of shrine was beginning to give way to the solid variety with niches; and the drawing conforms with the new type.

One frequently reproduced illustration is more suspect: this is the drawing preserved in a fire-damaged manuscript in the Cotton Collection.[10] It is labelled 'The forme of the shrine of Tho Becket of Canterburye', and the very absence of the word 'Saint' implies a post-Reformation date. The manuscript itself is a compendium of documents of widely ranging date, the latest of which is datable to the early seventeenth century; the drawing of the shrine and its accompanying text are probably mid-sixteenth century.

The drawing may have been copied from an earlier document. It was done first in pencil, then inked over, which might imply the uncertainties of a copyist. A large stone base is depicted, with five round-arched apertures in the side and three in the end, surmounted by a plain rectangular gabled object, presumably the actual reliquary, with three prominent finials on the apex of the roof; the finials are labelled with their materials and weight. The end ones were of silver gilt, weighing 60oz., while the central one was heavier at 80oz. The text below the drawing also stresses the value of the precious materials contained in the shrine:

> Al aboue the stoneworke was first of wood Jewells of gold set with stone *covered with plates of gold,* wrought uppon with gold wier then agayn with Jewells of gold as *brooches, images, angels, rings,* 10. or 12. together cramped with gold into the ground of gold The *spoils of which filled two* chests such as .6. or .8. men could but

[9] CVMA Inventory No. 5761: St Mary's Nettlestead, window n.V.

[10] BL, Cotton MS Tiberius E.viii, fo. 278v (following the most recent refoliation of the MS).

> conuay on out of the church at *one side was a stone with* an Angell of gold poynting therunto offred ther by a king of France *which King Henry put* into a ring and wear it on his thomb.[11]

Most curious of all is a small sketch at the bottom of the page, apparently depicting an open chest, with four longbones laid lengthways and a circle in the middle. Was this intended as a depiction of the innermost chest within the reliquary or, as some have suggested, of a repository in which the bones of the saint were covertly buried against the king's wishes? The words written on the side of the chest give some credence to the latter idea: 'This chest of iron cont*ained the* bones of Thomas Becket *scull and* all with the wounde *of his death* and the pece cut *out of his scull layde in the same wounde*.'

The drawing is worthy of attention as evidence for continued interest in the physical setting of saints' cults in the post-Reformation period. It is, however, fairly clear that it was simply based on verbal description, probably that of John Stow, whose *Annals* of *c.*1538 were translated from the Latin to provide the text accompanying the drawing. It must reluctantly therefore be dismissed as first-hand graphical evidence for the form of the shrine.

The shrine inaugurated in 1220 was the work of Walter of Colchester (†1248), who attended the translation,[12] and of Elias of Dereham.[13] Walter was one of an important family of craftsmen who had become monks at St Albans in the early thirteenth century. He was recognised by his contemporaries as an outstanding artist (*pictor et sculptor incomparabilis*, as Matthew Paris called him),[14] and had produced a wonderful rood screen at St Albans.

Despite Thomas Cromwell's efforts to obliterate the cult, some physical elements have survived. The shrine was raised on a large platform with three steps, around which was a rectangular band of pink marble at pavement level.[15] This is still in place, and the wear marks left by the feet of pilgrims, perhaps kneeling on the bottom step, are apparent. The groove cuts through one of the thirteenth-century decorative roundels, so there is no doubt that the stones are in their original position. The Purbeck marble steps, on the other hand, were recycled after 1538 as part of the pavement beneath where the shrine had formerly stood, and these blocks are also worn. Other fragments are less certain. A few pieces of pink marble, including fragments

[11] The ends of the lines are missing, having been damaged by the fire of 1731, but the text (here italicised) may be supplied from the Latin version given in an engraving in Dugdale's *Monasticon* and from John Stow's *Annals*, *s.a.* 1538.

[12] Matthew Paris, *Chronica Maiora*; ed. Luard, iii. 59–60: *Walterus, monachus et sacrista ecclesiæ Sancti Albani, mirabilis artifex, cuius documento omnia tractabantur.*

[13] For Elias, canon of Salisbury, see R. Allen Brown, H. M. Colvin, and A. J. Taylor, *The History of the King's Works I, The Middle Ages* (London, 1963), 99–101; A. Hastings, *Elias of Dereham, Architect of Salisbury Cathedral* (Much Wenlock, *c.*1997); N. Vincent, 'Dereham, Elias of', *DNB*, xv. 868–9.

[14] *GA*; ed. Riley, i. 280.

[15] T. Tatton-Brown, 'The Trinity Chapel and Corona Floor', *Canterbury Cathedral Chronicle*, 75 (1981), 50–6.

of triple-shaft capitals in the Museum of Canterbury, have been identified as remains of the actual shrine-base,[16] but these are fairly uninformative as to its design.

Although the shrine has vanished, its splendid architectural setting remains, together with the tombs of the Black Prince (†1376), Archbishop Courtenay (†1395), and Henry IV (†1413), who were buried between the arcade columns, close to the saint. Another survival is a sizeable area of the *opus Alexandrinum* pavement on the west side of the site of the shrine. Christopher Norton has suggested that elements of this pavement might date from the early twelfth century and that it was recycled from Anselm's 'Glorious Choir'.[17]

THE HEAD OF ST THOMAS AND OTHER HEAD SHRINES

No attempt was made at the time of the 1220 translation to suggest that Thomas's body was incorrupt. This meant that some fragmentation of the remains could take place almost at once. In any case, the piece of bone sliced from the saint's skull was already detached: known as the *corona* (crown) it was displayed in the newly completed Corona chapel at the extreme east end of the cathedral.[18] The earliest treasurers' accounts for the *corona* date from 1198–9,[19] perhaps indicating the date at which the incomplete chapel came into use.[20] The part standing for the whole, the relic was known as Becket's 'head': it therefore conformed with a developing trend in the thirteenth century for the head of a saint to be separately enshrined. The saint's head presumably remained in the Corona until 1548, and Erasmus may have been confused when he reported seeing it in the crypt. He had probably been shown the head of St Dunstan, separately enshrined since 1508.[21] The relic seems to have been displayed on the altar platform at the east end of the Corona, where marks of the original altar are still discernible in the pavement;[22] and a possible fragment of the head-shrine pedestal, in pink marble, at the time of writing ignominiously lies on the floor of the entrance

[16] W. Urry, 'Some notes on the two resting places of St Thomas Becket at Canterbury', in *Thomas Becket, Actes du Colloque International de Sédières, 19–24 août 1973*, ed. R. Foreville (Paris, 1975), 195–209, at 204–6.

[17] C. Norton, 'The luxury pavement in England before Westminster', in *Westminster Abbey: The Cosmati Pavements*, ed. L. Grant and R. Mortimer, Courtauld Research Papers, No. 3 (Aldershot, 2002), 7–27, at 15; T. Tatton-Brown, 'The two great marble pavements in the sanctuary and shrine area of Canterbury Cathedral and Westminster Abbey', in *Historic Floors: their Care and Conservation*, ed. J. Fawcett (Oxford, 1998), 53–62.

[18] In 1287/8 the *custos coronæ* was Peter de Ickham: J. Greatrex, *Biographical Register*, 207.

[19] Nilson, *Cathedral Shrines*, 147, 211–15.

[20] The upper stages of the chapel were roughly finished off in the sixteenth century and altered again in the eighteenth century.

[21] *Erasmus, Pilgrimages to St Mary and St Thomas*, trans. J. G. Nichols, 2nd edn. (London, 1875), 42. For the removal of Dunstan's skull in 1508 see Nilson, *Cathedral Shrines*, 32.

[22] See plan in Tatton-Brown, 'Trinity Chapel and Corona Floor', 54–5.

lobby to the cathedral library where the librarian Bill Urry, having discovered it in the precincts, deposited it many years ago.

An inventory of the relics at Canterbury Cathedral made on 2 February 1315/16 mentions three other head reliquaries: those of St Blaise 'in a silver head, gilded'; of St Fursa 'in a silver head, gilded and enamelled'; and of St Austroberht 'in a silver head enamelled and gilded'. All three were kept in a great reliquary *armoire* (*in magno armariolo reliquiarum*) near the high altar.[23] Its position is known from the archiepiscopal register of Henry Chichele, who had requested to be buried on the north side of the choir between the 'place of the relics' and the entrance to the choir from the 'vestibule' to the high altar.[24] Surprisingly, St Swithun's head is not specifically mentioned in the inventory; it had also been at Canterbury since it was taken there by Archbishop Ælfheah on his translation from Winchester in 1006. According to Eadmer, it had been placed in the high altar of Canterbury Cathedral;[25] by the end of the fourteenth century at least part of it had found its way to Évreux.[26] But the inventory does mention the 'body' (*corpus*) of the saint, so perhaps the compiler of the inventory was confused about the nature of the relic.

Head relics were found in many other churches. Lincoln boasted a head reliquary (*chef*) allegedly containing relics of St Ursula and the 11,000 Virgins. There was a chapel of St Richard's head at Chichester, where on at least two occasions Edward I made oblations *ad capud dicti sancti*.[27] At York and Lincoln in the later thirteenth century both St Thomas and St Hugh had separate head reliquaries independent of the main shrine. The heads of SS. Oswald and Wulfstan at Worcester were separately enshrined. In 1319, for example, Bishop Thomas of Cobham (1317–27), writing to the sacrist, mentioned offerings *ad feretrum et ad capud sancti Wolstani*, which were evidently not one and the same.[28] In 1394–5 timber was purchased *pro quodam trabe ad capita sanctorum Oswaldi et Wulfstani*.[29] The final reference to the head relics occurs shortly before the Reformation, in an inventory of

[23] BL, Cotton MS Galba E.iv, printed in *Inventories of Christchurch Canterbury*, ed. J. Wickham Legg and W. H. St. John Hope (Westminster, 1902), item II (ed. St John Hope), pp. 9–94. The editor states (p. 10) that the inventory was one of two 'compiled probably for and under the direction of Henry of Eastry, prior from 1285 to 1331'.

[24] ... *ad partem borialem chori nostri inter locum reliquiarum et introitum chori de vestibulo ad summum altare ibidem*: *The Register of Henry Chichele, Archbishop of Canterbury 1414–1443*, ed. E. F. Jacob, 2 vols., Canterbury and York Soc., vols. 45 and 42 (Oxford, 1943 (vol. i) and 1937), i. 123 (document dated 21 April 1432).

[25] Eadmer, *De reliquiis S. Audoeni*, 365–6.

[26] J. Crook, 'The rediscovery of St Swithun's head at Evreux', in the *Cult of St Swithun*, ed. M. Lapidge, Winchester Studies, 4.ii (Oxford, 2003), 61–5.

[27] BL, Add. MS 7956, fo. 55 (Wardrobe Book, 25 Ed. I), cited in A. J. Taylor, 'Edward I and the shrine of St Thomas of Canterbury', *JBAA*, 132 (1979), 22–8, at 23, n. 9 (oblations made in 1297).

[28] *The Register of Thomas de Cobham, Bishop of Worcester, 1317–27*, ed. E. H. Pearce, Worcestershire Historical Soc. (1930), 21.

[29] Account roll of William de Merstone, *tumbarius* 1394–5, Worcester Cathedral Library, MS C.459a. Merstone was *tumbarius* from Christmas 1394 to Michaelmas 1404. I am grateful to Dr Joan Greatrex for this information and transcription.

*c.*1535 enumerating objects in the care of the 'Tumbary', including 'Seynt Oswalde and seynt Wlstans hede w^{t} selver and gylte, A myter for seynt Oswalds hed w^{t} stonys sett ther ynn'.[30] A fifteenth-century 'sacrist's ledger' also lists as separate items the *capud beati Oswaldi archiepiscopi, capud beati Wlstani.*[31] The head of St Chad at Lichfield was also separately enshrined, and a special shrine-keeper is attested in 1481, the *custos capitis sancti Cedde.*[32] The *chef* was kept on an altar dedicated to the saint. Many other examples of head reliquaries could be cited: the head of St Piran, the patron saint of Cornwall, was displayed within the 'old church' on the coast at Perranzabuloe, south of Perranporth, and attracted local pilgrimage.

Head reliquaries were evidently still considered *de rigueur* for a saint's cult in the later middle ages. One was provided for St Osmund at the time of his belated canonisation in 1457. Its construction by the goldsmith 'John [the] Jew' is mentioned in some detail in a fragmentary and damaged financial account.[33] The reliquary was evidently of silver gilt, adorned with precious stones, including 'xx grete stonys for the mytre and the fote ... xxvi stonys for the mytre ... xvi stonys for the Crowne'. Its total cost was a huge £52 1*s* 8½*d.* The stone base of one head shrine from the fourteenth century has survived, that of St Hugh of Lincoln.[34] The main cult of the saint developed in the thirteenth century, however, and we should now explore its complexities.

ST HUGH OF LINCOLN

The fact that the great Carthusian bishop Hugh of Lincoln (1186–1200) was canonised in 1220, the very year that Becket was translated, is no more than a happy coincidence, but it must have given a boost to the contemporary enthusiasm for local saints' cults. Bishop Hugh had died in London on 16 November 1200 and his body was borne in procession back to Lincoln, as described in considerable detail by his chaplain and close confidant, Adam of Eynsham.[35] Adam was present when the bishop's entrails were removed and his body embalmed with spices (*multis aromatibus*) to reduce the effects of putrefaction during the long journey. Adam recalled that all the witnesses were astonished that Hugh's internal organs remained so clean: they seemed 'purer than glass' (*uitro purior*).[36] The arrival of the body, described both by Adam and in a second-hand account by Gerald of Wales, was a prestigious *adventus* ceremony: the procession was met by two kings, two archbishops,

[30] BL, Harley MS 604, fo. 118.

[31] Worcester Cathedral Library, MS Mun A22.

[32] J. Hewitt, 'The Keeper of St Chad's Head in Lichfield Cathedral', *Arch. J.*, 33 (1876), 71–82.

[33] Register II, MS, Salisbury Cathedral Archives, fo. 41v, printed in Malden, *St Osmund*, 217–18.

[34] For the head cult see below, pp. 264–6.

[35] Adam of Eynsham, *Magna Vita*, bk. iv, caps. 19–20; ed. Douie and Farmer, ii. 217–32. The Life was probably completed within fifteen years of the bishop's death (ibid., i. p. xii). Adam died in 1233.

[36] ibid., ii. 218–19.

twelve bishops, and a bevy of counts, barons, abbots, and priors. At the cathedral, vast multitudes of faithful surged forward to kiss the *feretrum*, and once the bier reached the choir there was scarcely room for the canons to stand in their stalls. Although Gerald of Wales was not present, he was full of praise for the splendour of the occasion, judging it the first of St Hugh's posthumous miracles.[37]

But Adam of Eynsham's account must be more reliable as he was an eye-witness to the whole sequence of events, culminating in the entombment at Lincoln. He records various miracles which occurred during the four-day northward journey via Hertford, Biggleswade, Buckden, Stamford, and Ancaster; and he relates how he personally vested the dead bishop in his episcopal robes for the last time, how the body miraculously assumed a ruddy hue, and how Hugh was finally laid to rest. The bishop had decreed that his tomb should lie close to the altar of St John the Baptist, a figurehead Carthusian saint to whom he had a particular devotion: Adam recalled that Hugh had commanded, 'Place me before the altar of the patron saint I have so often mentioned, the precursor of Our Lord, in any fitting place near a wall, in order that my tomb may not take up too much of the pavement and obstruct or injure those who pass by, as I have seen happen in so many great churches.'[38] Gerald of Wales confirms that Hugh was buried near the altar of St John the Baptist, on the left (north) side.[39] The *Magna Vita* also records that the bishop had given very specific instructions about his burial: he had asked to be 'securely hidden in two coffins, one of lead and the other of stone, so he would not be visible, neither would it be possible for ornaments to be taken.'[40]

Some of the *miracula* drawn up in support of Hugh's canonisation also mention the chapel and provide information about the monument itself. Whilst the actual coffin was well below pavement level, over it was a superstructure of *foramina* type, allowing suppliants to get a little closer to the venerated body.[41] One miracle indicates that the superstructure was made of 'marble' (perhaps Purbeck) panels, cemented together.[42]

[37] *Gerald of Wales*, vii. 83–147, at 114–17. Gerald added these *Miracula* 'before 1223', some years after the composition of the main text *c.*1213: Gransden, *Historical Writing, I*, 310.
[38] Adam of Eynsham, *Magna Vita*, bk. iv, cap.16; ed. Douie and Farmer, ii, 192: *Ante aram … sepedicti patroni mei precursoris Domini, ubi congruentius uidebitur spatium, secus murum aliquem ponetis me, ne pauimentum loci tumba, ut plerisque in ecclesiis cernimus, importune occupet, et incedentibus offendiculum prestet aut ruinam.* Cf. ibid., bk. iv cap. 20; ii. p. 232: *Sepultus est, sicut ipse nobis preceperat, secus parietem non procul ab altari sancti Iohannis Baptiste, et sicut uisum est propter accessum confluentis populi magis congruere, a boreali ipsius edis regione.*
[39] *Gerald of Wales*, *Distinctio ii*, cap. 4; ed. Dimock, vii. 123.
[40] Adam of Eynsham, *Magna Vita*, bk. iv, cap 16; ed. Douie and Farmer, ii. 192: … *in sepulchro duplici, plumbeo scilicet et lapideo, utroque solidissime obserato … nec uidere illud quisquam, nec sua sibi ornamenta preripere ualuisset.*
[41] See above, p. 195.
[42] ibid. For the cement, see the miracle of the cure of John of Plumgard, who cured his skin cancer by applying to the lesions scrapings of the mortar with which the tomb was fixed together (*cæmentum, quo lapides tumulis iungebantur, cultello suo abrasum*): *Gerald of Wales*; ed. Dimock, vii. 81–147, at 141.

It is at this point that the interpretative difficulties arise, owing to uncertainty over the location of the Baptist's chapel. It is reasonable to suppose, particularly in view of the Carthusian associations of the latter saint, that it was one of the chapels at the cathedral's east end, which Bishop Hugh himself had rebuilt from 1192.[43] This conjecture is supported by the fact that when that east arm was again remodelled in 1256–*c.*1280 as the Angel Choir, the central chapel of the square-ended chevet was dedicated to John the Baptist. It is likely that the dedications simply replicated the previous arrangement. Bishop Hugh may therefore have chosen to be buried in the most prestigious chapel of his short-lived east arm. The latter's unusual polygonal plan, first observed during building works in 1791, is approximately known from a rather inadequate excavation carried out in November 1886 under the watchful eyes of Precentor Edmund Venables.[44] Peter Kidson has plausibly suggested that St Hugh, with his enthusiasm for saints, had intended this unusually shaped axial chapel, resembling a corona, as a reliquary chapel for his Norman predecessor Remigius, whose canonisation he was seeking in the 1190s.[45] At that time Gerald of Wales was, presumably at Bishop Hugh's request, compiling Remigius's *Vita*. The bishop must then have been confident that Remigius would be canonised, and Hugh's choice of a grave on the north side of the chapel would have assured him a place near a major new saint—though in the end, the canonisation attempt failed. But even leaving Remigius aside, one might have expected that Hugh would wish to be buried, as founder and patron, within the new works that he had initiated and which were perhaps scarcely complete at his death.

The conjecture that Bishop Hugh was buried in the axial chapel of his new works is supported by a discovery made during Precentor Venables's excavation of 1886. An empty lead-lined stone coffin was revealed within the foundations of the north-east wall of the late twelfth-century chapel, a place conforming with the description in the *Magna Vita*.

The discovery did not, however, come as a surprise to the excavators, for this was close to the spot which in 1540,[46] and again two centuries later,[47] had been identified as the site of the final shrine of St Hugh, destroyed on 11 June 1540. Here a monument had been erected in the post-Restoration period by Bishop Fuller (1667–75). Venables believed that it covered a tomb

[43] For much of what follows I am indebted to Jennifer S. Alexander, 'The Angel Choir of Lincoln Cathedral and the shrines of St Hugh', *JBAA*, 148 (1995), 137–47.

[44] [Edmund Venables], 'The recent discovery of the Foundations of the Apse of St. Hugh's Cathedral, at Lincoln, by the Rev. The Precentor of Lincoln', *Reports and Papers of the Associated Architectural Socs.*, xviii, pt. ii (1886), 87–95. The discoveries of 1791 had been sketched (from notes and memory) by John Carter.

[45] P. Kidson, 'St Hugh's Choir', in *Medieval Art and Architecture at Lincoln Cathedral, BAA Trans.*, vol. 8 for 1982 (Leeds, 1986), 29–42, at 32–4.

[46] *Chapter Acts of the Cathedral Church of Lincoln, A.D. 1536–1547*, ed. R. E. G. Cole, Lincoln Record Soc., 13 (1917), 36, n. 1.

[47] Browne Willis, *A Survey of the Cathedrals of Lincoln, Ely, Oxford, and Peterborough* (London, 1730), preliminary plan.

in which the saint's bones had been reinterred after the destruction of the shrine. Thus, he was both disappointed and puzzled to find that the lead-lined coffin contained 'a decaying mass of linen and silken vestments so arranged as roughly to simulate the shape of a human body', but not a trace of bone.[48] Photographs of the excavation and of the tomb were taken at the time, but were not published until thirty-six years later.[49]

Precentor Venables had not paid sufficient attention to the documentary record. It is in fact clear that St Hugh's body was moved more than once during the thirteenth century. In 1220 petitions for Hugh's canonisation were successful, and Pope Honorius III gave the customary instruction that the new saint should be removed from his existing grave and more honourably located.[50] There is evidence that his injunctions were heeded, for Thomas Wykes later recorded, in a part of his chronicle written *c.*1275–82,[51] that Hugh was translated in 1219.[52] Wykes was an Augustinian canon of Osney, an abbey within the diocese of Lincoln, and there is no reason to distrust his testimony, which he presumably found in one of the Osney chronicles. A translation in 1220, following the injunctions in the papal bulls relating to the canonisation, would indeed be expected. Unfortunately, some later accounts imply that Hugh's body was not elevated until a later translation in 1280, and this led Precentor Venables and some more recent scholars to argue that the saint's bones had remained in their *foramina* tomb for a further sixty years.[53] However, Jennifer Alexander has adduced evidence in support of Thomas Wykes's chronology: she has analysed the evidence of charter witness lists showing that during the early thirteenth century two different individuals, Philip and Adam, concurrently exercised the functions of chaplain *de tumba sancti Hugonis* (of the *tomb* of St Hugh) and chaplain *de feretro sancti Hugonis* (of the *feretrum* of St Hugh). This indicates that the tomb and shrine were separate.[54] She suggests, furthermore, that the first shrine was located in the north-east chapel of the north-east transept, which was enlarged at that period.[55] Any archaeological evidence for this conjecture was almost certainly removed during the remodelling of the chapel by James Essex in 1772.

[48] Venables, 'Recent discovery', 95.
[49] Cole and Johnston, 'St Hugh'.
[50] *Gerald of Wales*; ed. Dimock, vii. 243–7 (Appendix I), at 246: *Cum autem venerabile corpus ejus a loco in quo est transferri oporteat et honorificientius collocari* ...; ibid., *Cum venerabile corpus beati Hugonis a loco in quo est transferendum sit et dignius collocandum* ...
[51] E. D. Kennedy, 'Wykes, Thomas', *DNB*, lx. 640–1.
[52] 'The Chronicle of Thomas Wykes', in *Annales Monastici*, iv, ed. H. R. Luard, RS, 36d (1869), 6–319, at 61.
[53] e.g. Stocker, 'Mystery, 89–124.
[54] Alexander, 'Angel Choir', 144, citing twenty-nine examples of this distinction from the *Registrum Antiquissimum*, ed. C. W. Foster and K. Major, 10 vols., plus 2 vols. of facsimiles, Lincoln Record Soc. (1931–73).
[55] Precentor Edmund Venables, 'The shrine and head of St. Hugh of Lincoln', *Arch. J.*, 50 (1893), 37–61, at 39, believed that the transept chapel was that of John the Baptist in which Hugh had first been buried—an error perpetuated by James Dimock: *Gerald of Wales*; ed. Dimock, vii. 223, n. 3.

The translation of 1220 seems to have been eclipsed by that of 1280, which is better documented, even though not all the documents have the same reliability. Perhaps the earliest account is a bald statement in a *memorandum* concerning the consecration of Thomas Bek as bishop of St David's that St Hugh was translated on the same day. Likewise an annal in William Rishanger's *Chronicle* states that in 1281 [*sic*] the venerable body of bishop Hugh was raised into 'a higher place',[56] a phrase which need not imply that he had not previously been elevated.

The later accounts seem to have been embroidered in such a way as to ignore the elevation of 1220. Thus, the author of a detailed description in the *Annals of the Carthusian Order* assumed that the body was being translated for the first time in 1280. The annal says that Archbishop John [Peckham] of Canterbury and Oliver Sutton, bishop of Lincoln, came to the tomb where the saint had been buried 'nearly eighty years before' (i.e. in December 1200) and discovered the almost intact (*quasi integrum*) body. When they felt the head, however, it came off, revealing a neck which was as ruddy as that of a recently dead man.[57] A somewhat similar addition of miraculous elements is found in another *Vita* published by Dimock as an appendix to the Rolls Series edition of Gerald of Wales's works.[58] Neither the annal nor the Life are consistent with the evidence that a tomb and a shrine co-existed from the time of Hugh's canonisation in 1220, though it is not impossible that the separate treatment of the body and the head dates from the second translation in 1280.

The later documentary sources are, however, of value for the light they shed on the form and position of the shrine at the time they were composed. Thus, the Carthusian Annals state that the body was placed in a *capsula* decorated with gold, silver, and precious stones, prepared in order to retain the body in perpetuity (*ad conservationem perpetuandam corporis præparata*), which was firmly fixed to the high marble *fabrica* which raised the monument by a suitable height.[59] Another account, from a Life of the saint edited by the Carthusian hagiographer Laurence Surius (†1578), states

[56] *Chronica Willelmi Rishanger, quondam monachi S. Albani*, ed. H. T. Riley, RS, 28.2 (1865), 99, *s.a.* 1281: *Hoc anno translatum est in locum eminentiorem venerabile corpus Beati Hugonis, quondam Episcopi Lincolniensis.*

[57] *Translatio corporis S. Hugonis Lincolniensis episcopi*, in *Catalogus Codicum Hagiographicorum Bibliothecæ Regiæ Bruxellensis, pars I, Codices Latini Membranei*, ed. Hagiographi Bollandiani (Brussels, 1886), 191–3, at 192: ... *post matutinas devote cantatas, ad tumbam sancti præsulis marmoream accedentes, corpus ipsius, quod fere octoginta annis, ut præmittitur, iacuerat tumulatum, quasi integrum reppererunt. Caput vero gloriosi corporis cum coepissent palpare, a corpore discingebatur, et collum rubeum velut hominis recenter mortui apparuit.* This *translatio* account, from a C15 MS (Brussels 298–306) is incomplete: the end was published by A. Poncelet, 'La Translation de S. Hugues de Lincoln', *Analecta Bollandiana*, 31 (1912), 463–5. The Carthusian annals were previously printed from the same MS by Charles le Couteulx, *Annales Ordinis Cartusiensis*, 8 vols. (Montreuil (France), 1887–91); for this passage see vol. iv (1888), 338–49 (*s.a.* 1280).

[58] *Gerald of Wales*; ed. Dimock, vii. 217–22 (Appendix F), at 221–2: 'Indulgences by Hugh and others to contributors to Lincoln Cathedral, and Translation of St. Hugh, Oct. 6, 1280'.

[59] *Translatio corporis*, ed. Hagiographi Bollandiani, 192.

that the body was finally placed in a casket (*theca*) decorated with gold, silver, and precious stones; and this casket was 'honourably placed in a suitably and sufficiently elevated place, not far from the most sacred head of that saint, next to the altar of blessed John the Baptist in the church of Lincoln'.[60] It would, however, be rash to infer from this account that the body and the head formed separate focuses of veneration from as early as 1220; and, as we shall see in the following chapter, the cult of St Hugh's head may not have taken off until the 1330s. There is some evidence that the main shrine containing Hugh's body was refurbished in 1310, two years after a protective grille had been placed around it.[61] The precious decoration and a few further details about the reliquary may be gleaned from the Lincoln manuscript known as the 'Welbourn Chantry Book', which states that John Welbourn, treasurer of Lincoln from 1350 to 1380, repaired the *feretrum*.

> As keeper of St Hugh he had the two upper sides of the same saint's *feretrum* repaired using pure gold plate, including a tabernacle and an image of St Paul standing within it on the north side, which things had previously been painted, and he even provided a new wooden canopy for the same.[62]

Both the Carthusian Annals and the Life of the saint printed by Surius indicate that the final shrine was not far from the head reliquary, which stood next to the altar of St John the Baptist. This provides a reference point for the chapel, because the masonry substructure of the head reliquary survives, at the junction between the central and northern chapels of the chevet. This is indeed not far from the shrine location proposed in this chapter. Furthermore there is good evidence for its final position: a contemporary *memorandum* appended to a copy of the 1536 royal injunctions concerning shrines copied in the cathedral's Treasurer's Book states that 'There were at that time [i.e. when shrines were destroyed according to Henry VIII's order] two shrines in that cathedral church; the one of pure gold, standinge on the back syde of the highe aulter neare unto Dalysons tombe : the place wyll easlye be knowen by the irons yet fastned in the pavement stones there.'[63] This statement is further supported by John Leland (†1552), who wrote that 'S. Hughe liethe in the body of the est parte of the chirche above [i.e. east of] the highe altare'.[64] It seems reasonable to

[60] *Gerald of Wales*; ed. Dimock, vii. 217–22 (Appendix F) at 222: *Tandem sacrum corpus in theca, auro, argento, et preciosis lapidibus ornata, reconditum est; ipsaque theca, loco congruo satisque sublimi e marmore structo, honorifice collocata est; non longe a sanctissimo ejus capite, quod juxta altare beatissimi Johannis Baptistæ in Lincolniensi ecclesia reposuerunt.*

[61] Cole and Johnston, 'St Hugh', 63. Their source is not given, and it seems possible that what was involved was the later refurbishment by John Welbourn.

[62] ibid., 47–72: *Qui eciam ut Custos Sancti Hugonis, fecit reparari ii. costas superiores feretri eiusdem, cum uno tabernaculo et i. ymagine Sancti Pauli stantis in eodem ex parte boreali, cum plato de auro puro, quæ fuerunt pro antea depictæ; et eciam canopeum novum de ligno pro eodem.*

[63] *Chapter Acts of the Cathedral Church of Lincoln, A.D. 1536–1547*, ed. Cole, 36, n. 1.

[64] Leland, v. 121–2.

suppose that the location was still well enough remembered in the mid-seventeenth century for Bishop Fuller to erect the present table-top monument in the correct place.

Let us summarise: the body was first laid to rest in 1200 in the north wall of Bishop Hugh's own chevet, then was elevated in 1220 and placed in an enlarged chapel in the north transept where it reposed until 1280. Finally it was moved once again into a prestigious position behind the high altar in the Angel Choir, over the site of the bishop's original tomb, an economy which would explain why after 1280 there are no further references to separate officers of the tomb and the shrine. Such are Jennifer Alexander's conclusions, and they seem plausible, involving the reluctant dismissal of David Stocker's ingenious argument that the shrine was located on top of the reredos of the high altar.[65] Needless to say, the debate would be avoided if there were any material evidence for the shrine, such as any indication of the pulley for the cover. At Winchester the rope passed through a pierced central key-stone of the vaulting, but the off-centred location proposed for the Lincoln shrine would obviously not allow this. Nor is any obvious disturbance evident in the vault above the proposed location, but such evidence might have been removed during post-medieval repairs.

Concerning the fate of the body at the Reformation, Canon Cole believed that it had been reinterred in the chapter house, where in 1919 the master mason told him that thirty years previously (1889) a headless corpse in episcopal vestments had been discovered in a tomb in the chapter house that was disturbed during building works.[66] Precentor Venables had, of course, been summoned, but he does not appear to have made the connection with St Hugh. Nevertheless, Canon Cole convinced himself that 'this headless body, still lying under the chapter house floor, is that of St. Hugh'. As for the head shrine, the surviving shrine-base and principal references date from the fourteenth century and will be studied in further detail in the next chapter.

THE DEVELOPMENT OF OTHER CULTS UNDER THE INFLUENCE OF BECKET

Becket's translation had an immediate knock-on effect on other, often older cults. Canterbury Cathedral's neighbours, the monks of St Augustine's Abbey, seem to have reacted rapidly to Becket's translation by promoting the cult of their own patron, Augustine himself. The events were recorded in a late fourteenth-century chronicle compiled by the St Augustine's monk William Thorne, who incorporated an earlier chronicle down to 1228 (now lost) written by an early thirteenth-century predecessor, Thomas Sprott.[67] It

[65] Stocker, 'Mystery'.

[66] Cole and Johnston, 'St Hugh', 71–2.

[67] Printed in Roger Twysden, *Historiæ Anglicanæ Scriptores Decem* (London, 1652), cols. 1758–2202 at 1793ff. For Sprott and Thorne see A. Gransden, *Historical Writing in England II, c.1307 to the Early Sixteenth Century* (London, 1982), 346.

is an unlikely tale of conspiracy and intrigue. Sprott says that immediately after the 1091 translation Abbot Wido had gone secretly to the new tomb-shrine and had removed the head and larger bones of the archbishop, hiding them in a stone coffin within the east wall nearby; he had placed the smaller pieces within the base of the tomb-shrine, and one small fragment in a lead coffer on top of the monument. The true location of the relics was secretly passed down amongst a select group of brethren. Then, Sprott continued, in 1221 the prior, John Marsh, opened up the east wall, discovered the coffin, and placed the bones in various receptacles: the larger bones were placed in a silver shrine; the lesser ones which had been discovered in the shrine-base were placed under a marble tomb; the third part, namely the small fragments which had been left in the shrine after the secret reburial in 1091, were put under the central window in the east part of the church. Abbot Hugh III (1220–5) had the head kept outside the shrine and placed in a head reliquary. All this sounds most improbable, and requires ignoring the suggestion of an earlier hagiographer, Goscelin, that Augustine's body was reasonably intact when it was first exhumed.[68] It seems more likely that the St Augustine's monks concocted a spurious tradition of the lost relics of their saint precisely in order to be able to bring about the 'miraculous discovery' of an early Canterbury archbishop whose cult would rival that of St Thomas in the cathedral. Tim Tatton-Brown has suggested that a new porphyry pavement may have been laid at the time of this translation, fragments of which were discovered in archaeological excavations at St Augustine's.[69] But Sprott's account must relate to a refurbishment of the saint's tomb, rather than his reliquary; it is hard to imagine that the monks were without a shrine of the saint from 1091 until the 1220s.

Three years later another dubious cult was relaunched at Dorchester-on-Thames, where the canons claimed to have rediscovered the relics of the Apostle to Wessex, St Birinus. It was a bold claim, contradicting Bede's statement that Hæddi, bishop of the West Saxons, had taken Birinus's body to Old Minster, Winchester when the bishopric was transferred to that church in 676.[70] The early tenth-century *Secgan* mentions that Birinus lay in the *Ealdan mynstre* at Winchester and makes no reference to Dorchester; and in the early thirteenth century the relics had recently been rehoused in the present Winchester Cathedral, probably in the south-east chapel. But in 1224, spurred on by a desire to claim a prestigious local saint, the canons of Dorchester petitioned Pope Honorius III, claiming that they possessed the true relics of the saint.[71] Archbishop Stephen Langton was appointed to

[68] See above, p. 135.
[69] Tatton-Brown, 'Pilgrimage shrines', 90–107, citing D. Sherlock and H. Woods, *St Augustine's Abbey: Report on Excavations 1960–78*, Kent Archaeol. Soc. Monograph Ser., iv (1988), 135–7.
[70] Bede, *HE*, iii.7; ed. Colgrave and Mynors, 232–3.
[71] The events are recorded in an addition to John of Tynemouth's abbreviated version of the *Vita S. Birini*; *Nova Legenda Anglie*, ed. Horstmann, i. 118–22.

examine the case. The canons ingeniously overcame the problem of Bede's version of events by claiming that the chronicler had been misinformed, and that the body Hæddi had taken to Winchester was in fact that of another local worthy called 'Bertinus', whose name had been confused with that of Birinus. A tomb was opened up revealing a bishop in pontificals, and a miracle obligingly occurred when a local hermit heard a heavenly voice confirming that Birinus was indeed buried on the Thames-side site.[72] The cult appears to have remained a very local affair, but in the early fourteenth century a new shrine-base was created, parts of which survive in a modern reconstruction, as described in the following chapter.

Finally, it should be noted that in 1220 work began on the new cathedral at Salisbury. By 1226 the Trinity chapel at the east end of the cathedral was complete, and Bishop Richard Poore ordered the body of 'blessed Osmund' together with those of Osmund's successors, Bishops Roger and Jocelyn, to be carried down the hill from Old Sarum. Osmund's disarticulated bones were probably 'buried' in a stone coffin within the plinth wall of the colonnade on the south side of the chapel, beneath the *foramina* tomb-shrine that had been created when the bishop's body was moved into the extended retrochoir at Old Sarum in the late twelfth century.[73] It seems likely that the bishop and his canons envisaged that Osmund would rapidly be canonised, and in 1228 they presented a petition to Pope Gregory IX. It failed. Later attempts to secure Osmund's canonisation were equally unsuccessful; so the saint remained, as it were, on the side-lines, being translated and moved to a new shrine in the centre of the Trinity chapel only in 1457.[74]

THE SAINTS OF EVESHAM: WIGSTAN, ECGWINE, AND OTHERS

In Chapter 4 we examined the growth of the cult of St Wigstan, whose body was translated from the crypt at Repton to Evesham in the early eleventh century by King Cnut. The cult may have received a boost in the second quarter of the twelfth century, when Prior Dominic wrote the *Vita* and *Miracula* of the saint.[75] But in 1207 Wigstan's *feretrum* was one of those smashed to pieces when the Norman tower collapsed (those of SS. Ecgwine, Odulf, and Credan miraculously survived the catastrophe).[76] Owing to malfeasance on the part of Abbot Robert Norreis, deposed in 1213, it was some time before repairs began. These are recorded in a *History* of the abbey

[72] For a summary of the development of the cult, see Love, *Three Saints' Lives*, lxxii–lxxiv.
[73] T. Tatton-Brown, 'The burial places of St Osmund', *Spire: 65th Annual Report of the Friends of Salisbury Cathedral* (Salisbury, 1999), 19–25; idem, 'Pilgrimage shrines', 96–7.
[74] See below, pp. 280–1.
[75] Published in *Evesham Chronicle*; ed. Macray, 325–37.
[76] Thomas of Marlborough, *History*, bk. iii, pt. iv, para. 436; *Thomas of Marlborough: History of the Abbey of Evesham*, ed. J. Sayers and L. Watkiss, OMT (Oxford, 2003), 416–19.

compiled by his eventual successor, Thomas of Marlborough, who had risen to fame within the monastery: he was appointed principal dean of the Vale of Evesham (1206), then sacrist (1217), prior (1218–29), and finally abbot, a post that he held until his death in 1236. Thomas's interest in his abbey's saintly cults is demonstrated by the fact that the *History* begins with the Life and *Miracula* of St Ecgwine, copied and partially rearranged from Prior Dominic's early twelfth-century text. His involvement was also practical. In 1217, whilst sacrist under Abbot Randulf (1214–29), Thomas supervised the creation of a new shrine (*feretrum nouum*) for St Wigstan;[77] and as prior he had a *thronum*, presumably a shrine-base, made for it. At the same time he designed a 'royal image' for the shrine, presumably a statue of the saintly prince rather than Henry III, which was made after he became abbot.[78] In 1233 he dedicated a chapel to St Wigstan, in which one may assume the reliquary was displayed.[79]

Marlborough also repaired the *feretrum* that Godric had constructed for St Ecgwine in the mid-eleventh century, which implies that its miraculous survival was not as complete as hagiographical conventions dictated.[80] The 'flowers and precious stones' were renewed; what the *flores* can have been is uncertain, but 'flowers', apparently of metal, also adorned the candlesticks around Becket's shrine.[81] Marlborough also created a shrine-base (*thronum*) to support the repaired *feretrum*, and the saint's cult was further enhanced by a window in the presbytery portraying St Ecgwine's story.[82]

Marlborough's use of the word *thronum* is interesting. It seems that he chose it as the closest Latin term to denote a new kind of shrine-base: the solid basal structure with niches which at this period seems to have been supplanting the earlier type supported on pillars, perhaps under the influence of the cult of St Thomas, whose shrine of 1220 appears, as we have seen, to have been of the type with prayer niches.

ELY AND THE SAINTLY FOURSOME

At Ely, the remains of the four saintly women seem to have been located behind the high altar of the Romanesque church. As noted in an *addendum* to the *Liber Eliensis*, there they remained until the thirteenth century, when Bishop Northwold undertook the remodelling of the Norman east end. The reconstruction of the choir clearly demanded changes in the liturgical arrangements; though it remains arguable as to

[77] ibid., bk. iii, pt. v, para. 521; ed. Sayers and Watkiss, 488–9.
[78] ibid., bk. iii, pt. v, para. 529; ed Sayers and Watkiss, 496–9: *Fecit etiam thronum feretro sancti Wistani et imaginem regiam eidem throno proposuit, quam perfecerat postquam factus est abbas.*
[79] ibid., bk. iii, pt. v, para. 544; ed. Sayers and Watkiss, 508–9.
[80] ibid., bk. iii, pt. v, para. 524; ed. Sayers and Watkiss, 492–3. For Godric's creation of the *feretrum* see above, pp. 75–6.
[81] Nilson, *Cathedral Shrines*, 51, citing 'Customary of the Shrine of St Thomas', fo. 9.
[82] Thomas of Marlborough, *History*, bk. iii, pt. v, para. 524; ed. Sayers and Watkiss, 492–3.

whether the prime purpose of the reconstruction was to provide improved space for the veneration of St Æthelthryth.[83]

For our purposes, the most important fact is that the shrine was reconstructed. It remained in its original relation to the high altar, i.e. immediately behind it. As patron, Bishop Northwold elected to be buried at the feet of the saint. Fragments of the monument are said to have survived, and they appear to be contemporary with the new works.[84] The survivals comprise a fragment of arcading enclosing a projecting gablet, and five fragments of a basal slab, with remains of an asymmetrical array of water-holding bases, suggesting that the monument was of the pillared variety, with four major shafts on each side supporting a three-bay arcade, and three smaller shafts set back at the centre of each bay. Needless to say, the identification of the fragments is tenuous.

There is some written evidence for the embellishment of the shrine in the fifteenth century: in 1455 the cover over the *feretrum* appears to have been renewed, and a carpenter and a 'graver' were procured to do the work, together with two painters. Eleven ells of linen cloth were purchased, presumably to line the cover.[85] This is really not much to go on, and as for the form of the shrines of the other three female saints of Ely, there is little or no evidence.

EDWARD THE CONFESSOR

The cult of Edward the Confessor owes its existence mainly to Henry III.[86] In Chapters 6 and 7 we studied the first slow beginnings of the cult at Westminster in the early twelfth century, followed by the saint's eventual canonisation in 1161, nearly a century after his death, and his translation two years later. We saw, too, how Ailred of Rievaulx reworked Osbert of Clare's workaday *Vita* into a more original narrative containing episodes that would nourish the artistic expressions associated with the cult. But even after 1163 Edward's cult never seems to have achieved the popular status that its initiators may have hoped for. All changed in the early years of Henry III's reign, when he developed a passionate devotion to the Confessor. In 1220 he had himself crowned a second time in the abbey church, and his adoption of Edward as patron seems to have occurred towards the end of that decade (previously he had wanted to be buried in the new chancel of the Temple Church). Not for nothing was his first-born son baptised by the name of Edward in 1239, and the Confessor even featured prominently in wall-paintings in Henry's bedroom in the Palace of Westminster, the so-

[83] P. Draper, 'Bishop Northwold and the cult of St Etheldreda', in *Medieval Art and Architecture at Ely Cathedral, BAA Trans.*, vol. 2, for 1976 (Leeds, 1979), 8–27.

[84] For a conjectural reconstruction of the shrine, see *VCH Cambridge and the Isle of Ely*, iv. ed. R. B. Pugh (1953), p. 71.

[85] ibid., iv. 72, citing Stewart, *Architectural History of Ely Cathedral*, 130.

[86] Binski, *Westminster Abbey*, 93–101.

called 'Painted Chamber'. By the 1240s Henry had assumed the role of patron of the abbey church that his Norman and Plantagenet predecessors had largely neglected, and had decided to rebuild it as a worthy setting for his own saintly *patronus*, buried there. As a result, the church would eventually become a royal mausoleum for the monarchs of England, though there are no indications that this was envisaged when the remodelling of the church began, a building project that was not quite complete at Henry's death.

The inception, and indeed the progress, of the remodelling was recorded by the St Albans monk Matthew Paris, who wrote that in 1245 the king, inspired by his devotion to St Edward, ordered St Peter's church at Westminster to be enlarged.[87] The cult was pursued even more energetically during the construction works, and in 1247 Henry ordered his magnates to attend the translation feast of the saint.[88] By then Henry's new Lady chapel, whose foundation stone was laid on the eve of his second coronation at Westminster in 1220,[89] must surely have been complete. It had to be integrated into the new works (whose form it may have constrained to a certain extent), and in 1256 its vault and roof were taken down prior to raising it still higher as part of the new works.[90] The thirteenth-century Lady chapel survived until it was replaced by the structure always known as 'Henry VII's Chapel'.

But the construction of the saint's new earthly home had begun four years before the start of work on the church: in 1241 Henry had chosen workmen 'from London' to create the shrine.[91] At that time, the Confessor's relics still reposed in the *locellum humile* of 1163. As already suggested, the illustrators of the *Estoire de Seint Aedward le Rei*, probably completed by 1250, may have portrayed the *foramina* shrine of 1163 as a model for the Confessor's original tomb. One illustration perhaps shows the kind of shrine they imagined the abbey was soon going to acquire.[92] It portrays a masonry substructure supporting the actual reliquary; we are evidently looking at the end of the monument, so there is just one *foramen*. The reliquary has foliate crockets and finials; its ends are embellished with statuary, presumably in bas-relief. The shrine is flanked by statues depicting the well-known story of St John appearing as a palmer to whom Edward gives a ring—elements of the Edward legend that featured in Ailred of Rievaulx's Life of the saint as well as in the *Estoire*.

[87] Matthew Paris, *Chronica Maiora*; ed. Luard, iv. 427: *Eodem vero anno* [1245], *dominus rex, quam habuit adversus sanctum Ædwardum, submonente, ecclesiam Sancti Petri Westmonasterii iussit ampliari.*

[88] ibid., iv. 640.

[89] The first stone of the Lady chapel had been laid on 16 May 1220: Matthew Paris, *Chronica Maiora*; ed. Luard, iii. 59. Cf. Ralph of Coggeshall, p. 188.

[90] For the Lady chapel, see Binski, *Westminster Abbey*, 10–13; also B. Harvey, 'The monks of Westminster and the old Lady chapel', in *Westminster Abbey, the Lady Chapel of Henry VIII*, ed. T. Tatton-Brown and R. Mortimer (Woodbridge, 2003), 5–31.

[91] Matthew Paris, *Chronica Maiora, s.a.* 1241; ed. Luard, iv. 156.

[92] Cambridge University Library, MS Ee.3.59, p. 55. Even though a shrine is clearly depicted, the text appertaining to the drawing still refers to the *sarcu*.

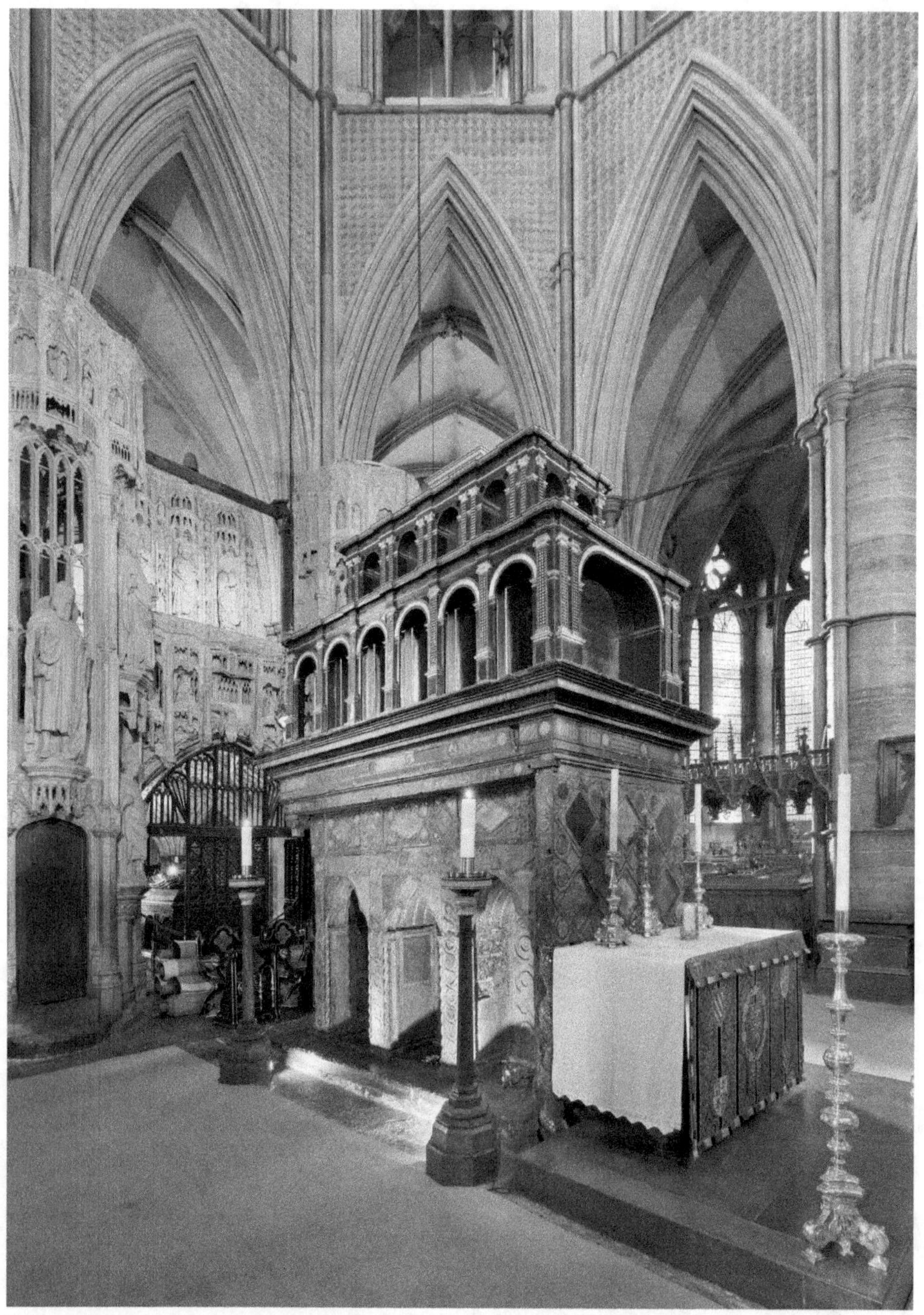

PLATE 8.4 WESTMINSTER ABBEY The shrine of Edward the Confessor, from the north-west.

The new shrine, within the chapel of St Edward immediately behind the high altar, was intended as the focus of the abbey church, and it was next to this monument that Henry III would elect to be buried. The original inscription around the shrine-base, known from a pre-Reformation transcription,[93] stated that it was the work of one '*Petrus ... civis Romanus*'; the Cosmati pavement in the choir is signed '*Odoricus*', and it has generally been assumed that both works were by the Italian marble-worker Pietro de Oderisio, though this identification has been challenged.[94] The inscription indicates that the shrine was completed in 1269, but Paul Binski has shown that accounts for the metalwork suggest that the decoration may not have been finished for a further twelve years.[95] Even so, the monument appears to have been sufficiently complete to be dedicated on 13 October 1269, a date recorded by numerous chroniclers.

Though in many ways a foreign hybrid, Edward the Confessor's monument is the finest of the medieval shrines to survive, albeit in a mid-sixteenth century reconstruction carried out during the reign of Queen Mary. Its original form was worked out by J. G. O'Neilly in 1958, and his reconstruction remains plausible.[96] Working upwards, it appears to have consisted of four steps, then an arcaded Purbeck marble base with Cosmati decoration supporting an upper slab; next, an inscribed band; finally a plinth on which the reliquary reposed. Whilst the Cosmati decoration and spiral pillars are 'clearly recognisable as Roman work',[97] the form of the shrine-base is emphatically local, in the tradition of English medieval high shrines, as, indeed, is the use of Purbeck marble. The reliquary or *feretrum* may well have been the one portrayed in *La Estoire de Seint Aedward le Rei*, for there is no reason to suppose that it was renewed at the same time as the shrine-base. At the west end of the new shrine-base was a reredos, against which stood an altar. The present altar there dates from 1902; O'Neilly thought that a monument in the south ambulatory was the original altar, but not all scholars accept this identification.[98]

Henry must have hoped that Edward would blaze forth as a national royal saint, outshining England's proto-martyr, perhaps even the great

[93] The inscription, of which only a fragment survives, was recorded, in an annotated version of Flete's history of the abbots and priors of Westminster, by the fifteenth-century monk Richard Sporley: BL Cotton MS, Claudius A.VIII, quoted in Binski, *Westminster Abbey*, 99.

[94] *Grove Dictionary of Art*, ed. J. Turner, 34 vols. (London, 1996), xxiv. 782–3, entry for Pietro de Oderisio by P. C. Claussen. The argument against Pietro di Oderisio's involvement is presented by J. Gardner, 'The Cosmati at Westminster: Some Anglo-Italian Reflections', in *Skulptur und Grabmal des Spätmitterlalters in Rom und Italien*, ed. J. Garms and A. M. Romanini (Vienna, 1991), 201–16.

[95] Binski, *Westminster Abbey*, 100–1.

[96] J. G. O'Neilly and L. E. Tanner, 'The Shrine of St. Edward the Confessor', *Archaeologia*, 100 (1966), 129–54, based on O'Neilly's 'prolonged and minute examination' undertaken in 1958.

[97] Claussen, 'Pietro de Oderisio', 783.

[98] T. Tatton-Brown, 'The pavement in the chapel of St Edward the Confessor, Westminster Abbey', *JBAA*, 153 (2000), 71–84, at 74.

Becket. Yet by the early fourteenth century Edward's fortunes were already waning, and he was replaced as the patron saint of England by a figure of doubtful authenticity, the eastern soldier-saint George. Finally it should be noted that Henry III's own tomb, with its huge slabs of purple porphyry, is itself as opulent as a shrine.

ST RICHARD OF CHICHESTER

The development of the cult of St Richard de Wych, bishop of Chichester (1244–53) is particularly well recorded. He died on 3 April 1253, and in his will left his soul to the Holy Trinity and the Blessed Virgin, and his body to be buried in the cathedral nave, near to the altar of Blessed Edmund the Confessor, next to one of the piers.[99] Richard had dedicated St Edmund's altar himself. It was at the east end of the north aisle, in a chapel formed by removing part of the aisle wall, and other chapels had similarly been formed further along the aisle at the same time. According to his biographer John Capgrave, Richard's sanctity was popularly recognised even before his burial: whilst his body was being carried to the church, people counted themselves happy if they touched the bier or even the hem of his vestments.[100] Further miracles occurred at the tomb, and scarcely had Pope Urban IV been elected than he was visited by two Chichester canons pressing for Richard's canonisation. The pope proclaimed Richard a saint and celebrated mass for him on St Vincent's Day, 1262. The bull did not include the usual instruction that the saint's body should be disinterred and elevated, and so the references to indulgences stated that these would be obtained at the *sepulchrum*.[101] But on 16 June 1276 Archbishop Robert Kilwardby, in the presence of the king and many bishops and nobles, translated the body into a silver and silver-gilt reliquary (*capsa argentea et deaurata*).[102] It was also studded with jewels, some of which were soon taken off but were replaced on Edward I's orders.[103] The saint's head was removed during the translation and was placed in a silver *chef* in the chapel of St Mary Magdalen. The main reliquary was placed on a platform and was protected by an iron grille, fragments of which are thought to survive.[104] Edward I evidently had a special devotion to the saint.

[99] W. H. Blaauw, 'Will of Richard de la Wych', *Sussex Archaeol. Collections*, 1 (1848), 164–92, at 166: ... *et corpus meum sepeliendum in maiori ecclesia Cicestrensi in navi eiusdem ecclesie prope altare beati Edmundi confessoris iuxta columpnam.*

[100] J. Capgrave, Life of St Richard 3:19; *AASS, Aprilis I*, 278F–282D at 282B: *felicem se quicque reputans, si vel feretrum tangat, vel vestimentorum sacrorum fimbriam contrectet.*

[101] The bull is printed in *AASS, Aprilis I*, 315A–317C.

[102] *Thomae Walsingham, quondam monachi S. Albani Historia Anglicana*, ed. H. T. Riley, 2 vols., RS, 28.1 (1863–4), i. 16. *Chronica Willelmi Rishangeri*, ed. Riley, 89, *s.a.* 1276. 'Osney Annals', in *Annales Monastici*, iv, ed. H. R. Luard, RS, 36d (1869), 3–352, at 268–9.

[103] *The history and constitution of a cathedral of the old foundation, Illustrated from documents (hitherto almost entirely unpublished) in the registry and muniment room of the cathedral of Chichester*, ed. C. A. Swainson (London, 1880), 47.

[104] T. Brighton, 'Art in the Cathedral from the Foundation to the Civil War', in *Chichester Cathedral; an Historical Survey*, ed. Mary Hobbs (Chichester, 1994), 69–84, at 79–80.

Six years after the translation the king and queen were again in Chichester and on 31 March 1296, just before St Richard's feast, they offered clasps (*firmacula*) that the goldsmith William of Faringdon had created at a cost of 103*s* 8*d* and 106*s* 8*d* respectively; Prince Edward offered one costing 100*s*. A lady called Edilina offered two golden clasps at the shrine on behalf of the princesses Maria and Elizabeth, costing 36*s*.[105] Another craftsman, Master Robert the Norman, provided three clasps costing £4 6*s* which were offered on behalf of the king's other daughters, Eleanor, Joan, and Margaret.[106]

The shrine platform did not survive the Reformation. Destroyed by order of Thomas Cromwell, it was reinstated in 1905 and is now a renewed focus for veneration of the saint.[107] The nearby watching loft survived, however, until it was taken down in 1820.[108]

HEREFORD: THOMAS CANTILUPE

The cult of St Thomas Cantilupe, a member of an influential Anglo-Norman family and bishop of Hereford from 1275–82, developed at the very end of the thirteenth century.[109] Bishop Thomas had died in Italy on 25 August 1282, aged around sixty; he was returning from a journey to Rome where he had sought the pope's release from a ban of excommunication imposed by Archbishop Peckham as a result of a dispute over ecclesiastical jurisdiction.[110] His body was taken to the monastery of San Severo, near Orvieto, where it was boiled up and dismembered,[111] only the bones and heart returning to England. The chronicler remarks laconically that 'the body was cooked': *corpus coctum fuit*, a grisly practice that was banned by Pope Boniface VIII in 1300.[112] The bones were initially buried beneath the floor of the Lady chapel of his cathedral, where the bishop's grave was marked by a large ledger stone.[113] Within a few years his successor, Richard Swinfield (1282–1317), was promoting his cult. The rapid creation of local episcopal saints by their successors in the see was, as we have noted, a feature of cults in Merovingian Francia and Anglo-Saxon England. But by the thirteenth century the papacy was claiming

[105] *Records of the Wardrobe and Household, 1285–1286*, ed. B. F. Byerly and C. R. Byerly, HMSO (London, 1977), 200–1, items 1992, 1995.

[106] ibid., 201, item 1997.

[107] T. Tatton-Brown, 'Destruction, Repair and Restoration', in *Chichester Cathedral; an Historical Survey*, ed. Mary Hobbs (Chichester, 1994), 143–56, at 143 and 153–5.

[108] Wall, *Shrines*, 127, merely observes that the watch-loft 'was removed so late as 1820'.

[109] The most complete recent account of the cult is Jancey, *Thomas Cantilupe*.

[110] For Bishop Thomas's life, see The Revd William Wolfe Capes's introduction to *Registrum Thome de Cantilupo*, ed. R. G. Griffiths and W. W. Capes, Canterbury and York Soc., 2 (London, 1907), i–lxxi.

[111] *Worcester Annals*, 355–562, at 483. The chronicler adds that a miraculous fountain sprang up in the place where the water used for the boiling had been thrown.

[112] Dom I. Barrett, 'The relics of St Thomas Cantilupe', in Jancey, *Thomas Cantilupe*, 181–5, at 181.

[113] *Compendium Vitæ [S. Thomæ de Cantilupe] ex Processu Canonizationis ex codice Vaticano 4015*, para. 38; *AASS*, *Octobris I*, 599D–609A, at 608.

exclusive right to canonisation,[114] and the process was beginning to take far longer. In 1286 Swinfield instructed his agents in Italy to find out whether any miracles had occurred at San Severo, and to determine the pope's views about the former bishop (*quid dominus papa senciat de episcopo supradicto*).[115] Meanwhile on 3 April 1287 he moved Thomas's bones to a new monument in the north transept of Hereford Cathedral: the prospective saint showed his willingness to cooperate by causing the heavy stone marking his former resting place in the Lady chapel to be easily removed by a couple of mere lads, and miracles occurred as soon as Thomas's remains were placed in the new tomb.[116] There are some indications that the prospective saint was initially venerated both at his old tomb and his new tomb-shrine, for on no fewer than three occasions (1289, 1293, and 1295) Swinfield had to resolve an internal dispute between the priory treasurer and the cathedral chapter over the division of the wax which pilgrims offered at the 'tombs' in the plural (*ad tumbas*).[117] The process of canonisation, which has been analysed in detail by Ronald Finucane,[118] took some thirty-four years to achieve, despite the enthusiastic support of Edward I and Edward II, and Bishop Swinfield spent much of his private income in pursuit of what appears to have become a personal obsession.[119] As early as April 1289 he was writing to the pope urging for Cantilupe to be canonised with speed, in view of the number of miracles already taking place.[120] Swinfield presumably also canvassed the four other bishops who, in November 1294, appealed to the pope, stressing that people were flocking to the tomb in search of a cure.[121]

A key stage in the canonisation progress was an enquiry held in 1307, when witnesses were called to London to give evidence. The transcript of the commission of enquiry survives at the Vatican,[122] and is the main source of the miracle accounts published by the Bollandists in *Acta Sanctorum*. Something of the flavour of the enquiry may be gleaned from Meryl Jancey's account of the questioning of one of the witnesses, Cantilupe's servant Hugh le Barber.[123]

[114] The first pope specifically claiming this right appears to be Alexander III *c.*1172: C. Norton, *St William of York* (York, 2006), 193.
[115] *Registrum Ricardi de Swinfield, episcopi Herefordensis*, ed. W. W. Capes, Canterbury and York Soc., 6 (London, 1909), 68.
[116] *Compendium Vitæ S. Thomæ*, para. 38; *AASS, Octobris I*, 608C.
[117] *Registrum Ricardi de Swinfield*, ed. Capes, 230–1, 297–9, 315–16.
[118] R. C. Finucane, *Miracles and Pilgrims: Popular Beliefs in Medieval England* (London, 1977), 173–88 (cap. 10: 'The Changing fortunes of a curative shrine: St. Thomas Cantilupe'.
[119] ibid., 490–1 (how the bishop was unable to contribute to the war in Scotland owing to the sums he had spent on the canonisation process, dated 1313).
[120] ibid., 281–2.
[121] *Registrum Ricardi de Swinfield*, ed. Capes, 234–5.
[122] Vat. Cod. Lat. 4015, partially printed in the *Compendium Vitæ S. Thomæ*; *AASS, Octobris I*, 599D–609A.
[123] M. Jancey, 'A Servant speaks of his master: Hugh le Barber's evidence in 1307', in Jancey, *Thomas Cantilupe*, 191–291 (Appendix).

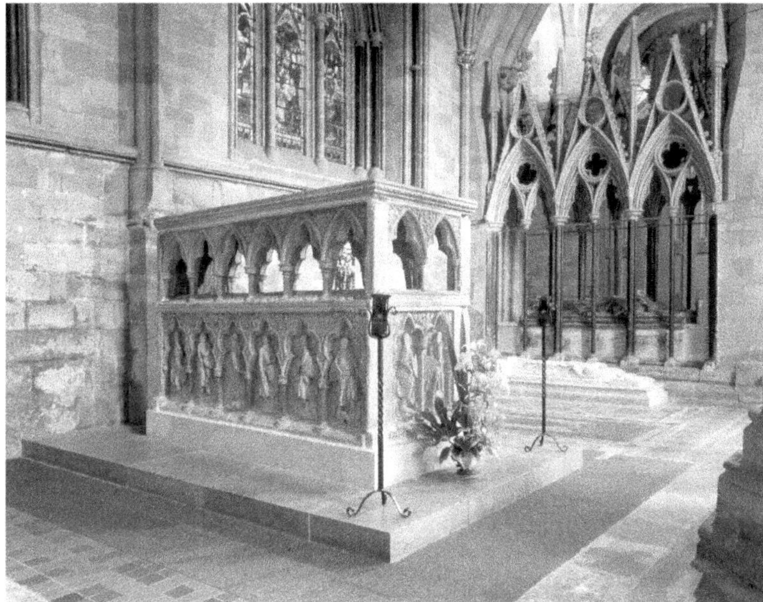

PLATE 8.5 HEREFORD CATHEDRAL The tomb-shrine of St Thomas Cantilupe in the north transept before the addition of a canopy in 2008.

By 1320, when the exiled Avignon Pope John XXII announced Cantilupe's sanctity and established 2 October as his feast-day, Swinfield's long episcopate had come to an end. The translation of St Thomas's relics to a new shrine did not take place until October 1349, when the tomb was opened and the bones carried to their final shrine, back in the Lady chapel.[124] Thus, rather as with St Hugh of Lincoln, the relics ended up at the site of the original burial.

Although Bishop Thomas was not officially a saint during the sixty-two years that his body had rested in the north transept, the monument into which Richard Swinfield placed his remains in 1287 evidently served as a tomb-shrine and is often called the bishop's 'shrine' today. It presumably survived the attentions of Thomas Cromwell's commissioners because it was so modest an affair compared with the opulent mid-fourteenth-century shrine in the Lady chapel. The monument is in two stages. The base, standing on a modern plinth, is decorated with a blind arcade of six cusped arches on each side and two at the west end separated by attached half-shafts. The east end is undecorated, for until 1857 the monument stood tight against the east wall of the transept. Each arch contains the seated image in bas-relief of a knight Templar, six on each side and two at the west end, making fourteen in all, and there is naturalistic foliage in the spandrels. This decoration is entirely consistent with the 1287 date provided by the documentary evidence.

[124] See below, pp. 275–6.

This substructure supports a Purbeck slab, formerly with a brass of the saint, and two attendant figures of which only one, portraying St Ethelbert (another Hereford saint), has survived. As Nicola Coldstream has finely written, 'The imagery of Cantilupe's monument … is … of Paradise: the saint, represented in brass, lies within the Paradise garden, defended against sin by Christ's battalions.'[125] The upper half consists of an arcaded canopy, again with foliate spandrels; at the top is a slab whose raised lip suggests that it was intended to support a *feretrum* containing the saint's remains (a similar lip was also found in the twelfth-century shrine of St Alban, as noted above).

The structure was first studied in detail in 1930 by the indefatigable editor of the Woolhope Club, George Marshall,[126] though some of his findings have been invalidated by more recent research undertaken when the shrine was reconstructed in 1998. Marshall believed that the monument was of two phases, the earlier of which was simply a table-tomb surmounted by the top slab with its brass inlay, and that the arcaded canopy was added a few years later. The argument relied especially on two vertical strips of plain masonry at the west end, which he took as evidence that the side panels were moved out slightly when the upper stage was added, but the recent investigations have shown that these strips were there from the outset. They may have compensated for an error in the dimensions of the central slab, which was a Purbeck marble import (the main body of the shrine used local stone).

Even though the monument predates Cantilupe's canonisation by several decades, his disarticulated bones probably lay in a receptacle on top of the uppermost slab from the time the monument was inaugurated. Fragments of iron embedded in the top slab at either end have plausibly been interpreted as guides for a lid which could be lowered over the container. So the casket containing the bishop's bones was perhaps displayed for about sixty-two years in a way which reflected aspirations that he should be regarded as a saint; rather as at Winchester the coffers containing the bones of pre-Conquest monarchs and bishops, never canonised, were on display within the cathedral. From 1349 the bones were again located in the Lady chapel, thereby assuring the preservation of the empty monument at the Reformation. It may not, indeed, have been disturbed until 1857, when Sir George Gilbert Scott moved it slightly westwards away from the wall of the transept.

Apart from the monument itself, we also have the evidence of miracle stories (many supplied by witnesses at the 1307 commission of enquiry) to help in building up a picture of the 'shrine' of Thomas Cantilupe in the years preceding his long-delayed canonisation in 1320. Several miracles were minutely described that were said to have occurred at the saint's *tumulus*; all arguably post-date the translation of the relics from the Lady chapel to the north transept in 1287, an event which seems to have brought about a

[125] N. Coldstream, 'The Medieval Tombs and the Shrine of St Thomas Cantilupe', in *Hereford Cathedral: a History*, ed. G. Aylmer and J. Tiller (London, 2000), 322–30, at 329.

[126] 'The Shrine of St. Thomas de Cantilupe in Hereford Cathedral', *Trans. of the Woolhope Naturalists' Field Club* (1930), 34–50.

resurgence of interest in the saint.[127] These miracles included the cure in that year of a hunchback, John of Holaurton, whom the witness saw

> ... placing his head within a certain hole adjoining the aforesaid tomb, and forming part of it; and when he had maintained the said head in the said hole for a length of time such as might be required to recite the Lord's prayer three times, together with the Ave Maria, he withdrew his head from it.[128]

It would seem then that sick people inserted their heads through the arches of the upper stage, which are precisely the right height; this would also have allowed them to kiss the brass effigy of the saint on the middle slab.

The undoubted success of the cult, even before the canonisation, provided funds that were employed in the architectural development of the cathedral. The fabric accounts for one year during this period have survived, showing that in 1290–1 offerings of £178 10*s* 7*d* were deposited at the tomb; by far the largest proportion of the church's income for building operations.[129] Unfortunately, income at his tomb had suffered a sad decline well before Cantilupe was proclaimed a saint, and the final translation of 1349 may have been delayed still further by the Black Death.

As for the mid-fourteenth-century shrine in the Lady chapel, we have little information. A list of jewels removed from the *feretrum* in 1538 mentions 'an image of the Trinity of gold with a diadem on his head with grene stones and rede, one oche on his creste with v. stones and iij. perles', and 'a table of gold with Jesus and Our Lady'.[130] These were presumably some of the decorative plates adorning the sides of the casket.

AN EXPATRIATE SAINT: ST EDMUND, ARCHBISHOP OF CANTERBURY

For real insight into papal involvement—one might almost say, interference—in the matter of canonisation, we must leave the shores of England, to study what one writer has somewhat optimistically called 'a shrine of an English saint, which has survived all the destruction of the sixteenth century, and exists to-day with a continuous and unbroken tradition'.[131] Edmund Rich, archbishop of Canterbury, spent his last days at

[127] *Miracula S. Thomæ de Cantilupe ex Processu Canonizationis*; *AASS, Octobris I*, 610A–96D. An addition to one miracle, published by Papebroch, makes the distinction between the tomb in the Lady chapel and the new one in the transept: ibid., 624B (note g).

[128] ibid., 625E: *ponentem caput suum intra quoddam foramen lapideum, propinquum dicto tumulo et sibi adhærens: et cum tenuisset dictum caput intra dictum foramen tanto tempore, quod potuisset dixisse ter orationem dominicam cum salutatione beatæ Mariæ, extraxit inde caput ....*

[129] P. E. Morgan, 'The Effect of the Pilgrim Cult of St Thomas of Cantilupe on Hereford Cathedral', in Jancey, *Thomas Cantilupe*, 145–52.

[130] *L & P Henry VIII*, 38.ii (1538), p. 507 (item 1208).

[131] B. Ward, *St Edmund, Archbishop of Canterbury, his Life, as told by old English writers* (London, 1903), x.

Pontigny, a choice inspired by the fact that his illustrious predecessor and patron, Thomas Becket, had sought refuge there some seventy-five years previously, during the first two years of his exile in France (November 1164 to November 1166). Edmund died at Soisy-Bouy, at dawn on Friday 16 November 1240. As he had requested, his body was taken to Pontigny, where it lay in the church for four days while the tomb was being prepared. No sooner had the body been laid in the earth than miracles began to occur—within twenty-eight days the archbishop of Sens had ordered an examination of the corpse, which was, needless to say, found to be incorrupt; and three months after his initial burial (surely one of the fastest transitions from grave to unofficial shrine) the miraculously preserved body was elevated and placed in a 'more fitting tomb', probably in the eastern chapel of the abbey church. Thus in the mid-thirteenth century the tomb-shrine of St Edmund formed a focus of pilgrimage and holy veneration, well before his official canonisation. In spite of opposition from the French royal court, the examiners proposed, following the usual formula, that the body of the prospective saint should no longer lie under a bushel but be placed on a candlestick, and after the Papal Commission had reported favourably the pope declared in the church of St John the Baptist, Lyon, that Edmund should 'be enrolled in the company of saints'. This decree of canonisation was announced on '*Gaudete*' Sunday, the second before Christmas, 1246.

The cult of St Edmund survived the tumult of the Wars of Religion, when the body was allegedly hidden within the abbey cellarage and invading Huguenots mistakenly destroyed the opulent tomb of a former abbot, taking it for the shrine; likewise the church survived the French Revolution, being adopted as a parish church. The relics were again spared. A new shrine was created in 1825, but the present Baroque monument, dominating the church of Pontigny, was inaugurated in 1872.[132]

THE THIRTEENTH-CENTURY *FORAMINA* MONUMENT OVER THE GRAVE OF ST SWITHUN AT WINCHESTER

Foramina tomb-shrines of the type introduced in the previous chapter continued to be created well into the thirteenth century. On 29 December 1885 the dean of Winchester, George Kitchin, partly opened up a Romanesque doorway in the north transept of his cathedral, the so-called 'Pilgrims' Door', blocked at the Reformation. Within the fill were fragments of statuary, remains of monuments, cable-shafted Purbeck marble: all, it would seem, the spolia of the Reformation.[133] It is likely that amongst this material were two pieces of Purbeck marble which attracted little interest

[132] ibid., 217–33.
[133] G. W. Kitchin, letters to *The Hampshire Chronicle*, dated 2 January 1886.

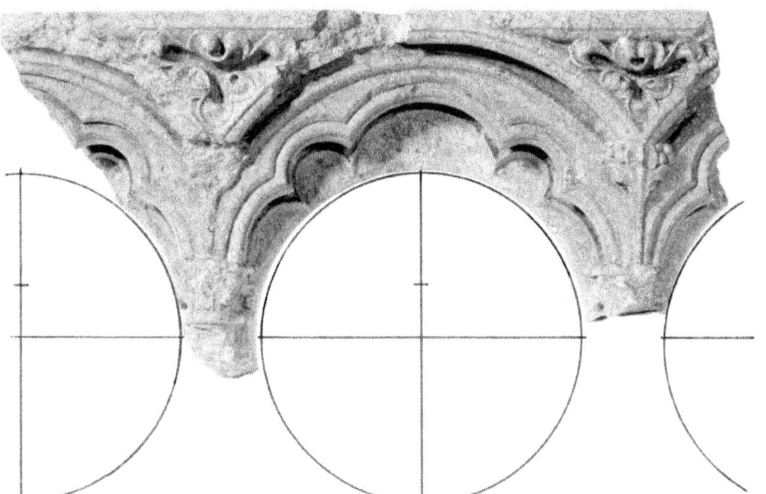

PLATE 8.6 WINCHESTER CATHEDRAL A surviving fragment of the thirteenth-century tomb-shrine over the original grave of the saint, showing the geometry of the monument.

until 1924, when J. D. Le Couteur and his exceptionally talented Winchester College pupil Douglas Carter published a paper in which they attempted a drawn reconstruction of the shrine of St Swithun; at the time it was not realised that the shrine destroyed at the Reformation dated only from 1476.[134] Le Couteur and Carter interpreted the Purbeck fragments as an extremely implausible round-headed arcade at the top of the shrine; a more recent examination has shown that the pieces in fact derived from a panel pierced with circular holes. I have argued more fully elsewhere that they came from a tomb-shrine of the 'port-hole' type, which was erected over the site of St Swithun's final grave in the mid-thirteenth century, when the tomb chapel which stood at the north-west corner of the nave was rebuilt.[135] During the excavation of the Old Minster site this chapel was also investigated: the floor of the chapel bore the imprint of a monument measuring 2.1m long by 0.75m wide at the west end, tapering to 0.65m at the east, dimensions comparable to St Osmund's tomb-shrine at Salisbury and the one at Ilam. It seems likely that the Winchester fragments derived from a similar structure, at a time when the reliquary containing the saint's bones was located on the 'feretory platform' within the Romanesque apse, to which the only, very limited, pilgrim access was the 'Holy Hole' beneath the platform. The 'Chapel of St Swithun', as it was known until the Reformation, would have provided a more accessible focus of veneration of the saint.

[134] J. D. Le Couteur and J. H. M. Carter, 'Notes on the Shrine of St Swithun formerly in Winchester Cathedral', *Antiq. J.*, 4 (1924), 360–70.
[135] J. Crook, 'The typology of early medieval shrines; a previously misidentified "tomb-shrine" panel from Winchester Cathedral', *Antiq. J.*, 70.i (1990), 49–64.

TWO MINOR CULTS: ILAM AND WHITCHURCH CANONICORUM

A rare survival of a thirteenth-century tomb-shrine is found at the much rebuilt parish church of the Holy Cross at Ilam (Staffs). The tomb, free-standing in the middle of the south chapel of 1618, is attributed to St Bertram or 'Bertelin/Bettelin' (*recte* Beorhthelm), said to have been an eighth-century Mercian prince who became a hermit after his Irish princess was devoured by wolves in the surrounding woods (scenes from the legend appear on the church's twelfth-century font). The hogs-back top of the tomb protrudes above the pavement, and is sheltered by a rectangular monument with three quatrefoil openings on each of the long sides and one at each end. The openings are rebated as if for glazing, and a sepia drawing by J. C. Buckler dated 1826 in the William Salt Library, Stafford, shows the quatrefoils apparently blocked up, though it is not clear that the infill is of glass.[136] Photographs at the National Monuments Record show that in the nineteenth century the monument was further protected by means of a metal hearse, presumably added during Sir George Gilbert Scott's restoration. The monument was dismantled and reassembled with the grave slab at a higher level *c.*1870.[137]

The hogs-back tomb and the stone superstructure are unlikely to be of

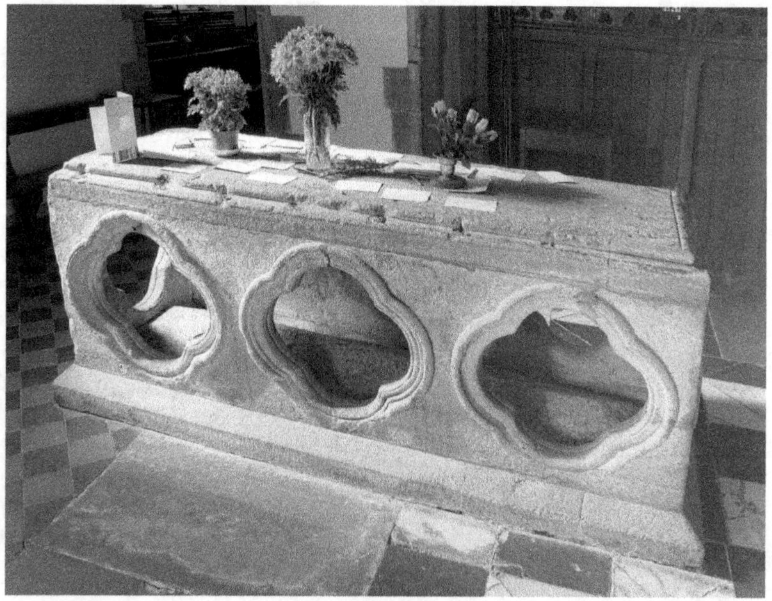

PLATE 8.7 ILAM (STAFFS) The tomb-shrine of St Bertram, constructed over the hogs-back tomb of the saint.

[136] Stafford, William Salt Library, ref. WSL Sv V.6b.

[137] J. Blair, 'Above-ground or below-ground', in *Local Saints and Local Churches in the Early Medieval West*, ed. A. Thacker and R. Sharpe (Oxford, 2002), Appendix 2, 490–3.

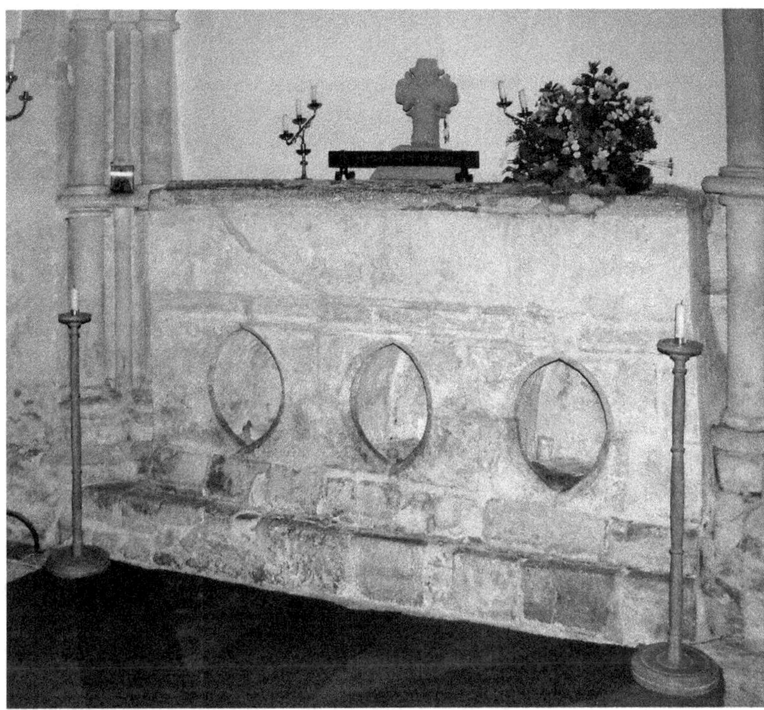

PLATE 8.8 WHITCHURCH CANONICORUM (DORSET), CHURCH OF ST CANDIDA
The shrine of St Hwita in the north transept.

the same date, given that the coffin-lid has been hacked away in order to accommodate the vertical slabs of the monument surrounding it. The form of the hogs-back would suit a twelfth-century date, but the mouldings of the top slab of the monument, with roll and fillet, are best attributed to the mid-thirteenth century. Needless to say, it is by no means certain that the monument is in its original position, given the date of the present south chapel, though this might have replaced an earlier one.

The structure presumably owes its survival to the fact that this was a very local cult, not mentioned in any of the medieval lists of saints' burial-places, and to the fact that it is not evidently a shrine. It is of course the form of the thirteenth-century superstructure that is of most interest.

A rather different kind of shrine-base is found tucked away in the hinterland of the Dorset coast at Whitchurch Canonicorum. There a cult developed of a certain 'St Wite' (*recte* Hwita, though known as St Wita or St Candida to Latinists) about whom nothing at all is known: post-medieval local traditions identified her as a Christian woman martyred by the Danes, but more recently it has been suggested, on no better evidence, that she was a West Saxon anchoress.[138] She also gave her name to a holy well at

[138] C. Waters, *Who was St. Wite?* (Bridport, 1980).

Morcombelake, about a mile from the church. The saint's name could simply derive from the common toponym 'White Church', rather than the other way around.[139] Despite the uncertainty about her identity, Hwita's cult was sufficiently developed for a monument to be constructed (or perhaps incorporated from an earlier shrine) as an integral part of the north wall of the transept when it was rebuilt in around 1220, though the arrangement has been further altered by the reconstruction of much of the wall *c.*1500.[140]

In its present form, the shrine comprises a rectangular monolithic limestone coffin (measuring 2055 × 610mm, 330mm high and capped by a lid 105mm thick), supported on a solid base, rising 670mm above the pavement. The front of the base is faced in two courses of slabs set vertically and pierced by three vesica-shaped openings into which people still place prayer-slips addressed to the saint—and cures are claimed to this day. When the coffin was opened in 1900 it was found to enclose a lead casket 740mm long and 200mm high, bearing the inscription +HIC. REQUIESCT. RELIQU.SCE.WITE.

It seems unlikely that the vesica openings ever gave access to a coffin *below* the monument, and the shrine is perhaps best regarded as a thirteenth-century confection that made use of a pre-existing, possibly twelfth-century, coffin that might originally have been embedded in the floor. As John Blair has pointed out, the monument might, however, have been remodelled, perhaps even in the reign of Mary Tudor.[141] Despite the vesica port-holes, this cannot be called a 'tomb-shrine'; rather it should be regarded as an early form of high shrine where the openings providing pilgrim access are still low down in the base, rather than at convenient 'work-top' height as are increasingly found in the high shrines of the fourteenth and fifteenth centuries.

THE SHRINE OF ST DAVID, 1275

The shrine of St David in the cathedral city that bears his name, at the westernmost tip of Pembrokeshire, has several affinities with that of St Hwita. It is located on the north side of the presbytery, and is double sided, allowing limited access by means of arcaded niches both from the main vessel and the aisle.[142]

Although the greater part of the monument appears to have been reconstructed, probably since the Reformation, and has been subject to various drastic modifications and conservation works, enough identifiable elements of the original structure survive to indicate that it was erected in

[139] John Blair also mentions the possibility that Hwita is a back-formation from the name of the church: 'A Handlist of Anglo-Saxon Saints', in *Local Saints and Local Churches in the Early Medieval West*, ed. A. Thacker and R. Sharpe (Oxford, 2002), 494–562, at 539.

[140] For the church, see *The County of Dorset*, RCHM I (West Dorset) (1952), 260–2.

[141] Blair, 'Above-ground or below-ground', 494.

[142] This shrine is the subject of a new study, J. Crook, 'The Shrine of St David', to be published in *The Condition of Menevia*, ed. Jonathan Wooding and Wyn Jones, forthcoming.

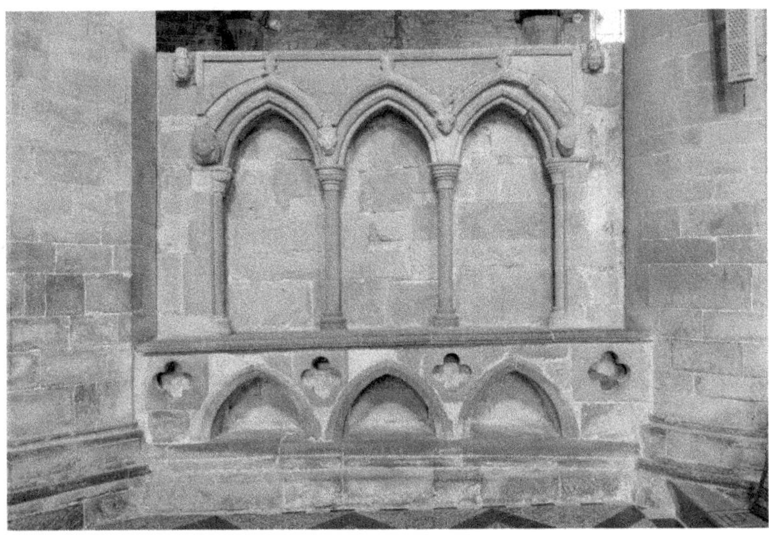

PLATE 8.9
ST DAVID'S
CATHEDRAL
South side of the shrine of St David.

the late thirteenth century, presumably shortly after the miraculous rediscovery of the saint's supposed bones in 1275. It is likely to have been complete by 1284 when Edward I and Queen Eleanor came to St David's 'on pilgrimage'.[143]

The two sides of the monument may be considered completely independently. On the presbytery side, the bottom half consists of an arcaded structure on a step, comprising three steeply arched niches which penetrate the monument to about half its depth. They are similar in function though not in form to the vesica-shaped openings in the shrine of St Hwita. The niches are separated by four quatrefoil openings, the central two of which contain hollow receptacles presumably for offerings. The bottom half resembles an altar, and is capped by a slab like the *mensa* of an altar, now in many reassembled pieces. Set well back from the front face are three blind arches, separated by shafts. A description by an Elizabethan writer states that these contained images of St David flanked by St Patrick and another saint (perhaps St Denis): nothing is now visible, but the images might have been painted on plaster that has not survived.[144] The north side of the shrine, facing the aisle, is also articulated by three niches, but these are round-headed and are not aligned to those on the south side. Indeed, the spacing of the niches on the two sides is completely independent.

The big question is of course where the reliquary might have been

[143] *Annales Cambriæ*, ed. J. Williams ab Ithel, RS, 20 (1860), 109, *s.a.* 1284: *causa peregrinationis*.

[144] The Elizabethan account was relayed by the disgraced antiquary William Wotton to Browne Willis, who published it in his *Survey of the Cathedral Church of St. David's and the Edifices belonging to it, as they stood in the year 1715* (London, 1717), 13 and 69.

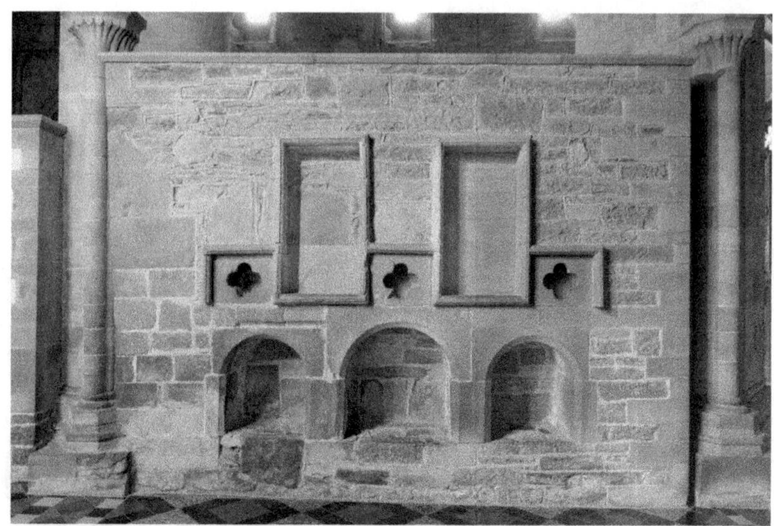

PLATE 8.10
ST DAVID'S CATHEDRAL
North side of the shrine of St David.

located. The most likely answer is that it was not a full-length reliquary intended to give the impression of a whole body, but a small casket containing disarticulated bones. The existence of this *feretrum* is known from accounts of its being carried about the locality in procession from time to time; normally it was perhaps parked on the *mensa*. Thus by placing their heads in the niches, before or after placing an appropriate donation in the quatrefoil money-boxes, pilgrims could place themselves under the tutelage of the saint.

Interestingly, the shrine of St David spawned a clone: the shrine of St Caradoc, which faces north into the north transept. This shrine is single sided, backing on to the choir stalls. It lacks a superstructure, and resembles a table-tomb with two low pointed arches separated by quatrefoil openings, an arrangement similar to that of the south side of the shrine of St David.

ST WILLIAM OF YORK

The elevation of the relics of St William of York in 1284 was an important stage in the long evolution of the cult which culminated in the construction of his final shrine in 1472.[145] William FitzHerbert was archbishop from 1141–7 and again in 1154 for a few months until his sudden death, perhaps by poison. He was buried in a reused Roman sarcophagus (now to be seen in the crypt) on the central axis of the nave, just west of the crossing. Within a very few years a fire that broke out in the city spread to the minster, and a

[145] For my account of the cult I am indebted to two admirable works: Christopher Norton's *St William of York* and Christopher Wilson's *The Shrines of St William of York* (York, 1977).

beam collapsed on the coffin-lid, breaking off the bottom half, but the flames miraculously left the body undamaged. William's successor, Bishop Roger, then began the first remodelling of the east end of the minster, though there is no evidence that this was specifically intended as an enhancement of the area around William's tomb. The cult developed in 1177 when a series of miracles were recorded at the tomb,[146] evidence of a popular cult that developed nearly fifty years before the 'official' canonisation by Pope Honorius III; by 1177 he was already being called *beatus* or *sanctus*. As Christopher Norton has suggested, the cult may have been encouraged above all by Archbishop Roger acting as impresario, perhaps working through Paulinus of Leeds.[147] But the papal bull of canonisation was issued on 18 March 1226, after the pope had ordered an enquiry led by Bishop John of Ely and the abbots of Fountains and Rievaulx.[148] The official promotion of the cult was presumably a response to the recent elevation of St Thomas of Canterbury; indeed, a second group of miracles was recorded at the turn of the century, including the miraculous oozing from the tomb of oil with saintly powers, a phenomenon recorded *c.*1223 by Matthew Paris.[149]

Somewhat surprisingly, the saint's body was not elevated immediately after his canonisation, as was the usual practice. The bull does not, as was usual, say that the body was to be raised from the earth (despite the usual reference to the candle not remaining beneath a bushel),[150] and although an altar of St William was founded in 1230, it does not appear to have been near the tomb.[151] The delay in elevating the relics may have resulted from a second phase of building works: the great transept was being constructed. In fact the translation did not take place until 1284, and again it is possible that the forthcoming reconstruction of the nave, begun in 1291 but perhaps already planned, prompted the raising of the saint's bones.

St William's translation is fully recorded in the liturgical readings for that feast-day, 8 January.[152] The third reading describes how the expenses were met by Anthony Bek in return for his election as bishop of Durham. The translation was enthusiastically supported by Edward I and Queen Eleanor, and during the planning stage the king miraculously survived a fall from a high place, which he attributed to the saint's intervention. Then came the translation. Archbishop William and Bishop Bek processed into the cathedral by night whilst the canons chanted the litany; they prostrated themselves over the tomb, and then the slab was lifted revealing the saint, his vestments imbued with the holy oil previously observed. They removed

[146] Norton, *St William*, 150–7.
[147] ibid., 163–4, 178, 186; see also ibid., 229–38, Appendix B 'Paulinus of Leeds and the family of Ralph Nowell'.
[148] ibid., 149, 197–201
[149] Matthew Paris, *Chronica Maiora*; ed. Luard, iii. 77.
[150] *Hist. Church of York*, iii. 127–30.
[151] ibid., iii. 141–2.
[152] *Breviarium ad usum insignis ecclesie Eboracensis*, 2 vols., ed. S. W. Lawley, Surtees Soc., 71, 75 (Durham, 1880–3), i. cols. 179–85: *In translatione S. Wilelmi Episcopi*.

the paten and chalice that had been placed beside (*iuxta*) the corpse and, starting with the head (which eventually would be enshrined elsewhere) they placed the holy bones in a receptacle (*capsula*) which was provisionally stored in a safe place. There was a tidying-up operation next morning, and the bishop's vestments were retained as contact relics. During matins early the following day a minor miracle occurred when a stone fell from one of the pillars on to the head of a servant dozing at the foot of the lectern (*basi[m] pulpiti in quo legi solet evangelium*), who was unscathed. This was the day appointed for the translation. The king and queen and a great company of counts and barons assembled, and the king himself and one of the bishops bore the reliquary casket in procession around the choir to its final resting place behind the high altar. After the ceremony the king distributed alms to the poor as was his custom.[153]

The form of this first, late thirteenth-century shrine, replaced in 1472, is not known. Amongst those who visited it was Margery Kempe, who came to York in 1413 and 1417. A few years later, in 1421–3, the famous St William window was created (pl. 1.4). This purports to show the monument, but its architectural character is contemporary with the window, suggesting that the artist was not attempting a realistic depiction. What is shown is a two-stage high shrine in two bays, with a quatrefoil base, lateral prayer niches, and a gabled top. An altar at the west end was framed by the diagonally placed corner shafts of the monument, and above it the west gable was ogival with crockets, features that had not yet entered the architectural vocabulary in 1284. One of the images shows that the monument was fitted with taps from which pilgrims could draw the holy oil that was an enduring feature of the cult.

The head removed in 1286 was separately enshrined, and was displayed in the choir. The saint's *chef* took the familiar form of a mitred bust supported by angels, one of which needed repair in 1371.[154] The wonderful York inventory dated by its editor to *c.*1500 shows that the head reliquary was richly adorned and attracted expensive gifts, such as jewels, precious coins, and coral.[155]

THE SURVIVING SHRINE OF ST FRIDESWIDE AT OXFORD

The most significant thirteenth-century English shrine to have survived, albeit as a reconstruction of incomplete fragments, is that of St Frideswide of Oxford. In the previous chapter we traced the earlier history of the cult, culminating in the elevation of the relics into a *feretrum* in 1180. The arrangements made at that time probably persisted unchanged until 1289,

[153] *Tribute to an Antiquary: Essays presented to Mark Fitch* (London 1976), 93–125 at 100, 113.
[154] *The Fabric Rolls of York Minster*, ed. J. Raine, Surtees Soc., 35 for 1858 (Durham, 1859), 126: *pro emendacione unius angeli supportantis capud S. Willelmi, 3s. 4d.* Further repairs to the *chef*, including repairs to the mitre, took place in 1481–2: ibid., 86.
[155] ibid., 212–34, at 224–5.

when the relics were again translated. Until then, as noted in the previous chapter, they were perhaps located in the square reliquary chapel postulated by John Blair over the original grave. This chapel appears to have been enlarged in two phases in the thirteenth century. Blair has suggested that in a first phase the Lady chapel was built alongside the north aisle of the chancel, prolonging the southern half of the chapel by two bays; later the two northern bays of the chapel were extended eastwards. The only visible evidence for the latter phase comprises the piers and responds of the thirteenth-century arcade between the new chapel and the adjacent Lady chapel to the south, for the area was remodelled in the fourteenth century (probably in 1338) when the present 'Latin chapel' was created.[156]

On stylistic evidence, the thirteenth-century phase dated from the last years of the century, and it is a reasonable inference that the extension to the chapel was intended as a larger, more prestigious setting for the cult, and that the enlargement of the chapel and the creation of a new shrine were related events. The account of the 1289 translation reads as follows:

> The old shrine (*feretrum*) of St Frideswide of Oxford was translated, and with due honour was placed in a new and more precious shrine in the same church, and near the site where it had previously been located, which *feretrum* indeed had long been prepared beforehand.[157]

It will be noted that the text yields no clue either to the earlier or the new position of the shrine. If, however, as Blair has argued, the new shrine simply stood somewhat to the east of its earlier position, this would indeed be 'near' the previous site. Later references to the shrine provide some further clues: in 1346 Lady Elizabeth Montague set up a chantry chapel 'in the chapel of blessed Mary, next to the shrine of St Frideswide'.[158] Unfortunately the Montague tomb has moved since the mid-fourteenth century, though a site in the Lady chapel, in the second bay from the east, is a likely possibility. Another indication of the possible site of the shrine is the structure usually identified as a 'watching loft' under the eastern arch between the Latin chapel and the Lady chapel; but this loft (assuming that this is what it is) would have provided the shrine-keeper with a view towards both the north and the south. It would have been perfectly consistent, indeed, with the position adopted when the shrine was reconstructed in the later nineteenth century, i.e. in the easternmost bay of the Lady chapel. Nevertheless, the

[156] D. Sturdy, 'Excavations in the Latin Chapel and outside the east end of Oxford Cathedral, 1962/3', *Oxoniensia*, 53 (1988), 75–102, at 94–5. R. K. Morris, 'The Gothic Mouldings of the Latin and Lady Chapels', ibid., 169–83, at 175–8. Blair, 'St Frideswide's monastery, problems and possibilities', ibid., 245.

[157] *Annales Monastici*, iv, ed. Luard, 318: ... *translatum est vetus feretrum Sanctæ Fritheswythæ Oxoniæ, et cum honore quo decuit collocatum est in novo et pretiosiori feretro in eadem ecclesia, et prope situm quo prius fuerat collocatum, quod quidem feretrum diu ante fuerat præparatum.*

[158] Registers of the Diocese of Lincoln, vol. I, fo. 75, cited in Blair 'St Frideswide's monastery: problems and possibilities', 251.

present position of the shrine, now relocated in the easternmost bay of the Latin chapel, seems the most plausible. It would have provided plenty of room for pilgrim circulation. Furthermore, it is not far from a window featuring three female saints, located in the second bay of the Latin chapel: the window might have been intended to enhance the shrine area.

Perhaps all one can confidently say is that the shrine was certainly located within the north-eastern chapels of the church, and certainly not in an axial position behind the high altar. As John Blair has emphasised, the later development of the north-eastern chapels seems to result from a desire to provide increasing tomb space in the general area of the shrine so that 'rich and favoured' people could lie *ad sanctum*.[159]

More importantly, a significant amount of the shrine-base survives. Most of the pieces were discovered in 1875 in the lining of a well, and were reconstructed at that time.[160] Other fragments were discovered in 1985 during excavations in the cloister;[161] most of them had been used in the infill of a structure which has been identified as a short-lived, timber belfry, probably demolished in 1545–6,[162] but another fragment was recovered from the rubble fill of a stairway leading out of the cloister.[163]

The shrine was reconstructed yet again in 2001–2, when the extra pieces were incorporated, and this description is based on the new reconstruction. Raised on steps, the lowest part of the shrine comprised a solid base adorned with a single frieze of quatrefoils, reconstructed (with additions) as seven units by four. Each quatrefoil encloses either a floral motif or a human head, some of the latter depicting crowned nuns, undoubtedly intended as portraits of the saint. The quatrefoil frieze is quite shallow, and a substantial plinth was postulated in both the nineteenth-century and the latest reconstruction, although the form of the lost original is not known. Above this substructure comes a moulded slab: again, this had to be supplied anew by the restorers, but there can be little argument that it would have been a feature of the original.

The next stage is better represented, consisting of a Purbeck marble canopy which is plausibly reconstructed as two bays long. This finely carved work includes naturalistic foliage, through which wimpled faces peek, in a probable allusion to the saint's sylvan life at Binsey. Of the original structure only the actual arches survive, and their present supports comprising quatrefoil shafts with appropriately lobed bases and capitals are entirely conjectural. In the nineteenth-century reconstruction the canopy was raised on rectangular stone piers which were unashamedly out of character but

[159] Blair, 'St Frideswide's monastery: problems and possibilities', 251–5.
[160] Wall, *Shrines*, 67–8.
[161] C. Scull and others, 'Excavations in the Cloister of St. Frideswide's Priory, 1985', *Oxoniensia*, 53 (1988), 21–73, at 48–9 and fig. 29.
[162] M. Biddle, 'Wolsey's bell-tower', ibid., 205–10.
[163] J. Munby, 'Christ Church, Priory House: Discoveries in St. Frideswide's dormitory', ibid., 185–93, at 191.

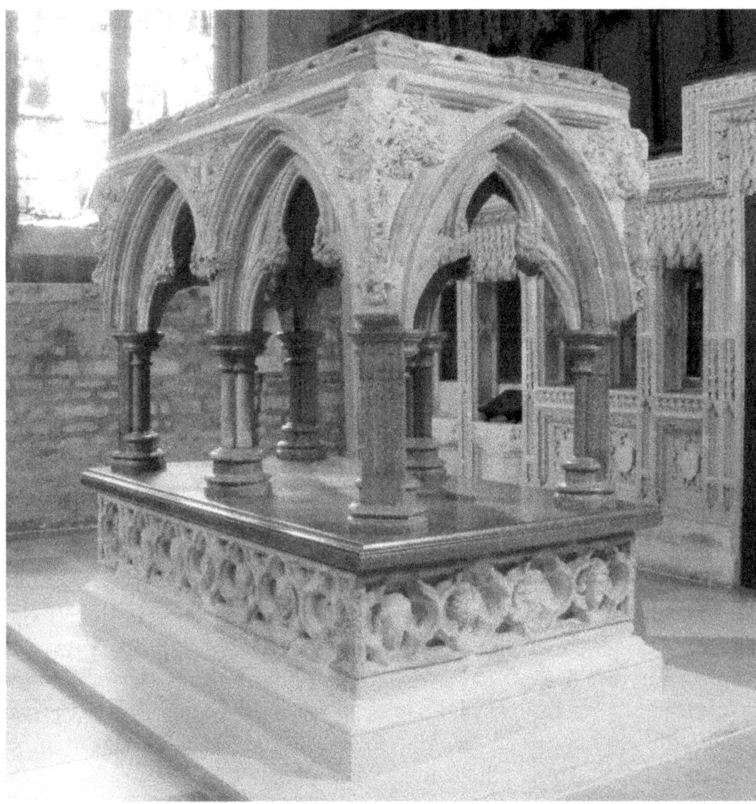

PLATE 8.11 OXFORD CATHEDRAL The thirteenth-century shrine of St Frideswide.

intended to provide some idea of the size of the monument. Another slab at the very top of the monument must, I think, be postulated, supported by the arcaded superstructure.

All that survives of the original structure are some of the Purbeck marble quatrefoils of the base and the Purbeck arcade; the fact that not a single fragment of the quatrefoil shafts has been located might render their existence suspect. But if the arcade had simply sat on the middle slab, this would have made a very low structure indeed.

The major question is of course where the reliquary might have been located within this monument. Perhaps the best analogy is the tomb of Bishop Cantilupe of Hereford, constructed, as we have seen, just two years before the shrine of St Frideswide. There an arcaded canopy surmounts a solid base, though the proportions of the two elements are different, the base at Hereford with its human figures being taller, and the arcading of the canopy comprising a greater number of small arches. But the general concept is similar, and we have suggested above that Cantilupe's *feretrum* was placed on top of the uppermost slab of the monument; likewise the reliquary containing St Frideswide's bones could have been raised on high; it seems unlikely that it was placed *within* the monument, as the broad arches would have provided very little protection.

ROBERT GROSSETESTE: A SAINT MANQUÉ

The tomb of Robert Grosseteste in Lincoln Cathedral bears witness to a saint's cult which never came off; that is to say, after the papal appropriation of the right to canonise, either the request was not made, or it failed. In an earlier age he would no doubt have become a saint through popular acclaim. Grosseteste's career developed as scientist, theologian, teacher at Oxford, and, finally, bishop of Lincoln from 1235, a see which he occupied until his death on 9 October 1253 at the age of sixty-five or so.[164] He was buried in the south-east transept of his cathedral, in front of the altar of St Stephen, where his monument has been reinstated. At his death 'the air was filled with strange sounds of bells and perturbations of nature'. The bishop appears rapidly to have become the focus of a local cult, and his successors and the chapter of Lincoln attempted no fewer than five times between 1254 and 1307 to secure his canonisation, without success.[165]

The nature of the monument has been convincingly investigated by David Stocker.[166] It appears to have been constructed immediately after the bishop's death, and its design seems to reflect the aspirations of the Lincoln clergy. The failure to elevate Grosseteste to the sainthood ensured its survival at the Reformation, and in the early 1540s John Leland observed that 'Robert Grosted lyethe in the hygheste southe isle with a goodly tumbe of marble and an image of brasse over it.'[167] Although the monument was almost certainly demolished by Parliamentarians in the late summer of 1644,[168] it had previously been drawn by Sir William Dugdale;[169] the remains of the monument were also discussed and illustrated, in the form of a 'flat-pack' drawing, by Richard Gough.[170] Finally, a number of pieces of the monument actually survive.

As originally built, the monument resembled a table-tomb, with three trefoil-headed niches on each of the long sides and similar single niches at the ends. The triple niches were separated by shaft-clusters, and it is highly probable that there were angels in low relief in the spandrels.[171] There were

[164] R. W. Southern, 'Grosseteste, Robert', *DNB*, xxiv. 79–86.

[165] R. E. G. Cole, 'Proceedings relative to the Canonization of Robert Grosseteste, Bishop of Lincoln', *Associated Architectural Societies' Reports and Papers*, xxxiii (1915–16), 1–34.

[166] Stocker, 'Tomb and shrine'.

[167] Leland, v. 122.

[168] The Royalist broadsheet *Mercurius Aulicus*, 16 September 1644, states that at Lincoln in particular 'all the monuments and tombes' had been 'laid … even with the earth'.

[169] BL, Loan MS 38, fo. 105v ('Dugdale's Book of Monuments'). Reproduced in Stocker, 'Tomb and shrine', fig. 1.

[170] R. Gough, *Sepulchral Monuments in Great Britain …* (London, 1786), vol. I, pt. I, pl. XVI facing p. 47.

[171] Two of the angel spandrels survive, and their dimensions and design conform with Dugdale's drawing, though he does not depict the angels: Stocker plausibly argues that Dugdale simply omitted the intricacies of the detail.

shafts at the corners, and their bases, together with those of the shaft-clusters, were integral with the basal slab, which was formed of eight stones. The top of the monument consisted of a lower, moulded slab, on which was placed a slightly smaller slab, also moulded: both mouldings were adorned with foliate sprays typical of the mid-thirteenth century. On top of the upper slab was a half-length brass depicting the bishop. It is surely unlikely that this was an original feature, and it might have been a later addition.

Stocker rightly relates this monument to contemporary or slightly earlier shrine-bases, notably the shrine of Edward the Confessor, which must have been under construction when the Lincoln monument was being made. But the monument differs from later thirteenth-century shrine-bases such as that of St Thomas Cantilupe, St Frideswide, or St David in that it was constructed *over* the undisturbed tomb of the prospective saint; Grosseteste's tomb was indeed opened (twice!) in 1782.[172] It is therefore a tomb-shrine, similar in form and function to the tomb of Thomas Becket, the monument at Ilam, or the tomb-shrine over the empty grave of St Swithun. This raises the question of what would have happened had the pope agreed to Grosseteste's canonisation. Is it possible that the curious arrangement of two superposed top slabs reflects an intention eventually to raise the top of the monument, perhaps by an additional arcade, to provide a space within which the elevated relics could be displayed? If so, the shrine of St Thomas Cantilupe provides the best parallel.

Robert Grosseteste's tomb, with its shrine-like echoes, is one of a group of similar monuments whose construction bears witness to the hope that their occupants might be sanctified. In York Minster the tomb of Archbishop de Grey certainly looks like a shrine, but an actual cult developed around the tomb of Archbishop Richard Scrope, a political 'martyr' of 1405, in the same church.[173]

LITTLE ST HUGH OF LINCOLN

In the mid-thirteenth century St Hugh of Avalon had been joined by his namesake 'Little St Hugh', another example of a boy allegedly ritually killed. He had almost certainly been murdered, and his body was discovered in a well, but the suggestion that he was crucified by members of Lincoln's influential and wealthy Jewish community—a gloss reminiscent of St William of Norwich—must surely be regarded merely as an expression of local anti-Semitism resulting from envy.

The shrine of this saint has partially survived in the cathedral's south choir aisle. Until the Commonwealth it appears to have been more or less complete. In the early eighteenth century the antiquary Browne Willis was shown a pre-Commonwealth manuscript in Lord Hatton's library containing

[172] Stocker, 'Tomb and shrine', 144.
[173] See below, p. 279–80.

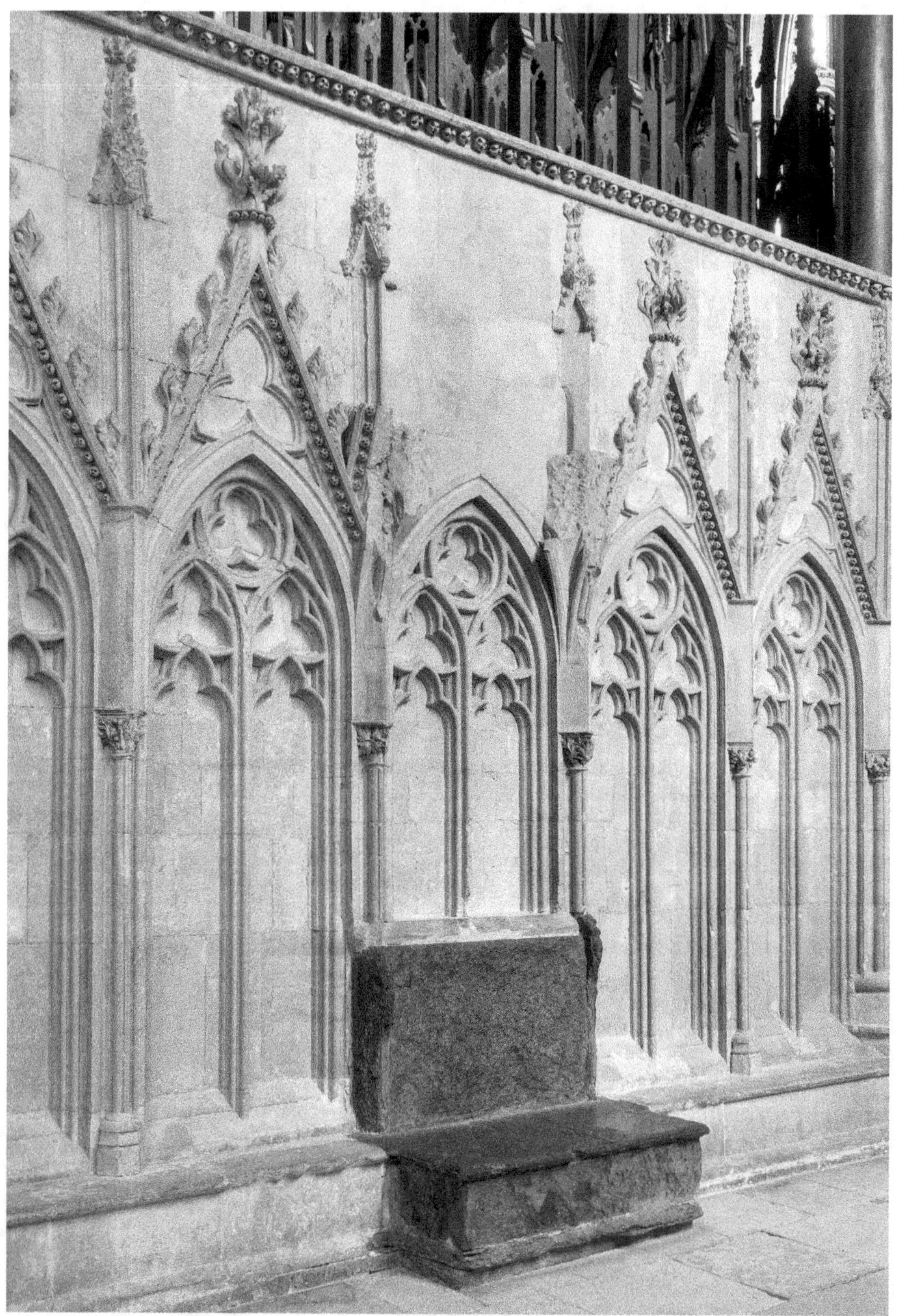

PLATE 8.12 LINCOLN CATHEDRAL The remains of the shrine of Little St Hugh.

'Draughts of all the most remarkable Tombs and Gravestones in this Cathedral'.[174] He noted in particular what he took to be 'A beautiful Shrine of Bishop St. *Hugh* of great height in pyramidical fashion'.[175] This drawing he showed to William Stukeley, who copied it as an engraving in his *Itinerarium Curiosum*.[176] It is clear from the latter depiction that the monument in question was in fact the shrine attributed to 'Little St Hugh', in the south choir aisle.[177]

The shrine was investigated in 1791, when a lead coffin beneath the monument was opened and its contents drawn by Samuel Grimm.[178] The coffin did indeed contain a small skeleton, to which the desiccated skin still clung.

The monument has been fully analysed by David Stocker.[179] The 'beautiful shrine' seen by Browne Willis was the central part of a larger structure comprising five bays of decorative arcading on the south (aisle) side of the choir wall between the second and third piers working from the crossing. The shrine itself consisted of a short chest oriented east–west and projecting into the aisle; only the stubs of the end panels survive. On the front of the chest were three narrow trefoil openings, separated by heraldic shields in the spandrels, while the ends had wider trefoil openings. Towering above was a tall vaulted canopy (part of which survives) supported on circular shafts, with crocketed gables on the three sides enclosing foiled arches. There were pinnacles at the corners, and the monument culminated in a spire whose gabled and pinnacled form echoed on a smaller scale the shape of the canopy below. On stylistic evidence the ensemble dates from the end of the thirteenth century, and Stocker points out the affinity with the Eleanor crosses, notably the Waltham cross of 1291–5. David Stocker plausibly argues that the cult was promoted by Edward I just after the expulsion of the Jews in 1290, in further justification of his action.

[174] Browne Willis, *A Survey of the Cathedrals of Lincoln, Ely, Oxford, and Peterborough …* (London, 1730), 4. Pencilled notes in Richard Gough's copy of Browne Willis in the Bodleian Library (Gough Eccl. top. 66(1)), pp. 49, 51, state that 'Mr Willis shew'd it [the drawing of the shrine] at A.S. (the Society of Antiquaries) in 1722.'

[175] ibid., 8.

[176] W. Stukeley, *Itinerarium Curiosum or, An Account of the Antiquities and remarkable Curiosities in Nature or Art observed in travels through Great Britain*, 2nd edn. (London, 1776), Centuria I, plate 29.

[177] Willis also transcribed (ibid. 9–31) a lengthy description of all the pre-Commonwealth monuments recorded by Robert Sanderson, and Sir William Dugdale made a record of the cathedral's monuments on 10 September 1641, shortly before the cathedral was 'so miserably ravaged and desecrated by the Abhorrers of Idols, that not one Brass Plate or Monument escaped the Rage of these Reformers' (ibid., 5). The 'pyramidical monument' of the drawing was, however, not mentioned in this comprehensive list, presumably because it was not recognised as a tomb or shrine.

[178] BL, Add. MS 15541, Grimm Drawings, Nos. 115–16. 115: 'The Crucified child in his stone coffin & lead wrapper in the aisle of the choir of Lincoln Minster Aug 25th 1791. S. Grimm'. 116: Close-up of the head.

[179] D. Stocker, 'The Shrine of Little St Hugh', in *Medieval Art and Architecture at Lincoln Cathedral*, *BAA Trans.*, vol. 8, for 1982 (Leeds, 1986), 109–17.

JOHN OF BEVERLEY

As previously noted, John of Beverley's relics were first elevated in 1037; thereafter there were two focuses of veneration within the church, the tomb—which of course did not move—and the shrine, which appears to have remained close to the high altar, which changed position as the church was altered and enlarged. The loss of any vestiges of these early phases means that any interpretation of the architecture of Beverley Minster before the late thirteenth century remains highly schematic. The cult evidently suffered a severe knock after a disastrous fire in 1188; the tomb and reliquary were relocated in 1197 and translated again. Then at around the time of the start of the Interdict (1213) the central tower collapsed, the event which led to the eventual reconstruction of the whole church.

It is in this context that towards the end of the thirteenth century the canons gave thought to the creation of a new shrine. Fortunately their contract with the goldsmith Roger of Faringdon has survived, providing a good deal of information about what a major reliquary looked like at this time. It was to be 5½ft long, 1½ft broad, and of proportionate (say 2½ft) height (1664 x 457 x 763mm). It was to be beautiful and fitted with plates (*platis*). It was to have 'columns of mason's work' (*cum ... columpnis de opere cementario*) and figures of cunning and beautiful work (*ymaginibus subtilis operis et decori*), the number and size being at the Chapter's discretion, to be placed all over the shrine, with canopies and pinnacles in front and rear, and other devices appropriate for a shrine of this sort and beauty, such as belongs to goldsmiths' work'.[180] The phrase 'columns of masons' work' is confusing; but the general context and the last words quoted here indicate that the entire contract related to the reliquary rather than a supporting shrine-base. The implication must be that the columns were a metal interpretation of the kind of shafts normally created by masons.

Where was the reliquary placed? It has been suggested that it was displayed on top of the reredos.[181] Even though the stair at the north end would have provided limited access, the position seems unlikely for the focus of veneration of a major saint. However, from the early fourteenth century St John appears to have been revered mainly at his tomb, so Beverley may provide an instance where the *feretrum* was not readily available to suppliants. Furthermore, during Archbishop William Melton's visitation in 1325 it was noted that at Rogationtide the *feretrum* was moved from the altar for four or five days (presumably because it was carried around in procession), which supports the idea that it was a prestigious display object rather than one to which pilgrims normally had ready access.[182] That there

[180] *Memorials of Beverley Minster: The Chapter Act Book of the Collegiate Church of S John of Beverley AD 1286–1347*, ed. A. F. Leach, 2 vols., Surtees Soc., 98 (1898) and 108 (1903), ii. 299–301.

[181] Coldstream, 'Decorated shrine bases', 21–2.

[182] *Memorials of Beverley Minster*, ed. Leach, ii. 60.

were two focuses of veneration is so apparent from accounts of Queen Isabella's visits to Beverley. She gave 7*s* on 8 October 1318, which was probably a donation at the relics though this is not recorded.[183] Ten days later she came again, this time to make an offering on behalf of Edward II. She presented a 'nut' (*unam nuchteam*, presumably a jewel) to the *feretrum*, but 7*s* to the tomb (*tumba*).[184] On a subsequent visit she gave about 7*s* to the *feretrum* and nothing else.[185]

So let us take stock. By the beginning of the thirteenth century new types of high shrines were developing in England that were quite different from those found on the Continent at the same period. There, the pillared variety of shrine continued with little change: at Clairvaux, for example, the shrine of St Bernard was of this form, supported on columns and over 8ft high (*octo circiter pedes supra terram attolitur, et marmores columnulis vestitur*).[186] But in England the pillars were being replaced by solid bases, first enclosing prayer niches, later with niches at higher level. The design of shrines was increasingly architectural, and it is perhaps this feature that distinguishes the physical setting of the cult of saints in England from practice on the Continent, where reliquaries tended simply to be displayed on or behind altars rather than being elevated on specific monuments. The decoration of English shrine-bases would continue to evolve in line with larger-scale architectural styles, but their general shape was now established and would endure to the end of the middle ages. The tendency continued apace in the fourteenth century and to the end of the middle ages, as we shall see in the final chapters of this book.

[183] ibid., ii. 362.
[184] ibid., ii. 364.
[185] ibid., ii. 37, dated 3 July 1323.
[186] *AASS, Augusti IV*, 354–5, at 354D.

9 THE FINAL FLOWERING

Saints' cults in the later middle ages

With a few late exceptions, the development of English shrines reached its high point in the late thirteenth and early fourteenth centuries. During this period a number of shrines were renewed that survived until the Reformation. Significant fragments of several of these late medieval monuments have been discovered, in some cases in sufficient number for them to be re-erected. Construction of new shrines in the fifteenth century was more sporadically pursued, but the final shrines of Osmund of Salisbury, Swithun of Winchester, and William of York are important examples from the end of the middle ages.

Perhaps the new construction of so many shrines in the fourteenth century reflects a particular interest in relics at that time. Nicola Coldstream suggests that a fresh enthusiasm for saints' cults was sparked off by the elevation of Edward the Confessor under Henry III in 1269.[1] The momentum was maintained during the following century. Some insight into attitudes at the start of the period may be had from the great inventory compiled for Prior Henry of Eastry at Christ Church Canterbury in 1315–16.[2] As well as a staggering quantity of vestments and ornaments that were normally kept in the vestry, the major and minor relics displayed within the church are carefully listed. The tally begins with whole bodies, *corpora*, which must have been disarticulated skeletons: the bones of St Thomas 'in his reliquary' (*in feretro suo*), those of St Ælfheah ('in his reliquary, next to the high altar'), and the remains of St Dunstan ('next to the high altar, on the south side'). Then come St Oda and St Wilfrid, whose *feretra* were disposed to the south and north respectively *ad coronam* (near Becket's head reliquary), probably flanking the altar of the rotunda; St Anselm's remains

[1] Coldstream, 'Decorated shrine bases', 26.

[2] BL, Cotton MS Galba E.iv, fos. 112–186v; J. Wickham Legg and W. H. St. John Hope, *Inventories of Christchurch* [*sic*] *Canterbury* (London, 1902), 9–94, at 79–94 for the relics.

were near the altar of St Peter in the chapel in what is now called 'Anselm's Tower'; St Ælfric's lay near the chapel of St John the Divine; St Blaise reposed behind the high altar. Behind or alongside this altar was a great reliquary cupboard (*magnum armariolum*), whose contents allegedly included the whole body of St Ouen, in a new *feretrum*, though the 'body' must surely have been a collection of disarticulated bones.[3] Finally, three *corpora* were housed in chests raised on beams over altars: St Salvius (Salvy) of Valenciennes, St Wulgan,[4] and, rather surprisingly, St Swithun. The latter can scarcely have been a 'body' in any sense of the word, given that the main relic was at Winchester. Canterbury had, on the other hand, possessed the saint's head since 1006, though by the end of the fourteenth century it was also claimed by Évreux Cathedral.

Also displayed in the reliquary armoire were the head reliquaries of SS. Blaise, Fursey, and Austroberht.[5] Eleven arm reliquaries follow, perhaps also kept in the armoire: these included quite recent saints, such as Richard of Chichester, translated only forty years previously (1276), and St Hugh of Lincoln, finally translated in 1280.[6] Some of the contents of the armoire were more dubious, such as 'Aaron's rod'. The same reservations might be expressed about many of the relics housed in containers called *filacterii*: the blood of St Stephen and the stones with which he was put to death, bones of the Holy Innocents, and fragments of the Blessed Virgin's clothing. Finally, a large and disparate collection was accommodated in other receptacles. In a big oblong ivory casket with a domed lid (*in scrinio magno eburneo rotundo in capite oblongo*) were contact relics of St Thomas: two of his mitres, a hair shirt, and fragments of his bed, together with smaller items separately wrapped in two bundles of white cloth. Amongst these were dust from his body and more fragments of clothing, including his raincoat, '*capa pluvialis*'. Then there were the *tabulæ*: relics mounted on boards, including a set of relics of Roman saints. Yet more *scrinia* followed, each containing between ten and twenty fragments, all of which were presumably carefully labelled. Some of the more unlikely relics may have been brought back from the Holy Land and accepted in good faith: a piece of the stone on which Our Lord ate having summoned his disciples from their boat; the tree into which 'Abraham' [*recte* Zacchaeus] climbed in order to see the Lord; part of the socket into which the Cross of Calvary was inserted. Though Christ Church could boast a staggering collection, relic lists from other churches suggest that similar enthusiasm was to be found throughout the land.

This was the period when the shrines of major local saints had achieved a certain measure of standardisation. The table type, typified by the twelfth-

[3] The 'Great Armoire' was located within the presbytery arcade on the north side, in the bay now occupied by Archbishop Howley (ibid., 11, n. 2), and this is where Erasmus saw various relics shortly before the Dissolution.

[4] Identified as the patron of Lens, near Douai: Farmer, *Dictionary*, s.n.

[5] See above, p. 219.

[6] ibid.

century shrine of St Alban and the shrine illustrated in the windows of the Trinity chapel at Canterbury, had given way to two-stage monuments. Initially the lower storey was pierced with niches, perhaps deriving from the tomb-shrine tradition—we noted several examples in the thirteenth century. Then in the fourteenth century the lower stage increasingly became a solid base, the earlier niches surviving as vestigial decoration such as foiled motifs, as might also be found on table-tombs of the period. The niches were transferred to the upper storey, where they were at more convenient 'work-top' height.

THE TOMB-SHRINE OF ST WILLIAM OF YORK

As we saw in the previous chapter, St William's body was finally elevated in 1284 and moved to a shrine behind the high altar. As usual, the saint's original tomb in the nave remained an alternative, perhaps more accessible focus of veneration. The nave was being remodelled from 1291, but this was a protracted process and the design was modified during the early fourteenth century. The east end of the nave was certainly complete by the time Archbishop William Melton (1317–40) donated £20 towards the 'new building' of St William's tomb.[7] Christopher Wilson considers that 'The 1330s seem the most likely years for such a gift',[8] and this would suit the style of the monument, fragments of which have survived.[9]

It was a late example of a tomb-shrine built over an empty grave, rather like the thirteenth-century monument over Swithun's long-vacated tomb already discussed. But fashions in shrines had developed. *Foramina* bases were out-dated, and in many ways William's new tomb-shrine resembled a typical fourteenth-century high shrine, the sort of monument provided for a saint whose relics had been elevated from the tomb. It was a two-stage structure, measuring around 3500 × 1250mm on plan. The lower storey was essentially a hollow box, with four nodding ogee arches on each of the long sides and two at the ends. In the spandrels between the arches was figurative sculpture of decidedly non-religious, even 'irreverent' subjects (Wilson's word). It is of course the open nature of the lower storey that distinguishes it from the solid bases of contemporary high shrines, and the open arches were presumably intended to provide limited access to the lid of the empty coffin. In the Romanesque nave the coffin-lid may have protruded above the pavement; it was buried by the higher pavement of the Gothic nave, though the top might perhaps have been left exposed beneath the cenotaph so that people could touch it. 'Tide marks' on the masonry suggest that the

[7] *Hist. Church of York*, ii. 388–421 (Stubbs's Lives of the Archbishops of York), at 417: *Tumbam vero Sancti Willelmi sumptibus xx. librarum renovabat.* The author, Thomas Stubbs, was probably a fourteenth-century Yorkshire friar.

[8] Wilson, *St William*, 25, n. 37.

[9] Some of the fragments are illustrated in ibid., 14–17 figs. 7–8, 10–12. They were discovered in the minster precincts, mainly in the eighteenth century.

sarcophagus was partly submerged by the steps of two successive monuments which rose around it, though it always remained at the same level until the Reformation, when it was completely buried beneath the floor, still in the same location. There were marks of colonettes on the top of the coffin-lid and other associated wear patterns, all of which could be clearly distinguished from the wear patterns that had formed when the coffin was enclosed within the fourteenth-century monument. It seems, therefore, that there had been an earlier monument over the tomb. It is likely, also, that the tomb remained in the same position throughout its history.[10]

The arcaded substructure supported a flat slab, above which was a canopy-like second storey with twelve supports featuring statuettes of saints within tall niches with nodding ogee canopies. This superstructure was presumably entirely ornamental, given that the body was enshrined elsewhere. The whole monument was coloured and gilded.

TWO SHRINES OF FEMALE SAINTS: ST WÆRBURH AND ST EADBURH OF BICESTER

We traced the early history of the cult of the royal nun St Wærburh (Werbergh or Werburg), in Chapter 3, where it was noted that the saint's remains may not have reached Chester until the early tenth century. The relics were translated again in 1095, when Goscelin was commissioned to write her Life, but nothing is known about how her relics were displayed until the fourteenth century, when a new shrine was created. Smashed up at the Reformation, the lowest part was recycled in the early seventeenth century, first as part of the tomb of Bishop Downham, then (in 1635) as the base of the bishop's throne on the south side of the choir.[11] Other fragments were discovered during George Gilbert Scott's restoration in 1873; and in 1888 the architect Sir Arthur Blomfield reassembled all the available pieces into the present assemblage, placing it at the west end of the Lady chapel; originally it probably stood between the high altar (then further west than it is today) and the rectangular ambulatory of the new presbytery that was created over a long period during the thirteenth century.

The monument as restored consists of a base with niches, an intermediate slab, and a traceried, box-like top storey, reconstructed in a very schematic way. Only two bays long by one bay wide, it looks truncated; could the original monument have been intended to be longer, perhaps with four niches per side? But in broad terms it is clear that it conformed with the emerging type of high shrine, a design perhaps ultimately deriving from Thomas Becket's shrine of 1220.

The inauguration of the monument is unrecorded, but the flowing,

[10] Christopher Norton and Stuart Harrison, *pers. comm.*

[11] *VCH Cheshire*, v, pt. ii, 'The City of Chester: Culture, Buildings, Institutions', ed. C. P. Lewis and A. T. Thacker (Woodbridge, 2005), pp. 185–204 (Major buildings: Cathedral and Close), at 191.

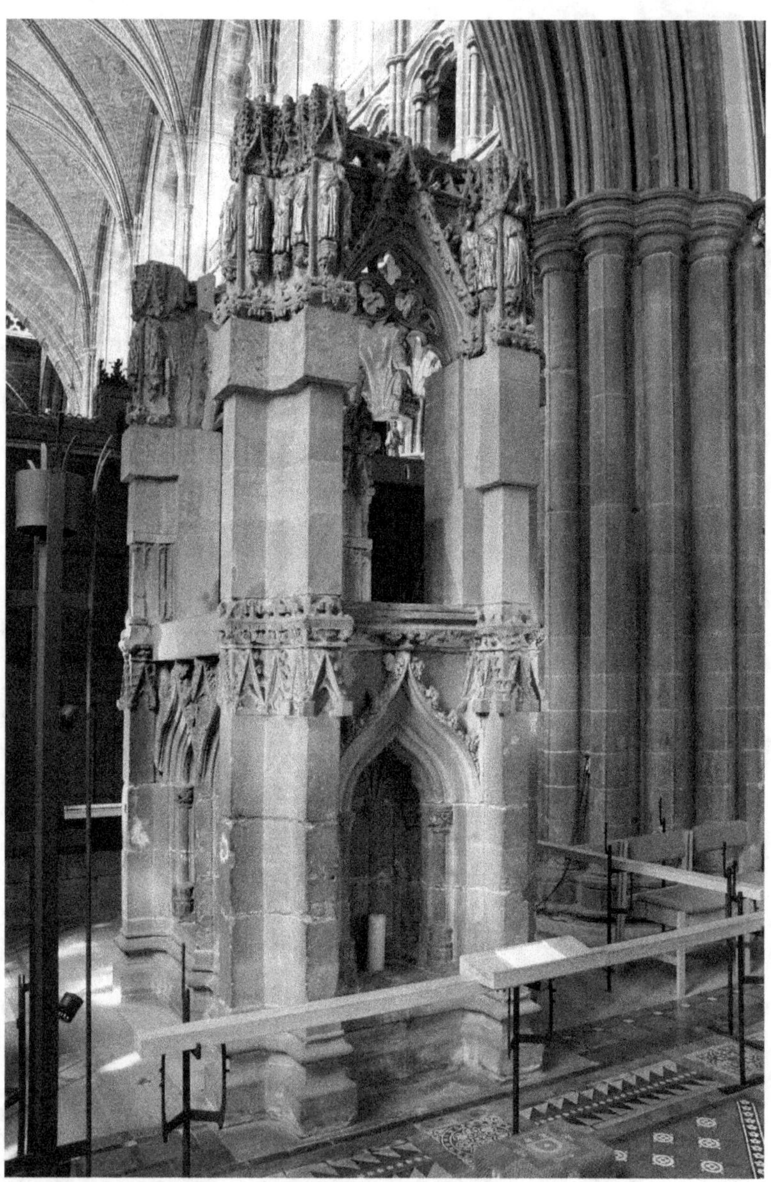

PLATE 9.1 CHESTER CATHEDRAL The shrine of St Wærburh.

quasi-Flamboyant tracery of the upper lights is paralleled at Chester by the windows of the nave and south transept, remodelled from around 1323. Even this seems a little early for the style of the miniature bases of the lower niches, and a date of *c.*1340 is perhaps most likely.

What remains uncertain is how the relics were accommodated within the monument. There was never any tradition that Wærburh's body had remained incorrupt, and the disarticulated bones presumably still lay in a smallish reliquary, just as they had since the saint was elevated in the early eighth century.[12] The Elizabethan antiquary Henry Bradshaw recalled in his Life of the saint that during the great Chester fire of 1180 her shrine, carried through the streets, miraculously extinguished the blaze, but this late occurrence of a hagiographical *topos* can scarcely be taken as evidence for the way the relics were kept in the late twelfth century.[13]

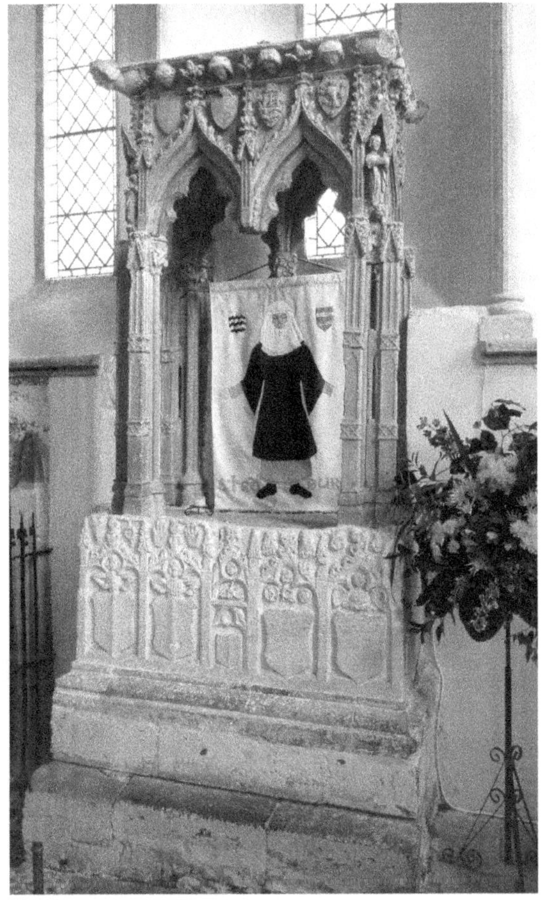

PLATE 9.2 STANTON HARCOURT (OXON) Remains of the fourteenth-century shrine of St Eadburh of Bicester.

Coincidentally, fragments also survive of the early fourteenth-century shrine of another seventh-century royal nun, St Eadburh of Bicester. Eadburh is said to have been a daughter of Penda of Mercia, who died in the mid-seventh century, though Bede makes no mention of her. She became a nun at Aylesbury,[14] probably rising to the rank of abbess; her relics were later translated to the minster at Bicester, perhaps at the time an Augustinian priory was founded there in 1182. The shrine at Bicester was built or rebuilt in the early fourteenth century; at the Reformation it seems to have been acquired by Sir Simon Harcourt and was transferred to Stanton, to be used as an Easter Sepulchre. Other parts of the shrine were incorporated in a tomb in the Harcourt chapel.[15]

The result is a monument of disparate parts. It sits on a tall stone step. The lowest element is a limestone base made up of three slabs adorned with five bays of arcading in very shallow relief, comprising ogee-headed niches containing angels holding shields, presumably once painted. This might be of fifteenth-century date, though is perhaps better interpreted as new-built

[12] See above, p. 62.
[13] H. Bradshaw, *The Hole Lyfe and History of Saynt Werburge very frutefull for all Christen people to rede* (London, 1521), cap. 20.
[14] Though it is not impossible that her convent was at Adderbury ('Eadburh's burg').
[15] 'Stanton Harcourt: Church', in *VCH Oxford*, xii. 289–93.

after the shrine came to Stanton *c.*1537. Above is a tall superstructure just two bays wide and one bay deep. Rectangular corner shafts adorned with gablets support two steep ogee arches, still retaining polychromy. The heraldic shields in the spandrels are carved in relief: Coldstream dates the heraldry to 1294–1317. Finally, at the top is a cornice with human heads. Presumably this superstructure formed a canopy over what must have been quite a small reliquary; it can never have been claimed that the monument accommodated a whole-body cult.

THE HEAD OF ST HUGH OF LINCOLN

A cult focused on the detached head of Bishop Hugh of Lincoln seems to have developed in the early fourteenth century. There is some evidence, already noted, that the head and body were separately housed from the 1220 translation,[16] though the date of the narrative edited in the seventeenth century by Surius is uncertain, and the description might merely reflect the arrangement in that editor's own day. In fact, the earliest secure reference to a separate focus of veneration seems to be an account compiled in 1334 of cash taken when the money-boxes at the *feretrum* and the *caput* were opened and the contents distributed to various cathedral officials. These annual records of the *aperturæ* continue until 1532, with a gap between 1450 and 1510.[17]

One event involving this secondary centre of devotion is well recorded, namely the theft of the head during the episcopate of John Bokyngham (Buckingham) 1363–98. The event may be more precisely dated to 1363 × 1365 by a royal charter dated February 1365 referring to the 'recent' theft, in which 'the head of St Hugh, stripped of gold and silver, had been stolen by the aforesaid thieves and carried hence'; following the inquest into the crime the king restored the head to the dean and chapter.[18] Gerald of Wales embellished the story: the skull was thrown into a field where it was guarded by a crow until it could be taken back to the cathedral.[19] The *custos* of the shrine, John Welbourn (treasurer of Lincoln Cathedral, 1350–80), who, as we have seen, repaired the main shrine of St Hugh, paid for the repair of the head-shrine: 'after the theft and damage to the head of St Hugh, he had it repaired and decorated anew with gold, silver, and precious stones'.[20]

On this evidence the reliquary might have simply been a *chef* in the form of a human head, created by covering a skull in plates of silver-gilt. Such an

[16] See above, pp. 224–5.

[17] E. Venables, 'The shrine and head of St. Hugh of Lincoln', *Arch. J.*, 50 (1893), 37–61, at 51. He prints sample accounts on pp. 56–59 (Appendix B).

[18] *Foedera*, ed. T. Rymer, vi (London, 1727), 433: ... *capud sancti Hugonis ... auro et argento exornatum, per dictos latrones furatum et abinde asportatum ...*

[19] *Gerald of Wales*, vii. 222, n. 2.

[20] Welbourn chantry-book: Lincolnshire Archives, Lincoln Cathedral Archives, Ref. D. & C., A.1.10: *Qui eciam, post furacionem et spoliacionem capitis Sancti Hugonis, de novo fecit cum auro et argento et lapidibus preciosis ornari et reparari.*

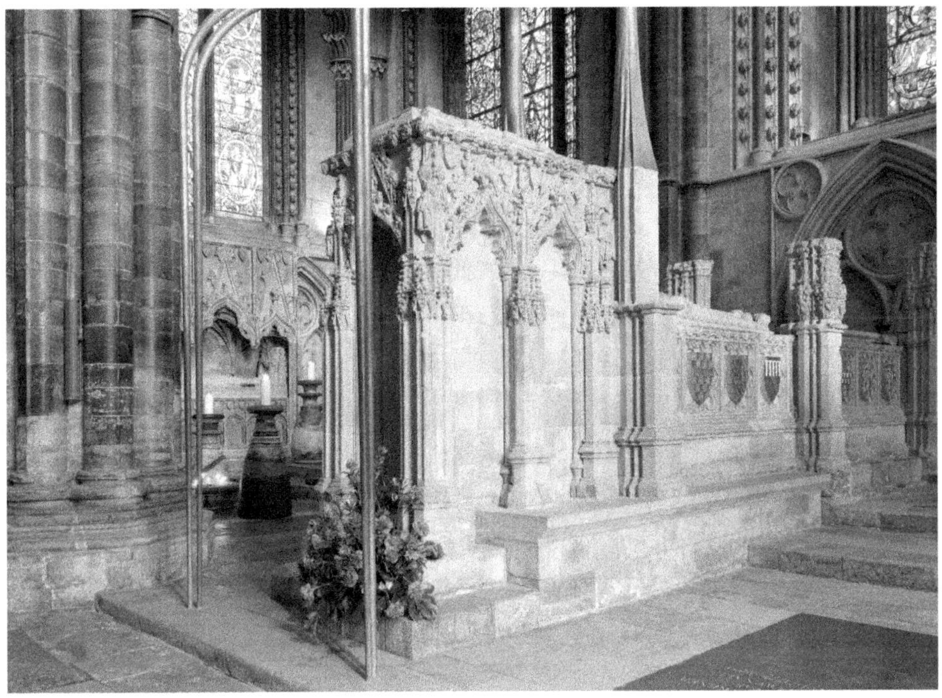

PLATE 9.3 LINCOLN CATHEDRAL The head shrine of St Hugh.

object, combining opulence with portability would have been an obvious target for Henry VIII's commissioners. The king had specifically written to the bishop of Lincoln, Dr John Longland (1521–47), in October 1541, noting that shrine coverings survived 'in sundrye places of [his] realme' and ordering that they should be removed;[21] the bishop had in turn forwarded the letter to his cathedral chapter, who undertook to carry it out.[22] The royal order for the destruction of St Hugh's shrine, issued by Thomas Cromwell on 6 June 1540 and copied in the Lincoln Chapter Acts book, specifically mentions only the main shrine,[23] but an extract from the book, inserted into the acts for 1520, evidently dates from the destruction of the head shrine and includes 'Relikes, jewels and other stuff belonging to seint hugh's head delivered to Sir William Johnson the xxvij[th] day of November ... and FFURST the hede of seint hugh closed in siluer gilt and enamelled. *Item* the mytre of hugh of siluer gilt and enamelled ....'[24]

Whereas the main shrine was totally demolished in 1540, the destruction of the head shrine involved only the removal of the *chef* itself and its precious

[21] *L & P Henry VIII*, xvi. 517–18.
[22] *Chapter Acts of the Cathedral Church of Lincoln, A.D. 1536–1547*, ed. R. E. G. Cole, Lincoln Record Soc., 13 (1917), 56.
[23] Printed in Cole and Johnston, 'St Hugh', 66–7.
[24] Printed in Venables, 'The shrine and head of St. Hugh', 56 (Appendix A).

adornments, and perhaps also the destruction of the shrine's superstructure, for it is unlikely that the head merely stood on the top of the monument as seen today. The survival of the supporting base is surprising and is presumably due to the fact that it was integral with the tomb of Bishop Henry Burghersh. The tomb and the shrine-base are almost certainly contemporary. As we have seen, the earliest evidence for separate enshrinement of the head seems to date from the 1330s. Burghersh died in 1340, which is consistent with the date of the monument on art-historical evidence.[25] This means that the monument pre-dates the theft of the reliquary and its restoration.

Like the shrine of St Eadburh of Bicester, the base comprises two bays of recesses on the north side balanced by shallow arcaded panels on the south, with a single niche at the west end. It is richly decorated with nodding ogees, censing angels, and crockets, all of which were presumably originally richly coloured. It seems likely that the monument rose still higher and was surmounted by some sort of openwork structure enclosing the head reliquary, an effect which is partly replicated by the metalwork which now rises above the shrine. When it was surmounted by the rich *chef* of St Hugh it must have been a splendid monument indeed.

ST BIRINUS OF DORCHESTER

As we saw in the previous chapter, during the 1224 the canons of Dorchester-on-Thames miraculously rediscovered the relics of the founder of their church, St Birinus. In his *Polychronicon* the Chester monk Ranulph Higden (†1364) attempted to reconcile the rival claims of Dorchester and Winchester, explaining that the Dorchester canons maintained that the body which had gone to Winchester was a different individual.[26] By then the putative saint was displayed in a new shrine at Dorchester, which continued to bring revenue to the canons until the Reformation: £5 *per annum* at the time of Henry VIII's great survey of ecclesiastical revenue, the *Valor Ecclesiasticus*.[27]

The reliquary appears to have been reconstructed in 1320,[28] and this must have been the *feretrum* of wondrous workmanship known to Higden.[29] It must have been removed by Henry VIII's commissioners at the Reformation, but fragments identified as coming from the demolished shrine-base were used as infill of a doorway in the west wall of the north transept. They were discovered in 1858,[30] and were incorporated in the

[25] Coldstream, 'Decorated shrine bases', 19.
[26] *Polychronicon Ranulphi Higden, monachi Cestrensis*, vi, ed. J. R. Lumby, RS, 41 (1876), 4. See above, pp. 227–8.
[27] 'The offeringe to Seynt Berren v^{li}', in *Valor Ecclesiasticus*, ed. J. Caley and J. Hunter, 6 vols. (1810–34), ii. 170.
[28] H. Addington, *Some Account of the Abbey Church … at Dorchester* (Oxford, 1860), 137.
[29] *Polychronicon*, vi. 4: *feretrum mirandi operis super locum primæ sepulturæ apud Dorcestram hodie cernitur.*
[30] W. C. Macfarlane, 'A Short Account of the Restoration of the North Aisle' (1882), printed as a repaginated appendix in J. H. Parker, *The History of Dorchester, Oxfordshire* (Oxford and London, 1882).

present monument in 1964. The most significant survivals are a few fragments of fine lierne-vaulted work in freestone, presumably from the niches, though the nineteenth-century accounts refer to the discovery of Purbeck marble pieces which were also thought to come from the shrine. The survival of the niche heads indicates at least that the shrine-base was of the solid variety, though of course one cannot tell whether the niches were in the lowest storey (as at Chester) or higher up as in later examples.

LONDON, OLD ST PAUL'S

In Chapter 7 we left the relics of St Earconwald, the late seventh-century bishop of London, in a new shrine behind the high altar of Old St Paul's, whither they had been translated on 14 November 1148. The church was reconstructed in the second half of the thirteenth century; progress was slow, and the official 'measurement', presumably marking the completion of the building works, took place *c.*1315.[31] The shrine was to stand in the bay beyond the high altar, i.e. in the fifth of the eight bays of the thirteenth-century 'New Work', and its foundation stone was laid by Bishop Gilbert de Segrave in 1313. It is interesting that the saint was no longer at the high altar but further east, a change of emphasis of the sort seen at Winchester in the following century, when Swithun's body was finally disassociated from the high altar. Work on the reliquary was recorded in 1319,[32] and the saint's relics were translated into the new monument in 1326.[33]

The shrine then had a costly make-over in 1339. 'William de Leleford, archdeacon of Colchester and canon of St Pauls, in 1335 had given forty pounds for the ornamentation of the shrine. Three London goldsmiths were retained for a whole year for the work, beginning at Candlemas, the master smith at eight shillings and the other two at five shillings a week each.'[34] Further embellishments took place during a six-week period finishing in October 1401, when John Grantham the goldsmith, Herebright the painter, and their colleagues worked on the shrine.[35] It is regrettable that the shrine was not mentioned in an inventory taken in 1402.[36]

The appearance of the final reliquary was depicted by Wenceslaus Hollar

[31] R. K. Morris, 'The New work at Old St Paul's Cathedral and its place in English thirteenth-century architecture', in *Medieval Art, Architecture and Archaeology in London*, ed. L. Grant, *BAA Trans.*, vol. 10, for 1984 (Leeds, 1990), 74–100, at 75.

[32] Coldstream, 'Decorated shrine bases', 24, citing W. R. Lethaby, 'Old St Pauls', *The Builder*, 139 (1930), 193.

[33] *Chronicles of the Reigns of Edward I and Edward II*, ed. W. Stubbs, 2 vols., RS, 76 (1882–3), i. 311: *corpus beati Erkenwaldi fuit amotum ab illo loco ubi prius translatum fuit prope magnum altare, usque ad novam capellam beatæ Mariæ, et in novo feretro honorifice collocatum.*

[34] Wall, *Shrines*, 105.

[35] ibid., 106–7.

[36] 'Two Inventories of the Cathedral Church of St. Paul, London, dated respectively 1245 and 1402 ...', ed. W. Sparrow Simpson, *Archæologia*, 50, pt. ii (1887), 439–524, at 500–18. The shrine is mentioned in a short inventory of 1445/6, but in little detail (ibid., 518–20).

in an engraving of 1651.[37] William Dugdale claimed that this drawing was 'a true presentation from the very originall draught, made for a direction to the Smith that wrought [the grille]'. His comments appear, however, to refer only to the 'grille' rather than the *feretrum*, and it is by no means certain that the 'original draught' included the shrine. In other words, Hollar's view of the latter may be imaginary, particularly as the monument depicted is almost two-dimensional, perhaps six inches deep at the most. Perhaps Hollar misinterpreted an earlier drawing showing the elevation of one end of the reliquary. It stood on a plain altar dedicated to the saint, located within a three-sided, railed enclosure (*clausura*) set against a wall. This was presumably the east side of the high altar reredos, as noted by Dugdale: 'The *Shrine* of Saint *Erkenwald* … stood on the East side of the wall above the high altar.'[38] But if Hollar's drawing was indeed based on a surviving original, and assuming it was deeper than the shallow object shown in the engraving published by Dugdale, it was a huge house-shrine, with three tall window-like lights in the western face beneath a gable. The lights resembled Decorated windows, with trefoil heads to the sub-lights, a quatrefoil at the top, and trefoils in the spandrels; they were separated by pilasters with niches for statuary. Within the crested gable was a group of irregular foiled shapes. The gable ended in a pinnacle, and was linked by tracery to two flanking pinnacles at the corners of the body of the reliquary. Along the longer side were free-standing buttresses, linked by bridges to the body of the shrine. As Nicola Coldstream has pointed out, the reliquary displays 'every influence of Westminster'.[39]

THE SHRINE OF ST ALBAN

The finest example of a fourteenth-century shrine was reconstructed from more than two thousand fragments of Purbeck marble and freestone forming the blocking of the three arches on the east side of the shrine chapel behind the Great Screen. Much of this material had been discovered in 1847–53 by that indefatigable local researcher, the Revd Henry Nicholson, and further discoveries were made early in February 1872. It was realised that there were enough pieces of stone for a reconstruction to be attempted, and the following month the painstaking work began. It was undertaken by George Gilbert Scott's Clerk of Works John Chapple and J. T. Micklethwaite, the abbey architect and Scott's deputy for the major refurbishment of the church then in progress.[40] One hundred and twenty years later a second

[37] Reproduced in *Medieval Art, Architecture and Archaeology in London*, ed. L. Grant, *BAA Trans.*, vol. 10, for 1984 (Leeds, 1990), pl. XVb.

[38] W. Dugdale, *The History of St Paul's Cathedral in London* (London, 1658), 20. See also Hollar's plan dated 1657, ibid., 161, which shows the shrine (*Tum: S. Erckenwaldi*) in this location.

[39] Coldstream, 'Decorated shrine bases', 24.

[40] J. T. Micklethwaite, 'The Shrine of St Alban', *Arch. J.*, 29 (1872), 201–11.

reconstruction took place, in conjunction with an archaeological excavation beneath the shrine. In general terms the exercise confirmed the accuracy of the nineteenth-century reconstruction, though some alterations were made. The monument gained greatly in stability, the nineteenth-century brick core being replaced by a lightweight steel frame. The reconstruction was accompanied by conservation and cleaning, architectural components (though not sculptural detail) that in the original had been either missing or represented in alien materials such as wood were replaced by resin replicas, and a canopy was placed on top of the monument.

We have already noted the evidence for the pillared shrine inaugurated by Abbot Simon, completed by 1183. It stood behind the high altar of the Romanesque church, presumably in the apse. But in 1257 alarming cracks were discovered at the east end of the church, the event which prompted the reconstruction of the presbytery. During the preliminary works, when the two east bays and apse of the Romanesque chevet were demolished, the workmen also undertook soundings between the matutinal altar of St Oswine and the altar of Wulfstan, and located a tomb beneath the place where, as Matthew Paris tells us, 'the old painted *feretrum*' had been placed together with a certain 'tomb' with marble columns, which place and tomb were called the 'old tomb of St Albans'; it was believed to be the site of the saint's original tomb.[41] Just where this tomb could have been located is uncertain, but the reference to the matutinal altar implies an axial position, presumably west of the high altar and perhaps in the choir. It sounds as though the position of the pre-1183 shrine continued to be marked by a secondary focus of devotion to the saint.

When we study the cult in the early fourteenth century we are on firmer ground. John de Maryns began his short abbatiate in 1302 and, according to the *Gesta Abbatum*, soon resolved to move the shrine-base into the enlarged presbytery, whilst retaining the twelfth-century *feretrum*, which he adorned at great expense (more than 160 marks, which he laid out in cash 'without many courtesies').[42] In the end, he built a completely new shrine-base. Magnificently restored in the 1990s, the monument is one of the finest achievements of the Dorset marblers, and is built of Purbeck marble and Totternhoe stone, the latter being a hard form of chalk. Four bays long and one (broader) bay wide, it measures 2600 × 950mm externally, excluding the buttresses. The height from floor to the top slab was originally about 2660mm (it is slightly less today as the bottom step is embedded in the pavement). The base is raised, as usual, on two shallow steps (each no more than 115mm), the lowest of which survived the Reformation and remained

[41] ... *ubi quoque collocatum fuerat antiquum feretrum pictum, et quædam tumba marmorea cum columpnis marmoreis, qui locus et tumba dicebatur vetus tumba s. Albani.* Matthew Paris, *Chronica Maiora*; ed. Luard, v. 608.

[42] *GA*; ed. Riley, ii. 207: *Tumbam autem Sancti Albani, et feretrum, amovere fecit, honorifice istud decorando; et expensas exposuit, sine multis curialitatibus, plus quam centum sexaginta marcas in pecunia numerata.*

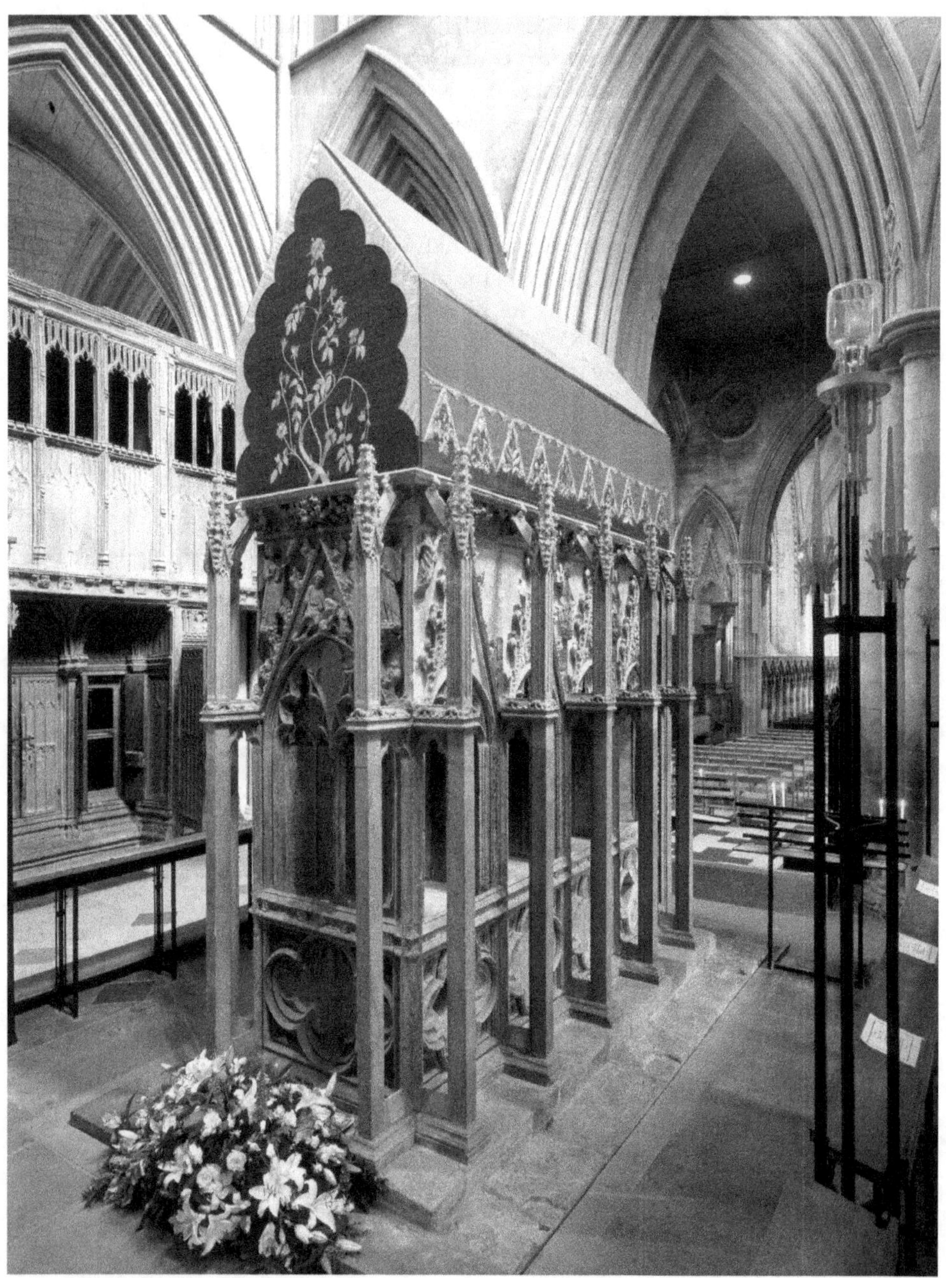

PLATE 9.4 ST ALBAN'S ABBEY The fourteenth-century shrine of St Alban.

in place for over three centuries, forming a 'frame' marking the position of the shrine.[43] The lowest element is a quatrefoil base, with an elongated and subdivided quatrefoil at each of the ends. Three of the plain Purbeck marble surfaces enclosed by the quatrefoils are rather incongruously pierced by unadorned lozenge-shaped holes through which recent pilgrims to the shrine posted a curious collection of memorabilia.[44] Then comes a chamfered mid-slab, 767mm above the top step, at exactly the right height for kneeling people of average size to place their heads into the niches. These are each 430mm wide at the front, and around 450mm deep. They have walls of panelling, with reticulation in Caen stone at the top, rising to the remains of exquisitely carved miniature lierne vaults (the freestone still retaining its alternating colours of red and blue). These niches are surrounded by mouldings terminating in decorated cinquefoil heads contained within tall ogee gables. The spandrels between the gables are adorned with images of at least one king (presumably Offa, the legendary founder, as he is shown holding a model of a church), and bishops or priors (sadly defaced, some almost totally hacked off) with censing angels at the ends. The monument is topped by a slab supporting a *feretrum* (replaced in 1993 by a modern replica), making a total height from floor to apex of about 4000mm. The bays of the monument are further articulated by free-standing buttresses, linked to the body of the shrine by bridge-like fliers. These buttresses, suggested by projections at the foot of the shrine-base and by surviving fragments, were (as wooden replicas) a feature of the nineteenth-century restoration, and their aesthetic importance became apparent during the reconstruction process.[45]

The finest sculpture is reserved for the two ends. At the east end is another figure of King Offa holding a model of a church and, above it, a scene that Sir Charles Peers and William Page identified as the 'scourging of St Alban': the saint stands between two bearded figures, who seem to be pulling at his hair.[46] At the west end is a scene showing the execution of the saint, with censing angels. This must have stood, as today, at some distance from the shrine altar. Nevertheless, a celebrant at that altar would have had the scene of Alban's martyrdom both 'before his face and in his heart', just like his predecessors who celebrated mass at the high altar with Abbot Simon's *feretrum* behind it.[47] Indeed, given that the shrine-base supported the twelfth-century *feretrum*, retained by Abbot John, a celebrant would have been able to see the same scene twice: in repoussé metal above, and carved in stone in front of him.

[43] Biddle, 'Remembering St Alban', 124–5.
[44] Crook, *Architectural Setting*, 38–9. As restored, the openings are in the end bays on the south side and the westernmost bay only on the north.
[45] M. Biddle, 'The Shrine Restored', *The Alban Link*, Newsletter of the Fraternity of Friends of St Alban's Abbey, No. 39 (September 1933), 13–20, at 16–19.
[46] *VCH Hertfordshire*, ii, ed. W. Page (1908), 495.
[47] See above, p. 205.

THE SHRINE OF ST AMPHIBALUS

As noted in Chapter 7, the *feretrum* containing the alleged bones of this entirely fictitious saint reposed on the lateral screen wall of the retrochoir at St Alban's Abbey from 1186. Again we have the authority of the *Gesta Abbatum* that in the time of Abbot William (1214–35) the reliquary was moved to the 'middle of the church' where it was surrounded by a grille. It formed part of an ensemble of two altars: one dedicated to Amphibalus himself and the other to the Holy Cross, suggesting a location in front of the rood screen at the east end of the nave.[48] This is confirmed by the account of how in 1323 part of the south nave arcade collapsed, bringing down a beam (presumably one of the tie-beams of the roof) on to Amphibalus's shrine.[49] The *feretrum* was undamaged, but the marble 'columns' were broken.[50] It would seem, then, that the tomb was of the 'table' variety like the twelfth-century shrine of St Alban, in other words, a slab supported on pillars.

The shrine was then moved to a position described as 'very unworthy' (*nimis abjecto*) behind the altar of St Hugh,[51] possibly the north aisle of the presbytery. Finally, in the time of Abbot Thomas de la Mare (1349–96) the *feretrum* was placed on a 'most beautiful new stone shrine-base' (*tumba*), created by the sacrist Ralph Whitchurch.[52] Abbot Thomas expended £8 18*s* 10*d* in repairing and adorning the east side of the *feretrum* with images and silver-gilt plates. The new location of the monument (just called 'the place where we see it today' in the *Gesta*) was specified in notes on altar positions within the abbey church compiled *c.*1435:

> Near the Chapel of the Blessed Virgin, there stands within an enclosure [which was] becomingly adorned with panelling through the care of Abbot Hugh de Eversden, the shrine (*scrinium*) of Saint Amphibalus, honourably placed upon a tomb of white stone modelled in openwork (*opus interrasile*) at the cost of Ralph Whitchurch, Sacrist.[53] [—] In the interclose extending

[48] *GA*; ed. Riley, i. 281–2.

[49] ibid., ii. 128.

[50] ibid., ii. 129: *contritis columnis marmoreis tumbæ suæ, capsam ligneam, in qua eiusdem reliquiæ continebantur, in nullo lædebat.*

[51] *VCH Hertfordshire*, ii. 487, citing BL, Cotton MS Nero D.vii, fo. 23.

[52] *GA*; ed. Riley, iii. 384–5: *Feretrum etiam Sancti Amphibali de loco nimis abjecto, retro videlicet, altare sancti Hugonis primitus situatum, a loco [recte in loco?] ubi nunc cernitur per dictum abbatem est translatum; et super tumbam perpulchram lapideam, industria Domini Radulphi Witechurche, tunc sacristæ,* [385] *honestius collocatum. Cuius etiam frontem orientalem idem abbas imaginibus et laminis argenteis et deauratis nobiliter reparavit; octo libris, octodecem solidis, decem denariis, in eodem opere profusis.*

[53] *Chronica Monasterii S. Albani: Annales Monasterii S. Albani a Johanne Amundesham Monacho (ut videtur) conscripti*, ed. H. T. Riley, 2 vols., RS, 28 (1870), i. 431–50, Appendix D. *De altaribus, monumentis, et locis sepulchrorum, in ecclesia monasterii Sancti Albani, quædam annotationes* [BL, Harley MS 3775, fo. 129a], at 433: *Est etiam inter clausum, prope capellam Beatæ Virginis, decenter cælatura industria Abbatis Hugonis adornatum, scrinium Sancti Amphibali, super tumbam albi lapidis, operis interrasilis, sumptibus Radulphi Whytchirche, sacristæ, honorifice repositum …*

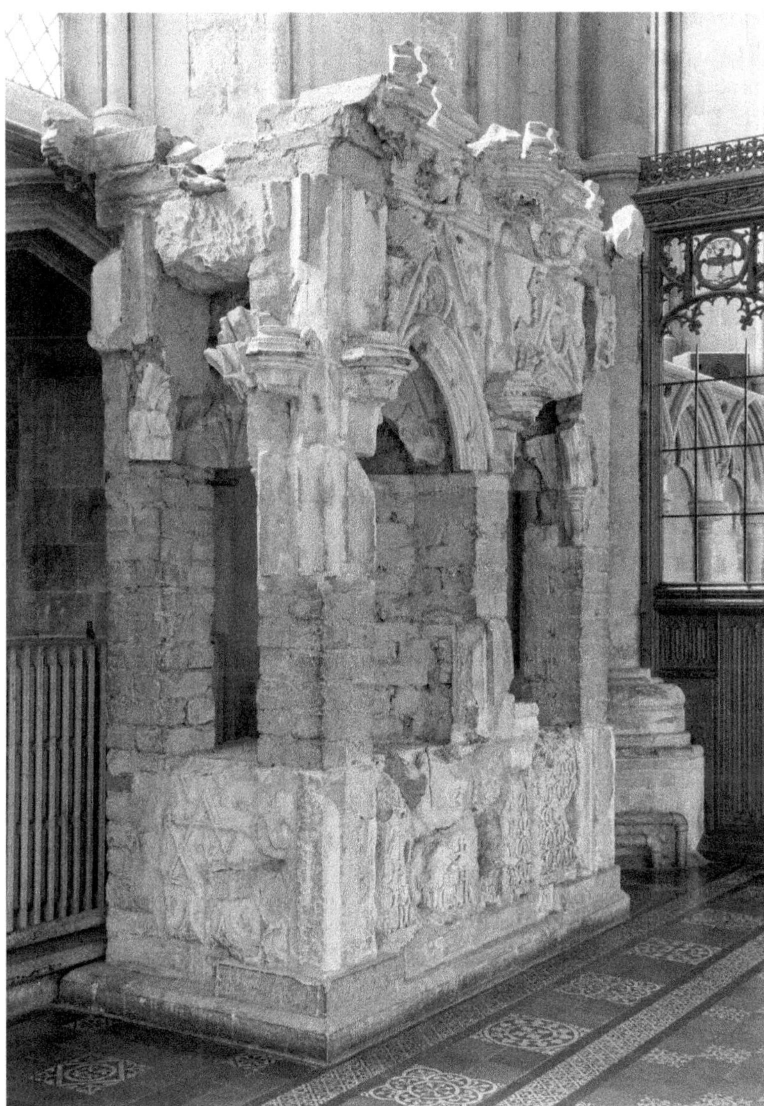

PLATE 9.5
ST ALBAN'S ABBEY
The fourteenth-century shrine of St Amphibalus from the south-west.

from the Saint's Chapel to the Chapel of Saint Mary are three Altars; namely the Altar of Saint Amphibalus at the head of his shrine (*feretrum*), the altar of Saint Edmund, King and Martyr, on the north side; and of Saint Peter on the south side.[54]

[54] ibid., 447. *In intercluso inde usque Capellam Sanctæ Mariæ sunt tria altaria; altare, videlicet, Sancti Amphibali, ad caput feretri eiusdem; altare Sancti Edmundi, Regis et Martyris, ex parte boreali; et Sancti Petri, ex parte australi, cum eorum imaginibus et historiis depictis; ubi fit frequens devotio populi eorum utrisque festis, per Sacristam Monasterii solemniter celebratis.*

In 1872, together with the very much greater number of fragments from St Alban's shrine, pieces of worked Totternhoe stone were discovered in the blocking of the eastern arches of the Saint's chapel; other pieces were retrieved from the fill of the north and north-east windows of the Lady chapel vestibule.[55] There can be no doubt on grounds of style that these derived from the shrine-base created by Ralph Whitchurch (they even bear his initials, RW). The pieces were reconstructed and the shrine-base now stands at the east end of the north choir aisle.

As reconstructed, the shrine base is just two bays long, measuring 1830 × 870mm, and 2450mm high, but these dimensions (and indeed the assumption that it was a two-bay structure) should be treated with circumspection given the poor survival of the material, which is built up on rather crude modern brickwork. Perhaps about fifty per cent of the medieval stonework survives. The lowest part of the monument is a chest, about 585mm high, on a 150mm plinth. The chest is adorned with intersecting fretwork, the *opus interrasile* of the description, a term usually reserved for silverwork; the west end is decorated with a star motif and fleurs-de-lys and the inscription 'Amphib …'. There are more fleurs-de-lys and quatrefoils above, and the initials of Ralph Whitchurch.

The niche floors are 700mm above the pavement (there are no steps in the reconstruction, though these would seem likely originally). Some of the niche heads are well preserved, taking the form of miniature lierne vaults. These vaults tilt forward, and there are remains of polychromy. Their surrounding arches take the rather unusual form of an ogee moulding surmounted by a cinquefoil. The monument was evidently well adorned with statuettes: two at each end, and one in the central spandrel, all in very shallow niches.

ST OSWINE OF TYNEMOUTH

As noted above, St Albans had a prominent altar to St Oswine, a king of Deira (644–51), who was murdered during a dynastic feud and thereafter was regarded as a saint. The relics were, however, located at Tynemouth Priory, a monastery which in the late eleventh century had become a cell of St Albans. Hugh Candidus's mid-twelfth-century list of saint's resting places mentions the cult: *Et in Tinemuthe sanctus Osuuius* [recte *Osuuinus*] *rex*,[56] a saint missing from the earlier *Secgan*. Veneration of Oswine at Tynemouth had started in 1065 with the discovery of the saint's relics, which Bishop Æthelwine of Durham raised from a tomb, placing them 'in a shrine' (*in scrinio*).[57] In 1110

[55] 'The shrine of St Amphibalus', in Ridgway Lloyd, *An Architectural and Historical Account of the Shrines of St Alban and St Amphibalus in St Alban's Abbey* (Langley and London, 1873), 17–24.

[56] *The Chronicle of Hugh Candidus, a Monk of Peterborough*, ed. W. T. Mellows, Friends of Peterborough Cathedral (Oxford, 1949), 60.

[57] *Florentii Wigorniensis monachi Chronicon ex Chronicis*, ed. B. Thorpe, 2 vols., English Historical Society (London, 1848–9), i. 222.

Richard, abbot of St Albans, moved the relics from the old oratory of St Mary into the new church and placed them in a new *feretrum*.[58] Circumstantial detail in the saint's Life shows that the *feretrum* was raised on a slab supported on pillars,[59] but its location within the Norman church is uncertain. When the east end of the church was rebuilt *c.*1200 the shrine was presumably relocated. Thomas Walsingham, abbot of St Albans, records that in 1346–9 his predecessor, Thomas de la Mare, when prior of Tynemouth, moved the shrine, which up to then had been attached to the high altar (*altari majori connexum*), and put it 'in the place where it now stands'. De la Mare's object was to create an environment that would 'allow people coming there to pursue their devotions more quietly, freely, and capably near to the martyr'.[60]

It seems possible that until it was moved by Prior de la Mare the shrine was located within the recess or *loculus* that was formed in the east wall of the thirteenth-century chevet, immediately behind the high altar. It is often assumed that the prior moved the shrine into the Lady chapel on the north side of the presbytery, but it has not previously been noted that the doorway leading into the fifteenth-century east chapel (the 'Percy chapel') is stylistically of earlier date than the chapel itself and was pierced through the above-mentioned recess. The doorway is probably of fourteenth-century date, to judge from the sculptural detail of the royal heads carved in its spandrels. Furthermore, disjunctions in the side walls at the west end of the Percy chapel suggest that there was a predecessor building on the same site. It is therefore suggested that Prior Thomas constructed an axial shrine chapel that was subsequently replaced by the Percy chapel, perhaps when interest in the cult waned in the fifteenth century.

ST THOMAS CANTILUPE

In Chapter 8 we followed the slow development of the cult of St Thomas Cantilupe, at Hereford. Bishop Richard Swinfield's hope that his predecessor would be canonised was realised only in 1320, and immediately work began on his final shrine in the Lady chapel. Penelope Morgan, formerly Honorary Librarian of Hereford Cathedral, has summarised the main outlay on the new monument.[61] By December 1320 a London goldsmith called John of Werlyngworthe was making various ornaments for the shrine; Purbeck marble was supplied by Adam of Corfe in March 1321, and the same year

[58] Matthew Paris, *Chronica Maiora*; ed. Luard, ii. 138

[59] *Vita Oswini Regis*, in *Miscellanea Biographica*, cap. 22, ed. J. Raine, Surtees Soc., 8 (1838), 1–59, 36: *lapidem amplexus est cui theca eius superposita erat …*

[60] *GA*; ed. Riley, ii. 379: *Et ante omnia, decorem domus Dei cupiens, feretrum Sancti Regis et Martyris Oswini, altari majori connexum, dimovit a loco, et in loco quo modo stat fecit magnifice collocari; et advenientes quietius, liberius, et capacius possent circa martyrem suas devotiones continuare.*

[61] P. E. Morgan, 'The Effect of the Pilgrim Cult of St Thomas of Cantilupe on Hereford Cathedral', in Jancey, *Thomas Cantilupe*, 145–52, at 150–1.

William Sprot of London received £80 for latten ('*Electrum*'). The chief worker on the shrine appears to have been another London craftsman, Michael the image-maker, who received payments for fashioning the shrine according to an agreement and for his travelling and accommodation expenses to and from Hereford.[62] But by the time Cantilupe was translated to his final resting place in 1349 the cult was no longer the draw for pilgrims that it had been in its heyday in the late thirteenth century.

THE SHRINE OF ST BEDE

The present tomb of the Venerable Bede (†835), on the south side of the Galilee chapel at the west end of Durham Cathedral, dates only from 1831, following the opening of the tomb described by the librarian James Raine.[63] It confidently proclaims in jingling Latin, *Hac sunt in fossa Bedæ venerabilis ossa* ('In this grave are the bones of the Venerable Bede'), the inscription that featured on the medieval monument. The saint's bones, brought to Durham from Jarrow *c.*1022, had first been placed in the same coffin as Cuthbert, but were removed at the 1102 translation and enshrined nearby. According to Reginald of Durham, a new *feretrum* of the purest gold and silver adorned with precious stones was provided in 1165 by Hugh de Puiset.[64] In 1370 the relics were moved by Prior Forcer to the Galilee Porch at the expense of Richard of Barnard Castle, who wanted to be buried next to the saint.[65] No subsequent reconstructions of the shrine are recorded, and it is reasonable to suppose that from then on the arrangement was as described in the well-known *Rites of Durham*, compiled in the late sixteenth century:

> There was on ye south syde betwixt two pillers a goodly monumt all of blew marble [Frosterley marble] ye hight of a yeard from ye ground, supported with .v. pillers, in every corner one, & vnder ye mydest one ... [The tomb had] a fair couer of wainscott verie curiously gilted and appointed to drawe vp and downe over the shrine as they list to showe the sumptuousness therof. [66]

And elsewhere:

> There are two stones that was of Sayncte Beede's shrine in the galiley of blewe marble, which after the defacinge therof was browght into the bodye of the church and lyeth nowe over against the estmost Toumbe of the Neivells ioined both together, the vppermost stone of the said shrine hath .iiij. holes in euery corner,

[62] For Adam of Corfe, see J. Harvey, *Medieval Craftsmen* (London, 1975), 130, 133.
[63] J. Raine, *A Brief Account of Durham Cathedral with Notices of the Castle, University, City Churches, Etc.* (Newcastle, 1833), 79ff.
[64] Reginald, *Libellus*, Continuatio; ed. Raine, 169.
[65] [W. H. D. Longstaffe], 'The Hereditary Sacerdotage of Hexham', *Archaeologia Aeliana*, n.s., 4 (1860), 11–28, at 25.
[66] *The Rites of Durham*, ed. J. T. Fowler, Surtees Soc., 107 (1903), 44.

> for Irons to stand and to be fastned in to guyde the covering whene yt was drawe vp or letten downe, wherevpon did stand Saincte Beedes shrine. And the other ys a playne marble stone, which was loweste, and dyd lye aboue a litle marble tombe, whereon the lower end of the .v. small pillars of marble did stande; which pillers did also supporte the vppermost stone …[67]

The *Rites* also record the inscription on the lower slab, which credits Hugh de Puiset with the construction of the *feretrum*, which was evidently retained.[68] But the shrine-base, apparently of the pillared type, sounds very outdated for the 1370s. It seems likely that the shrine-base was also recycled, simply being moved into the Galilee from the choir.

When Charles Wall was writing his *Shrines of British Saints* he asked Dean Kitchin to send a description of two stones in the fourth bay of the south nave arcade, which seemed to answer to the description in the *Rites*.[69] One of them is said still to bear the marks of the corner holes, exactly as described. Indeed, the author of that part of the *Rites* presumably based it on the archaeological evidence of the two slabs, all that remains of the monument destroyed in November 1541.

'QUASI-SHRINES' OF ARCHBISHOPS OF CANTERBURY

A number of archiepiscopal tombs in Canterbury were destroyed after 1548 because it was claimed that they were 'superstitiously abused'; they therefore functioned like shrines. They included the tomb of Archbishop Robert Winchelsea (†1313) in the south-east transept, and that of Archbishop Bradwardine (†1349) on the south side of St Anselm's chapel. Attempts to canonise Winchelsea were unsuccessful, but it seems that an unofficial cult was still flourishing at the time the shrines were destroyed. Archbishop Arundel's (†1414) tomb in a chantry chapel on the north side of the nave that he rebuilt was also destroyed at the Reformation, probably more as a result of his opposition to Lollardy than because he, too, was regarded as a saint. Two archiepiscopal 'quasi-shrines' survived the reformers. At the entrance to St Anselm's chapel is the tomb of Simon Meopham (†1333). It is built of shiny black Tournai marble, contrasted with lighter-coloured Purbeck marble and cream-coloured Caen stone, and encloses the archbishop's coped coffin.[70] It has something of the appearance of a tomb-shrine, with its niches giving access to the coffin-lid. The monument must have upstaged the reliquary of St Anselm, of which little is known, but which

[67] ibid., 87.
[68] ibid., 45–6.
[69] Wall, *Shrines*, 114.
[70] For a fuller description and discussion, see C. Wilson, 'The Medieval Monuments', in *A History of Canterbury Cathedral*, ed. P. Collinson, N. Ramsay, and M. Sparks (Canterbury, 2002), 451–510, at 466–7.

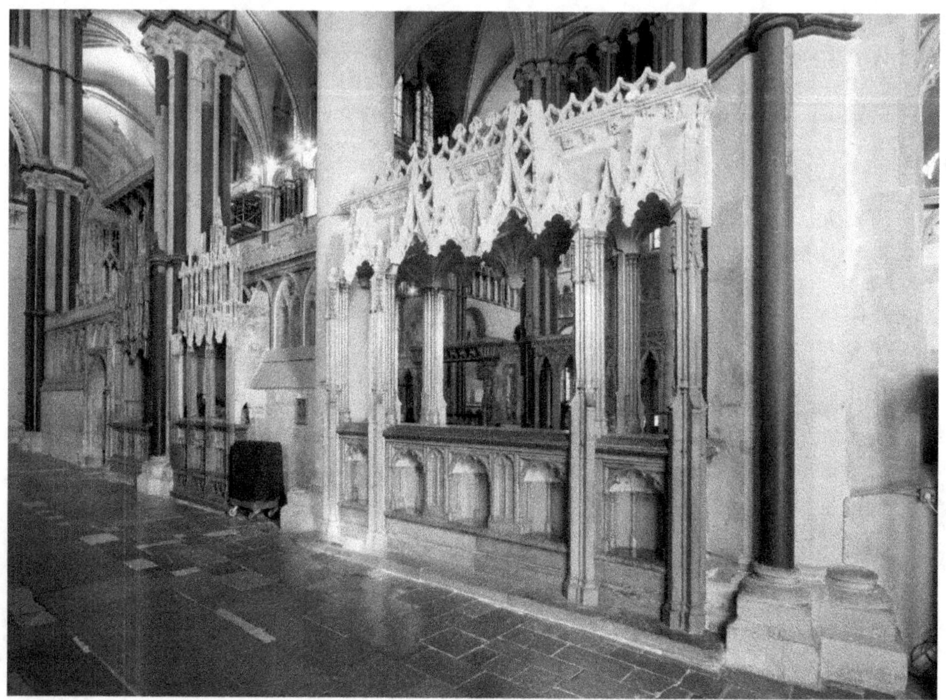

PLATE 9.6
CANTERBURY CATHEDRAL
The tomb of Archbishop Simon Sudbury.

was most probably located behind the altar at the east end of the chapel. Furthermore, three years after Meopham's death, a large window was inserted into the south wall of the chapel, presumably to shed more light on the tomb.[71] Indeed, Tim Tatton-Brown has argued that the tomb was perhaps originally intended as a new, more visible shrine for St Anselm, but that it was never completed and was taken over as Meopham's tomb.[72]

There is no suggestion that Meopham was ever the focus of veneration. But on the other side of the presbytery aisle, within the arcade and flanking the high altar, is the tomb of Archbishop Simon Sudbury, famously murdered in 1381 during the Peasants' Revolt. He was therefore regarded by many as a martyr, and his tomb seems to reflect this.[73] It encloses his headless corpse (the head is claimed by St Gregory's church, Sudbury, although recent dating techniques suggest that this is a nineteenth-century replacement), and the actual head within the coffin is represented by a lead ball. On the aisle side of the monument are five polygonal niches with freestone heads, of exactly the size and height that would be found in a shrine-base, allowing the faithful

[71] R. Willis, *The Architectural History of Canterbury Cathedral* (London, 1845), 115–16, citing accounts for making the window in 1336.
[72] Tatton-Brown, 'Pilgrimage shrines', 105–6.
[73] ibid., 471–2.

to say a prayer at the tomb. Those that commissioned the tomb could not have made a more overt statement of the sanctity of the deceased archbishop. Above the base is a high canopy, which Wilson convincingly argues formerly enclosed Sudbury's effigy. In this regard the monument parts company with medieval high shrines of this period.

THE FIFTEENTH CENTURY

It is often maintained that during the century or so before the English Reformation, the popularity of cults centred on relics was waning in favour of new cults devoted to images. Thus Eamon Duffy: 'Where early medieval devotion to the saints was focused on their relics, late medieval devotion focused in images.'[74] At the Reformation, much of the polemic of the reformers was directed against images. As we shall see in the final chapter, documents such as Henry VIII's two sets of Injunctions seem to lay equal emphasis on images and shrines. The great set-piece denunciations of popish cults involved images as much as relics, notorious examples being the Boxley Rood, and the Welsh 'idol' Darvell Gadarn. Likewise the Blood of Hailes attracted the commissioners' censure because they suspected it of being a trick. Shrines of local saints were of course destroyed, but less was made of the superstitious aspects of the cults, and of course it is usually supposed that the reformers' main motives were financial.

The decline in enthusiasm for saints' cults seems to be reflected in offerings made at their shrines. Ben Nilson has examined shrine revenues at a number of English cathedrals, and illustrated his findings by a series of revealing graphs. He concludes that offerings reached their highest levels in the 1370s or 1380s; by 1400 they were back to the levels they had reached before the Black Death, and thereafter there was 'a long-term, relatively shallow deterioration of about 1% per year until the very end of accounts, when the declining trend becomes more serious'.[75]

But shrine offerings do not show the whole picture. In fact, during the fifteenth century a number of cults received a significant boost: shrines were rebuilt, and the cult of saints appears to have undergone a revival.[76] At the start of the century, indeed, an unofficial cult developed at York that might well have eclipsed that of St William. It was devoted to Archbishop Richard Scrope, who, having joined the Percys in an attempt to dethrone Henry IV, was executed by the king's command outside the city on 8 June 1405. He was soon regarded as a martyr. Clement Maidstone composed a Life, including several conventional miracles,[77] and liturgical readings and prayers

[74] Duffy, *Stripping of the Altars*, 167.
[75] Nilson, *Cathedral Shrines*, 171.
[76] As noted by Nigel Ramsay and Margaret Sparks, 'The Cult of St Dunstan at Christ Church, Canterbury', in Ramsay, *St Dunstan*, 311–23, at 321.
[77] 'Miscellanea Relating to the Martyrdom of Archbishop Scrope'; *Hist. Church of York*, ii. 304–11.

were composed for him. An attempt at canonisation in 1462, following the accession of Edward IV, came to nothing.[78]

Scrope's tomb is quite conventional for the period, and certainly does not resemble a shrine, though this did not prevent the compiler of the great York Inventory of *c.*1500 from once referring to it as a *feretrum* (elsewhere he correctly calls it a *tumba*).[79] The front is adorned with four bays of quatrefoils enclosing armorial shields, and above a moulded top slab is a marble slab with a brass. The monument seems to have attracted as many, perhaps more, gifts as the shrine of St William. In 1509 the treasurer, Robert Langton, inserted into the 1500 inventory a list (in a barbaric mixture of Latin and English) of ex-votos found at the tomb. As well as the usual coins, girdles, belts and so on, there were silver images of whole men, hearts, teeth, breasts, legs and feet (*leges and futes argenti*), reflecting health concerns; numerous silver ships and anchors, presumably left by seafarers seeking protection; and representations of livestock deposited by farmers hoping for success.[80]

ST OSMUND'S CANONISATION AND FINAL SHRINE

Other, older cults were receiving a boost at this period, notably that of St Osmund. As we have seen in previous chapters, the first campaign to canonise the Norman bishop of Old Sarum was initiated by Richard Poore, who translated his body into the Trinity chapel of the new cathedral in 1226. It was probably placed in a temporary tomb-shrine in full expectation that Osmund's relics would soon be gloriously enshrined, perhaps in the middle of that chapel. A new attempt at launching the canonisation process occurred in around 1370; renewed efforts were thwarted by the successive deaths of three popes in the early fifteenth century, and it took all the efforts and, above all, financial backing of that great churchman Bishop Beauchamp (1450–81) to bring about the canonisation, announced in a letter from the pope to Henry VI dated 1 January 1456/7.[81]

In the bull of canonisation issued a week later (8 January 1457) the pope decreed that Osmund's 'venerable tomb' should be transferred to a worthier place (*in digniori loco*),[82] but it is clear that the bishop and canons aspired to an altogether more glorious monument than the *foramina* tomb-shrine. So in July 1457 the body was moved to a new position, but the shrine may have been a temporary affair; only in November 1471 did a London goldsmith called Edward Bowden provide a design for a new silver shrine, and an

[78] J. W. McKenna, 'Popular canonisation as political propaganda: the cult of Archbishop Scrope', *Speculum*, 45 (1970), 608–23.
[79] *The Fabric Rolls of York Minster*, ed. J. Raine, Surtees Soc., 35 (1858), 212–34, at 220: *in fine orientali feretri domini Ricardi Scrope*.
[80] ibid., 226.
[81] However, for Nilson, *Cathedral Shrines*, 22, 'the bishop did not bear the brunt of the cost'.
[82] Malden, *St Osmund*, Appendix, 224–35, at 234 (the bull of canonisation).

assessment was made of the amount of precious metal and jewels offered at the temporary shrine which could be used for the definitive monument.[83] By 1473 the canons had 'laid foundations in [Purbeck] marble and begun to make a silver shrine'.[84] The shrine was still being embellished in 1485 when funds available from the sequestration of one of the prebends were diverted to the work, and further adornments were being added so late as 1492/3.[85]

Although the financial details of the construction of the shrine are adequately recorded, the surviving documentation provides very little idea of what the monument looked like, and no vestiges of it have been discovered. Even its location is uncertain, though the most likely place is in the centre of the Trinity chapel where, after the Reformation, a Tournai marble grave slab was placed, perhaps (as at St Alban's Abbey) in order to perpetuate the memory of where the shrine had stood. The slab is marked with Osmund's death date 1099 (MXCIX), but it is clear from the style of lettering that this inscription was a post-medieval addition.

THE SHRINE OF ST WILLIAM OF YORK

In around 1470 the long process of remodelling the east arm of York Minster in Perpendicular style was coming to an end after one hundred and eleven years, and in 1472 the cathedral was reconsecrated to mark the completion of the works. It is in this context that a new shrine-base was created for St William of York. The best evidence for the date is a donation made in 1471 when the rector of Lythe, near Whitby, left 10*s* in his will 'to the construction of the marble base for the *feretrum* of St William'.[86] The work has been attributed to Robert Spillesby, Clerk of Works 1466–73,[87] and it is regrettable that the York fabric rolls of the period do not directly mention the shrine, the only reference being to cleaning the *feretrum* in 1470–1.[88] However, amongst sundry expenses a payment is recorded for a twenty-eight-day journey made by Spillesby and his man 'for the marblers' (*pro les merblers*),[89] and as the shrine is made of Teesdale marble it seems likely, as Wilson suggests, that specialist marblers (perhaps in London given the time taken over the journey) were required for the construction of the shrine.

Enough components of the shrine-base have survived to permit a plausible reconstruction to be drawn.[90] It is assumed that it was raised on at least one step. The width of the niche canopies indicates that the structure

[83] S. Eward, 'St Osmund: The Building of the Shrine', *Salisbury Cathedral News*, 148 (April 1992), 5–7, citing 'Machon Register', MS, Salisbury Cathedral Archives, fo. 39.
[84] Eward, 'St Osmund', 6.
[85] Nilson, *Cathedral Shrines*, 23, n. 73, citing Salisbury Cathedral Archives, 'Account of the Warden of the Shrine of St Osmund', 1493/4.
[86] Wilson, *St William*, 19.
[87] ibid., 20.
[88] *Fabric Rolls of York Minster*, ed. Raine, 77.
[89] Compotus Roll of Simon Browne, Clerk of Works, Nov 1469–Nov 1470; ibid., 72–4, at 73.
[90] Wilson, *St William*, fig. 13 (p. 18).

was probably four bays long. The lowest stage consisted of a quite shallow quatrefoil base, so that a kneeling person could rest his elbows on the middle slab. Then came the prayer niches, which were canted and roofed with vaults (there are four different patterns, including fan vaulting). Each bay was separated from its neighbour by an elaborate buttress incorporating niches for statuary, between the pinnacle-like heads of which rose the highly decorated ogee canopies over the niches. There was presumably an altar at the west end, which was flanked by wings projecting at an angle from the corner of the monument. Of all this the principal surviving elements are a part of the base, one of the buttresses, the vault of one of the niches, and a length of cornice.

The York Inventory of *c.*1500 gives a vivid picture of the way the shrine was adorned.[91] The entries are headed *Circa feretrum S. Willelmi portabile*, but as only this shrine and the head-shrine are listed, the *feretrum portabile* was presumably the reliquary containing the saint's body, standing on the high shrine base of the 1470s. Around the shrine were five silver-gilt images, adornments of coral and chalcedony in silver mounts (*precularia*), small crosses, belts, brooches and buckles, and other items whose Latin names caused problems for the compiler of the list.

THE FINAL SHRINE OF ST SWITHUN OF WINCHESTER

Almost exactly contemporary with the work at York is the final shrine of St Swithun. Until the mid-fifteenth century the relics reposed behind the high altar of Winchester Cathedral in the great silver-gilt reliquary that had been presented by King Edgar shortly after the saint's elevation: an astonishing survival. The *feretrum*, raised high on the feretory platform of Bishop Henry of Blois, perhaps on its own shrine altar, must have dominated the monks' view east from the choir.

All this changed at the death of Cardinal Beaufort, bishop of Winchester, in 1447. Although his will, dated 20 January 1446, gives little detail,[92] it is likely that he had discussed with his executors his grand scheme for the construction of a new 'Great Screen' behind the high altar. During the quarter-century following his death a major reordering of the east end of Winchester Cathedral took place, with three major elements: the construction of the Great Screen, the preparation of a shrine for St Swithun, and the building of a chantry chapel for the deceased cardinal. Even though the shrine was not mentioned in Beaufort's will, his executors were in no doubt that it was 'gyfyne by my lorde Cardinall Bewford'.[93] As early as

[91] *Fabric Rolls of York Minster*, ed. Raine, 212–35, at 224.

[92] *Testamenta Vetusta*, ed. N. H. Nicolas, 2 vols. (London, 1826), 249–55 (English translation).

[93] Winchester Cathedral Archives, Ledger Book I, fo. 76v, published in Greatrex, *Common Seal*, item 321, pp. 103–4.

January 1452 the prior and convent had agreed to create a new silver-gilt 'frontal' which was to be the centrepiece of the Great Screen;[94] the materials listed for its construction included 47lb 7¼oz. of silver from the old *feretrum* (*de antiquo feretro*), which was to be replaced by a new one paid for out of Beaufort's estate. So despite the lack of references in the will either to the shrine or to the screen, there is little doubt that what the prior and convent agreed with the bishop's executors soon after his death was an integrated project. The proposed screen would conceal the old feretory area and make it redundant; the reliquary, no longer visible, had therefore to be moved elsewhere. An additional factor was the construction of the cardinal's chantry chapel in the retrochoir, whose position was perhaps determined by the fact that he would end up alongside the new shrine.

The decision to melt down the Anglo-Saxon reliquary meant that the relics had to be rehoused whilst its replacement was under construction, and for about twenty years the bones were stored in an ivory casket in the sacristy (probably the room now used as the cathedral's Morley Library). Meanwhile, work went ahead on the screen, the tomb, and the shrine-base, the last two probably being the work of the same Purbeck marble workshop.

The inauguration of the shrine is described in detail in a *memorandum* preserved in the archiepiscopal register of Cardinal John Morton, and the account is so important that it merits quoting in full.

> In 1476, on 14 July, the eve of the feast of the translation of St Swithun, bishop and confessor, before the first vespers of that feast, some of the brethren of the cathedral church of Winchester carried off a certain ivory coffer, decently covered with a cloth, in which the relics of blessed Swithun had been stored by the sacristan, and in which the said precious relics had lain for about twenty years, and they placed it with great reverence on the high altar. And very shortly afterwards the reverend father [Waynflete], head of the aforesaid church, came to his throne and the office of vespers was devoutly celebrated; and as certain of the brethren recall, having also celebrated Mattins before the dead of night, according to the custom of the church, the brethren of the same church retired to bed, apart from two or three who kept guard in a watching chamber around the relics. On the very next day indeed, at the appointed hour, they came together in the choir of the said church to form a solemn procession, including the bishops of Winchester and Chichester and the bishop of Winchester's suffragan [probably William Westkarre, bishop of Sidon], who was present, also the prior of the house of canons regular of Mottisfont, the abbot of Hyde near Winchester, and the prior of the monastic church of Winchester, all wearing pontificals; the monks and ministers of the said church, clothed in albs and copes as custom demands on such solemn occasions.

[94] ibid., fo. 77r; Greatrex, *Common Seal*, item 322, p. 104.

Thus lined up in due order and rank the abbot of Hyde and the prior of the church of Winchester, kneeling before the high altar, took up on their shoulders the aforesaid ivory coffer with the glorious relics as already described, which had been placed on a certain bier, and when everyone had left the church in procession they went round the greater part of the city. And in the middle of the said procession the abbot going in front and the prior following behind honourably carried the relics in this manner: on one side the noble Lord William Downley, count of Arundel, and on the other side, as some assert, Lord Stourton, had knelt down with the aforesaid coffer on their shoulders. There were there a great concourse of people and a crowd which could not be counted, who followed the procession. The bishop of Winchester celebrated mass. After the Gospel had been read and the Offertory made, the bishop of Chichester preached to the people in English. Once Mass was over, the prelates dressed in pontificals devoutly carried the precious relics from the altar, to the place where they now lie, with joyful singing accompanied by joyous organs and many other kinds of music and instruments musically played; and in procession making their way to the place where a marble tomb [had] been constructed for the glorious saint, upon which a silver and gilt reliquary had previously been placed; those prelates who were capable of it climbed up a ladder which had been erected from the ground to the reliquary on the east side, and while they were standing at the top the bishop of Winchester and the prior inserted the coffer containing the glorious relics into the reliquary through a certain hatch that had been made for this purpose on the east side. Then the bishop of Winchester 'entered' the reliquary and, having kissed [the relics] with great devotion came out again, as did all the other prelates, one after another, as well as certain lords. After this the hatch was closed, the ladder was taken away, and when outpourings and prayers to God and his glorious saint, blessed Swithun, had been made, all those who were there went away.[95]

[95] Register of Archbishop John Morton, *s.a.* 1476, MS, Lambeth Palace Library, vol. I, fo. 204v, printed (with errors) in D. Wilkins (ed.), *Concilia Magnæ Britanniæ et Hiberniæ* (London, 1737), iii. 610ff. The marginal title reads *Processio Episcopi Wintoniensi in honorem reliquiarum sancti Swithin*[*i*] *Episcopi reconditurum in Cista eburnea fere viginti annos*. The Latin text reads as follows: *Anno Domini millesimo quadringentesimo septuagesimo sexto mensis vero Julii die quartodecimo qui est vigilia Translationis sancti Swithuni episcopi et confessoris ante primas vesperas eiusdem festi* ***Quidam*** *de confratribus ecclesie cathedralis Wintoniensis quandam cistam eburneam pallio decenter coopertam In qua beati Swythuni reliquie recondebantur a sacrista, Ubi fere per viginti annos dicte preciose reliquie pausabant deportantes; magna cum reverentia super magnum altare collocaverunt;* ***Postea*** *vero absque magno intervallo, reverendus pater prefate ecclesie antistes in sua sede aderat ac officium vesperarum devote executus est. Quibus et matutinis etiam ut quidam de confratribus retulerunt ante noctis tenebras secundum morem ecclesiasticum solemniter decantatis eiusdem ecclesie confratres preter duos aut tres in excubiis circa reliquias vigilantes*

As well as this literary evidence, there is a considerable amount of physical evidence for the position of the shrine. The central boss of the retrochoir vault is pierced with a hole, and above the vault the remains of an iron pulley are attached to a beam, indicating the way the wooden cover over the *feretrum* was raised by means of a counterbalance. In the corresponding position in the crypt a mass of flintwork survived until 1886, similar to that underpinning the chantry chapels on either side; this reinforcement to the crypt vault was necessary to cope with the extra loading caused by the shrine.

Most exciting of all, enough fragments of the monument have survived for a reconstruction to be made. They have been discovered in a variety of locations. The first pieces to be found were removed by Dean Kitchin on 31 December 1885 from the infill of the 'Pilgrims' Door' in the angle of the north transept and nave. Even at the time they were found the dean wondered whether they formed part of a shrine. Then in 1907 three fragments of a Caen stone cornice, adorned with carved human heads, were discovered in the foundations of a stone staircase on the south side of the retrochoir when it was replaced. In both cases the fragments were discovered together with other spolia likely to have resulted from destruction at the Reformation. In 1990 five fragments of worked Purbeck marble with delicate small-scale attached shafts, capitals, and bases were discovered in the footings of a collapsed wall built on the site of the monastic dormitory

quieti se dederunt. ***In die vero*** *sequenti hora congrua convenerunt in choro dicte ecclesie ad solempnem processionem faciendam Episcopi Wintoniensis & Cicestrensis ac suffrageneus Episcopi Wintoniensis qui adtunc erat, etiam Prior domus Canonicorum Regularium de Mottesham* [*sic*], *Abbas de Hida iuxta Wintoniam et prior conventualis ecclesie Wintoniensis pontificalibus induti monachique & ministri prefate ecclesie albis vel capis secundum formam in tanta solempnitate consuetam vestiti. Qui gradatim in ordine debito constituti Abbas de Hida et prior ecclesie Wintoniensi ad magnum altare accedentes, prefatam cistam eburneam cum gloriosis reliquiis ut prefertur pallio coopertam, Et super quodam portatili positam suis humeris imposuerunt & omnes more processionali ecclesiam exeuntes maiorem partem civitatis devote circuerunt, Et in medio chori processionalis, dictus Abbas precedens et Prior subsequens huiusmodi reliquias honorifice baiulabant, ex uno latere nobili viro domino Willelmo Downley, Comite de Arundell, et ex altero latere ut quidam asseruerunt Domino de Storton incedentibus, ac prefatam cistam super humeris suis deportantibus. Interfuit denique magna procerum caterva & populi quasi innumerabilis multitudo que processionem sequebantur.* ***Antistes*** *Wintoniensis Missam celebrabat, lecto Evangelio et Offertorio finito, Episcopus Cicestrensis sermonem habuit ad populum in vulgari. Post missam finitam, prelati pontificalibus induti, pretiosas reliquias ab altari devotissime accipientes, ad locum ubi iam requiescunt cum magno gaudio vocis, iubilo organorum uno, ac diversorum generum musicarum, & instrumentorum modulamine detulerunt, Et modo processionali pervenientes ad locum, ubi tumba marmorea gloriosi sancti construitur, super quam capsa argentea, et deaurata per prius fuerat collocata;* ***De prelatis*** *qui commode poterant scalam ligneam ab humo usque capsam extendentem ex parte orientali ascenderunt, Et in summo existentes Episcopus Wintoniensis & prior ibidem, cistam cum gloriosis reliquiis in capsam per quoddam hostium ob hanc causam in parte orientali eiusdem capse apertum intromiserunt.* ***Deinde*** *Episcopus Wintoniensis in capsam introivit & cum magna devotione osculatus exiit, Sicque alii prelati unus post alium, et quidam magnates fecerunt. Quibus peractis, clausum est hostium & scala removebatur Fusisque ad Deum et eius sanctum gloriosum beatum Swythunum precibus qui aderant, recesserunt.*

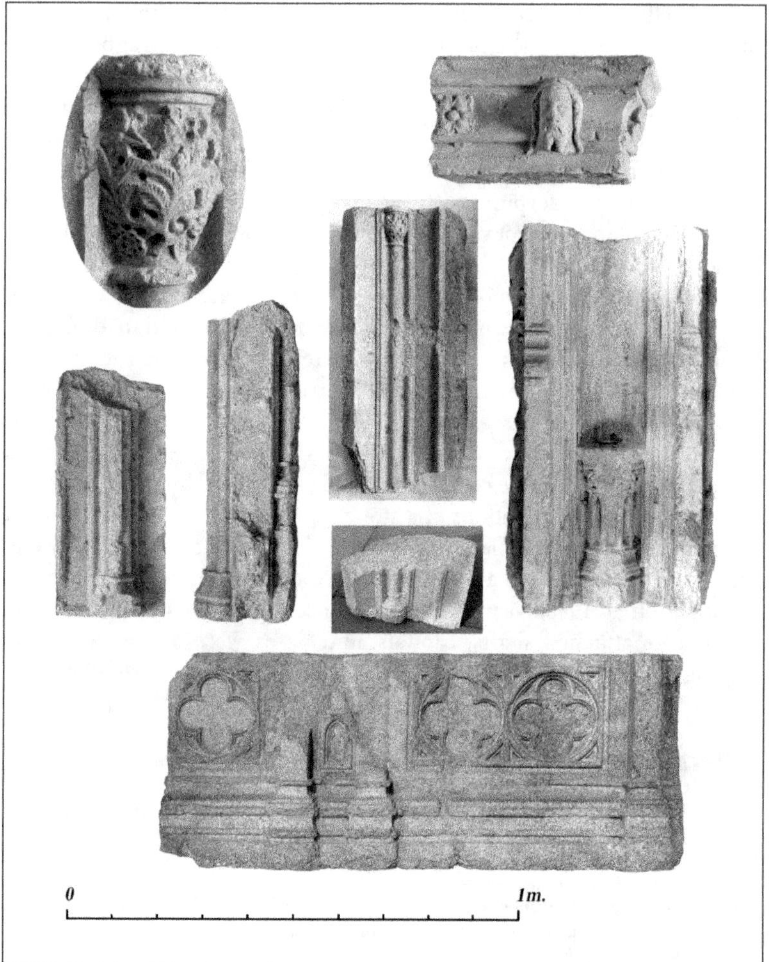

PLATE 9.7 WINCHESTER CATHEDRAL CLOSE Fragments retrieved from walls in the Cathedral Close and excavations, identified as being from the final shrine of St Swithun, inaugurated in 1476.

(demolished *c.*1540), and other similar pieces were retrieved in 1994 from the footings of a cross-wall that appears to have been built on the site of the dormitory soon after it was demolished. Finally, a large Purbeck marble niche that had been reused as an internal feature of the Deanery bakehouse, built soon after the demolition of the monastic rere-dorter (which it overlies) *c.*1540, was retrieved.

It was possible to establish, through analysis of the dimensions of the various pieces and stylistic comparison, that all the Purbeck fragments derived from the same monument, and thanks to an institutional link between Winchester Cathedral, Portsmouth University, and the University of Bamberg, a three-dimensional computer model of the shrine has been created. In the summer of 2007 the fragments were scanned by two German

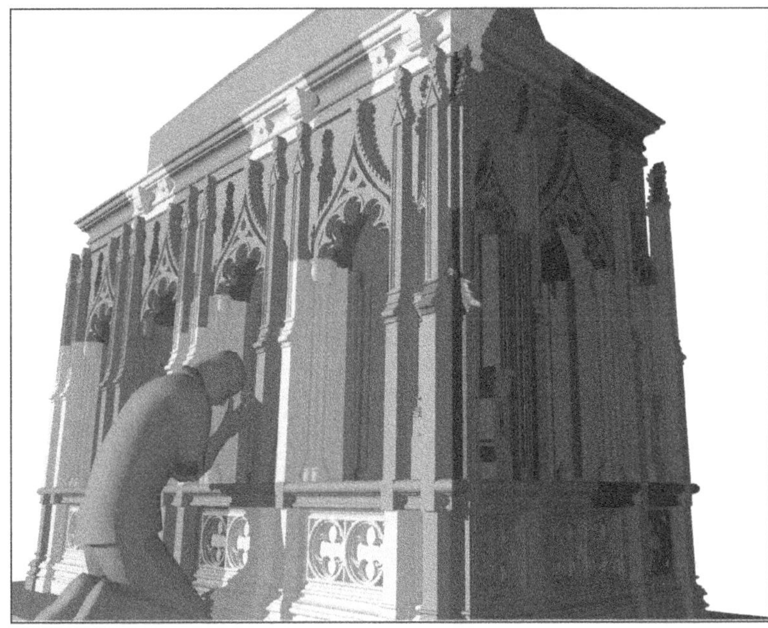

PLATE 9.8
THE FINAL SHRINE OF ST SWITHUN
Detail from a computer reconstruction. Surviving elements discovered to date are shown in light tone.

post-graduate students, Christian Schalk and Christine Barz,[96] and after much discussion and experimentation the various pieces were electronically reassembled in a small number of alternative configurations.

Based on comparative evidence, the most probable configuration is that shown in Plate 9.8. The shrine was raised on at least one step. The lowest stage comprised the quatrefoil base, supporting a slab which, for a kneeling individual, would be at elbow height. The next stage consisted of a series of prayer niches, four on each of the long sides of the monument, and at each end a single large niche flanked by two smaller statuary niches. The heads of the niches were probably of freestone rather than Purbeck marble, and a possible fragment, in Caen stone, also survives in the cathedral's lapidarium. Then there was a top slab, with a projecting cornice around it, probably represented by the three fragments described above. The *feretrum*, whose great size is apparent from the 1476 description, stood on the top slab.

The detailing of the Purbeck fragments is in several respects similar to that of the nearby chantry chapel of Cardinal Beaufort, and it is likely that both monuments were created by the same team of marblers. Interestingly, the freestone may have been worked by a different team; the Caen stone elements of the chapel are inaccurately matched with the Purbeck work. Given this poor matching it is even possible that a surviving freestone niche head in the

[96] C. Barz and C. Schalk, 'Der Schrein des Hl. Swithun, Winchester Cathedral, England : Aufnahme der Bruchstücke und Rekonstruktion', unpubl. thesis, Institute for Archaeology, Otto-Friedruch University, Bamberg, Germany.

cathedral collections, though an imperfect match for the width of the Purbeck niches, also derives from the 1476 shrine.

In the long term it is the author's hope that the shrine may be reassembled in its original position in the retrochoir, thus bringing to eight the list of saints' shrines that have been put together again in modern times.[97]

THE CULT OF ST DUNSTAN AT GLASTONBURY

In 1508 another new shrine was set up in the abbey church at Glastonbury, allegedly containing the bones of St Dunstan. The monks of Glastonbury had long claimed that the relics had been brought from Canterbury in 1012, though the assertion was later refuted by Eadmer.[98] The new shrine was set up in a conspicuous position, and its inauguration attracted a large number of people, both clerics and laity, including the nobility. Needless to say, Canterbury still laid claim to the relics, and Archbishop Warham was appalled by the proceedings at Glastonbury.[99] In order to settle the matter, he ordered an investigation of Dunstan's alleged tomb, and on 20 April 1508, after the church had been closed, a select band of brothers began their search. Their excavations continued throughout the night. Then a little before daybreak they came across a stone *feretrum* measuring about 7ft. by 1ft. 6ins. (2135 × 457mm) containing a coffer (*arca*) clad in lead, studded with nails, and bound with iron straps.

Needless to say, a full set of bones was discovered in the tomb at Canterbury with a lead plate on its chest stating that it was the archbishop. The monks of Glastonbury were sceptical and were summoned by Warham to proffer evidence for their claim. Something of a climb-down ensued, and eventually, thanks to Warham's influence, part of Dunstan's skull remained on permanent display in the cathedral as a manifestation of his presence there.

The final shrine of St Dunstan was the last important monument related to the cult of saints for which there is evidence. Within thirty years Henry VIII's commissioners had begun their onslaught on the medieval shrines of England.

97 The others are the shrines of SS. Alban, Amphibalus, Frideswide, Wærburh, Eadburh, Birinus, and Melangell.

98 R. Sharpe, 'Eadmer's Letter to the monks of Glastonbury concerning St Dunstan's disputed remains', in *The Archaeology and History of Glastonbury Abbey, Essays in honour of the ninetieth birthday of C. A. Ralegh Radford*, ed. L. Abrams and J. P. Carley (Woodbridge, 1991), 205–15 (a translation into English of Eadmer's text, from *Memorials of St Dunstan*. 412–22).

99 The proceedings are known from Warham's correspondence with Glastonbury, printed in *Memorials of St Dunstan*, 426–39.

THE FATE OF SHRINES AT THE REFORMATION 10

The English Reformation is one of the most fascinating episodes in the religious history of our island, with its interplay of orthodoxy and heterodoxy and its rapidly changing definitions of what was heretical. These changes were closely linked to the personalities of the time: men such as Sir Thomas More, Thomas Cranmer, Thomas Cromwell; above all, Henry VIII and, indeed, his queens. Such was the initially somewhat flexible mould in which a new church was formed. The subject has generated a vast literature, but in this chapter the Reformation is examined simply from the point of view of the cult of saints, more particularly those saints who were venerated through their relics (the veneration of images, though they were also the subject of pilgrimage, falls outside the scope of this book). A key element in the reform of the Church of England was the purging of 'superstition', and the cult of saints was an easy target, expressing itself as it did in physical objects and unambiguous human activities such as pilgrimage, lighting of candles, and offerings made at shrines. Before looking at the fate of individual shrines and relic cults, let us take a broad view of changing attitudes to relic cults during the two decades leading up to the key year of 1538. These attitudes evolved quickly, and clergy and laity alike were obliged continually to modify their professed views in order to steer the narrow course between conservatism and reform. When one considers that the king himself eventually retreated from the progressive views that in 1540 would ultimately lead to the execution of Thomas Cromwell, it is evident that they had to choose their path carefully.

For the general picture, all researchers in this field are indebted to Eamon Duffy.[1] He focuses more on images than shrines, and we have already noted his view that by the sixteenth century images had become the more widespread vehicle for saints' cults. This may well be true of parish churches, but perhaps not of the ancient cult centres that are the subject of this book.

[1] Duffy, *Stripping of the Altars.*

The evidence that he deploys to such good effect in his masterly survey of the cults of the late middle ages demonstrates equally well that relic cults were still active right up to the fateful year of 1538, which saw the almost total annihilation of saintly relics. Whereas images could be re-erected after the demise of Cromwell, and again during the short-lived Catholic revival under Queen Mary, relics—with a few exceptional survivals—had largely vanished for ever.

At the start of Henry VIII's reign, those who expressed doubts about the efficacy of pilgrimage or the veneration of saints and relics were condemned as 'Lollards', which by then was a catch-all term for heretics. In 1509, for example, Elizabeth Sampson of Aldermanbury appeared before Archbishop Warham (1503–32) accused of saying that 'It was better to give Alms at home to poor people than to go on Pilgrimages; and that Images were but Stocks and Stones.'[2] Two years later Archbishop Warham tried six men and four women, mainly from Tenterden, accused of Lollardy. Amongst other accusations they were said to have maintained 'That Pilgrimages to holy and devout Places be not profitable, neither Meritorious for man's soul'. Most of those accused abjured and 'were enjoyned to carry a Faggot in Procession and to wear on their Cloaths the Representation of one in flames, as a publick Confession that they had deserved to be burnt', but four men and one woman were actually burnt at the stake.[3] It is a cruel irony that by the late 1530s such opinions would become orthodox, but not before Latimer's friend and mentor the Cambridge reformer Thomas Bilney, fellow of Trinity Hall, had been burned at Norwich on 19 August 1531. Amongst the charges levelled against him were that throughout the 1520s he had preached against the value of pilgrimages and the veneration of saints and images; people would do better to 'stay at home and give much alms'. So late as 1535 Robert Vaws, the parson of Over Wallop (Hants), was indicted for 'refusing to allow his parishioners to maintain lights before images in the parish church, saying that such activities were 'but pomp and pride, and the saints shall do us no good'. He added that 'The saints which they buy of the carvers were not set up for sacrifice, but to be laymen's books.'[4] Yet at the same time Friar Arthur, a Canterbury friar, was accused of preaching against those 'new preachers' whose sermons discouraged pilgrimage: it was better to give a penny to St Thomas's shrine than a noble (a gold coin worth 6*s* 8*d*) to the poor, because one activity was spiritual, the other corporeal. Evidently preachers had to be fully abreast of the latest orthodoxies if they were to keep out of trouble. The problem in 1535 was second-guessing the attitude of the king and his vicegerent Thomas Cromwell: a point made by the Lord Chancellor, Sir Thomas Audley, discussing William Marshall's recently published translation of Bucer's *Das*

[2] Gilbert Burnet, *The History of the Reformation* (London, 1679), i. 29.
[3] ibid., 27–8.
[4] *L & P Henry VIII*, 8 (1535), pp. 7–8 (item 20).

einigerlei Bild, whose main thrust was against the 'worship of images'.[5] Although the book claimed to be printed with royal licence, Audley commented that, 'It were good that preachers and people abstained from opinions of such things until the King has put a final order by the report of those appointed for searching and ordering the laws of the Church.'

A little more than a year would pass before Convocation issued the Ten Articles in July 1536. The members' minds must have been focused by the forceful sermon preached by Latimer at the opening of Convocation, and the sarcastic response drawn up by the more conservative clergy in the form of a list of 'erroneous opinions' worthy of reformation.[6] They challenged the view that 'images, as well of the crucifix as of other saints, are to be put out of the church, and the reliques of saints in no wise to be reverenced', or that 'saints are not to be invocated or honoured; and that they understand not, nor know nothing of our petition, nor can be mediators or intercessors betwixt us and God'. Some of the erroneous propositions were parodied: thus some of the reformers were claimed to have held that 'our lady was no better than another woman, and like a bag of pepper or saffron when the spice is out; and that she can do no more with Christ than another sinful woman'; 'it is much available to pray unto saints, as to hurl a stone against the wind; and that saints have no more power to help a man, than a man's wife hath to help her husband'; 'holy water is more savoury to make sauce with than the other, because it is mixed with salt; which is also a very good medicine for an horse with a galled back; yea, if there be put an onion thereunto, it is a good sauce for a gibbet of mutton'.[7] The Ten Articles proposed a conservative, softly-softly approach: images would be permitted, provided the people were instructed that the saints they represented were 'representers of vertue and good example ... kindlers and stirrers of mens minds ... [which] make men oft to remember and lament their sins and offences', but censing of images must cease, and people must not be allowed to kneel before images or offer to them.[8] No mention was made of relic cults, however.

These conservative rulings were expanded in the first Injunctions of August 1536, formulated by Thomas Cromwell in the name of the king, and the proper use of relics was spelled out more clearly. The clergy were directed not to 'set forth or extol any images, relics, or miracles for any superstition or lucre, nor allure the people by any enticement to the pilgrimage of the saint'; they should be instructed that 'it shall profit more their soul's health, if they do bestow that on the poor and needy, which they would have bestowed upon the said images or relics'.[9]

[5] As Duffy discusses, *Stripping of the Altars*, 386, Bucer's book had been written in 1530 to justify the destruction of all images at Strasbourg.

[6] *Concilia magnæ Britanniæ et Hiberniæ*, ed. David Wilkins, iii (London, 1737), 804–7, discussed by Duffy, *Stripping of the Altars*, 392–4.

[7] Wilkins, *Concilia*, iii. 84–7, items 22, 39–41, 63.

[8] ibid., iii. 817–23.

[9] 'First Royal Injunctions of Henry VIII, 1536', in *Visitation Articles*, ed. Frere, ii. 1–11, at 5–6.

Within two years Cromwell was inveighing more strongly against relic cults, in the second Royal Injunctions of 1538. The faithful should not 'repose their trust and affiance in any other works devised by men's phantasies besides Scripture; as in wandering to pilgrimages, offering or money, candles, or tapers to images or relics, or kissing or licking the same'.[10] These injunctions were relayed by diocesan bishops, often with a slant which reflected the degree to which they espoused the new ideas. Eamon Duffy has perceptively analysed the conservative 'spin' which Edward Lee, archbishop of York, could put on the Injunctions, comparing them with the injunctions of the reformist bishop Nicholas Shaxton of Salisbury (1535–9).[11] Regarding images, Shaxton decreed that the people should no longer be allowed 'to kneel to them, nor worship them, nor offer candles, oats, cake-bread, cheese, wool, or any other such things to them' and the priest should 'instruct and teach them, how they ought and may use them; that is to say, only to behold, or look upon them, as one looketh upon a book'.[12] Shaxton's injunctions are particularly revealing in that he apparently had first-hand experience of cults of dubious relics within his diocese: 'namely of stinking boots, mucky combs, ragged rochets, rotten girdles, pyld purses, great bullocks' horns, locks of hair, and filthy rags, gobbetts of wood, under the name of parcels of the holy cross, and such pelfry beyond estimation'.[13] These holy objects were to be brought to his episcopal manor of Ramsbury, together with any available documentation, so that the bishop could examine their authenticity: the bishop promised to return any authentic relics, and to provide instructions as to how such true relics should be used, 'that is to say, as memorials of them whose relics they be, in whom and by whom Almighty God did work all that ever they virtuously wrought; and therefore only he ought in them all to be glorified, lauded, and praised'. In these dealings Shaxton seems to have shown himself more reticent than Henry VIII's commissioners, who at that very time were destroying shrines and disposing of relics with little evident concern whether or not they were authentic.

Shaxton's views were apparently shared by the mayor and corporation of his city. Early in June 1537 they realised that the annual feast of St Osmund would soon be coming round again. Osmund was one of those saints affected by the 'Act for the abrogation of certain holydays' which had been issued by Cromwell and Convocation in mid-July the previous year.[14] In an alleged attempt to increase agricultural production hitherto lost 'through the superstitious observance of the said holydayes in not taking th'oportunitie of good and serene wheather, offered upon the same in time

[10] 'Second Royal Injunctions of Henry VIII, 1538'; ibid., ii. 34–43, at 37.

[11] Duffy, *Stripping of the Altars*, 414–15.

[12] 'Shaxton's Injunctions for Salisbury Diocese, 1538', in *Visitation Articles*, ed. Frere, ii. 53–60, at 57.

[13] ibid., ii. 59–60.

[14] Wilkins, *Concilia* 1737, iii, 823–4.

of harvest', all holy days between 1 July and 29 September became normal working days, and the feast of the Translation of St Osmund (16 July) fell within this period. Yet the saint's shrine still stood in the Trinity chapel of Salisbury Cathedral. Foreseeing trouble, the mayor and his brethren sought the advice of the vicar general, drawing a parallel with the cult of Edward the Confessor, a saint with whom Cromwell was presumably more familiar:

> It has been the custom upon the even of St. Osmunde, 15 July, which saint lies in the cathedral church as St. Edward does in Westminster, to keep a solemn watch like that kept in London on midsummer even, and to keep the morrow as a holiday. Now that St. Osmund's day is commanded not to be kept they beg to know that is to be done as regards the said watch.[15]

Salisbury, though, seems to have been conservative, despite Shaxton's best efforts. In August 1538 the town's vice-bailey, John Goodall, denounced to Cromwell 'the privy practices of certain priests in Sarum, who in confession forbid white meats in Lent, the reading of the New Testament in English, and the company of those of the new learning'. The same month a rumour had arisen that Henry VIII had seen an angel (according to some, the spirit of Jane Seymour) asking him to go on pilgrimage to St Michael's Mount.[16]

The following year (15 April 1539), the mayor and his 'brethren' again denounced practices in Salisbury Cathedral, and even Shaxton seems to have been worried:

> John Goodall, the vice-bayly, about 3 p.m., seeing the people kneeling and kissing an image of Christ standing on an altar on the north side of the choir, wherein, unknown to him, was the Sacrament, told one of the priests to take it away, it being the King's commandment that no such kissing of images should be suffered, but only creeping to the cross and kissing it on Good Friday and 'Estryn morow' which both were passed, for it was 3 p.m. The priests being not over ready to take it away, and the people fast pressing to kiss it, Goodall commanded his servant to take it down. This was done in obedience to the King's proclamations, but they interpret it as dishonour to the Sacrament and against the King's proclamation that all laudable ceremonies should be kept until otherwise ordered. They exaggerate the thing so far that they gather thereof that Goodall has a heretical opinion of the Sacrament, and con[d]emns the King's proclamation, though he has done more to set forth the injunctions and things contained in the proclamation than all of them.[17]

[15] *L & P Henry VIII*, 12.ii (1537), pp. 17–18 (item 52).
[16] ibid., 13.ii (1538), p. 23 (item 62).
[17] ibid., 14.i (1539), p. 373 (item 777).

THE DESTRUCTION OF SHRINES

As noted above, the first, popular attacks on images had occurred in the 1520s, with an increasing spate in the early 1530s. Such activities, which could now be regarded as specifically sanctioned by Henry VIII's Injunctions of 1538, took on an official character, with the destruction of shrines forming an integral part of the dissolution of the major monasteries, so many of which harboured the principal local saints of the realm. Within the larger monasteries there were some who realised what was in store: thus at St Albans as early as August 1536 the keeper of the shrine there, Robert Morton, reported having heard the prior say that 'now the King had pulled down the little houses, he would pull down the great ones'.[18]

The *modus operandi* of the commissioners had been established shortly after 1535, when Thomas Cromwell was commissioned to carry out a general visitation of the churches, monastery, and clergy.[19] The earliest list of questions to be put by the commissioners makes no specific reference to relics or relic cults, apart from enquiring whether 'jewels and reliques' had been listed in an inventory, but it is clear from the subsequent reports that the visitation of the monasteries, which would lead to their dissolution within four years, was concerned not only with their internal organisation, income, and worth, but also with their moral state, including activities which went under the general heading of 'superstition'. The glee with which the commissioners would report on the morals of monks and clergy, and on their encouragement of various forms of 'idolatry', suggests that these features were regarded as a convenient justification for the closure, first of the smaller religious houses (with an income of less than £200) in 1536, then of the larger religious houses two years later.

These concerns are apparent in a surviving summary of the findings of two of the commissioners, Dr Richard Layton and Dr Thomas Leigh, in the province of York and the combined diocese of Coventry and Lichfield; and this is followed by another similar record for Norwich diocese. In each case the moral faults (mostly sexual) of the prior, brethren, sisters, etc. are noted, followed by a note on 'superstitions', usually the presence of relics, together with the name of the founder and the value of rents and debts.[20] A few examples must suffice. The smaller priories came in for the most censure as regards morals: at Thurgarton ten monks were named as 'sodomites'. This was a catch-all term for most sexual misdemeanours, though some of the monks there admitted to improper relationships with boys. At Garendon five brethren were similarly charged, 'one with ten boys'. Others had sexual relationships with women. They included the prior of Pontefract, James Thwaites, who was accused of fornicating with two married women, and

[18] ibid., 11 (1536), pp. 142–4 (item 354).
[19] ibid., 8 (1535), p. 24 (item 75).
[20] ibid., 10 (1536), pp. 137–44 (item 364).

was apparently the subject of an attempt on his life from his brethren. Nuns were no better, it seems, many being accused of incontinency, and some having given birth, including Margery Shacklady of St Mary's, Chester, who had had a child from a priest (*peperit ex presbytero*). Such evidence of malpractice must have facilitated the closure of the smaller houses in 1536. But it is the astonishing tally of local relic cults that concerns us here: at Repton (where Thomas Rede, the sub-prior, and three others were named as 'sodomites' *per voluntarias pollutiones*, i.e. self-abuse) it was noted that 'a pilgrimage is made to St. Guthlac and his bell, which they put upon people's heads to alleviate headache'. Virgin's milk was found at six of the northern monasteries and the 'girdle of St Mary' at no fewer than eleven of them, the last being regarded as useful for women during their confinement. The major monastic centres contained more plausible relics: it was noted that Durham Cathedral Priory possessed the bodies of St Cuthbert and St Bede, and the Cross of St Margaret (supposed to be good for those lying-in); while at Lichfield Cathedral Priory pilgrims were still drawn to the shrine of St Chad. Perhaps the main point to emerge from this extraordinary list is that of the one hundred and twenty-one northern monasteries enumerated, fifty-five possessed relics of various degrees of plausibility: a useful counterbalance to the impression given by other documents of the Reformation period that by the sixteenth century images of saints outweighed corporeal relics.

During their visitation of the religious houses and churches, the commissioners reported on many other implausible relic cults. In August 1535 Richard Layton sent a bag of relics to Cromwell, including, from Maiden Bradley, 'strange things, such as God's coat, Our Lady's smock, part of God's supper, *pars petre super qua natus erat Jesus in Bethlehem*', Our Lady's red silk girdle from Bruton, and Mary Magdalen's girdle from Ferley [Farleigh].[21] The following month, an inventory of the relics at Worcester Cathedral Priory included '"St Oswalde and St. Ulstan's hede with selver and gylte." A mitre for St. Oswald's head. An arm of St. Edmund the Bishop', and many other smaller relics.[22] Not to be outdone, four days later, on 11 September another commissioner, Thomas Thacker, reported having confiscated various images from St Mary's, Ipswich, and a relic of the Virgin's milk,[23] and a fortnight later Thomas Leigh reported the veneration at Chertsey of the arm bone of St Blaise, through which they give wine in cases of illness, adding 'there is also an image of St. Faith, before which they place a candle on behalf of sick persons, and hold that if the candle remain lighted till it is consumed, the sick person will recover, but if it goes out he will die'.[24] Then in October, Dr Richard Layton, chief of the commissioners sent to Canterbury, was undeterred by a lucky escape from a fire in his chambers at

[21] ibid., 9 (1535), pp. 49–50 (item 168).
[22] ibid., 9 (1535), pp. 99–101 (item 297).
[23] ibid., 9 (1535), p. 114 (item 340).
[24] ibid., 9 (1535), pp. 154–5 (item 472).

the prior's lodgings at the cathedral priory.[25] The following morning he sent for the abbot of St Augustine's, telling him to prepare to give up the shrine of the Apostle to the English, and noting, *en passant*, that 'The prior of Dover and his monks are as bad as others. Sodomites there is none, for they have no lack of women ….'[26] Bury St Edmunds supplied unlikely relics, and John ap Rice wrote to Cromwell in November that he had found 'much superstition' amongst the relics, such as 'the coals that Saint Lawrence was toasted withal, the paring of St. Edmund's nails, S. Thomas of Canterbury penknife and his boots and divers skulls for the headache, pieces of the Holy Cross able to make a whole cross of, other relics for rain, &c.'.[27]

Implausible relics were also found in some parish churches. Wisborough Green in Sussex possessed a large number, which 'sage men of the parish claimed had been used and offered unto time out of mind':

> A crucifix, the foot silver, the middle a crystal containing a little quantity of Our Lady's milk, with two other bones. Relics of the tomb and vestments of St Thomas of Canterbury; of the hair shirt and bones of St James; of the cloak in which St Thomas the Martyr was martyred, and his blood; of the Holy Sepulchre; of SS Sebastian and Sylvester; of St Peter's beard and hair; of St Giles; of the Mount of Olives; of the stones with which St Stephen was stoned; of the rochet of St Edmund, archbishop of Canterbury. St James' comb. A chymer of St Thomas of Canterbury.[28]

Some of the relics reflected the growth of new cults, popular in the pre-Reformation period, such as St Blaise (Blasius), one of the so-called 'Fourteen Holy Helpers'—a group of early saints whose popularity emerged in the Rhineland in the fourteenth century. Blaise was thought to have been an Armenian bishop, put to death under the emperor Licinius in the early fourth century. As well as the arm bone at Chertsey, another of his bones was allegedly found at the nunnery of Minster-in-Sheppey, where it was 'set in silver and gilt with stones'.[29] St Blaise was also venerated by means of numerous images, and in Ashford (Kent) after the prohibition of images of Thomas Becket the parishioners 'transposed' his statue into one of St Blaise by replacing the crozier with a new attribute, a woolcomb, representing the instrument with which St Blaise was allegedly done to death.[30]

The confiscation of implausible relics from minor religious houses was merely the prelude to the wholesale destruction of relic cults, culminating in the great destruction of shrines in 1538. By the autumn of 1535

[25] *Memorials of the Cathedral and Priory of Christ in Canterbury*, ed. C. E. Woodruff and W. Danks (London, 1912), 217.
[26] *L & P Henry VIII*, 9 (1535), p. 226 (item 669).
[27] ibid., 9 (1535), p. 261 (item 772).
[28] ibid., 13.ii (1538), p. 36 (item 101).
[29] ibid., 10 (1536), pp. 219–20 (item 562).
[30] ibid., 14.i (1539), pp. 480–1 (items 1052–4). Such 'transposing' is discussed by Duffy, *Stripping of the Altars*, 419–20.

Cromwell's purpose was clear, however, and Dr Pedro Ortiz wrote to the empress from Rome telling her that 'The rents of many churches are taken away, and it is said that they will take away images, shrines [*templos*], and the principal temporalities of the Church.' The following months saw the dissolution of the smaller monasteries, several of which possessed saints' cults, such as Bromholme, whose famous rood was confiscated by Richard Southwell early in February 1537.[31] Another relic cult was at Bridlington, where Cromwell gave orders to the Duke of Norfolk that the shrine of St John should be taken down;[32] during the suppression of the monastery Norfolk ordered the removal of its gold decoration, sending it to the king.[33] The same day (5 June 1536) he told Cromwell that he had also asked Henry VIII what should be done with the remaining silver, adding a message to the vicar general which reveals something of Cromwell's character: he would be welcome to lodge at his house in York, where if Cromwell did not 'lust to dally with his wife, he [had] a young woman with pretty proper tetins'.[34]

Discontent at this first spoliation of relic cults seems to have been muted. However, during the Pilgrimage of Grace, Robert Aske is reported as having condemned 'the violation of relics by the suppressors, and the unreverent demeanour of the doers thereof …'.[35] Perhaps in order to counter such popular feelings, as well as linking relic cults with discredited smaller monasteries, Cromwell also orchestrated a powerful propaganda campaign, whipping up popular hostility towards the cult of saints by demonstrating how the people had been deceived by unscrupulous monks. In February 1538 Jeffrey Chamber wrote to Cromwell describing the 'Rood of Grace' at Boxley:

> On defacing the late monastery of Boxley and plucking down the images, found, in the Rood of Grace, which has been had in great veneration, certain engines and old wire, with old rotten sticks in the back of the same, which caused the eyes to move and stir in the head thereof, like unto a lively thing, and also the nether lip in likewise to move as though it should speak, which was not a little strange to him and others present.

He had showed it to the people of Maidstone, and intended bringing the image to London.[36]

The image was first brought to Westminster where its workings were demonstrated to King Henry and his jeering courtiers: 'The King hardly knew whether more to rejoice at the exposure or to grieve at the long deception.'[37] A few days later, on 24 February, John Hilsey, the future bishop of Rochester in succession to Fisher (who had been deprived of the bishopric the previous

[31] *L & P Henry VIII*, 12.i (1537), p. 145 (item 317).
[32] ibid., 12.i (1537), pp. 574–5 (item 1257).
[33] ibid., 12.ii (1537), p. 12 (item 34).
[34] ibid., 12.ii (1537), pp. 12–13 (item 35).
[35] ibid., 12.i (1537), pp. 2–9 (item 6).
[36] ibid., 13.i (1538), p. 79 (item 231).
[37] ibid., 13.i (1538), p. 120 (item 348).

year, and would be executed in June), preached at London, with the image opposite him; the image was made to perform again: it 'turned its head around, rolled its eyes, foamed at the mouth, and poured forth tears down its cheeks',[38] before being cut to pieces and put in the fire.[39] The event was widely reported in numerous surviving letters,[40] and was described by Charles Wriothesley in his Chronicle, who commented that the monks of Boxley 'had gotten great riches in deceaving the people thinckinge that the sayde image had so moved by the power of God, which now playnlye appeared to the contrarye'.[41]

Such animated images may not have been uncommon. At St Alban's Abbey the monks seem to have erected an image of the saint near to the shrine. So late as the beginning of the seventeenth century an elderly monk recalled the image: 'one [monk] being placed to govern the wyres, the eyes would move and head nodd according as he liked or disliked the offering, and that being young he had many times crept into the hollow of it ...'.[42]

Another image which attracted attention was the Welsh image of Darvell Gadarn. On 6 April the commissioner Ellis Price wrote to Cromwell asking what should be done with this image, to which people came daily 'somme withe kyne, other with oxen or horsis, and the reste with money'; as many as five or six hundred pilgrims had offered to the image the previous day.[43] This image, too, was brought to St Paul's, where it was burned on 22 May. As an additional refinement a heretic friar, Friar Forrest, was slowly roasted alive over the smouldering image.[44]

The public destruction of images may have been a familiar sight during this period, as Bishop Hugh Latimer (1535–9) implies in a letter sent to Cromwell on 13 June 1538 when he urged him to destroy the great miracle-working statue of St Mary at the centre of Worcester Cathedral 'with great noise' (*cum sonitu*).[45] He added, 'She herself hath been the devil's instrument to bring many, I fear, to eternal fire; now she herself, with her old sister of Walsingham, her young sister of Ipswich, with their other two sisters of Dongcaster [Doncaster] and Penryesse [Penryth], would make a jolly muster in Smithfield. They would not be all day in burning.'[46] Latimer continued

[38] Letter, Nicholas Partridge to Henry Bullinger, in *Original Letters relative to the English Reformation*, ed. H. Robinson, 2 vols., Parker Soc., 23 and 28 (1846–7), ii. 608–10 (letter cclxxix).

[39] ibid.

[40] *L & P Henry VIII*, 13.i (1538), p. 239 (item 644); pp. 283–4 (item 754), and *Original Letters*, ed. Robinson, ii. 604–10 (letters cclxxvii–cclxxix).

[41] Wriothesley, *Chronicle*, i. 74.

[42] James G. Clark, 'Reformation and reaction at St Albans Abbey, 1530–58', *EHR*, cxv no. 461 (April, 2000), 297–328, at 324.

[43] *Letters relating to the Suppression*, ed. Wright, 190–1 (item 95).

[44] Wriothesley, *Chronicle*, i. 80.

[45] When the garments clothing the statue were removed, 'she' was found to be a huge image of a bishop, 'like a giant, almost ten foot long'. The statue was finally burned in the churchyard in 1560. Quoted in Ute Engel, *Worcester Cathedral: an Architectural History* (Worcester, 2007), 195.

[46] *L & P Henry VIII*, 13.i (1538), p. 437 (item 1177). Holograph letter, Latimer to Cromwell, dated Hartlebury, 13 June 1538.

by urging Cromwell to destroy the shrines of St David, St Wulfstan, and Bishop John of Coutances.

The famous liquefying blood of Hailes, England's answer to St Januarius, was the focus of one of the most active late medieval pilgrim cults. The abbot of Hailes pre-empted its destruction by seeking Cromwell's advice: he was minded to remove this relic, lest he should himself be accused of renewing it with 'drake's blood'.[47] The way in which the imposture was achieved was described by Lord Herbert:

> Another great imposture was at Hales in Gloucestershire, where the blood of Christ brought from Jerusalem was showed in a chrystal vial, and was said to have this property: That if a man was in a mortal sin, and not absolved, he could not see it. Therefore, every man that came to behold this miracle was forced to continue to make presents till he bribed Heaven to give him the sight of so blessed a relic. This was now discovered to be the blood of a duck renewed every week, and one side of the vial was so thick that there was no seeing through it, but the other was transparent. It was so placed near the altar that anyone in a secret place behind could turn which side he pleased outward.[48]

Although the relic itself had been removed by March 1538,[49] the shrine which enclosed it was still standing six months later, and Abbot Stephen wrote to Cromwell, asking that it should be taken down, perhaps hoping that he would thereby increase the chances that his abbey would be allowed to remain.[50] Meanwhile Bishop Hugh Latimer, at Hailes, was subjecting the relic to a detailed examination:

> Have been boulting and sifting the blood of Haylles all this forenoon. It was wondrously closely and craftily enclosed and stopped up, and cleaves fast to the bottom of the little glass. It seems to be an unctuous gum and compound of many things. It has a certain unctuous moistness, and though it seem somewhat like blood while it is in the glass, yet when any parcel of the same is taken out it turneth to a yellowness and is cleaving like glue.[51]

The monastery of Hailes was dissolved early in January 1539.[52] The Blood of Hailes was also taken to St Paul's Cross, where Bishop Hilsey again preached, showing the relic to the crowd, and 'affirmed the same to be no bloud, but honie clarified, and coloured with saffron, as it had beene evidentlie proved before the king and his counceil'.[53]

[47] ibid., 13.i (1538), p. 119 (item 347).
[48] Wriothesley, *Chronicle*, i. 76.
[49] *L & P Henry VIII*, 13.i (1538), p. 207–8 (item 564); p. 214 (item 580).
[50] ibid., 13.ii (1538), p. 158 (item 409).
[51] ibid., 13.ii (1538), pp. 272–3 (item 709); cf. ibid. 273 (item 710).
[52] ibid., 15 (1540), p. 8 (item 19). Cf. *Letters relating to the Suppression*, ed. Wright, 236–8 (item 116).
[53] ibid., 237, footnote, citing Holinshed.

The dissolution of the major monasteries in 1538 was accompanied by the destruction of almost all of England's premier shrines. Amongst the first was the shrine of St Edmund at Bury St Edmunds, where the commissioners reported to Cromwell as follows:

> Pleasith it your lordshp to be advertysed, that wee have ben at saynt Edmondes Bury, where we found a riche shryne whiche was very comberous to deface. We have takyn in the seyd monastery in golde and sylver m.m.m.m.m. markes, and above ...[54]

Having finished their work at Bury, the commissioners announced their intention of continuing to Ely, presumably to take down the shrine of St Æthelthryth.

The most spectacular shrine to be destroyed was that of St Thomas of Canterbury. In April 1538 Nicholas Partridge had received reports at Frankfurt that it was expected that St Thomas would soon be 'performing miracles' at St Paul's Cross,[55] and within four months the shrine had been demolished. On 8 September John Hussey, secretary to Arthur Plantagenet, Lord Lisle, the English Deputy in Calais, wrote to Lady Lisle that the commissioner for the destruction of the Canterbury shrine, Richard Pollard, 'hath so much ado with St Thomas shrine in offering and praying, that he cannot yet intend to follow worldly causes, but I trust when he hath prayed and received the offering and relics, he will be at leisure'.[56] According to one report the gold and silver filled twenty-six wagons;[57] Professor Barrie Dobson has called it 'the greatest collection of earthly treasure ever seen in medieval England'.[58] Whether the saint's bones were burnt or buried remains a controversial topic to this day; in a lively book on the fate of Becket's body John Butler has convincingly argued that the story of the burning of the bones originated at the Vatican in October 1538 and quickly gained acceptance in Catholic Europe, having 'no independent corroboration in contemporary English documents'.[59]

From Canterbury, Pollard continued to Winchester where, together with Thomas Wriothesley and John Williams, he pulled down St Swithun's final shrine, which had been in existence only since 1476. His letter to Cromwell was written in the cathedral in haste early on Saturday 21 September.

> Pleasith your lordship to be advertisid, that this Saturdaye, in the mornyng, aboutes thre of the clok, we made an ende of the shryne

[54] ibid., 144–5 (item 67).

[55] *Original Letters*, ed. Robinson, ii. 608–10, at 609 (letter cclxxix). *L & P Henry VIII*, 13.i (1538), pp. 283–4 (item 754).

[56] ibid., 13.ii (1538), p. 119 (item 303). *The Lisle Letters*, ed. M. St. Clare Byrne, 6 vols. (Chicago, 1981), v. no. 1217.

[57] *L & P Henry VIII*, 13.ii (1538), p. 49 (item 133).

[58] B. Dobson, 'The Monks of Canterbury in the later middle ages', in *A History of Canterbury Cathedral*, ed. P. Collinson, N. Ramsay, and M. Sparks (Oxford, 1995), 69–153, at 150.

[59] J. Butler, *The Quest for Becket's Bones* (New Haven and London, 1995), chapter 7 ('Burned or Buried'), 109–33.

> here at Wynchestre. There was in it no pece of gold, ne oon ring, or true stone, but al greate counterfaictes. Nevertheles we thinke the sylver alone thereof woll amounte nere to twoo thousande markes.[60]

At Winchester, too, the fate of St Swithun's relics is uncertain. Unlike Becket, the bones of a pre-Conquest saint cannot have been regarded as politically controversial, and it might have been expected that they would have been reburied, as were the remains of St Cuthbert. This is certainly what one contemporary account suggests, thought by Thomas Milman, in his study of the fate of Becket's bones, to have been written by Thomas Derby, clerk to the privy council, in 1539: Milman thought the document was 'a scheme or plan for a sermon at St. Paul's Cross, to be preached as a public vindication of the late proceedings of king Henry VIII'. The passage in question maintains that,

> St Swythan and other reliques wheraboute abuse of ipocrasy was be layde save, and not, as it is untruely surmitted, brent [burnt], but according to reason collocate secretely, wher ther shal be no cause of superstition giuen by them, as some say that for the like cause the body of Moyses was hyden lest the Jues shuld fall to idolatry.[61]

There can have been little local official resistance to the destruction of the shrine of St Osmund of Salisbury, where both the bishop, Nicholas Shaxton, and the mayor and town council were ardent reformers, as we have already noted. Demolition of the monument took some considerable time and was undertaken by the cathedral's workmen: John Sylvester and John Somer received 2*s* 8*d* for working for over a week *circa demolicione scrinii sci Osmundi* in January 1539, and later in the year Somer and his workmate continued the task for a further fortnight.[62]

Salisbury was, of course, a secular cathedral, so the destruction of the shrine did not go hand-in-hand with the spoliation of a monastery prior to its dissolution. So, too, was Chichester Cathedral, where the shrine of St Richard was located on a feretory platform behind the high altar. A special commission was issued by the king on 14 December 1538 to Sir William Goring and William Erneley, to destroy the shrine and bones of 'a certain bishop ... which they call St Richard, which was still the subject of much superstition, and a certain kind of idolatry'; the place where the shrine stood was to be demolished down to the ground, and the main shrine, together with other reliquaries, was to be conveyed to a treasury in the Tower of

[60] *Letters relating to the Suppression*, ed. Wright, 218.

[61] Henry Salisbury Milman, 'The Vanished Memorials of St. Thomas of Canterbury', *Archaeologia* 53 (1892), 211–28, at 221–2.

[62] S. Eward, 'St Osmund: the destruction of the shrine', *Salisbury Cathedral News*, 149 (May 1992), 10–11. J. M. J. Fletcher, 'Bishop Richard Beauchamp, 1450–1481, *Wilts. Archaeol. Mag.*, 48 (1938), 161–73, at 165.

London.[63] The commissioners worked fast, and within a week an inventory of the shrine and relics had been taken: the saint's bones were found to be in 'a long coffin' containing fifty-seven pieces of silver and gilt.[64] The lower dais survived the destruction, and Bishop Day (†1556) chose to have his tomb placed on it, on the north side. Day had objected to the 'plucking down' of stone altars in 1550 and was deprived the following year; during the reign of Mary he reinstated the rood screen and may have hoped to restore St Richard's shrine.[65]

Some shrines in secular cathedrals lasted a little longer: the shrine of St Wærburh of Chester seems to have survived until 1539.[66] Not until 6 June 1540 was the commission issued for the destruction of 'a certain shrine and divers feigned relics and jewels in Lincoln Cathedral, by which simple people are deceived and brought into superstition and idolatry',[67] perhaps because of the conservative views of Bishop Longland. The commissioners arrived in Lincoln on the 11th, and 2,621oz. of gold, 4,285oz. of silver, and a great number of pearls and precious stones were removed from the cathedral. The commissioners noted two shrines: the gold shrine of St Hugh and the silver shrine of Sir John Dalderby, which had been previously listed in an inventory made in 1536.[68]

So effective were the activities of the commissioners, that, with a very few exceptional survivals, discussed below, the vast majority of relics, and their reliquaries and shrines, had perished by 1542: some may have enjoyed a temporary reprieve, like the shrine of St Augustine of Canterbury, which had by special permission been given to the church of Chilham (Kent), but this was short-lived.[69] The precious metals and jewels from shrines swelled the royal coffers, and the consequence is that examples of English medieval reliquaries are rare indeed. True, Edward VI's articles to parish clergy of 1547 enquired whether their churches still contained 'any misused images, with pilgrimages, clothes, stones, shoes, offerings, kissings, candlesticks, trindles of wax, and other such like: and whether there do remain not delayed and destroyed any shrines, covering of shrines, or any other monument of idolatry, superstition and hypocrisy', but apart from asking whether those

[63] Wilkins, *Concilia*, iii. 840. Cf. 'The Early statutes of the Cathedral Church of the Holy Trinity, Chichester, with observations on its constitution and history', ed. M. E. C. Walcott, *Archaeologia*, 45 (1877), 143–234, at 176.

[64] *L & P Henry VIII*, 13.ii (1538), p. 464 (item 1103).

[65] T. Tatton-Brown, 'Destruction, repair and restoration', in *Chichester Cathedral, an Historical Survey*, ed. M. Hobbs (Chichester, 1994), 143–56, at 143–4.

[66] R. V. H. Burne, *Chester Cathedral, from its founding by Henry VIII to the Accession of Queen Victoria* (London, 1958), 35.

[67] *L & P Henry VIII*, 15 (1540), pp. 364–5 (item 772).

[68] W. Dugdale, *Monasticon Anglicanum*, ed. T. Caley and H. Ellis, 6 vols. (London, 1817–30), vi, pt iii, pp.1278–86, item lxviii: 'The register and inventary of all jewels, vestments, and other ornaments to the revestry of the cathedral Church of Lincoln belonging, made by Master Henry Lytherland, Treasurer of the same church, in the year of our Lord God, 1536, 28 Hen. VIII. (Ex Regist. Dec. et Capit. Eccles. Cath. Linc.).'

[69] *L & P Henry VIII*, 18.ii (1543), pp. 291–378 (item 546) and p. 302.

clergy who had formerly spoken in favour of 'feigned relics' had not recanted, relics are hardly mentioned.[70] Images could subsequently be reinstated during the Catholic revival under Mary, to be removed at the start of Elizabeth's reign, and the survival, retention, or reinstatement of a number of images is attested in the surviving Act Book for the visitation of the northern province,[71] but no mention is made of relics. As far as English churches were concerned, they had vanished from the scene.

SURVIVAL OF MAJOR RELICS

A few major relics, whose authenticity was more or less established, appear to have survived. The most spectacular example is the body of Edward the Confessor, whose high shrine in Westminster Abbey was destroyed in 1536, four years before the surrender of the monastery in January 1540. The saint's body was removed from its opulent *feretrum*, which was melted down, but Henry VIII refrained from annihilating the remains of his royal predecessor; the Confessor was reburied within the church, perhaps on the site of the shrine. The abbey was restored during the reign of Queen Mary, in November 1556, and within four months the diarist Henry Machyn recorded that 'The xx day of Marche [1557] was taken up at Westmynster agayn with a hondered lyghtes kyng Edward the confessor in the sam plasse wher ys shryne was, and ytt shalle be sett up agayne as fast as my lord abbott [Abbot Feckenham] can have ytt don ...'.[72] Machyn records that the work was completed by April 1557, when he viewed the shrine 'nuw set up'.[73] J. G. O'Neilly has shown that the present structure betrays evidence of haste in construction, several elements being wrongly reassembled.[74] O'Neilly suggests, furthermore, that the wooden superstructure or canopy, which originally would have covered the *feretrum*, was not renewed during Abbot Feckenham's time, but that it dated from earlier in the sixteenth century and escaped the destruction of the shrine-base.[75] In the Marian reconstruction which has survived to this day the canopy serves no practical purpose, for the coffin (presumably provided in 1536) containing the body of the saint was replaced within the monument itself, in the space between the head of the vaulted niches and a new oversailing freestone cornice with a classical moulding which was added for the purposes of the reconstruction.

Another saintly body to survive was that of St Cuthbert, which until 1538 had been enshrined in its Anglo-Saxon light chest within the opulent high shrine, 'exalted with most curious workmannshipp of fine and costly marble,

[70] 'Royal Articles of Edward VI', in *Visitation Articles*, ed. Frere, ii. 103–13, at 105.
[71] PRO, State Papers 12/10: *The Royal Visitation of 1559*, ed. C. J. Kitching, Surtees Soc., vol. 187, for 1972 (Gateshead, 1975).
[72] *The Diary of Henry Machyn*, ed. J. G. Nichols, Camden Soc., o.s., 42 (1848), 130.
[73] ibid., 132.
[74] J. G. O'Neilly and L. E. Tanner, 'The Shrine of St. Edward the Confessor', *Archaeologia*, 100 (1966), 129–54.
[75] ibid., 150–4.

all limned and guilted with gold'.[76] This stood on the feretory platform behind the high altar. The body was violently removed from the shrine (during which one of the leg bones is supposed to have been broken), was stored in the vestry (or perhaps in the cloister garth), and in 1542 was buried in a new grave cut into the feretory platform, in exactly the place where the shrine had stood. The lining of the grave incorporated fragments of the plinth of the final shrine which were removed in 1899 and which until recently stood on the feretory pavement. There is little evidence to support the charming legend that the body was reburied elsewhere in the cathedral in a place known only to three Benedictines who continue to pass the secret down the generations; the objects found with the remains of the body are sufficient proof of its authenticity. Similar traditions existed at Hereford, and have been suggested at Canterbury in the complex arguments over the fate of Becket's bones. Better authenticated are the remains of St Chad of Lichfield, claimed by the Roman Catholic cathedral in Birmingham since its consecration in 1841. The documentation for the movements of the relics since the Reformation was printed and discussed by John Hewitt in 1876.[77]

It is possible that the reliquary of St Augustine escaped immediate destruction. When the commissioners visited Chilham Church in 1543 they discovered that the incumbent, Dr Willoughby, still retained an object called 'St Austin's shrine' which had been taken thither on the destruction of the abbey.[78] Dr Willoughby, a participant in the conspiracy against Cranmer of 1543, had evidently retained the relic hoping for better times.[79] But even the relics of the first archbishop of Canterbury met their end.

SURVIVAL OF INDIVIDUAL RELICS

In view of all this activity, it is surprising that any relics survived the activities of the various commissioners. But there were undoubtedly some individuals whose belief in the efficacy of relics was powerful enough to overcome their fear of royal retribution. Most of the accounts which have come down to us concern the unfortunate individuals who happened to be caught. In 1539, for example, Sir John Rogke, a priest of Reading, was accused of possessing 'a relic named St. Anastasius' hand, knowing that his Majesty had sent visitors to the said abbey to put down such idolatry'.[80] At around the same time a north-country beggar was accused of retaining relics from Tynemouth Priory. He had described to one of the witnesses against him how he had watched the commissioners roughly casting aside the bones from which they had stripped the gold and silver; they gave him some bones,

[76] *The Rites of Durham*, ed. J. T. Fowler, Surtees Soc., 107, for 1902 (Durham, 1903), 3–4.
[77] J. Hewitt, 'The Keeper of St Chad's Head in Lichfield Cathedral', *Arch. J.*, 33 (1876), 71–82, at 73–8.
[78] *L & P Henry VIII*, 18.ii (1543), item 546, see also p. 319, item xi.
[79] For more on this subject see Potts, 'Tombs', 97–112, at 104–5.
[80] *L & P Henry VIII*, 14.ii (1539), p. 96 (item 256).

covered with silver, inviting him to strip it off in order to decorate his dagger; but he seems to have retained the relics in their adorned state, as well as other bones that they had cast away.[81] Relics were still available as late as 1547, when Thomas Monday, a London parson, and Thurston Hickman, a former monk of the Charterhouse, were sentenced to be hanged, drawn and quartered for treason because they had attempted to smuggle various relics to John Foxe, another Charterhouse monk who had become a parish priest but then had fled to Louvain to become a monk again. The relics included the left arm of John Houghton, the martyred last prior of the Charterhouse, and 'other baggage that they called reliques'.[82]

When the shrine of St Thomas Cantilupe of Hereford was about to be destroyed in around 1538, relics of that saint were removed for safekeeping. Their fate has been chronicled by Dom Illtud Barrett.[83] After the Reformation a custodian of the relics was appointed, the first known of whom was the Revd William Ely, ordained during the reign of Queen Mary; and as late as the mid-seventeenth century the relics were carried through the streets of Hereford in order to avert the plague. At around that time several of the relics, which had been dispersed during the Commonwealth period, were transferred to the relative safety of the Continent; an arm bone, for example, eventually found its way to Bruges. The saint's head was translated *c.*1670 to the English Benedictine house which had been founded at Lamspring, in the diocese of Hildesheim, Germany. After the suppression of that monastery by the Prussian government in 1803 the relic was lost for nearly eighty years, until it was rediscovered in 1881, languishing at the top of a cupboard behind the high altar reredos of the former abbey church, by a monk of Downside, Dom Gilbert Dolan. The relic is now preserved in the Latin chapel of the abbey church of Downside. A tibia of St Thomas is now venerated at Stonyhurst College, having been preserved until 1835 at Holywell in North Wales.

Another relic which appears to have been illegally concealed was the shrine and bones of St Eanswyth of Folkestone. As we have seen,[84] the lead coffer and relics appear to have been crammed, perhaps hastily, into a cavity in the north wall of the chancel of the abbey church, where they were discovered some three hundred and fifty years later. Walling up treasures was one way of evading their confiscation, and in September 1538 the commissioners reported from Glastonbury that 'we have dayly fownde and tryede oute bothe money and plate hyde and muryde up in wallis, vauttis, and other secrette placis as well by thabbott as other of the conventt'.[85] The

[81] ibid., 14.ii (1539), p. 281 (item 750).
[82] Wriothesley, *Chronicle*, i. 184–5.
[83] 'The Relics of St Thomas Cantilupe', in Jancey, *Thomas Cantilupe*, 181–5, drawing on Father John Morris, 'English Relics', *The Month*, 44 (Jan–April 1882), 112–26, and E. Horne, in *The Clergy Review*, 28 (1947), 91–104.
[84] Above, pp. 68–9.
[85] *Letters relating to the Suppression*, ed. Wright, 257–8.

abbot of Glastonbury was hanged, drawn and quartered for treason, including this accusation, soon after.

An admittedly unlikely relic that was discovered immured within a former monastery precinct is the so-called 'Hand of St James' at Reading Abbey.[86] The small, mummified hand was discovered by a workman digging in the abbey ruins, and eventually found its way to the Roman Catholic church of St Peter, Marlow, where it is preserved in a glass and brass casket. Needless to say, the authenticity of the relic is dubious, and it is hardly surprising that in 1960, when a pilgrimage to venerate the relic was planned, the Catholic bishop of Northampton 'positively [forbade] the public veneration of the relic'. Quite apart from the question of the primary authenticity of the relic displayed at Reading since the twelfth century as one of its principal holy treasures, there is no way of telling whether the surviving hand is the relic still attested there at the dissolution. 'Saynt James hande' was near the top of an 'Inventorye off the Relyques off the howse off Redyng' compiled at Reading Abbey by Dr John London on 18 September 1538, who told Cromwell that he had 'lokyd them upp behind the high awlter' and had the key in his keeping.[87] It might therefore be thought improbable that the commissioner should have mislaid such an important relic. However, another hand, that of St Anastasius, was also listed by Dr London, and yet, as we have seen, was illegally retained by Sir John Rogke, so such appropriation was evidently possible. The small size of the relic has suggested to some people that the hand might be that of Henry I's second wife, Queen Adeliza, who was also buried at Reading.[88]

But the most fascinating account of the illegal retention of relics concerns the so-called 'foot of St Philip' in St Swithun's Priory, Winchester, which by 1585 had reached the abbey of St Andrew, Bruges.[89] The abbot hoped to offer the relic to a bearer of the same name, Philip II of Spain, and the documentation relating to its authentication has survived in the Spanish national archive at Simancas, providing a valuable insight into the way relics could be preserved, despite the best efforts of the reformers.

According to the *Annales Wintonienses*, the relic had been brought to the priory by Bishop Peter des Roches in 1231: *Obtulit [episcopus] pedem Sancti Philippi.*[90] it is likely therefore that the warrior prelate brought it back from his crusade to the Holy Land in 1227–31. On the eve of the dissolution the foot was normally kept in the 'sacristy' (almost certainly, the walled-off area in the south transept known as the 'Treasury of Henry of Blois'); there it was

[86] The story of the relic is discussed by the Revd Brian Taylor, 'The Hand of St James', *Berks. Archaeol. Jnl.*, 75 (1994–7), 97–102, to whom I am indebted for the details here given.
[87] BL, Cotton MS Cleopatra E.iv, fos. 264–5 (formerly fos. 223–4), quoted in *Letters relating to the Suppression*, ed. Wright, 226.
[88] Taylor, 'Hand of St James'.
[89] The fascinating story was published by Peter Bogan, 'Dom Thomas Figg and the foot of St Philip', *Winchester Cathedral Record*, 61 (1992), 22–6, reporting on research by the Revd Dr Michael Williams.
[90] *Winchester Annals*; ed. Luard, 86.

listed with other relics preserved in the sacristy, and itemised as 'sayncte philyps Fote coveryd with plate of gold & with stones'.[91] Nearly fifty years later, Thomas Figg, an elderly English monk living in exile at Bruges, shed light on how the relic had reached Belgium, and his account is worth quoting extensively for the exceptional insight it also gives into the methods of the commissioners:

> He had been educated from boyhood in the said monastery of Winchester, and in due course had been appointed and instituted one of the three custodians [*custodes*], who had in their care the relics of the saints of the same monastery, and he was officially a custodian at the time when his highness King Philip of Spain took Mary Queen of England to wife in the same monastery, where for a long time previously the aforesaid foot of St Philip the Apostle had been kept in the vestry enclosed in a silver-gilt reliquary decorated with precious stones, valued together in common estimation £100 sterling. Once a year, namely on the actual Feast of St Philip, it was solemnly and reverently carried to the high altar, lying on a cushion of red silk with two tapers lit, to be venerated by the people. The witness most often carried it like this. But in the time of Henry VIII, of England, the king, motivated by hatred of saints, who were no longer to be revered or invoked, decreed that the holy places were not even to be called by their names, and on that account the name of the Most Holy Trinity was imposed on the said monastery. But at Henry's death, and in the reign of the aforesaid Queen Mary, wife of his Highness Philip, king of Spain, the original name of St Swithun was restored to the said monastery. King Henry, proceeding from one impious and outrageous deed to another, one day ordered the said church and monastery to be plundered of its silver, jewels, relics and all its goods by certain commissioners sent to this end. No-one was allowed to enter the church with these commissioners apart from the senior custodian, who was allowed into the vestry, and was compelled to open the chests of ornaments and repositories of jewels. He watched the commissioners frenziedly taking, stealing and violently carrying off gold and silver, and indeed throwing the relics of saints on the ground to be burned. From these relics the senior custodian secretly picked up and carried away the said foot of St Philip the Apostle, faithfully looking after it until his death. First, however, he had drawn up his will, appointing William Benyan, a layman, as executor, to whom he entrusted the said foot for safe-keeping. Before that same executor in due course died, he gave custody of the foot to his wife Margaret, who was acquainted with and well known by the witness [Thomas Figg], to whom moreover she sent the foot without request or demand. The witness knew and recognised that it was the foot of St Philip and accepted it with joy,

[91] BL, Harley MS 358, fo. 17v, printed in J. Strype, *Memorials of Cranmer* (Oxford, 1840), ii. 709, Appendix XVI.

> keeping it faithfully in a certain casket. When he fled from England for fear of the heretics he left the foot with a young man called Ambrose Edmunds (who subsequently died in prison for his Catholic faith) so that might send it on to him at the first available opportunity. In this way the witness received the foot in these parts [i.e. at Bruges] eighteen years ago.

The story was complicated by the involvement of another English refugee, Lady Anne Hungerford, a prominent figure amongst the exiled Catholic community in Bruges, and further documents are concerned with charting the movements of the relic until it was finally delivered to the abbot of St Andrew's, Bruges. From there, once it had been properly authenticated by order of Philip II's secretary, the relic eventually reached the Escorial in 1592.

SURVIVAL OF SHRINES

As well as secreting relics, some cathedral and church authorities appear to have attempted to preserve fragments of demolished shrines, perhaps in the hope that one day they might be reconstructed. The shrine of St Alban, for example, was broken into over two thousand fragments in 1539, which were used in the construction of a wall separating the former feretory area from the Lady chapel, which was converted into a school. That so many of the pieces were used in a single archaeological context could suggest that those who treated them thus hoped in fact that they might one day be reassembled; and indeed in 1847 (the first discovery of some elements) and more particularly in 1872, they were retrieved and put together like a jigsaw when the shrine was first reassembled. Likewise at Oxford, the remains of the shrine of St Frideswide were discovered in the lining of a well.

By the time of the Elizabethan visitation of 1559, relics, reliquaries, and shrines had disappeared for ever from the great majority of churches and cathedrals. On the other hand, a number of images had been reinstated during the reign of Queen Mary. Images still stood, for example, in the church of Rotheborne,[92] and an image of Our Lady at Beynton had 'byn used for pilgrymage'.[93] At Doncaster images had survived in the vestry, and were described as 'not destroyed'.[94] One or two parishioners had retained images: at Chester, it was said of Mistress Dutton, of St Peter's church that she 'kepith secreatly a Roode, too pictures and a masse boke', and of Peter Fleicher that he 'hathe certin ymages whiche he kepithe secreatlye';[95] and at Bridlington the images were also 'secretly kepte'.[96] Those at Osmotherley church had been 'convayed awaye' but the parishioners did not know by whom.[97]

92 PRO, State Papers 12/10, fo. 109v; *The Royal Visitation of 1559*, ed. Kitching, 73.

93 ibid., fo. 100v; p. 69.

94 ibid., fo. 97v; p. 67.

95 ibid., fos. 134r and 135r; p. 85.

96 ibid., fo. 100v; p. 69.

97 ibid.

EPILOGUE
ENGLISH SHRINES TODAY

A new interest in shrines is evident today, not just as historical vestiges of the religious practices of the past, but as focuses of spiritual activity, where pilgrims can reflect, pray, or light votive candles, a practice that would have been viewed with disgust a century ago. When John Chapple laboriously reconstructed the shrine of St Alban in 1872 it was a personal research project, led by antiquarian considerations, and the monument was principally a tourist attraction for many years. The same could be said of the shrine of St Frideswide, fragments of which were discovered in 1875 and pieced together. The reconstruction of the shrine of St Birinus at Dorchester in 1964 remained something of a curiosity.

Things were very different when the St Albans shrine was again rebuilt in 1990–3 in honour of the twelfth centenary of the foundation of King Offa's abbey church. The dedication service was held on 6 May 1993 in the presence of Queen Elizabeth the Queen Mother, and the Very Revd Peter Moore introduced the prayers of rehallowing with the following words:

> From the time of Constantine and Gregory of Tours the use of candles at shrines has been an established custom. Though this holy, thoughtful use degenerated, it is our intention now to encourage a return to the hope and prayer of the first pilgrims, whose faith shone in the light of their candles, as token and reminder of him who is the Light of the World.

The initiative proved a success, and St Alban is now firmly at the centre of the abbey's campaign to raise its profile by setting England's proto-martyr at the forefront of that great church's life. According to a publicity leaflet, 'We want to draw and welcome increasing numbers of worshippers and visitors to the national shrine of Britain's first Christian martyr.'[1] Thus Alban has been established as the *persona* of the abbey, just as Swithun of Winchester represented the priory there at the time of the monastic reforms of the tenth century.

[1] *A Vision for St Albans Cathedral*, publicity leaflet, 2011.

The example set by St Albans has been followed in many other churches. In 1999 the *foramina* tomb-shrine of St Osmund at Salisbury was returned to its original site on the south side of the Trinity chapel, displacing the black Tournai marble slab which was set in the middle of the chapel on the presumed site of the saint's final shrine. Candles burn constantly to east and west of the slab, and pilgrims can light votive candles at the tomb-shrine. The shrine of St Frideswide was reconstructed in 2002 and acts as a focus for prayer in Oxford Cathedral. At Hereford, the tomb of St Thomas Cantilupe was embellished in 2008, with the addition of a new superstructure in the form of a gabled canopy supported on slender colonettes, and the east side of the transept is devoted to the cult, with tapestries depicting the saint's life and miracles, and opportunities for lighting candles, reflection, and prayer. At Dorchester-on-Thames, 'one of the future tasks of the Dorchester Abbey Preservation Trust is a sensitive re-assessment and completion of this project so that the shrine can be used as a focus for ecumenical worship'.[2] At the time of writing, an appeal has been launched for a complete refurbishment of the shrine of St David, with the aim of placing Wales's national saint at the centre of his cathedral.

For many centuries after the Reformation the cult of saints was viewed with abhorrence, disdain, or amusement. There seems to be a new interest amongst clergy and laity alike in promoting the native cults of England and Wales. Erasmus would have been astonished.

[2] Dorchester Abbey website, www.dorchester-abbey.org.uk/history3.htm, accessed 27 April 2011.

GLOSSARY

Adventus. The ceremonial 'arrival' of a saint, as the body or relics were carried into a church.

Analogium. Term used by early writers to denote a monument created over a saint's grave (cf. *memoria, tropaion*).

Brandea. Contact relics: objects made holy through contact with a saintly body or bones.

Capsa (or diminutive *capsella*, occasionally *capsula*). A casket for the relics of a saint, cf. *theca, scrinium*.

Cella, cella memoria. A burial chamber. Synonymous with Gk. *hypogeum*.

Chef. A head reliquary; a decorated, suitably shaped container for the skull of a saint.

Cista. A chest.

Confessio. An underground chamber or crypt housing the body of a saint.

Confessor. A person, usually a priest or bishop, who has become regarded as a saint having lived an exemplary life of witness to the Christian faith.

Contact relics. Objects imbued with sanctity through contact with corporeal (bodily) relics. In Latin, called *brandea, sanctuaria*.

Cripta, crypta. A vault, usually an underground chamber or 'crypt'.

Domuncula, domunculus. Diminutives of *domus*: a monument resembling a 'little house' over the grave or body of a saint.

Elevatio, elevation. The exhumation and 'raising up' of a saint's body.

Ex-votos. Ritual objects left by pilgrims to a shrine; including wax or clay models of body parts cured or to be cured by the saint.

Fenestella. Diminutive form of *fenestra* (window). A window-like opening providing access to or a view of relics.

Feretrum. A bier (stretcher) used to carry the body of a saint; by extension, a chest-like container for a saint's body.

Foramina. Plural of *foramen*, a cavity or aperture. The round or oval openings in the sides of a tomb-shrine providing access to the tomb or relics within.

Hagiography. Writing about saints.

Hagiology. The study of the cult of saints.

High shrine. The typical shrine of the later middle ages, comprising a reliquary supported on a tall stone shrine-base with niches in the sides.

Hypogeum. (Gk. 'under ground'). A burial chamber, cf. Latin *cella*.
Inventio. The (usually) miraculous discovery of the body of a potential saint, occasionally referred to as the *revelatio* (literally, 'unveiling').
Locellus. A receptacle for housing saintly relics: often synonymous with *scrinium*, *theca*, etc .(*q.v.*).
Loculus. Diminutive of Latin *locus*: a niche or cavity to house the bones of a saint.
Martyr. Literally 'witness', from the Greek. In a Christian context, one who has given up his/her life for the faith.
Martyrium. A monument marking the grave of a martyr.
Memoria. A funerary monument.
Miracula. A written account of the miracles performed by a saint.
Pallium. A cloth, typically one placed over saintly relics or shrines.
Passio. A narrative recounting the suffering (passion) and death of a saint.
Porticus. A 'porch'. In Anglo-Saxon architecture, an annex, usually rectangular, added to the side(s) of a church.
Refrigerium. A commemorative meal eaten at the tomb of a deceased relative.
Relics. The physical remains of a saint, the subject of veneration. Most commonly his or her bones. Secondary relics, also called *contact relics* (*q.v.*), are objects (for example, items of clothing) that have achieved similar holiness through contact with the saint, or with his relics.
Reliquary. A container to house or display relics.
Sacellum. A small underground cavity, typically a burial chamber.
Sanctuaria. Synonymous with *brandea*. Contact relics: objects made holy through contact with a saintly body or bones.
Scrinium. A box or casket; in this context one housing saintly relics.
Sepulchrum. Latin for a sepulchre or tomb.
Shrine. From Latin *scrinium*, a box or casket. The term originally referred to a reliquary, but by extension can refer to the whole monument housing a saint's remains (the way the term is used in this book) or even to a church. In this book a distinction is made between *tomb-shrines* and *high shrines* (q.v.).
Theca. Gk. equivalent of *scrinium*.
Tomb-shrine. A monument, often with *foramina* (port-holes) constructed over the grave of a saint.
Topos. A literary commonplace.
Transenna. A vertical slab closing the front of a tomb.
Translation. The moving of a saint's body or relics, usually to a more prestigious location.
Tropaion. A funerary monument (Gk. equivalent of *memoria*).
Tugurium. A small hut; in a hagiological context, a monument resembling a small house, built over a saint's grave.
Vita. A written account of the life of a saint.

SELECT BIBLIOGRAPHY

This select list is not intended as a full bibliography of the cult of saints in England and Wales, but includes the more important sources and studies used in the preparation of this book, together with recent publications. Other, incidental, references are supplied in the footnotes to the main text.

PRIMARY SOURCES

MEDIEVAL HISTORIANS AND CHRONICLERS

Alcuin. *Alcuin: The Bishops, Kings, and Saints of York*, ed. P. Godman, OMT (Oxford, 1982).

Bede. *Bede's Ecclesiastical History of the English People*, ed. B. Colgrave and R. A. B. Mynors (Oxford, 1969).

Eadmer. *Edmeri Cantuariensis cantoris noua opuscula de sanctorum ueneratione et obsecratione*, ed. A. Wilmart, *Revue des sciences religieuses*, 15 (1935), 184–219 and 354–79.

Egeria. *Itinerarium Egeriæ: Peregrinatio Ætheriæ*, ed. O. Prinz (Heidelberg, 1960), 20; *CCSL*, 175 (*Itineraria et alia Geographica*), 27–90; *Egeria's Travels*, trans. J. Wilkinson, 3rd edn. (Warminster, 1999).

Flores Historiarum, ed. H. R. Luard, 3 vols., RS, 95 (1890).

Gerald of Wales. *Giraldi Cambrensis Opera*, ed. J. S. Brewer, J. F. Dimock, and G. F. Warner, 8 vols., RS, 21 (1861–91).

Gervase. *The Historical Works of Gervase of Canterbury*, ed. W. Stubbs, 2 vols., RS, 73 (1879–90).

Gildas. *Gildæ sapientis, De Excidio et Conquestu Britanniæ*; *Chronica Minora Saec. iv. v. vi. vii.*, vol. iii, ed. T. Mommsen, *MGH, Auctores Antiquissimi*, xiii, pt. i (Berlin, 1898), 25–85.

Goscelin. *Goscelin of Saint-Bertin, The Hagiography of the Female Saints of Ely*, ed. R. C. Love, OMT (Oxford, 2004).

John 'Florence' of Worcester. *The Chronicle of John of Worcester*, ii, *The Annals from 450 to 1066*, ed. R. R. Darlington and P. McGurk, trans. J. Bray and P. McGurk, OMT (Oxford, 1995); iii, *The Annals from 1067 to 1140 with the Gloucester Interpolations and the Continuation to 1141*, ed. and trans. P. McGurk, OMT (Oxford, 1998).

Leland. *The Itinerary of John Leland in or about the years 1535–1543*, ed. L. Toulmin Smith, 5 vols. (London, 1906–10).

Matthew Paris. *Matthæi Parisiensis ... Chronica Maiora*, ed. H. R. Luard, 6 vols. and index, RS, 57 (1872–83); *Matthæi Paris ... Historia major*, ed. W. Wats (London, 1640).

Orderic Vitalis. *The Ecclesiastical History of Orderic Vitalis*, ed. M. Chibnall, 6 vols. (Oxford, 1969–80).

Symeon of Durham. *Symeonis Monachi Opera Omnia*, ed. T. Arnold, 2 vols., RS, 75 (1882–5); *Libellus de exordio atque procursu istius, hoc est Dunhelmensis, ecclesie*, ed. D. Rollason, OMT (Oxford, 2000).

William of Malmesbury, *Gesta Pontificum Anglorum: the History of the English Bishops*, ed. and trans. M. Winterbottom and R. M. Thomson, 2 vols., OMT (Oxford, 2007).

— *De Gestis Regum Anglorum*, i, ed. and trans. R. A. B. Mynors, completed R. M. Thomson, and M. Winterbottom, OMT (Oxford, 1998); ii, *General Introduction and Commentary*, by R. M. Thomson in collaboration with M. Winterbottom, OMT (Oxford, 1999).

Wykes, Thomas. 'The Chronicle of Thomas Wykes', *Annales Monastici*, iv, ed. H. R. Luard, RS, 36 (1869).

SAINT'S LIVES AND MIRACLE ACCOUNTS

St Æthelwold. *Wulfstan of Winchester: The Life of St Æthelwold*, ed. M. Lapidge and M. Winterbottom, OMT (Oxford, 1991).

St Anselm. *The Life of St Anselm, Archbishop of Canterbury, by Eadmer*, ed. R. W. Southern, rev. edn. (Oxford, 1962).

St Augustine of Canterbury. *Historia translationis S. Augustini episcopi Anglorum apostoli, auctore Goscelino*; *Pat. Lat.*, clv. cols. 13–46.

St Bregwine. 'Eadmer's Life of Bregwine, Archbishop of Canterbury, 761–764', ed. B. W. Scholtz, *Traditio*, 22 (1966), 127–48.

St Cuthbert. *Vita S. Cuthberti, auctore anonymo*, in *Two Lives of Saint Cuthbert*, ed. B. Colgrave (Cambridge, 1940), 60–139; *Vita Cuthberti, auctore Beda*, in ibid., 142–307; *Bedas Metrische Vita Sancti Cuthberti*, ed. W. Jaager (Leipzig, 1935); *Reginaldi monachi Dunelmensis Libellus de Admirandis Beati Cuthberti Virtutibus*, ed. J. Raine, Surtees Soc., 1 (London, 1835); *Capitula de Miraculis et Translationibus S. Cuthberti*, in *Symeonis Monachi Opera Omnia*, ed. T. Arnold, 2 vols., RS, 75 (1882–5), i. 229–61.

St Dunstan. *Vita S. Dunstani, auctore 'B'*, in *Memorials of St Dunstan Archbishop of Canterbury*, ed. W. Stubbs, RS, 63 (1874), 3–52; Osbern, *Vita Dunstani*, in ibid., 69–161; Eadmer, *Vita et Miracula S. Dunstani*, in ibid., 162–249; William of Malmesbury, *Vita S. Dunstani*, in *William of Malmesbury, Saints' Lives*, ed. M. Winterbottom and R. M. Thomson, OMT (Oxford, 2002), 157–303. *Eadmer of Canterbury: Lives and Miracles of Saints*

Oda, Dunstan, and Oswald, ed. and trans. A. J. Turner and B. J. Muir, OMT (Oxford, 2006), 41–159.

St Earconwald, *The Saint of London: The Life and Miracles of St. Erkenwald*, ed. and trans. E. Gordon Whatley (Binghampton, New York, 1989).

St Ecgwine. *Byrhtferth of Ramsey: The Lives of St Oswald and St Ecgwine*, ed. M. Lapidge, OMT (Oxford, 2009).

St Edith. 'La Légende de Ste Édith en prose et en vers par le moine Goscelin', ed. A. Wilmart, *Analecta Bollandiana*, 56 (1938), 5–101; 265–307.

St Edmund of Bury. Abbo of Fleury, *Passio Sancti Eadmundi*, in *Memorials of St. Edmund's Abbey*, ed. T. Arnold, 3 vols., RS, 96 (1890–6), i. 3–25; *Hermanni archidiaconi liber de miraculis S. Eadmundi*, in ibid., i. 26–92; *Samsonis Abbatis opus de Miraculis S. Ædmundi*, in ibid., i. 107–208.

St Edward the Confessor. 'La Vie de S. Édouard le Confesseur par Osbert de Clare', ed. M. Bloch, *Analecta Bollandiana*, 41 (1923), 5–131; Ailred of Rievaulx, *Vita S. Edwardi regis et confessoris*, *Pat. Lat.*, cxcv. cols. 737–90; *Vita Ædwardi regis: The Life of King Edward who rests at Westminster*, ed. F. Barlow, 2nd edn. (Oxford, 1992); *Passio Edwardi*, ed. C. F. Fell, *Edward King and Martyr*, Leeds Texts and Monographs, n.s., 3 (Leeds, 1971), 1–17.

Gundulf of Rochester. *The Life of Gundulf, Bishop of Rochester*, ed. R. Thomson, Toronto Medieval Latin Texts, 7 (Toronto, 1977).

St Guthlac of Crowland. *Felix's Life of Saint Guthlac*, ed. B. Colgrave (Cambridge, 1956).

St Hugh of Lincoln. Adam of Eynsham, *Magna Vita S. Hugonis*, ed. D. L. Douie and D. H. Farmer, 2 vols., rev. edn., OMT (Oxford, 1985); *Vita S. Hugonis, auctore Giraldo Cambrensis*, in *Giraldi Cambrensis Opera*, ed. J. S. Brewer and J. F. Dimock, 8 vols., RS, 21 (1867–91), vii. 83–147; *Appendix* D, 'Legends of St Hugh', in ibid., 172–87, and miracles, in ibid., 188–92.

St Ithamar. 'The Miracles of St Ithamar', ed. D. Bethell, *Analecta Bollandiana*, 89 (1971), 421–37.

St Mildred of Minster-in-Thanet. 'Goscelin of Canterbury's account of the Translation and Miracles of St. Mildreth (*BHL* 5961/4): An Edition with Notes', ed. D. W. Rollason, *Medieval Studies*, 48 (1986), 139–210.

St Osmund. *The Canonization of St Osmund*, ed. A. R. Malden, Wiltshire Record Soc. (Salisbury, 1901).

St Oswald. *Byrhtferth of Ramsey: The Lives of St Oswald and St Ecgwine*, ed. M. Lapidge, OMT (Oxford, 2009).

St Remigius of Lincoln. *Vita S. Remigii episcopi Lincolniensis, auctore Giraldo Cambrensis*, in *Giraldi Cambrensis Opera*, ed. J. S. Brewer and J. F. Dimock, 8 vols., RS, 21 (1867–91), vii. 3–80.

St Swithun. Lantfred of Winchester, *Translatio et Miracula S. Swithuni*, in *The Cult of St Swithun*, ed. M. Lapidge, Winchester Studies, 4.ii (Oxford, 2003), 217–333; Wulfstan of Winchester, *Narratio Metrica de S. Swithuno*, in ibid., 335–551.

St Thomas Becket. *Materials for the Study of Thomas Becket*, ed. J. C. Robertson, *et al.*, 7 vols., RS, 67 (1875–85).

St Wilfrid of Hexham. *Vita Wilfrido episcopi, auctore Eddio Stephano*, in *Historians of the Church of York and its Archbishops*, ed. J. Raine, 3 vols., RS, 71 (1879–94), i. 1–103; *Vita Wilfridi, auctore Fridegoda*, in ibid., 105–9; *The Life of Saint Wilfrid by Edmer*, ed. B. J. Muir and A. J. Turner (Exeter, 1998); *The Life of Bishop Wilfrid by Eddius Stephanus*, ed. B. Colgrave (Cambridge, 1927, reprinted 1985).

St William of Norwich. *The Life and Miracles of St William of Norwich by Thomas of Monmouth*, ed. A. Jessopp and M. R. James (Cambridge, 1896).

St Wulfstan of Worcester. *The Vita Wulfstani of William of Malmesbury, to which are added the extant abridgements of this work and the Miracles and Translation of St. Wulfstan*, ed. R. R. Darlington, Camden Soc., 3rd ser., 40 (1928); *The Vita Wulfstani of William of Malmesbury*, in *William of Malmesbury, Saints' Lives*, ed. M. Winterbottom and R. M. Thomson, OMT (Oxford, 2002), 10–155.

PLACES

Abingdon. *Chronicon Monasterii de Abingdon*, ed. J. Stevenson, 2 vols., RS, 2 (1858).

Battle Abbey. *The Chronicle of Battle Abbey*, ed. E. Searle, OMT (Oxford, 1980).

Bury St Edmunds. *The Chronicle of Bury St Edmunds, 1212–1301*, ed. A. Gransden (London, 1964); *Memorials of St. Edmund's Abbey*, ed. T. Arnold, 3 vols., RS, 96 (1890–6).

Canterbury, Christ Church. C. E. Woodruff and W. Danks (eds.), *Memorials of the Cathedral and Priory of Christ in Canterbury* (London, 1912).

Canterbury, St Augustine's. Thomas of Elmham, *Historia Monasterii S. Augustini Cantuariensis*, ed. C. Hardwick, RS, 8 (1858).

Croyland (Crowland). *The Chronicle of Croyland Abbey by Ingulph*, ed. W. de Gray Birch (Wisbech, 1883).

Durham. *Durham Episcopal Charters*, ed. H. S. Offler, Surtees Soc., 179 (1968); *Registrum Palatinum Dunelmense*, ed. J. D. Hardy, 4 vols., RS, 62 (1873–8); *The Rites of Durham*, ed. J. T. Fowler, Surtees Soc., 107 (1903).

Ely. *Liber Eliensis*, ed. E. O. Blake, Camden Soc., 3rd ser., 92 (1962).

Evesham. *Chronicon Abbatiæ de Evesham*, ed. W. D. Macray, RS, 29 (1863); *Thomas of Marlborough: History of the Abbey of Evesham*, ed. J. Sayers and L. Watkiss, OMT (Oxford, 2003).

Glastonbury. *The Chronicle of Glastonbury Abbey*, ed. J. P. Carley (Woodbridge, 1985).

Hexham. *[De] Sanctis Ecclesiæ Haugustaldensis, auct. Ælredo, abbate Rievallensi*, cap. 11, in *The Priory of Hexham, its Church, Endowments, and Annals*, ed. J. Raine, Surtees Soc., 44 (1864), 173–203.

Melrose. *Chronica de Mailros*, ed. J. Stevenson (Edinburgh, 1835).

Peterborough. *The Chronicle of Hugh Candidus, a Monk of Peterborough*, ed. W. T. Mellows, Friends of Peterborough Cathedral (Oxford, 1949).

St Albans. *Gesta Abbatum Monasterii Sancti Albani*, ed. H. T. Riley, 3 vols., RS, 28.iv (1867–9); *Alban and St Albans. Roman and Medieval Architecture, Art, and Archaeology*, ed. M. Henig and P. Lindley, *BAA Trans.*, 24 (Leeds, 2001).

Winchester, New Minster. *Liber Vitæ: Register and Martyrology of New Minster and Hyde Abbey, Winchester*, ed. W. de Gray Birch, Hampshire Record Soc. (London and Winchester, 1892).

Winchester, St Swithun's. *Annales Wintonienses*, in *Annales Monastici*, ii (Winchester and Waverley), ed. H. R. Luard, RS, 36 (1865), 3–125; *Chartulary of Winchester Cathedral*, ed. A. W. Goodman (Winchester, 1927).

Worcester. *Annales Prioratus de Wigornia*, ed. H. R. Luard, *Annales Monastici*, iv, RS, 36 (1869), 355–564; *Registrum sive liber irrotularius et consuetudinarius prioratus Beatæ Mariæ Wigorniensis*, ed. W. Hale Hale, Camden Soc., o.s., 91 (1865); *The Register of Bishop William Ginsborough, 1303 to 1307*, ed. J. W. W. Bund, Worcester Historical Soc. (Oxford, 1907).

York. *Historians of the Church of York and its Archbishops*, ed. J. Raine, 3 vols., RS, 71 (1879–94).

SECONDARY SOURCES

Alexander, J. S., 'The Angel Choir of Lincoln Cathedral and the shrines of St Hugh', *JBAA*, 148 (1995), 137–47.

Bailey, R. N., 'The Anglo-Saxon Church at Hexham', *Archaeologia Aeliana*, 5th ser., 4 (1976), 47–67.

— 'St. Wilfrid. Ripon and Hexham', in *Studies in Insular Art and Archaeology*, ed. C. Karkov and R. Farrell, American Early Medieval Studies, i (Oxford Ohio, 1991), 3–25.

Barlow, F., *The English Church, 1000–1066: A Constitutional History* (London, 1963).

— *Edward the Confessor* (London, 1970).

Bates, D., *Bishop Remigius of Lincoln, 1067–1092* (Lincoln, 1992).

Battiscombe, C. F. (ed.), *The Relics of St Cuthbert* (Oxford, 1956).

Biddle, M., 'Alban and the Anglo-Saxon Church', in *Cathedral and City: St Albans Ancient and Modern*, ed. R. Runcie (St Albans, 1977), 23–42, 138–42.

— 'Archaeology, Architecture and the Cult of Saints in Anglo-Saxon England', in *The Anglo-Saxon Church*, ed. L. A. S. Butler and R. K. Morris (CBA Research Report, 60, 1986), 1–31.

— *The Tomb of Christ* (Stroud, 1999).

— 'Remembering St Alban: the site of the shrine and the discovery of the twelfth-century Purbeck marble shrine table', in *Alban and St Albans: Roman and Medieval Architecture, Art and Archaeology*, ed. M. Henig and P. Lindley, *BAA Trans.*, vol. 24, for 1999 (Leeds, 2001), 124–61.

Bidwell, P., 'A Survey of the Anglo-Saxon crypt at Hexham and its reused Roman stonework', *Archaeologia Aeliana*, 5th ser., xxxix (2010), 53–145.

Binski, P., *Westminster Abbey and the Plantagenets: Kingship and the Representation of Power, 1200–1400* (New Haven and London, 1995).

Blair, J., 'St Frideswide's monastery: problems and possibilities', in 'Saint Frideswide's Monastery at Oxford: Archaeological and Architectural Studies', ed. J. Blair, *Oxoniensia*, 53 (1988), 220–58.

– 'Above-ground or below-ground', in *Local Saints and Local Churches in the Early Medieval West*, ed. A. Thacker and R. Sharpe (Oxford, 2002), Appendix 2, 490–3.

— 'A Handlist of Anglo-Saxon Saints', in ibid., 494–562.

Blockley, K., Sparks, M., and Tatton-Brown, T., *Canterbury Cathedral Nave: Archaeology, History and Architecture*, Archaeology of Canterbury, n. s., i (Canterbury, 1997).

Bonner, G., Rollason, D., and Stancliffe, C. (eds.), *St Cuthbert, his Cult and his Community to A.D. 1200* (Woodbridge, 1989).

Britnell, W. J., and Watson, K., 'Saint Melangell's Shrine, Pennant Melangell', in *Pennant Melangell*, ed. W. J. Britnell, *The Montgomeryshire Collections*, 82 (1994), 147–66.

Brooke, C. N. L., 'Princes and Kings as Patrons of Monasteries: Normandy and England, 1066–1135', in idem, *Churches and Churchmen in Medieval Europe* (London, 1999), 139–57, reprinted from *Il Monachesimo e la Riforma Ecclesiastica (1049–1122), Miscellanea del Centro di Studi Medioevali*, 6 (Milan, 1971), 125–52.

Brooks, N., *The Early History of the Church of Canterbury: Christ Church from 597 to 1066* (Leicester, 1984).

— and Cubitt, C. (eds.), *St Oswald of Worcester, Life and Influence* (Leicester, 1996).

Brown, P., *The Cult of the Saints* (London, 1981).

Brown, P. D. C., and McWhirr, A. D., 'Cirencester, 1965', *Antiq. J.*, 46 (1966), 240–54.

Cabrol, F., and Leclercq, H. (eds.), *Dictionnaire d'Archéologie Chrétienne et de Liturgie*, 15 vols. (Paris, 1903–53).

Caviness, M. H., *The Early Stained Glass of Canterbury Cathedral, c.1175–1220* (Princeton, 1977).

Clapham, A. W., 'Note on the Burial Chamber [at Glastonbury]', in C. R. Peers, A. W. Clapham, and Dom E. Horne, 'Glastonbury Abbey Excavations, 1928', *Proc. Somerset. Archaeol. and Nat. Hist. Soc.*, 74 (1928), 5–6.

Coldstream, N., 'English Decorated Shrine Bases', *JBAA*, 129 (1976), 15–34.

— '*Cui bono*? The Saint, the Clergy and the New Work at St Albans', in *Medieval Architecture and its Intellectual Context: Studies in honour of Peter Kidson*, ed. E. Fernie and P. Crossley (London, 1990), 143–9.

— 'The Medieval Tombs and the Shrine of St Thomas Cantilupe', in *Hereford Cathedral: a History*, ed. G. Aylmer and J. Tiller (London, 2000), 322–30.

Cole, R. E. G., and Johnston, J. O., 'The Body of St Hugh', *Associated Architectural Soc. Reports and Papers*, 36.1 (1921–2), 47–72.

Craster, H. H. E., 'The Red Book of Durham', *EHR*, 40 (1925), 504–32.

Crook, J., 'The Romanesque East Arm and Crypt of Winchester Cathedral', *JBAA*, 142 (1989), 1–36.

— 'The typology of early medieval shrines – a previously misidentified "tomb-shrine" panel from Winchester Cathedral', *Antiq. J.*, 70.i (1990), 49–64.

— 'King Edgar's reliquary of St Swithun', *Anglo-Saxon England*, 21 (1992), 177–202.

— 'St Swithun of Winchester', in *Winchester Cathedral: Nine Hundred Years*, ed. J. Crook (Chichester, 1993), 57–68.

— '"A worthy antiquity": the movement of King Cnut's bones in Winchester Cathedral', in *The Reign of Cnut*, ed. A. R. Rumble (Leicester, 1994), 165–92.

— 'The Architectural Setting of the Cult of St Cuthbert in Durham Cathedral (1093–1200)', in *Anglo-Norman Durham*, ed. D. Rollason, M. Harvey, and M. Prestwich (Woodbridge, 1994), 235–50.

— *The Architectural Setting of the Cult of Saints in the Early Christian West, c.300–1200* (Oxford, 2000).

— 'The medieval shrines of Rochester Cathedral', in *Medieval Art, Architecture and Archaeology at Rochester*, *BAA Trans.*, vol. 27, for 2002 (Leeds, n.d.), 114–29.

— '*Vir Optimus Wlstanus*: The post-Conquest commemoration of Archbishop Wulfstan of York at Ely Cathedral', in *Wulfstan, Archbishop of York*, Proc. of the Second Alcuin Conference (York, 15–18 July 2002), Studies in the Early Middle Ages, 10, ed. M. Townend (Turnhout, 2004), 501–24.

— 'The Physical Setting of the Cult of St Wulfstan', in *St Wulfstan and his World*, ed. J. S. Barrow and N. P. Brooks, Studies in Early Medieval Britain, 4 (Aldershot, 2005), 189–217.

Curry, I., 'Aspects of the Anglo-Norman Design of Durham Cathedral', *Archaeologia Aeliana*, 5th ser., 14 (1986), 31–48.

Delehaye, H., *Sanctus: Essai sur le culte des saints dans l'antiquité*, Subsidia Hagiographica, 17 (Brussels, 1927).

— *Les origines du culte des martyrs, Subsidia Hagiographica*, 20, 2nd edn. (Brussels, 1933).

Douglas, D. C., *William the Conqueror: The Norman Impact upon England* (London, 1964).

Draper, P., 'Bishop Northwold and the cult of St Etheldreda', in *Medieval Art and Architecture at Ely Cathedral, BAA Trans.*, vol. 2, for 1976 (Leeds, 1979), 8–27.

Duffy, E., *The Stripping of the Altars: Traditional Religion in England, c.1400–c.1580*, 2nd edn. (New Haven and London, 2005).

Eales, R., and Sharpe, R., *Canterbury and the Norman Conquest: Churches, Saints and Scholars* (London, 1995).

Farmer, D. H. (ed.), *The Oxford Dictionary of Saints*, 3rd edn. (Oxford, 1992).

Finucane, R. C., *Miracles and Pilgrims: Popular Beliefs in Medieval England* (London, 1977).

Flight, C., *The Bishops and Monks of Rochester*, Kent Archaeol. Soc. Monographs, 6 (1997), 55–69.

Fouracre, P., and Gerberding, R. A., *Late Merovingian France: History and Hagiography, 640–720* (Manchester, 1996).

Fowler, J. T., 'On an examination of the grave of St Cuthbert in Durham Cathedral Church, in March, 1899', *Archæologia*, 57 (1900), 11–28.

Frend, W. H. C., '*Ecclesia Britannica*: Prelude or Dead End?', *Jnl. of Ecclesiastical History*, 30 (1979), 129–44.

Gasquet, F. A., and Bishop, E. (eds.), *The Bosworth Psalter* (London, 1908).

Geary, P. J., *Furta Sacra: theft of relics in the central Middle Ages* (Princeton, 1978).

Gee, L. Lewes, '"Ciborium" Tombs in England, 1290–1330', *JBAA*, 132 (1979), 29–41.

Grabar, A., *Martyrium; recherches sur le culte des reliques et l'art chrétien antique*, 2 vols. plus album (Paris, 1943, reprinted London, 1972).

Gransden, A., *Historical Writing in England, I, c.550–c.1307* (London, 1974).

— 'Cultural Transition at Worcester in the Anglo-Norman Period', *Medieval Art and Architecture at Worcester Cathedral, BAA Trans.*, 1 (1978), 1–14.

Greenwell, W., 'Durham Cathedral', *Trans. Architectural and Archaeol. Soc. of Durham and Northumberland*, 2 (1883), 163–233.

Guy, C., 'Excavations at Worcester Cathedral, 1881–1991', *Trans. Worcester Archaeol. Soc.*, 3rd ser., 14 (1994), 1–73.

Hall, R. A., 'Rescue excavations in the crypt of Ripon Cathedral', *Yorks. Archaeol. Jnl.*, 49 (1977), 59–63.

Hayward, P. A., 'Translation-narratives in post-Conquest hagiography and English resistance to the Norman Conquest', *Anglo-Norman Studies*, 21, Proc. of the Battle Conference for 1998, ed. C. Harper-Bill (Woodbridge, 1999), 67–93.

[*The*] *Heads of Religious Houses, England and Wales*, 3 vols. (Cambridge, 1972–2008); i [940–1216], ed. D. Knowles, C. N. L. Brooke, and V. C. M. London; ii [1216–1377], ed. D. M. Smith and V. C. M. London; iii [1377–1540], ed. D. M. Smith.

Heaton, R. B., and Britnell, W. J., 'A Structural history of Pennant Melangell Church', *The Montgomeryshire Collections*, Jnl. of the Powysland Club, 82 (1994), 103–26.

Heslop, T. A., 'The Canterbury Calendars and the Norman Conquest', in *Canterbury and the Norman Conquest: Churches, Saints and Scholars*, ed. R. Eales and R. Sharpe (London, 1995), 52–85.

Hope, W. H. St. John, 'On the great Almery for relics of late in the Abbey Church of Selby, with notes on some other receptacles for relics', *Archaeologia*, 60 (1907), 411–22.

— 'Recent discoveries in the Abbey Church of St Austin at Canterbury', *Arch. J.*, 32 (1917), 1–27.

Horstmann, C. (ed.), *Nova Legenda Anglie: as collected by John of Tynemouth, John Capgrave, and others, and first printed … by Wynkyn de Worde a.d. mdxui*, 2 vols (Oxford, 1901).

Jackson, E. D. C., and Fletcher, E. G. M., 'Excavations at Brixworth, 1958', *JBAA*, 3rd ser., 24 (1961), 1–15.

— 'The apse and nave at Wing, Buckinghamshire', *JBAA*, 3rd ser., 25 (1962), 1–20.

James, M. R., 'On the Abbey Church of S. Edmund at Bury', *Cambridge Antiquarian Soc. Octavo Publications*, 28 (1895), 115–212.

Jancey, M. (ed.) *St Thomas Cantilupe, Bishop of Hereford: Essays in his Honour* (Hereford, 1982).

Johnson, G. A. L., and Dunham, K., 'The Stones of Durham Cathedral; a Preliminary Note', *Trans. Archit. and Archaeol. Soc. of Durham and Northumberland*, n.s., 6 (1982), 53–6.

Kahn D., *Canterbury Cathedral and its Romanesque Sculpture* (London and Austin, Texas, 1991).

Kemp, E. W., *Canonization and Authority in the Western Church* (Oxford, 1948).

Kirschbaum, E., *The Tombs of St. Peter and St. Paul* (London, 1959).

Klukas, A. W., 'The architectural implications of the *Decreta Lanfranci*', *Anglo-Norman Studies*, 6 (1983), 136–71.

— 'The continuity of Anglo-Saxon liturgical tradition as evident in the architecture of Winchester, Ely, and Canterbury Cathedrals', in *Les Mutations Socio-Culturelles au Tournant des XIe–XIIe siècles*, Colloque international du Centre National de la Recherche Scientifique, 11–16 July 1982 (Paris, 1984), 111–23.

Knowles, Dom. D. [M. C. Knowles], *The Monastic Order in England*, 2nd edn. (Cambridge, 1966).

Korhammer, P. M., 'The Origin of the Bosworth Psalter', *Anglo-Saxon England*, 2 (1973), 173–87.

Lapidge, M., (ed.), *The Cult of St Swithun*, Winchester Studies, 4.ii (Oxford, 2003).

Le Blant, E., *Inscriptions Chrétiennes de la Gaule*, 3 vols. (Paris, 1856–92).

Levison, W., 'St. Alban and St. Albans', *Antiquity*, 15 (1941), 337–59.

Liebermann, F., *Die Heiligen Englands: angelsächsisch und lateinisch* (Hannover, 1889).

Love, R. C., ed., *Three Eleventh-Century Anglo-Latin Saints' Lives*, OMT (Oxford, 1996).

Loyn, H., *The English Church, 940–1154* (Harlow, 2000).

Lucius, [P.] E., *Die Anfänge des Heiligenkults in der christlichen Kirche* (Tübingen, 1904).

McAleer, P., *Rochester Cathedral, 604–1540* (Toronto, 1999).

Maître, L., 'Remarques sur les tombeaux percés d'une fenêtre', *Revue Archéologique*, 5th ser., 4 (Sept–Oct 1914), 265–85.

Maltby, H. J. M., 'Excavations of the Abbey Ruins, Bury St. Edmunds', *Proc. Suffolk Inst. of Archaeol.*, 24 (1949), 256–7.

Mason, E., *St Wulfstan of Worcester, c.1008–1095* (Oxford, 1990).

Mayr-Harting, H., 'Functions of a twelfth-century shrine: the miracles of St Frideswide', in *Studies in Medieval History presented to R. H. C. Davis* (London, 1985), 193–206.

Meyer, W., *Die Legende des hl. Albanus des Protomartyr Angliæ in Texten vor Beda*, Abhandlungen der Königlichen Gesellschaft der Wissenschaften zu Göttingen, n.s., viii.1 (Berlin, 1904).

Milner, J., *The History, Civil and Ecclesiastical, and Survey of the Antiquities of Winchester*, 2 vols. (Winchester, 1798–9).

Morgan, P. E., 'The Effect of the Pilgrim Cult of St Thomas of Cantilupe on Hereford Cathedral', in *St Thomas Cantilupe, Bishop of Hereford: Essays in his Honour*, ed. M. Jancey (Hereford, 1982), 145–52.

Nilson, B, *Cathedral Shrines of Medieval England* (Woodbridge, 1998).

Norton, C., *St William of York* (York, 2006).

Offler, H. S., 'Hexham and the Historia Regum', *Trans. of the Architectural and Archaeol. Soc. of Durham and Northumberland*, 2 (1971), 51–62.

Parsons, D., 'The Pre-Conquest Cathedral at Canterbury', *Arch. Cant.*, 84 (1969), 175–84.

Quirk, R. N., 'Winchester Cathedral in the Tenth Century', *Arch. J.*, 114 (1957), 28–68.

Radford, C. A. Ralegh, 'Two Scottish Shrines: Jedburgh and St. Andrews', *Arch. J.*, 112 (1955), 43–60.

— 'The bishop's throne in Norwich Cathedral', *Arch. J.*, 116 (1959), 115–32.

— 'The Church of Saint Alkmund, Derby', *Derbys. Archaeol. Jnl.*, 96 (1976), 26–61.

— and Hemp, W. J., 'Pennant Melangell: the Church and the Shrine', *Archæologia Cambrensis*, 107 (1958), 81–113.

Raine, J., *St Cuthbert: with an Account of the State in which his Remains were Found upon the Opening of his Tomb in Durham Cathedral in the year MDCCCXXVII* (Durham, 1828).

— *A Brief Account of Durham Cathedral with Notices of the Castle, University, City Churches, Etc.* (Newcastle, 1833).

— 'On the Architectural History of the Cathedral Church of Durham', *Proc. Archaeol. Institute*, Durham Meeting, Aug. 1852, 2 vols. (London, 1858).

Ramsay, N., Sparks, M., and Tatton-Brown, T. (eds.), *St Dunstan: his Life, Times, and Cult* (Woodbridge, 1992).

Ridyard, S. J., '*Condigna Veneratio*: Post-Conquest attitudes to the saints of the Anglo-Saxons', *Anglo-Norman Studies*, 9, Proc. of the Battle Conference for 1986, ed. R. Allen Brown (Woodbridge, 1987), 179–206.

— *The Royal Saints of Anglo-Saxon England* (Cambridge, 1988).

Rodwell, W., *The Archaeology of Wells Cathedral: Excavations and Structural Studies, 1978–93*, English Heritage Archaeological Reports, 21, 2 vols. (London, 2001).

Rollason, D. W., 'Lists of Saints' Resting-Places in Anglo-Saxon England', *Anglo-Saxon England*, 7 (1978), 61–93.

— 'The Search for Saint Wigstan', University of Leicester, Vaughan Papers, No. 27 (Leicester, 1981).

— 'The cult of murdered royal saints in Anglo-Saxon England', *Anglo-Saxon England*, 11 (1983), 1–22.

— 'Relic-cults as an Instrument of Royal Policy *c.* 900–*c.* 1050', *Anglo-Saxon England*, 15 (1986), 91–103.

— *Saints and Relics in Anglo-Saxon England* (Oxford, 1989).

Sawyer, P. H. (ed.), *Anglo-Saxon Charters: An Annotated List and Bibliography* (London, 1968).

Scott, G. G. [Sr.], 'Re-opening of a Roman basilica under the chancel of Wing Church', *Records of Bucks*, 5, no. 3 (1880), 147–8.

Sharpe, R., 'The Date of St. Mildreth's Translation from Minster-in-Thanet to Canterbury', *Medieval Studies*, 53 (1991), 349–54.

— 'The setting of St Augustine's translation, 1091', in *Canterbury and the Norman Conquest: Churches, Saints and Scholars, 1066–1109*, ed. Richard Eales and Richard Sharpe (Hambledon, 1995), 1–13.

— 'The Late Antique Passion of St Alban', in *Alban and St Albans: Roman and Medieval Architecture, Art, and Archaeology*, ed. M. Henig and P. Lindley, *BAA Trans.*, 24 (Leeds, 2001), 30–7.

Sigal, P. A., 'Naissance et premier développement d'un vinage exceptionnel: l'eau de saint Thomas', *Cahiers de Civilisation Médiévale*, 44 (2001), 35–44.

Southern, R. W., *Saint Anselm and his Biographer* (Cambridge, 1966)

— *Saint Anselm: a Portrait in a Landscape* (Cambridge, 1990).

Stancliffe, C., *St Martin and his Hagiographer* (Oxford, 1983).

— and Cambridge, E. (eds.), *Oswald: Northumbrian King to European Saint*, (Stamford, 1995).

Stenton, F. M., *Anglo-Saxon England*, 3rd edn. (Oxford, 1971).

Stephens, G. R., 'Caerleon and the martyrdom of SS. Aaron and Julius', *Bulletin of the Board of Celtic Studies*, 32 (1985), 326–35.

Stocker, D., 'The Shrine of Little St Hugh', in *Medieval Art and Architecture at Lincoln Cathedral*, *BAA Trans.*, vol. 8, for 1982 (Leeds, 1986), 109–17.

— 'The Mystery of the Shrines of St Hugh', in *Saint Hugh of Lincoln*, ed. H. Mayr-Harting (Oxford, 1987), 89–124.

— 'The Tomb and Shrine of Bishop Grosseteste in Lincoln Cathedral', in *England in the Thirteenth Century: Proceedings of the 1984 Harlaxton Symposium*, ed. W. M. Ormrod (Harlaxton, 1985, reissued Woodbridge, 1986), 143–8.

Sulser, W., 'Die St. Luziuskirche in Chur', *Frühmittelalterliche Kunst in den Alpenländern*

Sumption, J., *Pilgrimage: an Image of Mediæval Religion* (London, 1975).

Tatton-Brown, T., 'Canterbury and the architecture of pilgrimage shrines in England', in *Pilgrimage: The English Experience from Becket to Bunyon*, ed. C. Morris and P. Roberts (Cambridge, 2002), 90–107.

Taylor, H. M., 'Corridor crypts on the Continent and in England', *North Staffs. Jnl. of Field Studies*, 9 (1969), 17–52.

— 'The Anglo-Saxon Cathedral Church at Canterbury', *Arch. J.*, 126 (1969), 101–30.

— *Repton Studies 1: The Anglo-Saxon Crypt, 1974–76*, privately printed (1977).

— *Repton Studies 2: The Anglo-Saxon Crypt and Church*, privately printed (1979).

— 'St. Wystan's Church, Repton, Derbyshire: a reconstruction essay', *Arch. J.*, 144 (1987), 205–45.

— *St Wystan's Church, Repton; a Guide and History* (Derby, 1989).

— and Taylor, J., *Anglo-Saxon Architecture*, i–ii (Cambridge, 1965); iii, by H. M. Taylor (Cambridge, 1978).

Thacker, A. T., 'The Social and Political background of early Anglo-Saxon Hagiography', unpubl. D.Phil. thesis, Oxford, 1976.

— 'Kings, Saints, and Monasteries in Pre-Viking Mercia', *Midland History*, 10 (1985), 1–25.

— 'Lindisfarne and the Origins of the Cult of St Cuthbert', in *St Cuthbert, his Cult and his Community*, ed. G. Bonner, D. Rollason, and C. Stancliffe (Woodbridge, 1989), 103–22.

— 'Cults at Canterbury: Relics and Reform under Dunstan and his Successors', in *St Dunstan: his Life, Times, and Cult*, ed. N. Ramsay, M. Sparks, and T. Tatton-Brown (Woodbridge, 1992), 221–45.

— '*Membra Disjecta*: the division of the body and the diffusion of the cult', in *Oswald: Northumbrian King to European Saint*, ed. C. Stancliffe and E. Cambridge (Stamford, 1995), 97–127.

— 'Saint-making and relic collecting by Oswald and his communities', in *St Oswald of Worcester: Life and Influence*, ed. N. Brooks and C. Cubitt (Leicester, 1996), 244–68.

— 'The making of a local saint', in *Local Saints and Local Churches*, ed. A. T. Thacker and R. Sharpe (Oxford, 2002), 45–73.

Theobald, J., 'Some account of Saint Peter's church in the East, Oxon., from an old MS', *Archaeologia*, 1 (1770), 151–5.

Thomas, A. C., *Bede, Archaeology, and the Cult of Relics*, Jarrow Lecture 1973 (Jarrow, 1973).

Thomas, C., *Christianity in Roman Britain to A. D. 500* (London, 1981).

Thorpe, J. (ed.), *Registrum Roffense* (London, 1769).

Toynbee, J. M. C., *Death and Burial in the Roman World* (London, 1971).

— and Ward Perkins, J., *The Shrine of St Peter and the Vatican Excavations* (London, 1956).

Vauchez, A., *La Sainteté en Occident aux derniers siècles du Moyen Âge: d'après les procès de canonisation et les documents hagiographiques* (Rome and Paris, 1981).

Wall, J. Charles, *Shrines of British Saints* (London, 1905).

Wallace-Hadrill, J. M., *Bede's 'Ecclesiastical History of the English People': A Historical Commentary* (Oxford, 1988).

Watkins, C. F., *The Basilica or Palatial Hall of Justice and Sacred Temple; its Nature, Origin, and Purport: and a Description and History of the Basilican Church of Brixworth* (London, 1867).

Whittingham, A. B., 'Norwich Saxon Throne', *Arch. J.*, 136 (1979), 60–8.

Wilkinson, J., *Jerusalem Pilgrimage, 1099–1185*, Hakluyt Soc. (London, 1988).

Williams, A., *The English and the Norman Conquest* (Woodbridge, 1995).

Willis, R., 'The Architectural History of Winchester Cathedral', *Proc. Archaeol. Institute* (1845), 1–80, reprinted by Friends of Winchester Cathedral (Winchester, 1980).

— *The Architectural History of Canterbury Cathedral* (London, 1845).

Wilson, C., *The Shrines of St William of York* (York, 1977).

Woodman, A. Vere, 'Wing Church', *Records of Bucks.*, 16, pt 5 (1960), 367–8.

— 'Wing Church', *Records of Bucks.*, 17, pt 2 (1962), 130–1.

Wormald, F., *English Kalendars before A.D. 1100*, Henry Bradshaw Society, 72, for 1933 (London, 1934).

Wright, T. (ed.), *Three Chapters of Letters Relating to the Suppression of Monasteries*, Camden Soc., o.s., 26 (1843).

INDEX

Already Published

The Art of Anglo-Saxon England
Catherine E. Karkov

English Medieval Misericords: The Margins of Meaning
Paul Hardwick

English Medieval Shrines
John Crook

Thresholds of Medieval Visual Culture: Liminal Spaces
Edited by Elina Gertsman and Jill Stevenson

The Marvellous and the Monstrous in the Sculpture of Twelfth-Century Europe
Kirk Ambrose

Early Medieval Stone Monuments: Materiality, Biography, Landscape
Edited by Howard Williams, Joanne Kirton and Meggen Gondek

The Royal Abbey of Reading
Ron Baxter

www.ingramcontent.com/pod-product-compliance
Lightning Source LLC
LaVergne TN
LVHW020504100826
845148LV00003B/696

* 9 7 8 1 7 8 3 2 7 0 9 3 4 *